T0214599

Communications
in Computer and Information Science   **858**

Commenced Publication in 2007
Founding and Former Series Editors:
Phoebe Chen, Alfredo Cuzzocrea, Xiaoyong Du, Orhun Kara, Ting Liu,
Dominik Ślęzak, and Xiaokang Yang

More information about this series at http://www.springer.com/series/7899

Daniel A. Alexandrov · Alexander V. Boukhanovsky
Andrei V. Chugunov · Yury Kabanov
Olessia Koltsova (Eds.)

Digital Transformation and Global Society

Third International Conference, DTGS 2018
St. Petersburg, Russia, May 30 – June 2, 2018
Revised Selected Papers, Part I

 Springer

Editors
Daniel A. Alexandrov ⓘ
National Research University Higher School
of Economics
St. Petersburg, Russia

Alexander V. Boukhanovsky
Saint Petersburg State University
of Information Technologies
St. Petersburg, Russia

Andrei V. Chugunov
Saint Petersburg State University
of Information Technologies
St. Petersburg, Russia

Yury Kabanov ⓘ
National Research University Higher School
of Economics
St. Petersburg, Russia

Olessia Koltsova ⓘ
National Research University Higher School
of Economics
St. Petersburg, Russia

ISSN 1865-0929   ISSN 1865-0937   (electronic)
Communications in Computer and Information Science
ISBN 978-3-030-02842-8   ISBN 978-3-030-02843-5   (eBook)
https://doi.org/10.1007/978-3-030-02843-5

Library of Congress Control Number: 2018958515

This Springer imprint is published by the registered company Springer Nature Switzerland AG
The registered company address is: Gewerbestrasse 11, 6330 Cham, Switzerland

Preface

The International Conference on Digital Transformation and Global Society (DTGS 2018) was held for the third time from May 30 to June 2, 2018, in St. Petersburg Russia. It is a rapidly developing academic event, addressing the interdisciplinary agenda of ICT-enabled transformations in various domains of human life. DTGS 2018 was co-organized by the ITMO University and the National Research University Higher School of Economics (St. Petersburg), two of the leading research institutions in Russia.

This year was marked by a significant rise in interest in the conference in academia. We received 222 submissions, which were carefully reviewed by at least three Program Committee members. In all, 76 papers were accepted, with an acceptance rate of 34%. More than 120 participants attended the conference and contributed to its success. We would like to emphasize the increase in the number of young scholars taking part in the event, as well as the overall improvement in the quality of the papers.

DTGS 2018 was organized as a series of research paper sessions, preceded by a poster session. The sessions corresponded to one of the following DTGS 2018 tracks:

- ESociety: Social Informatics and Virtual Communities
- EPolity: Politics and Governance in the Cyberspace
- EHumanities: Digital Culture and Education
- ECity: Smart Cities and Urban Governance
- EEconomy: Digital Economy and ICT-Driven Economic Practices
- ECommunication: Online Communication and the New Media

Two new international workshops were also held under the auspices of DTGS: the Internet Psychology Workshop, chaired by Prof. Alexander Voiskounsky (Moscow State University) and Prof. Anthony Faiola (The University of Illinois at Chicago), as well as the Computational Linguistics Workshop, led by Prof. Viktor Zakharov (St. Petersburg State University) and Prof. Anna Tilmans (Leibniz University of Hannover). The agenda of DTGS is thus becoming broader, exploring the new domains of digital transformation.

Furthermore, we would like to mention several insightful keynote lectures organized at DTGS 2018. Prof. Stephen Coleman from the University of Leeds gave a talk on the role of the Internet in restoring and promoting democracy. The lecture was partially based on his recent book *Can the Internet Strengthen Democracy?* (Polity: 2017), which was translated into Russian and published by the DTGS team before the conference. Dr. Dennis Anderson (St. Francis College, USA) shared with the participants his vision of the future of e-government and its role in society, while Dr. Christoph Glauser (Institute for Applied Argumentation Research, Switzerland) presented the tools to evaluate citizens' expectations from e-government and the ways e-services can be adjusted to serve people's needs. The keynote lecture by Prof. Anthony Faiola was devoted to e-health technologies, especially to the potential of mobile technologies to facilitate health care.

Finally, two international panel discussions were arranged. The first one – "Cybersecurity, Security and Privacy" — was chaired by Prof. Latif Ladid from the University of Luxembourg. Panel participants Dr. Antonio Skametra (University of Murcia), Dr. Sebastian Ziegler (Mandat International, IoT Forum, Switzerland), and Dr. Luca Bolognini (Italian Institute for Data Privacy and Valorization) shared their opinion on the future of privacy protection in relation to the changes of the EU personal data regulations. The second panel moderated by Dr. Yuri Misnikov (ITMO University) and Dr. Svetlana Bodrunova (St. Petersburg State University) was devoted to the online deliberative practices in the EU and Russia. Prof. Stephen Coleman, Prof. Leonid Smorgunov (St. Petersburg State University), Dr. Lyudmila Vidiasova (ITMO University), Dr. Olessia Koltsova, and Yury Kabanov (National Research University Higher School of Economics) took part in the discussion, expressing their views on the role of virtual communities in maintaining democratic practices and better governance.

Such a plentiful scientific program would have been impossible without the support and commitment from many people worldwide. We thank all those who made this event successful. We are grateful to the members of the international Steering and Program Committees, the reviewers and the conference staff, the session and workshop chairs, as well as to the authors contributing their excellent research to the volume.

We are happy to see the conference growing in importance on the global scale. We believe that DTGS will continue to attract an international expert community to discuss the issues of digital transformation.

May 2018

Daniel A. Alexandrov
Alexander V. Boukhanovsky
Andrei V. Chugunov
Yury Kabanov
Olessia Koltsova

Organization

Program Committee

Artur Afonso Sousa	Polytechnic Institute of Viseu, Portugal
Svetlana Ahlborn	Goethe University, Germany
Luis Amaral	University of Minho, Portugal
Dennis Anderson	St. Francis College, USA
Francisco Andrade	University of Minho, Portugal
Farah Arab	Université Paris 8, France
Alexander Babkin	Crimea Federal University, Russia
Maxim Bakaev	Novosibirsk State Technical University, Russia
Alexander Balthasar	Bundeskanzleramt, Austria
Luís Barbosa	University of Minho, Portugal
Vladimír Benko	Slovak Academy of Sciences, Ľ. Štúr Institute of Linguistics, Slovakia
Sandra Birzer	Innsbruck University, Austria
Svetlana Bodrunova	St. Petersburg State University, Russia
Radomir Bolgov	St. Petersburg State University, Russia
Anastasiya Bonch-Osmolovskaya	National Research University Higher School of Economics, Russia
Nikolay Borisov	St. Petersburg State University, Russia
Dietmar Brodel	Carinthia University of Applied Sciences, Austria
Mikhail Bundin	Lobachevsky State University of Nizhni Novgorod, Russia
Diana Burkaltseva	Crimea Federal University, Russia
Luis Camarinha-Matos	University of Lisbon, Portugal
Lorenzo Cantoni	University of Lugano, Italy
François Charoy	Lorraine Laboratory of Research in Computer Science and its Applications, France
Sunil Choenni	Research and Documentation Centre (WODC), Ministry of Justice, The Netherlands
Andrei Chugunov	ITMO University, Russia
Iya Churakova	St. Petersburg State University, Russia
Meghan Cook	SUNY Albany, Center for Technology in Government, USA
Esther Del Moral	University of Oviedo, Spain
Saravanan Devadoss	Addis Ababa University, Ethiopia
Subrata Kumar Dey	Independent University, Bangladesh
Alexey Dobrov	St. Petersburg State University, Russia
Irina Eliseeva	St. Petersburg State University of Economics, Russia
Anthony Faiola	The University of Illinois at Chicago, USA

Isabel Ferreira	Polytechnic Institute of Cávado and Ave, Spain
Olga Filatova	St. Petersburg State University, Russia
Enrico Francesconi	Italian National Research Council, Italy
Diego Fregolente Mendes de Oliveira	Indiana University, USA
Fernando Galindo	University of Zaragoza, Spain
Despina Garyfallidou	University of Patras, Greece
Carlos Gershenson	National Autonomous University of Mexico, Mexico
J. Paul Gibson	Mines Telecom, France
Christoph Glauser	Institute for Applied Argumentation Research, Switzerland
Tatjana Gornostaja	Tilde, Latvia
Dimitris Gouscos	University of Athens, Greece
Stefanos Gritzalis	University of the Aegean, Greece
Karim Hamza	Vrije Universiteit Brussel, Belgium
Alex Hanna	University of Toronto, Canada
Martijn Hartog	The Hague University of Applied Sciences, The Netherlands
Agnes Horvat	Northwestern University, USA
Dmitry Ilvovsky	National Research University Higher School of Economics, Russia
Marijn Janssen	Delft University of Technology, The Netherlands
Yury Kabanov	National Research University Higher School of Economics, Russia
Katerina Kabassi	TEI of Ionian Islands, Greece
Christos Kalloniatis	University of the Aegean, Greece
George Kampis	Eotvos University, Hungary
Egor Kashkin	V. V. Vinogradov Russian Language Institute of RAS, Russia
Sanjeev Katara	National Informatics Centre, Govt. of India, India
Philipp Kazin	ITMO University, Russia
Norbert Kersting	University of Muenster, Germany
Maria Khokhlova	St. Petersburg State University, Russia
Mikko Kivela	Aalto University, Finland
Bozidar Klicek	University of Zagreb, Croatia
Ralf Klischewski	German University in Cairo, Egypt
Eduard Klyshinskii	Moscow State Institute of Electronics and Mathematics, Russia
Andreas Koch	University of Salzburg, Austria
Olessia Koltsova	National Research University Higher School of Economics, Russia
Liliya Komalova	Institute of Scientific Information for Social Sciences of Russian Academy of Sciences, Moscow State Linguistic University, Russia
Mikhail Kopotev	University of Helsinki, Finland
Ah-Lian Kor	Leeds Beckett University, UK

Evgeny Kotelnikov	Vyatka State University, Russia
Artemy Kotov	National Research Center Kurchatov Institute, Russia
Sergey Kovalchuk	ITMO University, Russia
Michal Kren	Charles University, Czech Republic
Valentina Kuskova	National Research University Higher School of Economics, Russia
Valeri Labunets	Ural Federal University, Russia
Sarai Lastra	Universidad del Turabo, USA
Sandro Leuchter	Hochschule Mannheim University of Applied Sciences, Germany
Yuri Lipuntsov	Moscow State Universuty, Russia
Natalia Loukachevitch	Moscow State University, Russia
Mikhail Lugachev	Moscow State University, Russia
Olga Lyashevskaya	National Research University Higher School of Economics, Russia
Jose Machado	University of Minho, Portugal
Rosario Mantegna	Palermo University, Italy
Ignacio Marcovecchio	United Nations University Institute on Computing and Society, Macao, SAR China
João Martins	United Nations University, Portugal
Aleksei Martynov	Lobachevsky State University of Nizhny Novgorod, Russia
Ricardo Matheus	Delft University of Technology, The Netherlands
Tatiana Maximova	ITMO University, Russia
Athanasios Mazarakis	Kiel University/ZBW, Germany
Christoph Meinel	Hasso Plattner Institute, Germany
Yelena Mejova	Qatar Computing Research Institute, Qatar
András Micsik	SZTAKI, Hungary
Yuri Misnikov	ITMO University, Russia
Harekrishna Misra	Institute of Rural Management Anand, India
Olga Mitrofanova	St. Petersburg State University, Russia
Zoran Mitrovic	Mitrovic Development & Research Institute, South Africa
John Mohr	University of California, USA
José María Moreno-Jimenez	Universidad de Zaragoza, Spain
Robert Mueller-Toeroek	University of Public Administration and Finance Ludwigsburg, Germany
Ilya Musabirov	National Research University Higher School of Economics, Russia
Alexandra Nenko	ITMO University, Russia
Galina Nikiporets-Takigawa	University of Cambridge, UK; Russian State Social University, Russia
Prabir Panda	National Institute for Smart Government, India
Ilias Pappas	Norwegian University of Science and Technology, Norway
Mário Peixoto	United Nations University, Portugal

Dessislava Petrova-Antonova	Sofia University St. Kliment Ohridski, Bulgaria
Anna Picco-Schwendener	University of Lugano, Italy
Edy Portmann	University of Fribourg, Switzerland
Devendra Potnis	University at Tennessee at Knoxville, USA
Yuliya Proekt	Herzen State Pedagogical University of Russia, Russia
Dmitry Prokudin	St. Petersburg State University, Russia
Cornelius Puschmann	Alexander von Humboldt Institute for Internet and Society, Germany
Rui Quaresma	University of Evora, Portugal
Alexander Raikov	Institute of Control Sciences of the Russian Academy of Sciences, Russia
Aleksandr Riabushko	World Bank, Russia
Manuel Pedro Rodriguez Bolivar	University of Granada, Spain
Alexandr Rosen	Charles University, Czech Republic
Gustavo Rossi	National University of La Plata, Argentina
Liudmila Rychkova	Grodno State University, Belarus
Luis Sabucedo	University of Vigo, Spain
Fosso Wamba Samuel	Toulouse Business School, France
Nurbek Saparkhojayev	Kazakh National Research Technical University named after K.I. Satpayev, Kazakhstan
Demetrios Sarantis	National Technical University of Athens, Greece
Carolin Schröder	Centre for Technology and Society, Germany
Olga Scrivner	Indiana University, USA
Patrick Shih	Indiana University, USA
Alexander Smirnov	SPIIRAS, Russia
Artem Smolin	ITMO University, Russia
Stanislav Sobolevsky	New York University, USA
Thanakorn Sornkaew	Ramkhamheang University, Thailand
Fabro Steibel	Project Sirca2 (FGV/UFF), Singapore
Zhaohao Sun	University of Ballarat, Australia
Stan Szpakowicz	University of Ottawa, Canada
Florence Sèdes	University of Toulouse 3, France
Irina Temnikova	Qatar Computing Research Institute, Qatar
Neelam Tikkha	MMV, RTMNU, India
Alice Trindade	University of Lisbon, Portugal
Rakhi Tripathi	FORE School of Management, India
Aizhan Tursunbayeva	University of Molise, Italy
Elpida Tzafestas	National Technical University of Athens
Nils Urbach	University of Bayreuth, Germany
David Valle-Cruz	Mexico State Autonomous University, Mexico
Natalia Vasilyeva	St. Petersburg State University, Russia
Cyril Velikanov	MEMORIAL NGO, Russia
Antonio Vetro	Nexa Center for Internet and Society, Italy
Gabriela Viale Pereira	Danube University Krems, Austria

Lyudmila Vidiasova   ITMO University, Russia
Alexander Voiskounsky   Lomonosov Moscow State University, Russia
Ruprecht von Waldenfels   University of Jena, Germany
Catalin Vrabie   National University of Political Studies and Public
                                  Administration, Romania
Ingmar Weber   Qatar Computing Research Institute, Qatar
Mariëlle Wijermars   University of Helsinki, Finland
Vladimir Yakimets   Institute for Information transmission Problems
                                  of RAS, Russia
Nikolina Zajdela Hrustek   University of Zagreb, Croatia
Victor Zakharov   St. Petersburg State University, Russia
Sergej Zerr   L3S Research Center, Germany
Hans-Dieter Zimmermann   FHS St. Gallen University of Applied Sciences,
                                  Switzerland
Thomas Ågotnes   University of Bergen, Norway
Vytautas Čyras   Vilnius University, Lithuania

Additional Reviewers

Abraham, Joanna   Mavroeidi, Aikaterini-Georgia
Abrosimov, Viacheslav   Melnik, Mikhail
Balakhontceva, Marina   Metsker, Oleg
Belyakova, Natalia   Mityagin, Sergey
Bolgov, Radomir   Nagornyy, Oleg
Bolgova, Ekaterina   Naumov, Victor
Borisov, Nikolay   Nikitin, Nikolay
Burkalskaya, Diana   Papautsky, Elizabeth
Chin, Jessie   Routzouni, Nancy
Churakova, Iya   Semakova, Anna
Derevitskiy, Ivan   Sergushichev, Alexey
Derevitsky, Ivan   Sideri, Maria
Duffecy, Jennifer   Sinyavskaya, Yadviga
Eliseeva, Irina   Smoliarova, Anna
Funkner, Anastasia   Steibel, Fabro
Gonzalez, Maria Paula   Trutnev, Dmitry
Guleva, Valentina Y.   Ufimtseva, Nathalia
Karyagin, Mikhail   Vatani, Haleh
Kaufman, David   Virkar, Shefali
Litvinenko, Anna   Visheratin, Alexander
Marchenko, Alexander   Zhuravleva, Nina
Masevich, Andrey

Contents – Part I

E-Economy: IT & New Markets

E-Society: Social Informatics

Contents – Part II

International Workshop on Internet Psychology

International Workshop on Computational Linguistics

E-Polity: Smart Governance and E-Participation

Information Systems as a Source of Official Information (on the Example of the Russian Federation)

Roman Amelin[1]([✉]), Sergey Channov[2], Tatyana Polyakova[3], and Jamilah Veliyeva[2]

[1] National Research Saratov State University named after N. G. Chernyshevsky, 83 Astrakhanskaya Street, Saratov 410012, Russia
ame-roman@yandex.ru
[2] The Russian Presidental Academy of National Economy and Public Administration, 23/25 Sobornaya Street, Saratov 410031, Russia
[3] Institute of State and Law Russian Academy of Sciences, 10 Znamenka Street, Moscow 119019, Russia

Abstract. The article analyzes the role of state information systems in building a democratic information society. The information available through such information systems is official information. Citizens trust such information, plan and base their actions on it. Meanwhile, unlike special state portals, the information systems of individual state and municipal bodies are not always distinguished by high quality of the data. Even if some information is actually present in the system, it may not be detected by a simple search query. This is misleading users. To solve this problem, technical, organizational and legal measures are needed. The authors formulate a presumption of authenticity of official information. A citizen has the right to rely on official information as a reliable one, his behavior based on such information should be regarded as conscientious. A classification of state information systems on the legal significance of the information contained in them is proposed. The authors make some proposals on the development of international legislation on guarantees of access to government information.

Keywords: Information society · Official information · Right to information
State information system · State register · Reliability of information
Quality of information

1 Introduction

The discussion on the right of access to information contained in public information systems is part of a more general scientific discussion on the right of access to information on the activities of government bodies.

This work was supported by grant 17-03-00082-ОГН from the Russian Foundation for Basic Research.

Now it is a general principle that official documents, whether of state or local government authorities, shall be public. The rule is of long standing, having made its first appearance in a Freedom of the Press Act in 1766 in Sweden [1, p. 150]. Only two centuries later, other countries followed the example of Sweden: Finland (1951), USA (1966), Norway, Denmark (1970), France (1978), etc. In the second half of the twentieth century, the right to information in the field of public administration received new content and significance, moved to the attention of lawyers of various countries [2, p. 45]. This was promoted by the development of the doctrine of the rights and freedoms of the individual, as well as the unprecedented improvement of computing and communication tools. This right is of a dual nature. It is a form of personal freedom to receive information, as well as a means of realizing the important principle of a democratic state, the principle of participation in the management of its affairs, which implies, among other things, openness and transparency of the public administration [3, p. 27]. As pointed out by Toby Mendel, public bodies hold information not for themselves but for the public good, and therefore this information should be available to the public, if it is keeping secret is not a priority. The consent of state bodies to provide such information is not sufficient for the effective realization of this right. The active activity of these bodies in the publication and dissemination of key categories of information, even in the absence of a request, is important [4].

In the Russian legal science, the discussion about the importance of legislative support for this principle was activated after the adoption of the Constitution of the Russian Federation in 1993. Part 2 of Article 24 enshrined the duty of public and local authorities, their officials to ensure that everyone had the opportunity to get acquainted with documents and materials that directly affected his rights and freedoms.

Initially, the right to access information on the activities of state bodies was considered an element of the right to information (alongside such elements as the right of creation, the right of distribution, the right of transfer, etc.) [5, pp. 219–220]. Later, the opinion of its independent status and position in the group of basic information rights, such as freedom of thought, of speech, of the press, began to prevail [6]. And while freedom of thought, speech, and press require non-interference of the state in their implementation, the right to information is a reflection of direct cooperation, communication between the state and an individual, where the state acts as an active participant, ensuring all conditions for a person to exercise his/her right [7, p. 91].

The conditions for real ensuring the right to access the information appeared in the Russian Federation in 2009 when the adoption of Federal Laws "On providing access to information on the activities of courts in the Russian Federation" [8] and "On providing access to information on the activities of state and local government bodies" took place (Law on Access to Information) [9]. For the first time, the principles of access to such information, the ways of access and the procedure for providing information, legal guarantees for the protection of the right to access the information were established. The law also established a wide range of types of information that must be placed in the Internet.

Today, the practice of providing government information through the system of state websites and portals is common in most countries. France launched its open data portal, data.gouv.fr, in December 2011, allowing public services to publish their own data. A new version of the data.gouv.fr portal was launched which adds a social and collaborative dimension by opening up to citizens contributions. It now also allows civil society organizations to enhance, modify and interpret data with a view to coproduce information of general interest [10]. Portal www.bund.de is the main web-resource providing citizens and enterprises of Germany with online access to government structures and services, etc.

2 State Information Systems

There is a large number of information systems (IS) that are created and maintained by state and local bodies. They provide information to citizens through the Internet, but do not belong to special government portals. The credibility of the information in such systems is a crucial issue for building of the information society [11].

Unlike unified state portals, the information systems of individual state bodies solve certain specialized tasks in the sphere of public administration and can be initially oriented at gathering and processing information that is necessary for state bodies, rather than providing it to citizens.

But if you do not take into account law enforcement agencies, military and other security agencies, most state information systems (SIS) in a democratic society operate on the principle of openness. This means that most of the information in these systems (or all information) is available to citizens. The exception is mostly personal data and commercial secrets [12]. In the Russian Federation there are several dozens of unified information systems of the federal level, the information in which is open.

In addition, many normative acts regulate the disclosure of information by state bodies, which are budgetary institutions. For example, each state university in the Russian Federation should create a special section on its website with certain types of reports and data. There are laws that require public authorities to disclose certain types of information (for example, on inspections) without clarifying the specific method of providing them [13].

It should be noted that the information systems at the Federal level in the Russian Federation have long ceased to play the role of simple tools for working with information. State information systems become an instrument of legal regulation. We wrote about this in our paper [14]. The bottom line is that the law increasingly places the obligation on individuals to provide some information not just to the controlling bodies, but to special state information systems. After that, the algorithms and capabilities of the information system itself begin to influence the nature of legal relations related to the collection of such information, its use for the purposes of state accounting and control, as well as the activities of controlled entities. This is how the prophecy of Lawrence Lessig comes true, that the right will be embodied «in the code and in the machine» [15]. But with this growing role of unified federal information systems, the quality of information processing in regional and local government bodies remains low. This is due to financial and personnel problems. In particular, in fulfilling the requirement of legislation on the publication of open data, a public authority can post ordinary Microsoft Word text documents that have simply been converted into an XML format by standard tools [16], which is completely pointless in terms of the possibility of their further use.

Meanwhile, in accordance with the Russian law on information [17], information contained in government information systems is official. Similar provisions are in the laws of other countries. And in general, citizens tend to rely on information, if the information is placed on the official information resource of a certain state body.

3 Presumption of Authenticity of Official Information

"Official" means "established by the government, administration, official, etc., or coming from them". A citizen who perceives some information as official expects that he/she has the right to rely on it, that the use of such information guarantees the recognition of the good faith of his/her behavior.

In general, legislation and jurisprudence of the Russian Federation in general supports this conclusion. The Law on Information states that "information in any state information system is official and authorized state bodies are obliged to ensure the reliability and relevance of the information contained in such information system, access to this information in cases and in the manner prescribed by law, as well as protection of this information from unauthorized access, destruction, modification, blocking, copying, provision, distribution and other illegal actions" [17].

This rule serves as the basis for refusing to enter knowingly unreliable information into the state information system. In addition, on the basis of specified rules any person may request an exception from SIS inaccurate (irrelevant) information, challenging the legitimacy of state authority, expressed in inclusion in the SIS of false information (or omission resulting in the failure of updating outdated information). As the court pointed out in the case "The people against Thermal Protection Ltd" [18], the reliability of information placed in a single state register is one of the principles of its formation, and its users have the right to receive reliable information. This right is violated if, as a result of the actions of the company and/or the actions of the registering body, inaccurate information will be placed in the state registration resource.

Unfortunately, Russian legislation does not contain requirements regarding the completeness of information in state information systems, as well as ways to protect a person who has suffered from unreliable official information. Practice confirm only the right of a person to demand the exclusion of inaccurate information from the SIS, while the burden of proving the unreliability of the information lies on that person.

We believe that if certain information is declared as official and the law fixes the duty of the state to ensure the reliability of such information, this must be followed by a presumption of its authenticity.

Significantly this means that a person has the right: (a) to rely on such information, (b) expect other persons' legal actions and decisions based on the presumption of authenticity of this information, (c) claim compensation for harm resulting from the use of unreliable official information.

There is a certain tendency to recognize the legitimacy and conscientiousness of the person's actions based on the use of official information.

So, according to the Resolution of the Plenum of the Supreme Arbitration Court of the Russian Federation [19], the tax benefit may be recognized as unfounded if the inspection proves that the taxpayer acted without due diligence and caution and he/she should have been aware of violations committed by the counterparty (in particular, due to the relationship of interdependence or affiliation taxpayer with a counterparty). The Ministry of Finance of the Russian Federation explains that one of the circumstances that testifies to the manifestation by the taxpayer of diligence and caution in choosing a counterparty is the use of official sources of information characterizing the activities of the counterparty [20]. At the same time, in practice, official sources of information (in particular, free services of the Federal Tax Service of Russia) will only partially help to avoid tax claims and prove law-abiding in court, and additional actions need to be taken to check counterparties.

Of course, courts are not ready to apply this approach to all state information systems. There are several thousand such IS in the Russian Federation. The largest of them are: Unified portal of state services, Personal account of the taxpayer, SIS of housing and communal services, etc. They are designed to inform users of their rights and responsibilities. But the lack of information about the penalty for violation of traffic rules in the personal account on the Unified portal of state services is currently not the basis for the citizen not to pay such a fine. And this situation is linked with a more general problem of the reliability of lack of information on official websites and information systems.

4 The Problem of Reliability of Lack of Information

An ordinary citizen estimates the authenticity of information as its completeness. Accordingly, if a citizen trusts a certain site (registry, another information system) as a source of official information, he/she bases his/her actions not only on the information posted on this site, but on the information that does not exist there (or the citizen could not find it).

The situation can be illustrated by the following example. In 2008, in the Russian Federation, during the liberalization of business legislation undertaken by President Dmitry Medvedev, the law "On the Protection of the Rights of Legal Entities and Individual Entrepreneurs in the Implementation of State Control (Supervision) and Municipal Control" was adopted [21]. In accordance with this law, the annual plan of planned inspections should be brought to the attention of interested persons by means of posting the plan on the official website of the state or municamental supervisory authority. A businessman received a notice from regional divisions of Rosreestr that his co-op will be checked for the implementation of land legislation according to theplan. The entrepreneur appealed to the consolidated audit plan posted on the website of the Altai Territory Prosecutor's Office, where there was no data on his co-op. Various overlays of inter-agency data transmission caused the above noted situation. The entrepreneur notified Rosreestr that "he does not intend to appear anywhere or give anything". The court did not support his position [22].

This situation could theoretically be resolved in favor of the entrepreneur, since his right to access to information was violated as a result of inaction of the state body. However, everything is not so unambiguous, when the information on the site is actually posted, but not found by standard search tools. For example, on many websites of government agencies of the Russian Federation, information is actually present, but the search engine of the site in response to a query produces a negative result.

In our opinion, talking about real provision of access to information is only valid when, having received a negative answer from the search engine, the user will be able to refer to it as a legal fact, that is, the circumstance causing, in accordance with the legal norms, the occurrence, change or termination of legal relations [23, p. 471]. In other words, the law should provide the user with a guarantee of reliability of lack of information (negative information). Technically, this can be solved by providing the user with an automatically generated electronic document containing the search query string, the date of access to the site, the system response to the request and the current version of the search engine manual. The document must be certified by an electronic digital signature and have evidentiary value in the court. To date, the legislation of Russia and other countries does not provide for such mechanisms that guarantee the reliability of negative information [24].

5 The Problem of Information Quality in State Information Systems

The problem of reliability of lack of information is part of a more general problem of information quality in state information systems.

Unlike federal unified state portals, the relevance and completeness of information available through the information systems of regional and local agencies often leaves much to be desired. This is due to a number of objective reasons. First of all, there are financial and personnel restrictions in the sphere of work with information. But a more important reason is that the information system and related technological processes of information gathering and processing could often be designed without taking into account the goal of ensuring 100% authenticity of the information [24]. Even in the State Automated System "Elections", which has been in operation since 1990 and is one of the most reliable state information systems in Russia, the error of the voters list is 300 thousand people [25, p. 16].

Some information systems that are created and maintained by government agencies receive information from external sources that are very difficult to control. For example, in 2015, the Russian Federation created an information and analytical system "All-Russian vacancy base "Work in Russia"", which is filled with employers [26]. The bodies of the employment service are obliged to evaluate the information in the system for completeness, reliability and compliance with the established requirements. However, it is quite obvious that it is not possible to check the availability of each vacancy, and it is not advisable to conduct such checkup. There are other systems that are filled at the subjective discretion (including those intended for internal use by government bodies, for example, for organizing document circulation or simply messaging). Some systems are under implementation and testing. However, under Russian law, all such systems are public, and therefore they are the source of official information. The law also obliges to ensure access to all unclassified information that is at the disposal of the state body. A citizen who plans his actions on the basis of information obtained from such a system, as a rule, does not have an opportunity to assess the "internal kitchen" of the public authority that affects the quality of information in the IS.

Of course, this problem is not unique to the Russian Federation. In the United States, government agencies are more independent in making decisions about their own information programs and the information systems they have created. In particular, they independently established a policy of using information systems. For example, the PACER (Public Access to Electronic Records) information system is used as the main service of electronic justice in the United States. It was created on the initiative of the Judicial Conference (the national decision-making body for the US federal courts) [27]. All federal courts support the PACER database with respect to information on cases in its jurisdiction. Karl Malamud notes that developers of the system abuse the monopoly position and the price policy makes the system accessible only to wealthy people, and the fee is not collected for the result (obtaining the necessary document), but for a search query (which may not give the desired result). In addition, there is no liability for placing information in the system, which leads to the possibility of manipulating electronic documents. There was a precedent for removing more than 1,000 documents from PACER, and their restoration, even after numerous appeals and complaints from the Congress, depended solely on the goodwill of the court staff [28].

6 Types of State Information Systems Based on the Possibility of Ensuring the Authenticity of Information

Information systems of state bodies (including those containing open information, which can be accessed via the web interface) vary significantly both in respect of the types of information placed in them, its sources and legal significance, and the capacity of authorized bodies to ensure the reliability of information [29]. We propose to distinguish three groups of such information systems.

1. SIS, the information in which has a legal value. In other words, the information is reliable and reflects the legal status de facto because it is located in such an information system. This category includes, in particular, various state registers. Even if the information is entered in the register illegally (including cases of falsification), it is impossible to speak about its unreliability - especially if the entry in the register is the primary document. The owner of the real estate is a person whose information is entered in the register of rights, limitations of rights and encumbrances of immovable property until the contrary is established (and the entry in the register has not been changed accordingly). Information in such SIS records is a legal fact. It is equally a legal fact, the only evidence of the existence of a registered right. Information in such systems is official, its completeness, relevance and reliability are guaranteed by the state. For the stability of legal relations, reliable legal protection is important. It is no accident that Article 285.3 of the Criminal Code of the Russian Federation provides criminal liability for falsification of state registers.
2. Information in second category state information systems is not primary and has no legal value but it has three important features: (a) the information in these systems is

intended to inform citizens and other persons about their rights, duties, etc.; (b) the reliability of the information is important for the sustainability of legal relationships related to the use of it; (c) state bodies and other persons providing the formation and maintenance of an information system have the ability to control the quality of the information. As an example, the Russian Federal Information System of State Final Certification can be cited. This system contains information about the results of the state final certification. The universities use it to check the information provided by the applicants [14]. Obviously, the situation in which information in the system is unreliable will lead to a violation of the constitutional right of the applicant for education, in connection with which special guarantees are needed. We believe that the information in such SIS should be official information. It may differ from reality (through the fault of the information provider or the operator, due to an error in the software, etc.), but harm reduction guarantees should be provided for its users. The law should establish the duty of the authorized bodies and the GIS operator to take measures to ensure the reliability of information, measures of responsibility for violation of this obligation. Only timely updating of the database (in the sphere of state and municipal management) and maintaining it up-to-date can ensure the confidential nature of the information contained in it and the possibility of unconditional use by the subjects of law as the initial grounds for committing legally significant actions.

3. There are information systems that are public, but at the same time objectively can not meet strict quality criteria for the information contained in them (for example, the above-mentioned all-Russian vacancy database). It seems obvious that such systems should not be considered as a source of official information.

7 Conclusions and Prospects

The development of a democratic information society is largely built on the idea of openness of the governmental information. However, openness is not enough if a citizen can not trust such information in such a way as to confidently and safely base his actions on it, including actions that entail significant legal consequences [30].

Of course, the key measures to ensure such a state are of an organizational and technical nature. State information systems, the organization of processes for collecting, processing and providing information should be improved. But the law plays a necessary role in this system of measures, a sort of facade of the building in which a citizen sees a real guarantee of protecting his/her interests.

In this regard, we consider it very important to develop the category of an "official information" in international law. The consolidation of this category in national legislation is necessary. It is also necessary to recognize the presumption of reliability of such information, which gives its users appropriate rights. The very first step in this direction is the practice of recognizing as illegal the decision of a state body, according to which unreliable information receives official status (including by posting in the state information system). A person should be able to claim compensation for harm caused by such an unlawful decision. Ultimately, any citizen or other entity should have a guarantee of recognition of good faith behavior, if this behavior is based on information received from the government through a request, by accessing a site or the information system of this body.

Classification of information systems, depending on the objective possibilities to ensure the quality of information (a kind of gradation of "officiality") is also important for solving this problem. We offer a three-level gradation: (1) information systems with right-establishing information; (2) information systems of official information; (3) information systems that provide information witch is available to the public authorities without guaranteeing its reliability. Within the boundaries of one information system or information resource, all categories can occur. The marking of relevant sections and education of citizens (users of official information) about the consequences of using a particular category are necessary.

The issue of the legal meaning of derivative information, which is formed as a result of automatic processing of primary information (including various summaries, reports, search results, etc.) is relevant. The official status of such information depends both on the status of the primary information (it is obvious that the right-establishing information can be obtained only if all the initial data belong to the same category) and on the characteristics of the data processing algorithm. (An incorrect algorithm for processing a search query can produce incorrect negative information, even if all the source information is complete and reliable). This issue deserves further study.

References

1. Elder, N.C.M.: Government in Sweden: The Executive at Work. Elsevier Science, Amsterdam (2013)
2. Travnikov, N.: The main stages of the formation of individual rights in the information sphere. Mod. Law **2**, 43–47 (2016). (in Russian)
3. Gritsenko, E., Babelyuk, E., Proskuryakova, M.: Development of the right to access to information in the field of public administration in Russian and German constitutional law. Comp. Const. Rev. **5**, 10–27 (2015). (in Russian)
4. Mendel, T.: Freedom of information: a comparative legal survey. UNESCO, Paris (2008). http://unesdoc.unesco.org/images/0015/001584/158450e.pdf
5. Bachilo, I., Lopatin, V., Fedotov, M.: Information Law. Legal Center Press, St. Petersburg (2001). (in Russian)
6. Fedoseeva, N.: The right of citizens to access to information in the Russian Federation. Civ. Law **3**, 6–11 (2007). (in Russian)
7. Sheverdyaev, S.: The right to information: to the question of the constitutional and legal essence. Law Polit. **10**, 91–100 (2001). (in Russian)
8. Federal Law No. 262-FZ of December 22, 2008: On providing access to information on the activities of courts in the Russian Federation
9. Federal Law No. 8-FZ of 09.02.2009: On providing access to information on the activities of state bodies and local self-government bodies
10. eGovernment in France, February 2015, Edition 17. European Commission (2015). https://joinup.ec.europa.eu/sites/default/files/document/2015-04/egov_in_france_-_february_2015_-_v.17_final.pdf

11. Amelin, R., Channov, S., Polyakova, T.: Direct democracy: prospects for the use of information technology. In: Chugunov, A.V., Bolgov, R., Kabanov, Y., Kampis, G., Wimmer, M. (eds.) DTGS 2016. CCIS, vol. 674, pp. 258–268. Springer, Cham (2016). https://doi.org/10.1007/978-3-319-49700-6_24
12. Sundgren, B.: What is a public information system. Int. J. Public Inf. Syst. 1, 81–99 (2005)
13. Bundin, M., Martynov, A.: Russia on the way to open data. In: Current Governmental Initiatives and Policy. Conference. dg.o 2015. Digital Government and Wicked Problems: Climate Change, Urbanization, and Inequality. Arizona State University, USA, 27–30 May 2015, pp. 320–322. ACM, New York (2015)
14. Amelin, R., Channov, S.: State information systems in e-government in the Russian Federation: problems of legal regulation. In: Proceedings of the 2nd International Conference on Electronic Governance and Open Society: Challenges in Eurasia (EGOSE 2015), pp. 129–132. ACM, New York (2015)
15. Lessig, L.: Code and Other Laws of Cyberspace. Basic Books, New York (1999)
16. Begtin, I.: How can you not publish public data and why not all XML files are equally useful (2013). https://habrahabr.ru/company/infoculture/blog/201260/
17. Federal Law No. 149-FZ of July 27, 2006: On information, information technologies and information protection
18. Decree of the Federal Arbitration Court of the Volga region from 27.02.2014 in case No. A65-11193 (2013)
19. Decree of the Plenum of the Supreme Arbitration Court of the Russian Federation of 12.10.2006 No. 53: On evaluation by arbitration courts of the justification of receiving a tax benefit by a taxpayer. Bull. Supreme Arbitr. Court. Russ. Fed. 12 (2006)
20. Danilov, S.: Due diligence: show and prove. Pract. Account. 9, 44–47 (2016). (in Russian)
21. Federal Law No. 294-FZ of 26.12.2008: On protection of the rights of legal entities and individual entrepreneurs in the exercise of state control (supervision) and municipal control
22. Demin, P.: Why controllers are in no hurry to post plans for inspections on the Internet (2010). (in Russian). http://www.altapress.ru/story/49647
23. Perevalov, V. (ed.): Theory of State and Law: A Textbook for Universities. Norma, Moscow (2004)
24. Ziemba, E., Obłąk, I.: The survey of information systems in public administration in Poland. Interdiscip. J. Inf. Knowl. Manag. 9, 31–56 (2014)
25. Churov, V.: The development of electronic technology in the electoral system of the Russian Federation. In: Digital Administration Law in Russia and in France. Conference Proceedings, Moscow, Canon+, pp. 15–20 (2014). (in Russian)
26. Decree of the Government of the Russian Federation No. 885 of August 25, 2015: On the Information and Analytical System All-Russian Vacancy Database "Work in Russia"
27. PACER Policies and Procedures (2014). https://www.pacer.gov/documents/pacer_policy.pdf
28. Malamud, C.: Memorandum of Law. A national strategy of litigation, supplication, and agitation (2015). https://yo.yourhonor.org
29. Homburg, V.: Understanding E-Government: Information Systems in Public Administration. Routledge, New York (2008)
30. Cordella, A., Iannacci, F.: Information systems in the public sector: the e-Government enactment framework. J. Strateg. Inform. Syst. (2010). https://doi.org/10.1016/j.jsis.2010.01.001 (2010)

Blockchain and a Problem of Procedural Justice of Public Choice

Leonid Smorgunov[(✉)]

St. Petersburg State University, Universitetskaya nab., 7/9,
St. Petersburg 199034, Russia
l.smorgunov@spbu.ru

Abstract. In public policy theory there is a problem of just procedure which could be used in obtaining a fair result in decision. Blockchain as a network of distributed registers is often positioned as an institution ensuring the fairness of decisions by voting on the basis of a consensual procedure. Consensus is achieved in the blockchain interactions through various algorithms (Proof of Work, Proof of Stake, Byzantine Fault Tolerance, Modified Federated Byzantine Agreement) that provide different rules for a procedural justice. Current political theory distinguishes between pure, perfect and imperfect procedural justice. The article analyzes the political ontology of the pure procedural justice of blockchain-technology. This ontology relies not on the legal nature of interaction in the network, but on the technical and social immediacy of trust, cooperation and co-production. The empirical basis of the study is the analysis of cases of using blockchain-voting on the platform of "Active Citizen" (Moscow).

Keywords: Blockchain · Procedural justice · Reputation
Autonomous identity · Trust · Reciprocity · Collaboration · Active citizen

1 Introduction

Network technologies of distributed data (registers) were first used in the financial sphere (2008), and then began to expand to services, trade, local government, art, and other areas. However, the social and political nature of this technology has not yet been explored. Moreover, the available research reveals only certain aspects of the socio-political nature of blockchain technology, and are primarily descriptive and hypothetical. Moreover, the studies are dispersed between different branches of knowledge, and that reduces their effectiveness, taking into account the humanitarian and technical nature of distributed data technology. In this respect, it is important to develop the foundations for a new synthesized scientific direction of "digital social humanitaristics".

Within the framework of research on the potential of blockchain in reconstructing political reality, the issues of involvement, participation and "citizenship" of the population in the digital space of local communities has become especially important. Over the past 3 to 5 years, practical experience in the use of distributed networks in addressing issues of territorial development and public policy, including Russia (the Active Citizen platform, Moscow, based on the Ethereum concepts) has been

D. A. Alexandrov et al. (Eds.): DTGS 2018, CCIS 858, pp. 13–23, 2018.
https://doi.org/10.1007/978-3-030-02843-5_2

accumulated. While these platforms are aimed mainly at informing citizens about the existing problems of local development and assessing public opinion on pressing issues, the popularization of mobile applications that provide easier access to information also creates opportunities for using e-voting mechanisms to make mostly non-political decisions (for example, voting for the best name for a street or a metro station). It seems that this stage of development of electronic platforms (including the blockchain system) can be defined as the stage of "learning", which involves raising awareness, competence and engaging citizens in "smart" networks for making political decisions. An important indicator of the success of the use of blockchain platforms in political processes at the local level is the possibility of "being heard" for different social groups, and the absence of direct control by political institutions. The question arises about the readiness of the political system to move to new principles of digital state governability, or the need for such a transition. As civil involvement promotes the development of "liquid democracy" in local communities, when the subjects of politics choose and vote only for matters of major importance, this implements a "flashing" of the political agenda.

The technology of network distributed databases (blockchain) has been the subject of research since 2008 [16]. In subsequent works, a number of theoretical and practical questions for the use of blockchain in various spheres of human activity and its interactions with other people are described, in particular in the field of finance [1, 22]. In recent years, particular attention has been paid to the philosophical, social and political theories of the blockchain [3, 10, 12, 14, 21, 23]. The role of knowledge, information and trust in new blockchain technologies and their impact on society is studied [6]. The perspectives of this methodology and its applicability have been formed almost everywhere, where it is a question of large data, transactions, registers, and virtual communication flows. Much attention is paid to the administrative problems of the blockchain, with emphasis on the challenges, risks and limitations of this technology [7, 8, 19, 20]. In the theoretical perspective of analyzing the possibilities of blockchain in governance, the decentralized network design, reducing transaction costs, transparency of operations and confidentiality, increasing the speed of ongoing processes, reliability and security, as well as increasing the degree of "awareness" of decision-making, achieved by the possibility of tracking all the stages of the workflow cycle, are especially important for the public sector at the present stage. Primary research on ontological questions of blockchain (philosophical, political, sociological) formed the idea of a transition from an institutional governance architecture with representation and hierarchy (centralism), to a procedural one, based on a humanitarian and technical platform of networked cooperation with free identification organized by anarchy, and distributed knowledge. Along with the optimistic position regarding the political, social and technological effectiveness of the blockchain-technology, there is a well-founded judgment about the risks and challenges that arise for a society associated with the de-institutionalization of interactions, the instability and imbalance in the development of public life, and the use of new technologies by criminals and terrorists. One of the central issues in the optimistic and critical areas is the lack of clarity regarding the new nature of the organization, and hence governance and governability in distributed networks, including their use in the public sphere.

All these problems are important and promising for the theory of public choice. *This article raises only one significant issue*, which, in our opinion, lies at the basis of solving other problems - *the nature of the decision-making process in the blockchain*. In this respect, the blockchain is a new institutional technology of public choice, which provides pure procedural justice based on such organization principles as publicity, initial disinterest, and consensus. In this sense, we use the concept of John Rawls about the kinds of perfect, imperfect and pure procedural justice. Rawls wrote: "Pure procedural justice is obtained when there is no independent criterion for the right result: instead there is a correct or fair procedure as such that the outcome is likewise correct or fair, whatever it is, provided that the procedure has been properly followed" [16: 75]. Rawls believed that the principles of justice he derived as fairness, when applied to the basic institutional structure of society ensure in real application, a pure procedural justice for the cooperation of people. Consequently, *the task of the paper is not to define the blockchain technology as a model of pure procedural justice, but to justify the principles on which the real use of blockchain gives a just result*.

The example of the "Active citizen", of course, is not a textbook to describe this process or to find new approaches and reflections. However, it allows us to describe gradually the introduction of new technological rules into public policy in Russia. Blockchain algorithms are similar to the basic conditions for Rawls' pure procedural justice. Their reconstruction makes it possible to understand that blockchain is not only a technology, but also an institution of interaction. At the same time, Rawls emphasized that real procedural justice is achieved not in the course of developing rules, but in the process of following them. This is why the paper describes two mutually intersecting topics. On the one hand, as the rules of blockchain promote procedural justice. On the other hand, how these rules are developed step by step in practice (on the platform "Active citizen").

2   Blockchain in Russia: Active Citizen (Moscow)

In Russia, blockchain technology began to penetrate many spheres of economic life in 2016. Many politicians and businessmen are engaged in stimulating its use, beginning with the Russian Prime Minister Dmitry Medvedev. Today we have some experience of using this technology in the banking sector, in public administration, in electoral processes, as well as statements about its imminent implementation. The "National Public monitoring" in the upcoming presidential elections in Russia will take advantage of blockchain technology. This system will store all the data from 100,000 independent observers. Also, the technology will help to make the exit-polls from polling stations as honest and transparent as possible. This is a joint project of VtSIOM and 2chain. The project will be one of the world's first electoral studies using this technology. In December 2017, the opening of the Blockchain Competences Center of Vnesheconombank (VEB) and NITU "MISiS" in Moscow took place. This is the first specialized expert center in Russia to introduce blockchain technologies in public administration. The international companies Ethereum, Bitfury, Waves, E & Y, PwC became partners and residents of the Center. In connection with the Center, there have been meetings of government working groups on the implementation of blockchain in the public administration, training courses for officers and specialists of government agencies, and international seminars and conferences on blockchain topics. Recently "Sberbank" and "Alfa-Bank" held the first interbank payment in Russia with the help of technology of distributed registries ("blockchain"). Minpromtorg of Russia (Ministry of Industry and Trade) together with the Vnesheconombank (VEB), launched a project in November 2017 in a test mode accounting for forest resources on the basis of blockchain technology. Monitoring the condition of forest areas will be done by drones.

This is only a small part of the projects that have already been noted in the Russian information space. One of the important areas of use of the blockchain is the *"Active Citizen"* platform, which was initiated in Moscow to involve citizens in the choice of prioritized areas for the development of urban life in the capital, and to address topical current issues. This platform is part of the system of interaction between the city authorities and citizens, called system of joint decisions "Together" (see Table 1).

Table 1. Moscow Mayor' Portal

Joint decisions "Together" (www.mos.ru)		
Moscow – Our City	Active Citizen	Crowdsourcing Platform
www.gorod.mos.ru	www.agmos.ru	www.crowd.mos.ru
1178221 registered	2035198 registered	140285 participants
2254630 problems	3509 polls	88857 proposals

The joint decision system, formed by the mayor of Moscow for citizens' participation in the affairs of the city, includes a number of platforms related to the open government, open data, government services, as well as platforms for organizing the direct participation of citizens in public policy. Platforms for participation are composed of three main elements. This is the platform "Moscow - Our City", aimed at finding practical solutions to city problems. Currently, it has 1,178,221 registered users. Since its inception, 2,254,630 problems have been solved in urban life. The second platform is a platform for crowdsourcing. It is designed to identify interesting ideas and create projects relating to the city. The latest data on this platform speak of 16 projects implemented and 88,857 proposals and ideas received. The third platform is "Active Citizen". It was established in 2014 on the initiative of the Government of Moscow. Today 2,035,198 people are registered, and through it 3,509 polls have been conducted.

The "Active Citizen" is a platform for conducting open referendums in electronic form, created on the initiative of the Moscow Government in 2014. The project allows people to conduct citywide and local voting on a wide range of topics. Every week, Muscovites are invited to discuss important issues for the city. On the platform, you need to register, and to participate in a local vote, you must specify your address. For the passage of each vote, the participant is awarded points. Having gained 1000 points, you attain the status of "Active Citizen" and the opportunity to exchange them for city services (parking hours, visits to theaters and museums) or useful souvenirs. Bonus points can be earned also if you visit the application more often, invite friends, and share information about the passed votes in social networks.

To solve the task of ensuring the transparency of the project, a number of tools have been implemented that allow users to monitor the progress of voting and monitor the reliability of the results obtained. In particular, each user who participated in the voting can:

- check the correctness of recording their vote;
- in online mode, monitor the overall dynamics of voting results.

For these purposes, *anyone can install a special program based on the system of the Ethereum, that is, everyone can become a member of the network of blockchain.* This program allows network participants to see in real time those questions which have passed, or are still being voted on, as well as the appearance of new votes. The system allows anyone to become a member of the blockchain network. not only as a resident of Moscow, but also as an organization. Blockchain, as indicated by the organizers of the program, allows for a number of additional functions:

- check the chronology of the appearance of votes and confirm their uniqueness;
- see the distribution of votes on issues;
- see the voices of real people (personal data is encrypted).

It is argued that the more people become members of the network, the higher the trust in the data stored in the system. Blockchain also gives the opportunity to control all votes in the "Active Citizen". The user installs on his personal computer a distribution program "Parity UI" to create a node of the blockchain network and starts receiving votes from the "Active Citizen" site in real time. Viewing the content of voting on a particular issue in the blockchain allows each participant of the distributed network to receive information about the question ID, the title of the question (CurrentVersionTitle), the number of voters on the issue (VoterCount), the resulting versions of the survey (AllExistingVersions), and the number of votes for each of the answers in the general list (CurrentVersionResults). Judging by the number of nodes, confirmation of which is required by the application, at present this program is used by more than five hundred and fifty thousand users of "Active Citizen", including organizations (Higher School of Economics) and the Data Processing Center of the Information Technology Department of the Moscow Government.

In 2018, this system in Moscow offered the use of multi-apartment housing blocks for citizens to vote. For this purpose, the "Electronic House" project is being implemented. This project is based on the possibility of Ethereum to form decentralized autonomous organizations (DAO).

In these last two cases of using blockchain technology to monitor the progress of voting and to make decisions, a number of characteristics of distributed networks that are related to the problem of procedural justice are seen. First of all, this is *the honesty of the conditions* of the emerging consensus, determined by the technological characteristics of distributed networks, and a small degree of identification in connection with the cryptographic protocols of recording and presenting users. Secondly, it is the acceptance of the terms of interaction that ensure the implementation of *the principle of reciprocity* in the exchange of goods, decisions, knowledge and supervision. In this respect, the blockchain is a platform of collaboration for reciprocal benefits, whether it concerns finances, things, norms or regulation. Fair interaction conditions, together with the principle of reciprocity, create a form of procedural justice in which incentives for genuine collaboration arise.

3   Blockchain and the Fairness of the Conditions for Collaboration

In the process of using the Ethereum, various problems arose associated with the protection of its ecosystem. In this regard, not everything is perfect with regards to ensuring the integrity of the participants. However, security issues do not remove from the agenda the issue of securing such a reputation for the blockchain, which is related to its perception as an honest system of cooperation. Dhillon Vikram, David Metcalf, and Max Hooper wrote: "On the other side were those committed to the ideals of decentralization and immutability. In the eyes of many in this camp, the blockchain is an inherently just system in that it is deterministic, and anyone choosing to use it is implicitly agreeing to that fact. In this sense, the DAO attacker had not broken any law" [24: 76]. Blockchain as a technology of distributed networks based on cryptographic protocols which provides a number of conditions for an honest procedure for interaction in solving various tasks of creating and sharing resources, including finance, goods, services, information, knowledge, norms and regulations. First of all, such conditions include *reputation, autonomous identity* and *trust*.

Reputation means the ability to judge the value of a counterparty of a transaction, based on a variety of information sources. As a rule, this process of obtaining information is costly and is included in the transaction costs. Ethereum uses reputation management in the process of concluding smart contracts or creating and operating decentralized autonomous organizations. Technologically, as Ethereum's White Paper states: "The contract is very simple; all it is, is a database inside the Ethereum network that can be added to, but not modified or removed from. Anyone can register a name with some value, and that registration then sticks forever. A more sophisticated name registration contract will also have a "function clause" allowing other contracts to query it, as well as a mechanism for the "owner" (i.e. the first registrant) of a name to change the data or transfer ownership. One can even add reputation and web-of-trust functionality on top" [11]. Reputation in the blockchain is formed in the process of interaction P2P on the basis of cryptoprotocols, and is confirmed by the possibility of open checks and obtaining of various scores and the crypto currency itself. As many developers and users of distributed networks point out, the reputation is directed against abuse that can arise here in the form of various forms of breach of honesty. These include: collusion—shilling attack; reputation cashing; strategic deception; faking identity. The advantage of the blockchain system for reputation is the invariability of information about the user and the impossibility of forging it. According to the developers of the new protocol (PoS – Proof of Stake), it allows to ensure honest behavior to achieve the Nash equilibrium, thus neutralizing attacks such as selfish mining [13: 10].

Reputation in the "Active Citizen" system is built on the basis of three main processes. *Firstly*, there is activity in the discussion and voting of issues put forward by citizens or the government for discussion. For this, each participant receives a certain number of points (a kind of crypto currency that can be spent on services or goods). *Secondly*, points are set for activity to attract attention to this system and other users of networks. *Thirdly*, on the basis of previous forms of activity, a citizen can reach the status of "expert", and participate in the discussion, offering his "valued" opinion.

Autonomous identity in the blockchain is akin to the Rawlsian idea of the "veil of ignorance", when negotiators do not include their status characteristics in the process of weighing their preferences, and cannot form an opinion that is interested in others. "People", - W. Reijers et al. writes, - "interacting through blockchain applications could theoretically operate through a "veil of ignorance" – in the sense that they could enjoy a high level of "pseudo anonymity" and the technology would be structurally incapable of discriminating against them on the basis of who they are" [18: 140]. Of course, anonymity in addition to the positive sides generates a number of threats for the use of so-called dark networks [2, 15]. However, here we only pay attention to the conditions of anonymity as the quality of the initial state from which the possibility of a trusted consensus grows. Although the open "Active Citizen" platform can use cryptographic protocols for the participants, the registration process implied is still a departure from anonymity, because it includes verification. A unique participant ID is a random number that is assigned to a user once, and forever, when registering with the Active Citizen project. This identifier is used by the user himself to check the results of his vote in a common array of open data with all voting results. Also, a unique user ID may be asked for, to provide project support staff with additional verification of the user. However, the proposed blockchain system for monitoring the voting process (Parity UI) is based on the anonymity of the participants. In the blockchain you can check the chronology of the appearance of votes and confirm their uniqueness. You can see the distribution of votes on issues and look at the voices of real people (personal data is encrypted). But more importantly, the more members of the network become members of the network, the higher the trust in the data stored in the system. Blockchain allows the control of all votes in Active Citizen.

In this respect, *trust* is the third important condition for cooperation. Blockchain provides a specific mode of trust, based on technology. Therefore, it is often pointed out that the blockchain network organizes cooperation almost without trust, meaning socially organized trust. It produces "consensus without requiring centralized trust" [9: 5]. Trust in technology means that the procedural justice provided by the blockchain is determined by consensus, which is based on almost apodictic truth, not authority or power. Such trust combined with autonomy ensures the objectivity of public choice. From Rawls, "one consequence of trying to be objective, of attempting to frame our moral conceptions and judgments from a shared point of view, is that we are more likely to reach agreement" [17: 453].

4 Reciprocity for the Blockchain Community

It is known that cryptocurrency provides mutual benefits better than fiat money. The norms of reciprocity arising in the blockchain networks are provided by a proof of work (PoW), a proof of stake (PoS), Byzantine Fault Tolerance, Modified Federated Byzantine Agreement and are included in the system of qualities of the blockchain community. However, reciprocity is not only the principle of allocation of resources, but also of a public choice based on pure procedural justice. Reciprocity in public choice means that the interacting parties in the decision-making process will be pre-occupied with recognizing the claims of all parties to the agreement and will form a solution based on the compatibility of claims.

There is a difference in understanding the reciprocity between the economic and social approach. The economic approach links reciprocity with the circulation of money in the process of realizing the obligation to give, receive and return. The social understanding of reciprocity is based on the concept of gift and responsibility of the reciprocal response, which links the participants of the commune. Sometimes the social understanding of reciprocity on the basis of the blockchain is connected not with the obligation to repay the debt, but with a sharing economy or sharing community. "'Communal sharing' would then refer to more open and evolving groups than households... It would be characterized by sharing activities (by giving access to them) within the boundaries of a community, and by the possible voluntary nature of belonging to this community. It is important to stress that the action of sharing does not necessarily lead to debt relations (contrary to reciprocity)" [4: 14]. Blockchain creates conditions for reciprocity, introducing a system of associative currency for communal sharing. The first example of such currency was Bitcoin which could be used for communal sharing.

The "Active Citizen" system does not use cryptocurrency. This is written in its basic rules. The accrued scores for activity are only a factor of a certain incentive, and not a mutual exchange between citizens. However, the already existing experience of developing blockchain voting for multi-family houses could use communal sharing and associative money, such as a time bank. The Bank of Time is a socio-economic model based on the principles of mutual assistance and the initial equality of all participants and using non-market mechanisms for charity. In Russia in 2006 appeared the first Bank of Time. This was initiated by the Nizhny Novgorod businessman and head of the private charity foundation "Beginning", Sergei Ivanushkin, whose idea was supported and further developed by the leaders of the Nizhny Novgorod Volunteer Service. Currently, the Time Bank is located in a number of Russian cities. In 2017 on the basis of combining the idea of a time bank with the technology of blockchain, an international Chronobank system emerged (see: https://chronobank.io/).

5 Blockchain as an Institution for Collaboration

In this regard, the question arises: what does the new blockchain technology produce concerning interrelations between people? Partnership or collaboration? Of course, at first glance, partnership is collaboration. Often these terms are used interchangeably.

Meanwhile, practice of partnership and collaboration makes it possible to divide the content of these forms of interaction and find their distinctive features. To compare these forms of mutual activity, we will use the work of Ros Carnwell and Alex Carson, who conducted a large analytical work to clarify these terms, based on the practice of interaction in the field of health and social protection [5: 11, 14–15].

Partnership characteristics: trust and confidence in accountability; respect towards specialized expertise; teamwork; crossing professional boundaries; members of the partnership share some interests; suitable management structure; common goals; open community within and between partner organizations; goal agreement; reciprocity; empathy.

Characteristics of *collaboration*: intellectual and cooperative efforts; knowledge and expertise are more significant than roles and positions; joint commitment; team-work; participation in planning and decision-making; non-hierarchical relations; joint examination; trust and respect for parties; partnership; interdependence; strong network communication; low wait times for a response.

As can be seen from the listed characteristics of the two principles of interaction, partnership and collaboration have some common, mutually intersecting characteristics of organizational, social, psychological and ethical plans. However, a comparative analysis of characteristics suggests that partnership is a more institutionalized and formalized type of interaction than collaboration.

The differences between these terms should be taken into account when comparing the contexts in which these relationships arise. Somewhere, the general dividing line lies in the difference between "being together" (being partners) and "acting together" (collaborating) [5: 10]. For a clearer division of these concepts, it can probably be said that partnership is a joint activity based on distributed (often equal) rights and duties aimed at achieving common goals, whereas collaboration is a joint activity based on the unconditional desire of the interacting parties to work together to achieve joint interests. The partnership is loaded with external legal conditions for joint activities, while collaboration implies an internal willingness to act together on the basis of mutual assistance and responsibility.

Mostly, the blockchain is a base for collaboration than partnership although some mixed features can be found during network interrelations. Collaboration through blockchain is based on the pure procedural justice. Blockchain is an institutional arrangement for collaboration, primarily because it reduces the costs of interactivity and the making of a complete agreement. However, this is not enough to assess the prospects for a new social and political association, which is promised by the protagonists of distributed networks. Given the collaborative type of cooperation, it can be said that the blockchain promises a new type of coordination of social actions, especially in the economy. As S. Davidson, P. De Filippi, and J. Potts write, "blockchain-based coordination may enable new types of economic activity that were previously not able to be governed by firms, markets or governments, because the transaction costs were too high to justify the expected benefits" [9: 16].

In public policy, the effect can be even more striking due to the fact that the new technology creates a space of fairness for honest decisions and mutual responsibility for their implementation. Not only economic opportunism can be reduced, but also opportunities to use the desire to become a free rider when resolving public issues.

However, these are only forecasts. By its basic parameters of pure procedural fairness, the detective should show its nature in practice. As Rawls wrote, "a fair procedure translates its fairness to the outcome only when it is actually carried out" [17: 75]. The "Active Citizen" program creates the conditions for such an effect. Expanding the use of the blockchain procedure will contribute to a more rational understanding of its initial opportunities and democratic direction.

6 Conclusion

Distributed data technology is gaining popularity in the economy and public policy. In the latter, it is used in the processes of voting, making decisions, determining agenda, policy evaluating, and other areas. The general belief of researchers is that the blockchain is not just a technology that increases the effects of economic production and political interaction but is an institution that creates new opportunities for the coordination of interactions. In the economy, the blockchain opposes opportunism and transaction costs. In politics, this technology provides honest conditions for public decisions. The main problem of procedural fairness is how to institutionalize fair conditions for public choice. In this respect, the blockchain, as a new institution, creates a space of opportunities for pure procedural fairness, ensuring reputation, autonomy, trust and reciprocity for participants in interaction. On this basis, collaboration arises that, without undermining the differences, contributes to a fair result. The experience of the Moscow "Active Citizen" project using blockchain demonstrates the promise of this technology in public policy. This program creates conditions for the effectiveness of learning for citizens, and for public officials to act honestly.

Some further reflections could be added. What is a blockchain? Technology or institution? Arguing about this, we must, probably, think in terms of techno-social knowledge without breaking technology and social relations. What is a bitcoin (e-coins)? Currency, money, commodity, security, assets, good or gift? In our opinion, rather narrow is the consideration of electronic money in terms of market exchange. It is probably necessary to look at this process as a system of reciprocity. What is a smart contract, based on consensus? Probably, this is only not a new form of legality, but a new form of communal sharing. What is blockchain governance? Definitely, block-chain is a technological instrument for reducing the transactional costs, but it is also new form of coordinative activity.

Funding. The author disclosed receipt of the following financial support for the research, authorship, and/or publication of this article: This work was supported with a grant from the Russian Foundation for Basic Research (grant 18-011-00756 A "Study of citizens participation and building digital government").

References

1. Antonopulos, A.: Mastering Bitcoin: Unlocking Digital Crypto-Currencies. O'Reilly Media, Sebastopol (2014)
2. Bancroft, A., Reid, P.S.: Challenging the techno-politics of anonymity: the case of cryptomarket users. Inf. Commun. Soc. **20**(4), 497–512 (2017)
3. Bjerg, O.: How is bitcoin money? Theory Cult. Soc. **33**(1), 53–72 (2016)
4. Blanc, J.: Making sense of the plurality of money: a polanyian attempt. In: SASE 29th Annual Meeting (Society for the Advancement of Socio-Economics), Lyon, France (2017)
5. Carnwell, R., Carson, A.: The concepts of partnership and collaboration. In: Carnwell, R., Buchanan, J. (eds.) Effective Practice in Health, Social Care and Criminal Justice: A Partnership Approach. Open Universities Press, Maidenhead (2008)
6. Clemons, E., Dewan, R., Kauffman, R., Weber, Th.: Understanding the information-based transformation of strategy and society. J. Manag. Inf. Syst. **32**(2), 425–456 (2017)
7. Cusumano, M.: Technology strategy and management: the bitcoin ecosystem. Commun. ACM **57**(10), 22–24 (2014)
8. Danaher, J., Hogan, M., Noone, Ch., et al.: Algorithmic governance: developing a research agenda through the power of collective intelligence. Big Data Soc. **4**(2), 1–21 (2017)
9. Davidson, S., De Filippi, P., Potts, J.: Blockchains and the economic institutions of capitalism. J. Inst. Econ. (Online), 1–20 (2018)
10. Dos Santos, R.: On the philosophy of bitcoin/blockchain technology, Is it a chaotic, complex system? Metaphilosophy **48**(5), 620–633 (2017)
11. Ethereum White Paper. A Next-Generation Smart Contract and Decentralized Application Platform. https://github.com/ethereum/wiki/wiki/White-Paper#applications. Accessed 17 Mar 2018
12. Greengard, S.: Internet of Things. MIT Press, Cambridge (2015)
13. Kiayias, A., Russell, A., David, B., Oliynykov, R.: Ouroboros: a provably secure proof-of-stake blockchain protocol. In: Katz, J., Shacham, H. (eds.) CRYPTO 2017. LNCS, vol. 10401, pp. 357–388. Springer, Cham (2017). https://doi.org/10.1007/978-3-319-63688-7_12
14. Manski, S.: The building the blockchain world, Technological commonwealth or just more of the same. Strat. Chang. **26**(5), 511–522 (2017)
15. Moore, D., Rid, T.: Cryptopolitik and the darknet. Surviv. Glob. Polit. Strat. **58**(1), 7–38 (2016)
16. Nakamoto, S.: Bitoin: a peer-to-peer electronic cash system. https://bitcoin.org/bitcoin.pdf. Accessed 21 June 2018
17. Rawls, J.: A Theory of Justice. Harvard University Press, Cambridge (1999)
18. Reijers, W., O'Brolchain, F., Haynes, P.: Governance in blockchain technologies & social contract theories. Ledger **1**(1), 134–151 (2016)
19. Scott, B., Loonam, J., Kumar, V.: Exploring the rise of blockchain technology: towards distributed collaborative organizations. Strat. Chang. **26**(5), 423–428 (2017)
20. Sherin, V.: Disrupting governance with blockchains and smart contracts. Strat. Chang. **26**(5), 499–509 (2017)
21. Swam, M., De Filippi, P.: Towards a philosophy of blockchain: a symposium. Metaphilosophy **48**(5), 603–619 (2017)
22. Swan, M.: Blockchain. O'Reilly Media, Sebastopol (2015)
23. Velasko, P.: Computing ledgers and the political ontology of the blockchain. Metaphilosophy **48**(5), 712–726 (2017)
24. Vikram, D., Metcalf, D., Hooper, M.: Blockchain Enabled Applications: Understand the Blockchain Ecosystem and How to Make It Work for You. Apress, Orlando (2017)

Competence-Based Method of Human Community Forming in Expert Network for Joint Task Solving

Mikhail Petrov[1,2], Alexey Kashevnik[1,2(✉)],
and Viktoriia Stepanenko[2]

[1] ITMO University, 49 Kronverksky Pr, St. Petersburg, Russia
{161307,189562}@niuitmo.ru
[2] SPIIRAS, 39, 14th Line, St. Petersburg, Russia
{161307,189562,174725}@niuitmo.ru

Abstract. Expert networks that are the community of professionals have become more popular in/over the last years. The paper presents a method of human community forming in expert network for joint task solving that is based on competence management approach. Related work analysis has been implemented and the requirements for the method development have been identified. The proposed method allows user to find the best possible community of experts for the reasonable time that is related to the number of experts and the number of skills in the competence management system.

Keywords: Competence management · Expert community forming
Joint task solving · Expert network

1 Introduction

Expert networks are the community of professionals in certain area that are joined together by an information system. This information system has to solve the following main tasks: expert community forming for joint task solving, experts rating determination, support of experts' professional and scientific activity, and searching for colleagues by interests. Modern publications in the areas of expert networks, human resource management, and competence management consider a set of tasks related to identifying the human competencies and its application to task solving. The task of a dynamic expert community forming for joint work on a project is not solved at the moment. Further investigation of the community forming problem is very important since it is a well-known fact that the project results highly depends on community performance. The formed community should satisfy with the skill requirements to the task, support the communication among participants, and provides ability to deal with emerging problems. Automatic or semi-automatic community composing methods can simplify a decision making process related to expert community management (Tables 1 and 2).

D. A. Alexandrov et al. (Eds.): DTGS 2018, CCIS 858, pp. 24–38, 2018.
https://doi.org/10.1007/978-3-030-02843-5_3

Table 1. Identified selection criteria for resource management

Criteria for selecting resources	[2]	[3]	[4]	[5]	[6]	[7]	[8]	[9]	[10]	[11]	[12]	[14]	[15]	[16]
Limiting criterions														
Compliance of the scope of work with resources	✓			✓	✓									✓
The community limitation	✓	✓									✓		✓	
Resource compatibility	✓		✓				✓	✓					✓	✓
Compliance with deadlines		✓												
Resource availability		✓	✓	✓	✓			✓			✓			
The competence importance for the task									✓		✓			
Prefiltering of the resources		✓			✓					✓	✓	✓		
Differentiation of the required and desirable task competence			✓				✓				✓			
Optimization criterions														
Maximizing the community competence	✓	✓							✓	✓	✓			✓
Maximizing the effectiveness of resources (quality/cost)		✓	✓											✓
Minimizing the cost of resources				✓	✓	✓	✓	✓				✓	✓	
The effectiveness of resources limitation		✓	✓		✓	✓								

The paper presents a method for human community forming in expert networks for joint task solving that is based on ontology-based competence representation of expert network participants [1]. The method will be implemented in the competence management system. It considers time, which expert could spend on task solving, cost of his/her work, and the degree of psychological influence on other expert as input data. Basic idea of the suggested community forming method is following: according to set restrictions, described input data, and task requirements the groups are composed; the next step is to calculate the optimality coefficient, which shows if the formed community could be optimized or not (for example, the number of community members could be reduced without performance quality loss). The estimation result of optimality

Table 2. The identified requirements to the methods considered

Method requirements	[2]	[3]	[4]	[5]	[6]	[7]	[8]	[9]	[10]	[11]	[12]	[14]	[15]	[16]
Binary matrix usage	✓		✓					✓						
Iterative solution finding		✓	✓	✓		✓	✓			✓	✓		✓	✓
Finding several solutions		✓			✓				✓	✓	✓			
Graphs usage for representing constrains				✓				✓					✓	✓
Finding solution in a reasonable computational time				✓				✓		✓			✓	✓
Considering resource change probability					✓									
Discrete competence levels usage					✓	✓				✓	✓	✓		
Different competences types usage							✓			✓	✓	✓	✓	✓
Construction of multi-level competences structure							✓							
Usage of fuzzy logic		✓				✓		✓	✓					

coefficient is displayed to the manager in the descending order as a list. Using the list the manager will be able to make a decision about the community for the task solving.

The rest of the paper is organized as follows. Section 2 considers the related works in the studied/investigated area. In the third section one can find a list with identified requirements to community forming methods and criteria for choosing resources. The developed method is represented in details in the fourth section. The conclusion summarizes the paper.

2 Related Work

The section considers the modern research in the area of resource management and existing methods for expert community forming over the last 10 years

Algorithms, which form a community for joint task solving taking into account time and budget constraints, required competencies for the task, and the degree of influence each expert on another one in the composed group were selected for analysis. All algorithms discussed in the paper could be divided into two big groups. The first group of algorithms takes into account most of the parameters/characteristics, listed above. However, they do not form a team, or community to complete a task, but create a plan or a sequence, which define the order of task performing and allocated resource (human resource as a rule) [4, 5, 7–9, 14]. The second group includes algorithms for expert community forming, but these algorithms often ignore important parameters as a degree of influence as budget restrictions etc. [2, 3, 6, 10–12, 15, 16].

Approaches presented in the paper [2] describe distribution of personnel between departments that perform certain work. The approaches are applicable to different variants of problem formulation and divided into three groups. The first group considers the number of places in a department that is strictly defined, and the number of experts that is enough to occupy all the positions. Besides, the number of places in a department may not be fixed, but limited by its maximum value. In these variants, internal and external part-time experts can also be considered. In the approaches of the first group, the required distribution of personnel is represented as a binary matrix. This matrix determines the inclusion of experts in the departments. The competencies of experts and the scope of work of the departments are presented as vectors. The required distribution of personnel should correspond to constraints given by equalities and inequalities, which are determined by each considered variant. The second group of approaches also takes into account the compliance of experts' required qualification and the cost of work. For this purpose vectors that contain bonus and penalty coefficients for competency excesses and deficiencies, as well as vectors of nominal and increased pay (for scope of work exceeding nominal) are additionally introduced. The most complex approaches which are considered in the third group include the following factors: compliance of the scope of work with the personnel capabilities, the expert qualification, the cost of their work, and the compatibility of experts in the departments. Experts' compatibility is presented as a matrix in which the columns and rows correspond to specific experts, and their intersection is a number from -10 to 10, indicating how one expert affects another by hindering or helping. The remaining factors are presented in the same form as in the approaches of the first and second groups. Considering experts' cost of work and the degree of influence on each other is an advantage of this algorithm. Nevertheless, the algorithm does not take into account time for a task.

Authors of the paper [3] deal with the selection methods for different types of resources in project management. These methods are used to find the optimal set of resources for each project or their combination. For this purpose, options of resource sets pertaining to each project are created or generated. The creation of resource sets occurs manually, semi-automatically or automatically, depending on the preferences and capabilities of the person who manages resources. Then, the options that do not meet the optimality criteria are removed. The following conditions are used as the criteria of optimality: compliance with implementation deadlines and budgets, availability of resources, increased quality and efficiency. The remaining options are sorted according to the priority of projects, their absolute usefulness (the difference between the numerical positive effects and the amount of risks and costs) or relative usefulness (the ratio of absolute usefulness to the amount of risks and costs). The described methods can be generalized to the case of fuzzy values. This algorithm finds an optimal solution taking into account time and budget constraints, expert availability, but does not consider an influence degree.

The model presented in the paper [4] considers the scheduling problem for various types of tasks, considering the requirements for efficient distribution of available resources and time, needed to achieve the set goals. The action planning for Russian segment crew of the International Space Station is offered as a scenario for this model. This plan satisfies the following conditions and limitations: using only available resources, support the accuracy of temporal relations between flight operations, presence of all necessary operations in the plan, restriction on total time of functioning of experts. The plan in the paper is a three-dimensional binary matrix containing a list of cosmonauts, discrete moments of time and planned operations. The cosmonauts' competences are represented in the form of vectors with values from 0 to 1. The availability of cosmonauts, resources and operations at each point in time and the need for resources for each operation are formalized as corresponding two-dimensional binary matrices. The model also takes into account the priority of operations defined by a vector that contains a fixed priority of the operation or the limit of the priority value that should be strived when placing operations in the plan. The optimal plan should be minimally deviated from the constraints given by equalities and inequalities. To develop the plan the authors use the device of genetic algorithms. The key feature of the algorithm is a resource availability and task priority consideration. But the resulting plan does not include a formed community for a task, but the sequence of tasks and allocated human resources.

Presented in the paper [5] methods are aimed at planning the medical services for patients at home. These methods are aimed at assigning patients to specialists, and generating the schedule for the specialists appointed to visit patients. In the first phase, these methods find a suitable solution, and in the second phase they optimize it. In the proposed methods the patients are presented as a complete directed weighted graph. In this graph the vertices represent patients, and the arcs represent possible trajectories between patients. Each arc is labeled with a distance. Both a patient and a specialist have a vector of competences, denoting required and acquired competences respectively. There is also a vector showing the number of visits of a specialist with each skill required to the patient disease, and a vector showing timetable. The following restrictions are taken into account in finding solutions: compliance of specialists' skills with patients' requirements, limited daily workload for specialists, limited the number of specialists for each patient. Optimization and required competencies analysis are the main features of the algorithm. Nevertheless, it does not form a community.

The authors of the paper [6] developed a reinforcement learning model to optimize human resource planning for a high-tech industry. The proposed model determines the optimal number of skilled workers that should be assigned for training other workers. One of the main attribute of workers is a knowledge level. There are three of them: the first level called new-hired, the second level called semi-experienced and the last one is described as fully experienced. The model considers the amount and cost of workers of all knowledge levels, the complexity of learning of the first and second level workers, represented by variables and coefficients. It should maximize the profit and minimize the cost for work. The model finds several solutions for all given states (periods of time) using probability of workers' transitions between states, which makes it more flexible. This algorithm takes into account knowledge levels of workers and forms a community according to them. However, the main idea of the algorithm is to form a balanced group, which includes high-level and low-level workers, but not a community for a specific task. This algorithm does not consider an influence degree among workers.

Genetic algorithms presented in the paper [7] solve the problem of scheduling jobs on a single machine that requires flexible maintenance under human resource competence and availability constraints. The first one is based on the sequential strategy. It generates the integrated production and maintenance schedules, and then assigns human resources to maintenance activities. The second algorithm is based on a total scheduling strategy and consists of generating integrated production and maintenance schedules that explicitly satisfy human resource constraints. The main task of both algorithms is to find an operation sequence of given job sets to minimize the objective expressed by the sum of tardiness. Each job that has to be processed on a single machine has a duration time for each competency level. The algorithm considers required competencies and resource availability, but the main goal is to create a sequence of actions, but not a community.

Human resource allocation problem is considered in the paper [8]. Authors use the inverse optimization method to solve the problem in order to take competency disadvantage and adjustment requirement into consideration. For this purpose the authors construct a competency indicator system, create a disadvantage structure identification model and apply the inverse optimization of human resources. The competency indicator system contains values and coefficients of psychology, attitude, skill and knowledge indicators of workers. The disadvantage structure identification model contains three competency levels. The lower level represents indicators from the competency indicator system. The values of the top and the middle levels are evaluated using these indicators and evaluation weight vectors. The inverse optimization should determine working hours' allocation plan of each kind of human resources for each kind of job so that the cost is as small as possible. The constraint parameters are total working hour needed for each job. Psychology, competence, skill and knowledge coefficients, a weight of coefficients are taken into account in the algorithm. Nevertheless, the result of computing is a sequence of actions without forming a community of experts.

Fuzzy resource-constrained project scheduling problem is presented in the paper [9]. Authors discussed a combinatorial NP-hard problem of constructing a special plan for performing a number of precedence related tasks subject to limited uncertain resources. The authors constructed the fuzzy heuristic-based approach to obtain a near optimal solution in a reasonable computational time. In the paper a project is characterized by 4 components: the set of projects activities, precedence constraints in this set, the set of renewable resources available at every moment and the set of project performance measures. The mathematical programming formulation of fuzzy scheduling problem is based on the binary matrix that represents whether each activity is completed in each period of time. The main objective of the scheduling is minimization of project completion time subject to the constraints on the precedence relationships and on renewable resource availability. The precedence relationships are given in a directed fuzzy graph; resource availability in each period of time is given in a resource binary matrix. The algorithm takes into account an order of tasks, optimizes results, and creates not a community of experts for a task, but a sequence of actions.

Method proposed in the paper [10] allows users to make a team for the chosen project and select a project manager. It consists of three steps: evaluation of the personnel's knowledge competence score for the project, organizing project team via genetic algorithm developed and selecting a project manager for this project. The project is represented as a set of keywords. The personnel's knowledge includes information about publications (reports, papers, patents etc.), which they published before. The aim of the first step is to evaluate personnel's knowledge and relations with other experts. To achieve this goal authors get a personal knowledge score via a fuzzy inference system. The next point is to assess the familiarity among personnel. The familiarity evaluation is calculated taking into account the number of co-authors of publications and average intervals of their publications. The second step is devoted to composing a group using the generic algorithm. The main goal is to find experts, who have knowledge about each keyword of the project. At the end, a project manager could be selected from the group formed with the following actions: calculate knowledge competence score, degree centrality and closeness centrality for M keywords, which are related to the formed group; assign the weight for the knowledge competence score, degree centrality and closeness centrality according to the type of the chosen project. The project manager could be a person, who has the highest weighted average of properties, listed above. The algorithm allows user to find the leader of the formed team, taking into account the influence degree. Required competencies are represented as keywords, but the algorithm does not consider time and budget restrictions.

The ranking and clustering algorithm based on principles of clustering analysis of experts (Scott-Knott algorithm) is discussed in the paper [11]. The core idea of the described algorithm is to divide all experts for a job position into the two non-overlapping homogeneous groups: the first one is the group with experts, who are qualified enough for a specific job, another one contains the experts who do not meet job requirements. The algorithm is the following. Firstly, the experts are sorted by the means of the gap score (gap between required and actual competence) in ascending order. After that, the group sorted from the first step is separated into two subgroups. The next step is to compute the coefficient reflecting the sum of squares between subgroups and to find the partition maximizing the coefficient. Then, the algorithm estimates the variance by dividing the sum of squares by the corresponding degree of freedom. The resulting value is compared with Pearson's chi-squared test. If the value is less than Pearson's chi-squared test, then all means belong to a homogeneous group. The algorithm runs, until chi-squared test is significant or the homogeneous group cannot be split (the resulting new groups are not significantly different). The detailed information and equations for the described algorithm one can find in the paper [11]. This algorithm finds the homogeneous group of appropriate experts for a task, but does not take into account their intercommunication.

There is another algorithm for the process of group forming, presented in papers [12, 13]. By means of the algorithm, it is possible to assign several tasks for several experts. In other words, the user can compose the project (several tasks) and find the group of experts, which could complete the project. The algorithm takes as input the set of available expert profiles and the set of project activities to be solved. The activities are represented as a combination of knowledge required for the task, temporal constraints and a number of required group members. These requirements are subdivided into two groups: strict requirements (i.e. an expert must have knowledge) and soft requirements (the requirements are desirable, but not necessary; the expert, who possesses them, has an advantage). The algorithm allows a user to get a list of possible teams for a task or a project (a set of tasks), but does not consider the degree of their influence on each other.

Personnel recruitment task is reviewed in the paper [14]. At the beginning the list of competences required for the completing the task/job should be identified, for each competence the user assigns a weight that is the number, which shows the importance of the competence chosen for the task. The next step is to reveal an expert's competence via a survey. At the last stage the user can get a score, which shows if the expert examined meets task requirements or not. The authors described the distance function for calculation this a score. Input data for the distance function include a set of all competences, a set of competence verification procedures, a set of verification procedure accuracy, a vector with the expert competence grades, a weight vector. Output data shows if the expert examined can take a job interview for a position. There is also another scenario: an expert meets the requirements for a high-level position; nobody meets the requirements, but it is possible for them to get training; requirements for the position are too high and must be reviewed. This algorithm takes into consideration the competence degree of importance for a task. Nevertheless, the algorithm only makes recommendations for a human resource manager and does not form a community of experts.

The group formation process for generalized task is presented in the paper [15]. The suggested algorithm allows a user to find a group for a specific task, using concepts of a generalized task and an expertise network. The authors define the concept of the generalized task as a set of required skills and the number of required experts. However, the feature of this definition is that the required number of experts is assigned to each declared required skill in the set (not to the whole set). The expertise social network is an undirected and weighted graph, where each node represents an expert, who possesses a set of skills, each edge shows the connection between experts, and a weight reflects a collaboration cost between experts. The collaboration cost could be high or low. A low collaboration cost is assigned to the connection between two experts, who are co-authors of many publications. Considering skill requirements, communication costs among experts and generalized tasks the procedure suggests forms an appropriate group for completing the task. The general idea of the procedure is to find a group of experts with the lowest communication cost. The algorithm computes the degree of interaction between experts via the amount of the common scientific publications. It serves as a basis for forming an effective community of experts. However the algorithm does not consider time and budget limits.

The group formation algorithm is presented in the paper [16]. The algorithm is using the knowledge of the grade, which shows how well group members work together. This knowledge is represented as a synergy graph. The authors denote the synergy graph as vertexes, which correspond to a group of experts, unweighted edges and a list with Normal distributions. The last one shows the capability of the group of experts to solve tasks. The goal of the algorithm is to compose an effective group from a synergy graph. The number of the group members should be defined in advance. The algorithm computes an approximation of the optimal group: at the first stage, a random group is generated and several experts are chosen. Next, simulated annealing runs in order to optimize this random group: replace one expert with another, who is not currently in the group. Once an optimal group is found, the algorithm learns a synergy graph to quantify synergy within a group. Using this algorithm it is possible to find the most cohesive group of experts, not taking into account time and budget limits.

3   Identification of Requirements

Tables 1 and 2 present a summary of the papers analyzed, which concern the methods for forming groups of objects. The most commonly used requirements and criteria are extracted from the analyzed papers. To unify and simplify the identification of the most common criteria, these requirements and criteria are formulated in terms of resource management. Table 1 represents the identified criteria for selecting resources and show which paper uses these criteria. Tables 2 represents the identified requirements to considered methods and show which paper uses these requirements.

Based on the analysis of existing groups of resource forming methods, the following requirements have been identified:

- Usage of discrete competence levels;
- Usage of binary matrix to represent the formed community of experts;
- Consecutive improvement of the found solution;
- Presentation of alternative results that meet the requirements;
- The formed community of experts should be able to solve the task at the given time most effectively and qualitatively; consist of available experts, free at the time of formation of the group; not exceed the available budget, i.e. the total payment for the experts' work should not exceed the specified value; be formed according to compatibility of experts.

It should be noted that discussed algorithms either focus on interaction within the forming group of experts, neglecting time and budget limits, or other way round ignore the degree of influence, but consider other parameters as a resource availability, budget and time restrictions, competence degree of importance for a task etc.

The algorithm proposed in this paper unifies the following important parameters and allows user to get an optimal list with community of experts for a task, which takes into account the degree of influence, time and budget restrictions, and required competencies for a task.

4   The Method for Forming a Community of Experts for Task Solving

The developed method is aimed at forming the community of experts to jointly solve a task. The task is specified as a set of competencies that the community of experts should have to solve this task. The project manager specifies the set of competencies in the competence management system [1]. The list of skills that experts can possess is a set, see (1).

$$S = \{S_n,\ n = 1..N\}, \tag{1}$$

where N is the number of skills in the system. Also, each skill S_n corresponds to the maximum level of possession SM_n.

The incoming task is formally defined, see (2)

$$T = \{t, t, C_{max}\}, \tag{2}$$

where t is the following set, see (3).

$$t = \{t_n,\ n = 1..N\}, \tag{3}$$

in which t_n – is the level of skill S_n possession required for the task; τ is the following set, see (4).

$$t = \{t_n,\ n = 1..N\}, \tag{4}$$

where τ_n is the work time required by the task that the expert who possesses skill S_n should spend to solve the problem associated with this skill; C_{max} is the maximum cost of work for the task solving. The list of available experts is a set, see (5).

$$P = \{P_m,\ m = 1..M\}, \tag{5}$$

where M is the number of experts in the system. Also, the experts are given the following characteristics. Experts' competencies are represented in (6).

$$L = \begin{pmatrix} l_{11} & \cdots & l_{1N} \\ \vdots & \ddots & \vdots \\ l_{M1} & \cdots & l_{MN} \end{pmatrix}, \tag{6}$$

where l_{mn} is the possession level of skill S_n of expert P_m. The work cost of the experts is represented by a matrix, see (7).

$$C = \begin{pmatrix} c_{11} & \cdots & c_{1N} \\ \vdots & \ddots & \vdots \\ c_{M1} & \cdots & c_{MN} \end{pmatrix}, \tag{7}$$

where c_{mn} is the cost of applying skill S_n of expert P_m per hour of work. Reconcilability of experts is presented in the form of a matrix, see (8).

$$R = \begin{pmatrix} r_{11} & \cdots & r_{1M} \\ \vdots & \ddots & \vdots \\ r_{M1} & \cdots & r_{MM} \end{pmatrix}, \tag{8}$$

where r_{ij} is a degree of influence of expert r_i on expert r_j, $r_{ij} \in (\frac{1}{10}$ to $10)$. If one expert does not have any influence on another (neither positive nor negative), then its degree of influence is equal to one. If the influence is negative, then the degree of influence is less than one (e.g., if $r_{12} = \frac{1}{2}$, then the first expert worsens the productivity of the second twice); if the influence is positive, then the degree is more than one (if $r_{12} = 2$, then the first expert improves the performance of the second twice).

An activity diagram of the method for forming a community of experts is shown in Fig. 1. To satisfy the requirement of presenting alternative results, a decision list is created, in which all the found variants of the experts groups are saved. To compare the results of the found groups, the group's optimality coefficient Opt is introduced. The coefficient is calculated by the formula (14). At the beginning of the algorithm $Opt = 0$.

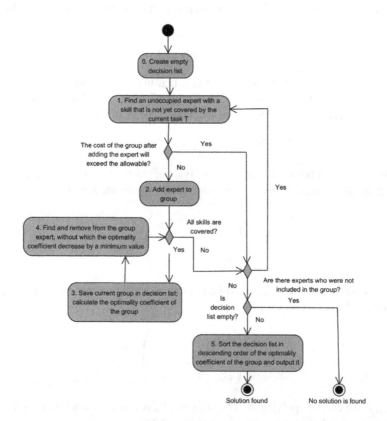

Fig. 1. An activity diagram of the method for forming a community of experts

Every time after the addition of the next expert, the community is checked to see if there are skills necessary to perform the task that none of the experts in the community possesses. If there are such skills, then the search of experts continues. If no experts are available and no decisions are found, then the task is considered impossible.

The community satisfies the criteria of the problem if two conditions are satisfied. First, there should not be skills necessary to perform a task that no expert from the formed community possesses at the required level. Second, the cost of the community should not exceed the maximum cost of work for the task solving. If the formed community satisfies both conditions, then this variant is stored in the decision list, and the group's optimality coefficient is calculated for it. After that the method changes the group. For each expert in the group, the coefficient of community optimality without this expert is calculated. The expert that causes the maximum coefficient is considered the least effective and is removed from the group. After that, new experts are added to the group, if necessary. When there are no available experts to add to the group, all saved decisions are sorted by decreasing the group's optimality coefficient and displayed to the user. The found decisions are represented as a binary matrix, see (9).

$$
D = \begin{pmatrix} d_{11} & \cdots & d_{1M} \\ \vdots & \ddots & \vdots \\ d_{F1} & \cdots & d_{FM} \end{pmatrix},
\tag{9}
$$

where F is the number of found decisions. The lines represent decisions, columns represent available experts. The value of cell d_{fm} at the intersection indicates whether expert P_m participates in decision d_f.

The group's optimality coefficient (*Opt*) is calculated on the basis of the community cost, aggregate competence of experts, and reconcilability of experts in the group. The community cost is calculated by the formula, see (10) and (11).

$$
\text{Cost} = \sum_{i \in K} \sum_{j \in N} x_{ij} c_{ij} \tau_j,
\tag{10}
$$

$$
x_{ij} \begin{cases} 1, & l_{ij} \geq \max_{j \in N}(l_j) \; and \; t_j > 0 \\ 0, & \text{otherwise} \end{cases},
\tag{11}
$$

where K is the number of experts in the group.

Thus, if the expert possesses the skill required to solve the task better than the other experts in the community (i.e., his level of possession of this skill is not lower than the maximum level of possession of it among all the experts in the group), then the cost of applying this skill by this expert is multiplied by the time of work required for the skill and is added to the total amount.

Aggregate competence of experts is calculated by the formula, see (12).

$$
\text{Levels} = \sum_{i \in K} \sum_{j \in N} x_{ij} \frac{l_{ij}}{t_j}
\tag{12}
$$

Thus, if the expert possesses the skill required to solve the task with better possessing level than the other experts in the group, then its level of possession of this skill is divided into the level of possession required by the task and is added to the total amount.

Reconcilability of experts in the community is calculated by the formula, see (13).

$$\text{Reconcilability} = \prod_{i \in K} \prod_{j \in K} r_{ij} \tag{13}$$

Thus, the degrees of the experts' influence in a community are multiplied among themselves. The result shows how the composition of the community as a whole affects its performance.

The community's optimality coefficient is calculated by the formula, see (14).

$$\text{Opt} = \frac{\text{Levels} * \text{Reconcilability}}{\text{Cost}} \tag{14}$$

Thus, the optimality of the experts' community is directly proportional to the aggregate competence and reconcilability of the experts in the community and inversely proportional to the cost of work of the experts' group.

With the group's optimality coefficient, the time required to solve the task by the formed community is calculated and displayed to the user for each found decision. This time is calculated by the formula, see (15).

$$\text{Time} = \sum_{i \in K} \sum_{j \in N} x_{ij} \tau_j \tag{15}$$

Thus, if the expert possesses the skill required to solve the task with better possessing level than the other experts in the group, the time that he has to spend to solve the part of the task associated with this skill is added to the total amount.

To evaluate the complexity of the method, we should consider the loops it contains:

1. A cycle including blocks 1 and 2 is performed M times.
2. The condition check after block 2 is executed N times.
3. Blocks 3 and 4 are executed F times. The group's optimality coefficient is calculated K times in block 4.
4. The decision list is sorted once.

The calculation of the group's optimality coefficient in the cycle of block 4 is performed the greatest number of times, so the complexity of the method is determined by the complexity of this calculation.

In the process of calculating the optimality, each skill of each expert in the community is checked, as well as the reconcilability of the experts with each other, therefore this calculation of optimality has a complexity $O(K^2 + KN)$. The calculation is executed $F * K$ times, so the complexity of the method is equal to $O(FK(K^2 + KN))$.

Since the method only scans the list of experts once, then $F \leq M$. It is also obvious that $K \leq N$, since each expert in a community has at least one skill required to solve a task that other experts in the community do not have.

Thus, if we replace F to M and K to N, then the method has complexity $O(M \times N3)$.

5   Conclusion

This paper presents the method for expert searching for joint task solving. A user defines a task to be solved. Based on this task and expert competencies the presented method searches for the groups of experts to solve the task. Based on the conducted state-of-the-art it could be noticed that freely available at the moment algorithms do not consider time, which an expert has to spend on a task solving, total cost restriction for a task (project), and the influence degree between experts. The method proposed in this paper fulfils these requirements and allows the user to make the right decision and find a good group of experts for the task solving. Moreover, group optimization is another key feature of the method that allows user to find a cheaper or more effective group.

For the future work the proposed method is going to be implemented in competence management system of Technopark of ITMO University.

Acknowledgements. The presented results are part of the research carried out within the project funded by grants # 16-29-12866 and # 18-37-00377 of the Russian Foundation for Basic Research, by the Russian State Research # 0073-2018-0002, and by ITMO University (Project #617038).

References

1. Smirnov, A., Kashevnik, A., Balandin, S., Baraniuc, O., Parfenov V.: Competency management system for technopark residents: smart space-based approach. In: Internet of Things, Smart Spaces, and Next Generation Networks and Systems. LNCS, vol. 9870, pp. 15–24 (2016). https://doi.org/10.1007/978-3-319-46301-8_2
2. Brumsteyn, Y.M., Dudikov, I.A.: Optimization of personnel distribution between organizations divisions on the basis of competence approach. Casp. J. Manag. High Technol. **2**, 45–58 (2015)
3. Brumsteyn, Y.M., Dudikov, I.A.: Optimization models of resources selection for management of the project sets taking into account the dependence of the quality results, risks and expenses. Vestn. AGTU. Ser. Manag. Comput. Sci. Inform. **1**, 78–89 (2015)
4. Orlovskiy, N.M.: Research of mathematical model for optimum plans formation of experts group functioning. Mod. Probl. Sci. Educ. **3**, 128 (2014)
5. Yalçındağ, S., Cappanera, P., Scutellà, M.G., Şahin, E., Matta, A.: Pattern-based decompositions for human resource planning in home health care services. Comput. Oper. Res. **73**, 12–26 (2016). https://doi.org/10.1016/j.cor.2016.02.011
6. Karimi-Majd, A., Mahootchi, M., Zakery, A.: A reinforcement learning methodology for a human resource planning problem considering knowledge-based promotion. Simul. Model. Pract. Theory **79**, 87–99 (2017). https://doi.org/10.1016/j.simpat.2015.07.004
7. Touat, M., Bouzidi-Hassini, S., Benbouzid-Sitayeb, F., Benhamou, B.: A hybridization of genetic algorithms and fuzzy logic for the single-machine scheduling with flexible maintenance problem under human resource constraints. Appl. Soft Comput. **59**, 556–573 (2017). https://doi.org/10.1016/j.asoc.2017.05.058
8. Zhang, L.: An inverse optimization model for human resource allocation problem considering competency disadvantage structure. Procedia Comput. Sci. **112**, 1611–1622 (2017). https://doi.org/10.1016/j.procs.2017.08.248

9. Knyazeva, M., Bozhenyuk, A., Rozenberg, I.: Resource-constrained project scheduling approach under fuzzy conditions. Procedia Comput. Sci. **77**, 56–64 (2015). https://doi.org/10.1016/j.procs.2015.12.359

10. Wi, H., Oh, S., Mun, J., Jung, M.: A team formation model based on knowledge and collaboration. Expert. Syst. Appl. Int. J. **36**, 9121–9134 (2009). https://doi.org/10.1016/j.eswa.2008.12.031

11. Bohlouli, M., Mittas, N., Kakarontzas, G., Theodosiou, T., Angelis, L., Fathi, M.: Competence assessment as an expert system for human resource management: a mathematical approach. Expert Syst. Appl. **70**, 83–102 (2016). https://doi.org/10.1016/j.eswa.2016.10.046

12. Tinelli, E., Colucci, S., Di Sciascio, E., Donini, F.: Knowledge compilation for automated team composition exploiting standard SQL. In: Proceeding SAC 2012 Proceedings of the 27th Annual ACM Symposium on Applied Computing, pp. 1680–1685 (2012)

13. Tinelli, E., Colucci, S., Donini, F., Di Sciascio, E., Giannini, S.: Embedding semantics in human resources management automation via SQL. Appl. Intell. **46**, 1–31 (2016). https://doi.org/10.1007/s10489-016-0868-x

14. Rizvanov, D., Senkina, G.: Ontological approach to supporting decision-making management of the competencies of the organization. Vestn. RSREU **4**, 79–84 (2009)

15. Li, C., Shan, M.: Team formation for generalized tasks in expertise social networks. In: IEEE Second International Conference on Social Computing (SocialCom), pp. 9–16 (2010). https://doi.org/10.1109/socialcom.2010.12

16. Liemhetcharat, S., Veloso, M.: Modeling and learning synergy for team formation with heterogeneous agents. In: AAMAS 2012 Proceedings of the 11th International Conference on Autonomous Agents and Multiagent Systems, vol. 1, pp. 365–374 (2012)

EParticipation in Friedrichshafen: Identification of Target Groups and Analysis of Their Behaviour

David Hafner⊙ and Alexander Moutchnik$^{(\boxtimes)}$⊙

RheinMain University of Applied Sciences,
HSRM, DCSM, PF 3251, 65022 Wiesbaden, Germany
alexander.moutchnik@hs-rm.de

Abstract. 'eParticipation' means the involvement of citizens in the political process via information and communication technologies. This paper analyses the identification of target groups in eParticipation and the elaboration of their behaviour. Research and analysis was conducted on a target population in Germany. Second and third generational citizens were the focus of the analysis. The city of Friedrichshafen was chosen due to its inherent electronic and network infrastructural advantage. It is assumed that this city's mode of connectivity will be established in the whole country in the years to come. The research methodology was quantitative; a survey was conducted to collect statistical data. Questions for the survey were derived from literature-based research in adjacent areas. Topics in the survey include 'eGovernment', 'technology-acceptance' and 'target group behaviour'. Survey locations were chosen close to administrative institutions, aiming to elicit responses from long-term citizens of Friedrichshafen. In total 249 people were surveyed. This represents a confidence level of 94%. Four distinctive target groups of adults were identified and categorized according to experience: "First-time Voters", "Amateur Voters", "Professional Voters" and "Expert Voters". Research results showed a strong tendency of the respondents towards eParticipation provided its direct political impact was being limited. Moreover, the strongest concerns about an online election were voter-manipulation and vote-buying. Local administrations and politicians can use findings from this research to implement technologies and to encourage their target audience to participate electronically in the political discourse.

Keywords: eParticipation · eGovernment · eDemocracy · Democracy
Target group · Group behaviour · Germany · Technology acceptance

1 Introduction

"The role of citizen in our democracy does not end with your vote." Barack Obama, Victory Speech, November 7th 2012 [1].

The idea, that people have the power to actively shape their country, is the guiding principle of a democracy. With the development and advancement of the internet, the evolution of a neo-democracy will follow. This online political involvement of the

© Springer Nature Switzerland AG 2018
D. A. Alexandrov et al. (Eds.): DTGS 2018, CCIS 858, pp. 39–50, 2018.
https://doi.org/10.1007/978-3-030-02843-5_4

citizenry is called eParticipation. The political concept remains the same, but the way people communicate and participate, changes. The United Nations [2, p. 49] stated that "eParticipation is [...] an evolving concept", which means an enhancement of the role of citizens.

The German government and local institutions are deploying more electronic services [3] to serve the people's demand for convenience. These technological developments caused a demand for political change; an "interactive network shifting from an elite democracy to a participatory democracy" [4, p. 489]. Such a shift is complex and requires effort from the leading parties and patience by the public for the transition. The German Chancellor Angela Merkel referred to the internet as "virgin soil" in a press conference with Barack Obama on June 19, 2013. This statement and its implications contain the views of some administrative bodies and show the need for transformation.

One measurement for the progress in digitalization of administrations is the eParticipation Index (EPI). It shows the utilization of eServices in a country. Germany is ranked 27 out of 188 on the EPI. That is a relatively low rank compared to other European countries such as Italy and Finland (both share rank 8) and strong industrial nations such as Japan (rank 2) [2]. From looking at the EPI, it seems as if Germany is facing more problems than other countries in getting its citizens involved via information and communication technology. Esteves and Joseph [5, p. 119] speculate that there is a lack of "studies beyond the citizens' perspective". In this context, the OECD states that "barriers to greater online citizen engagement in policy-making are cultural, organisational and constitutional, not technological" [6, p. 9].

This study examines the potential for different forms of eParticipation and its target groups in Friedrichshafen.

Friedrichshafen is a town in southern Germany with a population of nearly 60 000 [7]. Since the advent of the T-City project from Deutsche Telekom, the town is considered one of the most technologically advanced cities in Germany. Approximately 98.4% of the citizens are now connected to the internet [8]. These infrastructural settings make the town an ideal place for research in the field of technology usage. It is the prototype model for each future city in Germany. People in this town are familiar with technological change and its potential benefits. The administration in this region is more developed than in other neighbouring regions. The regional administration can assert that its citizens have greater intrinsic experience with eParticipation as a democratic process, even though they may not be aware of the terminology. As a consequence, conclusions drawn in this research may correlate well to neighbouring regions assuming similar cultural, political and legal conditions.

eParticipation is a relatively young research field which offers numerous opportunities to conduct research [9, 10]. This paper aims to bridge the information gap in literature between eParticipation and target group behaviour [11]. The research within seeks to examine this relationship in local settings [12–14]. In addition, eParticipation is a broad, multi-disciplinary research field. The majority of research is conducted through comparative case studies, qualitative interviews or project reports [15–17]. There is a lack of quantitative studies [18]. Models from published research papers are examined and taken into account when formulating hypotheses and deriving questions. Researchers can benefit from this quantitative research as it is based on real-life settings and delivers results based on field data. This proceeding offers the chance to review these concepts and strengthen their applicability.

2 Hypotheses About EParticipation and Group Behaviour

Based on literature research, seven factors are identified that influence eParticipation:

- H1: eParticipation is influenced by the form of eGovernment (eGovernment Portal → eDiscussion → eParticipation → eVoting → eElection) [19].
- H2: eParticipation is influenced by the hierarchical level of the institution [20].
- H3: eParticipation is influenced by the scale of the impact [21].
- H4: eParticipation is influenced by the level of trust of citizenry in the political process and the government [22].
- H5: eParticipation is influenced by the socio-economic context of the region [23].
- H6: eParticipation is influenced by an individual citizen's experience with technology [24].
- H7: Participatory groups can be identified, and a profile of their behaviour can be identified for each target group.

3 Research Approach and Methodology

In the methodology of similar studies, questions are derived from previously elaborated hypotheses [25]. The structure of the questionnaire allows participants to flow through various categories from general to specific, and from the least politically sensitive questions to the most sensitive ones. The first part of the questionnaire includes nominal questions where respondents are asked for relevant characteristics and can choose one specific answer. The second part includes interval questions to measure the agreement in factors that might influence eParticipation.[1]

---

[1] [H1]: eElection: I think it is good to perform elections online; eVoting: I think it is good to perform votes online; eParticipation: I think it is good to carry out local council meetings online; eDiscussion: I think it is good to conduct political surveys online; eGovernment Portal: I think it is good if information exchange with the community council takes place online. [H2]: Community level: I think it is good to elect the mayor online; Community level: I think it is good to elect the Chancellor online. [H3]: I think it is good to build a playground; I think it is good to elect the mayor online. [H4]: Safeguards from vote buying: I am afraid that votes are bought; Secrecy of the votes cast: I am afraid that someone can find out for whom I vote; Identification: I am afraid that someone can find out who I am; Manipulation: I am afraid that the election gets manipulated; Auditability: I am afraid that there is no physical proof of vote as ballot papers disappear; Misinformation: I am afraid that electors are misinformed. [H5]: Gender, age, education. [H6]: Technology Knowledge: I find it easy to operate a computer.

The data collection took place in Friedrichshafen's public areas. Spots for surveying were selected according to the potential of meeting long-term local citizens: the areas around Friedrichshafen's town hall, the local city office, the district's administration office and the local graveyard. A period of five working days, from Monday the 19th until Friday the 23rd of December, 2016 was used for data collection. Usually, the distribution of questionnaires would take place from eight o'clock in the morning until five o'clock in the afternoon. While conducting the surveys, it turned out that the term eParticipation was largely unknown to the citizens. A total of 249 responses was collected. Using Yamane's transformed sample size formula, an error of 6.3% has to be accepted which means a confidence level of 93.7% was achieved.

4   Participants' Characteristics

First part of the analysis is the examination of variance in demographic characteristics. The results are compared to statistical data from the community of Friedrichshafen. In case such information about local settings is not available, data from the district Bodenseekreis or nation-wide statistics are used for comparisons. 57% of the survey participants are males (142 respondents) and 43% females (107 respondents). This does not quite reflect the gender distribution in Friedrichshafen, where the ratio was 50% women and 50% men [26]. From a total of 249 respondents, 88% own a computer, which can be either a laptop or a personal desktop computer. Approximately 84% are owners of a smartphone. Almost 90% of the respondents have private internet access. The prevailing age-group of respondents was between 26 and 35 years old. The second largest group comprised citizens born in or before 1960; it includes the widest age-range compared to the other groupings. When the survey was conducted, it was difficult to involve non-voting citizens born after 1998 due to their young age.

Next step was the comparison of respondents' educational levels with the educational distribution in Germany. National statistical data was used for comparison, as there is no region-specific data available. 57% of respondents graduated from vocational school. 17% held a bachelor's degree and 12% held a master's degree. Furthermore 12% of respondents had an uncategorized educational level and 2% of the respondents refused to answer this question. The distribution between vocational, bachelor and master level education corresponds well to the educational distribution in greater Germany.

To begin the analysis, target groups are identified by optimal scaling in SPSS. This is illustrated in Fig. 1.

The two-dimensional diagram in which four groups of participants can be identified: "First-time Voters" (1), "Amateur Voters" (2), "Professional Voters" (3) and "Expert Voters" (4).

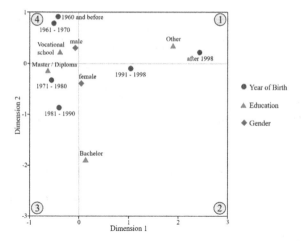

Fig. 1. Optimal scaling: target group identification. Source: Own elaboration

5   Target Group Behaviour Determination Concept

The basic idea for determination of group behaviour is the allocation of weights, determined by the group fit, to the respondents' ratings. These weights are correlated to the demographic markers of target groups. The results can be used to create distinctive profiles of target group behaviour. These profiles are compared to the sample profile and among one another. Figure 2 provides an overview of the concept.[2]

By this procedure, unique group profiles of target group behaviour are statistically determined. These four profiles are described in the following text.

---

[2] In the first step, for each respondent the fit of demographic markers with the target group characteristics is examined. For every fit, the weighting factor is increased by one. For instance, respondent one fits to the target group with two demographic markers representing age and education. Therefore, the weight of 2 is noted in the weight column. In the calculation step, the respondent's rating of a question is multiplied by the weight. It results in weighted ratings for each respondent and each factor in the right-hand columns. Referring to the given example, the previously determined weight of 2 is multiplied with the respondent's rating (2) of the question. A weighted rating of 4 is noted. Step one and two are repeated for all questions and respondents. The third step sums all of the weighted ratings of one target group. The fourth step calculates the group's weighted rating for each factor. Divide the sum of the weighted ratings by the sum of the weights. These steps are repeated for each group. By this procedure, unique profiles of group behaviour are statistically determined. It is possible that there is no correlation between markers and target groups. This occurred with the second respondent. In his case the weight 0 is allocated, which means answers given by the respondent do not influence the group behaviour profile of the examined target group.

	Demographic Markers			Weight	Rating	Calculation	Weighted Rating
	Age	Gender	Education				
Respondent 1, Q. 1	✖		✖	2	2	2 x 2	4
Respondent 2, Q. 1				0	5	0 x 5	0
Respondent 3, Q. 1	✖	✖	✖	3	2	3 x 2	6
Respondent 4, Q. 1		✖		1	3	1 x 3	3
✖ = fit of demographic marker and group characteristic				$\sum$ 6			$\sum$ 13

Weighted Group Rating: $\sum$ Weighted Ratings / $\sum$ Weights → 13 / 6 = **2.17**

Fig. 2. Target group behaviour: evaluation concept. Source: Own elaboration

5.1   First-Time Voters

The group of "First-time Voters" is defined by two demographic markers: born after 1998 and no specified educational level. Generally, they prefer small mobile devices over fixed and bulky computers [27]. They are quick to absorb the most recent advances in technology. The group's technology knowledge, tested by asking for the respondent's ability to operate a computer, is moderate. However, this result may not represent the group's most preferred technology as most of the members might be more experienced with mobile technologies such as smartphones and tablets.

Their interest in politics is moderate and eParticipation is least known. "First-time Voters" prefer traditional offline means of conducting elections. However, they are comfortable casting their votes online. In comparison to the other groups, "First time Voters" have got fewer reservations to perform votes online. Even though the group is proficient at acquiring technological knowledge, the rating of non-participation in online council meetings is even stronger than the average sample rating. Interestingly, this group which comprises members who grew up with information and communication technology does not support political online surveys as strongly as the other groups. Nevertheless, the group's rating indicated a positive attitude towards such political online surveys.

Online information exchange with the local administration should be increased to involve this "First-time Voters" group in politics. The weighted group rating for this question is more positive than the average rating of the sample.

When introducing an eElection system, this group might be prepared to relinquish part of their privacy and the secrecy of their vote in order to protect against vote-manipulation. Manipulation of the vote cast is the group's greatest concern. On the second rank comes the fear of vote-buying. The fear of vote-buying is stronger compared to the average rating of the entire sample. The group is unconcerned about the lack of auditability. The rating shows that the group is concerned about voters getting fed with malicious or fake information. This rating almost matches with the average ratings from all groups.

5.2   Amateur Voters

The second group, called "Amateur Voters", is defined by three demographic characteristics. Members of this group are female, born between the years 1991 and 1998 and
have successfully finished their bachelor degree studies. It fills the gap between "First-
time Voters" and "Professional Voters". 90% of the group members own a computer,
which is about 10% more than the "First-time Voters". The share of computer ownership
is higher than the share of smartphone and tablet ownership. 91% have internet access.
When looking at the raw data of the group, it can be discovered that every member owns
at least one device, either a smartphone, a tablet, or a computer. In addition, group
members are more familiar with using a computer than the average survey respondent.
The reasons might be related to their educational background and their relatively young
age. In regards to political interest, the weighted group rating is similar to the average.
There is some resistance to conducting national elections online. While there are
reservations regarding online elections, a positive attitude towards casting votes online
was measured. Members are opposed to the election of the Chancellor online, but they
support voting on local topics. When performing political surveys online, a large share
of this group is most likely to participate. Among the four groups, "Amateur Voters" are
most concerned about the vote-manipulation if it takes place online. This group's rating
to conduct political online surveys is quite positive compared to the other groups. This
positive correlation shows a desire to get involved in the political decision making. The
last level of eParticipation, the exchange of information, has also received a positive
correlation. It shows that people in this group want to interact locally with their community council through information and communication technology. The group ratings
and the averages from the sample nearly match in each of the six dimensions of fear. The
group's strongest fear in regards of eElection is manipulation. Second strongest concern
is the fear of vote-buying. The third greatest fear is misinforming the voters. The group
feels uncertain about the auditability of the vote cast caused by missing ballot papers.
Ratings for the secrecy of the vote cast and identification of voters are both slightly
above the neutral position. This indicates fewer concerns. Nevertheless, both evaluations are slightly below the average.

5.3   Professional Voters

"Professional Voters" are the third group and comprise citizens of Friedrichshafen
whose year of birth is between 1971 and 1990. The educational level of the members is
relatively high as they have obtained a master's degree or a diploma. This group has
reached the top values in the categories of computer ownership, about 92%, and
internet access, almost 93%. These ratios might be related to the group members'
education which leads to better job opportunities with higher remunerations. Computers and internet access are an integral part of their careers which impacts their
private lives. Furthermore, they are the group with the greatest interest in politics. Their
knowledge about eParticipation is significantly higher compared to the three other
groups. Overall, "Professional Voters" show the most positive attitude towards eParticipation. A relationship between the different levels of eParticipation is discovered.
The positive correlations imply that the ratings for all eParticipation levels differ

equally from the average rating. This is the only group with a positive attitude towards conducting online elections in regards to lower administrative levels. This rating is a major departure from other groups which are indifferent or prefer offline elections. Based on their group rating, elections on national level should preferably take place offline. The group tends to agree that votes may be cast online. However, local council meetings should not be carried out online. Online surveys are accepted by the group as political tools. Members also agree to increase information exchange with the community council through information and communication technologies. The fear of manipulation is the group's strongest concern followed by the fear of vote-buying. Citizens of Friedrichshafen who belong to the group of "Professional Voters" are least concerned about the secrecy of the vote cast and they are unconcerned about the secrecy of their identity. They are more concerned about the lack of auditability than the average respondent. This group may not trust a digital system which is not based on physical proof of vote submission. The group is less concerned about misinformation of the voters in comparison to other groups and the average respondent rating. However, the group is seriously concerned about manipulation and vote-buying. When introducing an eElection system to this group, it can help to communicate its technical specifications to convince them to participate in an election online.

5.4   Expert Voters

The fourth group are males born before 1970 who graduated from vocational school. Due to the members' long-life experience and the number of elections they experienced, this group is called "Expert Voters". They own significantly fewer devices (85% computer, 80% smartphone or tablet) than the other groups. Additionally, their 88% ratio of internet access is the lowest among the three adult groups. This is reflected by their comparably low computer knowledge. It can be assumed that the low technology experience is related to the group's age characteristics. Members of this group are against carrying out elections online, no matter if it is local or national. The group members' interest in politics is close to the average rating. Based on results from the correlation analysis, reservations regarding eParticipation in general are expected and confirmed by the weighted rating. "Expert Voters" have a negative attitude towards of eElection on local and national level. It differs from the other three groups in terms their weighted rating of online vote casts. The rating of online vote casting in the community shows uncertainty. All three ratings relate to submitting one's vote online. However, there is a clear tendency towards conducting political surveys and exchanging information online. These are the two forms with low personal involvement referring to the stage model of eParticipation. Even though this group differs in most ratings from the other groups, carrying out local council meetings, is surprisingly close to the average. "Expert Voters" is the group with most experience in elections and vote casts. This might be the reason why they are less concerned about manipulation of the voting process. But, manipulation of the eElection is still their strongest fear. Second biggest is the fear about vote buying. The group is marginally concerned about misinformation of the voters. The low rating in regards of lacking auditability is surprising as it could be expected that this generation values the physical proof of ballot papers high. The weighted rating does not reflect this assumption as it is very close to the average.

There is a marginal tendency that this group is not concerned about their identification in an eElection. In addition, they show few concerns about the secrecy of the vote cast if it is performed online. In comparison to the other three groups, members of this group are late followers. The adaptation to the fast-moving technology development takes the longest due to their age and their areas of interest.

6 Verification of Hypotheses

The hypotheses tests show that statistical findings support the interpretation of the weighted group ratings. The correlation analyses and the weighted group ratings complement each other.

- The hypothesis **H1,** eParticipation is influenced by the form of eGovernment, can be verified.
- **H2**: eParticipation is influenced by the hierarchical level of the institution. The impact of the hierarchy of eGovernment is tested by comparing elections on national and local level. The average sample rating shows that citizens in Friedrichshafen prefer to elect a mayor online compared to the Chancellor. H2 is verified.
- **H3**: eParticipation is influenced by the scale of the impact. The submission of a vote in an election has a different impact than the submission of a vote in a vote cast. At the end of an election, a representative is in charge to shape the community's future for a limited period of time. The outcome of a vote cast can directly impact the citizen in one case and not impact the citizen at all in another case. Both factors show significant differences in the average sample ratings and on group specific level. H3 is verified.
- **H4**: eParticipation is influenced by the level of trust of citizens in process and government. The correlation analysis result reveals that eParticipation is negatively related to four dimensions of mistrust. eParticipation decreases if the concerns about vote buying, secrecy of the vote cast, auditability, and misinformation increase. The H4 is partially verified.
- **H5**: eParticipation is influenced by the socio-economic context. Correlation is discovered in the ratings of the two variables age and eParticipation. It is also illustrated by the segmentation of four target groups. These four groups can be distinguished by their unique behaviour profiles which are a strong indicator for the influence of socio-economic characteristics. Consequently, the H5 is verified.
- **H6**: eParticipation is influenced by citizen's experience with technology. Correlation between the expertise in computer usage and the readiness for eParticipation is measured. The H6 is verified.
- **H7**: Participatory groups can be identified. Four distinct target groups are identified by optimal scaling of demographic factors. The groups can be distinguished by their behaviour which verifies the H7.

7 Discussion, Conclusion and Outlook

It can be concluded that "Professional Voters" will readily adopt eParticipation and the group of "Expert Voters" represents slight reluctance to vote digitally. Politicians and researchers can use this finding to develop group specific measurements based on their preference profiles. In case the city of Friedrichshafen aims to increase eParticipation among relatively young citizens, the integration of mobile technology is the key to this target group. The group profiles show that the dominant fear of eElections is related to manipulation and vote-buying. The city administration of Friedrichshafen should start their eParticipation initiative with low impact eServices such as online surveys and improved offerings of online information exchange. In the next step, they can move on to online vote casting which will likely be supported by the public. In general, all four groups show readiness to participate in these three categories of eParticipation.

This research is not all encompassing and leaves some open points for subsequent research:

- The first point is the influence of technological conditions on eParticipation. It should be considered to examine this factor in a separate research group as it turned out to be more complicated than expected. Aiming to get reliable data, the identification of factors that define technological conditions should be a priority. Furthermore, the development of an evaluation metric should be emphasized.
- Secondly, the models used in this study can be tested in other regions. The research community can benefit from multiple sets of field data. It offers a great chance to compare the results and draw more comprehensive conclusions.
- The third suggestion is to use an alternative approach to answer the same research question. By using the qualitative approach deeper insights into *why* citizens want or do not want to participate online in the political discourse may be revealed.

Obama's quote from 2012 that "the role of citizen in our democracy does not end with your vote" shows the need to increase political involvement of the public. eParticipation offers a great chance for a new way of equal collaboration between a government and its citizens. From field research we know that citizens in Friedrichshafen show a readiness to get involved in politics via information and communication technology. One of the participants summarized the current situation in Friedrichshafen as follows: "the citizens are ready to use technology to get politically involved, but the politicians do not know how to deal with our multiple and differing needs and wants"[3]. Current developments show that in reference to the transition model of an eGovernment, the cultural gap is closing. The next step is to transform political procedures into a participative democracy, to make a true eDemocracy a reality. Leaps of technology come faster and in several years, governments may recognize the value of eParticipation. In a foreseeable future, law makers may mandate total participation in an eDemocracy.

---

[3] "Wir sind eigentlich dazu bereit politisch aktiv zu sein, aber von den Politikern weiß doch keiner wie er dann mit unseren vielen unterschiedlichen Wünschen und Bedürfnissen dann umgehen soll." – Johannes Fauth, Friedrichshafen 22.12. 2016.

References

1. Barack Obama, President Obama's Full Acceptance Speech. McCormick Place, Chicago, Illinois: The White House: Office of the Press Secretary. http://abcnews.go.com/Politics/OTUS/president-obamas-full-acceptance-speech/story?id=17661896. Accessed 20 Apr 2018
2. United Nations E-Government Survey 2016. E-Government in Support of Sustainable Development, United Nations Department of Economic & Social Affairs, New York (2016)
3. Wagner, S.A., Vogt, S., Kabst, R.: The future of public participation: empirical analysis from the viewpoint of policy-makers. Technol. Forecast. Soc. Change **106**, 65–73 (2016). https://doi.org/10.1016/j.techfore.2016.02.010
4. Jho, W., Song, K.J.: Institutional and technological determinants of civil e-Participation: solo or duet? Gov. Inf. Quart. **32**(4), 488–495 (2015). https://doi.org/10.1016/j.giq.2015.09.003
5. Esteves, J., Joseph, R.C.: A comprehensive framework for the assessment of eGovernment projects. Gov. Inf. Quart. **25**(1), 118–132 (2008). https://doi.org/10.1016/j.giq.2007.04.009
6. Promise and Problems of E-Democracy: Challenges of Online Citizen Engagement. OECD Publications Service, Paris (2003)
7. Stadtmarketing Friedrichshafen (2015). https://www.friedrichshafen.de/fileadmin/user_upload/images_fn/Wirtschaft_Verkehr/Stadtmarketing/Imagebroschuere_Stadt_Friedrichshafen.pdf. Accessed 22 Feb 2018
8. Groupe Speciale Mobile Association GSMA 2016. The Mobile Economy, London (2016)
9. Zheng, Y., Schachter, H.L., Holzer, M.: The impact of government form on e-participation: A study of New Jersey municipalities. Gov. Inf. Quart. **31**(4), 653–659 (2014). https://doi.org/10.1016/j.giq.2014.06.004
10. Madsen, C.Ø., Kræmmergaard, P.: Channel choice: a literature review. In: Tambouris, E., et al. (eds.) EGOV 2015. LNCS, vol. 9248, pp. 3–18. Springer, Cham (2015). https://doi.org/10.1007/978-3-319-22479-4_1
11. Siau, K., Long, Y.: Synthesizing e-government stage models – a meta-synthesis based on meta-ethnography approach. Bus. Process Manag. J. **11**(5), 589–611 (2005). https://doi.org/10.1108/02635570510592352
12. Dobnikar, A., Nemec, A.Ž.: eGovernment in slovenia. Informatica **31**, 357–365 (2007)
13. Freschi, A.C., Medaglia, R., Nørbjerg, J.: A tale of six countries: eparticipation research from an administration and political perspective. In: Macintosh, A., Tambouris, E. (eds.) ePart 2009. LNCS, vol. 5694, pp. 36–45. Springer, Heidelberg (2009). https://doi.org/10.1007/978-3-642-03781-8_4
14. Pederson, K.: e-Government in local government: challenges and capabilities. Electro. J. e-Government **14**(1), 99–116 (2016)
15. Bolgov, R., Karachay, V.: E-participation projects development in the e-governance institutional structure of the Eurasian economic union's countries: comparative overview. In: Chugunov, A.V., Bolgov, R., Kabanov, Y., Kampis, G., Wimmer, M. (eds.) DTGS 2016. CCIS, vol. 674, pp. 205–218. Springer, Cham (2016). https://doi.org/10.1007/978-3-319-49700-6_20
16. EU eGovernment Action Plan 2016–2020. Accelerating the digital transformation of government. European Commission, Brussels (2016)
17. Burkhardt, D., Nazemi, K., Ginters, E.: Best-practice piloting based on an integrated social media analysis and visualization for e-participation simulation in cities. Proc. Comp. Sci. **75**, 66–74 (2015). https://doi.org/10.1016/j.procs.2015.12.214
18. Yusuf, M., Adams, C., Dingley, K.: A review of e-government research as a mature discipline: trends, themes, philosophies, methodologies, and methods. Electr. J. e-Government **14**(1), 18–35 (2016)

19. Prosser, A.: Transparency in eVoting. Transform. Government: People, Process. Policy **8**(2), 171–184 (2014)
20. Irimie, R.C.: Egovernment: transforming government engagement in the European Union. Mediterranean J. Soc. Sci. **6**(2), 173–188 (2015). https://doi.org/10.5901/mjss.2015.v6n2s2p173
21. Candiello, A., Albarelli, A., Cortesi, A.: Quality and impact monitoring for local eGovernment services. Transform. Government: People, Process Policy **6**(1), 112–125 (2012). https://doi.org/10.1108/17506161211214859
22. Axelsson, K., Lindblad-Gidlund, K.: eGovernment in Sweden: new directions. Int. J. Public Inf. Sys. **2**, 31–35 (2009)
23. Kabanov, Y., Sungurov, A.: E-government development factors: evidence from the russian regions. In: Chugunov, A.V., Bolgov, R., Kabanov, Y., Kampis, G., Wimmer, M. (eds.) DTGS 2016. CCIS, vol. 674, pp. 85–95. Springer, Cham (2016). https://doi.org/10.1007/978-3-319-49700-6_10
24. Chugunov, A.V., Kabanov, Y., Zenchenkova, K.: E-participation portals automated monitoring system for political and social research. In: Chugunov, A.V., Bolgov, R., Kabanov, Y., Kampis, G., Wimmer, M. (eds.) DTGS 2016. CCIS, vol. 674, pp. 290–298. Springer, Cham (2016). https://doi.org/10.1007/978-3-319-49700-6_27
25. Gulati, G.J., Williams, C.B., Yates, D.J.: Predictors of on-line services and e-participation: a cross-national comparison. Gov. Inf. Quart. **31**(4), 526–533 (2014). https://doi.org/10.1016/j.giq.2014.07.005
26. Statistisches Landesamt Baden-Württemberg (2015). http://www.statistik-bw.de/BevoelkGebiet/Bevoelkerung/99025010.tab?R=GS435016. Accessed 22 Feb 2018
27. Ochara, N.M., Mawela, T.: Enabling social sustainability of e-participation through mobile technology. Inf. Technol. Dev. **21**(2), 205–228 (2015). https://doi.org/10.1080/02681102.2013.833888

Social Efficiency of E-participation Portals in Russia: Assessment Methodology

Lyudmila Vidiasova[1](✉), Iaroslava Tensina[1], and Elena Bershadskaya[2]

[1] ITMO University, Saint Petersburg, Russia
bershadskaya.lyudmila@gmail.com, tensina.yaroslava@mail.ru
[2] Penza State Technological University, Penza, Russia
bereg.50@mail.ru

Abstract. The paper presents a methodology for e-participation portals social efficiency assessment based on the United Nations (UN) approach. The system of indicators frames a political decision-making cycle and covers 3 dimensions of social efficiency such as political, technological and socio-economic. The methodology developed involves factors that are available from open sources. The authors present results of the methodology approbation on 5 e-participation portals in Russia. The findings have revealed the portals studied show the least progress in socio-economic dimension of social efficiency compared to political and technological ones.

Keywords: E-participation · Social efficiency · Assessment tool · Indicators
Decision-making cycle

1 Introduction

E-participation assessment issues arose several years ago when e-participation tools (counting e-petition portals, e-consultation activities and even e-voting) were becoming more and more popular. However, the impacts of such tools are still not obvious and raise such questions as: Do these tools provide the proper options for various sorts of participation? Do these tools really involve citizens into decision-making? Is it possible to measure their social efficiency in some valid way based on available open data?

With the purpose to answer these questions, this paper presents a framework for e-participation tools assessment focusing on social efficiency. Understanding the importance of a country's context, the methodology has been developed and tested on the Russian e-participation portals. At the same time, its application can be of interest for other countries where e-participation portals provide a certain level of data openness.

The paper consists of six sections. Section "State of the Art" presents an overview of current research field. The methodological section illustrates the main notions and categories being used in the study. Section 4 shows the results of e-participation portals' assessment based on the methodology proposed. Section 5 summarizes conclusions received, and the discussion section stresses some limitations of the current research and highlights the future steps.

© Springer Nature Switzerland AG 2018
D. A. Alexandrov et al. (Eds.): DTGS 2018, CCIS 858, pp. 51–62, 2018.
https://doi.org/10.1007/978-3-030-02843-5_5

2   State of the Art

In previous works [29] there were several attempts to illustrate a variety of techniques for e-participation evaluation. While some institutions focus on a unique methodology creation [16, 26], the others concentrate their efforts on case description [24]. In addition to the variation in focusing, there is a wide range in terms of conceptual framework. For instance, there are 3-level [26] and 5-level [25] structures of e-participation, as well as a complex of their dimensions involving democratic, project and socio-technical criteria proposed by Macintosh [15], institutional factors [10], active actors and contextual factors [17], information exchange and influence on political decision [24].

In scientific literature when it comes to assessing social effects from e-participation, the term "creation of values" is used more often. In case of e-participation portals operation public values should be mentioned – as they are created in completely different ways regardless of those that can be found in the private sector [18]. The process of value creation is described through the steps of a behavioral model [14], as well as relations between inside and out actors [11].

Based on literature review the following large groups of indicators have been found in order to describe some points of e-participation social efficiency:

- Regulation framework and legitimation [3, 7];
- Usage level, popularity, usability [8];
- Deliberation possibilities [1, 20];
- Multichannel accesses [12];
- Users' activities and satisfaction [13, 23];
- Openness and transparency [21, 30];
- Possibilities for information sharing [5];
- Social media involvement [4, 9, 19, 22].

Concluding from literature review research teams usually develop their own tools, not referring to the positive experience of their predecessors, and try to cover the measurement of specific components that they are interested in. The results of local cases assessment are not translated into evaluating projects of a wider scale. Current literature on e-participation involves the development of a new evaluation system. Both scientists and politics agree that it is crucial to develop such a reliable evaluation system: scientists have to understand the practice of e-participation to provide the proper recommendations addressing officials' needs to build a positive dialogue with citizens.

ICT usage in governmental practices has a long history in Russia. The very first attempts were taken during the Administrative reform (2006–2010) and E-Russia program (2002–2010). Then there appeared such state programs as Information Society, Open Government, Open Data, etc. The previous investigations [2, 28] showed the importance of institutional factors and the political will in the development of such initiatives. Additionally, the texts of strategic documents and regulations in the sphere of G2C electronic interaction reflect the following indicators used in Russian practice:

e-participation channels, administrative level, citizen satisfaction, citizens' involvement, statistical indicators, indicators of technology infrastructure assessment, publication of open government data, cybersecurity, evaluation of different types of electronic participation, social and economic effects.

E-participation tools began operating in Russia in 2011, and there were several initiative projects at first. The government paid attention to citizens' engagement in policy-making in 2013, when the first e-petition portal (Russian public initiative) was launched. There is no single vision or unified strategy on e-participation development [6], however some activities and performance indicators could be found in the state documents [28].

At the moment, there is no comprehensive methodology for assessing the efficiency of the e-participation system. In existing methods very little attention is paid to the relationship between stakeholders and social effects achieved. The next sections of the paper describe the methodology developed for e-participation assessment and its approbation on the Russian portals. The methodology developed was aimed to solve a theoretical task - to link the evidences of e-participation development with social effects appeared.

3   Methodology for E-participation Portals Assessment

The present research describes e-participation as a set of methods and tools that ensure electronic interaction between citizens and authorities in order to consider the citizens' opinion in terms of decision making at state and municipal level. From this point of view e-participation social efficiency presents the ability to realize publicly stated goals, achieve results that meet the needs of population and are accessible to those who are interested in them.

From the point of view of state and municipal government projects, social efficiency is viewed as a positive consequence of an investment project's implementation that manifests itself in improving the quality of life, with an increase in the volume or supply of new services, increasing access, timeliness and the regularity of their provision. In this study social efficiency means the ability to achieve policy stated goals, get results that meet the citizens' needs and accessible to those who are interested in them, with the fullest use of conditions and factors.

The methodology developed for e-participation social efficiency has been created for evaluating Russian e-participation portals that refer to e-decision making category of international Measurement and Evaluation Tool for Engagement and e-Participation (hereinafter METEP) [16]. The possibility to measure real effects in decision-making determines the choice of this category.

The general scheme of interaction between citizens and government can be presented as an attempt to find an optimal balance between the decisions a government makes considering citizens' interests and opinions regarding the content of procedures and the consequences of such decisions.

The methodology for e-participation social efficiency assessment concentrates on 3 interrelated processes:

1. Creation of e-participation tools by a government (or non-government organizations) and ensuring universal access to them;
2. Usage of the portal by citizens, creation of content (citizens' contribution and its quality);
3. Incorporation of citizens' opinions in political decisions (improving the quality of decision-making).

The efficiency of each process ultimately affects the efficiency of participation in general. Understanding this interaction scheme leads to the need to assess the efficiency of participation at each stage of the decision-making cycle.

3.1 Stages of Political Decision-Making

General scheme of interaction between citizens and government can be presented as an attempt to find some optimal balance between the government decisions in the interests of citizens and the citizens' opinions regarding the procedures and consequences of such decisions. Accordingly, the state and citizens, as the main actors of political participation, are linked among themselves by three interrelated processes. First, it is the process of state creation of e-participation tools and ensuring universal and equitable access to them (accessibility and inclusiveness). On this basis, the process of using such instruments by citizens and the creation of appropriate content on their part unfolds. A special role here is played by the quality of the contribution and their awareness (participation of the first type). The cycle of interaction is closed by the process again on the side of the state, which is aimed at incorporating the opinions of citizens in the decision. The key aspect of this process is the government ability to analyze citizens' contribution and optimally use it in improving both the quality and legitimacy of decisions. The effectiveness of each process ultimately affects the effectiveness of participation in general. Understanding the scheme of such interaction between the state and citizens leads to assess the effectiveness of participation at each stage of decision-making agenda.

The methodology developed corresponds to the international methodology of the policy decision cycle, which includes 5 consecutive stages [27]:

1. Agenda setting – providing information to the public on the political decisions proposed by creating prerequisites for organizing citizens' contribution (publication on e-participation portals petitions, citizens' initiatives, availability of tools for public discussion).
2. Policy preparation – analysis of public contribution, collection of different opinions, proposals, criticism, voices from a portal's audience as well as attracting new users to them.
3. Inclusion of citizens' contribution in decision – formulation of citizens' ideas and their transfer to responsible authorities.
4. Policy execution – authorities' response on citizens' applications, voting etc., implementation of decisions adopted.
5. Policy monitoring – monitoring of political decisions implementation, indicating citizens' feedback on the decision-making outcomes.

3.2 Dimensions of Social Efficiency

As mentioned above social efficiency assessment includes three interrelated dimensions: political, technological and socio-economic. These dimensions allow to assess comprehensively the availability, use and effects of e-participation portal.

The indicators of the political dimension assess how legitimate the portal is and what political values are created while using portals (transparency of power decisions and creation of platforms for deliberation).

The technological dimension creates a basis for measuring the potential readiness of the target audience to use the portal, as well as the level of activity at the portal expressed in the amount of messages and comments.

The socio-economic dimension makes it possible to draw conclusions about the efficiency of the submitted applications/initiatives/petitions, as well as the formation of cohesive real communities of citizens, dedicated to the activities of portals and the problems raised there.

3.3 System of Indicators

To assess the social efficiency of e-participation portals, a methodology for evaluating portals has been developed. The methodology includes a system of 27 indicators that reveal three dimensions at each decision-making stage, a description of procedures and methods for data collection as well as formulas for calculating indicators.

According to the methodology, for each indicator the estimated portal can receive from 0 to 1 points. Table 1 presents the set of indicators for the assessment. The set of indicators was created on the base of large indicators groups revealed from literature review, as well as results of expert consultation on the specific of Russian e-participation portals development.

The following principles have been considered in choosing the research methods for data collection:

- uniformity of indicators scale, the calculation of their normalized values,
- openness and accessibility of data collection,
- verification possibility of the procedure for estimating and calculating control indicators.

The methodology aims to collect objectively observable characteristics that determine the achievement of the social efficiency. At this stage, the methodology includes no positions related to subjective characteristics revealed by interview methods or opinion polls.

To obtain data for each indicator, the following traditional methods were applied: official statistics, keyword search, web analytics, expert evaluation. In addition, two methods for data analysis were used to conduct the assessment: (1) automated research of network communities formed around e-participation portals (with the use of a web-crawler configured to collect data on the relationships between users of communities), and (2) automated monitoring of e-participation portals via the information system created by the authors.

Table 1. System of indicators for assessing e-participation portals' social efficiency. Source: the authors' methodology

Stage	Dimension	Indicators	Social effects
1. Agenda setting	Political	Legitimacy, regulation framework	Openness Citizens' awareness with participation opportunities
	Technical	Internet usage Easy search of the portal	
	Socio-economic	Registration in ESIA (single inf.system for the Russian citizens) Information sharing about the portal	
2. Policy preparation	Political	Possibilities of deliberation	Active citizens' involvement Sense of community
	Technical	Users' support at all stages Opportunities for participation people with disabilities Multichannel participation Links with other tools and resources	
	Socio-economic	Citizens' activity in publications Growth of network activity Nature of citizens' contribution	
3. Inclusion of citizens' contribution in decision	Political	Officials' responsibility for a response Obligation to the inform public on citizens' contribution analysis	Democratic values generation
	Technical	Usability and interface Personal data security	
	Socio-economic	Voting activity Additional tools for citizens' opinions collection	
4. Policy execution	Political	Problem solving/petition's support	Justice and fairness of decision-making Transparency
	Technical	Publication of review's history	
	Socio-economic	Users' satisfaction	
5. Policy monitoring	Political	Transparency of results and G2C interaction Confirmation of influence on political decisions	Trust in government Citizens' satisfaction
	Technical	Ranking of citizens and their input Access to archiving	
	Socio-economic	Time saving for G2C interaction	

All indicators presented were reduced to a single scale from 0 to 1. To calculate the level of social efficiency for each portal, the integral estimates for each dimension were calculated with the final indicator of social efficiency being as an integral measure of the three dimensions (additive function).

The evaluation of the dimension is defined as the ratio of the sum of the indicators in stage n to the maximum possible number of indicators for stage n, multiplied by 100%. In its turn, the score for each *stage* is calculated as the arithmetic sum of the measurement estimates with a 1/3 coefficient for each dimension.

As an integral evaluation (eParticipation Impact Index), the arithmetic sum of estimates of parameters is taken (taking into account coefficient k for each stage). The coefficients for calculating the final indicator are set for each stage: 0.1 – for the first stage, 0.2 – for the 2 and 3 stages, 0.25 – for the 4 and 5 stages.

The final ranking of social efficiency assessment portals is made by recalculating the index in accordance with the groups of 5 levels of social efficiency development:

1. Level 1 - Very low – 0–24,9%
2. Level 2 - Low – 25–49,9%
3. Level 3 - Medium – 50–69,9%
4. Level 4 - High – 70–89,9%
5. Level 5 - Very high – 90–100%

Thus, when assessing the social effectiveness of the e-participation portal, it is assigned the appropriate level of development, in accordance with the estimates received in the range presented.

4   Results of E-participation Portals Social Efficiency Assessment

For the approbation of the proposed methodology, five portals have been chosen: the Russian public initiative, Change.org (Russian segment), Our Petersburg, the Beautiful Petersburg, and Open Penza. Approbation was carried out in autumn 2017. All these portals belong to the category of e-decision-making portals. At the same time, the research interest was focused on measuring the portals created on government or initiative base, as well as the portals address federal, regional and municipal levels issues.

- The portal «*Russian Public Initiative*» (hereinafter RPI, https://www.roi.ru/) is a platform for the publication of citizens' initiatives. The portal was developed by the authorities' will. For published initiatives, citizens can leave the votes "for" or "against". If initiatives overcome the necessary threshold of votes (100 thousand for the federal level, and 5% of the population for the regional and municipal), it is submitted for a discussion to an expert group and depending on the results can go to the authority in charge.
- The portal «*Change.org*» (https://www.change.org/) is a world-wide platform for civil campaigns where citizens publish petitions, disseminate information about them, interact with addressees of petitions and actively involve supporters.

- The portal «*Our Saint Petersburg*» (https://gorod.gov.spb.ru/) was created on the initiative of the governor of Saint Petersburg. The portal allows citizens to send messages about city problems, and then transfer them to the responsible authorities.
- The portal «*Beautiful Petersburg*» (http://красивыйпетербург.рф) - a platform of civic activists' movement for improving the city. The platform appeared before the official portal and quickly became quite popular.
- The portal «*Open Penza*» (http://open-penza.ru/) collects information about the state of the city management and beautification, demonstrating problem points. Through the Internet portal the citizens send applications and can monitor their decisions. This site also includes a unified database on all city problems.

The indicators were assessed using the web portal analytics, automated monitoring system for e-participation portals, automated tool for network communities' analysis, official statistics and experts' scores.

During the web analytics the indicators detected were registered in the form of screenshots identifying the features revealed. The automated monitoring system created at ITMO University (http://analytics.egov.ifmo.ru) allowed real-time data downloading on submitted initiatives/petitions/appeals, number of votes, as well as measuring increase/decrease of users' activity. The authors developed the automated module for data collection, processing and visualization for each studied portal. The implementation of the modules is presented in the user's interface, which is open for access after registration in the system.

For network communities' analysis a web-based research center in the field of sociodynamics and its applications (http://socio.escience.ifmo.ru/) was used. The tool allowed to find and analyze information about messages and their authors in social networks, as well as relations between community members. The researchers found out the communities belonged to the portals studied and set a web-crawler for data collection in these specific groups. Both websites of Rosstat (http://www.gks.ru/) and the Ministry of Communications and Mass Communication (http://minsvyaz.ru) were used as statistic data sources. In addition, the qualitative analysis of documents posted in the following sections: "Resolved" (Beautiful Petersburg), "Decisions made" (RPI), "Already solved problems" (Our St. Petersburg), "Victories" (Change.org), "Solved problems" (Open Penza), was conducted.

The indicators' scores were recorded in a spreadsheet, then the estimates by dimensions, stages and the final value were calculated. Table 2 presents the results of calculating indicators for the stages of political decision-making, the final value and the corresponding level of e-participation social efficiency.

Table 2. Results of e-participation portals' assessment, 2017. Source: the authors' collected data

Portal	Stage 1	Stage 2	Stage 3	Stage 4	Stage 5	Final	Level
RPI	67,67	25,31	55,50	33,39	46,00	42,77	2
Change.org	42,67	53,78	61,00	56,67	50,00	53,89	3
Our St. Petersburg	67,33	11,42	50,00	59,33	75,00	52,60	3
Beautiful Petersburg	42,33	30,89	45,83	37,33	58,33	43,49	2
Open Penza	59,50	10,75	33,83	45,67	66,67	42,95	2

The «RPI» portal demonstrated a high indicator (67.7%) of the "Agenda setting" implementation, a little more than a half (55%) for the 3rd stage development, only ¼ level of "Inclusion of citizens' contribution in decisions" stage, 1/3 of the possible level at the Policy execution stage, and slightly less than half (46%) of Policy monitoring. In general «Change.org» portal had higher scores than the previous portal: only the first stage achieved 42% out of 100%, the remaining stages were at the level of 50–61%. The portal «Our St. Petersburg» received high scores for all stages, except for the analysis of the citizens' contribution in decisions (11.4%), where the lowest indicators were obtained in the socio-economic dimension. The indicators of the «Beautiful Petersburg» were almost equal at all stages at the level of 30–40%. However, this portal demonstrated high scores at the political and socio-economic dimension at Policy monitoring stage. The «Open Penza» had the lowest scores for Policy preparation (10.7%).

Less difference in indicators was recorded among technological dimensions in stages 1–4 (see Fig. 1). The greatest spread of indicators was noted in the assessments of socio-economic indicators for all stages. These results in combination with equal weighting coefficients of measurements have led to the conclusion that the value of the final indicator was determined by the achievements of e-participation portals on socio-economic and political dimensions.

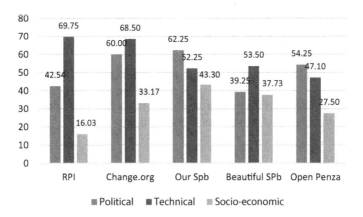

Fig. 1. Distribution of e-participation marks by 3 dimensions of social efficiency. Source: the authors' collected data

Based on the results, the portals «Change.org» and «Our St. Petersburg» showed the medium level of e-participation social efficiency while the rest portals had a low level.

5   Conclusion

The study conducted underlines that the term "social efficiency" is a quite complex and it is still difficult to operationalize in accordance with the research tasks. From this point of view this phenomenon is unlikely to be measured without decomposition into subsystems and dimensions. In this research the authors have proposed a 5 stage and 3-dimensional view on e-participation portals social efficiency.

From the country perspective there should exist a single e-participation program with the proper performance indicators. Since there is no such a program in Russia, the methodology proposed is based on the international practice incorporating the aims of information society stated in the federal programs.

Moreover, there is also an issue of data availability as the research topic cannot be covered by statistic data only, and there are no comprehensive opinion polls with main stakeholders conducted in Russia. To overcome this challenge, the authors have developed a special research tool for collection open data from e-participation portals and also paid attention to social network communities that gathered active citizens - real users of e-participation portals.

For the validation of the methodology developed and its approbation the expert survey was conducted. 15 experts from public administration, research institutions, IT companies and NGOs were interviewed about the conceptual framework, the completeness of indicators set, the mathematical basis and the approbation results. In general, the experts confirmed the high level of the approbation, they agreed that the results corresponded the observed picture. Thus, the portals have much to strive for.

According to experts the methodology presented is original, has a scientific novelty. The following recommendations were proposed:

- add different weights to the three dimensions;
- prescribe the typology of portals that are to be evaluated using the developed methodology;
- request information from the portals developers from their back office;
- involve experts for a qualitative assessment of portals.

6   Discussion

The research has some limitations. The number of indicators is limited, and some indicators are linked with the other data sources. However, the portals themselves do not provide all the necessary data to draw a picture of e-participation efficiency. We understand that some data on social effects' measurement could be collected through public opinion polls. At the same time, when we speak about the efficiency of a specific portal, it's really hard to get the audience of that particular portal.

The study revealed the achievement of such social effects as openness and citizens' involvement in decision preparation. At the same time, the rest of the effects proposed in the methodology stay almost untouched or still unclear for interpretation.

The research results could not be generalized for all e-participation portals in Russia, but the methodology itself could be of interest for measurement each case one by one.

At the next stages it is important to test the methodology proposed on a larger sample and provide recommendations for the portals developers to build a better G2C dialogue.

Acknowledgements. This work was conducted with the support of RFBR grant No. 16-36-60035, "The research of social efficiency of e-participation portals in Russia".

References

1. Chugunov, A., Filatova, O., Misnikov, Y.: Online discourse as a microdemocracy tool: towards new discursive epistemics for policy deliberation. In: ACM International Conference Proceeding Series, 01–03 March 2016, pp. 40–49. ACM (2016)
2. Chugunov, A.V., Kabanov, Y., Misnikov, Y.: Citizens versus the government or citizens with the government: a tale of two e-participation portals in one city - a case study of St. Petersburg, Russia. In: ACM International Conference Proceeding Series, Part F128003, pp. 70–77. ACM (2017)
3. Civil Participation in Decision-Making Processes: An overview of standards and practices in Council of European Member States. European Center for Not-for-profit Law. European Center for Not-for-profit Law (2016)
4. Criado, J.I., Rojas-Martín, F., Gil-Garcia, J.R.: Enacting social media success in local public administrations: an empirical analysis of organizational, institutional, and contextual factors. Int. J. Public Sect. Manag. **30**(1), 31–47 (2017). https://doi.org/10.1108/IJPSM-03-2016-0053
5. Dawes, S.S., Gharawi, M.A., Burke, G.B.: Transnational public sector knowledge networks: knowledge and information sharing in a multi-dimensional context. Gov. Inf. Q. **29**(Suppl. 1), S112–S120 (2012). https://doi.org/10.1016/j.giq.2011.08.002
6. Dawes, S.S., Vidiasova, L., Parkhimovich, O.: Planning and designing open government data programs: an ecosystem approach. Gov. Inf. Q. **33**(1), 15–27 (2016). https://doi.org/10.1016/j.giq.2016.01.003
7. Gil-Garcia, J.R., Pardo, T.A., Sutherland, M.K.: Information sharing in the regulatory context: revisiting the concepts of cross-boundary information sharing. In: ACM International Conference Proceeding Series, 01–03 March 2016, pp. 346–349. ACM (2016)
8. Hagen, L., Harrison, T.M., Uzuner, Ö., May, W., Fake, T., Katragadda, S.: E-petition popularity: do linguistic and semantic factors matter? Gov. Inf. Q. **33**(4), 783–795 (2016). https://doi.org/10.1016/j.giq.2016.07.006
9. Harrison, T.M., et al.: E-petitioning and online media: the case of #bringbackourgirls. In: ACM International Conference Proceeding Series, Part F128275, pp. 11–20. ACM (2017)
10. Jho, W., Song, K.: Institutional and technological determinants of civil e-Participation: Solo or duet? Gov. Inf. Q. **32**, 488–495 (2015). https://doi.org/10.1016/j.giq.2015.09.003
11. Jorgensen, T., Bozeman, B.: Public values an inventory. Adm. Soc. **39**, 354–381 (2007). https://doi.org/10.1177/0095399707300703
12. Kawaljeet, K.K., Amizan, O., Utyasankar, S.: Enabling multichannel participation through ICT adaptation. Int. J. Electron. Gov. Res. **13**, 66–80 (2017). https://doi.org/10.4018/IJEGR.2017040104
13. Kipenis, L., Askounis, D.: Assessing e-Participation via user's satisfaction measurement: the case of OurSpace platform. Ann. Oper. Res. **247**(2), 599–615 (2016). https://doi.org/10.1007/s10479-015-1911-8
14. Luna-Reyes, L.F., Sandoval-Almazan, R., Puron-Cid, G., Picazo-Vela, S., Luna, Dolores E., G-G., J.R.: Understanding public value creation in the delivery of electronic services. In: Janssen, M., et al. (eds.) EGOV 2017. LNCS, vol. 10428, pp. 378–385. Springer, Cham (2017). https://doi.org/10.1007/978-3-319-64677-0_31

15. Macintosh, A., Whyte, A.: Towards an evaluation framework for e-Participation. Transform. Gov. People Process Policy **2**(1), 16–30 (2008). https://doi.org/10.1108/17506160810862928

16. Measuring and Evaluating e-Participation (METEP): Assessment of Readiness at the Country Level. UNDESA Working Paper (2013). http://workspace.unpan.org/sites/Internet/Documents/METEP%20framework_18%20Jul_MOST%20LATEST%20Version.pdf

17. Medaglia, R.: eParticipation research: moving characterization forward (2006–2011). Gov. Inf. Q. **29**, 346–360 (2012). https://doi.org/10.1016/j.giq.2012.02.010

18. Moore, M.H.: Creating Public Value: Strategic Management in Government. Harvard University Press, Cambridge (1995)

19. Picazo-Vela, S., et al.: The role of social media sites on social movements against policy changes. In: ACM International Conference Proceeding Series, Part F128275, pp. 588–589. ACM (2017)

20. Radu, R.: E-participation and deliberation in the European Union: the case of debate Europe. Int. J. E-Polit. **5**(2), 1–15 (2014). https://doi.org/10.4018/ijep.2014040101

21. Reggi, L., Dawes, S.: Open government data ecosystems: linking transparency for innovation with transparency for participation and accountability. In: Scholl, H.J., et al. (eds.) EGOVIS 2016. LNCS, vol. 9820, pp. 74–86. Springer, Cham (2016). https://doi.org/10.1007/978-3-319-44421-5_6

22. Sandoval-Almazan, R., Gil-Garcia, J.R.: Cyberactivism through social media: Twitter, YouTube, and the Mexican political movement "I'm Number 132". In: Proceedings of the Annual Hawaii International Conference on System Sciences, № 6480047, pp. 1704–1713 (2013)

23. Scherer, S., Wimmer, M.: Trust in E-participation: literature review and emerging research needs. In: Proceedings of the 8th International Conference on Theory and Practice of Electronic Governance, pp. 61–70, 27–30 October 2014, Guimaraes (2014)

24. Schroeter, R., Scheel, O., Renn, O., Schweizer, P.: Testing the value of public participation in Germany: theory, operationalization and a case study on the evaluation of participation. Energy Res. Soc. Sci. **13**, 116–125 (2015). https://doi.org/10.1016/j.erss.2015.12.013

25. Ter'an, L., Drobnjak, A.: An evaluation framework for eParticipation: the VAAs case study. Int. Sch. Sci. Res. Innov. **7**(1), 77–85 (2013)

26. UN E-government Survey (2016). https://publicadministration.un.org/egovkb/en-us/reports/un-e-government-survey-2016

27. Van Dijk, J.A.G.M.: Participation in policy making. Study of Social Impact of ICT (CPP № 55 A - SMART №2007/0068). Topic Report, pp. 32–72 (2010)

28. Vidiasova, L., Dawes, S.S.: The influence of institutional factors on E-governance development and performance: an exploration in the Russian Federation. Inf. Polity **22**(4), 267–289 (2017). https://doi.org/10.3233/IP-170416

29. Vidiasova, L.: The applicability of international techniques for E-participation assessment in the Russian context. In: Chugunov, A.V., Bolgov, R., Kabanov, Y., Kampis, G., Wimmer, M. (eds.) DTGS 2016. CCIS, vol. 674, pp. 145–154. Springer, Cham (2016). https://doi.org/10.1007/978-3-319-49700-6_15

30. Zheng, Y.: The impact of E-participation on corruption: a cross-country analysis. Int. Rev. Public Adm. **21**(2), 91–103 (2016). https://doi.org/10.1080/12294659.2016.1186457

Direct Deliberative Democracy: A Mixed Model

(Deliberative for Active Citizens, just Aggregative for Lazy Ones)

Cyril Velikanov[✉]

"Memorial" Society, Moscow, Russia
cvelikanov@gmail.com

Abstract. In this paper, I introduce and discuss a new model of governance, in which epistemic qualities of intrinsically elitist open deliberation are combined with normative qualities of aggregative democracy based on universal suffrage. In our model, these two approaches, typically considered as opposite to each other, are combined in a quite natural way. Namely, the process of deliberative policy-making in a community is open to every its member who is willing to participate (the "active" ones); while all others (the "lazy" ones) are provided with the possibility of either to cast their informed vote, or, at the end, to delegate their voting right to the whole community, through an IT system enforcing appropriate procedures and performing appropriate algorithms. Practical implementation of our model will be made possible through a combined use of (1) a procedural framework for Mass common Online Deliberation (MOD), which had been described in detail in our past papers; (2) an appropriately designed Computer-Assisted Argumentation (CAA) system; and (3) a system for collecting and taking into account individual preferences of every "lazy" citizen, in a way similar to the so-called Voting Advice Application (VAA) systems.

Keywords: Deliberative democracy · Mass online deliberation
Aggregative democracy · Computer-Assisted Argumentation · Implicit vote

1 Introduction

Our starting assumption is that the deliberative model of democratic governance is indeed superior, at least theoretically, to the aggregative one, i.e. to the model(s) based on immutable social choices of citizens. Deliberative model is, however, intrinsically elitist, for, not all people are capable to exercise the Habermassian "forceless force of the better argument" (Habermas [4, 5]), even when they have their vital interests to defend, or a valuable proposal to move. Such a real (or only imaginary) argumentative inability deters from deliberative participation many of those who otherwise would have something important to say.

In a series of my earlier papers I proposed a procedural model (further developed in Velikanov and Prosser [10]) called *Mass Online Deliberation* or "MOD", for a very large-scale common online deliberation on a given issue, which satisfies the basic requirements of *fairness*, *inclusiveness* (in some sense of the word), *productivity*, and *economy* of time and efforts required from the participants. Here, "common deliberation"

© Springer Nature Switzerland AG 2018
D. A. Alexandrov et al. (Eds.): DTGS 2018, CCIS 858, pp. 63–77, 2018.
https://doi.org/10.1007/978-3-030-02843-5_6

means an activity of deliberating all together, in one common "virtual room", rather than in several small groups in parallel (as e.g. in Deliberative Polling®, see Fishkin [3]). Such a large common deliberation can only progress if some necessary "housekeeping" activities are continuously performed in a way as to keep the "common deliberation space" noise-free (by filtering out spam and other irrelevant input) and, in addition, well-sorted, ranked and ordered. In our model, these activities are performed collaboratively by the participants themselves, facilitated and "orchestrated" by an appropriately designed IT system.

This "collaborative housekeeping" method is expected to make our basic deliberative model practically implementable—with virtually no impact, however, on its intrinsically elitist character. To abate this elitism, we need deploying additional efforts. In (Velikanov [9]), I proposed a method to increase inclusiveness of a public deliberation. It consists in bringing help and advice in argumentation to the least prepared deliberators by their more advanced peers. This can be seen as yet another collaborative activity, performed by participants themselves, while being facilitated and orchestrated by the system. In this way, everybody concerned with an issue can valuably take part in a common, fair and purposeful deliberation on the issue.

In a typical case, the deliberation outcome will be a short-list of alternative solutions to select from (for, reaching a full consensus on a controversial issue can be set as a theoretical goal only). Thus, the final step of selecting one winning alternative needs aggregating the choices (or the rankings) made by all participants in the deliberation. This step therefore is not deliberative but aggregative (see Mansbridge et al. [6]). I will not expand here on the aggregation algorithm to use, as this topic relates to voting systems, and as such had been extensively studied elsewhere.

What, then, will happen to those people who nevertheless will abstain, the "lazy" ones? Indeed, not all of them would abstain just because of laziness; many would abstain because of a feeling (often erroneous) of not being concerned, or of an extreme timidity, or of concrete circumstances of their life, etc. (Velikanov [8]). So, "lazy" is used here just as a shorthand expression for all those "deliberation abstentionists", whose proportion may turn out to be even higher than that of today's non-voters.

We should assume, however, that many of those abstentionists would become affected in future by the choice made by their more active peers; so, the basic democratic principle requires that their interests and preferences be taken into account as well. Hence, the final "vote" should be open to everybody, not just to the deliberators. To help every such voter in making a reasonable choice, the deliberators may collaboratively prepare a "profile" for every alternative, which will state to what degree the alternative satisfies every basic value and every common interest pertaining to the issue considered[1].

On the other hand, the community may ask every citizen to specify their *personal preference profile*, e.g. by filling a questionnaire where they state their preferences in terms of basic values and (typical) personal interests. Then, before casting their vote,

---

[1] Alternatively, if at the beginning of the process a list of *requirements* has been set up, which shall be satisfied, to a greater or lesser degree, by every alternative solution accepted to enter the final vote, then the profile of an alternative would take the form of a *requirements compliance vector*. In the subsequent sections of the paper, I will further expand on this idea.

they can compare their personal profile with the profile of every alternative, to find out the best match or, better, to rank the alternatives starting from the best match. The whole functionality is similar to what is known as Voting Advice Application (VAA), with a number of notable differences that will be discussed in Sect. 6 below.

What about those who have specified their profile, but have not cast their vote explicitly? My idea is to consider, for every such "lazy non-voter", the system-proposed "best match" with their personal profile as their *implicit choice*, which could enter the common aggregation process—indeed, if authorized by that non-voter[2].

In this way, we arrive at the highest possible inclusiveness of the democratic will-formation, while maintaining the largest possible participation in its deliberative phase. Thus, my model, which I call "Direct Deliberative Democracy", or "D3", has a mixed nature: it is direct and deliberative for active citizens, while remaining just aggregative for "lazy" ones. Moreover, as the "lazy non-voters" would "delegate" their voting power to the system (more precisely, to those participants who have specified every alternative's profile), my model can be considered as *representative* (in some sense of the word) with regard to those lazy people[3].

Below this introductory section, the paper is organized as follows. In Sect. 2, I present in more detail the multistage process of deliberative policy-making. In Sects. 3 to 5, I introduce the main three components of my model, resp. Mass Online Deliberation (MOD), Argumentative Facilitation, and Implicit Vote. The MOD component is the central one; however, its presentation here is just a short summary of (Velikanov and Prosser [10]). Argumentative Facilitation has been succinctly presented in my other paper (Velikanov [9]). The concept of Implicit Vote is the newest one, and therefore it is discussed here in more detail. In Sect. 6, I discuss a VAA-derived method of filling everyone's *personal preference profile*; the system will explore those preference profiles both for advising non-participants in taking the right choice, and for taking the most appropriate choice automatically in the name of every non-voter (implicit vote). At the end of Sect. 6, I discuss the issue of confidentiality with regard to personal preferences that will be stored and manipulated by the system.

---

[2] Or, if such an implicit vote is made compulsory by law, for every person that hasn't cast their vote explicitly.

[3] At the very end, we should also consider the case of those "laziest" people who have neither voted explicitly, nor filled their preference profile at all. This does not mean, however, that these people will not be *affected* by any direct or indirect effect of the solution chosen by all others. Should we, nevertheless, drop those people from any consideration in a given policy-making instance? Or, instead, we should try to *approximate* the preference profile of each of them, e.g. by considering known parameters of their *socio-economic status* (SES) and then define their "implicit preference profile" by averaging and extrapolating the profiles of people with similar SES who have explicitly specified their profiles? This is not a purely technical question, but a question of political theory as well. For, one thing is aggregating needs and preferences of those who *feel (or believe) themselves concerned* with an issue, and a quite different thing is taking into account *assumed* needs and preferences of all those who are supposed to be *affected* by the issue, though remain mute and inactive (cf. Sunstein [7]).

2 Multistage Deliberative Policy-Making Process

To better locate my proposed conceptual and procedural innovations within the overall process of online participatory and deliberative policy-making, let us consider every instance of the latter[4] as a multistage process, which progresses through the following stages:

1. discovering and formulating a *problem* to solve;
2. setting up *requirements* to be satisfied by every acceptable solution;
3. submitting *proposals* on how to solve the problem, discussing those proposals, and assorting them into a "short-list" of edited *alternatives*;
4. evaluating alternatives resulting from stage 3 against the requirements defined in stage 2, in order to fill, for every alternative, its *requirement compliance vector*;
5. and finally, selecting one "winning" solution among the alternatives, by collecting implicitly or explicitly expressed individual *rankings* of them, and then *aggregating*, for every competing alternative, all its rankings assigned by individual participants.

Each of the stages 1 to 4 is assumed to progress in a deliberative setting, which is either open to every member of the community concerned (esp. at stage 3), or somehow representing the whole community (at stages 2 and 4—see discussion below).[5] Stage 5 by its very nature is not deliberative but aggregative.

In addition, let us consider that every participant (including every "lazy" one) had specified their *personal preference profile* at the very beginning of the above five-stage process. This activity is therefore assumed to happen in a separate "Stage 0", prior to the Stage 1. Every participant's profile shall be kept strictly confidential and shall never be disclosed to other people. Let us consider, however, that *the system* (an IT system supporting the online participation process) may have algorithmic access to all those profiles—in the same way as browsers and mail servers keep track of your activities and manage this information in order to better personalize their services; we will use this feature in a similar way. A more detailed account of the whole subject will be proposed in Sect. 6.

Let us start with setting the basic requirements on participation in every stage. I argue that stage 1 (formulating a problem) and, yet more importantly, stage 3 (submitting,

---

[4] In my earlier papers, I have introduced a neologism *deliberandum*, which designates a specific instance of public deliberation on a given issue, within a given community, on a given online platform, and with a given time schedule. A deliberandum on an issue is a process quite naturally leading to a *referendum*, for selecting one solution among proposed alternatives. In my proposed design, such a referendum can be considered as the 5-th stage of the process.

[5] At some stages of this process, involvement of external experts (domain specific ones, legal ones, etc.) may often appear necessary. Their selection/accreditation is a very difficult issue, as they need a double recognition: recognition of their knowledge and skills by their professional community (epistemic), and recognition of their integrity by the deliberating community (normative). This issue needs separate consideration.

discussing, and elaborating alternative solutions) should, first of all, provide for *open-ness*. That is, each of these two stages should be open for participation to every eligible[6] citizen who wishes[7] to take part in.

For, in both these stages the main task is rather *creative* (and even *inventive* at stage 3) than evaluative, and open participation by its nature provides for richer cognitive diversity, crowd wisdom and crowd creativity, hence, for epistemically better results. It also provides for fuller citizens' satisfaction in *normative* terms, for, nobody could then rightfully claim, "you haven't given me an opportunity to submit my idea for public consideration, that's why you've come with a poor solution…"

This is the main reason why I am not considering James Fishkin's Deliverative Polling® as an acceptable option for both stages 1 and 3.

Stage 2 (setting up a list of requirements) is indeed less creative than evaluative; and stage 4 (defining requirement compliance vectors for the alternative solutions developed in stage 3) is purely evaluative. Hence, the basic requirement for these two stages is *representativeness*: every [cluster of] opinion[s] shall be represented in the panel of participants performing at this stage.

As per the concluding stage 5, it shall be as *inclusive* as possible. Namely, everyone is appealed to cast their vote; as for the abstentionists, according to my proposed concept of *implicit voting*, their vote is assumed to be the one calculated by the system as "the best match" with, or derived from, their personal preference profile.

Hereafter, our five stages are presented and discussed in more detail.

1. Discovering and formulating a problem to solve. In the overall (and presumably continuous or recurrent) process of open deliberative policy-making in a community, this stage relates to *agenda setting*. Hence, every its instance should normally lead to adding to the policy-making agenda a certain problem to solve as a new item, or to rejecting it as insignificant or inappropriate (or else, to postponing its further consideration because of its relatively low impact or low urgency).

Stage 1 is not time-critical, nor its particular outcomes (i.e. new items added to the agenda) need always be incontestable. For, if an insignificant, or a badly formulated, or even a false problem is put into the agenda, it will certainly not withstand deliberation at the subsequent stages. If, however, an important problem fails to enter the agenda at a given time, there remains a possibility to resubmit it at a later time.

Furthermore, a good agenda planning requires that no person is appealed to participate simultaneously in more than, say, 2 or 3 deliberations over different issues that are all of concern for them. For, otherwise, some people would abstain from deliberating over some issues just because they haven't got enough time for it.

---

[6] I assume that every instance of policy-making relates to a given *community*, which can be a territorial (country-state, region, city, municipality), or professional, or religious, etc. A citizen of a state who is not legally deprived of his/her civic rights is an *eligible* citizen; the same term can be applied to a member of a community. In this paper, I use the terms 'citizen' and 'community member' interchangeably, always assuming their eligibility.

[7] ὁ βουλόμενος in Ancient Athenian terms (literally, 'anyone who wishes', a shortened form of a longer expression signifying 'anyone who wishes among those who can', that is, among eligible Athenian citizens).

Free participation of citizens in agenda-setting is one of Robert Dahl's five basic criteria for a democratic process (Dahl [2]). There is no need, however, for the whole community to discuss every "citizen's request for consideration" in common. Rather, every specific request can be discussed within a circle of those strongly concerned with the issue, and different such requests can be discussed in parallel. On the contrary, the "vote of interest" in pushing a given problem toward the next stages of the community policy-making should involve the whole community—this is necessary for a good agenda planning, in order to avoid too large intersections of the community subsets involved in different deliberations.

The whole concept needs a further elaboration and an appropriate procedural implementation. For, several national platforms for "submitting citizens' proposals" exist in different European countries and elsewhere; most if not all of them, however, are used by citizens in a "submit and forget" way, with every specific request attracting just a handful of readers and supporters, thus making those systems inapt of serving the agenda-planning purpose. See more detailed discussion in (Velikanov and Prosser [10]).

2. Setting up a list of requirements. In any technological problem-solving process, a stage of setting up a list of requirements to be satisfied by any solution to a problem is typically considered as necessary. Similarly, this stage is very useful if not necessary when designing a process of societal problem solving. For, conflicting interests and differently ordered values of different citizens can be better assessed prior to discussing any specific proposal of a problem solution, in a stage of formulating "societal requirements". The latter can take the form of "this or that value shall be honored/promoted", or "this or that interest of (the group of) people concerned with the problem, or with direct or indirect effects of applying any of its solutions, shall be taken into account".

Do we really need at this stage an effective participation of the whole community, to formulate those requirements in a reasonably full and societally acceptable way? In my view, a representative subset of the community (a "panel") would suffice. "Representative" means here that every "cluster" of similar preference profiles (whether a large or a tiny one), significantly different from other clusters, should be represented by at least one panelist.

So, let us assume that a representative panel is selected, consisting of, say, a few tens up to a few hundred of citizens, who have accepted to take part in a (presumably not too long) deliberation at this stage. This deliberation aims at defining requirements on possible solutions, rather than at proposing specific solutions. We can proceed by dividing this panel into a number of small groups deliberating separately offline (i.e. face to face), as e.g. in J. Fishkin's Deliberative Poll®. Another option is to pool all the panelists into one common online "virtual room", to deliberate all together according to our MOD procedural model. I expect that the latter option, once a MOD system becomes available, will be definitely better than the former one.

3. Submitting and discussing proposals on how to solve the problem. Submitting proposals, deliberatively discussing and comparing them, and finally assorting them into a "short-list" of alternatives, is indeed the central stage of the whole process. It is also the stage at which crowd creativity would be most welcomed and most productive (submitting ideas, proposals or opinions). Hence, it shall proceed in an open setting, rather than by selecting any "representative" sub-community. It may involve a number of external experts in the field of the problem being discussed. In some cases, it may even be open to proposals from people with an advisory capacity only, who do not belong to the community concerned.

The way for a large number of people to deliberate all together on a given problem in an ordered and productive way, "in one common room", is extensively discussed in (Velikanov and Prosser, [10]). Our model is called *Mass Online Deliberation* (MOD); it is one of the three components of the general D3 model. The outcome of Stage 3 typically will be not one, but a short list of well-formulated and clearly distinct alternatives of how to solve the problem discussed. See Sect. 3 for more details.

The way for the least prepared people to take part in a deliberation on a par with their more advanced peers through the use of "argumentative facilitation" had been briefly presented in my 2017 conference paper [9]. It is the second component of D3 (see Sect. 4). I assume that, together with MOD, it will be primarily used in the stage 3— simply because no other stage comprises large common deliberation.

4. Evaluating alternatives against the requirements. Deliberation that takes place in stage 3 calls upon citizens' creativity; hence, it should not comprise too formal steps or elements. Rather, submitted proposals will be discussed in stage 3 in an informal way, and their evaluations by individual participants will take the simplest, rather intuitive form of "I like/dislike this proposal" and "its presentation is good/poor". Now, in stage 4, the community needs to assess those alternative proposals in a more formal and quantitative way, namely, the level of conformance of every alternative to every requirement that has been set in stage 2.

To perform this task, we have no need for a large and open participation. Rather, we need here a representative panel of citizens (and, possibly, experts) to do the job. As in stage 2, "representative" means here that every "cluster" of similar preference profiles, significantly different from other clusters, should be represented by at least one panelist; however, proportionality may be an issue at this stage, because of some aggregation mechanism to apply (see below).

What makes the difference with the stage 2, however, is that at this stage the system knows much more about every citizen who has participated in stage 3. Namely, for every active participant the system knows which proposed alternative (and which supportive or critical argument for it) they endorse, and how strong is this endorsement in comparison with other alternatives. This information can be considered by the system as complementary to the initial preference profile of the participant[8].

The procedure of stage 4 may be as follows. Every panelist assigns to every alternative its "requirements compliance vector"; then the system applies some aggregation method to all those vectors assigned by individual panelists. The outcome of the stage 4 is one aggregated requirements compliance vector for every alternative that has been

---

[8] The situation is somehow similar to what happens in a typical Deliberation Poll, when the same questionnaire filled by every participant after the deliberation is to be compared with the pre-deliberative one.

produced in stage 3, where each position in the vector corresponds to a requirement specified in stage 2.

5. Selecting one "winning" solution. The aim of this final stage 5 is to take a common decision on which of the alternatives produced in stage 3 is to be selected and applied. The process is like a referendum with several alternatives. Every citizen should cast their vote, presumably by ranking the alternatives in the decreasing order of their desirability to the voter. The system then selects one "winning" solution among the alternatives, by aggregating all those individual rankings, according to any appropriate method appropriate for this type of voting rule.

As per the types of vote, a number of cases may be considered separately:

(a) Every citizen who filled their preference profile at stage 0 (see Sect. 6) can now get a voting advice produced by the system. He/she will be presented with their profile, "translated" into a ranked list of the requirements (produced on step 2 above), and on the other side, with the requirements compliance vector for every alternative. The system will propose "the best matching choice", then the second best choice, and so on. This works much like a Voting Advice Application, a very popular type of interactive systems actually mostly used in the period of legislative elections. If the person explicitly casts their vote, they indeed may follow or not such a system-provided advice.

(b) If a person participated in stage 4, then they know quite well every alternatives' specific traits and characteristics; and if they participated in stage 3, they should also know main arguments pro and contra every alternative. They can now cast their vote in view of this detailed knowledge, regardless of whether they filled or not their preference profile at stage 0, and of how they filled it.

(c) If a person filled their preference profile at stage 0, but now in stage 5 abstains from explicitly casting their vote, then the system suggests them to cast their vote implicitly, by authorizing the system to rank the alternatives on that person's behalf, starting from the "best match", then continuing with the second best match, and so on. This is what I call *implicit vote*.

(d) If, in a given community, an implicit vote is made legally required in the absence of an explicit one, then in the case (c) the system will not ask the non-voter for an authorization, but will simply apply the method described.

(e) If a citizen neither filled their preference profile in stage 0, nor casted their vote explicitly in stage 5, then the system, in order to remain conformant with the legislation (d) or a stronger one, may apply an implicit vote based on some kind of extrapolation, e.g. by considering the votes of other citizens having the same set of socio-economic characteristics, or else, by considering same person's previous votes if any.

3   Mass Online Deliberation

In this section, a brief description of the MOD procedural framework is provided, with reference to (Velikanov and Prosser [10]), where it is described in more detail. In a typical case, a deliberation on a given issue (a *deliberandum*) comprises three distinct phases, namely, *ideation, consolidation*, and optional *reconciliation*, of which the first is the longest and by far the most complex. The procedure looks as follows.

Participants in a deliberation on a given issue submit their proposals. Other participants may post their comments, which may be supportive or critical arguments, or suggestions on what should be added/deleted/modified in a proposal, or simply editorial remarks. All those items of text posted by participants are collectively called contributions. They may also include additional information, reports on facts, etc.

The system "passes" every newly posted contribution through a number of procedural steps, starting with *anonymizing* it. Then, the contribution is sent to one *moderator*, randomly selected from among the participants; the latter either accepts or rejects it. In case of disagreement between the author and the moderator, the case is submitted to three *arbiters*, also randomly selected. An accepted contribution is then sent to three (or more) randomly selected *evaluators* (appraisers, reviewers) for an initial review. Each of them assigns it two distinct grades, one for its *quality* (of exposition of an idea contained therein), another for the reviewer's own approval or disapproval of the idea. After these initial steps, the contribution is de-anonymized and made available to the whole deliberating community, so that every participant can see and evaluate it, and comment on it.

During the deliberation (esp. in the *ideation* phase), the system regularly sorts the proposals (and maybe other types of contributions) into a few semantic clusters. This is done by algorithmically analyzing the distribution of (dis)approvals of different proposals by different participants. During the clustering process, the system may complement this information by requesting from selected participants additional evaluations, or an explicit comparison, of the least seen and least evaluated proposals, in order to increase reliability of the clustering results. In this way, proposals with similar *ideas* are put into the same cluster, and the total number of clusters will remain within the attention limits of individual participants (say, from 5 to 20).

Additionally, proposals in every cluster are *ranked* according to their average *quality* (the first of our two above-mentioned evaluation parameters); ranking is done in every cluster separately. In this way, the system may suggest to every participant to get acquainted with every idea or opinion by reading the best formulations of that idea, taken from the top of the corresponding cluster. Note that the system does not show explicitly the *popularity* of any proposal or of a cluster of proposal (and maybe even *hides* this information from the participants); hence, *minority opinions* remain visible on a par with the majority ones all the long of the deliberation.

In the subsequent *consolidation* phase, which progresses separately and independently in every cluster, a group of *editors*, somehow selected from among the participants who support at least some of the proposals in that cluster, performs an editorial work on the overall material of the cluster, with the aim to deliver one *consolidated proposal* per cluster.

Then, in the next (optional) phase of inter-cluster *reconciliation*, some of the consolidated proposals from different clusters may be "merged", aiming at delivering a *joint proposal*, on which the majority of supporters of those clusters would agree. This task may be performed by a group of volunteering editors from the clusters they intend to merge. At the end, if there remains more than one such joint proposal, a final vote should be conducted (phase (e), or stage 5 in D3).

As we have seen, large-scale deliberation needs performing a large amount of various "house-keeping" activities; in MOD, these are deliberately designed as system-orchestrated collaborative activities, whose performance is fairly distributed by the system among the participants. Automated tools can also be envisaged, depending on when the appropriate Natural Language Processing (NLP) methods reach their maturity.

An ICT-system to support and enforce the above-described interactive procedures and to implement related background algorithms has been specified on the architectural level; it still awaits its practical realization.

4   Argumentative Facilitation

According to my general programme stated above, we need to elaborate a method of enhancing argumentative capabilities of "ordinary citizens", once they have decided (or have been persuaded) to join a common deliberation on a given issue. This topic seems not yet having been dealt with extensively. For, while scientific research on argumentation in general and on various argumentation schemes (see e.g. Walton et al. [11]) flourishes, and a number of analytical tools have already emerged, a parallel research on, and development of tools for such a computer-assisted argumentation, or CAA, has not yet advanced to a comparable level. The few existing tools need to be adapted and tested in real-life large-scale experiments[9].

My basic idea is that, in order to assist participants (deliberators) in expressing and in understanding "better arguments", we need both an interactive CAA tool and a number of human agents ("argumentation coaches" or "facilitators"). Facilitators have a double role: first, to coach the "least capable" participants to develop better arguments in support of their proposals or opinions; and second, to assist the whole deliberating community in rebutting fallacious, populist and ill-intentioned arguments, thus greatly improving epistemic robustness of a deliberation.

Facilitators (coaches) could be external experts; a much better solution, however, would be to selected them internally, that is, from among the better-prepared participants (either at random, or, say, by ideological or other affinity). Such a coached participation in real deliberation would become a practical apprenticeship in acquiring argumentation skills—kind of continuous learning…

The coaching task is not easy to define and to organise procedurally: finding for a novice a "friendly coach" among the participants, procedurally organizing their interaction, incentivizing the coaches for their societally beneficial endeavours—these and many other issues are to be dealt with.

---

[9] "…so far, both in the AI literature and in argumentation studies generally, the direction of research has been almost exclusively on argument evaluation rather than on argument invention." (Walton and Gordon [12]). In the paper cited, the authors discuss two existing tools (Carneades and IBM Watson Debater); both, however, in their actual state seem to address experts rather than "average" deliberators.

Turning now to computer-assisted argumentation, we can plausibly expect existing or future CAA tools to become quite useful in the hands of "medium-level" deliberators, helping them not only to better formulate their own arguments, but also to provide help for their less capable peers. Those less capable deliberators, in contrast, would probably not be able to use the same CAA tools by themselves; though we can imagine that some simpler tools would do the job, at least partly, in this case as well.

In a deliberation on a normative or on a practical issue, individual statements (such as proposals, factual assertions, critical or evaluative statements, etc.) may belong to different logical modalities; a good deliberation procedure may allow or not the use of a given modality in a given context, or at a given stage of a deliberation process of a given type. Accordingly, use of various argument schemes in appropriate modalities will be governed by the deliberation procedure. Studying these dependencies will be necessary, first, for formulating a list of argumentation rules in a deliberation, and then, for designing appropriate CAA tools.

5   Implicit Voting

Now we approach the third component of my proposed model. The question is—can we propose a method for taking into account values, interests and preferences of those who have chosen *not* to participate? If we bring about such a method, this would greatly enhance normative correctness of our deliberative model as a whole, and its suitability to become institutionalized.

We can reasonably expect that our large-scale online deliberation procedure (MOD) enhanced with argumentative facilitation (AF) would become suitable for all those who decide to participate. What about those who will abstain nevertheless, the *non-deliberators*?

Indeed, they could join the process at the final stage 5, to tacitly compare and rank those few alternative solutions that have been proposed, discussed and finalized by the deliberation participants. Their personal rankings of the alternatives will be considered by the aggregation algorithm on a par with those provided by the deliberators.

The minimal involvement of such a person would be just letting the aggregation algorithm to take into account that person's preferences—on a condition, that he/she had made them known to the deliberation system. My idea is therefore to introduce a preliminary stage 0, in which the system learns every person's individual preferences, values and interests, e.g. in an interactive dialogue.

Such a dialogue can take the form of a multistep treelike questionnaire, carefully designed to minimize the total number of questions to put in every specific case. The resulting personal "preference profile" can be considered as defining the content of an implicit "mandate" given by a citizen to the whole community (or, more specifically, to the system, "representing" the community through appropriate procedures and algorithms)—rather than to one elected representative.

Indeed, information in the preference profile of every individual should be kept confidential (i.e. not accessible to others), while the deliberation system should be able to use it algorithmically, and the information owner should be able to have control on such a use. This is a solvable technical problem—see the end of Sect. 6.

In order to be able to translate a person's preferences into his/her implicit ranking of alternatives (in stage 5), we need an additional sub-stage 2a, in which every requirement is itself evaluated in terms of common values and typical personal interests.

The above-introduced concept, which we call *implicit voting*, can be considered as a normatively and epistemically superior replacement of the classical Universal Suffrage. For, it would much better deserve the interests and preferences of "abstentionists" than if they were drawn into casting an unprepared and thoughtless vote.

6   Personal Preference Profiles

In this section, I present my vision of what should contain a person's "preference profile" and how and when it should be defined. The whole topic indeed needs much more attention and a further investigation and development. Existing Voting Advice Applications (VAAs) should be carefully analyzed in view of our particular needs and requirements; this work is yet to be done.

1. Values vs. Interests. One of the basic principles of my proposed D3 model, and esp. of its Implicit Vote component, is that every fair and inclusive policy-making process shall take into account the *preference profile* of every person concerned. A person's preference profile is to be understood as a system of *values* and *interests*, which a person keeps, or adheres, or sticks to, partially ordered according to the person's *preferences*. If we try to define a procedural implementation of the above principle, then we need to specify as precisely as we can the basic notions of "values" and "interests", and also the span of the notion "a person concerned". There is indeed a large literature on the subject, which I cannot discuss here in much detail; instead, I propose a very succinct presentation of my approach.

Every person, as an individual and as a member of one or more communities (local, professional, ethnic, linguistic, religious, hobby-related, etc.) has values and (self) interests. Values, in general, pertain to the notion of goodness for every member of a given community that is, "what is good and what is bad with regard to everybody". Interests, in contrast, relate to needs, desires and expectations of an individual, most often including also his/her family members.

These two seemingly so different categories are, however, tightly coupled and intertwined; for, in many instances, community values condition personal interests and vice versa (see Chong [1]). Moreover, "values" of a closed community can appear as its specific interests with regard to, or opposing it to, the larger outer society. Hence, interests are opposed to values not by their object (material vs. moral or cultural), but by their *span*.

The above-proposed model serves well our purpose—to define and to structure the content of one's personal preference profile, which, after having been defined, could then be used in many subsequent instances of open deliberative and collaborative policy-making, in various communities of different size to which the person belongs.

2. Preferences. When people consider their own value-and-interest system, they can also state what is most important to them. This "importance" criterion is not, however, of a kind to establish a linear ranking; at best, we can assume that the system is partially ordered, comprising both comparable and incomparable elements.

Presumably, the total set of all possible values and interests is very large and rather diversified. Hopefully, not all of them would be useful in supporting a person's participation throughout all the different instances of policy-making. Moreover, as every such instance would deal with a policy pertaining to a specific field (of common actions, norms, institutions or dispositions), every given type of interests or values would appear as relevant in some fields and irrelevant in some others.

Hence, an interactive support system for helping a person to fill their preference profile should provide for an incremental such filling, by suggesting them to answer, in Stage 0 of every deliberandum, only those questions that are currently relevant. These new answers are combined with the answers they provided in the past, thus gradually enriching the person's preference profile. When a person had already answered a question on a specific interest or a value in some past policy-making instance, the system typically would not put the same question anew. In some cases, however, repeating the same question at a later time and on a different occasion may help the person to better understand their own internal preference system.

It goes without saying that any person should have full access to their personal preference profile, esp. for correcting or updating any preference every time they feel or consider that it has changed in their mind, e.g. as a result of opinion exchange in course of a deliberation.

3. An Interactive Support System. The above considerations show how difficult will be the task of guiding a person in filling and maintaining their preference profile, while keeping at minimum their efforts and time spent. The task is much more complex here as in typical VAAs, which are designed or tuned every time for a specific one-time use. Moreover, such a one-time use always consists in advising electors to cast a reasonable vote by selecting one among a short list of alternative candidates' or parties' programmes, which are at this time already presented in detail. In our case, on the contrary, citizens are invited to fill a relevant part of their preference profiles when alternatives are not yet proposed, only the problem to solve is stated.

An interactive system to support and guide citizens in incrementally filling their preference profiles must be able to store and manage a large number of those profiles on a permanent basis. The profile filling process, presumably organized as a series of questions put by the system, must be structured in such a way as to follow always the most appropriate branches of the overall "questions tree".

What makes the whole thing yet more complex is that, for every specific instance of policy-making, the relevant subset of values and interests (an issue-dependent "profiling template") shall be defined dynamically, and agreed upon by the community, to avoid any politically motivated bias, or any suspicion of citizens about such a bias. Hence, the task of defining every "issue-specific profiling template" should be left to the citizens' community (probably accompanied by experts), rather than to the experts alone, as yet another deliberative stage of the overall policy-making process.

Finally, an appropriate clustering algorithm should be implemented, for grouping individual preference profiles into distinct clusters, in order to perform a representative selection of panellists for steps 2 and 4 above.

Summing up, our VAA-like system should be designed for permanent operation and continuous updates, which makes it much more sophisticated than traditional VAAs.

4. Filling One's Preference Profile (Stage 0). A citizen should be able to fill in the issue-specific part of their preference profile at any moment before the final vote in Stage 5; our profile-filling system should provide for such a continuous operation. However, in order for a citizen to become eligible for joining a panel of Stage 2 or Stage 4, and for the system to perform a better clustering of profiles and to create more representative panels, it is desirable that everyone fills their profile as early as possible. At Stage 3 as well, if the system can access every participant's preference profile, it can use this information for a more efficient distribution of system requests to individual users. That is why we call "Stage 0" this possibly continuous activity.

5. Confidentiality and user data protection. Our model assumes collecting, storing and accessing by the system a large set of highly sensitive user data, starting with those describing a user's socio-economic status and then continuing with their responses to multiple questions concerning their values and interests. Every user will indeed be highly concerned with the confidentiality and protection of all these data.

On the other hand, most people would like to be seen by the community as stable and consistent citizens with unquestionable integrity, etc. Moreover, if the society decides to reward those citizens who have been e.g. the most active in performing various collaborative tasks during the policy-making process, the system should be able to find the right persons to reward.

This double-sided problem can be solved by assigning to every user in the system, through one-way enciphering, their *unique system-registered pseudonym*, whose physical owner can at any moment prove their ownership (e.g. to reclaim a prize), while this ownership remains otherwise unknown to the system. Every data related to the user preferences, or to their actions in course of policy-making process, will be assigned by the system to this "virtual social identity" of the user, with no reference and no possible access to the physical owner of the virtual identity.

Within the system, most of these data, and certainly the whole preference profile of the user, will be accessible to system algorithms, but not to other users (much like contextual advertising delivered by e.g. electronic mail agents to their users on the basis of their preferences discovered by analyzing their private correspondence).

7 Conclusion

In this paper we have introduced and discussed a number of concepts, which, taken together, define a practically implementable model of inclusive governance that satisfies both the requirements of normative correctness and of epistemic soundness. We have also outlined a procedural framework and a number of requirements for implementing such a model. We have identified a number of open questions and of (socio-) technological problems yet to investigate.

In this way, a large new multidisciplinary research and development programme is being launched, involving research in political theory, in argumentation theory and in informal logic, in political psychology, normative ethics and value theory, and yet others.

References

1. Chong, D.: Values versus interests in the explanation of social conflict. U. Pa. L. Rev. **144**(5), 2079–2134 (1996)
2. Dahl, R.A.: Democracy and Its Critics. Yale University Press, New Haven (1989)
3. Fishkin, J.S.: The Voice of the People: Public Opinion and Democracy. Yale University Press, New Haven (1995)
4. Habermas, J.: Legitimationsprobleme im Spätkapitalismus. Suhrkamp Verlag (1973). English transl: Habermas, J.: Legitimation Crisis. Translated by McCarthy, T. Beacon Press, Cambridge (1975)
5. Habermas, J.: Faktizität und Geltung. Surkampf Verlag (1992). English transl: Habermas, J.: Between Facts and Norms. Translated by W. Rehg. MIT Press, Cambridge (1996)
6. Mansbridge, J., Bohman, J., Chambers, S., Christiano, T., Fung, A., Parkinson, J., Thompson, D.F., Warren, M.E.: A systemic approach to deliberative democracy. In: Parkinson, J., Mansbridge, J. (eds.) Deliberative Systems: Deliberative Democracy at the Large Scale (Theories of Institutional Design). Cambridge University Press, Cambridge (2012)
7. Sunstein, C.: Choosing Not to Choose. Oxford University Press, New York (2016)
8. Velikanov, C.: Minority Voices and Voiceless Minorities. In: Proceedings of the CeDEM-11 Conference. Edition Donau-Universität Krems (2011)
9. Velikanov, C. Can Deliberative Governance Become Inclusive? In: Proceedings of the dg.o-2017 Conference. ACM Digital Library (2017)
10. Velikanov, C., Prosser, A.: Mass online deliberation in participatory policy making. Part I: rationale, lessons from past experiments, and requirements. Part II: mechanisms and procedures. In: Beyond Bureaucracy: Towards Sustainable Governance Informatisation. Public Administration and Information Technology (PAIT) Series, vol. 25. Springer International Publishing AG (2017)
11. Walton, D., Reed, Ch., Macagno, F.: Argumentation Schemes. Cambridge University Press, Cambridge (2008)
12. Walton, D., Gordon, Th.F.: Argument Invention with the Carneades Argumentation System. SCRIPTed **14**(2) (2017)

Identifier and NameSpaces as Parts of Semantics for e-Government Environment

Yuri P. Lipuntsov[(✉)]

Lomonosov Moscow State University, Moscow, Russia
lipuntsov@econ.msu.ru

Abstract. At present, a large number of information systems have been created that operate productively and provide information support of specific functions. Currently, a topical issue is to unite these information systems, create favourable conditions for their information interaction. This task is particularly important for the creation of an information infrastructure in the electronic government, which involves both large-scale state systems and applications automating local functions. The main part of system interoperability is defined by semantics – tools for transfer of meaningful data, information. Semantics in information space is defined by two components: identification of objects and NameSpace.

In different information spaces the problem of semantics provision is solved in a customized way. In semantic web, it is possible to use standard NameSpaces, or create your own one. An automatically generated URI is used as identifiers.

There are alternative options to reproduce semantics in the framework of information infrastructure. In practice, there are cases where identifiers are a profound business key containing information about individual elements of business logic, the result of which is the object described. The article describes examples of such practice and shows elements of the methodology for creating such identifiers.

The second semantics element is the namespace. In this field, serious groundwork has been made in different economy sectors. There is a tendency of interaction between separate dictionaries and development of uniform approaches. This can be implemented through creation of templates.

Currently, the prerequisites for combination of two elements of semantics definition are fulfilled: identifiers and namespaces. This would make it possible to move quickly towards the creation of an e-government information infrastructure.

Keywords: Semantic · Identifiers · NameSpaces · Codification system
Information modeling

1 Introduction

Many areas of activity have passed through an initial informatization stage, which offers an informative reflection of basic transactions. In order to automate specific functions, information systems have been created that describe the content of objects involved in transactions and processing conditions of these transactions. If we look at

© Springer Nature Switzerland AG 2018
D. A. Alexandrov et al. (Eds.): DTGS 2018, CCIS 858, pp. 78–89, 2018.
https://doi.org/10.1007/978-3-030-02843-5_7

an activity on the level of an entity, holding company, or economy sector, rather than on the level of a separate function, then a picture is beginning to emerge that reveals a large fraction of the participants of one activity and, at the same time, each participant's particular system. As a result of such informatization, systems are created according to individual methodology, and changes occurring with one participant are not immediately reflected by the actors in adjacent stages. This leads to inaccuracies and reprocessing that affects the effectiveness of the entire project. Transparency in the sequence of operations performed by various participants assumes data collection in a single format, whereby it is necessary to ensure identification a specific object involved in operations of different participants. In the merchandise logistics the ability to track goods from beginning to end is called Traceability. Traceability is an ability to track the history, application or location of an object [1]. When examining a product or services, tracking can refer to:

- origin of materials and parts
- processing history
- distribution and location of a product or service after delivery

Tracking the goods supply chain in logistics is based on providing a current information picture of the state of objects passing through the supply chain. For end users the tracking system makes it possible to monitor the status of the freight, and for managers the system allows to follow the status of transport vehicles, containers, and warehouse facilities.

The interconnection between the various categories of participants of a single activity can be distinguished not only in logistics, but also in other sectors of economic activity: construction, transportation, education, medicine, real estate objects, finances, etc. This article will present a methodological approach to creating an information infrastructure focused on a transparent reflection of the basic activity stages in various economy sectors.

Most of Europe's scientific research on the government information delivery implies usage the RDF format [2–5]. Semantic Web technologies can be used if there is a well-developed, well-established model that will not change for a long time. Such models can be classified as high-level abstraction dictionaries, for example, FOAF. Now we can speak as a formalized description some part of the domain activity, about 30–40%. At the same time, a significant part of the domain activity is cannot be structured, because it is constantly changing and has a significant impact on the structuring zone. Therefore, only the upper level ontologies can use the semantic web technologies. The part that involves a detailed description of the activity and the data delivery in a standard format, most likely should focus on traditional technology like relational models, XML format and others.

The most famous American experience of standardizing the government information turnover is NIEM [6]. In addition to the dictionaries of data standards, the technology of translating local source data to a standard form [7]. In addition, the idea of creating a system for exchanging messages is discussed periodically.

2 Conceptual Modeling

From the point of view of conceptual modeling one should describe a structure model and behavior model for creating applications [8, 9]. Aside from that, in a separate block [8] we present a section devoted to metamodels describing metamodeling principles and languages for assembling metamodels.

Implementation of large-scale projects in the field of information and communications technologies assumes the application of an architectural approach that describes the basic model classes and their framework form according to architecture layers. We will examine the models of basic architectural slices: layer of real world models and data layer. The real world is represented by the structure model where the make-up of organizational units and their subordination is mentioned, and the business processes model, describing the sequence of actions, dynamics of an entity. In addition to business processes, it is possible to examine the document flow model taking into account the self-sufficiency of such entity as document, which is especially important in government management.

Semantics in information space is defined by two components: identification of objects and name space. Object identifiers are created in registers that are developed, as a rule, for separate objects. These are usually governmental systems in which the current state of specific objects is tracked: physical persons, legal persons, real estate entities, etc. All operations involving these entities must obtain information about the entity from this source. The register maintains current information about the object, including its identifier.

NameSpace helps the information exchange participants coordinate the rules of transaction description. By using NameSpace, the information exchange participants can obtain information from other participants, carry out a series of actions as part of their business logic, and also publish data with the results of their activity for external data users. NameSpace offers an opportunity to describe transactions performed in a format that is understood by all information space participants. As a result of transactions, the state of an object may change. These changes should be reflected in the register.

The object identifier system reflects the structure of information space, while NameSpace allows to reflect the dynamics.

3 Registers of Core Components

A substantial portion of information required for use by government and corporate information systems relates to information about basic objects used in a combination of information systems, and for effective interaction of these systems it would be sensible to accumulate information about basic objects in single registers. When arranging data in such a way it is simpler to update information associated with the addition of new entries, changes in existing ones, and deletion of obsolete ones, since these operations must be performed solely in the registry. For correct operation in local systems it is necessary to set up connections between register entries and entries in local systems.

3.1   Methodological Aspects of Data Codification

One of the issues in intersystem exchange of data coming from different sources is identification of similar objects. Use of codification system is a promising tool for solution of this problem. A codification system makes it possible to compare data arriving from different sources and offer quality data to end users.

It should be noted that the codification system is an internal element; there is no need to present the entire system of codes to external users. Any information system assumes the use of an object naming system and their identification. If information exchange is proposed between systems, all participants in the exchange must adhere to a single naming and identification system. For a full-fledged exchange of data, a codification system must be developed to reproduce original data for all data suppliers, taking into account the fact that similar objects in various systems may have a different description.

Codification is an important element of many existing information exchange systems. Codification system are widely used in medical applications [10, 11].

A single center or a combination of coding centers may serve as issuers of identifiers used for different categories of objects. Identifiers assigned in one center may be found and reused elsewhere if there is no provision is made for a system of consultation between identifier elements. Arrangements are needed to ensure that the activity results of one code issuer will be known to other participants. Interaction among many systems requires development of identifiers that make it possible to use them in services beyond the limits of direct management [12].

The codification system is a derivation of business processes occurring as part of the knowledge domain. It assumes transformation of a business process which results in formation of a concept about the sequence of object transformations involving objects of other classes.

Let us examine the principles for creating a codification system on the example of the stock market. The business process of financial instrument issuance and circulation includes such elements as registration of securities issuance, going through the procedures of listing on the exchange, and trading on a regulated market after which specific participants become owners of securities.

Based on the business process a graphic representation of the ontology is created, which serves as the basis for creating a codification system (Fig. 1). A general representation of this model is laid out in the work [13].

The diagram reflects the primary basic entities and intersection entities. The primary basic entities include the issuer profile (Enterprise), financial tools (Tool), trading platforms (Exchange), sellers and buyers of tools (Owner). Intersection entities are obtained by combining two or several basic entities. A codification system is created based on the graphic representation of the knowledge domain. At first, the rules for codification of primary basic entities are developed and then the intersection entities are codified.

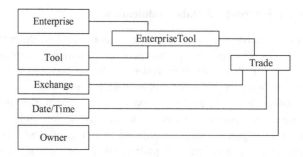

Fig. 1. Part of graph of stock market ontology

Codification of primary entities. Codification rules should be defined for each of the primary entities of the data model from Fig. 1. The code will allow unique identification of a separate example of an entity. To codify a specific entity we can apply keys used in the real world or generated in the system, i.e., surrogate codes. A system for codification of all data is built based on codes of basic entities.

The model of the knowledge domain Stock Market is used to collect data about the Russian stock market. In the data sources separate entities have a content key, which will be used in the repository. For the entity "Enterprise" we will use the Enterprise's four-character ticker, assigned by the Moscow Exchange [14]. In order to designate tools on the exchange, companies are assigned a ticker, which is thereafter used to generate the ticker of tools. Aside from companies, there is a ready-made code for designating the trading platform or exchange coming from the same source. For other primary entities—Tool, Date/Period, Financial Report—we will use surrogate keys.

Creating a surrogate key. The basis for creating a surrogate key is a field, or set of fields, based on which objects in external systems will be identified. For example, we can use a combination of two fields to codify lines of companies' financial reports—the form number and number of line on the report form.

An essential element of the coding system is the number of positions assigned to the code. The number of code positions for all objects of a single entity should be the same. If we take the number letters as equal to 26 and the number of numerals as 10, then the total number will be 36, a two-position code – will be 1,296, a three-position code – will be 46,656, a four-position code – will be 1,679,616, a five-position code – will be 60,466,176, and a six-position code – will be 2,176,782,336. The system for reserving airline tickets uses a 6 position coding system, allowing around two billion variations of the code.

Let us look at the primary entities of the Stock Market knowledge domain. "Tool" is a directory of tools: ordinary shares, preference shares, bonds, etc.—each object will be assigned a one-position code.

Codification of intersection entities. An intersection entity is obtained by combining several primary entities and/or intersection entities. The code for the intersection entity Enterprise Report, consisting of the Enterprise code, the Period code, and the Report code, will look as follows (Table 1).

Thus, a codification system is developed based on a graphic representation of the knowledge domain onthology.

In the practice of compiling data models, the methodology of creating templates is used, reflecting the basic directions that can be reflected as parts of the models. Directions reflected in an ontological representation of the coding system may include Objects, Time, Location, and Life Cycle.

Table 1. Intersection entity codes Enterprise Report

Trades
AVAZ.C.DGV.TRK.ADFT.VDWR
ACRN.C.DGR.TRK.GUMM.BREF
....

3.2   International Experience in Application of Codification Systems

In international practice codification systems in specific knowledge domains are rather widespread. Codification is used in the financial sphere: Financial Instrument Global Identifier, FIGI [15]. Airports use the IATA codification system [16], and for codification of marine ships and operators the International Marine Organisation (IMO) codes are used [17].

Public transport services actively use information systems. To improves an interoperability between the information processing systems of the transport operators and agencies in EU the European Standard "Public Transport Reference Data Model" [18] was developed. One part of the model is "Identification of Fixed Objects in Public Transport" devoted to the problem of identifying objects.

Global system for identification of legal entities. Codification systems for universal objects are known in international practice and have found application in many countries, including Russia. One of the most representative examples is the Global Legal Entity Identifier Foundation (GLEIF) [19]—a global system for identification of legal entities, which controls the designation of the Legal Entity Identifier (LEI) and can serve as an example for codification of objects used in many knowledge domains.

The use of a system for codification of legal entities was caused by economic necessity in 2008; the world community plunged into reverie about methods to prevent similar situations following financial woes. During the analysis it was found that the crisis situation had developed as a result of massed interventions on the part of specific participants, and it was impossible to identify them unambiguously in the registration system which was in use at the time. In trading practice, a sequence of figurehead might have been involved with real actors behind them.

To solve this problem, the Global Legal Entity Identifier Foundation was developed and adopted by resolution of the G 20 on the level of international standard ISO 17442 [20]. The goal in creating this identifier is to increase transparency in the financial sphere. The Global Legal Entity Identifier Foundation allows unique identification of the participants in financial transactions.

At the same time, a certain peculiarity accompanies this identification system. The thing is that ISO Technical Committees (TC) are oriented toward standardization according to specific sectors.

For example, such an object as 'legal entity' obtains the identifier Legal Entity Identifier (LEI) according to ISO 17442 which were prepared by the Technical Committee ISO/TC 68, Financial Services [21].

The codification system is a key factor in creating a semantic information space. The ideology of using the URI global identifier proposed by the semantic web is not always appropriate, since in some cases, for example, when arranging the Goods Tracking System in logistics, a strict methodology for setting up the code structure and determining the rules for codifying specific components is necessary [22]. Therefore there is a need to develop rules for setting up codification systems. For example, to generate the FIGI code for financial instruments, vessel codifications systems (IMO) use the legal entity code. Such rules are important since almost any codification system in a single knowledge domain uses objects supplied from another knowledge domain. Rules are required for links to adjacent codification systems.

The Zachman architecture as a set of 6 directions: Data; Transactions; Organizations; Locations; Events and Timing; Motivation. The identification is an important element of two directions: Data and Organizations. In the article the main place for identification describing is allocated to the objects (Data). The second direction, in which identification is an important element, is the "Organizations", which examines the participants performing the activates of business processes.

In the digital economy, a significant part of transactions can be performed by digital devices, and identification in this case becomes an essential element in the execution of individual business processes. A lot of works are devoted to the topic of identification of participants.

The document "Digital Identity Guidelines" [23] covers three categories of identification. For non-federated systems, agencies will select two components, referred to as Identity Assurance Level (IAL) and Authenticator Assurance Level (AAL). For federated systems, a third component, Federation Assurance Level (FAL), is included. FAL refers to the strength of an assertion in a federated environment, used to communicate authentication and attribute information to a relying party. This level of assurance is more reliable than IAL and AAL.

4 Standardization of Name Space for Information Exchange

How do Chinese companies work while constructing railroads in Russia, or how do Russian companies work while constructing a nuclear power station in Norway? Companies receive a set of standards, some of them to determine the procedure for information interaction with government agencies, suppliers, and contractors. These standards define a name space. Based on XML language, several thematic dictionaries have been developed, which establish the rules for data exchange in a given sphere of activity. Examples of such dictionaries in the commercial sector are ebXML (e Business XML), XBRL (Extensible Business Reporting Language), HR-XML (Human resource XML), and others. In the trade sector, including the international one, there are active use of standard, that define common syntactic rules for packet and interactive messages standard, used in the exchange between computer systems. These rules are adopted at the level of the international standard ISO 9735 [24]. The basic part of the standard is the Core Components Library developed and maintained by the United Nations Center for Trade Facilitation and Electronic Business (UN/CEFACT) [25].

4.1 Domain Dictionaries

Let us examine standards in the construction field in greater detail. In the construction sector many countries use the local version of the Industry Foundation Classes (IFC), from the BuildingSMART series of standards [26]. This is a modeling ideology that was initially developed for local projects but later achieved the level of international standards. Currently, more than 30 countries participate in the activities of buildingSMART International (bSI), a noncommercial organization whose activity is directed towards application of information standards in specifics sectors of activity and promotion in creating innovative, stable information assets using state-of-the-art software solutions focused on data exchange [27]. Through the efforts of bSI, an IFC specification is being developed and published—an open data model for describing data exchange in the field of construction and management of construction facilities. The current version IFC 4, published in March, 2013, has been adopted as ISO 16739: 2013 standard [28].

In addition, bSI offers two other ISO standards: the Information Delivery Manual (IDM), registered as ISO 29481, and the International Framework for Dictionaries (IFD), registered as ISO 12006 3. IDM clarifies the processes and information flow throughout the entire life cycle of an object. IFD is a standard for data dictionaries. BsDD (buildSMART Data Dictionary) is based on the IFD standard and reference library or database of objects and their attributes [29, 30].

In the case of BIM we see that information exchange is provided by the interaction of three components—terms, processes, and data. The Terms section presents the rules for setting up the three categories of classifiers:

- rules for describing various objects involved in the construction process: elements of buildings, equipment, materials, etc., and their interconnections;
- rules for describing the participants in an operational activity;
- rules for describing the stages of the project life cycle.

ISO 29481 standard is a methodology for information support of business processes carried out in the construction of facilities, indicating information required at each stage of described processes.

Standard ISO 16739 is a format for BIM data, allowing the exchange of data among software programs that are used by different participants of a construction project or in management of facility construction.

Terms provide a structure for object exchange: they describe the participants in the exchange and their functions, and describe the objects worked on in construction and performing separate operations. Processes describe the dynamics—the sequence of actions to be performed. The third standard makes it possible to reproduce an information reflection of the activity occurring in the real world and to exchange information.

Use of the BIM offers many advantages to participants in a construction activity, since all interested parties use one common model and delays from reprocessing or duplicating drawings for various stages of the construction activity are curtailed. All participating parties have access to the Common Data Environment (CDE) and, consequently, to preparation of documentation: more accurate work schedules and cost budgets can be prepared, since time and costs can be separated according to elementary actions of the construction project, thereby preserving the integrity of the entire project. Aside from that, maintenance and life cycle management are simplified after the construction phase, since detailed information about components is accessible in the information model.

4.2 Expansion of Branch Dictionaries for Adjacent Object Fields

Branch IFC data formats have been developed for the construction sector. In addition to the basic standards, expansions designed for support of infrastructure such as bridges, tunnels, roads, and rail lines. Railroad designers have adopted these construction standards: by using the IFC in Great Britain the HS2 (High Speed 2) project was developed. The project has to do with a high-speed rail network connecting London with Leeds and Birmingham with Manchester. The Chinese standard IFC Rail has important significance for the further expansion of the IFC for railroads. Working groups from bSI undertook an analysis of national standards, such as the Chinese IFC Rail, the Korean IFC Road, and the French IFC Bridge for possible inclusion in the IFC 4 expansion. These expansions may be included in the next version of the IFC.

4.3 Unification of the Dictionaries Used for Computerization of Various Functions

The second direction in information standardization in the field of railroad transport is the RailTopoModel. A large number of information systems function in the area of railroad management and service the operation of railroad transportation. In order to organize information exchange among the systems of the various countries of the European Union the RailTopoModel (RTM) project is being implemented [31]. This project is oriented toward developing a single semantics for unifying railroad transportation systems, including such systems as RINF—a description of infrastructure; ETCS—control and protection of trains; and INSPIRE—describing information about space.

RTM is a logical model of infrastructure data, oriented toward international standardization of description of railroad systems (topology of the network, infrastructure, and the entire life cycle of the operations). Interaction among the participants can be organized either through a central chain or point-to-point among the separate participants. In the case of RailTopoModel the second variant was chosen and the need arose to standardize the format to ensure interoperability, since RTM was not intended for exchanging data among participants. RTM is a model that can be used, for example, for organizing a storage facility, while for point-to-point data exchange a language is needed. Therefore the Expert Group International Railroading Union (UIC), in addition to RTM, is occupied with developing the RailML® format for data exchange. The RailML.org Project is presently developing a new version of RailML® (RailML® 3), corresponding to the requirements of the railroad industry and in full harmony with RTM [31].

Two projects in the IFC and TRM railroad object field have begun to interact [32] in order to join the railroad information picture at the construction and usage phases. In order to develop a common standard it is necessary to compare the two standards being used. The comparison criteria in this case can consist of such elements of description as modeling language, architectural model, exchange format, subject area, scope of application, level of implementation, compatibility of tools, issuing organization, and licensing. Based on this comparison further interaction will be built in so as to develop the rules of a single format for data presentation [33].

As we see, a great deal of work is proceeding in the area of standardizing name space to develop dictionaries in various subject areas; interaction is beginning among dictionaries. To reduce costs for coordinating separate directions it makes sense to create dictionaries according to templates. In templates one can separate the directions and assign rules for presentation according to direction. Sections can be separated for directions in creating templates of information models: Objects, Transactions, Roles, Time, Location, Purpose, and Life Cycle.

The use of templates will make it possible to develop unified rules for reflecting separate directions, which will ease the process of coordinating dictionaries and using common information exchange rules.

5 Conclusions

This article presents an overview of two elements defining the semantics of electronic government information space—identifiers and name space. A multitude of projects are being implemented in each of these directions: where a number of participants need to organize information interaction among a multitude of participants, name spaces are being developed; where the traceability of separate groups of objects must be ensured, a codification system is being built and identifiers are being assigned to those objects. Along with that, the task of a single description and identification is in the process of being resolved in each project, and if there is no single standard approach, then in each case the definition of one or another portion of the semantics must be resolved according to its own rules. It would be logical to begin movement toward comprehensive resolution of these tasks. On the one hand, transparent rules for creating codification rules are necessary, based on which codifiers suitable for use in conditions of active information circulation are created. On the other hand, in order to reflect the principal material, financial, and other economic flows, name spaces are being developed, oriented toward creating an environment for exchanging data among participants.

Creation of a transparent information space in various sectors of the economy is proceeding by means of standardization in the field of identifiers and name space. In this connection special attention should be given to using open standards in identifying the transparency of the state of objects that bear a relationship to various subject areas. This will help organizations and branches to achieve a global system for reflecting the basic information objects of basic subject areas. Resolution of these tasks will make it possible:

To provide a methodology for various sectors of activity for developing the requirements toward creating systems for tracking the movement of various categories of objects.

To create a methodology that can serve as a starting point for branch, regional, and local standards and guiding principles

To provide interoperability and seamless communication in value creation chains by providing consistent methods of identifying basic objects and exchanging data based on standards of relocation, transformations, and other events of these objects over the course of their life cycle.

References

1. ISO 9000 - Quality management. https://www.iso.org/ru/iso-9001-quality-management.html
2. Maali, F., Cyganiak, R., Peristeras, V.: A publishing pipeline for linked government data. In: Simperl, E., Cimiano, P., Polleres, A., Corcho, O., Presutti, V. (eds.) ESWC 2012. LNCS, vol. 7295, pp. 778–792. Springer, Heidelberg (2012). https://doi.org/10.1007/978-3-642-30284-8_59
3. Maali, F., Cyganiak, R., Peristeras, V.: Enabling interoperability of government data catalogues. In: Wimmer, Maria A., Chappelet, J.-L., Janssen, M., Scholl, Hans J. (eds.) EGOV 2010. LNCS, vol. 6228, pp. 339–350. Springer, Heidelberg (2010). https://doi.org/10.1007/978-3-642-14799-9_29
4. Koumenides, C., Salvadores, M., Alani H., Shadbol, N.: Global integration of public sector information. In: Web Science Conference, Raleigh, North Carolina (2010)
5. Omitola, T., et al.: Put in your postcode, out comes the data: a case study. In: Aroyo, L., et al. (eds.) ESWC 2010. LNCS, vol. 6088, pp. 318–332. Springer, Heidelberg (2010). https://doi.org/10.1007/978-3-642-13486-9_22
6. National Information Exchange Model. https://www.niem.gov
7. CAM XML validation. http://www.verifyxml.org/OpenXDX-page.html
8. Olive, A.: Conceptual Modeling of Information Systems. Springer, Heidelberg (2007)
9. Wieringa, R.: Real-world semantics of conceptual models. In: Kaschek, R., Delcambre, L. (eds.) The Evolution of Conceptual Modeling. LNCS, vol. 6520, pp. 1–20. Springer, Heidelberg (2011). https://doi.org/10.1007/978-3-642-17505-3_1
10. Fenna, D.W.J.: A comprehensive codification for the medical hospital information system. Med. Inform. **10**, 1 (1985). https://doi.org/10.3109/14639238509010024
11. HL7 Code Systems. www.hl7.org
12. Arms, W.: Digital Libraries. M.I.T. Press, Boston (2000)
13. Lipuntsov, Y.: Application of information model of interagency data-exchange for the aggregation and analysis of stock market data. In: XI International Scientific-Practical Conference Modern Information Technologies and IT-Education SITITO 2016, Aachen (2016)
14. Group Moscow Stock Exchange. http://www.moex.com
15. Financial Instrument Global Identifier. http://www.omg.org/spec/FIGI/
16. IATA Codes. http://www.iata.org/services/Pages/codes.aspx
17. IMO Identification Number. http://www.imonumbers.lrfairplay.com
18. Identification of Fixed Objects in Public Transport. www.transmodel-cen.eu/standards/ifopt
19. The Legal Entity Identifier Regulatory Oversight Committee. https://www.leiroc.org/
20. Financial services – Legal Entity Identifier. https://www.iso.org/standard/59771.html

21. ISO/TC 68 Financial services. https://www.iso.org/committee/49650.html
22. GS1 Global Traceability Standard GS1's framework for the design of interoperable traceability systems for supply chains. https://www.gs1.org/standards/traceability/traceability/1-3-0
23. Grassi, P., Garcia M.E., Fenton, J.L.: Digital Identity Guidelines. NIST Special Publication 800-63-3. https://dx.doi.org/10.6028/NIST.SP.800-63-3
24. ISO 9735:1988 Electronic data interchange for administration, commerce and transport (EDIFACT). https://www.iso.org/standard/17592.html
25. Core Components Library UN/ CCL for trade. https://www.unece.org/?id=3133
26. buildingSMART International Standards. https://www.buildingsmart.org/standards
27. Open Symbology. https://www.openfigi.com/
28. ISO 16739:2013 Industry Foundation Classes (IFC) for data sharing in the construction and facility management industries. https://www.iso.org/standard/51622.html
29. Building information models – Information delivery manual. ISO/TC 59/SC 13 Organization of information about construction works. https://www.iso.org/committee/49180.html
30. ISO 12006-3:2007 Building construction – Organization of information about construction works – Part 3: Framework for object-oriented information. https://www.iso.org/standard/38706.html
31. RailTopoModel. http://www.railtopomodel.org/en/
32. Collaboration between RailTopoModel, railML.org and IFC. https://www.buildingsmart.org/collaboration-railtopomodel-railml-org-ifc/
33. Augele, V.: Comparative Analysis of Building Information Modelling (BIM) and RailTopoModel/railML in View of their Application to Operationally Relevant. In: 8th RailTopoModel Conference, Paris (2017)

Digital Transformation in the Eurasian Economic Union: Prospects and Challenges

Olga Filatova, Vadim Golubev[⊠], and Elena Stetsko

St. Petersburg State University, St. Petersburg, Russia
{o.filatova, v.golubev, e.stetsko}@spbu.ru

Abstract. This paper discusses digital transformation in the Eurasian Economic Union and provides an analysis of possible risks. A classification of risks is proposed, existing forecasts of the development of the digital economy in Russia and the EEU are considered. The study makes account of existing economic disparities and political factors. The authors offer their scenarios of digital transformation within the EEU and the union's transition to e-government.

Keywords: Digital agenda · Digital transformation
Eurasian Economic Union · Risks · Forecasts · Scenarios

1 Introduction

An increasing use of digital technologies in various sectors of the economy, public administration, and people's daily life is a global trend, and it fully applies to the countries of the Eurasian Economic Union (EEU), a new integration association that emerged on the world's map in 2015. At present, the EEU consists of Russia, Belarus, Kazakhstan, Armenia and Kyrgyzstan. The EEU covers an area of more than 20 million square kilometers, with a population of more than 179 million people, which indicates that the EEU is becoming a major integration bloc in Eurasia and has a potentially self-sufficient market. However, as in any integration association, the countries constituting it are characterized by different levels of economic development. This dictates the following integration goals: creating a common market for goods, services and labor and modernizing national economies.

The need for EEU member-states to modernize their economies calls for a digital transformation. Digital platforms would go a long way to facilitating interaction between governments, businesses, and social services from different countries and boosting the union's competitiveness. Without digital transformation, the EEU may run the risk of disintegration.

In this regard, the purpose of this paper is to examine digital transformation as a tool of combating the risks faced by the EEU. A classification will be proposed of identified risks and possible ways to overcome them. Available forecasts of the development of the digital economy in Russia and the EEU will be analyzed taking into account risks stemming from existing economic disparities and political factors.

D. A. Alexandrov et al. (Eds.): DTGS 2018, CCIS 858, pp. 90–101, 2018.
https://doi.org/10.1007/978-3-030-02843-5_8

The research methodology is original in that it treats digital transformation as a precondition to overcoming disintegration risks and simultaneously as a set of risks itself. The risks and forecasts of how to mitigate them have both objective and subjective aspects. This creates avenues for further research.

The authors offer their scenarios of digital transformation in the EEU and its transition to electronic governance.

2   Theoretical Background and Research Methodology

This paper will employ neo-institutionalism as its theoretical basis drawing on the writings of its eminent proponents Ronald Coase, John Kenneth Galbraith, and Douglas North [5, 11, 17]. The EEU is an institution established on the basis of an interstate treaty ("rules of the game") with a view to obtaining mutual economic benefits. At the present stage, it is becoming increasingly clear that the commonly accepted Digital Agenda is certain to greatly facilitate the minimization of transaction costs and contribute to the economic modernization of the EEU.

We will also use a pragmatic approach to Eurasian integration, which is based on viewing it not as a goal, but as an instrument for solving the countries' economic problems, the main of which is modernization.

Methodologically, the research focuses on risks arising in the process of digital transformation. Most sociologists, e.g. Ulrich Beck, view our society as a risk society [1].

As a research methodology, we also use the concept of regionalism, proposed by Van Langenhof and Costea in 2005 [21]. According to these scholars, in terms of global integration a region goes through three stages: the first stage includes establishing basic economic relations within the region; the second stage involves political integration; and the third complete integration, in which the region as a whole acts as a participant in global relations. The EEU has not gone beyond the first stage yet despite some progress. Currently, the EEU is involved in developing an institutional, organizational and legal framework of digital integration. An important stage was completed in 2017 when the EEU member-states approved a strategic document entitled "The Digital Agenda in the Eurasian Economic Union" [19].

In addition to a traditional analysis of this and other official documents, we employed secondary data analysis and statistical analysis, as well as modeling and forecasting methods to identify risks and construct scenarios for the development of digital transformation in the EEU.

In terms of theoretical foundations, we draw on the works by Andrei Chugunov, Olga Filatova, Radomir Bolgov, Vitalina Karachay, Yuri Misnikov [2, 4, 10], that are devoted to the issues of the digital agenda in the Eurasian space. Since Eurasian integration has not yet acquired a generally accepted conceptual framework we also looked at similar processes taking place in the European Union [14].

3   The Digital Agenda and Digital Transformation in the EEU: Main Directions and Expected Results

On October 11, 2017, the EEU countries approved the main directions of the digital agenda of the EEU until 2025 [20]. The directions of development of the digital economy include:

- digital transformation of economic sectors and cross-sectoral transformation;
- digital transformation of markets for goods, services, capital and labor;
- digital transformation of management processes and integration processes;
- development of digital infrastructure and ensuring the security of digital processes.

Each direction defines a special range of cooperation issues in the development of the digital economy. The parties use a common framework of directions to systematize proposals for cooperation within the framework of the Digital Agenda, preparation and implementation of joint projects [13, 20].

Achieving the goals of the digital agenda should lead to the following results:

- accelerate the processes of free movement of goods, services, capital and labor resources within the EEU in the development of the digital economy;
- increase the competitiveness of economic entities and citizens of member-states through digital transformation in all spheres of society;
- create conditions for sustainable development of economies of member-states in transition to new technological and economic structures;
- set up comprehensive cooperation of economic entities in member-states on the basis of end-to-end digital processes, create and develop digital assets and sustainable digital ecosystems for economic entities of member-states;
- align the levels of preparedness of member-states for the development of the digital economy;
- include member-states in global, macro-regional and regional processes of digital transformation, taking into account the emergence of new opportunities and risks;
- form a digital market of the EEU and simplify access by economic entities in member-states to foreign markets;
- create innovative workplaces in digital and non-digital spheres of the economy and increase the involvement of businesses and citizens of member states in the digital economy;
- expand development opportunities and reduce risks for businesses, citizens and government bodies of member-states in the development of the digital economy.

It should be noted that the key difference between "digital transformation" and automation and informatization is the creation of new opportunities and new processes, rather than just enhancing the efficiency of existing processes. V.B. Khristenko, President of the EEU's Business Council said: "Digital transformation is the most global of all processes of globalization. There is no more pervasive and "all-encompassing" process in the global sense. If we can create an adequate digital agenda that will talk about what we can do, what resources we have; it will allow us to understand national interests, and also the fact that we can make real steps at the supranational level of the Eurasian space within the framework of digital transformation" [6].

In the broad sense, the process of digitalization is the process of transferring to the digital environment the functions and activities (business processes) previously performed by individuals and organizations. Digital transformation does not just imply introducing new information technologies; it implies the implementation of new business models. Therefore, we can say that the digital economy is a system of economic relations based on the use of digital information and communication technologies. This new system also assumes management innovations at the level of the entire integration association rather than individual member-states.

It is obvious that citizens of member states (civil society), business entities (business), and public officials in member-states should be the main beneficiaries of EEU integration.

However, along with the predicted advantages of digital transformation and the development of the digital economy within the framework of the EEU, serious risks also need to be taken into account. An analysis of these risks allows us to make several scenario forecasts for the future of digital transformation.

4 Risk Assessment of Digital Transformation in the EEU

We believe that the risks faced by the EEU that pertain to digital transformation can be placed at three levels:

1. General risks inherent in all countries and the integration association as a whole that emerge as part of digital transformation of the economy characterized by different rates of integration and political sovereignty.
2. Risks associated with the digital divide caused by the modernization and digitization of the economy.
3. Potential risks deriving from a particular e-government model.

Let's consider these risk groups in more detail.

4.1 General Risks

Common risks are described in the document "General approaches to the formation of the digital space of the Eurasian Economic Union until 2030" [12].

These risks derive from: the fact that EEU member-states are excluded from processes of digital transformation that are taking place at the global, macro-regional (OECD, SCO, EU, etc.) or regional levels, and the lack of a coordinated position within the EEU regarding its transformation. This leads to: the loss of consumers and new economic entities (first of all, technology entrepreneurs, principals); depreciation of traditional assets that have not gone through digital transformation; the exhaustion of competences and the drain of talents into the digital spaces and digital economies created by other global actors outside the EEU; domination of global digital platforms, whose owners direct changes; the emergence of additional gaps between countries and people [12].

Some experts also point out several other important risks including:

- difficulty of reforming corporate culture and business processes;
- a serious shortage of qualified ICT workers (according to the Ministry of Communications, Russian universities produce about 25,000 IT specialists every year. Currently, there are about 400,000 programmers working in Russia. In contrast, America has over 4 million programmers, 3 million work in India and 2 million in China" [3]);
- an unfavorable economic situation affecting private investment in fixed assets, including in the acquisition and introduction of new technologies;
- excessive government regulation of innovative processes in the economy;
- the use of unreliable, unsystematic, unusable data by businesses;
- an urgent need for relevant legislation [7].

Governments have an understanding of the need for digital transformation and the creation of national concepts for the development of the information society. The Russian Federation has passed its first pieces of legislation defining the digital economy (e.g. "Telemedicine Law"). Work is in progress as part of a EEU digital transformation project. The process of legislative regulation is accompanied by the creation of common digital platforms.

In October 2017, Tigran Sargsyan, Head of the Eurasian Economic Commission outlined concrete steps to implement the concept of digital transformation. It includes the creation of a special CT office and a plan for implementing this concept through specific initiatives of countries (or companies) participating in the EEU. "Digital transformation will be carried out through initiatives. Today the prime ministers approved the set of guidelines concerning such initiatives. It is presumed that a new office will be created headed by a chairman of the board, which will include experts from five countries to assess and develop recommendations regarding submitted initiatives" [18]. The procedure of working out the initiatives was also adopted by the Eurasian intergovernmental council as a practical guide in October 2017.

Thus, the EEU Digital Office is designed to oversee the implementation of digital platforms and monitor the development of legislation to ensure their successful operation.

4.2   Risks Associated with the Digital Gap

The risks associated with the digital gap can be divided into three types: the gap in the indicators of digital transformation within the EEU countries; the gap between the EEU and leading integration associations; and the predicted increase in the digital gap in the process of digital transformation in the EEU.

The gap in the indicators of digital transformation within EEU countries. This gap is best illustrated by the ranking survey conducted by the World Bank and the International Telecommunications Union, which used the Digital Implementation Index. It shows the implementation of digital technologies in each of the EEU countries. The quantitative results are shown in Table 1 [16].

Table 1. The gap in the indicators of digital transformation within EEU countries

Country	Digitalization implementation index. Total score	Business indicator	Indicator of people	Government indicator
Armenia	0,67	0, 48	0,82	0,72
Belarus	0,52	0, 43	0,76	0,36
Kyrgyzstan	0,49	0,37	0,60	0,50
Kazakhstan	0,63	0,32	0,73	0,83
Russian Federation	0,71	0,37	0,62	0,52

Table 1 demonstrates that each country faces its own challenges introducing digital technologies into public life, business and governance. Kyrgyzstan experiences the most problems. A serious problem common to the Russian Federation, Belarus and Kyrgyzstan is the reluctance on the part of officials to work in the new format. However, the business sector shows even lower digital performance in all the EEU than the public sector. This indicator suggests that the process of building an integrated digital economy will not be fast. By some estimates, it will take up to 10 years.

The gap between the EEU and leading integration associations. X. Navas-Sabater addressed this gap when he compared the ICT Development Index and the Network Readiness Index [16]. In the study countries are ranked according to these indices against their position in the global rating of competitiveness. While the dependence is indirect as the rating of competitiveness takes into account a multitude of indicators (inflation, tax rates, corruption, access to financing, tax regulation, political instability, inefficient state management, and currency regulation), but it does exist. Nevertheless, one cannot ignore a favorable factor: being at roughly equal stages with regard to digital transformation, the EEU countries can establish their own rules of the game and create their own economic opportunities and laws.

Increasing digital inequality as a result of digital transformation in the EEU. First of all, the digital transformation of the EEU space can lead to social imbalances as a result of the emergence of the so-called "enclaves" [9]. These enclaves will be "smart cities", high-tech hubs and financial centers (rent-charging centers). This process will consolidate the inequality that has developed in the industrial and post-industrial eras. For EEU countries, this is especially dangerous, because certain regions have not passed through the stage of industrialization. Thus, a new social division and social stratification may lead to an increase in social tension in the future. To overcome this risk, a new social system of relations within different social groups and between those groups and the elites should be built.

4.3   Potential Risks in Implementing Electronic Governance

Potentially, there are three groups of risks that pertain to implementing e-governance. They are associated with technology, time and management.

Technological risks imply that the digital products created for platforms of the digital economy are not fully functional. This needs to be tackled through the creation of effective expert services, consisting of representatives of stakeholders and program developers.

Temporal risks mean that there is a gap between the rate of the growth the digital economy in the world and in the EEU. This can make the EEU a periphery of the global economy and eventually cause the breakdown of the union as an inefficient international association. This can be tackled by investinig in digital transformation and education.

Management risks include a lack of political will on the part of governments and companies to introduce digital governance or even discuss it. These risks arise as a result of distrust, both in technology and in new, more transparent management models, which exclude reduntant intermediary links. Possible forms of tackling these risks may be the requirement that EEU officials and decision-makers go through digital literacy courses and an anti-corruption strategy.

5   Evaluation of Expert Forecasts

In order to build further scenario projections of the digital transformation of the EEU, it is also necessary to consider existing forecasts regarding the development of the digital economy in Russia and the EEU.

Analysts of Boston Consulting Group predict three main scenarios for Russia:

1. Stagnation (a Venezuelan Model). Unless the digital component of the economy is boosted, its share in GDP will continue to stagnate and increase the backlog from the leaders from 5–8 years today to 15–20 years in five years.
2. Moderate Growth (a Middle Eastern Model). This is possible in case of full-scale implementation of existing initiatives in public services, medicine, and education. They include optimizing existing online processes and eliminating their duplication offline. This scenario will eliminate a radical backlog and create an added value for the economy of 0.8–1.2 trillion roubles a year, while the digital economy can reach 3% of the GDP.
3. Intensive Digitalization (an Asian Model). The most ambitious and most complex scenario. Changes should occur both at the level of the state and individual industries and companies. Investments (both public and private) should grow in such promising areas as the Internet of Things, Big Data, and IT products and services with high export potential. This will increase the share of the digital economy to 5.6% of the GDP, as well as create large-scale intersectoral effects and added value in economic sectors to 5–7 trillion rubles a year. China made a breakthrough by following this scenario. It will soon be among the top ten digitization countries, despite the fact that it lagged behind Russia by 8 positions in 2011 [22].

EEU followed Russia in 2017 by adopting a digital economy development program. It is evidence of the fact that the EEU will move along an intensive path in the digitalization of the economy. The EEU will strive for the "Asian Model", combined with a more comfortable existence within the "Middle Eastern Model". This duel direction derives from the nature of the EEU. The serious breakthrough China has demonstrated in the digital economy in the last 5–6 years derives from the fact it is a unitary nation-state with a rigid authoritarian system of government, which gives China's undoubted advantage in terms of the speed of decision-making, whereas the EEU is an integration space consisting of sovereign states with their own national interests and capacities.

All EEU countries have a large share of the public sector in their GDP. According to the Federal Antimonopoly Service of Russia, in 2005–2015, the share of the public sector in the Russian economy grew from 35 to 70% of the GDP. In Kazakhstan, the share of the public sector in its GDP is now about 60%. In Belarus, it is estimated to be 70–75%, according to the EBRD. The global average is in the range of 30–40% [8]. This fact allows us to hope for a relatively fast decision-making processes in the area of the digital economy in every EEU country and the EEU as a whole.

There are two ways of building a digital economy: one that uses market mechanisms and the other that uses planned economy mechanisms. Being an integration project, the EEU has to combine elements of both.

The market approach to building a digital economy assumes that the state creates optimal conditions for the functioning of the digital economy and stimulates business to move into this new sector. Optimal conditions presuppose a set of interrelated measures of regulatory, legal, economic, and social nature as well as the availability of a technological base. Since the positive effect of the digital economy depends on its scale, a sufficient condition for the implementation of this approach is the existence of a sufficient number of privately owned economic entities.

Once in a new environment, private business, in cooperation with public institutions, stimulates the further development of the digital economy. A variety of growth points are formed. Gradually expanding, the growth points form a continuous "mosaic carpet" that fills all possible space, introducing the digital economy in all spheres of activity. This is the main advantage of the market approach.

The planned economy approach to building a digital economy involves the phased development of infrastructure under the leadership of the state and the purposeful "embedding" of different economic entities with the relevant sector of economy. The development of the infrastructural and technological basis for the digital economy occurs simultaneously (or even outstrips) the creation of conditions conducive to the development of private businesses (primarily small and medium-sized companies).

In the planned approach, technological development fulfills planned digital economy priorities. The remaining technologies either remain poorly developed or are imported. The main advantage of the second approach is the speed of construction and the universality of the created infrastructure [15].

We believe that the EEU has adopted a symbiotic or hybrid way of transition to the digital economy. It takes into account different rates of integration at the level of industries and enterprises in member-countries, and a catching-up type of development of social electronic services.

The positive factors of this approach include:

- a single plan coordinated between the governments of the EEU member-countries;
- an understanding shared by all participants (at least at the level of senior officials and experts) of the benefits of digital transformation and risks in the event of deepening the digital divide.

The negative factors include:

- differences in the levels of digitalization in the economy and social sphere;
- undeveloped digital legislation;
- a need for unification and access to social services for all citizens of member states.

Also, we must not forget that the digital economy can be the accelerator of only the real economy, which has tangible assets, economic ties and innovations. To date, the volume of intra-union trade most clearly demonstrates the weaknesses of economic intra-union integration. It has shown a negative trend since 2013. Currently, the volume of exports to third countries significantly exceeds the volume of mutual trade, an unchanging trend. At the end of the year, external exports exceeded the volume of all intra-union trade by 7.3 times (see Table 2 [8]).

Table 2. Volumes of intra-union and foreign trade of EEU Member-states (2015–2016)

Indicator	2015, $ bln	2016, $ bln	Dynamic 2016/2015, %
The volume of intra-union trade	45.6	42.5	−6.7
The volume of foreign trade:			
Export from the EEU	373.8	308.4	−17.5
Import into the EEU	205.5	201.3	−2.0
Foreign trade turnover in the EEU	579.4	509.8	−12.0

In addition, it is necessary to take into account political factors that affect EEU integration:

The Russian Federation. The desire to control the digital space of the EEU, including social networks and production chains. This can be interpreted by the rest of the members as a desire for political domination.

Armenia. The development of cooperation with the EU, the USA and China, including integration into their digital systems, and linking economic cooperation in the EEU with solving the Nagorny Karabakh problem.

Belarus. Active cooperation with the EU. Sale of digital technologies to third countries outside the EEU. Possible political bargaining for each new element of digital integration.

Kazakhstan. Possible preferences for digital integration in certain areas with China, the EU and the USA. Defending its own vision of the digital agenda for the EEU at the later stages of its implementation.

Kyrgyzstan. Low level of digitalization of the economy and the social sphere. Expectation of large financial subsidies and economic preferences in return to the unification of digital economic models. Using cheaper digital platforms (e.g., Chinese).

6 Discussion

Considering the abovementioned risks (technological, temporal and managerial) and expert forecasts, we propose three scenarios for the development of the digital transformation of EEU: optimistic, pessimistic and realistic.

The optimistic scenario involves overcoming all types of risks and implementing a program of transition to the digital economy within 5–8 years (an optimal period of closing a digital gap between developed countries and the Russian Federation).

The pessimistic scenario implies that the EEU is unable to overcome technological and managerial challenges. It can be assumed that weak links exist in the spheres of both state administration, business, and civil society.

In e-government, this scenario is characterized by low levels of citizen e-participation. The reasons include: a lack of trust in the effectiveness of the EEU, distrust of digital methods of participation, and a lack of technological reliability of e-government resources.

In e-business, the scenario demonstrates: slow rates of digitalization of industries and agriculture and slow law-making.

In civil society, the scenario is marked with: gaps in the volume and quality of social services, the unresolved nature of pension provision in the EEU, the poor quality of the digital services, especially in healthcare and education.

Implications include an economic backlog from such leading economies as the USA, EU and China, and the gradual erosion of the single economic space of the EEU.

The realistic scenario means that technological and managerial risks can be overcome by 50–60% while temporal risks remain unmet.

Managerial risks will remain unless a sufficient level of trust is achieved in digital management and digital technologies over the next ten years, which constitutes the period necessary for the elimination of the digital gap. Low rates of digitalization of the social environment, education and professional training will also play their role.

Technological risks will remain due to the already existing gap between the EEU and industrialized countries.

In terms of temporal risks, the digital gap between the EEU and developed countries will eventually grow less pronounced, but will persist in the short and even medium terms.

The realistic scenario will most likely see the creation of digital enclaves in the shortest possible time including high-tech industries, smart cities, online medical centers and universities. Continuous improvement of digital legislation and social policy will bridge the imbalances between residents of high-tech enclaves and the provinces. The development of this scenario will allow enough time to reduce a digital gap between EEU member-states and advanced countries and between enclaves and the provinces. The likely risk of this scenario is its failure to eliminate the digital divide between enclaves and the provinces, which will entail increased social tensions and conflicts.

We believe this scenario to be the most likely to be implemented, because all EEU member states are interested in digital enclaves even at the backdrop of increasing disintegration that may accompany their economic development. Digitalization has already become an integral part of successful business practices because it speeds up management and policy decision-making. The rate of decision-making determines the competitiveness of regions and countries; therefore, for lack of time for blanket digitalization of the economy governments will invest in the digitalization of individual industries and locations. This would involve creating digital platforms. So the question is not whether this scenario is implemented or not, but for how long the gap between digital enclaves and the provinces will remain.

The optimistic scenario is less likely due to the lack of investment and required technologies. The pessimistic scenario is more likely as the EEU countries strive for closer bilateral and multilateral ties (excluding Russia). However, an existing system preferential trade regimes between EEU countries would make it impossible for this geopolitical integration project to be terminated at least in the short or medium terms.

Acknowledgments. The research is conducted with the support of the Russian Science Foundation grant No. 18-18-00360.

References

1. Beck, U.: World Risk Society. Polity Press, Cambridge (1998)
2. Bolgov, R., Karachay, V.: E-governance institutions development in the eurasian economic union: case of the Russian Federation. In: ACM International Conference Proceeding Series. 9th International Conference on Theory and Practice of Electronic Governance; Montevideo; Uruguay (2016). https://doi.org/10.1145/2910019.2910044
3. Chigareva, I.: Historical parallels: the digital economy risks repeating the fate of small businesses. In: Forbes, 20 June 2017
4. Chugunov, A., Filatova, O., Misnikov, Y.: Citizens' deliberation online as will-formation: the impact of media identity on policy discourse outcomes in Russia. In: Tambouris, E., Panagiotopoulos, P., Sæbø, Ø., Wimmer, M.A., Pardo, T.A., Charalabidis, Y., Soares, D.S., Janowski, T. (eds.) ePart 2016. LNCS, vol. 9821, pp. 67–82. Springer, Cham (2016). https://doi.org/10.1007/978-3-319-45074-2_6
5. Coase, R.H.: The nature of the firm. Economica, New Series **4**(16), 386–405 (1937)

6. Design and analysis session "Digital transformation of the economy EEU: new threats and sources of growth consolidated business position." 09–10 Feb 2017, Report (2017). http://www.eurasiancommission.org/ru/act/dmi/workgroup/Documents/Материалы%20для%20изучения/отчет_ПАС_9-10.02.2017.pdf
7. Digitalization of the economy. In: Business and information technology (2017). http://bit.samag.ru/uart/more/67
8. Eurasian Economic Integration 2017. Eurasian Development Bank, St Petersburg (2017). http://eurasian-studies.org/wp-content/uploads/2017/05/EDB_Centre_2017_Report_43_EEI_RUS.compressed.pdf
9. Evstafiev, D.: The world of enclaves. Risks of the Industrial Revolution for the Eurasian Economic Union (2017). http://eurasia.expert/mir-anklavov-riski-novoy-promyshlennoy-revolyutsii-dlya-stran-eaes
10. Filatova, O., Golubev, V., Ibragimov, I., Balabanova, S. E-participation in EEU countries: a case study of government websites. In: Proceedings of the International Conference on Electronic Governance and Open Society: Challenges in Eurasia, eGose 2017, Russia, St. Petersburg, 04–06 September 2017, pp. 145–151. ACM, New York (2017). https://doi.org/10.1145/3129757.3129782
11. Galbraith, J.K.: Economics and the Public Purpose. Houghton Mifflin Company, Boston, Toronto, London (1973). 334 p
12. General approaches to the formation of the digital space of the Eurasian Economic Union until 2030. http://www.eurasiancommission.org/ru/act/dmi/workgroup/materials/Documents
13. Guidelines for the development initiatives within the framework of implementation of the EEU Digital Agenda. http://www.eurasiancommission.org/ru/act/dmi/workgroup/Documents
14. Hix, S., Hoyland, B.: The Political System of the European Union. Palgrave (2011)
15. Keshelava, A.V.: Introduction to the "Digital" Economy, vol. 1 (2017). vvedenie-v-cifrovuyu-ekonomiku-na-poroge-cifrovogo-budushhego.pdf
16. Navas-Sabater, H.: Prospects for obtaining digital dividends in the EEU (2016). http://www.eurasiancommission.org/ru/act/dmi/workgroup/Pages/2016-10-27.aspx
17. North, D.C.: Institutions, Institutional Change and Economic Performance. Cambridge University Press (1990). http://epistemh.pbworks.com/f/8.%20Institutions__Institutional_Change_and_Economic_Performance.pdf
18. Sargsyan: EEU countries will create a digital office. In: Satellite-Armenia 25 Oct 2017. https://ru.armeniasputnik.am/radio/20171025/9197820/sarkisyan-strany-eaehs-sozdadut-cifrovoj-ofis.html
19. Statement on the digital agenda of the EEC. http://www.eurasiancommission.org/ru/act/dmi/workgroup
20. The main directions of implementation of the EEU digital agenda until 2025. http://www.eurasiancommission.org/ru/act
21. Van Langenhove, L., Costea, A.-N.: The EU as a global actor and the emergence of third generation' regionalism. In: UNU-CRIS Occasional Papers, 0–2005/14. http://cris.unu.edu/sites/cris.unu.edu/files/O-2005-14.pdf
22. Who controls the development of the digital economy and how? In: Tadviser. The state. Business. IT (2017). http://www.tadviser.ru/index.php

Contextualizing Smart Governance Research: Literature Review and Scientometrics Analysis

Andrei V. Chugunov[1], Felippe Cronemberger[2],
and Yury Kabanov[1,3(✉)]

[1] ITMO University, St. Petersburg, Russia
chugunov@egov-center.ru
[2] University at Albany SUNY, New York, USA
fcronemberger@alumni.albany.edu
[3] National Research University Higher School of Economics,
St. Petersburg, Russia
ykabanov@hse.ru

Abstract. As research on smart governments continues to attract interest, the concept of smartness seems to be growing in scope and complexity. This paper uses the scientometrics analysis to examine literature on smart cities and governance and situate the research conducted on this topic. Results suggest that research on smartness is interdisciplinary and, although spread across a variety of domains, it remains scant on topics such as e-participation and e-governance. The findings shed light on the importance of on-going examinations of smartness at the theoretical and conceptual levels for practical research endeavors.

Keywords: Smart cities · Citizens participation · Scientometrics
Analytics · VosViewer

1 Introduction

Although governance is an already established object of study in public administration literature and social sciences, *smart governance* is a fairly recent construct, which does not have a defined meaning. The debate on smart governance goes as far as roughly 17 years ago [27], but only in the last 10 years does smartness appear to have become prevalent in research. Seemingly, this occurred as a spinoff of the growing interest in studying governments that seek to become sounder at delivering what they are expected or mandated to do. In literature, those governments are known to work towards "smart governance systems" [33] or are referred to as "smart governments" [4, 40].

On the one hand, as its name suggests, its emergence is quite symptomatic of times where technologies [42], cities [21] and growth [22] are discussed as a part of the smart era in a variety of domains: from business analytics [38] to the management of tourist attractions [51]. In this context, smart governance appears to reflect a brand new quality of governance, different from previous theoretical assumptions.

On the other hand, smart governance still seems to have a limited scope of usage within the academia. It is quite frequently mentioned in the context of the so-called

© Springer Nature Switzerland AG 2018
D. A. Alexandrov et al. (Eds.): DTGS 2018, CCIS 858, pp. 102–112, 2018.
https://doi.org/10.1007/978-3-030-02843-5_9

smart cities, which involve the ways in which local governments approach increasingly intricate public issues [5, 9, 13]. Thus, smart governance might only have a contextually narrow meaning, and does not go beyond the literature on smart cities. This argument can be even stronger if we grasp the connection of the concept with previous terms, such as e-government, e-governance and e-participation, which also refer to the use of ICTs in governance and for democratic purposes. According to Alam and Ahmed [2], for instance, smart governance is a result of adapting e-government and making IT relevant to ordinary citizens, a position that also reverberates in digital divide literature [28, 47]. In this context, one should not forget that smart governance might be a spinoff of research on e-governance [14], which has been steadily growing since the early 2000s and, quite frequently, overlaps with literature or falls within topics such as e-government and digital government.

Such apparent conceptual opacity of the term poses a hurdle to further theoretical and empirical work and raises several topical questions. First, does the smart governance concept have some peculiar meaning and research focus in comparison to e-governance or e-participation, or can they be used interchangeably? Secondly, how does smart governance relate to a broader "smartness" literature, especially in the context of smart cities research? In order to approach these questions, the paper provides a review of the recent publications devoted to smart governance and smart cities, in order to reveal key topics and issues in smart governance research. This is done in two ways. First, using a database of publications, we run a scientometrics analysis in order to determine the place of smart governance studies in the research domain. Secondly, having selected the most relevant literature, we attempt to conceptualize smart governance, especially in relation to e-governance and e-participation.

2   A Scientometrics Review on Smart Governance

In order to have a more general overview of the current state in smart governance research in context, we have conducted a scientometrics analysis of papers, indexed in the Web of Science database. The sample we collected is devoted to both smart governance and smart city research and retrieved using the following search request: TS=(smart) AND TS=(governance OR cit*). The sample contains 8774 items.

The descriptive analysis of the sample reveals that more than half of all items were published in 2016 and 2017, while since 2010 the interest in the issue has been growing exponentially (Fig. 1). Most of the publications (4775, or 54.4%) are proceedings papers, 3598 items (41%) are journal articles and 444 (5%) are book chapters. As for the areas of research, smart governance and smart city research appears to be a multidisciplinary domain, mostly occupied by technical issues (Fig. 2). Almost half of the publications are related to the spheres of computer science, engineering and telecommunications, while there is a place for urban studies, public administration, social sciences and business as well.

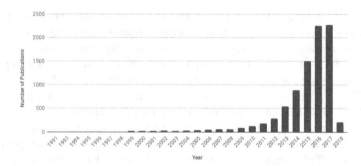

Fig. 1. Number of publications devoted to smart cities and smart governance, by year. Source: Authors' calculations based on the data from the Web of Science (webofknowledge.com)

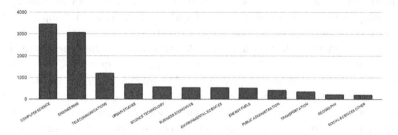

Fig. 2. Number of publications devoted to smart cities and smart governance, by research area. Source: Authors' calculations based on the data from the Web of Science

To run a bibliometric analysis, we use the *VosViewer*, software that helps to build and visualize networks based on publication data and keywords.[1] Based on the abovementioned bibliographic data we have developed a co-occurrence map, which denotes how often the keywords occur together in one publication. We use the author keywords, which occur at least 10 times in the sample. We have also developed a thesaurus to combine keywords with different spelling (i.e. *organization* and *organisation*), as well as the same keywords in various forms (i.e. *internet of things* and *IoT*). Overall, 172 keywords were found within the sample that match the abovementioned criteria. The clustering algorithm was set to form relatively large clusters of keywords (no less than 20), with the attraction value of "1" and repulsion value of "0"; association strength was selected as a normalization method.

The scientometrics map is presented in Fig. 3. The central concept used is definitely *smart city*, while *smart governance* occupies a relatively smaller size, adjacent to it. Overall, six clusters can be discerned, mostly related to technical, technological and engineering issues. The first cluster (**green**) is centered on big data and the different ways data can be used to make cities smart (i.e. machine learning, crowd-sensing, data-analytics). The adjacent **yellow** cluster is focused on social media, monitoring, and also

---

[1] http://www.vosviewer.com.

touches upon environmental issues (e.g. air pollution, waste and environmental monitoring). The **deep blue** cluster predominantly deals with the Internet of things, wireless sensor networks and cloud services, linked data, smart homes and intelligent transportation systems. The light **blue cluster** is mostly devoted to energy issues based on smart grids for energy efficiency.

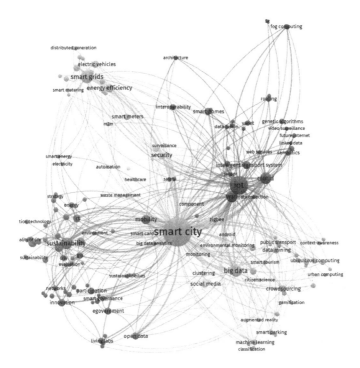

Fig. 3. Co-occurrence map of keywords. Source: Authors' analysis using the VosViewer software (http://www.vosviewer.com) (Color figure online)

The two clusters, which are less technical and more oriented towards governance and citizens' participation issues are the **red** and the **purple** ones (Fig. 4). The **red** cluster is centered upon the concepts of sustainability, smart growth and governance, with special emphasis on urbanization, urban planning and development. The **purple** cluster is the one that is the most related to smart governance, comprising the term, as well as others such as e-governance, e-government, participation, proving that these words are usually rather interchangeable. At the same time, there are some recent concepts here too, such as living labs and co-creation in the context of participation, smart community and knowledge management.

The general picture of the research domain looks as follows. First, its core is definitely the concept of smart city, while smart governance plays a peripheral role. The domain is split into several clusters of two basic types: a **technical** one, dealing with computing, engineering and programming, and a more **administrative** one, related to the issues of governance, participation, development and growth. They seem to be rather separated, and the prevalence of the former is evident, although public policies and citizens' participation are crucial for successful innovation implementation. The concept of smart governance is an indispensable part of the latter, denoting the public administration dimension of smart development. However, it is quite a small-scale component yet and seems to be used when e-governance and e-participation concern building smart cities. Even in this administrative cluster the concept of smart governance remains quite peripheral.

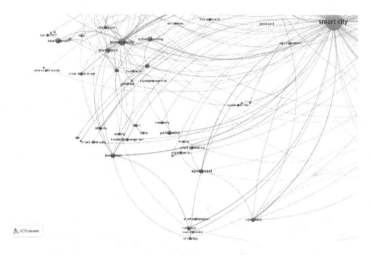

Fig. 4. Co-occurrence map of keywords (Smart Governance Cluster). Source: Authors' analysis using the VosViewer software (http://www.vosviewer.com) (Color figure online)

3 Contextualizing Smart Governance

3.1 Smart Governance and E-governance

As our literature review suggests, we may discern three major groups of authors dealing with smart governance issues: (1) researchers, working in the domain of e-government, open government and e-governance; (2) analysts and practitioners in charge of developing smart city projects on the global or national scales; (3) experts of the international organizations (e.g. the UN, World Bank) and consulting structures (e.g. Bloomberg, Deloitte, Gardner).

Speaking of the first [14, 23, 24] and the second [6, 36, 45] group, it is really hard to reveal any specific characteristics and definitions of smart governance vis-à-vis e-governance. In some cases, the authors use "classical" e-government/open government/e-governance models when describing the role of smart governance in the architecture and institutional environment of smart cities. To put it simply, a formula for smart governance is to add e-government (or open government/e-governance) to a smart city. At the same time, many articles emphasize the role of citizen participation by electronic and offline means. For instance, as put by J. Bell, "Smart governance or good governance are two sides of the same coin. The use of the Internet and digital technology is creating a progressive government-public partnership, strengthening government institutions and integrating all sections of society" [7]. According to Bell, the key functions of smart governance are: (1) the complex use of ICTs; (2) e-consultations with citizens and (3) e-data, or open government data [7].

There is a distinct direction of research, which can be entitled *Governance in Global Society*. This line of thought is especially prevalent in the activities of global consulting companies and analysts, working within the UN, World Bank, International Telecommunications Union etc., although there is academic research in this field as well. Here we can mention the book by H. Willke, attempting to place governance into the *global knowledge society* agenda. According to Willke, "Smart governance is ... the ensemble of principles, factors and capacities that constitute a form of governance able to cope with the conditions and exigencies of the knowledge society, ... [aiming] at redesigning formal democratic governance" [52: 165].

The activities of the Gardner Company should be mentioned as well. The Company developed the so-called *Hype Cycle* to assess the prospects of a certain technology (technology trigger, peak of inflated expectations, trough of disillusionment, slope of enlightenment, plateau of productivity), evaluating, among others, smart government technologies [30, 31]. In 2017 two reports were published to assess Digital Government [29] and Smart City [28] technologies.

Based on the literature review, we may draw a conclusion that smart governance is still lacking a specific research domain, which would be clearly different from the one of e-governance. Smart governance borrows a lot of models and assumptions from the previous research, but they are transferred to a relatively novel domain of smart cities, and, to put it broadly, smart society.

At the same time, the smart governance research agenda, reflecting the extensive literature on e-government, seems to respond to the consolidated notion that adopting ICT is not a terminal step to governments, but often where the efforts to govern those technologies to produce desired outcomes should begin [19, 24].

A relevant kick-off for the debate started from a number of reflections brought forth by Scholl and Scholl [48]. There, the authors present the central importance of information and its technologies to the development of models of smart governance. Authors highlight that "smart, open and agile government institutions" require both stakeholders' participation and an underpinning democratic drive". They moved off to set a research agenda for smart governance by looking at it as a result of various accomplishments in a number of scopes: economy, culture, education, and natural environment, among others. All of those would emerge from the evolution of research in e-government, leading to an open and smart government. As the authors suggest, smartness and openness are intertwined and continue to be considered as such [44, 46].

In a position paper about smart cities governance, Ferro et al. [18] imply that ICTs play a central role in creating an enabling infrastructure to the "transition process". In such transition, ICTs may enable production, distribution and governance processes, catalyze transformation and organization processes and inform the way people will make decisions and behave. Complementarily, Viale Pereira et al. [50] found that technologies positively influence governance in smart cities by providing support to information sharing and integration. This suggests that, as the relevance of studying smart cities emerges, research is increasingly valuing the importance of developing "smartness from within", that is, through a proper use of existing resources in face of existing problems and conditions.

The complexity of the issue continues to pose theoretical challenges to the discussion and encourages research that is more comprehensive and less deterministic on what smart governance is [11]. For example, Meijer and Bolívar [39] found that smart city governance is not a technological issue, but one that falls more within the socio-technical realm where complex institutional changes are taking place. To the authors, technology use and collaboration between citizens and a legit government should be in touch with an urban reality to ensure outcomes. Acknowledging the existence of multiple perspectives, the authors claim that the research agenda about smart city governance is still "confusing" and that it should evolve towards an understanding of institutional changes, public-value creation and the inevitable interplay with politics [39].

Thus, although smart governance literature is still quite narrowly concentrated on smart cities and technologies, there are certain trends that smart governance could become an umbrella term to encompass both e-government and e-governance, as its scope goes beyond ICTs towards a more comprehensive view of the governmental processes.

3.2 Smart Governance and E-participation

The issues of public participation, and e-participation in particular, appear to play a peripheral role in the literature on smart governance and smart cities. Based on the review, we propose that the presence of citizen participation in the smart governance literature falls under three different dimensions: (1) citizens' input into decision-making; (2) citizens' feedback (output) and (3) citizen-centric smart governance (Table 1). Citizens' input refers to initiatives where e-participation occurs with citizens' direct involvement. Such straight level of involvement may occur through initiatives such as living labs [20, 39], e-petitions [15] and participation in local communities [26]. That level of involvement may also be endorsed by internal administrative and managerial mechanisms that may foster collaborative governance practices and the development of knowledge networks. [16, 34].

Table 1. A summary of how citizen participation is portrayed in smart governance literature

Scope	Literature
Citizens' input into decision-making	
(a) Participation in urban planning, i.e. living labs, gamification	[15, 16, 20, 26, 34, 39]
(b) Collaborative smart governance: policy-making, e-participation	
(c) Participation in local communities	
Citizens' feedback	
(a) Evaluation of services	[12, 32, 35, 37, 39, 44, 48]
(b) Citizens and control of government: transparency and open government data	
Citizen-centric smart governance	
(a) Data-driven initiatives	[1, 3, 8, 10, 17, 25, 41, 49]
(b) Human-centric smart governance	

The citizens' feedback dimension relates to a more proactive stand taken by governments when they set out to consider citizens to their initiatives. Examples involve creating conditions for citizens to evaluate the services being provided, which may include a more open relationship of the government with its citizens [12, 48]. Similarly, initiatives to open government data are known to play a role in fostering citizen accountability [35, 37] and innovation [32].

Finally, the citizen-centric smart governance dimension involves a systematic and coordinated effort to jointly consider the interplay between human factors and technology factors as the key to maximize the results to citizens in a smart city [41]. This effort could be considered systematic because it involves engineering internal processes [43] and coordinated because it assumes that collaboration among a variety of stakeholders is needed [3, 25]. It is also important to state that those processes are being increasingly designed around data-driven practices [1, 49] and technologies support the data collection for those practices [8, 17].

Although the authors have touched upon many ways in which citizens can contribute to smart governance, the scope is still limited, and more effort is needed to place e-participation and democracy into the smart governance research agenda.

4   Conclusion

Both methods of analysis employed in this study – a bibliometric analysis and a more traditional literature review – show that smart governance is still an emerging concept within a fast-growing smart city body of literature. Therefore, further research is needed to assess the maturity of this research area.

At the moment, the concept appears to be seeking its own identity, key research foci and topics. While many studies show little difference between smart governance, on the one hand, and e-governance, open government, e-government, on the other, recent developments suggest that it may become an umbrella term that encompasses both ICT-related advancements of governance and the overall system of public administration.

We might argue that the maturity of concept and its greater heuristic value will be achieved under several circumstances. First, if the future research on smart cities is not directly split between technical issues and political, and social and administrative ones, a more holistic view on smart city development that takes both sides of the coin seriously is likely to address the importance of governance literature among scholars, experts and practitioners. Secondly, smart governance literature should take a more careful look at the questions of democracy and public participation, which is still a peripheral topic in the context of smart cities. A more nuanced approach towards integrating citizens' engagement into decision-making research in the public sphere may also expand the understanding of smartness in government. Complementarily, examining the e-participation research domain can open research avenues to assess the current developments in democratic governance and further contextualize the practical meanings of smart governance.

Acknowledgements. The research is conducted with the support of the Russian Science Foundation grant № 18-18-00360.

References

1. Abella, A., Ortiz-de-Urbina-Criado, M., De-Pablos-Heredero, C.: A model for the analysis of data-driven innovation and value generation in smart cities' ecosystems. Cities **64**, 47–53 (2017). https://doi.org/10.1016/j.cities.2017.01.011
2. Alam, M., Ahmed, K.: E-governance initiatives in Bangladesh. In: ACM International Conference Proceeding Series, vol. 351, pp. 291–295. ACM (2008). https://doi.org/10.1145/1509096.1509157
3. Amsler, L.B.: Collaborative governance: integrating management, politics, and law. Public Adm. Rev. **76**(5), 700–711 (2016). https://doi.org/10.1111/puar.12605
4. Anthopoulos, L.G.: Smart government: a new adjective to government transformation or a trick? In: Anthopoulos, L.G. (ed.) Understanding Smart Cities: A Tool for Smart Government or an Industrial Trick?. Public Administration and Information Technology, vol. 22, pp. 263–293. Springer, Cham (2017). https://doi.org/10.1007/978-3-319-57015-0_6
5. Anthopoulos, L.G., Vakali, A.: Urban planning and smart cities: interrelations and reciprocities. In: Álvarez, F., et al. (eds.) FIA 2012. LNCS, vol. 7281, pp. 178–189. Springer, Heidelberg (2012). https://doi.org/10.1007/978-3-642-30241-1_16
6. Batagan, L.: Methodologies for local development in smart society. Econ. Knowl. **4**(3), 23–34 (2012)
7. Bell, J.: Smart Governance for Smart Cities (2017). http://www.smartcity.press/smart-governance-for-smart-cities/
8. Benouaret, K., Valliyur-Ramalingam, R., Charoy, F.: CrowdSC: building smart cities with large-scale citizen participation. IEEE Internet Comput. **17**(6), 57–63 (2013). https://doi.org/10.1109/mic.2013.88
9. Caragliu, A., Del Bo, C., Nijkamp, P.: Smart cities in Europe. J. Urban Technol. **18**(2), 65–82 (2011). https://doi.org/10.1080/10630732.2011.601117
10. Cardone, G., et al.: Fostering participaction in smart cities: a geo-social crowdsensing platform. IEEE Commun. Mag. **51**(6), 112–119 (2013). https://doi.org/10.1109/mcom.2013.6525603
11. Castelnovo, W., Misuraca, G., Savoldelli, A.: Smart cities governance: the need for a holistic approach to assessing urban participatory policy making. Soc. Sci. Comput. Rev. **34**(6), 724–739 (2016). https://doi.org/10.1177/0894439315611103
12. Charalabidis, Y., Alexopoulos, C., Diamantopoulou, V., Androutsopoulou, A.: An open data and open services repository for supporting citizen-driven application development for governance. In: 49th Hawaii International Conference on System Sciences (HICSS), pp. 2596–2604. IEEE (2016). https://doi.org/10.1109/hicss.2016.325
13. Chourabi, H., et al.: Understanding smart cities: an integrative framework. In: 45th Hawaii International Conference on System Science (HICSS), pp. 2289–2297. IEEE (2012). https://doi.org/10.1109/HICSS.2012.615
14. Dawes, S.S.: The evolution and continuing challenges of E-governance. Public Adm. Rev. **68**(s1) (2008). https://doi.org/10.1111/j.1540-6210.2008.00981.x/full
15. Dumas, C.L., et al.: Examining political mobilization of online communities through E-petitioning behavior in We the People. Big Data Soc. **2**(2) (2015). https://doi.org/10.1177/2053951715598170

16. Emerson, K., Nabatchi, T., Balogh, S.: An integrative framework for collaborative governance. J. Public Adm. Res. Theor. **22**(1), 1–29 (2012). https://doi.org/10.1093/jopart/mur011
17. Farkas, K., Feher, G., Benczur, A., Sidlo, C.: Crowdsending based public transport information service in smart cities. IEEE Commun. Mag. **53**(8), 158–165 (2015). https://doi.org/10.1109/mcom.2015.7180523
18. Ferro, E., Caroleo, B., Leo, M., Osella, M., Pautasso, E.: The role of ICT in smart cities governance. In: Proceedings of 13th International Conference for E-democracy and Open Government, pp. 133–145. Donau-Universität Krems (2013)
19. Fountain, J.E.: Building the Virtual: Information Technology and Institutional Change State. Brookings Institution Press, Washington DC (2001)
20. Gascó, M.: Living labs: implementing open innovation in the public sector. Gov. Inf. Q. **34**(1), 90–98 (2017). https://doi.org/10.1016/j.giq.2016.09.003
21. Gascó, M., Trivellato, B., Cavenago, D.: How do Southern European cities foster innovation? Lessons from the experience of the smart city approaches of Barcelona and Milan. In: Gil-Garcia, J., Pardo, T., Nam, T. (eds.) Smarter as the New Urban Agenda, vol. 11, pp. 191–206. Springer, Cham (2016). https://doi.org/10.1007/978-3-319-17620-8_10
22. Geller, A.L.: Smart growth: a prescription for livable cities. Am. J. Public Health **93**(9), 1410–1415 (2003). https://doi.org/10.2105/ajph.93.9.1410
23. Gil-Garcia, J.R.: Enacting Electronic Government Success: An Integrative Study of Government-wide Websites, Organizational Capabilities, and Institutions. Springer, New York (2012). https://doi.org/10.1007/978-1-4614-2015-6
24. Gil-García, J.R., Pardo, T.A.: E-government success factors: mapping practical tools to theoretical foundations. Gov. Inf. Q. **22**(2), 187–216 (2005). https://doi.org/10.1016/j.giq.2005.02.001
25. Gil-Garcia, J.R., Zhang, J., Puron-Cid, G.: Conceptualizing smartness in government: an integrative and multi-dimensional view. Gov. Inf. Q. **33**(3), 524–534 (2014). https://doi.org/10.1016/j.giq.2016.03.002
26. Granier, B., Kudo, H.: How are citizens involved in smart cities? Analysing citizen participation in Japanese "Smart Communities". Inf. Polity **21**(1), 61–76 (2016). https://doi.org/10.3233/IP-150367
27. Griffith, J.C.: Smart governance for smart growth: the need for regional governments. Ga. St. UL Rev. **17**, 1019 (2000)
28. Helbig, N., Gil-García, J.R., Ferro, E.: Understanding the complexity of electronic government: implications from the digital divide literature. Gov. Inf. Q. **26**(1), 89–97 (2009). https://doi.org/10.1016/j.giq.2008.05.004
29. Hype Cycle for Digital Government Technology. Gartner (2017). https://www.gartner.com/doc/3770368/hype-cycle-digital-government-technology
30. Hype Cycle for Smart City Technologies and Solutions. Gartner (2017). https://www.gartner.com/doc/3776666/hype-cycle-smart-city-technologies
31. Hype Cycle for Smart Government. Gartner (2013). https://www.gartner.com/doc/2555215/hype-cycle-smart-government
32. Janssen, M., Konopnicki, D., Snowdon, J.L., Ojo, A.: Driving public sector innovation using big and open linked data (BOLD). Inf. Syst. Front. **19**(2), 189–195 (2017). https://doi.org/10.1007/s10796-017-9746-2
33. Johnston, E.W., Hansen, D.L.: Design lessons for smart governance infrastructures. Transforming American Governance: Rebooting the Public Square. Routledge, London and New York (2011)
34. Lee, J.: Exploring the role of knowledge networks in perceived E-government: a comparative case study of two local governments in Korea. Am. Rev. Public Adm. **43**(1), 89–108 (2013). https://doi.org/10.1177/0275074011429716

35. Linders, D.: Towards open development: leveraging open data to improve the planning and coordination of international aid. Gov. Inf. Q. **30**, 426–434 (2013). https://doi.org/10.1016/j.giq.2013.04.001
36. Lopes, N.V.: Smart governance: a key factor for smart cities implementation. In: IEEE International Conference on Smart Grid and Smart Cities (ICSGSC), Singapore, 23–26 July 2017. https://doi.org/10.1109/ICSGSC.2017.8038591
37. Lourenço, R.P.: An analysis of open government portals: a perspective of transparency for accountability. Gov. Inf. Q. **32**, 323–332 (2015). https://doi.org/10.1016/j.giq.2015.05.006
38. Marler, J.H., Cronemberger, F., Tao, C.: HR analytics: here to stay or short lived management fashion? In: Electronic HRM in the Smart Era, pp. 59–85, Emerald Group Publishing (2017). https://doi.org/10.1108/978-1-78714-315-920161003
39. Meijer, A., Bolívar, M.P.R.: Governing the smart city: a review of the literature on smart urban governance. Int. Rev. Adm. Sci. **82**(2), 392–408 (2016). https://doi.org/10.1177/0020852314564308
40. Mellouli, S., Luna-Reyes, L.F., Zhang, J.: Smart government, citizen participation and open data. Inf. Polity **19**(1, 2), 1–4 (2014). https://doi.org/10.3233/ip-140334
41. Nam, T., Pardo, T.A.: Conceptualizing smart city with dimensions of technology, people, and institutions. In: Proceedings of the 12th Annual International Digital Government Research Conference (2011). https://doi.org/10.1145/2037556.2037602
42. Park, C., Kim, H., Yong, T.: Dynamics characteristics of smart grid technology acceptance. Energy Procedia **128**, 187–193 (2017). https://doi.org/10.1016/j.egypro.2017.09.040
43. Patsakis, C., Laird, P., Clear, M., Bouroche, M., Solanas, A.: Interoperable privacy-aware E-participation within smart cities. Computer **48**(1), 52–58 (2015). https://doi.org/10.1109/mc.2015.16
44. Pereira, G.V., Macadar, M.A., Luciano, E.M., Testa, M.G.: Delivering public value through open government data initiatives in a Smart City context. Inf. Syst. Front. **19**(2), 213–229 (2017). https://doi.org/10.1007/s10796-016-9673-7
45. Pierre, J.: The Politics of Urban Governance. Palgrave Macmillan, Basingstoke (2011)
46. Recupero, D.R., et al.: An innovative, open, interoperable citizen engagement cloud platform for smart government and users' interaction. J. Knowl. Econ. **7**(2), 388–412 (2016). https://doi.org/10.1007/s13132-016-0361-0
47. Reddick, C.G.: Citizen interaction and E-government: evidence for the managerial, consultative, and participatory models. Transform. Gov. People Process Policy **5**(2), 167–184 (2011). https://doi.org/10.1108/17506161111131195
48. Scholl, H.J., Scholl, M.C.: Smart governance: a roadmap for research and practice. In.: Proceedings of iConference 2014 (2014). https://doi.org/10.9776/14060
49. Tenney, M., Sieber, R.: Data-driven participation: algorithms, cities, citizens, and corporate control. Urban Plan. **1**(2), 101–113 (2016). https://doi.org/10.17645/up.v1i2.645
50. Viale Pereira, G., Cunha, M.A., Lampoltshammer, T.J., Parycek, P., Testa, M.G.: Increasing collaboration and participation in smart city governance: a cross-case analysis of smart city initiatives. Inf. Technol. Dev. **23**(3), 526–554 (2017). https://doi.org/10.1080/02681102.2017.1353946
51. Wang, X., Li, X.R., Zhen, F.: Zhang, J: How smart is your tourist attraction? Measuring tourist preferences of smart tourism attractions via a FCEM-AHP and IPA approach. Tour. Manag. **54**, 309–320 (2016). https://doi.org/10.1016/j.tourman.2015.12.003
52. Willke, H.: Smart Governance: Governing the Global Knowledge Society. University of Chicago Press, Chicago (2007)

E-Polity: Politics and Activism in the Cyberspace

Is There a Future for Voter Targeting Online in Russia?

Galina Lukyanova$^{(\boxtimes)}$ ⓘ

St. Petersburg State University, 7/9 Universitetskaya nab.,
St. Petersburg 199034, Russia
g.lukiyanova@spbu.ru

Abstract. The use of targeting as election technology in campaigns increases in western democracies with each electoral cycle, and every time new forms and methods are being applied. During the last presidential campaigns of B. Obama, D. Trump, and E. Macron, targeting was actively used to improve the effectiveness of the impact on the target audience of voters. The Russian school of political consulting traditionally uses new western technologies, adapting them to the nature of the political process in Russia. This article examines the pattern of usage of different targeting methods during campaigns in the State Duma elections. The research involves expert interviews with political consultants who were professionally connected to the planning and conduct of election campaigns. Internet targeting is gaining its popularity among Russian political consultants to carry out targeted work with some groups of voters in social media. The development is slower than that in Western countries due to the lack of tried-and-tested tools, high financial costs, and indifference to politics of most Russian web users. The prospects for using microtargeting in Russian political campaigns are somewhat ambiguous due to the existing legislative restrictions and, in general, the need itself for such an in-depth method of agitation.

Keywords: Internet targeting · Political campaigns · Voter targeting

1 Introduction

Due to rapidly evolving information technology, most voters actively use plenty of digital devices in their everyday life. Traditional mass media, such as print media, television, and radio are losing their popularity, giving way to online sources of information, which is important to take into account when planning an election campaign [5, 19]. Thus, the widespread of the Internet and social media has prompted politicians to use this medium as an instrument of political struggle, and scientists, in turn, to revise the traditional models of pre-election communication. For the past years, there has been a rapid development in studying the possibility of using the Internet for campaigning, mobilizing and political socialization of people [2, 3, 6, 23]. Most studies have tended to focus on the role of digital media mainly in campaigns in liberal democracies [1, 6, 10, 15]. In many respects, this was facilitated by the last presidential campaigns of B. Obama, D. Trump, during which Internet-targeting was actively used to improve the effectiveness of the impact on the target audience of voters, which could

© Springer Nature Switzerland AG 2018
D. A. Alexandrov et al. (Eds.): DTGS 2018, CCIS 858, pp. 115–126, 2018.
https://doi.org/10.1007/978-3-030-02843-5_10

not be reached through traditional channels [20]. However, there still has been little discussion on adaptability and expediency of new digital technologies to election campaigns in non-Western democracies. The purpose of this research is to explore the features of the usage of different targeting methods during campaigns in the State Duma elections in Russia.

2 Theoretical Background

The trend towards digitization over the past decade have led both political and scientific community to an understanding of the need to rethink the consequences of the active introduction of digital technologies in election campaigns. Of scientific interest are the methods of politicians interacting with the electorate [12], the ways to turn the online audience into offline electorate [13], the differences in the use of social media by politicians of different levels [23], the technologies for formation of public opinion using social media [6].

Reflecting on the development of political consulting Cacciotto [3] lists three different phases in its history: the advent of mass media (1920s–1950s), television era (1960s–1980s), from tv to online (1990s–2000s) and the digital era after the American presidential election in 2008. As Cacciotto [3] states "today, we are seeing another new transformation with the rising importance of the Internet and digital technologies, the wide use of political marketing (and analytic measuring systems), and new and advanced techniques of segmentation and microtargeting of the constituency." Russian school of political consulting traditionally uses new Western technologies, adapting them to the specifics of the political process in Russia [8]. Nevertheless, the possibility of using online targeting in Russian election campaigns remains unclear. The authors mainly study the experience of the United States, not paying attention to the experience of Russia [24].

In recent years various approaches have been proposed to define targeting from a different perspective:

(1) Targeting as a separate full-fledged stage of targeted marketing. Kotler [11] defined targeting as a process of selecting the most attractive target segment after evaluating segments of the whole market. Leppäniemi et al. [13] examines targeting of young voters in the 2007 Finnish general election and describes it as a part of a digital marketing campaign.

(2) Targeting as an advertising strategy [21]. In this concept, the priority objectives are to maintain consumer relations and increase the value of the consumer message through the individual approach in the product positioning process, accurate approach of small target groups and in-depth feedback. Targeting allows spending the existing funds on advertising in the right manner without wasting money on a non-target audience, as well as increasing the efficiency of interaction with the audience. Focusing on G.W. Bush and the Republican Party in the 2000 election Knuckey and Lees-Marshment [10] describe positive advertising campaign appealed to three target groups: women, moderates, and independents. Minchenko [14] points out that one of the basic projects of the election campaign of E. Macron during the presidential race in 2017 in France was geographical targeting. France was divided into 60,000 zones, about 1,000 people in

each (size of an urban quarter). The voting history, demographic indicators, socioeconomic statistics, sociological survey data and information about the presence of volunteer agitators in the area were superimposed on these districts. Based on these data, the agitation priorities were determined, — from working schedule and public gathering locations to the frequency of meetings with the candidate and his representatives [14].

(3) In a narrower sense (which is more common, however) the term "targeting" is used as an Internet promotion technology allowing to separate a group of users with similar properties corresponding to the given criteria of the advertiser from all visitors of a website (a social networking service). Targeting can be performed in different forms and based on different criteria: geographical sociodemographic, time, thematic, contextual, behavioral, profile targeting [9].

Microtargeting is a new tool for political consultants all over the world [16]. This method is centered on singling out very narrow groups of voters and addressing them with a message based on the preliminary research of their behavior. To take advantage of new technologies, campaigns collect primary information from available sources: lists of registered voters, their party affiliation, voting history, credit card statements, network store bonus programs, health insurance data, newspaper subscriptions, and more. Information on each voter is used to create databases with segmentation of voters on the grounds of geography, demography, and socioeconomics. The voter profile can have up to 400 parameters which further determine the content of advertising messages for effective impact on the voter [15].

Microtargeting can be carried out in two ways of message delivery: the use of traditional means of mass-communication tools (mailings, door-to-door agitation, phone calls); the use of the Internet (email circulation, robocalls, Internet advertising, social networking media).

Microtargeting of voters was used widely for the first time during the presidential race in the United States in 2004 as part of the G.W. Bush's reelection campaign. The use of microtargeting to communicate with citizens was also successfully used in the B. Obama's presidential campaign in 2012 [2]. The election team developed a database that contained personal information of users who registered on the Obama's website via Facebook. The program developed by the Obama's election team allowed integrating all the collected databases to create a profile of each individual voter who could vote for B. Obama. The program analyzed the expectations and hopes of the voters to identify their positions on different political issues and made it possible to personalize messages to the voter. The system used in this campaign helps to organize the fieldwork in such a way so that volunteers in the door-to-door agitation could knock on the right door, ask the right questions when calling and bring up a topic that is relevant for the voter. Thus, the system allows collecting real information online, to use it for work with citizens in the future [17, 23].

Microtargeting played an important role in the presidential campaign of D. Trump and during the mobilization of UK citizens to take part in the referendum on withdrawal from the European Union [1, 20]. These two events were inextricably connected to Cambridge Analytica; a company engaged in microtargeting using "psychographic" profiling of users of various social networking services [16]. The campaign targeted 13.5 million persuadable voters in sixteen battleground states, discovering the hidden Trump voters, especially in the Midwest, whom the polls had ignored [18]. The positive aspect of the use of microtargeting is the opportunity of direct agitation of the voter and voter mobilization.

However, the application of microtargeting in some European countries is difficult due to legislation which limits the collection of personal data. Investigating restrictions on data-driven political micro-targeting in Germany, Kruschinsi and Haller [12] conclude that political micro-targeting highly depends on contextual factors within the system, budgetary and legal restraints, party structures and even individual decisions and knowledge of campaign leaders.

There are also other difficulties in applying this technology, such as: the cost of databases and related software; the need for precise wording of voter attitudes to increase the effectiveness of the message; the expediency of use of individual advertising; the incapability of the databases of covering all citizens, which could lead to "sagging" of voters; the negative effect of the use of confidential information.

3 Methods

The complexity of the problem and the lack of regulatory tools led to an expert survey of the political consultants who took part in the parliamentary election campaigns in Russia. An expert survey is a special survey in which the main source of information is competent persons whose professional activities are closely related to the subject of the research. The purpose is to obtain information on actual events in the form of opinions, assessments, and knowledge of the experts. The following criteria are taken into account when selecting respondents: professional competence; personal interest of the expert in taking the survey; analytical and constructive thinking of the expert.

The purpose of the expert survey is to identify the features of usage of different targeting methods during campaigns in the State Duma elections.

The following provisions were put forward as hypotheses of the research:

H1. Targeting as an election technology is practically not used in parliamentary elections in the Russian Federation;
H2. In the next few years, it is not possible to implement microtargeting during the election campaigns in Russia.

A guide was drawn up to meet the goal, which included eight main points to be discussed with the experts: work experience of the expert; the role of segmentation in the planning of the election campaign; the ways to segment the voters; special features of identifying the main target audiences; features of targeting voters in parliamentary elections; the key methods of Internet targeting; relevance of the use of microtargeting in the process of elections in Russia; prospects for the development of targeting as a key election technology.

The expert survey was conducted as an unstandardized interview and implied one-on-one communication according to a pre-planned scenario. Each interview allowed a deviation from the plan due to the nature of respondents' activity. This format allowed to provide trust-based relations with the expert and to allay the possible confidentiality-related fears of experts regarding the participation in the research. The anonymity of the interview played an important role due to the limited market of political consulting in Russia.

3.1 Sample

The survey was conducted in April–May 2017. The respondents were 7 experts whose professional activities were inextricably connected to planning and conduct of political campaigns: six political consultants (three of them with more than 10 years of experience, one strategist having 5 years of experience, and two having 3 years of experience) and one municipal parliamentarian who has repeatedly participated in elections at different levels (Table 1). The respondents were selected using the "snowball method."

Table 1. The description of experts

№	Experience (years)	Region	Level of elections
1	>3	St. Petersburg	Municipal elections, State Duma elections
2	>11	St. Petersburg, Leningrad region	Municipal elections, regional parliament elections
3	>5	Leningrad region	Municipal elections, regional parliament elections, State Duma elections, city mayors/governor elections
4	>4	St. Petersburg	Municipal elections, regional parliament elections, State Duma elections
5	>17	St. Petersburg, Cheboksary, Moscow, Ukraine	Municipal elections, regional parliament elections, State Duma elections city, mayors/governor elections
6	>10	Moscow, Kaliningrad, St. Petersburg	Municipal elections, regional parliament elections, State Duma elections, city mayors/governor elections
7	>11	Republic of Karelia, St. Petersburg, Leningrad region	Municipal elections, regional parliament elections, State Duma elections

Most of the selected experts had taken part in elections at different levels in the Northwestern Federal District: In the Republic of Karelia, St. Petersburg, Leningrad region, Kaliningrad region, Arkhangelsk region. All seven experts had been consultants or candidates in municipal elections and regional parliament elections, six had been engaged in the State Duma elections (both in single-seat districts and in party campaigns), three had had experience in election of governors (Kaliningrad region, Leningrad region, St. Petersburg) and city mayors (Cheboksary, Moscow). Party affiliation of clients of the experts was also different: four experts worked with the party and candidates of Edinaya Rossiya, three of Spravedlivaya Rossiya, two of the LDPR (Liberalno-demokraticheskaya Partiya Rossii), one of the consultants cooperates with representatives of the KPRF (Kommunisticheskaya Partiya Rossijskoj Federacii). The choice of experts having experience in election campaigning, mainly in the North-West Federal District, is accounted for by great extent of penetration of the Internet into everyday life of people living in large cities. According to the Public Opinion Foundation [5], the North-West Federal District, and in particular St. Petersburg, is leading among the other regions in terms of Internet use.

When processing and analyzing interview data, coding categories and data grouping were used, the latter being preceded by decoding of records. Data grouping performs three functions during the processing: facilitation of encoding process; development of the coding system; rearrangement of data. Coding is used to create a conceptual apparatus (system of categories) – a basis for the formulation of a concept. In the course of analysis, natural categories are distinguished - words, expressions, terms used by the respondents during the discussion; as well as constructed codes - the terminology created by the researcher for designating certain situations. When forming constructed codes, the transition to a system of concepts with greater logical volume and smaller content is used.

For the analysis of interviews, Fairclough's critical discourse analysis (CDA) was used as well [4]. CDA consists of three inter-related processes of analysis tied to three inter-related dimensions of discourse. These three dimensions are text, discourse practice, and sociocultural practice. Each of these dimensions requires a different kind of analysis: text analysis (description), processing analysis (interpretation), social analysis (explanation). It should be noted that the procedure of critical discourse analysis is interpretive; it should be regarded not as a particular succession of steps, but as a cycle of actions in which all of the three levels of analysis are interrelated and require constant correlation and comparison.

4   Results

The role of segmentation of voters during planning of the election campaign is determined by the experts highly ambiguously. On the one hand, two experts put the segmentation among the priority objectives in the formation of the strategy, reasoning that there is a risk to lose the campaign if the basic voters are chosen mistakenly. On the other hand, there is no need to carry out quantitative or qualitative research of segmentation, as the necessary target audiences in the conditions of Russian voting behavior have been identified already: "*As they were segmented ten years ago, nothing has changed. When political consultants come, they know very well who their main target audiences are. They exist a priori: old-aged pensioners, middle-aged women, workers, military, youth...*"

There are two main methods of voter segmentation. First, the main tool is the creation of a district passport, which includes the following information: map of the district, the voting turnout data and results of the past elections, characteristics of the voting district resident (gender and age, employment, ethnic makeup), information about polling stations and administrative division, local industrial enterprises and farms, higher education institutions and campuses, military units and corrections facilities, etc. The second method is a method of quantitative and qualitative research.

Public opinion polls identify polar attitudes to some problems or individuals that were not previously available as a segmentation source. Summing up the block of respondents' answers about the basic segmentation, the following features can be identified:

1. There are eight main segments of voters in Russia: old-aged pensioners, workers, state-paid workers, students, military, businessmen, villagers and unemployed.
2. Segmentation of voters by the image of the candidate and segmentation in the context of a problem is only relevant in the case of correct positioning.
3. Geographical segmentation is important in conditions of a large voting district. A division into city/village, downtown/suburbs, private sector, center/periphery will certainly occur.

A subtle moment in the strategy of segmenting the voters is understanding its level: experts consider it necessary not to dig too deep into the segmentation and to identify only 3–4 main target groups for further work. The risk is that agitation is conducted within one territory, the number of channels and sources of information is limited, and target audiences overlap – it is important *"not to overdo it."*

Communication with voters should necessarily focus on the target audience. All experts have identified old-aged pensioners and middle-aged women as their main audience: *"They who go to vote most often, are main voters. Who are they? Old-aged pensioners, housewives, middle-aged women. The proportion of the segments across the nation is the same – old-aged pensioners and housewives."* Respondents believe that taking due account of the voting behavior of Russian voters leaves no sense in targeting the other segments.

Targeting channels are also different, as well as segments, which the agitation message must be sent to. The Web has secured its role in election campaigns as one of the main dissemination channels.

Targeting on the Web requires much preparatory work. The first step is to identify proper reference resources of the region to understand the main categories of users in the area: regional forums, news sites, groups in social media. Facebook, where regional bloggers publish news material available to representatives of the media elite of the region is worth noting. Telegram becomes an important channel; it appears to be a *"fresh and perspective thing."* The most popular channels within the region should also be identified. For example, Instagram plays a big role in the territory of the Caucasian republics.

Depending on the segmented groups, authentic content must be generated. Two experts say that good content can sell itself without targeted and contextual advertising. For example, viral videos: The video "Medvedev dancing" has scored more than 15 million views, and the KPRF's "Putin vs. Medvedev" about 4 million. An important point is a work with a top of the news on Yandex.News, which is one of the main sources of news in the regions, and a top of selections on YouTube, which gained popularity thanks to the development of connection speed and increased availability of video content.

One of the most common criteria for targeting in political campaigns is geographical segmentation. Geographical targeting is less effective for municipal elections because *"it is difficult to identify voters living directly in the voting district,"* but the creation and use of regional and city groups in social media within a single-seat district were mentioned by three experts as one of the geotargeting techniques.

The main drawback of Web targeting in social media as a key election technology is noted by all seven experts: *"The audience of social networking services is not active in the elections"* (*"It would be great if active Web users (even if they have a civic position) would really be willing to go to the polling station. This is probably the main drawback of working with the Internet audience"*).

Two experts in the course of their work in the last parliamentary elections used MyTarget as a tool for targeting in social media. This is a popular advertising platform that combines the largest Russian and CIS social media (VKontakte, Odnoklassniki, MoiMir) with a total coverage of more than 140 million people. When assessing the efficiency of targeted advertising, respondents pointed to its high cost and low efficiency: *"We used targeted advertising on social media sites in the case for a parliamentary party within St. Petersburg with reference to their official website. The efficiency is not high enough and still depends on what party or candidate it [targeted advertising] refers to. After all, there is a great chance that having scrolled through some content of interest, the voter stumbles on a website of a political party he hates. Therefore, he or she remains out of the target. Moreover, it is unreasonably expensive: with a large number of settings, attracting one voter can cost 30–40 cents."*

Experts were asked to discuss the possibility of using microtargeting similar to Obama's or Trump's campaigns for the Russian election process. Two experts described a similar procedure widely used in Russian practice: gathering own database of residents of the district, based on the unsystematized collection of personal data in the course of door-to-door agitation, in-the-street meetings, meetings with the Deputy or the common practice of *"collecting mandates"*:

- In the first case, door-to-door agitation took place in two stages: At the first round, agitator tried to describe the residents of the apartment as much as possible, to record their opinion and reaction. At the second stage, this information was analyzed, and during the next conversation agitator focused on the subjects of concern to the voters while keeping clear of negatively minded residents;
- Collection of mandates, voter proposals, and wishes, in which the contact details are specified, and transfer of them to the headquarters allowed building two-way communication through the subsequent call of voters to discuss topical issues.

The following are identified as the main difficulties that complicate the use of microtargeting in Russia: (1) Legal restrictions on the transfer of personal data to third parties; (2) The technical complexity of processing of large arrays of data; (3) The high cost of one positive contact; (4) No specific need in applying microtargeting in the conditions of the Russian political process.

The last criterion is formed by the experts on the basis of two opinions. Firstly, the use of such precise technology does not seem to be relevant because of the limited democratic character of the election process: *"It is necessary to understand the political regime in this country; our 'dictocracy' has evolved in such a way that we know what can be done, and what should not be done. In particular, in election campaigns".*

Secondly, the Russian voters do not need a detailed segmentation in the context of some issues or legislative initiatives. *"There are visible problems in Russia: why would agitator need to know any local issues of voters, if, upon entering the main entrance, he sees that there are broken windows and walls that have not been painted for 30 years? Why use microtargeting in a country where a large proportion of the population lives below the poverty line?"*

However, the experts remained very positive as suggested *"that with the development and change of the political system this [microtargeting] will not be just possible, but necessary in the work of strategists and election teams."* Several experts suggested that no development of microtargeting would happen in the next 10–12 years due to the above reasons, but the prospect of using targeted advertising in social media seemed more optimistic.

To conclude, the specifics of different targeting methods in political campaigns in the Russian Federation were identified. Traditional segmentation techniques are used to divide voters into groups. The division by geographical, demographic and socioeconomic parameters is combined by political consultants with corporate, problem and personal targeting. The hypothesis, which is associated with the small-scale application of targeting as election technology is confirmed by two reasons. First, audiences selected for targeting in most campaigns are limited to active population groups: old-aged pensioners and middle-aged women. For instance, the Russian Public Opinion Research Centre (VTsIOM) in late June 2016 presented the poll data on the level of the Russians' awareness of the forthcoming elections to the State Duma [22]. One month before the voting, only 37% of all Russians gave the correct year and month (September 2016) of the election. This figure was noticeably higher with older age groups and lower with young people (47% - 60 years old and above versus 24% of 18–24-year-olds). The declared election turnout was 51% in the first half of June 2016. The planned turnout spread was as follows: elderly people (68%), rural residents (55%), women (55%); the smaller figure was shown by young people (43% - 18 to 24 years old), citizens of Moscow and St. Petersburg (37%), men (45%). As a result, the turnout for the elections to the State Duma of the 7th convocation amounted only to 47.88%. The survey data clearly illustrate that young people, being the main Internet users and the main audience of social networks, are characterized by low political activity. It is for that reason that the electoral consultants focus on pensioners and middle-aged women as target groups. In this context, the use of Internet targeting as the main electoral technology is not rational and not justified. Secondly, targeting (in particular, Web targeting) requires high financial and time investments, which is ineffective and, most importantly, not necessary in the Russian conditions. The hypothesis about microtargeting is only partially confirmed: On one hand, experts highlight several important reasons for the complexity of this technique and consider using microtargeting only within a long-term perspective. On the other hand, attempts are being made to develop databases of loyal voters as necessary tools are available.

5   Conclusion and Discussion

Parliamentary elections give an opportunity to political consultants to use a large arsenal of various tools and techniques, the choice of which is based on the candidate or party standing for election, the available resources and, in general, the situation in the political arena. Targeting is just one of the tools in the extensive set of political strategists. However, provided the appropriate training and openness to election procedures, targeting can play a decisive role.

Internet targeting is gaining its popularity among Russian political consultants to carry out targeted work with some categories of voters in social media. The development is slower than that in Western countries due to the lack of tried-and-tested tools, high financial costs and apolitical view of most Russian web users.

The prospects for using microtargeting in Russian political campaigns are somewhat ambiguous due to the existing legislative restrictions and, in general, the need for such an in-depth method of agitation. On the other hand, the results of the expert survey show that the existing political system in Russia is the main reason hindering the development of targeting and microtargeting tools as techniques for influencing the identified segments. While in liberal democracies the functions of elections comprise representation of diverse interests of the population, presentation of competitive alternative political programmes and alternation of power, the elections in electoral authoritarian regimes, such as Russia, are, as a rule, predictable and "orchestrated in a way that not only ensures the autocrat's survival in power but also contributes to regime consolidation" [7]. The current laws, the mentality of the Russian voter, the socioeconomic situation of the population and the non-transparency of the election procedures limit the applicability of these techniques. However, even within the existing political situation, the basic approaches to segmentation and targeting of voters can significantly improve the efficiency of communication between the candidate and its voters and make the agitation impact more powerful and focused. Moreover, the use of online targeting seems to be promising as a long-term strategy aimed, in the first place, at political socialization of the population, development of its political consciousness and political involvement.

A variety of limitations should be acknowledged. First, the results of this study are obviously limited to a single-case study of elections to the State Duma. Nevertheless, the performed research demonstrates the basic principles of segmentation and targeting that are used by political technologists in their work over parliamentary electoral campaigns. The experience of using the voter targeting online in other election campaigns is necessary. Second, this research is constrained to geographical limits. Although Internet penetration is most strongly marked in the large cities of Russia with the population over one million people, the experience of consulting in other regions would be useful for further analysis. Third, the present study is more focused on the issues of targeting application in the context of existing political framework than on assessing its efficiency and possible impact on voting results. In this connection, the research aimed at elaborating the criteria for the efficiency of targeting for electoral campaigns and developing the ways of turning the online audience into offline electorate is useful.

Acknowledgments. The reported study was funded by RFBR according to the research project № 18-011-00705 "Explanatory Potential of Network Theory in Political Research: Methodological Synthesis as Analytical Strategy." The author wishes to thank Ksenia Suzi for the assist, and three anonymous reviewers for comments on earlier versions of this article.

References

1. Balázs, B., Helberger, N., de Vreese, C.H.: Political micro-targeting: a Manchurian candidate or just a dark horse? Internet Policy Rev. **6**(4) (2017). https://doi.org/10.14763/2017.4.776
2. Bimber, B.: Digital media in the Obama campaigns of 2008 and 2012: adaptation to the personalized political communication environment. J. Inf. Technol. Polit. **11**(2), 130–150 (2014). https://doi.org/10.1080/19331681.2014.895691
3. Cacciotto, M.M.: Is political consulting going digital? J. Polit. Mark. **16**(1), 50–69 (2017). https://doi.org/10.1080/15377857.2016.1262224
4. Fairclough, N.: Media Discourse. Bloomsbury Academic, New York (2011)
5. Fond Obshchestvennoye Mneniye (FOM): Internet v Rossii: dinamika proniknoveniya. Leto 2017. http://fom.ru/SMI-i-internet/13783. Accessed 01 May 2018. (in Russian)
6. Gerodimos, R., Justinussen, J.: Obama's 2012 Facebook campaign: political communication in the age of the like button. J. Inf. Technol. Polit. **12**(2), 113–132 (2015). https://doi.org/10.1080/19331681.2014.982266
7. Golosov, G.V.: Russia's post Soviet elections. Europe-Asia Studies (2018). http://explore.tandfonline.com/content/pgas/ceas-russias-post-soviet-elections. Accessed 03 May 2018
8. Goncharov, V.E.: Stranstvuyushchiye Rytsari Demokratii. Politicheskiye Konsul'tanty v XXI veke. IVESEP, Saint Petersburg (2014). (in Russian)
9. Klever, A.: Behavioural Targeting: An Online Analysis for Efficient Media Planning? Diplomica Verlag, Hamburg (2009)
10. Knuckey, J., Lees-Marshment, J.: American political marketing: George W. Bush and the Republican party. In: Lilliker, D.G., Lees-Marshment, J. (eds.) Political Marketing: A Comparative Perspective, pp. 39–58. Manchester University Press, Manchester (2005)
11. Kotler, P., Keller, K.L.: Marketing Management, 13th edn. PrenticeHall, Upper Saddle River (2009)
12. Kruschinski, S., Haller, A.: Restrictions on data-driven political micro-targeting in Germany. Internet Policy Rev. **6**(4) (2017). https://doi.org/10.14763/2017.4.780
13. Leppäniemi, M., Karjaluoto, H., Lehto, H., Goman, A.: Targeting young voters in a political campaign: empirical insights into an interactive digital marketing campaign in the 2007 Finnish general election. J. Nonprofit Public Sect. Mark. **22**(1), 14–37 (2010). https://doi.org/10.1080/10495140903190374
14. Minchenko Consulting Homepage. http://minchenko.ru/analitika/analitika_71.html. Accessed 21 Sept 2017. (in Russian)
15. Murray, G.R., Scime, A.: Microtargeting and electorate segmentation: data mining the American national election studies. J. Polit. Mark. **9**(3), 143–166 (2010). https://doi.org/10.1080/15377857.2010.497732
16. Nix, A.: The power of Big Data and psychographics in the electoral process. Presented at the Concordia annual summit, New York (2016). https://www.youtube.com/watch?v=n8Dd5aVXLCc. Accessed 03 May 2018
17. Panagopoulos, C.: All about that base: changing campaign strategies in US presidential elections. Party Polit. **22**(2), 179–190 (2016). https://doi.org/10.1177/1354068815605676
18. Persily, N.: Can democracy survive the Internet? J. Democr. **28**(2), 63–76 (2017). https://doi.org/10.1353/jod.2017.0025
19. Pew Research Centre: State of the News Media (2018). http://www.pewresearch.org/topics/state-of-the-news-media/. Accessed 03 May 2018

20. Raynauld, V., Turcotte, A.: "Different strokes for different folks": implications of voter micro-targeting and appeal in the age of Donald Trump. In: Gillies, J. (ed.) Political Marketing in the 2016 U.S. Presidential Election, pp. 11–28. Palgrave Macmillan, Cham (2018). https://doi.org/10.1007/978-3-319-59345-6_2
21. Rossiter, J.R., Percy, L.: Advertising and Promotion Management. McGraw-Hill, Singapore (1987)
22. Russian Public Opinion Research Centre (VTsIOM): Vybory-2016: chto? gde? kogda? 23 June 2016. https://wciom.ru/index.php?id=236&uid=115748. (in Russian)
23. Schill, D., Hendricks, J.A.: Media, message, and mobilization: political communication in the 2014 election campaigns. In: Hendricks, J.A., Schill, D. (eds.) Communication and Midterm Elections: Media, Message, and Mobilization, pp. 3–23. Palgrave Macmillan, New York (2016). https://doi.org/10.1057/9781137488015
24. Volodenkov, S.V.: Total data as a phenomenon for the formation of political postreality. Herald of Omsk University. Series "Historical Studies" 3(15), 409–415 (2017). (in Russian). https://doi.org/10.25513/2312-1300.2017.3.409-415

Measurement of Public Interest in Ecological Matters Through Online Activity and Environmental Monitoring

Dmitry Verzilin[1,2](✉) ⓘ, Tatyana Maximova[3] ⓘ, Yury Antokhin[4,5],
and Irina Sokolova[6]

[1] St. Petersburg Institute for Informatics and Automation of the Russian
Academy of Sciences, St. Petersburg, Russia
modusponens@mail.ru
[2] Lesgaft National State University of Physical Education, Sport and Health,
St. Petersburg, Russia
[3] ITMO University, St. Petersburg, Russia
maximovatg@gmail.com
[4] Russian State Hydrometeorological University, St. Petersburg, Russia
antokhinyn@mail.ru
[5] Territorial Fund of Compulsory Medical Insurance of the Leningrad Region,
St. Petersburg, Russia
[6] St. Petersburg State University, St. Petersburg, Russia
i_sokolova@bk.ru

Abstract. Taking into account the global world trends in the development of digital technologies and their diffusion into the economic and social space, it is proposed to use indicators of social interest in ecological matters (environmental responsibility and environmental concerns) for the population of Russian regions. An original approach to the estimation of these indicators according to the online activity of the population was proposed. It was found out that the data on the number, prevalence and dynamics of search queries for keywords related to environmental pollution, cleanliness of water and air, reflect the degree of responsibility and concern of the population with the environmental situation in the region and can be considered as an indirect indicator of environmental ill-being. Dependencies have been established between indicators of environmental interest and environmental monitoring data.

Keywords: Ecological economy · Environmental assets · Environmental monitoring · Key word searchers · Online activity · Social ecology Socio-ecological systems

1 Introduction

Ensuring environmental safety is an urgent public problem. The society can make a significant contribution to a solution of this problem if the majority of its members realize the importance and necessity of preserving the environment, natural landscapes, and biodiversity, understand the severity and irreversibility of adversities resulting from

© Springer Nature Switzerland AG 2018
D. A. Alexandrov et al. (Eds.): DTGS 2018, CCIS 858, pp. 127–143, 2018.
https://doi.org/10.1007/978-3-030-02843-5_11

the violation of ecological balances. In order that the members of the society acquire ecologically responsible behavior, information about the state of the environment must be accessible to the society and in demand by the society. The availability of the information on the Internet facilitates its dissemination among active users, self-organization of interested users, formation of their conscious ecologically responsible behavior and the diffusion of patterns of such behavior in other sectors of society. The need for information about the environment reflects the ecological maturity of the society, its readiness to participate in environmental initiatives, in the formation of regional ecological policy and civil institutions for environmental protection. There are important questions: what is the degree of interest within Russian society in the ecological information, what factors can determine the need for it, how to assess regional differences in the attitude of the population towards various aspects of environmental problems, how the informational behavior of Internet users reflects the population's concern with the ecological situation in a region. From the standpoint of neo-cybernetics and the theory of socio-cybernetic systems, the questions arise of how much the self-organization of socio-cybernetic systems in the sphere of ecology and environmental protection are widespread, or such systems are largely emerging from managerial actions. The answers to these questions are of practical importance. They will allow to estimate, how much the society and the state structures are ready to follow principles of ecologically responsible behavior.

2 Literature Review

The problem of ecologically responsible behavior of the population, business and governments is widely discussed in academic community. A lot of intergovernmental, state and public initiatives are directed to a formation of ecological responsibility.

In scientific studies the following fundamental issues can be identified: the relationship between the condition of ecosystems and human well-being; development of ecological consciousness; evaluation of public opinion on the need and importance of environmental initiatives; analysis and compilation of regional practices for the management of environmental resources; processes of identification and adoption of managerial decisions in the sphere of natural resources use; approaches to the formation of environmental policy; economy and management of socio-ecological systems.

We can mention the report [50] prepared by an international working group as a fundamental work evaluating the relationship between the state of ecosystems and human well-being. The report was worked out to meet the needs of decision makers in scientific information on the relationship between ecosystem change and human well-being. Conceptual basics for interrelation of economy and ecology, the relationship between biodiversity and ecosystem services, their importance for human well-being, the foundations of state and regional ecosystem management were outlined in the TEEB publications (The Economics of Ecosystems and Biodiversity) [51, 52] presenting the most comprehensive survey of current thinking in this field to date.

Systematized data on the actual condition of the natural environment in Russia and the main achievements in the state regulation of environmental protection and nature management are published in the annual State Report [50]. The report is intended to provide the state government bodies, scientific, public organizations, and the population of Russia with objective systematic information on the environment, natural resources, and their protection.

Paradigms and ways to develop the ecological consciousness in an individual and society as a whole, factors of negative impact on the nature and health of people are discussed in detail in the book by Christopher Uhl [63]. In the works of Russian researchers considerable attention is paid to theoretical aspects of forming ecological culture. The factors essential for a formation of planetary ecological consciousness [65] and ecological consciousness of an individual were considered [61, 71]. Ecological culture is understood as an integral part of human culture [37]. For the development of environmental awareness and the spread of ecological culture, it is proposed to improve educational programs [65] focusing on two important sections: conservation and rational use of nature; and forming a healthy lifestyle [48]. The authors of [71] substantiate a position that the level of the ecological culture of the society and individual specialists has a direct impact on the ecological safety of biosystems and the rational use of natural resources. Ecological consciousness should be contrasted both with ecological pessimism and ecological anxiety propagating a sharp restriction of technical and economic development, and unrestrained optimistic views on the inexhaustible riches of nature [71].

The public opinion on the necessity and importance of environmental initiatives is evaluated in two main ways: evaluating the opinion of a regional public about a specific environmental initiative in the region and evaluating public opinion about the environmental situation as a whole.

For example, the purpose of the study described in [2] was to determine the value for the inhabitants of the surrounding ecosystems. A statistical analysis of the opinions of 589 respondents of urban and rural residents located in Otún River watershed, central Andes, Colombia was conducted. It was found out that in addition to economic benefits, the surrounding ecosystem also has relational values for the population. It was determined that the expression of values depends on socio-economic factors. For example, residence and education affect the expression of environmental values. It was concluded that the numerous values of ecosystems, expressed by rural and urban societies, should be included in environmental management to solve social conflicts and take into account the diverse needs and interests of various social actors.

Sociological surveys of VCIOM [17], the Levada Center [18] and the Public Opinion Foundation Group [70] are examples of assessing public opinion about the state of the environment. Surveys in 2017 revealed that Russians note an improvement in the environmental situation, but negative future forecasts continue to prevail over positive ones in their mind [17]. Concerns over the state of the environment measured over the period 1989-2017 are declining [18]. At the same time, 58% of Russians believe that the environmental situation in the country has deteriorated in recent years, most people are in anxiety about garbage and landfills, dirty water bodies and poor drinking water, enterprise emissions and air pollution [70]. Opinions about whether Russians do something to protect the environment are divided equally (46% at both sides) [70].

Researches pay a significant attention to the processes of justification and adoption of management decisions in the sphere of nature management, to interaction of the processes' participants roles. The study [8] presents a detailed analysis and compilation of regional practices for the management of environmental resources. As a result of a five-year monitoring of the water supply management in The Sacramento-San Joaquin River Delta, or California Delta (CALFED[1]), the authors have identified a new adaptive approach to managing environmental resources, which, in their opinion, is more efficient than the traditional hierarchical control. The authors of [8] argue that CALFED can be viewed as a self-organizing, complex adaptive network that uses a distributed information structure and decision-making in the management of environmental resources. Comparison of national REDD + (Reducing emissions from deforestation and forest degradation) policies in seven countries [11] allows us to conclude that politicians from economic considerations and personal benefits are not always interested in implementing specific policy measures.

The authors of [31] analyze the "bottom-up" management mechanism used in the program of "green infrastructure" in cities. The authors applied a combination of qualitative and quantitative methods for analyzing the actions and motives of various actors participating in the program: from local residents to those responsible for implementing environmental policy in the region. The analysis revealed vertical and horizontal interaction schemes between the participants, as well as the influence of information flows and public opinion on the management of the "green infrastructure" program.

Problems of information interaction in the development of environmental policy and decision-making were investigated in [1, 32]. Four variants of adaptive joint management were analyzed, involving experts, decision-makers, and regional activists [32]. Policy development was carried out in an interactive way. Environmental experts often expressed their concern about the gap between themselves and the decision-makers. In their turn, the experts often did not perceive information from ecological activists, no matter it could be valuable for substantiating the policy. Support for "green infrastructure" policy requires informed and evidence-based spatial planning for sectors and levels of management in forest, rural, and urban landscapes [1].

The State Report [50] indicates the need for a concept and program of environmental education of the population, state support for the environmental education literature and for environmental media. Ensuring the needs of the population, public authorities, economic sectors in environmental information is an important task of the State Program of the Russian Federation "Environmental Protection" [59].

Thus, practically in all of the cited works, we can trace the idea, firstly, about the need to increase the ecological literacy and responsibility of the government, business, and the population, and secondly, about the necessity of close interaction between these actors in the development and advance of the environmental policy.

Practical implementation of these ideas is carried out in many state and public projects and initiatives [12, 24, 56, 64 etc.]. Currently, developed countries pay serious attention to environmental protection. In recent years the costs of the environmental protection in the countries of the European Union are about 2.43% of GDP [21].

---

[1] The CALFED Bay-Delta Program, also known as CALFED, is a department within the government of California, administered under the California Resources Agency.

In Russia, expenditures on environmental protection amounted to 0,7% of GDP in 2014–2016 [14].

The growing concern of Russian citizens with environmental conditions is evidenced by thematic sites [54, 57, 45, 58, 60, 25, 55, 20 etc.]. Social ecology significantly changes the thinking style and contributes to the formation of ecological thinking and responsible attitude to the environment.

3 Theoretical Grounding and Methodology

The existing approaches to environmental policy formation are, as a rule, the approaches of the ecological economy. They provide, basically, an economic justification of the policy and assume the use of cost indicators for prevention of environmental damage and conservation of protected environmental zones. Adverse side products of economic activity and consumption are part of an economic system in Leontiev-Ford's industrial balance model [38, 39]. Methods for constructing monetary estimates of natural resources and estimation of damage from certain types of pollution are described in [28, 29, 53, 62]. A general approach to evaluating socio-economic results of economic activities aimed at the use, conservation and development of environmental assets, was described in [66, 68], where much attention was directed to integration data of socio-economic statistics, environmental monitoring, and aerospace remote sensing.

For the modern society and its ideas about the value of natural environment, the concepts of social ecology and socio-ecological systems constitute the most adequate theoretical basics for studying processes of environmental policy formation and involvement of population into these processes [3, 5, 9, 15, 30, 43, 46, 47, 50].

The concept of socio-ecological systems has recently let researchers combine social, environmental and institutional approaches to analyze how interaction between various social and environmental factors affects the state of the natural environment and human well-being [46, 47]. The general terminology of socio-ecological systems, the formulation of interdisciplinary problems, the statement of interdisciplinary tasks, methodological principles are at the stage of active development [15, 47]. The structure of a socio-ecological system compliant with the general model of the system, includes four functional subsystems: nature, worldview, management and technology [30]. Such a representation of a social-ecological system can be applied to different situations [30]. The formal seven-level classification of the structures of socio-ecological systems makes it possible to identify promising structures that provide for the adaptation and transformation of systems in the interests of the sustainable development [5]. The concept of environmental sustainability has a limited scope of application to social systems from the point of view of social theory including the social concept of well-being [3]. At the same time, the idea of the interrelationship between environmental sustainability and social well-being in the formation of a socio-ecological perspective can be used for adaptive management of environmental resources and making up environmental policies [3]. Linking sustainability and well-being is an example of an integrated approach to an analysis of environmental and social systems, with better understanding of how complex systems develop and how individuals and society act simultaneously as elements of the system and as agents of change in these systems [3]. Inclusion of scientific uncertainty in a rigorous theoretical decision-making system will help to improve the efficiency of environmental policy. The proposed combinations of social, environmental, institutional theories are necessary for scientific research of problems and changes in socio-ecological systems.

Digital transformation of society and economy alters the processes of information interaction in socio-ecological systems [7]. Communication in the cyber-environment (for example, social networks, information portals on environmental initiatives and the environment, Internet forums, etc.) contributes to the self-organization of system's elements [13, 49] and allows us to talk about the emergence of a new type of system, namely cyber-socioecological system. For a formalized description and analysis of processes in cyber-socioecological systems, neo-cybernetic approaches can be used [6, 40–42, 49, 67]. The peculiarity of such a system is that it does not have a centralized management and can produce a significant impact on the external environment [49], despite the fact that consolidated autocracies increasingly use the potential of the Internet [35]. But, as studies show, even a directive creation of a platform for online communication can initiate an increasing demand for its services if the members of society are interested in them of [34, 69]. The current level of digital technologies makes it possible to characterize the functioning of cyber-socioecological systems using heterogeneous data. The data on online activity of the population make it possible to assess the interest and concern of the population with a particular problem [67]. There are many evidences that semantics and prevalence of web search queries interrelates and even precedes social and economic changes. Economic conjuncture, changes in stock markets, unemployment, epidemics, consumer behavior, and etc. [4, 10, 22, 26, 27, 36] can be estimated and forecasted as a result of the analysis of search queries on the Internet. For example, the study of the [16] has shown that the growth of search queries related to the financial world, such as "debt", "market", "shares", etc. leads to a drop in the market. Most of the studies aimed at processing search data use multivariate statistical technique, however there is a lack of multidisciplinary methodology accumulating methods of statistics, sociology, and social psychology.

4 Empirical Analysis

Taking into account the global world trends in the development of digital technologies and their diffusion into the economic and social space, it is proposed to use indicators of environmental interest (environmental responsibility and environmental concerns) among the population of the territories as part of social indicators. An original approach to the estimation of these indicators according to the online activity of the population is proposed here.

We analyzed search patterns for ecology-related keywords in order to find over-tones in ecological interest specific to population of Russian cities. We distinguished four degrees of ecological interest in a descending order of altruism (Fig. 1).

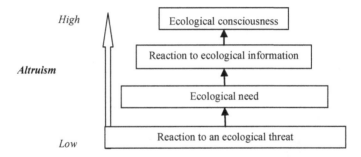

Fig. 1. Degrees of ecological interest. Source: author's contribution.

Online reactions to critical ecological threat occur in Russian cities with a high air pollution.

We analyzed the interrelation of the web search queries and ecological situation in large Russian cities arising concern in air pollution [50]. Keywords in search queries were related to the problem of high concentration of suspended solids.

In large Russian cities the administration occasionally introduces the so-called first regime of unfavorable meteorological conditions preventing the dispersion of harmful impurities in the ambient air. In this mode enterprises are required to limit or reduce the volume of their activities (emissions) according to Federal law 96, art. 19 [23]. In the cities with a high pollution such as Krasnoyarsk and Chelyabinsk unfavorable mete-orological conditions often result in exceeding the permissible concentrations of harmful substance in the ambient air. The website of Chelyabinsk Ministry of Ecology [44] releases intercomparison of meteorological conditions in the city with the level of air pollution. Usually, high concentration of suspended solids occurs at the first regime of unfavorable meteorological conditions.

We considered related time series including the duration of the first regime in Krasnoyarsk and Chelyabinsk and the intensity of search queries containing the key-word "smog" these cities. Specifically, we used the service WordStat of Yandex search system. This service provides data on the intensity of search queries for keywords and given Russian regions. Besides absolute intensity (the number of particular queries) the data contain relative regional intensity in fractions to the total number of queries in a region. We calculated the so-called affinity index as a ratio of the relative intensity in a city to the relative intensity in Russia. The affinity index characterizes the regional popularity of keywords in search queries. The values greater than 1 express a higher popularity as compared with the average popularity in Russia, while the value less than 1 stand for a lower popularity. We put together monthly or weekly affinity indices and corresponding duration (in days) of the first regime (Figs. 2 and 3). We observed higher online activities as a respond to an ecological threat. Actually, we got a sta-tistically significant regression ($p < 0.05$) with the correlation = 0.47 between affinity index and the duration of the first regime in Chelyabinsk. One more example of a reaction to an ecological threat is a rapid growth of online activity in the summer of 2016, when large-scale forest fires in Siberia and Ural caused smog in Russian cities (Fig. 4).

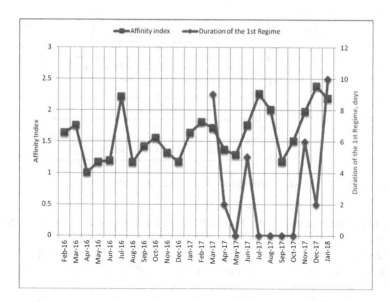

Fig. 2. Monthly affinity index (left axis) for the keywords "air pollution" (February 2016 – January 2018) and the duration in days (right axis) of the first regime (March 2017 – January 2018) in Krasnoyarsk. Source: author's contribution, data for affinity index obtained from the service WordStat of Yandex search system (https://wordstat.yandex.ru), data for the duration of the 1st regime obtained from the official portal of the Krasnoyarsk City Administration (http://www.admkrsk.ru/citytoday/ecology/Pages/NMU.aspx).

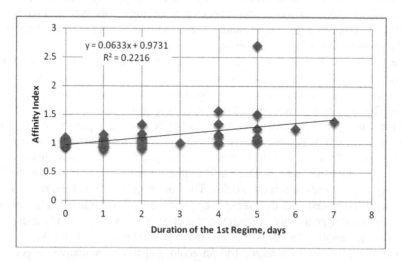

Fig. 3. Regression for the weekly affinity index ("smog", 20.02.2017 – 12.02.2018) and the duration in days of the first regime (same weeks) in Chelyabinsk. Source: author's contribution, data for affinity index obtained from the service WordStat of Yandex search system (https://wordstat.yandex.ru), data for the duration of the 1st regime obtained from the official portal of the Chelyabinsk City Administration (https://cheladmin.ru/ru/soobshcheniya-o-nmu).

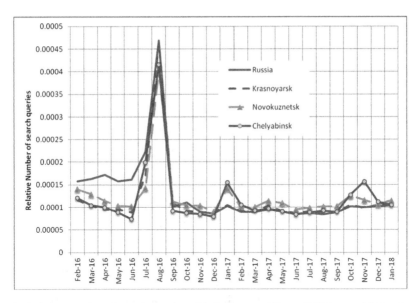

Fig. 4. Relative number of search queries with the keyword "smog" (February 2016 – January 2018) in Russia, Krasnoyarsk, Novokuznetsk and Chelyabinsk. Source: author's contribution, data obtained from the service WordStat of Yandex search system (https://wordstat.yandex.ru).

To illustrate the second level of altruism in online reactions, that is ecological need, we analyzed seasonal interest in St. Petersburg and Kaliningrad to the problem of water pollution (Figs. 5 and 6). There are obvious peaks of relative online activity related to purity of tap water and water bodies in spring and autumn (Fig. 5). We can see that the affinity index in Kaliningrad is usually greater than 1.

A vivid example of the next degree of altruism in ecological interest, that is a reaction to ecological information, addresses to various publications in mass media on air pollution in Krasnoyarsk during and soon after the visit of Russian President to the city where he proposed measures to deal with the city's problem of "Black sky" at 07.02.2017 (Fig. 7).

The absolute intensity of search queries increased almost seven fold at the event and remained rather high next week.

We can also examine the highest degree of altruism in more abstract interest to general ecological problems, for example to wastewater. However this interest characterizing ecological consciousness also depend on ecological needs and threats (Fig. 8, Fig. 9). We observe seasonal variations in both characteristics in Kaliningrad (Figs. 8, 9) and rather high values of affinity index in both cities during the whole period of observation.

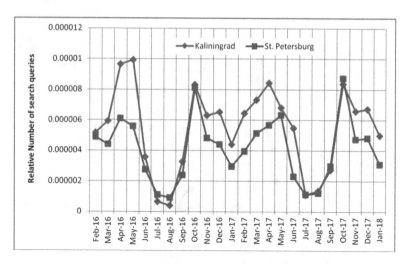

Fig. 5. Relative intensity of search queries with the keywords "water pollution" in St. Petersburg and Kaliningrad (February 2016 – January 2018). Source: author's contribution, data obtained from the service WordStat of Yandex search system (https://wordstat.yandex.ru).

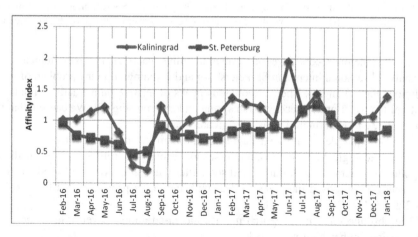

Fig. 6. Affinity index of search queries with the keywords "water pollution" in St. Petersburg and Kaliningrad (February 2016 – January 2018). Source: author's contribution, data obtained from the service WordStat of Yandex search system (https://wordstat.yandex.ru).

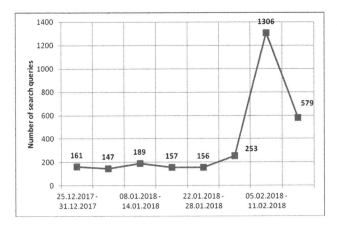

Fig. 7. Absolute number of search queries in Krasnoyarsk with the keywords "air pollution", weekly data. Source: author's contribution, data obtained from the service WordStat of Yandex search system (https://wordstat.yandex.ru).

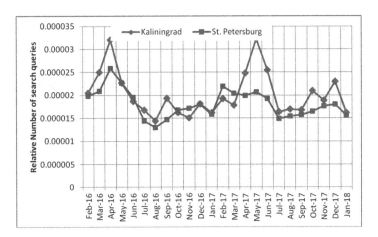

Fig. 8. Relative number of search queries with the keyword "wastewater" in St. Petersburg and Kaliningrad (February 2016 – January 2018). Source: author's contribution, data obtained from the service WordStat of Yandex search system (https://wordstat.yandex.ru).

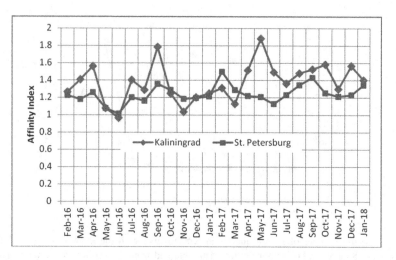

Fig. 9. Affinity index of search queries with the keyword "wastewater" in St. Petersburg and Kaliningrad (February 2016 – January 2018). Source: author's contribution, data obtained from the service WordStat of Yandex search system (https://wordstat.yandex.ru).

5   Discussions

We distinguished four degrees of ecological interest in a descending order of altruism. It was found out that the data on the number, prevalence and dynamics of search queries for keywords related to environmental pollution and cleanliness of water and air reflect the degree of responsibility and concern of the population with the environmental situation in a region and are an indirect indicator of environmental problems. For example, there was an increased popularity of search queries for the keywords "wastewaters", "water pollution" among the population of territories associated with the coastal zone of the Baltic Sea; for the keywords "smog", "air pollution" in industrial cities.

However, we observed manifestation of ecological altruism at different levels, in different situations, rather than quantitative characteristics of that. In our opinion, quantifying altruism needs additional consideration and studying with the aid of questionnaires involving psychological indicators.

Increasing the accessibility of environmental information will help to create an active public position among the population both in the matter of upholding their legitimate rights to a favorable environment and in practical participation in regional events to create a fair environment, prevent ecological violations. Taking into account the global trends in the digitalization of the society, increasing the importance of the Internet as a source of information for wider population, and in particular for young people, rising online activity of the population, it is advisable to develop Internet projects at the state, regional and municipal levels aimed at shaping the environmental consciousness of the population.

A promising interdisciplinary direction in the study of socio-economic systems is the development of methods for a comprehensive evaluation of socio-ecological systems with the aid of integrated data. These are data from online activity of the population, environmental monitoring, aerospace remote sensing of the Earth. The development of such methods will allow, firstly, to reasonably determine and select the sequence of tasks to be performed and the actions to be taken aimed at managing socio-ecological systems, and second, to justify compromise multi-criteria solutions when allocating limited resources of the system. Integration of socio-economic and environmental data within the boundaries of the socio-economic system, providing an interactive regime of environmental and economic monitoring (increasing the detail of observations and measurements, changing the composition of observable parameters, etc.) will serve as a basis for planning and clarifying the measures to ensure environmental safety.

Priority research should be aimed at the development of methodology and methods of evidence-based social ecology in the interests of developing an information base and tools for justifying management decisions in the field of ecology. We need multidisciplinary studies involving statistics, econometrics, sociology, and social psychology.

Acknowledgments. The research described in this paper is partially supported by the Russian Foundation for Basic Research (grants 15-08-08459, 16-07-00779, 17-08-00797, 17-06-00108), Russian Humanitarian Found (grants 15-04-00400), state research 0073–2018–0003, Vladimir Potanin Charitable Foundation grant GSGK-37/18.

References

1. Angelstam, P., Andersson, K., et al.: Solving problems in social-ecological systems: definition, practice and barriers of transdisciplinary research. Ambio **42**(2), 254–265 (2013). https://doi.org/10.1007/s13280-012-0372-4
2. Arias-Arévalo, P., Martín-López, B., Gómez-Baggethun, E.: Exploring intrinsic, instrumental, and relational values for sustainable management of social-ecological systems. Ecol. Soc. **22**(4), 43 (2017). https://doi.org/10.5751/ES-09812-220443
3. Armitage, D., Béné, C., Charles, A.T., Johnson, D., Allison, E.H.: The interplay of well-being and resilience in applying a social-ecological perspective. Ecol. Soc. **17**(4), 15 (2012). https://doi.org/10.5751/ES-04940-170415
4. Askitas, N., Klaus, F.: Zimmermann Google econometrics and unemployment forecasting. Appl. Econ. Q. **55**(2), 107–120 (2009)
5. Barnes, M.L., Bodin, Ö., Guerrero, A.M., McAllister, R.J., Alexander, S.M., Robins, G.: The social structural foundations of adaptation and transformation in social–ecological systems. Ecol. Soc. **22**(4), 16 (2017). https://doi.org/10.5751/ES-09769-220416
6. Becerra, G., Amozurrutia, J.A.: Rolando García's "Complex Systems Theory" and its relevance to sociocybernetics. J. Sociocybernetics **13**(15), 18–30 (2015)
7. Bershadskaya, L., Chugunov, A., Trutnev, D.: Information society development in Russia: measuring progress and gaps. In: Proceedings of the 2014 Conference on Electronic Governance and Open Society: Challenges in Eurasia, EGOSE 2014, pp. 7–13. ACM, New York (2014)

8. Booher, D.E., Innes, J.E.: Governance for resilience: CALFED as a complex adaptive network for resource management. Ecol. Soc. **15**(3), 35 (2010). http://www.ecologyand society.org/vol15/iss3/art35/

9. Bookchin, M.: Social Ecology and Communalism, 136 p. AK Press, Oakland (2007)

10. Bordino, I., Battiston, S., Caldarelli, G., Cristelli, M., et al.: Web search queries can predict stock market volumes. PLoS ONE **7**(7), e40014 (2012). http://journals.plos.org/plosone/article?id=10.1371/journal.pone.0040014

11. Brockhaus, M., Di Gregorio, M.: National REDD + policy networks: from cooperation to conflict. Ecol. Soc. **19**(4), 14 (2014). https://doi.org/10.5751/ES-06643-190414

12. Central Baltic Programme 2014–2020 project database. http://database.centralbaltic.eu/stats

13. Chugunov, Andrei V., Bolgov, R., Kabanov, Y., Kampis, G., Wimmer, M. (eds.): DTGS 2016. CCIS, vol. 674. Springer, Cham (2016). https://doi.org/10.1007/978-3-319-49700-6

14. Costs for environmental protection as a percentage of GDP. In: EMISS. https://fedstat.ru/indicator/57339

15. Cumming, Graeme S.: Theoretical frameworks for the analysis of social–ecological systems. In: Sakai, S., Umetsu, C. (eds.) Social-Ecological Systems in Transition. GES, pp. 3–24. Springer, Tokyo (2014). https://doi.org/10.1007/978-4-431-54910-9_1

16. Curme, Ch., Preis, To., H. Stanley, E., Moat, H.S.: Quantifying the semantics of search behavior before stock market moves. Proc. Natl. Acad. Sci. USA. **111**(32), 11600–11605 (2013)

17. Ecological situation in Russia: monitoring. Press Release No. 3430. https://wciom.ru/index.php?id=236&uid=116333. (in Russian)

18. Ecology. Poll 19–22 May 2017/ Levada Center. https://www.levada.ru/2017/06/05/ekologiya/. (in Russian)

19. Alcamo, J., et al.: Ecosystems and human well-being: a framework for assessment/ Millennium Ecosystem Assessment, 245 p. Island Press, Washington, D.C. (2003). Contributed by Bennett, E.M., et al.

20. Environmental problems of our time. https://ecoportal.info/category/ecoproblem/

21. Environmental tax revenues. In: Eurostat DataDatabase. http://appsso.eurostat.ec.europa.eu/nui/submitViewTableAction.do

22. Ettredge, M., Gerdes, J., Karuga, G.: Using web-based search data to predict macroeconomic statistics. Commun. ACM **48**(11), 87–92 (2005)

23. Federal Law No. 96-FZ of 04.05.1999 (as amended on 13.07.2015) "On the Protection of Atmospheric Air". http://www.consultant.ru/

24. FEE Annual Report 2016. https://static1.squarespace.com/static/550aa28ae4b0f34c8f7 87b74/t/591d6c0a59cc6827ccc15e9f/1495100465903/FEE_AnnualReport2016.pdf

25. Forum for ecologists. http://forum.integral.ru. (in Russian)

26. Ginsberg, J., Mohebbi, M.H., Patel, R.S., Brammer, L., et al.: Detecting influenza epidemics using search engine query data. Nature **457**(7232), 1012–1014 (2009)

27. Goel, S., Hofman, J.M., Lahaie, S., Pennock, D.M., Duncan, J.: Watts predicting consumer behavior with Web search. Proc. Natl. Acad. Sci. U.S.A. **107**(41), 17486–17490 (2010)

28. Gofman, K.G.: Economic mechanism of nature use in the transition to a market economy. Econ. Math. Methods **27**(2), 315–321 (1991). (in Russian)

29. Gofman, K.G.: Transition to the market and the ecologization of the tax system in Russia. Econ. Math. Methods, **30**(4) (1994)

30. Halliday, A., Glaser, M.: A Management Perspective on Social Ecological Systems: A generic system model and its application to a case study from Peru. Human Ecol. Rev. **18**(1), 1–18 (2011). http://www.humanecologyreview.org/pastissues/her181/halliday.pdf

31. Hauck, J., Schmidt, J., Werner, A.: Using social network analysis to identify key stakeholders in agricultural biodiversity governance and related land-use decisions at regional and local level. Ecol. Soc. **21**(2), 49 (2016). https://doi.org/10.5751/ES-08596-210249

32. Hermans, L.M.: Exploring the promise of actor analysis for environmental policy analysis: lessons from four cases in water resources management. Ecol. Soc. **13**(1), 21 (2008). http://www.ecologyandsociety.org/vol13/iss1/art21/

33. International Society of Ecological Economics (ISEE). http://www.isecoeco.org

34. Kabanov Yu., Sungurov A.: E-Government development factors: evidence from the Russian regions. digital transformation and global society. In: First International Conference, DTGS 2016, St. Petersburg, Russia, June 22–24, 2016, Revised Selected Papers. Chugunov, A.V., Bulgov, R., Kabanov, Y., Kampis, G., Wimmer, M. (Eds.), pp. 85–96 (2016)

35. Kabanov, Y., Romanov, B.: Interaction between the internet and the political regime: an empirical study (1995–2015). In: Alexandrov, Daniel A., Boukhanovsky, Alexander V., Chugunov, Andrei V., Kabanov, Y., Koltsova, O. (eds.) DTGS 2017. CCIS, vol. 745, pp. 282–291. Springer, Cham (2017). https://doi.org/10.1007/978-3-319-69784-0_24

36. Kristoufek, L.: Can Google Trends search queries contribute to risk diversification? Sci. Rep. **3**, 2713 (2013)

37. Krivosheyeva, Ye.S.: On the way to ecological consciousness. Bull. Krasnoyarsk State Agrarian University, **1**, 177–183 (2010). (in Russian)

38. Leontiev, V., Ford, D.: Interbranch analysis of the impact of the structure of the economy on the environment. Econ. Math. Methods, **Vol. VIII, 3**, 370–400 (1972). (in Russian)

39. Leontiev, V.: Impact on the environment and economic structure: the "input-output" approach. In: Economic Essays, pp. 318–339. Politizdat, Moscow (1990) (in Russian)

40. Mancilla, R.G.: Introduction to Sociocybernetics (Part 1): Third order cybernetics and a basic framework for society. J. Sociocybernetics **9**(1/2), 35–56 (2011)

41. Mancilla, R.G.: Introduction to Sociocybernetics (Part 2): Power. Cult. Inst. J. Sociocybernetics **10**(1/2), 45–71 (2012)

42. Mancilla, R.G.: Introduction to Sociocybernetics (Part 3): Fourth Order Cybernetics. J. Sociocybernetics **11**(1/2), 47–73 (2013)

43. McGinnis, M.D., Ostrom, E.: Social-ecological system framework: initial changes and continuing challenges. Ecol. Soc. **19**(2), 30 (2014). https://doi.org/10.5751/ES-06387-190230

44. Ministry of Ecology of Chelyabinsk region. http://www.mineco174.ru/

45. National map of environmental violations. https://ria.ru/ecomap/. (in Russian)

46. Ostrom, E.: A general framework for analyzing sustainability of social-ecological systems. Science **325**, 419–422 (2009). https://doi.org/10.1126/science.1172133

47. Ostrom, E., Cox, M.: Moving beyond panaceas: a multi-tiered diagnostic approach for social-ecological analysis. Environ. Conserv. **37**(4), 451–463 (2010). https://doi.org/10.1017/S0376892910000834

48. Rytov, G.L.: Concerning the necessity of ecological culture creation in mane and society. Izvestiya of the Samara Scientific Center of the Russian Academy of Sciences, **1**(4), 776–779 (2009) (in Russian)

49. Sokolov, B., Yusupov, R., Verzilin, Dm., Sokolova, I., Ignatjev, M.: Methodological Basis of socio-cyber-physical systems structure-dynamics control and management. Digital Transformation and Global Society First International Conference, DTGS 2016, St. Petersburg, Russia, June 22–24, 2016, Revised Selected Papers. Chugunov, A.V., Bulgov, R., Kabanov, Y., Kampis, G., Wimmer, M. (Eds.), pp. 610–618 (2016)

50. State report "On the state and protection of the environment of the Russian Federation in 2016": Ministry of Natural Resources of Russia; NIA-Nature. 760 p. (2017). (in Russian)

51. TEEB: The Economics of Ecosystems and Biodiversity Ecological and Economic Foundations. Ed. by Kumar, P.: Earthscan, London and Washington. 456 p (2010)
52. TEEB: The economics of ecosystems and biodiversity in local and regional policy and management. Ed. by Wittmer, H., Gundimeda, H.: Routledge, 384 p. (2012)
53. Temporary sample methodology for determining the economic efficiency of implementing environmental measures and assessing economic damage caused to the national economy by environmental pollution. Approved by the decision of the State Planning Committee of the USSR, Gosstroy USSR and the Presidium of the USSR Academy of Sciences on October 21, 1983 No. 254/284/134. Economics (1986). (in Russian)
54. The ECA initiative (interregional non-governmental organization). http://ecamir.ru/O-dvizhenii-EKA.html. (in Russian)
55. The Forum of the Ecological Initiative of Russia (2017). https://vk.com/ecoforum2017. (in Russian)
56. The Foundation for Environmental Education (FEE) is officially registered as a charity in England (registered charity number 1148274) under the address 74. http://www.greenkey.global/join-fee/
57. The interactive project "Landfill Map". http://www.kartasvalok.ru/request/171102-558
58. The network of initiative groups "Musora.Bolshe.Net". http://musora.bolshe.net/page/main.html (in Russian)
59. The State Program of the Russian Federation "Environmental Protection" for 2012–2020: Approved by Resolution of the Government of the Russian Federation of April 15, 2014 No. 326. http://programs.gov.ru/Portal/programs/passport/12. (in Russian)
60. Thematic maps on the environmental situation in St. Petersburg. http://gov.spb.ru/gov/otrasl/ecology/maps/. (in Russian)
61. Tobeyev, A.M.: The concept of ecological consciousness/Toboev A.I. The concept of ecological consciousness. Bullet. Omsk State Pedagogical University. Humanit. Res. 3(7). 23–26 (2015). (in Russian)
62. Transforming the economy: sustaining food, water, energy and justice: 2016 ISEE Conference/International Society of Ecological Economics (ISEE) Conference. (2016). http://www.isecoeco.org/isee-2016-conference/
63. Uhl, C.: Developing ecological consciousness: paths to a sustainable future, 288 p. Published March 14th 2013 by Rowman & Littlefield Publishers (2013). ISBN 1442218312
64. United Nations Environment Programme. https://www.unenvironment.org/explore-topics/environment-under-review/why-does-environment-under-review-matter
65. Veretennikov, N.Ya.: Globalization of environmental consciousness. In: Proceedings of the Saratov University. New episode. Series Philosophy. Psychology. Pedagogy. 14(2), 11–15 (2014). (in Russian)
66. Versilin D.N., Maksimova T.G., Antokhin Yu.N.: Development of digital technologies for multicriteria estimation of the state of ecological and economic objects. In: Statistics in the digital economy: teaching and use: materials of the international scientific and practical conference (St. Petersburg, 1–2 February 2018). SPb.: Publishing house SPbSEU. pp. 176–177 (2018). (in Russian)
67. Verzilin, D., Maximova, T., Sokolova, I.: Online socioeconomic activity in Russia: patterns of dynamics and regional diversity. In: Alexandrov, Daniel A., Boukhanovsky, Alexander V., Chugunov, Andrei V., Kabanov, Y., Koltsova, O. (eds.) DTGS 2017. CCIS, vol. 745, pp. 55–69. Springer, Cham (2017). https://doi.org/10.1007/978-3-319-69784-0_5
68. Verzilin, D.N., Maksimova, T.G., Antokhin, Yu.N.: Socio-economic and ecological indicators of the state of ecological and economic objects: genesis and development. In: Society: Politics, Economics, Law 2017. 12 (2017). http://www.dom-hors.ru/vipusk-12-2017-obshchestvo-politika-ekonomika-pravo/. (in Russian)

69. Vidiasova, L., Chugunov, A.: eGov Services' consumers in the process of innovations' diffusion: the case from St. Petersburg. In: Alexandrov, Daniel A., Boukhanovsky, Alexander V., Chugunov, Andrei V., Kabanov, Y., Koltsova, O. (eds.) DTGS 2017. CCIS, vol. 745, pp. 199–208. Springer, Cham (2017). https://doi.org/10.1007/978-3-319-69784-0_17
70. What in the environmental situation is most worried about people? And are they ready for ecological behavior?/Group of Companies Foundation Public Opinion. http://fom.ru/Obraz-zhizni/13693. (in Russian)
71. Zagutin, D.S., Nagnibeda B.A., Samygin, S.I.: Problems of development of social ecology in the aspect of ensuring industrial safety. In: Humanitarian, socio-economic and social sciences (2017). (in Russian)

Data-Driven Authoritarianism: Non-democracies and Big Data

Yury Kabanov[✉] and Mikhail Karyagin

National Research University Higher School of Economics, St. Petersburg,
Russia
{ykabanov,mkaryagin}@hse.ru

Abstract. The article discusses the problems of power asymmetry and political dynamics in the era of Big Data, assessing the impact Big Data may have on power relations and political regimes. While the issues of political ethics of the data turn are mostly discussed in relation to democracies, little attention has been given to hybrid regimes and autocracies, some of which are actively introducing Big Data policies. We argue that although the effects of Big Data on politics are ambivalent, it can become a powerful instrument of authoritarian resilience through ICT-facilitated repression, legitimation and cooptation. The ability of autocracies to become data-driven depends on their capacity, control powers and policies. We further analyze the state of the Big Data policy in Russia. Although the country may become a case of data-driven authoritarianism, it will be the result of the current discursive and political competition among actors. The ethical critique of Big Data should then be based on the empirical findings of Big Data use by non-democracies.

Keywords: Big Data · Political regime · Hybrid political regime
Authoritarianism · Authoritarian stability · Big Data policy · Russia

1 Introduction

The shifts in power relations are considered one of the key problems of the data turn [53], involving "both utopian and dystopian rhetoric" [7] on whether Big Data boosts economic and social growth or hinders privacy and democracy. The Snowden-inspired discussion on whether privacy is challenged by surveillance [5, 30], or the speculations on Donald Trump's victory via targeting in the social media open questions on what consequences Big Data has in relation to democracy. It challenges the ethics by manipulating people's behavior and undermining their autonomy in favor of those who process the data [20], making us, as put by Davis [12] "to consider serious ethical issues including whether certain uses of big data violate fundamental civil, social, political, and legal rights". He further argues that while Big Data, is "ethically neutral", its ethical values and problems are and should be attributed to individuals and organizations [2].

These ethical questions, we argue, need to be raised in the political domain. If Big Data poses challenges to the ethical values of privacy and human rights, pertinent to democracies, how can it be considered in relation to authoritarian countries?

© Springer Nature Switzerland AG 2018
D. A. Alexandrov et al. (Eds.): DTGS 2018, CCIS 858, pp. 144–155, 2018.
https://doi.org/10.1007/978-3-030-02843-5_12

The distinction between democracies and autocracies in relation to the Internet and Big Data usage is becoming blurred, first, because the former are compromised by surveillance and lose their "high moral ground" [3], being accused of "double standards" putting the very concept of Internet freedom under question [13]. At the same time, the latter are catching up with them in terms of technological development [13, 51]. Although the potential of Big Data to raise living standards and provide better governance in developing and non-democratic states cannot be denied, the process of its implementation is accompanied by developmental [21] and political issues, since, as argued by Cukier and Mayer-Schoenberger [11]: "big data could become Big Brother. In all countries, but particularly in nondemocratic ones, big data exacerbates the existing asymmetry of power between the state and the people". Although the data turn is still an emerging process, it is possible to elaborate on the impact of Big Data on the regime dynamics of authoritarian states.

A plethora of works has studied the influence of modern ICTs on the authoritarian rule. While there were some optimistic claims that the Internet facilitates democratization [15], a lot of research shows that ICTs, e-government and e-participation contribute to authoritarian resilience, introducing new instruments of legitimation, surveillance and repression [2, 19, 32, 36]. The discussion can be summarized here, if ICTs lead to the reinforcement of power or the redistribution of power [44]. The former is about how new technologies benefit those in power, making them stronger, while the latter can lead to power shifts in favor of other actors, e.g. citizens. Departing from this dichotomy, in this paper we discuss the ways Big Data and the data-driven instruments can contribute to authoritarian stability and subversion, thus summarizing a framework for a data-driven authoritarianism concept.

Secondly, we analyze the Big Data policy in Russia, which is considered to be an electoral authoritarianism [18], in order to find out how policy can moderate the effects of Big Data on political rule.

2   Big Data and the Regime Dynamics

The question, why the authoritarian regime survives, remains extremely important in comparative politics. It is emphasized that the logic of survival changes over time, and now the crucial role is played by nominally "democratic" institutions, such as parties or elections, turning a closed autocracy into various forms of hybrid regimes [16, 17, 29]. The general idea behind is to show the open and competitive nature of the regime to the population and international community, but, as summarized by Brancati [8], the effects of "democratic" institutions are different: for instance, they help to signal the strength of the incumbent, gather information about the public mood, monitor the elites, provide patronage and credible commitment. Despite all advantages, introducing such institutions is a risky enterprise for autocrats, since they can also be used for regime subversion, so, as Schedler [43] puts it, the dictator's institutional choice is inherently probabilistic. In line with this, ICTs are also a part of such institutional dilemma. The Internet is about institutional choice, first, because it can lead to changes in internal bureaucratic workflows and government – society, or more general, power relations [4]. Secondly, according to the dictator's digital dilemma, modern technologies pose controversial options for authoritarian countries, as they can either implement them and be at risk of losing the power, or not implement them, and thus lagging behind the technological progress [22, 27].

Recent studies have shown, however, that the dilemma is not so strict. Many developed autocracies have learnt to use the Internet for economic development and political legitimacy, at the same time using censorship and other control practices to suppress potential threats to the regime [2, 40]. This ambivalent strategy is shown in MacKinnon's networked authoritarianism [31], or Karlsson's "dual strategy of internet governance" [25], or the concept of "electronic authoritarianism" we used as for a contrasting term to "electronic democracy" [23]. The concept we use here - data-driven authoritarianism - has much in common with those findings on the Internet in non-democracies, but the meaning is a bit different. It is not about how authoritarianism is reflected in the Internet policy, rather about how innovative technologies (mostly Big Data) are becoming a part of the traditional authoritarian practices. It can thus be defined as the use of data-driven analytics and decision-making instruments to maintain authoritarian resilience and stability. Although these new instruments stem from the Internet, the outcomes are mostly related to the offline space.

To study how Big Data might be related to the regime stability, we take Gerschewski's "three pillars of stability" [17]: legitimation, cooptation and repression, as a framework. Legitimacy here refers to the public support of the regime, which can be based on either specific outcomes or general attitudes. The second pillar, cooptation, is the ability to "tie strategically-relevant actors... to the regime elite" [17: 22], while repression is a potential or real use of violence against opposition or population. These pillars, being intertwined and institutionalized, mutually reinforce each other and the regime.

If we consider this threefold disposition, what role, if any, will Big Data play? The simplest answer is that it can contribute to the repression pillar, mostly by raising the ability for surveillance. The data turn has opened new horizons for gathering information about citizens; make groupings and classifications, social profiles and predictions on their behavior [30]. The new analytics tools allow "the continuous tracking of (meta) data for unstated preset purposes" [48], now known as the dataveillance. It means that all the data can be collected and stored even if the goal is not specified. The clearest example here is China, which, according to several scholars, is moving towards a Big Brother 2.0 [51] or IT-backed authoritarianism [33] model, where the data is meant to assist in monitoring and controlling ideological loyalty and storing the individual archives of every citizen, which can affect his or her future. The surveillance – based repressions can be more targeted and predictive, meaning that an algorithm would be able to identify potentially dangerous groups for the regime.

However, Big Data is not only about the repression. The use of collected data can be used in more subtle ways, for instance, to strengthen the legitimacy of the regime. The argument that governments are introducing new technologies to aspire for legitimacy is quite widespread in the academia. They create, according to Chadwick [9], an "electronic face of government", introducing a symbolic dimension of power via websites. In autocracies such window-dressing is becoming even more evident, as the latter use ICTs to show its competency, modernity and openness either to the international audience, or to the population [26, 32]. The symbolic power of Big Data as a cutting-edge technology can be exercised by showing the adherence to the innovations through declarations and international forums, such as those Big Data Summits held in Singapore, China and the UAE, for example.

But here the symbolic power could be secondary, while the primary idea is to raise the regime stability using the new economy. To use data-driven innovations to boost innovations and growth seems to be a plausible rationale for Singapore and China, already experienced in combining advanced economy with illiberal political practices.[1] Other possible beneficiaries are the rentier states of the Middle East, which now seem to be diversifying their survival strategies, investing oil revenues for boosting innovations. "Data is the new oil" has become a slogan for Big Data programs in the UAE, Saudi Arabia and others, since the data-based model can be more resilient to market fluctuations.[2]

Another data-driven legitimacy instrument is related to governance and state capacity. As argued by Zeng [51], in China, the use of Big Data in the analysis and economic planning is crucial for achieving better outputs. In fact, Big Data can help the government to get clearer statistics on various sectors' performance. A thorough analysis of Big Data can lead to the algorithmic data-driven decision-making. It will allow the governments to meet some public expectations without direct public input and deliberation. The issues raised by data-driven policies, like the lack of transparency, privacy and accountability, as well as discrimination [28], can be even clearer in non-democracies without a developed civil society and public control. We are at the stage when data assists in "engineering the public" and manipulating public opinion on the individual targeted level, thus the public consent can be computed [46, 47].

The question on whether Big Data can co-opt the elites is more complicated and less obvious. For instance, Zeng [51] supposes that Big Data can be used in information wars among the elites, but he speaks of it more as of the challenge to the regime stability: "...the digital sources of data may be the game-changer for the power struggles in authoritarian regimes. If confidential data is highly concentrated in the hands of a few powerful individuals or agencies, it may seriously harm regime legitimacy and elite cohesion when misused". We would argue, however, the concentration of data better contributes to the elites' cohesion. The ability of the rulers to control the behavior of the selectorate by possible dissemination of compromising evidence, for instance, can be a strong instrument in maintaining stability in the broader authoritarian elites' coalition. Hence the control of Big Data can be a powerful tool of informal cooptation.

As in the case of other authoritarian institutions, the implementation of Big Data is also an issue of uncertainty. It can provoke the so-called data activism, either in the form of data-driven civic advocacy campaigns, or resistance against mass surveillance [34]. Also, the raise of the Big Data policy in authoritarian countries requires certain

---

[1] Beijing thinking big on switch to a big data economy. South China Morning Post. April 2017. URL: http://www.scmp.com/news/china/economy/article/2086229/beijing-thinking-big-switch-big-data-economy.

[2] Saudi Arabia turns to big data to boost business innovation. ComputerWeekly. November 2016. URL: http://www.computerweekly.com/news/450402173/Saudi-Arabia-turns-to-big-data-to-boost-business-innovation; UAE, Qatar and Saudi Arabia top connected countries in region. Gulf News. April 2017. URL: http://gulfnews.com/business/sectors/technology/uae-qatar-and-saudi-arabia-top-connected-countries-in-region-1.2019659.

changes in their attitude towards the data in general. The declaration to develop a data-driven economy and innovations can hardly be used without proper Internet development, regulation of information (including principles of information freedom) and Open Government Data policies [14]. The authoritarian regime is becoming more transparent for international and internal scrutiny, hence more vulnerable to pressures. But it seems it is a risk some autocracies would take, provided they have capacity to control the Internet and public behavior in general. In some cases, electronic participation can even become a part of the legitimacy pillar, when certain institutional constraints (identification on the Internet, self-censorship etc.) make citizens act in a loyal fashion [50], thus increasing the legitimacy of the incumbents. The political challenges of current information regulation and the Open Data can be minimized by bureaucratic inertia in meeting these requirements [24] (Table 1).

Table 1. The data-driven authoritarianism framework

Authoritarian stability			Challenges
Repression	Legitimation	Co-optation	
Surveillance Targeted repressions	Symbolic power of new technologies Economic output Data-driven governance Engineering the public consent	Control of elites Compromising evidence	Data – activism Freedom of Information Open Data

Surely, to avail themselves of Big Data benefits, autocracies need to meet several general requirements. First, they need to provide a sufficient basis for Big Data in terms of technological infrastructure (e.g., the Internet and the social media penetration), regulation and policies, as well as the political commitment to the idea of ICT development. The comparative data on this can be obtained from the Networked Readiness Index (World Economic Forum), a complex study on ICT development. Secondly, to use the dual strategy of Internet governance [25], they need to have enough tools to control it. Here we can refer to the Freedom on the Net Index (Freedom House), measuring the state of civil rights and censorship on the Internet. Table 2 shows that, in fact, the most developed non-democratic countries in terms of ICT, hence the most promising candidates for being data-driven autocracies, are at the same time imposing serious political restrictions on the Internet, which once more speaks well for the reinforcement argument.

These prerequisites - high levels of ICT development and the Internet control, are basic, but not sufficient. The government should further provide regulations to boost economic gains and reduce political costs. The most controversial measure is data localization, when a law prescribes the data to be stored within the national borders. According to the Albright Stonebridge Group [1], the strongest data localization laws are observed in China, Russia, Brunei, Nigeria, Indonesia and Vietnam. There is nothing explicitly authoritarian in it in such; many democracies (like the European countries) have also introduced localization measures after Snowden's revelations.

However, as some scholars argue, data localization benefits those countries aspiring for better control of their citizens [10] and for raising revenue of state-owned telecom companies [35], at the same time challenging the free flow of information and economic growth. It hence poses a dilemma for countries on whether to maximize the control over the data or to maximize the economic outcomes. This dilemma should be solved vis-à-vis other actors, primarily the private sector and the civil society.

We may summarize here that Big Data is in fact a valuable potential tool for the regime resilience. It does not alter the pillars of stability in principle, but strengthens

Table 2. ICT development and regulation in selected non-democracies countries

Country	Networked Readiness Index (score, ranking)[a]	Freedom on the Net status[b]
Singapore	6,0 (1)	Partly free
UAE	5,3 (26)	Not free
Qatar	5,2 (27)	N/A
Bahrain	5,1 (28)	Not free
Saudi Arabia	4,8 (33)	Not free
Kazakhstan	4,6 (39)	Not free
Russia	4,5 (41)	Not free
Oman	4,3 (52)	N/A
Azerbaijan	4,3 (53)	Partly free
China	4,2 (59)	Not free
Jordan	4,2 (60)	Partly free
Kuwait	4,2 (61)	N/A

[a]Networked Readiness Index 2016 (http://reports.weforum.org/global-information-technology-report-2016/networked-readiness-index/);
[b]Freedom on the Net 2016 (https://freedomhouse.org/report/table-country-scores-fotn-2016).

existing ones by innovational, data-driven techniques. If we need to evaluate what changes to power relations the data-turn brings – reinforcement or redistribution, then we assume the former is mostly probable. It does not necessarily imply the Orwellian scenario: Big Data can in fact be used for better policy-making and raising living standards. It just is that their regime stability will be rather strengthened, not eliminated, by the spread of Big Data. At the same time, the future of Big Data and its impact will depend on the regulation dynamics in each specific case.

3 Politics of the Big Data Policy in Russia

It is still unclear what the future of Big Data in Russia is. The market development is still "embryonic", as the analysts suggest, and covers mainly the banking sector, telecom and trade.[3] The major obstacle seems to be the regulation: the government has

---

[3] Big Data in Russia. Tadviser. URL: http://www.tadviser.ru/index.php/Статья:Большие_данные_(Big_Data)_в_Росси [in Russian].

only recently started to work out policies related to Big Data, and it is still in doubt as to how to adequately approach the problem [52]. At the moment the absence of a Big Data definition remains the key problem. The new Strategy of Information Society Development signed in May 2017 contains the notion of "Big Data processing", which remains quite vague, however.[4]

There might be certain concerns on the political outcomes of the Big Data policy in Russia. The Russian Internet-policy mode is quite in line with the abovementioned countries, which seem to have found the way out of the digital dilemma. The country is known for its surveillance strategies [45] and the dual policy of combining the nominal development of electronic government [6, 23] with elaborate censorship, propaganda techniques and active role in the Internet governance [37, 38].

Some implications of the future Big Data regulation can be discerned from the country's approach towards datafication, revealed in the personal or open government data policies. In 2014, Russia introduced the Data Localization law, stating that all personal data of the Russian citizens should be stored in the country for the sake of national security,[5] thus taking a data nationalism approach. Data localization, as put by Savelyev [42], constitutes a part of the Russian "digital sovereignty" strategy and "is mostly driven by national security concerns, covered in 'protection-of-data-subjects' wrap", like better law enforcement [42: 141], at the expense of possible economic losses. This tendency was further backed by the so-called "Yarovaya package", a set of new anti-terrorist amendments, among others, extending the period of personal communication data storage and facilitating the access and decoding of messages by the enforcement bodies, criticized to be the strictest data regulation law.[6]

However, Big Data is still waiting for proper regulation. The major step will be the final decision on who and how Big Data is to be controlled. The Big Data politics in Russia is not very specific to other cases, which are described by Sargsyan [41] as the competition between governments, which "pursue economic development, privacy and security, law enforcement effectiveness, enhanced surveillance, and the ability to track and oppress dissidents" and the companies that "maximize revenue by enabling data collection and analytics" [41: 2230]. At the moment, different actors are trying to take control over the agenda, and three competing discourses can be discerned.

The first one is the etatist discourse, based on the assumption that the government is the only actor able to regulate Big Data and protect citizens' privacy and security. Here we can mention the idea to establish the sole national operator of Big Data, based on Roskomnadzor (telecom authority). It is well in line with the logic of previous actions on data control for national security goals, although it leads to controversies on who is to pay for it, and how it will impact the innovation development.[7] The second approach

---

[4] Strategy of the Russian Federation on Information Society Development for 2017–2013. 2017. URL: http://kremlin.ru/acts/news/54477.

[5] Federal Law of the Russian Federation № 242, 21.07.2014. URL: http://www.consultant.ru/document/cons_doc_LAW_165838/ [in Russian].

[6] Russia is the Strictest. Vedomosti. January 2017. URL: https://www.vedomosti.ru/technology/articles/2017/01/12/672645-zakon-yarovoi [in Russian].

[7] The Law of the Big Brother. Vedomosti. May 2017. URL: https://www.vedomosti.ru/technology/articles/2017/05/16/689963-gosoperatora-bolshih-dannih.

can be called the market discourse, implying that Big Data operators such as banks, telecom companies and the social media will take responsibility for developing the market and protecting privacy. In April 2017, the largest Russian companies announced the establishment of the self-regulatory body in charge of Big Data (Big Data Association). In their view, the government should provide some minimum regulation not to interfere with the market by control and power abuse (Table 3).[8]

Table 3. Russian discourses on Big Data regulation

	Etatist	Market	Multistakeholderism
Key actors	The state	The market	All stakeholders, including the civil society
Rationale and priorities	National security, state control and law enforcement	Innovation, economic development	Interests' inclusion and consensus between privacy, security and innovation
Regulation	Law-based regulation, bureaucratic control	Competition-based instruments, minimum legal regulation	Laws, competition, public input
Solutions	National Big Data Operator	Big Data Association	Big Data Council

These two discourses are defining the Russian agenda on Big Data politics. The since major national ICT players are closely linked and loyal to the political elite [49], the argument should be taken mostly in the economic dimension. The government, being the leading player, needs to decide, what type of control – direct or indirect – it prefers, and how it weights national security against economic gains.

There is also a third alternative, which we can call a multistakeholderism discourse, where the government, the market and the society are equally responsible for data regulation. It stems from the idea of different actors' engagement in policy-making [39], and is partially realized in the Russian Open Data policy, where the civil society and expert community collaborate with businesses and the government (in the Open Data Council, for instance) to work out comprehensive recommendations on the Open Data release. Although the policy results remain quite ambivalent [24], the practice itself is quite promising. However, now there are no signals for this from all sides.

The outcomes of the abovementioned dilemmas are not yet clear in relation to the regime dynamics. In general, the previous steps of Russia in the sphere of the Internet policy and data localization support the reinforcement assumption in relation to Big Data: the government would benefit from taking control over Big Data. However, the country is still in search of the most suitable regulation model, while the question of finding a legal basis is just the first step in making Big Data an asset.

---

[8] Big, but not Given. Kommersant. April 2017. URL: https://www.kommersant.ru/doc/3260507.

4 Conclusion and Future Steps

While the assumption that technologies have positive and negative effects is quite trivial, the ambivalence of Big Data poses important ethical questions of democratic values' resilience. It seems to further erode the gap between democracies and autocracies, e.g. in how they implement data localization laws or introduce surveillance. But we argue that to analyze the causes and effects of the data-turn on politics, these cases should be, at least analytically, discerned. As more non-democracies are developing Big Data, they should be given more academic focus. From the ethical viewpoint, the issue of power asymmetry in non-democratic countries needs further elaboration, considering the responsibility and ethics of the governments, companies and the society. The positive empirical program in this context should concentrate on comparative unveiling the factors of Big Data policies adoption and dynamics in non-democracies, as well as the stability/subversion effects of data-driven politics on authoritarian rule.

Although Big Data can potentially be an empowering tool, we suppose that it favors the regime resilience in the data-driven format, enhancing the capacity to exercise repression, legitimation and cooptation instruments. However, the question remains open as to what pillar of stability Big Data serves most: will it incarnate the Orwellian scenario, or increase legitimacy via better decision-making and raising living standards? Or, in fact, facilitate the democratic changes due to the data activism?

In this regard, the Russian case needs further analysis. Now, the Big Data policy is still under development, encompassing the power play between various actors, mostly the government and the companies. While the present situation suggests that the state will take lead in Big Data, the consequences are hard to predict.

Acknowledgements. The research has been conducted within the project "Governance in Multi-Level Political Systems: Supranational Unions and Federal States (European Union, Eurasian Economic Union, Russian Federation)" as part of the HSE Program of Fundamental Studies.

References

1. Albright Stonebridge Group: Data localization: a challenge to global commerce (2015). http://www.albrightstonebridge.com/files/ASG%20Data%20Localization%20Report%20-%20September%202015.pdf
2. Åström, J., Karlsson, M., Linde, J., Pirannejad, A.: Understanding the rise of e-participation in non-democracies: domestic and international factors. Gov. Inf. Q. **29**(2), 142–150 (2012). https://doi.org/10.1016/j.giq.2011.09.008
3. Bajaj, K.: Cyberspace: post-Snowden. Strat. Anal. **38**(4), 582–587 (2014). https://doi.org/10.1080/09700161.2014.918448
4. Barrett, M., Grant, D., Wailes, N.: ICT and organizational change introduction to the special issue. J. Appl. Behav. Sci. **42**(1), 6–22 (2006). https://doi.org/10.1177/0021886305285299
5. Bauman, Z., et al.: After Snowden: rethinking the impact of surveillance. Int. Polit. Sociol. **8**(2), 121–144 (2014). https://doi.org/10.1111/ips.12048

6. Bershadskaya, L., Chugunov, A., Trutnev, D.: e-Government in Russia: is or seems? In: Proceedings of the 6th International Conference on Theory and Practice of Electronic Governance, ICEGOV 2012, pp. 79–82. ACM (2012). https://doi.org/10.1145/2463728. 2463747

7. Boyd, D., Crawford, K.: Critical questions for Big Data: provocations for a cultural, technological, and scholarly phenomenon. Inf., Commun. Soc. **15**(5), 662–679 (2012). https://doi.org/10.1080/1369118x.2012.678878

8. Brancati, D.: Democratic authoritarianism: origins and effects. Annu. Rev. Polit. Sci. **17**, 313–326 (2014). https://doi.org/10.1146/annurev-polisci-052013-115248

9. Chadwick, A.: The electronic face of government in the Internet age: borrowing from Murray Edelman. Inf Commun. & Soc. **4**(3), 435–457 (2001). https://doi.org/10.1080/13691180110069482

10. Chander, A., Le, U.P.: Data nationalism. Emory Law J. **6**(3) (2015). https://ssrn.com/abstract=2577947

11. Cukier, K., Mayer-Schoenberger, V.: The rise of Big Data: how it's changing the way we think about the world. Foreign Aff. **92**(28) (2013). https://doi.org/10.1515/9781400865307-003

12. Davis, K.: Ethics of Big Data: Balancing Risk and Innovation. O'Reilly Media Inc, Sebastopol (2012)

13. Deibert, R.: Cyberspace under siege. J. Democr. **26**(3), 64–78 (2015). https://doi.org/10.1353/jod.2015.0051

14. Deloitte: Big Data: mining a national resource (2015). https://www2.deloitte.com/content/dam/Deloitte/xe/Documents/About-Deloitte/mepovdocuments/mepov18/big-data_mepov18.pdf

15. Diamond, L.: Liberation technology. J. Democr. **21**(3), 69–83 (2010). https://doi.org/10.1353/jod.0.0190

16. Gandhi, J., Przeworski, A.: Authoritarian institutions and the survival of autocrats. Comp. Polit. Stud. **40**(11), 1279–1301 (2007). https://doi.org/10.1177/0010414007305817

17. Gerschewski, J.: The three pillars of stability: legitimation, repression, and co-optation in autocratic regimes. Democratization **20**(1), 13–38 (2013). https://doi.org/10.1080/13510347.2013.738860

18. Gel'man, V.: Authoritarian Russia: Analyzing Post-Soviet Regime Changes. University of Pittsburgh Press, Pittsburgh (2015)

19. Göbel, C.: The information dilemma: How ICT strengthen or weaken authoritarian rule. Statsvetenskaplig tidskrift **115**(4), 385–402 (2013)

20. Herschel, R., Miori, V.M.: Ethics & Big Data. Technol. Soc. **49**, 31–36 (2017). https://doi.org/10.1016/j.techsoc.2017.03.003

21. Hilbert, M.: Big Data for development: a review of promises and challenges. Dev. Policy Rev. **34**(1), 135–174 (2016). https://doi.org/10.1111/dpr.12142

22. Howard, P.N., Agarwal, S.D., Hussain, M.M.: The dictators' digital dilemma: when do states disconnect their digital networks? In: Issues in Technology Innovation, vol. 13. Brookings Institution (2011). https://doi.org/10.2139/ssrn.2568619

23. Kabanov, Y.: Electronic authoritarianism. E-participation institute in non-democratic countries. Politeia **83**(4), 36–55 (2016). [in Russian]

24. Kabanov, Y., Karyagin, M., Romanov, V.: Politics of Open Data in Russia: regional and municipal perspectives. In: Vinod Kumar, T.M. (ed.) E-Democracy for Smart Cities, pp. 461–485. Springer, Singapore (2017). https://doi.org/10.1007/978-981-10-4035-1_15

25. Karlsson, M.: Carrots and sticks: internet governance in non–democratic regimes. Int. J. Electron. Gov. **6**(3), 179–186 (2013). https://doi.org/10.1504/ijeg.2013.058405

26. Katchanovski, I., La Porte, T.: Cyberdemocracy or Potemkin e-villages? Electronic governments in OECD and post-communist countries. Int. J. Public Adm. **28**(7–8), 665–681 (2005). https://doi.org/10.1081/pad-200064228

27. Kerr, J.: The digital dictator's dilemma: Internet regulation and political control in non-democratic states (2014). http://cisac.fsi.stanford.edu/sites/default/files/kerr_-_cisac_seminar_-_oct_2014_-_digital_dictators_dilemma.pdf

28. Lepri, B., Staiano, J., Sangokoya, D., Letouzé, E., Oliver, N.: The Tyranny of data? The bright and dark sides of data-driven decision-making for social good. arXiv preprint arXiv: 1612.00323 (2016)

29. Levitsky, S., Way, L.: The rise of competitive authoritarianism. J. Democr. **13**(2), 51–65 (2002). https://doi.org/10.1353/jod.2002.0026

30. Lyon, D.: Surveillance, Snowden, and Big Data: capacities, consequences, critique. Big Data Soc. **1**(2), 2053951714541861 (2014). https://doi.org/10.1177/2053951714541861

31. MacKinnon, R.: China's "networked authoritarianism". J. Democr. **22**(2), 32–46 (2011). https://doi.org/10.1353/jod.2011.0033

32. Maerz, S.F.: The electronic face of authoritarianism: E-government as a tool for gaining legitimacy in competitive and non-competitive regimes. Gov. Inf. Q. **33**(4), 727–735 (2016). https://doi.org/10.1016/j.giq.2016.08.008

33. Meissner, M., Wübbeke, J.: IT-backed authoritarianism: Information technology enhances central authority and control capacity under Xi Jinpin. MERICS Papers on China, pp. 52–56 (2016)

34. Milan, S., Velden, L.V.D.: The alternative epistemologies of data activism. Digit. Cult. Soc. **2**(2), 57–74 (2016). https://doi.org/10.14361/dcs-2016-0205

35. Mishra, N.: Data localization laws in a digital world: data protection or data protectionism? The Public Sphere (2016). https://ssrn.com/abstract=2848022

36. Morozov, E.: The Net Delusion: The Dark Side of Internet Freedom. Public Affairs, New York (2012)

37. Nocetti, J.: "Digital Kremlin": power and the internet in Russia. Russie. NEI. Visions, no. 59 (3) (2011)

38. Nocetti, J.: Russia's 'dictatorship-of-the-law' approach to internet policy. Internet Policy Rev. **4**(4) (2015)

39. Raymond, M., DeNardis, L.: Multistakeholderism: anatomy of an inchoate global institution. Int. Theory **7**(3), 572–616 (2015). https://doi.org/10.1017/s1752971915000081

40. Rød, E.G., Weidmann, N.B.: Empowering activists or autocrats? The Internet in authoritarian regimes. J. Peace Res. **52**(3), 338–351 (2015). https://doi.org/10.1177/0022343314555782

41. Sargsyan, T.: Data localization and the role of infrastructure for surveillance, privacy, and security. Int. J. Commun. **10**, 2221–2237 (2016). ISSN 1932-8036 201 60005

42. Savelyev, A.: Russia's new personal data localization regulations: a step forward or a self-imposed sanction? Comput. Law Secur. Rev. **32**(1), 128–145 (2016). https://doi.org/10.1016/j.clsr.2015.12.003

43. Schedler, A.: The new institutionalism in the study of authoritarian regimes. Totalitarismus und Demokratie **6**(2), 323–340 (2009). https://doi.org/10.13109/tode.2009.6.2.323

44. Schlaeger, J.: E-Government in China. Digital information and communication technologies in local government organizational reforms in Chengu. Ph.D. dissertation, University of Copenhagen (2011)

45. Soldatov, A., Borogan, I.: The Red Web: The Struggle Between Russia's Digital Dictators and the New Online Revolutionaries. Public Affairs, New York (2015)

46. Treré, E.: The dark side of digital politics: understanding the algorithmic manufacturing of consent and the hindering of online dissidence. IDS Bull. **47**(1), 127–138 (2016). https://doi.org/10.19088/1968-2016.111

47. Tufekci, Z.: Engineering the public: Big Data, surveillance and computational politics. First Monday **19**(7) (2014). https://doi.org/10.5210/fm.v19i7.4901

48. Van Dijck, J.: Datafication, dataism and dataveillance: Big Data between scientific paradigm and ideology. Surveill. Soc. **12**(2), 197–208 (2014)

49. Vendil Pallin, C.: Internet control through ownership: the case of Russia. Post-Sov. Aff. **33** (1), 16–33 (2017). https://doi.org/10.1080/1060586x.2015.1121712

50. Wallin, P.: Authoritarian collaboration: unexpected effects of open government initiatives in China. Doctoral dissertation, Linnaeus University Press (2014)

51. Zeng, J.: China's date with Big Data: will it strengthen or threaten authoritarian rule? Int. Aff. **92**(6), 1443–1462 (2016). https://doi.org/10.1111/1468-2346.12750

52. Zharova, A.K., Elin, V.M.: The use of Big Data: a Russian perspective of personal data security. Comput. Law Secur. Rev. **33**(4), 482–501 (2017). https://doi.org/10.1016/j.clsr.2017.03.025

53. Zwitter, A.: Big Data ethics. Big Data Soc. **1**(2), 2053951714559253 (2014). https://doi.org/10.1177/2053951714559253

Collective Actions in Russia: Features of on-Line and off-Line Activity

Alexander Sokolov[✉]

Demidov P.G. Yaroslavl State University, Yaroslavl, Russia
alex8119@mail.ru

Abstract. The paper is devoted to the analysis of collective actions in modern Russia. The author analyzes the approaches to understanding collective action in the modern socio-political process. The transformation of collective actions and the emergence of a new phenomenon - on-line collective action are analyzed in the paper. The degree of significance of on-line collective actions and the possibility of their impact on the socio-political situation is analyzed.

The paper includes the survey of experts from 21 regions of Russia in 2014, 14 regions in 2015, 16 regions in 2017 with a limited 10–16 number of experts for each region. The author analyzes the regional features of the organization of collective actions. The study is made possible to reveal the gradual growth of the importance and influence of the Internet of forms of collective action. However, the forms still have much less influence than traditional forms of collective action.

The paper identifies the features of online collective action in comparison with off-line collective actions. The author reveals the peculiarities of the reaction of the authorities to collective actions, revealing the features of the reaction to online collective actions. The author identifies the features of organizing collective actions both in off-line and on-line spheres.

Keywords: Collective actions · Protest · Internet · Social networks
Civic activism · e-Participation

1 Introduction

Massive collective actions swept the whole world. Their examples can be found in various parts of the world, and are organized under different requirements and manifestos. For example: the movement Indignados ("Outraged") in Spain, the "Occupied" movement in various countries, the "Arab Spring", "colored" revolutions and others. They are well-organized collective actions of the big human masses. They generate well-developed information signals and information content, coordinate activities of various groups and use them to achieve a common goal [1].

Activists of collective actions can manage their activities and communication in social networks, building up that communication that meets their interests, including with regard to participation in a concrete collective action, thereby increasing the effectiveness of collective action and promoting the formation of a collective identity.

© Springer Nature Switzerland AG 2018
D. A. Alexandrov et al. (Eds.): DTGS 2018, CCIS 858, pp. 156–167, 2018.
https://doi.org/10.1007/978-3-030-02843-5_13

Mobilization through social networks is formed due to a culture of cooperation, sharing of social networking data and the possibility of self-expression.

Russian social and political practice demonstrates more and more examples of the successful organization of collective actions through Internet technologies, as well as the possibilities for influencing the decision-making process through the using of ICT.

In recent years, there has been a new surge in collective action in Russia, forcing the authorities to respond to the formulated demands. As a result, collective actions can be interpreted as an instrument of actualization of the alternative agenda.

2 Collective Actions: Deviation or Rational Behavior

Researchers do not always unambiguously interpret collective actions. Drury and Scott pointed out that certain mechanisms of hierarchical control are important for the normal functioning of society, without which it will become a victim of irrationality and violence, provoked by the crowd [2]. This was because the masses can only attract outcasts and deviants.

Kornhauser under the "mass" understood a large number of people who are not integrated into any social group, including classes [3]. He argued that the causes of the "mass society" phenomenon formation are the loss of control over society by elites, the formation of a political system based on the electoral process, and the increase in the atomization of society. In "mass society", mass movements lead to undemocratic destruction of the state.

Among the researchers of the late 20th century, collective action is understood with a less negative evaluation and note that collective action is a consequence of objective circumstances, human perceptions, motivational, emotional and behavioral dispositions [4].

Olson made an important contribution to the collective action's theory development [5]. He tried to compare the activity and concernment in protecting interests of individuals and groups of citizens (united by a common goal). However, he questioned the assertion that individuals united in groups will act as actively as individual citizens in a situation requiring interests' protection. This is due to the identified problem of "free rider" - even without taking active steps you can reap the benefits (to obtain protection of their rights) at the expense of the collective actions of others. At the same time, non-inclusion in collective action will be predetermined by the awareness of the collective action cost (in terms of time, resources, etc.).

In the 1980s, researchers suggested that only instrumental explanation of collective action is not enough. The category of collective identity was introduced - the more individuals identify themselves with the group, the more they are inclined to protest on behalf of this group [6].

Jenkins points out that identity is an understanding of who "we" and "other" are, and a similar understanding of "others" about oneself and "others" towards them [7]. Identity is a significant variable in the theory of collective action. A. Hirschman argued that individuals loyal to the group are oriented toward receiving services from it, and in difficult situations, they are ready to help their organization with their actions [8].

A number of researchers note that collective actions form and strengthen a collective identity. In particular, Drury and Reicher demonstrated how a disparate crowd in the process of countering the police was gradually structured, and gained the power [9].

Klandermans, himself, together with de Weerd, does not revealed a direct link between identification and participation, but suggest that group identification predetermines the willingness to act [10]. Therefore, they assume that the reason is identification.

Summarizing existing approaches to understanding collective action, we can agree with L. Medina's approach, which indicates that collective actions in contemporary literature mean a set of actions representing a certain system of organized individuals belonging to certain degree of organized groups [11]. To achieve their goals, individuals form coordination mechanisms, a set of action instruments, symbolic practices [12]. These actions are aimed at the transformation of social space, with which the participating individuals do not agree.

3 Collective Action and the Internet

As Le Bon observes, collective action is formed from the unification of disparate individuals who unite to express their discontent [13]. Collective actions can have different forms of organization and demonstrate their effectiveness. As noted by Bennett and Segerberg, they acquire special efficiency when interpersonal networks are supported by technological platforms that allow collective actions' coordination and scaling [14]. Networking allows you effectively ensure the collective production and distribution of information and identities in comparison with the distributed content and relationships, based on a hierarchical organization. At the same time, such collective actions are well organized and structured when they possess the necessary resources and mass support, based on interconnected individuals using technological media platforms.

In these conditions, communication between individuals creates a relationship between them that reinforce the organization of collective actions. At the same time, technological tools allow individuals to find those forms of action that are most convenient for them.

In an organized and structured collective action, individual mobilization is built through communication (network links) with key organizational units that serve as engines for mobilizing new participants in the movement [15]. Such social networks promote the dissemination and implementation of pre-defined collective identities fixed in the frames of this collective action.

Brady, Verba and Schlozman argue that there is a positive relationship between the ability of an individual to influence political processes and the use of digital technologies [16]. Social networks have facilitated the search and dissemination of information, and therefore reduced the cost of access to it and political participation. They provided an opportunity to search for information, but also to comment on it, discuss it in a convenient place and time. Users can join social movements without direct participation in rallies and other events. As a result, digital technologies reduce costs and create significant potential for democratization of political participation.

McCurdy emphasizes the importance for the collective action's success of disseminating information about these activities in the media and the Internet [17]. This is how the alternative information space is formed, which allows to actualize the problem and mobilize supporters.

Social media are also used to express their point of view. This political activity assumes greater involvement, greater activity in the collection and processing of information, depth of thinking [18]. At the same time, active expression of different points of view in social media can promote the collective action's development and protest activity. This is because the statement of opinion is connected not only with the information exchange, but also with its interpretation. Thus, political discussions, expressing opinions in social media contribute to the formation of political discussions that facilitate political education and motivate people to engage in political activity.

Constant communication and emerging experience of interaction makes it possible to form a collective identity in social networks, which is understood as a sense of attachment to a group that takes collective action on a common topical issue [19]. They also allow you to build relationships with those who are not familiar with in everyday life.

One of the most controversial issues in the study of Internet activism is the question of the Internet slactivism role (from the English "slacker" (slacker) and "activism" (activism)). Canadian journalist M. Gladwell argues "real social changes are impossible through social media, since the links in them are fragile and decentralized, uncontrollable, whereas in order to achieve their demands, protesters need a cohesive, disciplined well-organized core with central administration" [20]. A team of experts from Oxford, New York Universities and the University of Pennsylvania has proved that even those users who participate in the campaign, only by pressing the "repost" button, play a big role in Internet activity [21]. The experts managed to prove that peripheral players played a decisive role in increasing the coverage of protest messages and generating online content. Despite the evidence that the heart of the social movements are minorities, the success of the campaign depends more on the critical periphery activation.

Gladwell in the article "Little Changes. Why the revolution will not be tweeted" [22] concludes that online campaigns cannot lead to really meaningful, large-scale social and political changes that require active action from participants and their readiness to take high risks, including loss of work, housing and even life.

Tufekci believes that a live, non-Internet communication is needed for real change, by comparing those protests in Greensboro with the election campaign of the one Turkish leaders [23].

The argument of both experts is based on the fact that real changes in the social or political spheres are based only on real actions, and social media can either simply help in organizing or informing about the possibilities of such changes, or even reduce the campaign to the lack of result. Thus, Internet users, in online activity, consider their "public debt" to be fulfilled and do not seek to exit offline.

The success of social and political campaigns depends on many factors that determine the degree of goal achievement at different stages of its implementation.

Obviously, a campaign that has achieved the goal is successful, but campaigns organized with the help of Internet resources often do not have one goal. The purpose of the Internet campaign is to involve users in solving a particular problem or informing them about the existence of such a problem. However, events that precede or resolve a problem situation always occur outside the Internet field.

4   Data and Methods

The purpose of the paper is to identify the characteristics of the organization of collective actions in modern Russia, the ability of collective actions to influence on the political process and the reaction of the authorities to them. An additional goal is to identify the characteristics of on-line and off-line collective actions, as well as the features of the authorities' re-action on these two types of collective action.

We can highlight two main forms of collective actions. The first is civic activity, which is understood in the paper as purposeful, coordinated voluntary activity of citizens in the interests of realizing or protecting their legitimate rights and interests. The second - political activity of citizens, which is understood as those forms of civic activity that are oriented towards influencing the decision-making process by the authorities, the process of functioning of the authorities as a whole.

The author attempted to conduct an analysis of collective actions in Russia on the basis of expert's survey. The experts were duly represented by the authorities (about 35% of the sample respondents), leaders of NGOs and political parties (about 30%), business representatives, journalists and representatives of academic environment (about 35%). The criteria for selecting experts were: the degree of competence of the expert; awareness of socio-political processes in their region; different political views; the ability to assess the situation without prejudice. Each of the experts assessed the situation in his region, as well as in the country as a whole (if there was an appropriate question). The report includes the survey results of experts from 21 regions of Russia in 2014, 14 regions in 2015, 16 regions in 2017 with a limited 10–16 number of experts for each region (Table 1).

Table 1. Distribution of sample survey of experts

	Region	2017	2015	2014
1	Altai region	–	–	12
2	Vladimir region	–	–	12
3	Vologda Region	–	–	11
4	Voronezh region	11	12	11
5	Irkutsk region	10	11	14
6	Kaliningrad region	11	–	11
7	Kirov region	11	12	13
8	Kostroma region	11	11	10
9	Krasnodar region	–	10	10
10	Nizhny Novgorod Region	–	–	10

(*continued*)

Table 1. (*continued*)

	Region	2017	2015	2014
11	Novosibirsk region	–	15	10
12	Republic of Adygea	12	11	11
13	Republic of Bashkortostan	10	11	10
14	The Republic of Dagestan	11	13	12
15	The Republic of Karelia	–	–	11
16	Republic of Tatarstan	10	10	10
17	Rostov region	14	–	–
18	Samara Region	11	13	10
19	Saratov region	14	14	12
20	Stavropol region	10	–	–
21	Ulyanovsk region	10	10	10
22	Khabarovsk region	–	–	10
23	Yaroslavl region	16	12	13
	TOTAL	172	165	233

The representativeness of the sample regions was provided based on the principle of heterogeneity on the following selection criteria: geographical position; the economic development of the region; political system of the region; social and demographic structure of the region; ethnic and religious structure of the region; regional political and administrative regime.

The procedure of absentee polling experts with the written data collection was used for data collection. Experts were asked the following questions:

1. How much developed off-line and on-line civil activity in your region?
2. What types (forms) of civic activity are the most common in your region (off-line and on-line)?
3. How significant is the civic activity on the Internet in your region?
4. What factors contribute most to the growth of the effectiveness of civil campaigns for defending the rights of citizens in your region?
5. What problems can you single out in the development of civic activity in your region?
6. What civil associations are most active in your region?
7. How many partners, as a rule, unite in off-line and on-line coalitions of public organizations and civil activists in your region?
8. Appreciate, how important are the following principles of interaction for the functioning of civil society organizations and civil activists?
9. Evaluate the degree of activity of off-line and on-line protest actions in your region in 2017?
10. To what extent are the organizers of on-line and off-line protests oriented to the interests of the population of the region?
11. To what extent does the protest activity (off-line and on-line) affect the socio-political situation in the region?

12. How would you assess the changes in the direction of civic activity on-line in your region as a result of the state's activation in the regulation of the Internet environment?
13. How did the dynamics of civil on-line activity in your region reflect the activation of the state in the regulation of the Internet environment recently?
14. How does the state react to off-line and on-line forms of civic engagement?
15. To what extent do authorities in your region oppose off-line and online protest activities?

The software SPSS were used for the statistical data processing. It allows us to give a generalized assessment of the phenomenon, details of which comes from several independent experts.

5 Discussion

According to the expert survey data, the number of citizens who somehow took part in various forms of collective action has practically not changed in recent years (in 2015 - 5.94 points, 2017 - 5.66 points on a scale from 0 to 10 points, where "0 "- lack of civic activity, "10" - large-scale civic activity).

Based on the experts' answers, it can be stated that residents of the Russian Federation are more likely to show their civic position in the Internet than in reality (real life). Experts estimated the level of off-line collective actions activity at an average of 4.90 points, while on-line at 5.66 points. However, such a pattern cannot be traced in all regions of Russia. Among the regions included in the study, in the Saratov, Samara, Rostov, Voronezh, Irkutsk regions, the Republic of Adygea, the activity of citizens is, firstly, lower than the average, and secondly the same as in off-line and on-line. It can be assumed that the manifestation of citizens' activity on the Internet is largely connected with the Internet penetration in the regions. According to the Public Opinion Foundation, the penetration rate of the Internet is slightly lower than the Russian average in the Volga Federal District, the South and North Caucasus Federal Districts (65% and 69% respectively).

Residents of various regions participate in the collective on-line and off-line activities in different ways. On-line activities are more focused on discussing problems in various forums, participating in surveys and charitable actions (as a rule, activity ends here with the money transfer). In real life, people prefer to take part in public and political life by means of participating in elections, work in NGOs, and charitable events. It should be noted that in real life and in the network, citizens give a lot of energy to write various appeals to the authorities.

For 2015–2017, according to the expert interviews' results, the significance and impact of online collective action on the result of the initiative groups and citizens' activities has significantly decreased. If in 2015, the citizens' action in the Internet was recognized by just over 40% of experts, in 2017 it was only 32%. On the contrary, the proportion of respondents who consider low or no influence of on-line activists on the social initiatives promotion and implementation, increased. It is interesting that experts representing different social and professional groups look at the Internet civic activity's effectiveness in different ways. The poll showed that deputies of different levels, representatives of NGOs, media and scholars tend to believe in the efficacy or low influence of the Internet citizens' activity on the social and political life. In power bodies, business and political parties, just few people see the power or any sense in online civil activity.

The organizers of protest and non-protracted off-line and on-line public actions much more often believe in the effectiveness of collective on-line actions.

The mass media support, bloggers, the Internet community, broad support from the population or large social groups and the presence of a bright, active leader play an important role in increasing the effectiveness of collective actions, according to the consolidated opinion of experts.

The main problem of citizens' collective actions development, according to most experts, is low initiative and activity of citizens, as well as disunity of civil society institutions and civil activists. The process of involving citizens in public and political life in each region has its own characteristics, but the main difficulties in all regions are approximately the same.

Officially registered public associations, as well as formally unregistered associations of citizens (for example): local groups, social movements, Internet communities, etc., and mixed coalitions of registered and unregistered associations demonstrate the greatest activity, like three years ago.

At the same time, as a rule, no more than two or three partners (on average in the country) unite coalitions. However, data for 2014–2017 indicate an increase in the number of coalitions that unite four or more participants (partners). It is important to note that such alliances often take shape in on-line environment.

The most important principle of the public organizations and civil activists' cooperation is "common interest/purpose to the cause of civic engagement", "voluntary nature of participation" and "openness, development of the external relations system ". The first two principles are among the main ones during 2014–2017, the third principle was included in the top three for the first time.

Monitoring data indicate an increase in protest sentiments in the subjects of the Russian Federation. In 2014, the degree of readiness for protest actions of civil activists was estimated by experts at 2.44 points, in 2015 by 3.20 points, in 2017, already at 4.67 points (on a scale of 0 to 10, where "0" absence of protest actions, "10" - large-scale protest activity). It can be assumed that this was due to the emergence and active dissemination among the population of a new platform for expressing protest sentiments - the Internet. The study showed the activation of the social networks' use in the process of organizing protest actions.

The protest actions initiators began to focus more on the interests of society rather than in 2014 (growth from the value of −0.03 to 0.55). It is interesting that in the Ulyanovsk region, where the highest level of civil and protest activity is observed, the organizers are most attentive to the needs of ordinary people when planning their actions.

The study revealed regularity: the growth of protest activity in the regions increasingly destabilizes socio-political life. Perhaps this is due to the growing opposition of the authorities to various manifestations, primarily by creating administrative barriers to the street actions organization. The Republic of Tatarstan is an exception.

Here, stabilization of the regional life is recorded, with an average level of protest activity, and orientation of authorities to dialogue with protesters.

The role of the state in the Internet environment regulation is growing in Russia recently. In the expert environment, there was no unified and unequivocal opinion as to how this fact affects the dynamics of on-line collective actions. Most experts representing the Republic of Bashkortostan, the Kirov Region, the Stavropol Territory, the Republic of Adygea, the Rostov Region and the Voronezh Region, i.e. regions with low socio-political significance of Internet civic activity, are confident in the absence of state influence on the development of citizens' Internet collective actions in their region. It is interesting that this opinion was especially often observed by the participants of the survey, who did not take part in the civil activists' actions (both protest and non-protest actions). The relative majority of experts from the Republic of Tatarstan and the Saratov region are convinced of a slowdown in online collective action both because of adaptation to the new conditions, and because of fears among Internet activists for the consequences of their actions. Twenty-five percent of experts adhere to the opposite point of view, i.e. look at the actions of the state in the sphere of regulation of the Internet environment as a factor stimulating the growth of activity of on-line collective actions in the region.

Speaking about the state influence on the content side of on-line collective action, there is still a relatively consolidated expert opinion: the majority of respondents (62%) did not see qualitative changes, i.e. changes in its fillability. In addition, experts who do not participate in public actions expressed such an opinion more often than others did. About 15% of respondents believe that government intervention in the Internet space regulation has led to increased loyalty in the relations of online activists and authorities. Each fourth expert (23.3%) noted the radicalization and intensification of protest sentiments in the Internet environment. This opinion is especially widespread among organizers and participants of off-line and on-line protest actions, as well as representatives of Ulyanovsk and Kostroma regions.

According to the absolute majority of experts, state authorities in the regions, as well as at the federal level, monitor activities and actions of civil activists and initiative groups. However, the state is more lenient to the Internet activities than to off-line civic engagement. Therefore, it rarely responds to public actions and initiatives on the Internet.

Authorities of different subjects respond differently to various forms of off-line protest collective action. However, more often they either "slightly support them" (25.4%), or "actively support, seeing positive results of work" (22.5%), or "fear and provide minimal assistance to them" (13.6%). 13.6% of experts spoke against holding public civic actions. Representatives of the Ulyanovsk region (22.2%), the Saratov region (21.4%), the Republic of Dagestan (27.3%), the Republic of Bashkortostan (30.0%) and the Irkutsk region (20.0%) spoke more often about this. Experts from these regions have put either the highest or the lowest estimate of the civic activity (off-line) development level in their region. In addition, there is a high growth of protest actions among the listed subjects. It is particularly interesting that the assessments and characteristics of the state's reaction to various public actions exhibited by the participants in these actions and by outside observers are different, but not critical.

The activity of citizens in the Internet is somewhat less interesting to the authorities, and the authorities are not so worried about the actual off-line collective actions. Nevertheless, experts witnessed situations in which public authorities feared the Internet actions of civil activists, supported them, or counteracted them. Response and resistance of state bodies to the development and manifestations of Internet citizens' activity is quite often found, according to the results of the survey. About 30% of experts were able to recall the cases of state support of Internet citizens' activity.

6 Conclusions

Collective action is an effective way of protecting citizens' rights and interests. Modern sociopolitical practice demonstrates an increasing distribution and a larger scale of collective action. At the same time, there is no unambiguous interpretation of collective action. Conventionally, two approaches for collective action understanding can be distinguished: as deviant behavior and as rational behavior aimed at protecting one's rights and interests. Collective actions are especially effective due to the network structure and use of modern information and communication technologies (Internet and social networks). The Internet provides a wide range of tools for organizing and implementing collective actions: expressing opinions, forming communities, communicating, voting, finding solutions to problems and collecting funds.

Activists use social networks (sites) to build political communication, and quickly organize a collective action. This action is based on digital technologies to organize and coordinate protests. As a result, digital technologies provide resources that were previously concentrated in social movements. However, Internet technologies are not enough without off-line activity, but they are necessary to ensure the proper level and intensity of communication.

As the results of the study show, the population's activity in the regional sociopolitical sphere is stable for several years. The activities and actions of social activists are noticeable both in real life and on-line. The state is more lenient to the activity of citizens in the Internet than to off-line civic engagement. Therefore, it reacts less often to shares in the online environment. Based on the regional practice, it can be concluded that only the cooperation of the state and civil activists (even if they are focused on protest) stabilizes the situation in the regions. The obstacle and resistance to the civil and protest activity development are destabilizing the socio-political situation in the regions of the Russian Federation.

Such forms of activity as communication and discussion at forums on socially significant problems and charitable actions are especially popular In the Internet. Especially often, these forms of collective action are used in regions with medium and low on-line activity of the population. Appeals to the authorities, as a form of collective action, are distributed equally in the online and off-line environment of the majority of constituent entities of the Russian Federation. Perhaps the popularity of this form is associated with its low energy costs.

The study made it possible to reveal the gradual growth of the importance and influence of the Internet of forms of collective action. However, the forms still have much less influence than traditional forms of collective action.

Collective actions are organized, mainly, by a narrow number of leaders. This significantly reduces the potential for mobilizing citizens and resources, and consequently, on their outcomes. It was revealed that collective actions on the Internet are organized by a larger number of partner leaders than traditional collective actions. This allows them to cover more people, create an information agenda. As a result, the authorities have to listen more and more to the Internet forms of collective action.

However, more organizers of collective action on the Internet predetermine a greater disunity of activists, whose actions require greater coordination. Internet tools allow achieving the necessary coordination, however, it is not always sufficient to involve the broad masses of the population and to exert a significant influence on the authorities and to solve the problems that caused collective action.

We can conclude that despite Internet audience growth and attempts to include users in public and political activities, the Russian population does not yet perceive the Internet as a platform for achieving meaningful social changes, or it happens unconsciously, for example, in spontaneous discussions of emerging problems. Thus, social media, while playing a significant role in the organization of civil activists' communication, so far remain only as one of the tool for achieving social and political goals.

The question of the Internet campaigns independence in achieving socio-political goals remains open. We can conclude that at the moment, Internet activism mostly is a part of real campaigns and actions, but this situation can be radically broken with the development of electronic voting systems and the development of Internet tools for achieving socially significant goals (such as the "Russian Public initiative").

Acknowledgments. The research was sponsored by Russian Foundation for Humanities as part of the research project №17-03-00132 "Collective action of citizens for the protection and realization of the legitimate rights and interests in contemporary Russia".

References

1. Della Porta, D.: Comment on organizing in the crowd. Inf. Commun. Soc. **17**(2), 269–271 (2014). https://doi.org/10.1080/1369118X.2013.868503
2. Drury, J., Stott, C.: Contextualising the crowd in contemporary social science. Contemp. Soc. Sci. **6**, 275–288 (2011). https://doi.org/10.1080/21582041.2015.1010340
3. Kornhauser, W.: The Politics of Mass Society. Free Press, Glencoe (1959)
4. Brandstatter, H., Opp, K.-D.: Personality traits ("Big Five") and the propensity to political protest: alternative models. Polit. Psychol. **35**(4), 515–537 (2014). https://doi.org/10.1111/pops.12043
5. Olson, M.: The Logic of Collective Action: Public Goods and the Theory of Groups. Harvard University Press, Cambridge (1965)
6. Stürmer, S., Simon, B.: Pathways to collective protest: calculation, identification, or emotion? A critical analysis of the role of group-based anger in social movement participation. J. Soc. Issues **65**(4), 681–705 (2009). https://doi.org/10.1111/j.1540-4560.2009.01620.x
7. Jenkins, R.: Social Identity. Routledge, Abingdon (2004)
8. Hirschman, A.O.: Exit, Voice, and Loyalty. Responses to Decline in Firms, Organizations, and States. Harvard University Press, Cambridge (1970)

9. Drury, J., Reicher, S., Stott, C.: Shifting boundaries of collective identity: intergroup context and social category change in an anti-roads protest. In: British Psychological Society Social Psychology Section Conference. University of Surrey (1999). https://doi.org/10.1080/1474283032000139779

10. De Weerd, M., Klandermans, B.: Group identification and social protest: farmer's protest in the Netherlands. Eur. J. Soc. Psychol. **29**, 1073–1095 (1999). https://doi.org/10.1002/(SICI)1099-0992(199912)29:8%3c1073:AID-EJSP986%3e3.0.CO;2-K

11. Medina, L.F.: A Unified Theory of Collective Action and Social Change, Analytical Perspectives on Politics. University of Michigan Press, Ann Arbor (2007)

12. McAdam, D., McCarthy, J.D., Zald, M.N.: Comparative Perspectives and Social Movements: Political Opportunities, Mobilizing Structures, and Cultural Framing. Cambridge University Press, New York (1996)

13. Le Bon, G.: The Crowd: A Study of the Popular Mind. Batoche Books, Kitchener (2001)

14. Bennett, L., Segerberg, A.: The Logic of Connective Action: Digital Media and the Personalization of Contentious Politics. Cambridge University Press, Cambridge (2013)

15. Diani, M.: Social movement networks virtual and real. Inf. Commun. Soc. **3**, 386–401 (2000). https://doi.org/10.1080/13691180051033333

16. Brady, H., Verba, S., Schlozman, K.L.: Beyond SES: a resource model of political participation. Am. Polit. Sci. Rev. **89**(2), 271–294 (1995). https://doi.org/10.2307/2082425

17. McCurdy, P.: Social movements, protest and mainstream media. Sociol. Compass **6**(3), 244–255 (2012). https://doi.org/10.1111/j.1751-9020.2011.00448.x

18. Cho, J., Shah, D.V., McLeod, J.M., McLeod, D.M., Scholl, R.M., Gotlieb, M.R.: Campaigns, reflection, and deliberation: advancing an O-S-R-O-R model of communication effects. Commun. Theory **19**, 66–88 (2009). https://doi.org/10.1111/j.1468-2885.2008.01333.x

19. van Stekelenburg, J., Klandermans, B.: Individuals in movements: a social psychology of contention. In: Roggeband, C., Klandermans, B. (eds.) Handbook of Social Movements Across Disciplines. HSSR, pp. 103–139. Springer, Cham (2017). https://doi.org/10.1007/978-3-319-57648-0_5

20. Kuznetsov, D.: Sofa troops are recognized as an important part of the protest. https://nplus1.ru/news/2015/12/08/slackers-strike-back

21. Barberá, P., Wang, T.: The critical periphery in the growth of social protests. http://journals.plos.org/plosone/article?id=10.1371/journal.pone.0143611

22. Gladwell, M.: Why the revolution will not be tweeted. http://www.newyorker.com/magazine/2010/10/04/small-change-malcolm-gladwell

23. Tufekci, Z.: Online social change: easy to organize, hard to win. https://www.ted.com/talks/zeynep_tufekci_how_the_internet_has_made_social_change_easy_to_organize_hard_to_win

E-Polity: Law and Regulation

Legal Aspects of the Use of AI in Public Sector

Mikhail Bundin[1(✉)] , Aleksei Martynov[1] , Yakub Aliev[2],
and Eldar Kutuev[2]

[1] Lobachevsky State University of Nizhny Novgorod (UNN),
Nizhny Novgorod 603950, Russia
mbundin@mail.ru, avm@unn.ru
[2] Saint-Petersburg University of MIA, Saint Petersburg 198206, Russia
alievyak@yandex.ru

Abstract. At present, the use of artificial intelligence technologies (AI) have become a general trend even in the areas normally appertained by humans. Smart technologies are actually widely used to ensure functioning of many vital sectors of economy such as public transport, communications, nuclear energy, space, medicine, etc. Such tendency also evokes the question about the use of AI for public administration and not only from the point of view of technology or ethics but also from the legal point of view. In this article, the authors seek to suggest a number of ideas and assumptions about general and specific legal issues on the use of AI for public sector, such as legal status and responsibility of AI, public trust and influence on Human rights.

Keywords: Artificial intelligence · Legal aspects · Public administration
Smart government · Smart computing

1 Introduction

The development of science and technology, especially computer technologies related to the use of "supercomputers", allows for the use of the so-called artificial intelligence (hereinafter – AI) in various fields. Scientists have different views on the prospects for the use of AI for the benefit of the mankind [13, 19, 35].

S. Hawking noted: "the creation of full artificial intelligence could be the beginning of the end of the human race. It [artificial intelligence] will exist by itself and will start to change with increasing speed. People who are limited in this respect, as the slow biological evolution cannot compete with machines and will be re-placed" [5].

Other scholars argue that intuition, understanding, insight, creativity are inherent to a mankind [25, 26]. Human behavior, in turn, is characterized by unpredictability. The human intellect has qualities that still cannot be expressed in a programming language: curiosity, depth of mind, flexibility and mobility of mind, intuitive ability to solve complex problems. For the scientific community understanding of mechanisms of creativity, understanding, intuition, insight, today, is not possible. Therefore, while the human mind remains a mystery, it still has a right to claim exclusivity. Thus, from the point of view of philosophy, the prospects of creating a universal artificial intelligence is not comforting until the nature of a man remains a mystery.

© Springer Nature Switzerland AG 2018
D. A. Alexandrov et al. (Eds.): DTGS 2018, CCIS 858, pp. 171–180, 2018.
https://doi.org/10.1007/978-3-030-02843-5_14

CEO of SpaceX and Tesla Elon Musk believes that artificial intelligence is the biggest existential risk for all mankind. Elon Musk during the annual meeting of the World Government Summit called AI is the biggest risk we face as a civilization: "AI's a rare case where we need to be proactive in regulation, instead of reactive. Because by the time we are reactive with AI regulation, it's too late" [15].

It should be noted that artificial intelligence is becoming a part of everyday life and is widely used now in various areas and largely penetrates into the society [7, 17, 24]. More and more areas of human life have been linked to AI, or will soon be associated with the use of it. Generally, among those areas are considered to be: scientific research; IT industry; medical treatment and paramedics [22]; space industry; entertainment industry (computer games); legal work (preparation of legal documents (claims, complaints), investigation, detection and prevention of crimes; digital economy and promoting goods and services; smart weaponry, etc.

2 Current Practice of the Use of AI for Smart Government

We could name a few cases [2, 29, 31] when AI systems are used for the purpose of public administration. This could be partly explained by a certain conservatism of the latter as public sector is usually quite cautious about innovations. At the same time, some elements of implementing AI technologies already take place, or at least such measures are considered and obviously find support among scientists and politicians [1, 12, 18, 32, 33]. One example could be the use of AI software for recruitment and personnel training [5]. The general trend to replace public employees by robots is becoming more obvious, according to some suggestions, it could happen soon enough [14]. One of most recent and well-known cases is the use of different expert systems or AI assistants that can, based on the analysis of big data, offer a solution to a practical case. However, full autonomy of such systems is not being considered yet.

Among the most debated issue for public sector is the use of AI in legal profession. Large legal companies use it now and achieve excellent results by operating high level AI assistants capable of linguistic and text analysis. In particular, there are examples of AI systems used for analysis and drafting of legal documents (lawsuits, contracts), preparation of judicial decisions and for preparatory legal advice [8]. At the same time, their algorithm is based initially on the analysis of business processes of large law firms, not individual lawyers whose working process hasn't been studied yet [8].

Despite such encouraging results, there are many skeptics speaking against the possibility of applying AI for the interpretation of the law and a rule of law, which are sometimes ambiguous, contradictory, or simply devoid of rational meaning.

Another point to consider here is an issue of ethics - a possibility to take a deliberate unlawful decision by AI certainly needs further analysis. Surely, this problem will have even a vital importance for the implementation of AI for the whole public sector. Recent analytical reports in the United States contain explicit suggestions for state and municipal officials to undergo special training and to acquire skills in working with AI systems that can support decision-making [31].

3 Rationale for the Use of AI in Public Sector

Modern researches names numerous advantages and risks of using AI. The most obvious merits of AI are usually include:

1. More robust decision-making;
2. Possibility to analyze large datasets;
3. Functionality (24/7 readiness and functioning);
4. Lack of conflict of interests in decision-making.

Obviously all those characteristics of AI support its use in public sector. There is even a strong presumption that AI is now indispensable for planning actions in critical, emergency situations. Currently, the use of such systems for crisis management centers is a rather common practice and in fact, the center itself represents to some extend the AI system, which is based on the analysis of big data from different sources to provide the decision-making body with high-level analytical support.

As for the possible risks, they usually could be explained by childish fears of robots and machines taking control over humans. Surely, those risks should be evaluated and kept in mind and to some extend those fears may have a certain ground in the future. On the other hand, it is absurd to deny the positive effect of using AI systems in the management of vital social spheres. Modern medicine, communication, trade, banking, transport and even weaponry couldn't be imagined without a high level of automatization and mostly with the use of AI. Moreover, any progress in these spheres is closely connected with further implementation of AI technologies. This is explained by a high level of the complexity of newly developed control systems that couldn't be operated by human without help of AI. In fact, we should acknowledge that we now trust AI to control other complex mechanisms more than humans. This fact faces serious criticism especially in cases of the use of autonomous systems in war scenarios [16].

Such arguments are not new. At present, the possibility of using AI for public needs is largely discussed in the forms of smart government, municipality, city, etc. [2, 3, 29, 30]. What the scholars are actually talking about is a much deeper degree of automation in public sector by the use of highly intelligent systems that in the future we will be able to entrust the management of many areas, including state and municipal administration. How far we are from that? Whether we have an appropriate legal basis for this?

4 Problematics on Forming an Appropriate Legal Framework

Essential and more particular legal issues related to the use of AI in public sector are mainly interconnected with general principles of law that are initially designed for human beings not machines. Some of them are more urgent or could be regarded as contemporary problems and others are far from solution and depends greatly on other factors like IT technologies development. The authors seek to analyze some of them that could be relevant for public sector as well.

4.1   Legal Personality of AI

Of course, the main issue for lawyers, as well as for the whole humanity is the recognition of the legal personality of the AI [6, 13]. It is actually a complex philosophical problem about the existence of rationality of AI in comparison with a human one. Probably the solution of this issue lies far in the future. However, the today situation requires the scholars to start thinking about creating an appropriate conceptual apparatus, which defines AI and forms it can take. Actually, we could start by trying to answer such simple questions as "what information system or software or something else we should name and recognize as having AI or could the latter have different levels in terms of ability to make independent, rational decisions, to comprehend their effects or even to have its own ethical standards" [10]. This is issue was a core problem treated in Resolution of the European Parliament of the 16th February 2017 with recommendation for the Commission on Civil Law for Robotics. This document suggests several criteria to classify AI mechanisms for the purpose of civil law regulation:

- the acquisition of autonomy through sensors and/or by exchanging data with its environment (inter-connectivity) and the trading and analyzing of those data;
- self-learning from experience and by interaction (optional criterion);
- at least a minor physical support;
- the adaptation of its behavior and actions to the environment;
- the absence of life in the biological sense [23].

More prominent issue to this extend should be the necessity of adopting a certain certification system for AI technologies with different level of ability for autonomy in decision-making. In certain cases, we can already find fragmentary regulation and requirements for different AI mechanisms but a general approach is yet to be developed. Newly appeared neural systems make think of whether AI could be equal to human mind or even excel it and whether its decisions could be its own, not programmed or predicted by a developer or an operator etc. A positive answer to this may evoke reflection on a question of a legal personality of AI or at least about a specific legal status for it [34].

4.2   AI vs. Human Rights

Processing of information about individuals by AI systems is now not a question - it is a fact [7]. Obviously, the processing of huge amounts of information or 'big data' is associated with a deeper analysis performed by AI. On the other hand, the idea or concept of 'big data' directly contradicts basic principles of data protection and affects significantly individual privacy. The key ideas of the latter is an individual's right to control his data processing. Furthermore, data protection regulation usually contains right to object or withdraw as well as a principles of prohibition of combining data from different information systems, destined for different purposes and a general principle of information self-determination [7, 21]. The 'big data' concept in return is oriented on deep data analysis from many sources to create a new knowledge by finding deep inner links between data and new correlation that is directly opposes to the existing legal framework for data protection. In private sec-tor, it is for an individual to give his consent on data processing or to object it. In public sector, the use of information technologies is usually prescribed by law and an individual don't have a right to object it as well as the use of AI technologies to process data.

Therefore, the use of technologies of 'big data' and AI can be rightly perceived by citizens as another element of control over their actions and a direct threat to their rights first and foremost to the right to privacy. On the other hand, avoiding the usage of 'big data' technologies with AI could probably reduce the effectiveness of public administration in comparison with other sectors of economics. In the future, the use of AI systems in public sector may probably lead to another dilemma between individual rights and state interests for effective data processing and public management.

The answer to the last issue is possible to associate with a another one – the right of an individual not only to refuse his data processing in information system with AI, but presumably to insist on such data being processed by a human – the right to insist on a human interference. Even now, we can hear voices for replacement of public employees by robots in implementing simple administrative procedures and drafting documents [14, 15].

The General Data Protection Regulation (GDPR) also contains in article 22 a set of rules to protect humans in cases of automated individual decision-making and profiling. Firstly, a solely automated decision-making that has legal or similarly significant effects is allowed only when decision is:

- necessary for the entry into or performance of a contract; or
- authorized by Union or Member state law applicable to the controller; or
- based on the individual's explicit consent.

If a decision-making is falling under the provisions of art. 22 of GDPR an individual should have the right to be informed about such a data processing and to request human interference or challenge the result of it. The controller has to check regularly if the system are functioning as intended [21].

4.3   Liability of AI

The answer to this question has several levels or dimensions and is closely linked to the form of interaction between human operator and machine. Let's exclude a phase of relatively simple automatization of the data processing and move to the stage of a kind of intelligent assistant or an advisor. Actually, in most cases the employee, who formulates the problem for AI and makes the final decision, is considered responsible [9, 11]. If the decision-making algorithm is comparably simple and ethical issues are not involved, the task to control the machine is simple for a human operator and reasonably he is responsible for the decisions. Newly developed AI technologies destined for 'big data' analysis and for control over complex systems as transport, space industry, smart weapon, etc. are hardly being controlled by a human operator. More often, those systems are initially created to replace a human because of his inability to work in the space or because of extreme complexity of data analysis or other reasons. Even if there is an operator he could hardly suggest another decision than that obtained by a smart machine except obvious cases usually caused by malfunction [27]. This tendency for dependency is already visible in the use of intelligent assistants in everyday life, in business and other fields, which may lead to the same results in public sector. The problematics of recognition of a certain "legal personhood" for AI systems (software agents, assistants) is continuously and reasonably suggested by several researchers [4, 28].

There could be another aspect of the same problem. Whether an operator is entitled or not entitled to agree with AI and its suggestions. The operator's decision is final but in complex systems he is limited in abilities to understand and estimate AI decisions and usually prefer to rely on the machine [7]. Is he really responsible in this case for the result of data processing as it is impossible for him to evaluate clearly the consequences of it? Presumably, in this scenario the responsibility will be shared with AI system's developer or creator. The answer about whom to blame will be even more complicated if the AI system is fully autonomous and has abilities for self-education and self-development and can create its proper algorithms for decision-making differing from the initial ones.

4.4   Transparency and Open Data

The problematics of responsibility and interconnection between the AI machine and its creator could have another implication. The question here is whether we may predict AI actions and evaluated its inner programming algorithm. If yes, then its creator could be blamed for defects in its construction and design or probably its owner - for defect programming or reprogramming it. However, doing this requires more information on AI system functioning. If we imagine that to be an AI for public goal or used for public administration or management it will certainly lead to the question of transparency of those systems. Surely, if this system processes personal data or confidential information that can never be revealed to anyone but its algorithm of processing data and decision-making is another point. Normally, the legal and administrative procedures (course of actions) are prescribed by law and are subject to transparency principle. Therefore, the citizens and the court may have the right to evaluate the algorithm used for data processing by AI system. E.g., in France there is a number of decisions obliging to reveal the algorithm of the software used for public administration to evaluate it from the point of law [20]. In this case, the algorithm is perceived as an official document, because it essentially describes the procedure of decision-making process usually used by an authority and thus to be open. It could be easily presumed that the decision-making algorithms used in AI systems for public administration should be considered as open data.

4.5   Public Trust and AI

Another important legal issue is the problem of people's confidence in AI. While the areas of using AI for public goals are quite limited, in the future it presumably will be used in many critical social spheres to overcome such problems as unemployment, hunger, poverty, crime, etc. All this may raise the question of "trust" with AI in decision-making on vital social problems and potentially even the consideration of such decisions on the level of electoral procedures.

It is quite possible to consider the situation when the issue of using and replacing the traditional management of certain economy sectors or areas of management by AI systems can be the subject of a referendum or elections. In the future, this may become an integral procedure for legitimizing AI actions and decisions, as it is now the case with the appointment to important state posts.

In this case, the most important issues are to be:

1. The determination of the economy sector or an institution of public management, which can be replaced by a "smart machine".
2. Consideration of the choice of alternative AI systems offered by different developers or manufacturers.
3. The possibility of a referendum on the issue of a refusal to use AI and to return to the traditional "human" model of governance.

5   Conclusion

In conclusion, the authors have considered a need for a model of legal regulation for AI implementation for public administration and management. This consideration leads to identification and substantiation of several consequent and urgent steps in creating an adequate legal environment for the application of AI in public sector:

1. The introduction of a legal definition for AI, and AI based technology into law. Most relevant issue here should be development of criteria and gradation of AI systems, particularly, based on their autonomy in decision-making and self-development.
2. The adoption of a system of certification of AI technologies based on risk evaluation approach. The latter will require identifying specific parameters and requirements for creation, development, usage and implementation of AI technologies and designating responsible authorities or institutions as well as the procedure of their formation, liability and their overall status.
3. The determination of what AI technologies may be used for public administration and to what extent. Presumably, the following three levels of admission can be identified:

   - areas, where the application of AI is prohibited;
   - areas, where the application of AI is admissible;
   - areas, where such use is recommended or prescribed.

   In cases, where the application of AI is allowed, there should also be required to determine the legal effects and implications of its decisions or conclusions.
4. The establishment of an adequate responsibility for AI actions. Apparently, the subjects of responsibility may be developer, operator, user, owner, certification body, third person, if he or she intentionally or recklessly makes changes to the AI system.

5. The correlation of AI regulation with the existing legal categories and concepts – privacy, data protection, 'big data' and a possible formulation of the right to object AI data processing in some cases.

Surely, this is not a final and full list of legal issues that require solution in the face of the emergence and evolution of AI technologies. The authors initially aimed to determine the immediate and long-term goals for developing the law in this area because it will rely generally on the IT development and the perception of it by modern society.

References

1. "Megaphone" has presented the new digital public sector development. NTA, Russia (2017). https://www.nta-nn.ru/news/society/2017/news_573065/. Accessed 25 Apr 2018
2. AlDairi, A., Tawalbeh, L.: Cyber security attacks on smart cities and associated mobile technologies. Proc. Comput. Sci. **109**, 1086–1091 (2017). https://doi.org/10.1016/j.procs.2017.05.391
3. Aletà, N.B., Alonso, C.M., Arce Ruiz, R.M.: Smart mobility and smart environment in the Spanish cities. Transp. Res. Proc. **24**, 163–170 (2017). https://doi.org/10.1016/j.trpro.2017.05.084
4. Andrade, F., Novais, P., Machado, J., et al.: Contracting agents: legal personality and representation. Artif. Intell. Law **15**, 357 (2007). https://doi.org/10.1007/s10506-007-9046-0
5. Cellan-Jones, R.: Stephen Hawking warns artificial intelligence could end mankind. BBC UK (2014). http://www.bbc.com/news/technology-30290540. Accessed 25 Apr 2018
6. Čerka, P., Grigienė, J., Sirbikytė, G.: Is it possible to grant legal personality to artificial intelligence software systems? Comput. Law Secur. Rev. **33**(5), 685–699 (2017). https://doi.org/10.1016/j.clsr.2017.03.022
7. Costa, A., Julian, V., Novais, P.: Personal Assistants: Emerging Computational Technologies. Intelligent Systems Reference Library, vol. 132. Springer, Cham (2018). https://doi.org/10.1007/978-3-319-62530-0
8. Elman, J., Castilla, A.: Artificial intelligence and the law. TechCrunch (2017). https://techcrunch.com/2017/01/28/artificial-intelligence-and-the-law/. Accessed 25 Apr 2018
9. Hall-Geisler, K.: Liability in the coming age of autonomous autos. TechCrunch (2016). https://techcrunch.com/2016/06/16/liability-in-the-coming-age-of-autonomous-autos/. Accessed 25 Apr 2018
10. Hentschel, K.: A periodization of research technologies and of the emergency of genericity. Stud. Hist. Philos. Sci. **52**(Part B), 223–233 (2015). https://doi.org/10.1016/j.shpsb.2015.07.009
11. Hernæs, C.O.: Artificial Intelligence, Legal Responsibility and Civil Rights. TechCrunch (2015). https://techcrunch.com/2015/08/22/artificial-intelligence-legal-responsibility-and-civil-rights/. Accessed 25 Apr 2018
12. Information security doctrine of the Russian Federation. http://www.kremlin.ru/acts/bank/41460. Accessed 25 Apr 2018
13. Is Artificial Intelligence Protectable by Law? Should it Be? The Fashion Law (2016). http://www.thefashionlaw.com/home/is-artificial-intelligence-protectable-by-law-should-it-be. Accessed 25 Apr 2018
14. Makridakis, S.: The forthcoming Artificial Intelligence (AI) revolution: its impact on society and firms. Futures **90**, 46–60 (2017). https://doi.org/10.1016/j.futures.2017.03.006

15. Morris, D.Z.: Elon Musk Says Artificial Intelligence Is the 'Greatest Risk We Face as a Civilization'. Fortune (2017). http://fortune.com/2017/07/15/elon-musk-artificial-intelligence-2/. Accessed 25 Apr 2018
16. Pasquale, F.: The Black Box Society: The Secret Algorithms that Control Money and Information. Harvard University Press, Cambridge (2015)
17. Ponciano, R., Pais, S., Casa, J.: Using accuracy analysis to find the best classifier for intelligent personal assistants. Proc. Comput. Sci. **52**, 310–317 (2015). https://doi.org/10.1016/j.procs.2015.05.090
18. Preparing for the Future of Artificial Intelligence. The Whitehouse USA (2016). https://obamawhitehouse.archives.gov/sites/default/files/whitehouse_files/microsites/ostp/NSTC/preparing_for_the_future_of_ai.pdf. Accessed 25 Apr 2018
19. Rajan, K., Saffiotti, A.: Towards a science of integrated AI and robotics. Artif. Intell. **247**, 1–9 (2017). https://doi.org/10.1016/j.artint.2017.03.003
20. Rees, M.: CADA: le code source d'un logiciel développé par l'État est communicable! Next Impact (2015). https://www.nextinpact.com/news/93369-cada-code-source-d-un-logiciel-developpe-par-l-etat-est-communicable.htm. Accessed 25 Apr 2018
21. Regulation (EU) 2016/679 of the European Parliament and of the Council of 27 April 2016 on the protection of natural persons with regard to the processing of personal data and on the free movement of such data, and repealing Directive 95/46/EC (General Data Protection Regulation). EU (2016). http://eur-lex.europa.eu/legal-content/en/TXT/PDF/?uri=CELEX:32016R0679. Accessed 25 Apr 2018
22. Reisfeld, J.: AI's forthcoming transformation of medicine. In: SWE Magazine, vol. 63, no. 1. SWE (2017)
23. Report 27 January 2017 with recommendations to the Commission on Civil Law Rules on Robotics 2015/2103(INL). EU (2017). http://www.europarl.europa.eu/sides/getDoc.do?type=REPORT&reference=A8-2017-0005&language=EN. Accessed 25 Apr 2018
24. Revell, T.: AI takes on top poker players. New Sci. **233**(3109), 8 (2017). https://doi.org/10.1016/s0262-4079(17)30105-7
25. Reynolds, M.: AI learns to reason about the world. New Sci. **234**(3130), 12 (2017). https://doi.org/10.1016/s0262-4079(17)31149-1
26. Reynolds, M.: AI poetry is so bad it could be human. New Sci. **235**(3134), 14 (2017). https://doi.org/10.1016/s0262-4079(17)31357-x
27. Reynolds, M.: Teachers prevent fatal AI mistakes. New Sci. **235**(3142), 14 (2017). https://doi.org/10.1016/s0262-4079(17)31755-4
28. Sartor, G.: Cognitive automata and the law: electronic contracting and the intentionality of software agents. Artif. Intell. Law **17**, 253 (2009). https://doi.org/10.1007/s10506-009-9081-0
29. Sokolov, I., Drozhzhinov, V., Raikov, A., et al.: On artificial intelligence as a strategic tool for the economic development of the country and the improvement of its public administration. Part 2 On prospects for using artificial intelligence in Russia for public administration. Int. J. Open Inf. Technol. **5**(9), 76–101 (2017)
30. Terence, K.L., Hui, R., Sherratt, H.R., Sánchez, D.D.: Major requirements for building Smart Homes in Smart Cities based on Internet of Things technologies. Future Gener. Comput. Syst. **76**, 358–369 (2016). https://doi.org/10.1016/j.future.2016.10.026
31. The Administration's Report on the Future of Artificial Intelligence. The Whitehouse USA (2016). https://obamawhitehouse.archives.gov/blog/2016/10/12/administrations-report-future-artificial-intelligence. Accessed 25 Apr 2018
32. The National Artificial Intelligence Research and Development Strategic Plan. The Whitehouse USA (2016). https://obamawhitehouse.archives.gov/sites/default/files/whitehouse_files/microsites/ostp/NSTC/national_ai_rd_strategic_plan.pdf. Accessed 25 Apr 2018

33. The strategy of information society's development in the Russian Federation. The President of Russian Federation (2017). http://www.kremlin.ru/acts/bank/41919. Accessed 25 Apr 2018

34. Wettig, S., Zehender, E.: A legal analysis of human and electronic agents. Artif. Intell. Law **12**, 111 (2004). https://doi.org/10.1007/s10506-004-0815-8

35. Yaqoob, I., Ahmed, E., Rehman, M.H., Ahmed, A.I.A., et al.: The rise of ransomware and emerging security challenges in the Internet of Things. Comput. Netw. **129**(2), 444–458 (2017). https://doi.org/10.1016/j.comnet.2017.09.003

Internet Regulation: A Text-Based Approach to Media Coverage

Anna Shirokanova[1]([envelope])[iD] and Olga Silyutina[2][iD]

[1] Laboratory for Comparative Social Research,
National Research University Higher School of Economics,
Moscow, Russia
a.shirokanova@hse.ru

[2] National Research University Higher School of Economics,
St. Petersburg, Russia
oyasilyutina@gmail.com

Abstract. Internet regulation in Russia has vigorously expanded in recent years to transform the relatively free communication environment of the 2000s into a heavily regulated one. Our goal was to identify the topic structure of Russian media discourse on Internet regulation and compare it between political and non-political media outlets. We used structural topic modeling on 7,240 texts related to Internet regulation that appeared in the Russian media in 2009–2017. We discovered the non-linear dynamics and the larger share of political media covering Internet regulation over years and compared the topics specific to political and non-political media outlets. We found out that most topics had a different share between political and non-political media and that discourse on law belongs largely to the political media. We also identified four clusters in the topics of media coverage of Internet regulation in Russia related to the law, norms, politics, and business, and the time references of particular topics. In addition, we show the parallel dynamics of the topics on site blockings and political opposition and provide the background on legislation and public opinion on Internet regulation in Russia. Our results demonstrate a rather politicized nature of Internet regulation and its connection to a broader political context in Russia.

Keywords: Internet regulation · Russia · Structural topic modeling

1 Introduction

National Internet regulation and growing politicization of the Internet are a major current trend [19]. In the 2000s the Internet was hailed the 'liberation

A. Shirokanova and O. Silyutina—The authors would like to thank Ilya Musabirov and Stanislav Pozdniakov for their friendly critique and help with obtaining texts. The authors would also like to thank the anonymous referees for valuable comments and suggestions.

© Springer Nature Switzerland AG 2018
D. A. Alexandrov et al. (Eds.): DTGS 2018, CCIS 858, pp. 181–194, 2018.
https://doi.org/10.1007/978-3-030-02843-5_15

technology' [7] enabling the 'Arab Spring' and other protests across the world including Russia [5]. It was widely held that the Internet helped citizens circumvent government-controlled television [19] posing challenge to the states that relied on dominating the political narrative for legitimacy [26]. Soon after, many authoritarian governments went to reassert control online. Growing Internet adoption made the Internet as strategic to them as traditional media. As a result, a more reserved point of view came to life which goes "beyond a binary vision of the Internet as 'a new space of freedom' or 'a new instrument of control"' [20].

In Russia, a distinct 'web culture' [21] grew by the end of the 2000s, a 'parallel public sphere' [11] that was often critical of the government and establishment. At that time the Internet served as a substitute to the public sphere in Russia [20], the 'public counter-sphere' online [13]. This was partly due to the fact that online communication was relatively free as compared to the traditional media [26]. Shortly after the 'Arab Spring', the results of parliamentary and presidential elections in Russia gathered mass protest in the streets. This was the time of fast Internet adoption when over 50% of Russians went online. As was shown later, for the participants of street rallies in 2011–2012, engagement with online media "appeared to completely 'switch them off' from using state media for any news about domestic protests" [26].

Starting from 2012, the previously subtle Internet regulation policy, aiming at reducing the digital divide and employing pro-government bloggers, switched to securitization of the web and 'sovereigntist' cyber policy [19,21]. Obtaining digital sovereignty has been set as a goal in order to defend against the threats from US companies where the Internet is officially treated as a foreign policy tool that can be used against Russia [19]. As a result, Internet regulation has become part of the holistic policy of information security [16,19].

Russia's strict Internet regulation puts it way ahead of many other countries, but it also has a rich landscape of media with many audiences (see [26]) which makes this case interesting for analysis. Internet regulation in Russia started with 'russifying' the web in the late 2000s and continued with introducing the site blacklist in 2012, registering bloggers as official media in 2014, retaining and disclosing upon request all communications in 2016, and banning the anonymizing software in 2017. Even though Internet regulation was largely out of headlines until 2014 (e.g., this year a regular section appeared at the tass.com, the oldest news agency's website), it has already produced substantial media coverage.

The goal of this paper is to present the findings of an ongoing project on the Russian media coverage of Internet regulation. Previously, we focused on countries and country groups in this coverage [25]. In this paper, we scrutinize the topics derived from political and non-political media. Our research questions are as follows: What topics in Internet regulation do political and non-political media speak about in Russia? How often do they appear? Are there groups of these topics? Which topics refer to the past and which to the future?

We hypothesized that media coverage of Internet regulation would be growing over time but that the topics in political and non-political media would differ.

We expected to find more business- and law-related topics in non-political media. Moreover, we assumed a connection between the intensity of coverage of politically motivated topics and the time of Internet-related political events in the country. We used Integrum, the largest media collection in Russia, to obtain a corpus of texts related to Internet regulation and process them with automatic topic modeling algorithms. We identified the topics across the texts, their prevalence in political and non-political editions, traced the dynamics of publication and time references within topics, and grouped the topics into clusters.

1.1 Theoretical Framework

We adopt Van Dijk and Hacker's version of the structuration model as a framework for our research. It is based on the premise of 'continual interplay of politics and media' and on the principle 'politics first and media second' [28] where the political system structures media and then media use structures politics back. The advantage of this perspective is that it overcomes methodological individualism and provides a systematic view of actors involved in the process of Internet regulation. On the one hand, there are structures of a political system; on the other, there is political action. Whatever happens between the political system and individuals is channeled in three modalities, interpretations, facilities, and norms (see Fig. 1.2 in [28]). Moreover, this interaction is 'continually mediated by contagion and discourse in networks' [28]. It is this intermediary discourse that we approach in this paper. We look into two out of three modalities, facilities (power and domination axis) and norms (sanction and legitimation axis), putting aside the 'communication-signification' modality which would require semantic analysis and is out of scope of the paper.

This choice of framework also means that we prioritize political theories over communication theories. We employ the 'networked authoritarianism' [15] perspective explaining the dilemma of Internet development for dictators in the following way. Non-democratic rulers are torn between the drives to develop e-Economy and to stifle online political communication [8]. Recent empirical research demonstrates that nowadays autocracies are just as likely to develop the IT infrastructure and e-participation as democracies, but they put those under control and use instrumentally to consolidate the regime [2,15]. This willingness of authoritarian governments to develop the online infrastructure for business while trying to regulate political communication is our first theoretical point of departure.

Our second theoretical point is that this differentiated strategy of Internet regulation results in traceable differences in agenda-setting [17] between state-controlled and private media, political and non-political outlets.

To sum up, both autocracies and democracies nowadays have high shares of Internet population. In autocracies, there is a specific dilemma of balancing the benefits of economic globalization and e-commerce, and the damage to the regime from free political communication. The structuration framework helps to knit together both political system resources such as legislation and political action such as street rallies via media discourse that is the subject of this analysis.

1.2   Legislation and Public Opinion on Internet Regulation in Russia

Internet regulation started in Russia in the late 2000s with subtle steps in recreating the state on the web and paying bloggers to support the government [21]. This practice was similar to 'astroturfing' in China where paid Internet commentators post cheerleading messages that strategically distract the public from criticism or collective action [12].

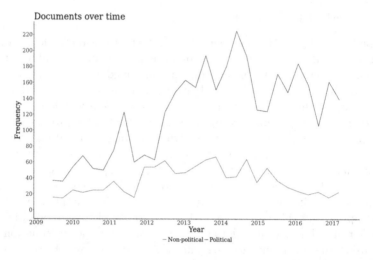

Fig. 1. Frequency of publications in documents from political and non-political media

In 2012, when massive rallies in Russia gathered more than 100,000 middle-class white collars [5] and the Internet penetration rate, having doubled in five years, approached 60% [20], the government adopted legislation that constrained the right to engage in organized public dissent.

The first Internet regulation law was also adopted in 2012 to introduce the legal possibility of Internet filtering and site blockings. In addition, the Federal Service for Supervision of Communications, Roskomnadzor, was launched that has the authority to shut down sites before the court order and maintains a 'unified registry' of blacklist sites. Another law in 2013 enabled the immediate block of any sites disseminating 'calls for riots or other extremist activity' or pirate content. New laws in 2014–2015 changed the status of popular bloggers into mass media ("the bloggers' law") and prescribed data localization of Russian website visitors. Two recent benchmarks are the 'Yarovaya laws' of 2016 that introduced data retention and on-demand access to personal communication of Russians and the ban on the use of software for blockage bypass i.e., online anonymizers, VPNs, and anonymous messengers, in June 2017. Thus, the introduction of Internet regulation in Russia has been really dynamic and has involved new, direct methods of control as compared with earlier practices [6, 21].

According to some reports, the Russian government gains the legitimacy of restrictive regulation from global companies that prefer to cooperate with it [27] but also from the opinion of majority of citizens [1]. The results of opinion polls, however, show not only support for but also ignorance of regulation. To name a few, 63% of Russians supported online censorship in 2012 (Levada Center poll) and 34% supported pre-court site blockings in 2013 (Levada Center). But in 2014, when the 'bloggers law' was passed, two our of three Russians never heard of it (Levada Center). A 2015 report [18] (VCIOM poll) said 35% of Russians were unaware of the website blacklist and 49% supported some Internet censorship but 26% would never justify a shutdown of the Internet in Russia. The month the 'Yarovaya laws' were passed, 62% of Russians reported they never heard of them; 13% supported them. In 2018, 52% preferred a global Internet to a national network (VCIOM poll). With about 70% Internet penetration, public opinion polls largely support further Internet regulation. However, the share of online censorship supporters is substantially higher among non-users [18]. The majority's consent is, thus, not necessarily informed or experience-based.

Small group protests against the Internet laws have been taking place since 2016. In 2017, one to two thousand came into streets against online censorship. In April and May 2018, the demonstrations in support of the 'free Internet' and Telegram, one of the popular messengers with end-to-end encryption, attracted more than 12 thousand participants. These acts of popular dissent demonstrate that public opinion on the Internet regulation may not be as overwhelmingly approving of the regulation as earlier public opinion polls showed.

2 Data and Method

Automated techniques can provide reproducible solutions for politicized topics like Internet regulation, which can be a problem for manually coded texts [10]. By deriving topic-specific words directly from the texts, 'they infer rather than assume' the content [23]. It is up to researchers then to establish the correspondence between topics and the constructs of theoretical interest [10].

In this research, we focused on popular traditional media having large audiences and obtained the data from a centralized archive of news agencies, national and regional media, Integrum. The search inquiry was '(regulat* OR govern*) AND (Internet NOT (Internet-site OR Internet-project*))'. The search spanned from 2009 till July 2017 and returned 7,240 documents. After pre-processing the data by tokenizing and lemmatizing the words, taking out numbers and Latin letters, and deleting stop-words, the final sample decreased to 6,140 documents which were used for analysis. Manually coded metadata included the type of source for each document based on its description: political or non-political. Pre-processing and the analysis were carried out in R.

To answer the research questions, we used structural topic modeling (STM). STM is part of the automatic classification algorithms [4]. It was implemented as a more versatile follow-up to the latent Dirichlet allocation algorithm, LDA [3]. Like LDA, each document in STM appears as a mixture of K topics. However, the

Fig. 2. Distribution of topics coverage over time, by months, 2009–2017

difference between STM and LDA consists in that STM allows topical prevalence to vary with user-specified covariates, which can be both an advantage and a weak point of STM as topics are likely to vary with covariates [22,23]. We also applied the fast greedy algorithm to detect clusters of topics that have higher chances of co-appearing [14].

Despite the wide use of topic modeling, there is no single measure for determining the effective number of topics in the model. It can be estimated with semantic coherence and exclusivity of models with different Ks and with subjective interpretation by researchers, especially for small corpora [29]. Semantic coherence represents the co-occurrence of the most probable words for the topic in each of its document. Exclusivity takes into account the words for a given topic which do not appear frequently in other extracted topics. It helps to balance the value of semantic coherence which can be inflated by frequent words found in each topic.

The fewer topics are chosen for the model, the broader they become [9] and this fact can be really useful for some research purposes. In our research we decided to compare models with 30 and 50 topics. The 50-topic model had better metrics. However, compared to the 30-topic model, substantively important topics such as 'Opposition' or 'Safe Internet League' were lost as they broke down into smaller topics. Given that Internet regulation can be legally supported only by the government, it is more important to see the connection between all opposition forces and governmental politics. Moreover, in mass media documents there is a lot of additional information not directly related to Internet regulation which can be blended with other topics to improve the interpretation of the model, which is why we settled on a 30-topic model.

One of the core features of STM is its ability to analyze relations with topics and covariates. To estimate the effect of each level of metadata we use a linear model with topic-proportion as outcome. We use the p-values for each estimated effect to retain only those topics which have significant relations with covariate's levels [23]. Thus, we got 24 topics which have significant effect from metadata.

To find out the relationship between topics, we conducted correlation analysis and created a network of positively correlated topics. It was further clustered by the fast greedy algorithm which uses maximization of modularity within clusters to effectively divide the non-directed network into groups [14]. In our case, we obtained four distinct clusters one of which consists of two topics and is not connected to the main part of network.

Lastly, we looked at each topic to find out connections between time periods and topics based not only on publication date but also on texts. This helps understand whether Internet regulation is discussed as a prediction for the future or as a process that has already started. We extracted mentionings of years using regular expressions. Then we connected them with our topics counting the number of mentionings of 5-years periods in documents from each topic.

3   Results

3.1   Dynamics and Topics

There is a trend of increasing interest to Internet regulation in Russian mass media till 2013–2014 and then a decrease in the frequency of documents by the end of the observed period (Fig. 1). The fluctuations in the data can be described by parallel events in the field of Internet regulation. The first peak in 2011 may relate to a report on Internet regulation commissioned by the Russian government and to post-election protests. Then there is a period of rapid growth, especially in political media outlets, from 2012 to 2013 when the 'blacklist' of sites and anti-piracy law were introduced. The highest peak to date in 2014 coincides with the 'bloggers' law' and first pre-court site blockings. The 2016 peak went parallel to the discussion and adoption of the 'Yarovaya laws' passed the same year. Thus, the first wave of media coverage has rather stabilized by now, which is especially visible when comparing the dynamics of political and non-political media outlets separately.

Moreover, Fig. 1 shows that there are many more political documents than non-political ones in our dataset, which could indicate the politicization of Internet regulation discourse in the Russian mass media. As mentioned above, the covariate used is the type of mass media which was the source for a particular document. Thus, we can also see that Internet regulation coverage is more popular among political media outlets in Russia.

Figure 2 demonstrates[1] that the earliest discourse related to Internet regulation in 2009 focused on the topic of Data centers. Remarkably, the Opposition topic has never been among the most covered in the media; however, it became popular in the middle of 2012. Site blocking has been the most discussed topic since 2012 and has had two more publication peaks in 2013 and 2017.

Figure 3 shows the co-dynamics of the Site blocking and Opposition topics which went parallel in 2012, 2014, and 2016. Thus, the Site blocking becomes a noisier and more debated topic whenever the Opposition topic activates. As the graph illustrates, the two topics had a common steep rise at the beginning of 2012, at the peak of protests for fair elections and the adoption of the 'single register' of banned sites proposed by the Safe Internet League (see [19,24]).

---

[1] See https://github.com/olgasilyutina/stm_internet_regulation for details.

Documents over time by topics

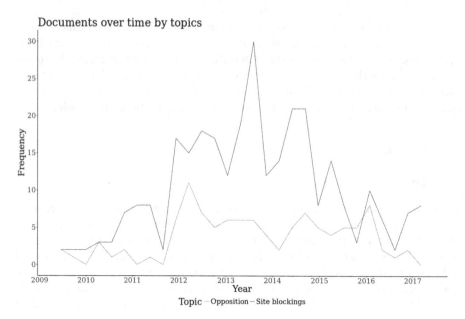

Fig. 3. Co-dynamics of Site blockings and Opposition topics

3.2 Topics and Metadata

We expected to find out more business- and law-related content in non-political media. Figure 4 illustrates all significant effects in the topics between political and non-political media, leaving us with 24 topics that had different shares between the two types of media. Non-political media have a larger share on the topics of Data centers (the largest effect), Online shopping, Education, Intellectual rights and Bitcoin, but also on Site blocking, and Cybersecurity and the US. We can make a conclusion that these topics are specific to non-political mass media sources. At the same time, Ukraine relations, Russian party politics and topics connected with new legislation are more typical for political outlets.

The network in Fig. 5 represents significant positive correlations between topics where the fast greedy algorithm provides us with four clusters. The top left red cluster shows the connection between the IT-related topics which discuss online markets along with Russian IT laws that regulate bitcoin, online shopping and intellectual rights. The green cluster represents the core topics of moral and ideological approach of the Russian government to Internet regulation. There we can see a topic on the Safe Internet League, an organization that unites a lot of high-rank politicians, business people and Internet activists who are aiming to 'eradicate dangerous content' [24]. The blue cluster displays the links between Russian customs and international Internet regulation context, particularly the Internet censorship in China and relations with Ukraine. We can assume then that Internet regulation in Russia is an important factor for foreign policy discourse in the media. The separate fourth cluster is about supervisory bodies like

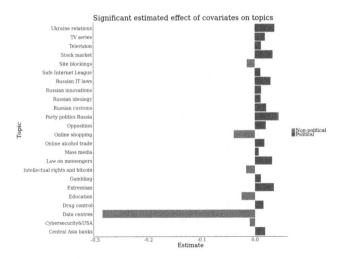

Fig. 4. Differences in topic distribution between political and non-political media

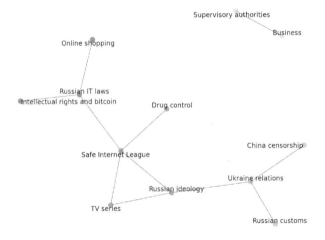

Fig. 5. The correlation network of topics (Color figure online)

Roskomnadzor and business. Internet business in Russia is largely dependent on supervisory authorities, and media discourse illustrates this pattern.

Lastly, Fig. 6 puts together the time-oriented content from each topic. The topics are on the left-hand side and 5-year time periods are on the right; the colors denote topics specific to political and non-political outlets (see Fig. 4). The graph shows that most publications in our corpus refer to 2011–2015, close to the publication date of the documents. In addition, there are more references to years 2006–2010 than to 2016–2020 across the topics. However, some topics refer more frequently to the future. Among them are Party politics in Russia, Online shopping and Site blockings. All topics refer to the years between 2006

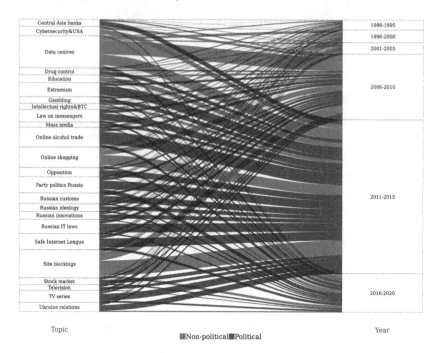

Fig. 6. Reference years mentioned in the texts, by topics

and 2015 most of the times, which confirms that the media mostly write about topics which can be considered breaking news at a particular moment in time or refer to the near past or future. We can also see that the proportion of topics specific to non-political outlets has decreased in 2011–2015 as compared to 2006–2010, which could be attributed partly to the growing variety of topics, partly to the politicization of the Internet regulation discourse.

4 Discussion

In this paper we used STM to identify the topics in Internet regulation coverage and compare them across political and non-political media in Russia. This approach to the coverage of a rather politicized issue helps avoid the problem of pre-selected topics' bias. As a result, we identified the approximate number and content of topics in the Russian media coverage of Internet regulation. The issue has been salient for the country recently due to intense legislation on the Internet which fits the global trend of politicization [19] and even 'balkanization of the Internet' [27] where governments take systematic efforts at regulating online communication as part of national legislation and jurisdiction.

The most obvious findings relate to the dynamics of coverage, which is not linear or constantly growing but rather a wave that fades away after a surge of interest in 2013. This runs counter to the legislation dynamics which has been no less intense, but may reflect the media logic of a new issue appearing on the agenda and then turning into an everyday topic. We tried to match the results of topic modeling and topic coverage with what is known about the Internet legislation in Russia, public opinion of Internet regulation, protests against Internet regulation, and major political events in the country. Even though we take caution in linking media coverage, legislation, and political events [26], we find multiple pieces of evidence that show the common dynamics of major political events and topics on regulation. Moreover, we discovered not only a larger share of coverage in political outlets, but also a larger proportion of political topics in the coverage in recent years, which is another indicator of the politicization of Internet regulation in Russia.

The more counter-intuitive findings relate to the differences in the topic coverage between political and non-political media. Site blockings and cybersecurity and the US, despite their possible relation to politics, turned out to be more specific to non-political outlets. Censorship in China or Internet supervisory bodies in Russia received equal attention from both political and non-political media. However, such topics and the law on messengers or IT laws were more common in political outlets. While we hypothesized that non-political outlets would rather cover business- and law-related issues on Internet regulation, this turned out to be only partly true. Indeed, business topics are either neutral or non-political, while law and legislation belong to the political media.

We also identified the links between specific topics where 12 topics join into four clusters on IT laws, normative core on Internet regulation in Russia, international relations, and business. The first three unite into a single segment. This structure of clusters is somewhat similar to the one we found earlier with another covariate [25], which corroborates such groupings of topics but also reflects more specific communities of topics which could be further investigated.

The contribution of this paper consists in revealing the structure of media discourse on Internet regulation in Russia between political and non-political media outlets. This is important in order to understand how media coverage works in rich media systems under non-democratic regimes. In particular, we found out how much, when, and what the media covered in Internet regulation during almost nine years. So far we have mostly looked into the 'hard facts', the dates and correlations of topics. The deeper dive into this data would entail semantic analysis which could tell the evaluation of the topics covered. However, this is another step of research and another research question.

Our exploration has also revealed a number of questions for future research. Putting major media outlets under state control opens a way for differentiated agenda-setting in covering Internet regulation. Therefore, looking not only at the political or non-political profile of the outlet but also at its ownership is one of the further ways to explain the dynamics of Internet regulation in Russia in the 2010s. We might hypothesize differences between private and state-controlled media not only in the agenda, but also in the semantics surrounding political aspects of Internet regulation (approval or critique of political actors, events, or legislation). Last, the timeline of topic coverage could be matched on a monthly basis with specific law adoption processes and public reaction in order to find out which laws spurred more coverage and activism and at what moment.

5   Conclusion

In this paper, we analyzed the media coverage of Internet regulation in Russia with automated topic modeling. We processed 7,240 texts and explored the scale of the discussion over years and the topics covered by political and non-political media. In this paper we answered the questions on which topics make part of the media discourse on Internet regulation, how they connect to each other and differ across political and non-political outlets, and to what time periods they refer. We found out that there are more texts on Internet regulation coming from political media outlets and that the wave of interest surged in 2012–2013 when first Internet regulation laws were passed. Further legislation in 2014–2017, though more constraining, did not provoke another rise in the number of publications on the topic. We extracted 30 topics according to political/non-political status of the media source using structural topic modeling and analyzed 24 topics having a significant connection to covariate levels (political or non-political). We found out that non-political publishers write more about Internet and its regulation from the perspective of online business, whereas political sources write more about laws and those spheres of Internet which government intends to regulate. Furthermore, we found that most coverage from 2009 to 2017 refers to the dates close to the publication date and only some of them, such as Party politics refer to the period of 2016–2020.

As our next steps, we will look into the temporal patterns of topic coverage, covariance of topics with external variables such as media ownership, and into text sentiments, which would help us distinguish structural divisions in the coverage of common topics on Internet regulation in Russia.

References

1. Asmolov, G.: Welcoming the Dragon: The Role of Public Opinion in Russian Internet Regulation. Internet Policy Observatory (2015). http://repository.upenn.edu/internetpolicyobservatory/8
2. Åström, J., Karlsson, M., Linde, J., Pirannejad, A.: Understanding the rise of e-participation in non-democracies: domestic and international factors. Gov. Inf. Q. **29**(2), 142–150 (2012). https://doi.org/10.1016/j.giq.2011.09.008
3. Blei, D.M.: Probabilistic topic models. Commun. ACM **55**(4), 77–84 (2012). https://doi.org/10.1145/2133806.2133826
4. Blei, D.M., Ng, A.Y., Jordan, M.I.: Latent Dirichlet allocation. J. Mach. Learn. Res. **3**, 993–1022 (2003)
5. Bodrunova, S.S., Litvinenko, A.A.: Four Russias in communication: fragmentation of the Russian public sphere in the 2010s. In: Dobek-Ostrowska, B., Głowacki, M. (eds.) Democracy and Media in Central and Eastern Europe 25 Years On, pp. 63–79. Peter Lang, Frankfurt am Main (2015)

6. Deibert, R., Palfrey, J., Rohozinski, R., Zittrain, J., Haraszti, M.: Access Controlled: The Shaping of Power, Rights, and Rule in Cyberspace. MIT Press, Cambridge (2010)

7. Diamond, L.: Liberation technology. J. Democr. **21**(3), 69–83 (2010). https://doi.org/10.1353/jod.0.0190

8. Göbel, C.: The information dilemma: how ICT strengthen or weaken authoritarian rule. Statsvetenskaplig tidskrift **115**(4), 386–402 (2013)

9. Greene, D., O'Callaghan, D., Cunningham, P.: How many topics? Stability analysis for topic models. In: Calders, T., Esposito, F., Hüllermeier, E., Meo, R. (eds.) ECML PKDD 2014. LNCS, vol. 8724, pp. 498–513. Springer, Heidelberg (2014). https://doi.org/10.1007/978-3-662-44848-9_32

10. Jacobi, C., van Atteveldt, W., Welbers, K.: Quantitative analysis of large amounts of journalistic texts using topic modelling. Digit. J. **4**(1), 89–106 (2016). https://doi.org/10.1080/21670811.2015.1093271

11. Kiriya, I.: The culture of subversion and Russian media landscape. Int. J. Commun. **6**, 446–466 (2012). http://ijoc.org/index.php/ijoc/article/view/1196

12. King, G., Pan, J., Roberts, M.E.: How the Chinese government fabricates social media posts for strategic distraction, not engaged argument. Am. Polit. Sci. Rev. **111**(3), 484–501 (2017). https://doi.org/10.1017/S0003055417000144

13. Koltsova, O., Shcherbak., A.: "LiveJournal Libra!": The political blogosphere and voting preferences in Russia in 2011–2012. New Media Soc. **17**(10), 1715–1732 (2015). https://doi.org/10.1177/1461444814531875

14. Lancichinetti, A., Fortunato, S.: Community detection algorithms: a comparative analysis. Phys. Rev. E **80**(5), 56–117 (2009). https://doi.org/10.1103/PhysRevE.80.056117

15. MacKinnon, R.: China's 'networked authoritarianism'. J. Democr. **22**(2), 32–46 (2011). https://doi.org/10.1353/jod.2011.0033

16. Marechal, N.: Networked authoritarianism and the geopolitics of information: understanding Russian Internet policy. Media Commun. **5**(1), 29–41 (2017). https://doi.org/10.17645/mac.v5i1.808

17. McCombs, M.: Setting the Agenda: Mass Media and Public Opinion. Polity Press, Cambridge (2014)

18. Nisbet, E.C.: Benchmarking Public Demand: Russia's Appetite for Internet Control. Internet Policy Observatory (2015). http://repository.upenn.edu/internetpolicyobservatory/9

19. Nocetti, J.: Contest and conquest: Russia and global internet governance. Int. Aff. **91**(1), 111–130 (2015). https://doi.org/10.1111/1468-2346.12189

20. Nocetti, J.: Russia's 'dictatorship-of-the-law' approach to internet policy. Internet Policy Rev. **4**(4) (2015). https://doi.org/10.14763/2015.4.380

21. Nocetti, J.: 'Digital Kremlin': power and the internet in Russia. Russie. Nei. Visions **59**, 5 (2011). https://www.ifri.org

22. Roberts, M.E., Stewart, B.M., Airoldi, E.M.: A model of text for experimentation in the social sciences. J. Am. Stat. Assoc. **111**(515), 988–1003 (2016). https://doi.org/10.1080/01621459.2016.1141684

23. Roberts, M.E., et al.: Structural topic models for open-ended survey responses. Am. J. Polit. Sci. **58**(4), 1064–1082 (2014). https://doi.org/10.1111/ajps.12103

24. Safe Internet League. http://www.ligainternet.ru/en/

25. Shirokanova, A., Silyutina, O.: Internet regulation media coverage in Russia: topics and countries. In: Proceedings of 10th ACM Conference on Web Science (WebSci 2018), 5 pages. ACM, New York (2018). https://doi.org/10.1145/3201064.3201102

26. Smyth, R., Oates, S.: Mind the gaps: media use and mass action in Russia. Eur. Asia Stud. **67**(2), 285–305 (2015). https://doi.org/10.1080/09668136.2014.1002682
27. Soldatov, A., Borogan, I.: Russia's surveillance state. World Policy J. **30**(3), 23–30 (2013). https://doi.org/10.1177/0740277513506378
28. Van Dijk, J.A.G.M., Hacker, K.M.: Internet and Democrac in the Network Society. Routledge, Oxford (2018)
29. Zhao, W., et al.: A heuristic approach to determine an appropriate number of topics in topic modeling. BMC Bioinform. **16**(Suppl. 13), S8 (2015). https://doi.org/10.1186/1471-2105-16-S13-S8

Comparative Analysis of Cybersecurity Systems in Russia and Armenia: Legal and Political Frameworks

Ruben Elamiryan[1] and Radomir Bolgov[2(✉)]

[1] Russian-Armenian (Slavonic) University, Public Administration
Academy of the RA, Yerevan, Armenia
rub.elamiryan@gmail.com
[2] Saint Petersburg State University, Saint Petersburg, Russia
rbolgov@yandex.ru

Abstract. The paper compares information security policies of two countries, Russia and Armenia. Provided the common historical past, two countries have a close cultural, historical and, partially, language basis. Moreover currently both countries tightly cooperate, particularly, in political, economic, and military fields. As cases for comparison, we choose countries – members to such international regional organizations, as Eurasian Economic Union (EEU) and Collective Security Treaty Organization (CSTO). In accordance with the Index of Democracy, Armenia and Russia are countries in democratic transition. However they have different approaches to information security – more liberal in case of Armenia and more centralized in case of Russia. We use two levels (legal and practical) to analyze cyber strategies, institutions and experience (policies) of two countries. First of all, we provide deep and comprehensive literature review on information security. The latter is performed on the following aspects of international information security: theoretical, legal, activities of international organizations, as well as Russia and Armenia positions on these issues. Second, we analyze key theoretical concepts (information security, information warfare, etc.) and approaches to them in academic and political communities. Third, we reveal basic doctrines and policy papers regulating information security policy in these states. One of the ways to evaluate information policy effectiveness is based on comparison of countries' positions in global rankings (e.g. ITU Global Cybersecurity Index). In addition the research considers official statistics data, experts' surveys, public opinion polls and media publications.

Keywords: Cyber security · Armenia · Russia

1 Introduction

The global information revolution led to multilevel structural transformations as a result of the development of a new technological paradigm. The process of developing of global technological communication networks completely transformed modern society, particularly in Western nations. Qualitatively, the new networked society

© Springer Nature Switzerland AG 2018
D. A. Alexandrov et al. (Eds.): DTGS 2018, CCIS 858, pp. 195–209, 2018.
https://doi.org/10.1007/978-3-030-02843-5_16

rejected a paradigm based on the method of "trial and error", by demonstrating the necessity of implementing a new paradigm based on scientific research. The formation and development of an information society with its new system of values gave birth to new symmetric and asymmetric challenges, both of which can threaten the vital interests of individual people, societies, nations, and states.

In this context, the main objective of the research is to understand in comparison the cybersecurity systems of Armenia and Russia, as well as to develop mechanisms to evolutionarily modernize the Armenia-Russia cooperation in the provision of information security to meet the demands of the current political, social, and economic realities.

This issue became especially urgent provided the increasing tendencies of global uncertainties and the necessity of tighter coordination and collaboration to provide information security for Armenia and Russia in the framework of both their bilateral relations and cooperation in the CSTO. The latter very often also determines the necessity to harmonize legal and political bases to provide multilateral information security.

2   Methodology and Scope of Research

The paper compares cybersecurity policies of two states, Russian and Armenia. The two countries have a common cultural, historical and, partially, language basis, as well as are members of the Collective Security Treaty Organization (CSTO). Given the principles of collective defense and collective security, both countries strive to protect and integrate their "own" cybersecurity systems to provide more systematic and comprehensive security architecture on national, regional and global levels. As cases for comparison, we choose countries, which collaborate strategically on wide range of issues both institutionally and on bilateral basis. Moreover in accordance with the Index of Democracy the two countries are in the process of democratic transition, but have different approaches to information security – more centralized in case of Russia and more liberal in case of Armenia.

We use two levels (legal and practical) to analyze cybersecurity strategies, institutions and experience (policies) of two countries. We analyze the priorities mentioned in cybersecurity strategies as well as terms, goals, and bodies in charge. First of all, we provide deep and comprehensive literature review on information and cybersecurity. The latter is performed on the following aspects of international cybersecurity: theoretical, legal, activities of international organizations, as well as Armenia and Russia positions on this issues. Moreover the literature review is complemented by bibliometric analysis. Second, we analyze key theoretical concepts (information security, information warfare, cybersecurity, critical cyber infrastructure) and approaches to them in academic and political communities. Third, we reveal basic doctrines and policy papers regulating information security policy in these countries. At the same time the study would be incomplete without understanding of implementation of the information security strategies. One of the ways to evaluate information policy effectiveness is based on comparison of countries' positions in global rankings (e.g. ITU Global Cybersecurity Index). In addition the research considers official statistics data, experts' surveys, public opinion polls and media publications.

3   Literature Review

We have found about 2,000 articles on "cyber security" topics in the bibliometric database "Russian Scientific Citation Index", while the publication activity continues to grow. We found more than 500 articles in bibliometric database "Russian Index of Scientific Citation" on the subject of "international information security", and the publication activity continues to grow. The term "international information security" is adopted by the set of the UN Resolutions. To clarify the thematic focus of the articles, the authors analyzed the dynamics of publication activity with breakdown by 2 time periods: 2000–2008 and 2009–2016 years. On average, the number of published articles in the second period is more than 3 times higher than the number of publications prior to 2008. This indicates an increase in the interest of the Russian scientific community in the issue.

Not less importance is paid to research of cybersecurity issues in Armenia. Though there is no specific database of Armenian Index of Scientific Citation, the issue is central due to difficult geopolitical situation, particularly, in the region of South Caucasus. Various Armenian think-tanks implement comprehensive researches on the issues of cybersecurity, specifically, National Defense Research University of the Ministry of Defense of the Republic of Armenia and Noravank Foundation.

Within the framework of this subject it is worth highlighting several areas:

- Theoretical aspects of international information security [1, 2];
- Activities of international organizations, incl. UN in ensuring information security [3];
- Russia's position on this issue and its activities in ensuring information security in the framework of international organizations, including UN [4–6];
- Cybersecurity and Information security of Armenia [7–9].

Much of this studies focus on international legal and institutional aspects of cyber security. Thus, Burton [10] sees the efforts of states to establish legal rules in the field of cyber security through the international organizations and coalitions. J. Harasta reveals the relationship between the national cybersecurity policy and the level of democracy [11].

The security concepts that give priority to ICT have both supporters and opponents in the military-political and expert communities of the states. Among the supporters it is worth noting Max Boot who considers the history of means of warfare in various countries over the past 500 years. Boot concludes that it is necessary to implement the concept of a "revolution in military affairs" in the United States, emphasizing the development of information technology [12]. Colin Gray believes that the introduction of new technologies to ensure national security (in particular, intelligence, command and operational management) transforms the security paradigm [13].

Murden is even more cyber-optimistic [14]. According to him, today we can speak about transformation of the nature of security and war. Here the author implies not so much a "revolution in military affairs", which means the emergence of new means of warfare, but rather a change in the political space that determines the specifics of armed conflicts. Under the impact of globalization and the revolution in military affairs, conflicts between states are replaced by clashes between states and their coalitions against terrorists and extremist groups. As a result, we can see a transformation of not only the means of conducting operations, tactics and strategy, but also the goals of military operations: for terrorist groups and networks, conventional political considerations do not always remain the main ones.

Frederic Kagan supports the opposite point of view. He considers the history of the development of military equipment in the last 50 years and only in the US (not around the world, as Max Boot). Kagan believes that the fascination with "exotic theories" (including the concept of cyber war) leads to underestimating the elements of "real power", i.e. conventional armed forces in the war with conventional weapons [15].

Betz and O'Hanlon support cyber-pessimistic point of view. They believe that ICT should not be exaggerated in the sense that the outcome of the battle is still not in cyberspace but in the real confrontation of forces [16, 17]. The consequences of asymmetric attacks, based on the use of cyber weapons, are unpredictable. Information technology can increase the combat capabilities of military equipment, but it can not replace the ability to make the right conclusions, which are increasingly difficult to do in the increasing volume of information. Also, the development of cyber weapons requires large financial costs and a long time.

As for cyberwar, a number of experts believe that the significance of this problem is exaggerated. Pollitt believes that, despite the vulnerability, while people are involved in the management, cyber attacks are unlikely to have great destructive consequences [18]. Schneier agrees that the threat does not come from the mythical cyber-terrorists but from ordinary criminals who use well-known bugs in software. This is purely technical but not political problem [19]. The problem is not in the unreliability of computer networks, but in the unreliability of staff. Lewis believes that cyber attacks are currently not carried out and in the near future will not bear any threat to critical infrastructure. Unauthorized intervention in the critical infrastructure cyber system can only lead to temporary malfunctions, but not a national catastrophe. For instance, national energy networks have many bypass and reserve control channels, and management organizations use various information technologies. Internet is practically not used in the critical infrastructure [20].

As typical examples of vigorous activity of the military-expert elite to agitate/justify a financing of ICT we consider publications of ex-first deputy of Minister of Defense Lynn [21], as well as General Clark (commander of NATO forces during the operation in Kosovo in 1999) and representative of business P. Levin [22].

The article by Clark and Levin describes an explosion of the Soviet gas pipeline in Siberia in 1982, allegedly due to the US intelligence activities that installed defective chips into the Soviet production chain [22]. However there are no reliable evidences of this point of view.

In secret communications systems of military departments, the use of the Internet is minimized. Although sometimes we can hear another point of view: 90% of military communications are carried out through commercial channels of communication, i.e. private users, banking system and the Ministry of Defense use the same channels of communication. Sources that could confirm or deny this are not available.

Lynn writes that in 2008 a laptop at one of the US military bases in the Middle East was attacked. The virus got into the computer through a flash device and quickly penetrated into military networks. As a result, the information from the laptop moved to foreign intelligence services. According to Lynn, this incident led to "the most large-scale leakage of data from the US military systems", as a result of which foreign intelligence services received information not only about the US, but also about their NATO partners [21]. Also, Lynn writes that the Internet was designed with low barriers for technological innovation, so security was in second place. Now, cyber threats coming from Internet cause the need to spend more money on providing computer security, incl. in military departments. This article roughly coincided with the building of US Cyber Command, whose head Keith Alexander is directly subordinated to Lynn.

4   The Concept of Cybersecurity

The terms "cyber security" and "cyber defense" are multifaceted, leading to differing interpretations of each. For instance, the UK National Cyber Security Strategy for 2016-2021 states that cyber security "refers to the protection of information systems (hardware, software and associated infrastructure), the data on them, and the services they provide, from unauthorized access, harm or misuse. This includes harm caused intentionally by the operator of the system, or accidentally, as a result of failing to follow security procedures" [23].

The Austrian Security Strategy defines cyber defence as "all measures to defend cyber space with military and appropriate means for achieving military-strategic goals. Cyber defence is an integrated system, comprising the implementation of all measures relating to ICT (Information Communication technologies) and information security, the capabilities of milCERT (Military Computer Emergency Readiness Team) and CNO (Computer Network Operations) as well as the support of the physical capabilities of the army" [24]. At the same time, France's Strategy on Information Systems and Defence views cyber defence as "the set of all technical and non-technical measures allowing a State to defend in cyberspace information systems that it considers to be critical" [25].

Thus, we see a diversified perception of cyber security. Some perceptions concentrate solely on the military dimension of the issue, while others include a systems approach with both civil and military dimensions.

Based on the above, the authors have developed the following definition of cyber security:

Cyber security is set of technical and non-technical (policies, security arrangements, actions, guidelines, risk management) measures allowing to provide social, ethnic and cultural evolutionary modernization of the critical cyber infrastructure, as well as protection of vital interests of human, society and state.

It is worth mentioning that both Russia and Armenia use comprehensive approach to information security. This means that none of the strategic documents in these countries use "cybersecurity" term, but include information-technical and information-psychological issues in one system.

5 Legal and Policy Framework of Cybersecurity in Russian Federation

Currently, Russia has more than 40 federal laws in the field of information, more than 80 presidential acts, and about 200 acts of the government of the Russian Federation. However, Russia does not yet have a separate information warfare strategy in the form of a policy paper. One of the key papers in this field is the Doctrine of Information Security, the first version of which was adopted in 2000. The new version was adopted in December 2016.

The adoption of this doctrine was preceded by a series of events throughout the 1990 s. Until the 2000's in Russia there was practically no clear government attitude to the problem of information security. Unlike the U.S. approach, in the Russian Doctrine, the provision of information security for individual, group and public consciousness is in the forefront. Today, a set of agencies are engaged in the development of the national idea of information warfare, particularly, Ministry of Defense, Federal Security Service and Department "K" of Interior Ministry, which is investigating crimes in high-tech field of information technology.

Two stages prior to the adoption of Doctrine of Information Security can be identified:

(1) 1991–1996: formation of the prerequisites and the legal framework. During this period, the Federal Law "On information, informatization and information protection" [18] and a number of other laws were adopted. So it is the accumulation of the positive experience of cooperation with the Russian participation in the international arena, associated with the acquisition of a new identity participant in international relations and media interest in the information domain. This period is characterized by discord in the role and place of Russia estimates in the information space, noticeable in the statements of different political parties, institutions and interest groups. The idealistic view on Russia's long term inclusion into the global information space was dominating. Copying of western experience in the field of information policy took place. A peak event was the presidential election in 1996 with the war of compromising materials in the information domain, and after which increasingly began to talk about the threats to the constitutional order and the dangers in the mental realm (which subsequently included into the Doctrine). At the end of the period a number of key political persons responsible for information security were replaced. In the same period, Russian troops defeated in information warfare in Chechnya.

(2) 1996–2000: formation of agencies to ensure information security. During this period, interdepartmental commission for information security was formed as part of the Security Council with the participation of Ministry of Internal Affairs, Federal Security Service, and others. Through the activities of these agencies the draft Doctrine of Information Security was prepared in 1997. However the power vacuum and the intensification of the contradictions within the ruling elites did not allow accepting the Doctrine. The financial and economic crisis in 1998 also delayed the adoption of the Doctrine.

Finally, in 2000, the Doctrine was approved. It is a set of official views on the goals, objectives, principles and main directions of ensuring information security of the Russian Federation. It serves as a basis for the formation of government policy in the realm of national information security, preparation of proposals to improve the legal, methodological, technical and organizational sides of Russian information security, as well as the development of targeted programs to ensure information security.

The information security is considered as the security of national interests in the information sphere, determined by a combination of balanced interests of the individual, society and government.

The doctrine spelled out the threats, sources of threats to the interests, methods of maintenance, as well as international cooperation in the field of information security. It allocated 4 types of threats: (1) threats to constitutional order and human rights in the information sphere, (2) threats to information security policy of the government, (3) threats to development of the domestic IT industry and (4) threats to security of information systems and networks.

However since 2000 there are many changes. Appearance of Web 2.0 and social media dramatically changed a national security that was demonstrated by the protests in the Arab countries in 2011 (so-called "Twitter revolutions"). In addition, the appearance of such new phenomena as smart phones, Internet of Things, Smart City, crypto currency and blockchain technology, which are also forced to rethink cybersecurity. Sanctions against Russia led to a policy of "localization of IT industry". Now the danger of cyber attacks for critical information infrastructure is being increasingly discussed by many experts. There are new policy papers related to the development of information technologies in Russia. The new version of the Doctrine of Information Security adopted in 2016 was an attempt to better reflect the changes that have occurred over the 16 years. The new doctrine paid greater attention to the use of computer technology in order to influence the Russian critical infrastructure. In addition, there is a component associated with the risks of using social media to influence public opinion. We are talking about the risks of not only extremist and criminal content, but in general any content that represents a threat to political and social stability.

As for the information warfare, this term was mentioned 2 times in the Doctrine of 2000 [26]. The Doctrine in 2016 does not contain mentioning of the term [27].

Russia's intention to develop a code of conduct in the field of international information security under the auspices of the UN is reflected in the Russian Foreign Policy Concept (Concept of Russia's foreign policy…, 2016). In addition, policy paper "Fundamentals of the Russian Federation's state policy in the field of international information security for the period up to 2020" as one of the directions to counter threats in information sphere states "the promotion of preparation and adoption of the UN international regulations governing the application of the principles and norms of international humanitarian law in the field of ICT usage" [28].

Russian policy papers almost do not contain the terms "cyberwar" or "cybersecurity". The preferred term is "information security" which is broader and includes cyber aspects. It is worth noting that we can find a term "cybersecurity", not "information security", in laws and policy papers of some post-Soviet countries (in particular Moldova) wishing to join the EU and NATO. Hypothetically, the terms differ from each other depending on the policy of the country.

6   International Aspects of Russian Information Security Policy

Russia has consistently emphasizes the legal regulation of cybersecurity issues at the national level, especially in recent years, if we look at the number of adopted policy papers. It adheres to the same approach at the international level: cyber security issues need to be regulated, as soon as possible and as detailed as possible. Russia has adhered to this approach for 15 years, offering its projects within the UN (in particular, the proposal to establish a special international court for cybercrimes). Russia was supported by China, India and Brazil. However, this approach counter to the position of the US, EU and Japan, which believed that cybersecurity issues need not be "over-regulated" in the prejudice of the freedoms of citizens and business. They proceeded from the priority of developing information security measures with regard to terrorist and criminal threats. At the same time, the threat of creating information weapons and the emergence of information warfare was viewed more as a theoretical one. Accordingly, the disarmament aspect of the problem of international information security also came to naught. Further discussion of this problem was proposed to be divided into regional and thematic forums (EU, G7, etc.). The representatives of this approach offer to move the discussion within the UN from military-political dimension to legal and economic ones. They believe that the issue of international legal regulation of the military and political aspects of information security has not yet been relevant. It seems necessary to first accumulate sufficient practical experience in regulating such problems [1].

These approaches were manifested while the discussion on Okinawa Charter of Global Information Society [29]. During the 53rd session of the UN General Assembly, Russia put forward a draft resolution on "Developments in the field of information and telecommunications in the context of international security", adopted by consensus in 1998 (UN General Assembly Resolution A/RES/53/70..., 1998). Another success, but a later one, is the UN General Assembly Resolution "Establishing a global culture of cybersecurity and assessing national efforts to protect critical information infrastructure" [30].

Some convergence of positions on these issues emerged at Munich Security Conference in February 2011, where most politicians and experts spoke in favor of the need for international legal regulation of cyberspace. Although no specific binding decisions were taken, a joint Russian-American report entitled "Working Towards Rules for Governing Cyber Conflict: Rendering the Geneva and Hague Conventions in Cyberspace" was prepared. The report points out the following problematic issues, for which the United States and Russia still do not have a common position, but on which the parties undertake to agree: is it possible to legislatively and technically "isolate" protected infrastructure from the "cloud" of unprotected objects in cyberspace, like Civil facilities are protected by international agreements during the war. Also, the parties must decide whether cyber weapons (viruses, worms, etc.) are similar to weapons banned by the Geneva Protocol (for example, poisonous gases). The conference also agreed to develop an international convention on cyberwar and establish an international tribunal on crimes in cyberspace. Within these structures, the parties will have to resolve these issues [31]. Russia's failure to conduct the initiatives on cybersecurity through the UN (since 1998) spurred it to include these issues on the agenda of the Shanghai Cooperation Organization (SCO). China and Kazakhstan since 2011 also see this organization as a tool for cyberspace monitoring. During the Russian presidency in SCO in 2014, information security was one of the priorities of the agenda that Russia defined in this organization. Among the main projects and initiatives on cyber security within the framework of the SCO it is worth mentioning:

- Strengthening of government control over the Internet as a consequence of protests in Arab countries.
- Building the cyber police (in 2011, this initiative was not implemented).
- Strengthening the cooperation on Internet security.
- Fighting the electronic financing of terrorism.
- Draft Code of Conduct in the field of international information security (in the letter of the SCO to the UN on September 12, 2011). Another format for promoting Russia's interests in cybersecurity is BRICS. Within the framework of this informal organization, the fight against cyber threats is called one of the four spheres of perspective cooperation. The ideas of the creation of the BRICS cyber threat center, as well as the "hot line" for informing and warning about cyber incidents are discussed.

7 Cybersecurity of the Republic of Armenia

There are several conceptual documents in the RA which can help in understanding the country's approach to cyber security: The Military Doctrine of the Republic of Armenia, National Security Strategy of the Republic of Armenia, Strategic Defence Review, and the Public Information Concept of the Armenian Ministry of Defence.

With regard to the cyber component of these documents, it should be noted that none of the above mentioned strategic documents contain information on cyber issues. These strategic documents do not bring clarity to the notion of critical cyber infrastructure either.

At the same time, for instance, the military doctrine of the RA sets official views with regard to, specifically, the military-technical dimension of military security of the RA. Moreover, the technical and infrastructural components, as well as the information systems, are viewed separately as components of military security.

Simultaneously, the research of the National Security Strategy of the Republic of Armenia concludes that cyber security is considered an instrument for effective functioning of information-psychological component of information warfare. For instance, it states, "Therefore, the Republic of Armenia aspires to… integrate into the international information area, to ensure professional promotion of Armenia and the Armenians, and to counter disinformation and propaganda" [32].

In this context, two other conceptual documents bring more clarification into Armenia's cyber policy: the Concept of Information Security of the Republic of Armenia and the Comprehensive Program of Measures to Provide Information Security of the Republic of Armenia, the latter of which is hereafter referred to simply as the "Concept".

The Concept discusses cyber issues twice, but only in the context of cyber-crime issues. At the same time it emphasizes five main fields of information security:

1. Protection of constitutional rights for humans and citizens to receive and use information, to provide spiritual development of the country, protection and development of social moral values, humanistic values, cultural and academic potential.
2. Information support to state politics to provide objective information to Armenian society and to the international community.
3. Development of modern information technologies to cover domestic demand and import to international markets.
4. Inclusion of the RA in international information space.
5. Protection of information resources from unsanctioned access, protection of information, communication, and telecommunication systems.

Thus, we see that cyber security issues are viewed in Armenia as a part of larger information security system. However, the realities of modern war, as well as international experience, necessitate separating and analyzing cyber security as an integral albeit unique component of a security system.

With this in mind, it is first necessary to discuss and to explore the critical cyber infrastructure of the RA, as well as to define the main threats. This will help develop an understanding of the cyber security system of the RA, as a precondition to developing Armenia-Russia relations.

Dave Clemente states that: "Critical infrastructure (CI) is generally understood to include the particularly sensitive elements of a larger ecosystem, encompassing the public and private sectors and society at large. This goes beyond physical infrastructure to include data – which can be considered a form of logical infrastructure or "critical information infrastructure" [33].

At the same time Swiss researcher Myriam Dunn Cavelty describes it in the following way: "[it] can be described as the part of the global or national information infrastructure that is essential for the continuity of critical infrastructure services. There is a physical component to it, consisting of high-speed, interactive, narrow-band, and broadband networks; satellite, terrestrial, and wireless communication systems; and the computers, televisions, telephones, radios, and other products that people employ to access the infrastructure" [34].

Based on these approaches, the definitions presented in the second part of this research, the reality of the RA and based on international experience the authors think that the RA cyber security infrastructure consists of the following components:

Armenia – Armenian Diaspora network, Government institutions, Management of natural resources (especially gold, copper, and molybdenum), Energy infrastructure (power generation and distribution infrastructure — specifically, the Metsamor Nuclear Power Plant), Water management (including water treatment and waste management waters), Education system as a precondition for human-capital resource management, Financial and banking systems, Telecommunications, Agriculture, Transport, Food industry, Health.

At the same time critical cyber infrastructure includes:

- Military and military-industrial fields
- State-society-private communication
- International cooperation.

A close examination of this system of critical cyber infrastructure reveals the most perilous symmetric and asymmetric threats and challenges to cyber security of Armenia:

- National level: This includes threats to low level cyber infrastructure, lack of high-quality cyber security specialists, brain-drain, and limited digital literacy of the population. Particular threats come from social media and social networks. Another serious threat is the limited level of democratic development. In this regard, Armenian scientist Margaryan [35] thinks that establishing the principles of 'good governance', run by strategic leaders, can become an effective measure to modernize the cyber security system in the region of the South Caucasus, not only on an information-technology level, but also to increase the responsibility of political leaders and maximize improvement of cyber security in the RA. The RA-Russia partnership should also include this component of cooperation and institutional development in the area of cyber security.
- Regional level: Being part of the South Caucasus and the Greater Middle East, Armenia faces a wide range of regional threats, particularly in cyber space. These issues deeply affect "human security", which is a comprehensive set of threats directed against personal cybersecurity, as well as to control human feelings, emotions psychological condition and ability to objectively percept the physical and virtual realities [9]. A large volume of information appears daily in conventional and social media and is aimed at influencing human perceptions in different countries. The countries of both South Caucasus and the Greater Middle East region strive to foster political stability and sustainable development. However, in our view, neither success nor failure in cyber operations can provide long-lasting sustainable development.

Armenia-Russia cooperation in cyberspace can support the transformation of state-centric cyber security architecture in the region to a human-centric system, making it more personal and cooperation-focused.

- Global level: Globalization and development of a networked society raises the issues of global cyber security due to the following:

- Vulnerability of the global cyber infrastructure, as a consequence of all the many actors involved in this process
- The threat of communication manipulation
- Underrepresentation in global cyber space
- Crisis of multiculturalism
- Dichotomy of traditional and modern values
- Threats to sovereignty

- Atomization of society, when a person only formally feels itself as a member of that society/state based on its current needs.
- International crime and terrorism, which are largely presented in cyber space.

All these issues should be included in the basis of the Armenia-Russia cooperation to transform national, regional, and global cyber security architecture, making them more peace-oriented and cooperative.

To conclude this part it is worth in comparison providing cybersecurity indexes for Armenia and Russia, as well as other CSTO member-states [36] (Table 1):

Table 1. CSTO cybersecurity indexes

Country Index/ Global ranking	Armenia	Belarus	Kazakhstan	Kirgizstan	Russia	Tajikistan	CSTO Avg.
2015	0.176/23	0.176/23	0.176/23	0.118/25	0.5/12	0.147/24	**0.215**
2017	0.196/111	0.592/39	0.352/83	0.270/97	0.788/10	0.292/91	**0.415**

8   Conclusions

Thus, we see that Russia and Armenia have rather different cyber strategies, objectives and capabilities to provide cybersecurity, which is normal given the geopolitical, political, economic and other differences between two countries. At the same time we see large room for cooperation on local, regional and global levels of international relations to promote common interests in cyberspace.

After the military operation in August 2008 in South Ossetia and Georgia we can see the Russia's Defense Ministry's intentions to create informational troops, whose functions should include all aspects of information warfare: from the psychological operations and propaganda (including the Internet) to security of computer networks and cyber attacks on the enemy's information systems. It should be noted that formation of a special kind of troops seems to be inappropriate for propaganda. It is worth to leave this for security services and business, if they interact intelligently. As A. Smirnov and P. Zhitnyuk believe, the technical aspects of cyber security are under monopoly of the Federal Security Service (FSB in Russian), since all structures are obliged to use means of information protection, certified by the FSB [37]. At the same time it would be advisable to create a joined regulatory authority in this field on the basis of representation of various departments. It is an interesting to look at Chinese experience, where the government interacts with business more actively than in Russia.

As for the discussion of the prospects for the aforementioned Cyber Command in Russia, so we conclude that the establishment of this agency would face not only be the objective difficulties (lack of funding, etc.). The cyber command was planned to be formed according to the American model, but it has not yet been created. The troops of information operations were established in 2014, but their formation was forced and not always rationalized. Initially it was planned to complete their formation by 2017. According to media publications, the formation of the troops was finally completed in February 2017.

When it comes to Armenia, the analysis of the above documents and normative acts allows to claim that:

Cyber space in Armenia is rather liberal. The principle is "allowed everything that is not prohibited", when prohibited are direct and clear criminal acts. For instance, the history of internet in Armenia could hardly remember a single case, when government blocked social media during anti-government demonstrations.

Similar to Russian approach, the Armenian side use wider concept of information security without specifying the concept of "cybersecurity". However it refers to the issue in different forms.

Armenia does not have any centralized body to coordinate cybersecurity or information security issues. However it is a question of further research, if this approach is negative or positive provided the development of networked forms of governance.

Despite the rather low level of Armenia in cybersecurity index, the Armenian related authorities rather effectively provide cybersecurity in the country, especially provided very high level of internet spread.

Armenia is open and develops multilevel cooperation with wide range of regional and global international organizations to better provide cybersecurity.

As for the future work, it is worth to elaborate a more comprehensive framework for cooperation between Russia and Armenia in cybersecurity given the membership of both countries in the CSTO, as well as collaboration, specifically, in financial and nuclear sectors. The sides also can work together to develop more unified and coherent international legislation in the sphere of regulation of cyberspace.

References

1. Fedorov, A.V., Tsygichko, V.N. (ed.): Informacionnye vyzovy nacional'noj i mezhdunarodnoj bezopasnosti (Information Challenges to national and international security); PIR-Center, Moscow (2001)
2. Bolgov, R., Filatova, O., Tarnavsky, A.: Analysis of public discourse about Donbas conflict in Russian social media. In: Proceedings of the 11th International Conference on Cyber Warfare and Security, ICCWS 2016, pp. 37–46 (2016)
3. Bolgov, R., Filatova, O., Yag'ya, V.: The united nations and international aspects of russian information security. In: Proceedings of the 13th International Conference on Cyber Warfare and Security, ICCWS 2018, pp. 31–38 (2018)
4. Demidov, O.V.: Obespechenie mezhdunarodnoj informacionnoj bezopasnosti i rossijskie nacional'nye interesy (Ensuring international information security and national interests of Russia). Secur. Index 1(104), 129–168 (2013)
5. Zinovieva, E.S.: Analiz vneshnepoliticheskih iniciativ RF v oblasti mezhdunarodnoj informacionnoj bezopasnosti (Analysis of Russian foreign policy initiatives in the field of international information security). Vestnik MGIMO-Universiteta (Bulletin of the MGIMO-University), 6(39), 47–52 (2014)
6. Shirin, S.S.: Rossijskie iniciativy po voprosam upravleniya Internetom (Russian initiatives on Internet governance). Vestnik MGIMO Universiteta 6(39), 73–81 (2014)

7. Kotanjian, H.: Complementarity in developing the national cybersecurity strategy of the republic of armenia: relevance of a strategic forum on cooperation in cyberspace. http://psaa.am/en/activities/publications/hayk-kotanjian/195-hayk-kotanjian-complementarity-in-developing-the-national-cybersecurity-strategy-of-the-republic-of-armenia-relevance-of-a-strategic-forum-on-cooperation-in-cyberspace-arm. Accessed 22 Feb 2018

8. Samvel Martirosyan, Hayastani tekhekatvakan anvtangutyuny ev kritikakan entakarutsvacqnery (2017). http://noravank.am/upload/pdf/Samvel_Martirosyan_21_DAR_03_2017.pdf. Accessed 22 Feb 2018

9. Elamiryan, R.G.: Human security in context of globalization: information security aspect. In: Proceedings of International Scientific Conference on The Problems of National Security in terms of Globalization and Integration Processes (interdisciplinary aspects), pp. 173–179 (2015)

10. Burton, J.: NATO's cyber defence: strategic challenges and institutional adaptation. Def. Stud. 15(4), 297–318 (2015). https://doi.org/10.1080/14702436.2015.1108108

11. Kessler, O., Werner, W.: Expertise, uncertainty, and international law: a study of the tallinn manual on cyberwarfare. Leiden J. Int. Law 26, 793–810 (2013). https://doi.org/10.1017/s0922156513000411

12. Boot, M.: War Made: Technology, Warfare and the Course of History, 1500 to Today. Gotham Books (2006). https://doi.org/10.5860/choice.45-0410

13. Gray, C.S.: How Has War Changed Since the End of the Cold War? Parameters, pp. 14–26. Spring (2005)

14. Murden, S.W.: The Problem of Force: Grapping with the Global Battlefield. Lynne Rienner Publishers, Boulder (2009). https://doi.org/10.1111/j.1949-3606.2010.00021.x

15. Kagan, F.: Finding the Target: The Transformation of American Military Policy. Encounter Books (2006). https://doi.org/10.14746/ps.2011.1.22

16. O'Hanlon, M.: Technological Change and the Future of Warfare. Brookings Institution Press, Washington (2000). https://doi.org/10.2307/20049760

17. Betz, D.: The RMA and 'Military Operations Other Than War': A Swift Sword that Cuts Both Ways. Taylor & Francis (1999)

18. Denning, D.: Activism, hacktivism, and cyberterrorism: the internet as a tool for influencing foreign policy. In: Networks and Netwars: The Future of Terror, Crime, and Militancy. Santa Monica, RAND, pp. 282–283 (2001)

19. Schneier, B.: Cyberwar. Crypto-Gram Newsletter, January 15 2005. http://www.schneier.com/crypto-gram-0501.html#10

20. Lewis, J.: Assessing the Risks of Cyber Terrorism, Cyber War and Other Cyber Threats. Center for Strategic and International Studies, Washington, DC (2002). http://csis.org/files/media/csis/pubs/021101_risks_of_cyberterror.pdf

21. Lynn, W.: Defending a New Domain. Foreign Aff. 89, 5 (2010)

22. Clark, W., Levin, P.: Securing the information highway. Foreign Aff. (2009). https://www.foreignaffairs.com/articles/united-states/2009-11-01/securing-information-highway

23. National Cyber Security Strategy 2016–2021, p. 15 (2016). https://www.gov.uk/government/uploads/system/uploads/attachment_data/file/567242/national_cyber_security_strategy_2016.pdf. Accessed 9 Feb 2018

24. Austrian Security Strategy: Security in a new decade - Shpaing security (2013). http://archiv.bundeskanzleramt.at/DocView.axd?CobId=52251. Accessed 9 Feb 2018

25. Information Systems and Defence – France's Strategy, p. 21 (2011). http://www.ssi.gouv.fr/uploads/IMG/pdf/2011-02-15_Information_system_defence_and_security_-_France_s_strategy.pdf. Accessed 9 Feb 2018

26. Doktrina informacionnoj bezopasnosti RF (Doctrine of Information Security of the Russian Federation) (2000). Razvitie informacionnogo obshchestva v Rossii. Tom 2. Koncepcii i programmy: Sb. dokumentov i materialov (Development of an information society in Russia. Volume 2. Concepts and Applications: Coll. documents and materials). St. Petersburg (2001)

27. Doktrina informacionnoj bezopasnosti RF (Doctrine of Information Security of the Russian Federation) (approved by. The President of the Russian Federation 05/12/2016 number 646). Rossijskaya gazeta (Rossiyskaya newspaper), 12 June 2016

28. Osnovy gosudarstvennoj politiki Rossijskoj Federacii v oblasti mezhdunarodnoj informacionnoj bezopasnosti na period do 2020 goda (Fundamentals of the Russian Federation's state policy in the field of international information security for the period up to 2020) (2013). Approved by the President of the Russian Federation, 24/7/2013, Pr-1753

29. Charter of Global Information Society (2000) http://www.mofa.go.jp/policy/economy/summit/2000/documents/charter.html. Accessed 22 Feb 2018

30. UN General Assembly Resolution A/RES/64/211: Creating a global culture of cybersecurity and the assessment of national efforts to protect critical information infrastructures (2010). http://www.un.org/ru/documents/ods.asp?m=A/RES/64/211. Accessed 22 Feb 2018

31. Working Towards Rules for Governing Cyber Conflict. Rendering the Geneva and Hague Conventions in Cyberspace. Advanced Edition Prepared by Russia-U.S. Bilateral on Critical Infrastructure Protection for the 2011 Munich Security Conference (2011). NY

32. National Security Strategy of the Republic of Armenia (2007). http://www.mil.am/media/2015/07/828.pdf. Accessed 9 Feb 2018

33. Clemente, D.: Cyber Security and Global Interdependence: What Is Critical? The Royal Institute of International Affairs – Chatham House, p. 1 (2013). http://www.worldaffairsjournal.org/content/cyber-security-and-global-interdependence-what-critical. Accessed 9 Feb 2018

34. Cavelty, M.D.: Cybersecurity in Switzerland, pp. 2–3. Springer, Heidelberg (2014). https://www.academia.edu/8979637/Cybersecurity_in_Switzerland. Accessed 22 Feb 2018

35. Margaryan, M.: «Good governance» in the context of information security of the Republic of Armenia. In: Proceeding of International Conference on Innovation and Development, Kiev, Ukraine, pp. 58–63 (2013)

36. Global Cybersecurity Index & Cyberwellness Profiles (2015). http://www.itu.int/dms_pub/itu-d/opb/str/D-STR-SECU-2015-PDF-E.pdf. Global Cybersecurity Index (GCI) (2017). https://www.itu.int/dms_pub/itu-d/opb/str/D-STR-GCI.01-2017-PDF-E.pdf. Accessed 22 Feb 2018

37. Smirnov, A., Zhitnyuk, P.: Kiberugrozy realnyie i vydumannyie (Cyber threats, real and imaginary). Russ. Glob. Aff. **2**, 186–196 (2010)

Assessment of Contemporary State and Ways of Development of Information-Legal Culture of Youth

Alexander Fedosov[✉]

Russian State Social University, Moscow, Russia
alex_fedosov@mail.ru

Abstract. The article is devoted to the analysis of results of levels of information-legal culture of modern youth. The research has been conducted among young Moscow residents during 2017 and is devoted to the issue of development of legal culture of school children and copyright compliance in respect of intellectual property items.

The survey was conducted by questioning. The questions were drawn up on the basis of expert polls of specialists in the sphere of copyright protection. The results of social research allowed to estimate the level of information-legal culture of youth in terms of copyright compliance for intellectual property.

Also the article suggests the ways of advancement of level of information-legal culture of pupils on the basis of development of upbringing and education methods, particularly within specialized training courses for secondary school.

For the courses the learning content is worked out, the ways of evaluation of level of information and legal culture of pupils are selected, the main methodical principals while executing the courses are formulated, and also the requirements for the level of grasping of learning content are set.

Keywords: Information-legal culture · Intellectual property
Legal culture of pupils

1 Introduction

Rapid development of information and communication technologies, which has global character, has led to the changes of social stereotypes of information transfer. The society, the main way of communication of which was language and writing, came to the creation of coding and transmitting devices. They extended the opportunities of social communication. Information and communication networks became an integral part of this phenomenon. The data in the global information networks has common characteristic, which is electronic form. It makes possible to copy, reproduce and spread information easily and with minimum expense. Intellectual property, introduced in electronic form, becomes the main type of property in post-industrial and information society and serves as the most important information source of the society, the principle source of sociocultural evolution [1].

Today the problem of copyright protection in the Russian Federation is actually important more than ever. It is connected not so much with definite gaps and omissions

© Springer Nature Switzerland AG 2018
D. A. Alexandrov et al. (Eds.): DTGS 2018, CCIS 858, pp. 210–223, 2018.
https://doi.org/10.1007/978-3-030-02843-5_17

in Russian legislation as mainly with low level of legal culture in the society in general. It's obvious that the formation of legal culture firstly of youth is primary target, facing the system of education.

Let's define the up-to-date concept of intellectual property, briefly examine the modern state of the problem of intellectual property protection in Russia and the state of legal culture of youth.

The notion "intellectual property" comprises the property, which becomes a result of intellectual activity, rights, related to the literary writings, works of art, scientific works, performing acting, recordings, radio and television, inventions, discoveries, trademarks, company names, new industrial product samples.

The intellectual property protection is a system of government measures, providing realization of person's exclusive right to own, dispose and use the intellectual object. The main function of intellectual property protection is to provide the author with an opportunity to decide how the intellectual object can be used – for practical and economic, cultural and aesthetic, hedonistic and other purposes. In this sense the protection is closely connected with the person's protection of intellectual object.

The term "intellectual property" for the first time was introduced in 1967 by the Convention Establishing the World Intellectual Property Organization (WIPO) [2]. In the legislation of the Russian Federation there are hundreds, if not thousands of regulatory legal acts of different levels: Federal laws, presidential decrees and orders, governmental decrees and orders, implementing guidance and other statutes of federal executive authorities, guiding interpretations of Supreme Court of the Russian Federation, Supreme Arbitration Court of the Russian Federation, statutory acts of constituents of the Russian Federation. The legal framework of the Russian Federation contains also international legal acts, recognized validly on the territory of Russia. The social orientation of all these acts is to take into account mutual right holders, society and state's interest in the results of intellectual activity as fully as possible. That determines the character of development of all legal framework of the Russian Federation.

For the first time the problem of intellectual property protection was introduced in the concept of post-industrial society, which stated the expansion of intellectual products in the society due to the beginning of the IT era of all spheres of social life. D. Bell and A. Toffler actualized the question about the value of information in the modern world. M. Castells introduced the term "information capitalism" and developed an idea of the role of information traffics in the organization of "innovative environment" of network society, and stated that informational way of development represents the new way of wealth creation [3–7]. H. Schiller proved the thesis that information should transform into goods, in other words the access to it more often would be possible only on commercial terms [8].

The growth of the value of intellectual products in the system of relations of a new society was also noticed by economic science, which started theoretical development of this problem in the 1990s. To a certain extent the short of economic research of intellectual property is considering the objects of intellectual property identical to material products. Sometimes it leads to deprivation of particularity of the results of intellectual activity as elements of economic relations of property. Lack of attention to the questions, connected with the control of intellectual property, causes essential economic damage to the society. Defense of rights to intellectual objects, which belong to certain states because of the fact that they don't possess exterritoriality in the past decade assumed great importance as far as it's obvious that military industry, science absorbing industry, international division of labor, national culture work for benefits to government only when there is powerful system of protection of results of spiritual activity.

Today in Russia distributed shadow market of intellectual property objects was formed. At the same time the lion's share of contempts is accounted for by objects of copyright: literary, audiovisual works (music, songs, video clips and films), software and databases.

According to the research results under the order of Business Software Alliance (BSA), the level of piracy in the sphere of software in 2016 was 39% world average. In absolute indicators it meant damage about US$ 48 billion for the software industry. In Russia there is still one of the highest level of piracy (64%, 2015), a Commercial value of unlicensed software is US$ 1,34 billion [9]. We can note that BSA and other organizations often make efforts to stop growth of piracy, including that they realize teaching programs and launch political initiatives, which are directed to reinforcement of copyright law and their practical implementation. All that is an effective obstacle for piracy.

The analysis of science literature showed that there are the following premises of poor development of intellectual property in Russia:

- insufficient development of legal framework, which regulates relations of possession, disposition and use of intellectual objects;
- corruption, connected with dirt-cheap sale of intellectual property of the Russian Federation to abroad;
- unworthy reward for academic work of authors of intellectual property, leading to "brain drain";
- unavailability of Russia to the competition on the market of high technology because of lack of legal norms, regulating the process of international cooperation in this sphere;
- uncontrolled usage of intellectual products, caused by the development of global communicative networks and activity of crackers and pirate (hacker).

It is necessary to emphasize that one of the main obstacle to the way of solving the problem of intellectual property protection is either law level of legal culture of the society in general or particularly of the youth as a social group which is much more connected with usage and distribution of intellectual property products. This is due to the contempt of ethical and legal norms of work with information, lack of knowledge and misunderstanding of principle theory of information law, intellectual property rights, basis of copyright, lack of skills to use the instruments, given laws and lack of idea about opportunities for intellectual property protection [10]. For overcoming these difficulties we need a system of law education and upbringing, where the system of general secondary education starts to play the main role.

In such a way the scientific interest of researching of the phenomenon of intellectual property is actively shown in the modern science. This is due to the extension of practical and utilitarian area of functioning of given kind of property. However it is possible to mention the lack of attention to the moral aspects of becoming and functioning of intellectual property.

2 Sociological Estimation of Contemporary State of Legal Culture of Youth in the Sphere of Using of Intellectual Property Items

The author did sociological research of the level of legal culture of youth, which is connected with appliance of means of information and communication technologies, particularly using of intellectual property items and respecting for copyrights.

The survey was conducted among young Moscow residents. The poll involved 504 individuals with quota sample (according to the gender, age, education, respondent's having of access to the Internet).

The survey was conducted by questioning. The questionnaire contained 33 questions, it's made in accordance with application tasks. It's necessary to notice that simple question formulations were used, they are clear not only for specialists in sphere of intellectual property but also unsophisticated in legal issues users. The answers to the questions were prepared in such a way that they reflect current opinions as far as possible. The list of questions was made by the expert poll of specialists in the sphere of intellectual property protection in order to prevent possible ambiguity in the answers and wrong question formulations.

Whether is youth informed of existing law in the sphere of intellectual property? With the help of questions about the knowledge the author determined the level of legal awareness of youth. The simplest and most popular way of measuring awareness is respondents' estimation of their knowledge. In order to define if it's possible to trust in respondents, the catch-question was framed. The fact is that the law "Protection of intellectual property and copyright in the Internet" doesn't exist. 19% of the respondents have noticed that they know such a law, 29,8% of the respondents have answered that know a little while 40,1% of respondents have said that they don't know it, 11,1% of respondents have noticed that this is the first time they've heard about it. In general it's possible to say that we can confide to the respondents.

It was offered to the young respondents to estimate their knowledge of main legal acts of the Russian Federation in the sphere of copyright protection, allied rights, legal protection of software for ECM and databases, legal protection of topology of IC chips, personal data security. The analysis of the results let us conclude that in general the youth isn't familiar with the legislation in the sphere of intellectual property.

As a part of study the respondents needed to estimate the following judgement: "Many young people don't know and don't understand the principle basis of copyright, they have no idea of possibility of intellectual property protection". 64,7% of respondents have agreed with the statement while 27% of respondents neither have agreed nor disagreed, and 7,9% of respondents have noticed that they disagree.

As one can see from Table 1, 41,7% of the respondents of the total number of respondents consider that it's impossible to break the law of intellectual property, 14,0% of respondents think that it's possible if "the law restricts private rights in the sphere of intellectual property" and 17,8% of the respondents have noticed that it's possible "in the name of benefit".

Table 1. The distribution of the responses for the question "How do you think if it is possible to break the law in the sphere of intellectual property?"

№	Possible replies	%
1	Yes, in the name of benefit	14,8
2	Yes, the law is unclear and so it's often broken	12,4
3	Yes, many laws contain in truth unrealizable norms	14,5
4	Yes, because of the fast replacement of laws	2,6
5	Yes, is the law restricts private rights in the sphere of intellectual property	14,0
6	No, a law is a law	41,7

One of the questions of the survey was formulated in such a manner to find out a youth's attitude to "pirates". The following question was offered to the respondents: "In your opinion the producer of pirate copy is ..." As the answers four alternatives were suggested. The distribution of answers is shown in Table 2.

Table 2. The distribution of the responses for the question "In your opinion the producer of pirate copy is ..."

№	Possible replies	%
1	Simple businessman	9,2
2	A man who makes the intellectual property products more accessible for customers	55,9
3	Simple criminal	34,2
4	It's difficult to define the opinion	12,5

As we can see 55,9% of the respondents consider that the producer of pirate copy is a man who makes the intellectual property products more accessible for customers, 34,2% of the respondents think that he is a simple criminal, 12,5% of the respondents have difficulty to give an opinion.

An youth's attitude to the piracy has compromise nature, which possibly can be determined not only by lack of pastoral work in this sphere on the part of the government but also patient position to pirate goods on the part of executive power and law enforcement agency.

It was important to us to find out what is the youth's attitude to introduction special courses, dedicated to information law, to the general school. Analyzing the respondents' answers to the question "How do you welcome the introduction of special courses to the general school?" we received the following distribution (Table 3).

As one can see the most number of respondents (58,1%) has answered "yes, facultative", while 16,9% of respondents consider that "high school student doesn't need it at this moment", 18,5% of respondents welcome the introduction of special

Table 3. The distribution of the responses for the question "Do you welcome the introduction of the course "Information law" to the general school?"

№	Possible replies	%
1	Yes, as part of education program	18,5
2	Yes, facultative	58,1
3	No, high school student doesn't need it at this moment	16,9
4	It's difficult to define the opinion	6,5

courses to the general school. It's difficult to define the opinion only for 6,5% of poll's participants.

The question "Do you think that it's possible to copy intellectual property items represented in electronic form?" was asked to the respondents. As the answers six alternatives were suggested. This is the distribution of answers (Table 4).

Table 4. The distribution of the responses for the question "Do you think that it's possible to copy intellectual property items represented in electronic form?"

№	Possible replies	%
1	Only within the law and right holder	34,7
2	Only within private use (without distribution), in spite of requirement of law and right holder	29,4
3	Within reasonable limits for friends and familiar people, in spite of requirement of law	15,3
4	Only for using on noncommercial objectives (at educational institutions, institutions of science, cultural institutions, etc.), in spite of requirement of law and right holder	8,9
5	For any purposes, including free distribution, totally ignoring requirement of law and right holder	6,5
6	It's difficult to define the opinion	5,2

As one can see 34,7% of the respondents of the total number of respondents consider that it's possible to copy intellectual property items only within the law and right holder, 29,4% of the respondents think that it's possible only within private use (without distribution), in spite of requirement of law and right holder, and 15,3% of the respondents say that it take place within reasonable limits for friends and familiar people, in spite of requirement of law. In general we can see that mostly young Moscow residents' consider copying and distributing of intellectual property items to be possible in spite of and contrary to legislative requirements, first of all within private use and within reasonable limits for friends and familiar people.

In such a way the found definitive estimation of level of information and legal culture of youth can be one of the reasons to introduce special educational courses to the general school, which should be directed to upbringing of legal culture of high school students, and also testify of pupils' position connected with the possibility to break and protect copyright law.

It's considered to be very important either creation of educational courses, dedicated to the basis of legislation in the sphere of intellectual property protection or introducing of the basis of legal culture of pupil, connected with the usage of means of information and communication technologies into the content of general educational discipline "informatics and information and communication technologies".

3   Content of Information and Legal Culture of a Pupil

Information and legal culture of a pupil is a part of the common information culture.

Information and legal culture means an integrative quality of personality necessary for the modern information society, which is characterized by a certain level of the formation of legal and ethical knowledge, abilities, skills and their implementation in the process of information activities. Information and legal culture is expressed in the existence of a complex of legal and ethical knowledge, abilities, skills and reflexive attitudes in the interaction with information environment. It's necessary to emphasize that the formation of such a culture of schoolchildren naturally involves into the strategy of development of the knowledge society, the information society, the rule-of-law state and the civil society in Russia. The modern school is the basis for the formation of the information society and the rule-of-law state.

The analysis of scientific literature [11–15] about information and legal culture made it possible to determine the set of knowledge and skills characterizing a person with a developed culture of such a type. In our opinion, the components of information and legal culture are:

- Existence of a definite information worldview, vision of general concepts (information society, information resources, information streams and arrays, patterns of their functioning and organization, information ethics, etc.);
- Skill to formulate their information needs and requests and present them to any data retrieval system, either traditional or automated [16];
- Ability to search independently various types of documents using both traditional and new information technologies, in particular information and intelligent systems and networks;
- Possessing the skills of analysis and synthesis of information (for example, drawing up simple and detailed plans, summary, annotating and abstracting, preparing reviews, compiling a bibliographical description, citations and references to scientific work, a list of used literature, etc.);
- Possessing technology of information self-dependence: the ability to use gain knowledge, found and gained information in the learning or other cognitive activities;
- Presence of a certain legal worldview, idea of the content of laws, statutory acts and other forms of legal regulation in the sphere of information circulation and production and application of ICT (for example, the legal basis for preparing documents, the basis of information law, information legislation);

– Presence of a certain ethical worldview, following the moral code while using information and ICT.

To organize the process of forming information and legal culture of pupils, it is necessary to determine the levels of its formation. In the most general terms, according to the acquirement of all the elements of legal culture it's possible to define the following levels: theoretical, special and empirical. In turn, according to the condition of the realization of legal research in the process of information activities, and this is an independent criterion for classifying information and legal culture, we can distinguish such levels: high, medium and low.

From the above, it can be concluded that information and legal culture (the legal culture of a pupil in the aspect of ICT use) is a complex personal education, a multifaceted and multilevel structure of qualities, properties and states that integrate a positive attitude toward working with information; presence of special knowledge about search, reception, processing, storage and transfer of information; a set of abilities and skills in working with information sources; presence of special legal and ethical knowledge in the sphere of information circulation and production and application of ICT.

In this way, today there is a need to form an information and legal culture, which is an element of the general culture of an individual. The formation of such a culture requires the introduction of various forms of educational integration, the implementation of interdisciplinary communications, and the use of various (effective) technologies for organizing the educational process using ICT.

The most effective way for the focused formation of information and legal culture of a pupil is introduction of the relevant training courses at the higher level of the general education school.

4 Selection of the Content of Legal Education and Training Within Learning Courses in General School

Under the content of legal training we will understand the set of knowledge in the field related to the legal side of the application of ICT, as well as the practical skills necessary for the implementation of technical and legal protection of intellectual property, personal information security.

The content of legal education of pupils should be directed to the formation of:

– basic knowledge in the field of law related to the application of ICT;
– knowledge of the features of legal protection of intellectual property;
– knowledge of the technical protection of intellectual property and personal information security;
– knowledge in the sphere of civil-law relations;
– responsible attitude towards compliance of ethical and legal norms of information activity;
– know-how of working with legislative acts in this field;
– skills of organization, morality, independence and courage in protection of their rights;

- legal organization of information activities connected with the usage of information technologies.

Legal education of pupils should fully satisfy the following didactic principles of training content selection [17]:

- The direction of the content of education for the main purpose of education which is the formation of a comprehensively and harmoniously developed personality;
- Scientific character in development of the content of education;
- Correspondence of the content of education with the logic and system appropriate for a particular science;
- Development of the content of education on the basis of the relationship between certain disciplines;
- Reflection of the connection between theory and practice in the content of education;
- Correspondence of the content of education with the achievement age of pupils.

In our opinion, the training content in the course of teaching pupils the basics of legal knowledge should have the following structure:

- Topic 1. The basics of intellectual property law;
- Topic 2. Legal framework for anti-piracy.
- Topic 3. Copyright protection in telecommunications networks.

The main goals of education and upbringing in the implementation of such a structure are:

- To show the spiral of intellectual property development in the evolutionary cycle of human rights development;
- To prepare pupils in the field of legal and technical protection of intellectual property, so it will provide them with the required level of knowledge in this field;
- To bring up the sense of respect for intellectual property rights.

The necessary condition for the introduction of a training course that implements these methodological principles in the system of teaching and educating pupils is to ensure the relationship with the subjects taught according to the state standard, in particular, with those disciplines in which it is possible to solve problems of general legal education. Obviously, there is a connection between courses that form information and legal culture with other school subjects, which allows to build an integral system of legal education.

5 Methods of Active Learning as an Effective Way of Forming Information and Legal Culture of a Pupil

In the formation of information and legal culture, three types of activity of a pupil should be demonstrated: thinking, activity and speech. We should note that depending on the type of methods used for active learning of pupils in the class, either one of the forms of activities or a combination of them can be realized.

The effectiveness of development of information and legal culture of pupils depends on what and how many of these activities are applied in the lessons. Thus, the lecture uses thinking (firstly memory), practical lesson uses thinking and activity, discussion uses thinking, speaking and sometimes emotional and personal perception, the role-play uses all the activities, an excursion uses only emotional-personal perception.

The author considers that applying the methods of active learning, it is necessary to use mainly the gaming technology. Gaming technologies in teaching pupils have their own specific character, which is expressed in the fact that their elements can be used both in the classroom and during the non-school hours. The leader can be either a teacher or a pupil, didactic material can be prepared by both the teacher and the learner. The effectiveness of development of information and legal culture of pupils in the classroom is determined by the form of the organization of games, the specific goal of the game (at the end it is supposed to receive the result, the formation of new knowledge, the systematization of knowledge, etc.). The important thing are the nearness of the game to real life conditions, the degree of independence of the organization of the game by high school students, the ability of high school students to take part in several roles, the selection of technical means, depending on the content of the game.

It is also important to note that a certain difficulty is caused by the possibility of development of motivating of pupils before playing the game. However, this task is facilitated by the usage of information technologies (in particular, multimedia technologies), educational technical equipment and other visual aids.

Didactic games are one of the methods of active learning of pupils. Taking into account the mechanisms of the computer-based learning process (integrity, step-by-step, etc.), it is advisable to use partially-searching (heuristic), games in which it is supposed to develop its own way of solving, creating its own algorithm (investigation games, logic games).

The most typical game situations are training role plays. At the heart of the role play usually lies an interpersonal conflict situation. The participants of the game take on roles and try to resolve the conflict in the course of dialogue. Although the actions of players are not regulated and formally free from rules, the game plot may contain general instructions of the form of implementation or presentation of the solution, and the game itself always contains "hidden" rules. Such rules are the instruction of the basic role characteristics, official position in the role, goals and real role prototypes or their generally accepted interpretation, ethical and service rules of behavior. All this imposes on the participants demands, which have an influence on the final result of their participation in the game. Simultaneously, in the absence of formal rules, these characteristics partially act for a directing function, determining possible options for the player's actions.

Role play has great teaching opportunities in forming of information and legal culture of pupils, helps to overcome difficulties in digestion of legal knowledge:

– A role play can be estimated as the most proper model of communication. In fact it implies imitation of reality in its most essential features. In the role play, as in life itself, the verbal and nonverbal behavior of high school students is interlinked in the most closely way. From this basic characteristic of the role play a number of other ones, making it an effective means of teaching oral speech follow.

- A role play has great opportunities for motivation and impulse. Communication, as you know, is unthinkable without a motive. However, in the teaching environment, it is not easy to provoke the student's motive to the utterance. The difficulty is the following: the teacher should describe the situation in such a way that there is such an atmosphere of communication, which in turn, causes the pupils to have an internal need for expressing their thoughts.
- A role play expects increase of the pupil's personal involvement in everything that happens. The learner enters the situation, though not through his "I", but through the "I" of the corresponding role.
- A role play helps the formation of educational cooperation and partnership among pupils.

Thus, the use of gaming technology (role plays, didactic games) increases the effectiveness of digestion the learning material, allows to create comprehensive knowledge about the subject, so the author emphasizes the use of active teaching methods.

In conclusion, we present the educational program and content of the teaching plan of the developed and approved training course "Information Law", which realizes the principles of formation of information and legal culture described above (Table 5).

Table 5. Educational program of the course "Information law"

Lesson number	Lesson topic	Kind of class activity	Form of control
Topic1. The Basics of intellectual property law (6 h)			
1	Introduction The history of intellectual property origin	Lecture with the elements of discussion	Essay on topic "Why do people break the intellectual property law?"
2	The world system of organization of protection of intellectual property	Lecture with the elements of discussion	"Open mike"
3	Legislation of the Russian Federation in terms of intellectual property	Lecture with the elements of discussion	General questioning
4	Information legislation and copyright law	Lecture with the elements of discussion. Working with legal acts	Making a table of legal acts
5	Basics of drawing up legal documents	Practical work	Recitation
6	Features of saving and protection of documents in office software	Practical work	Recitation

(*continued*)

Table 5. (*continued*)

Lesson number	Lesson topic	Kind of class activity	Form of control
Topic 2. Legal Framework for Anti-piracy (3 h)			
7	Software piracy and main methods of anti-piracy	Lecture with the elements of discussion. "Brainstorm"	Practical task solution
8	Software piracy and economics	Role play "Trail of pirate…"	Graphic work on topic: "Software pirate"
9	Software piracy and economics. Analysis of data in electronic worksheets. Search of the results of social studies on the Internet	Practical work	Recitation
Topic 3. Copyright Protection in Telecommunications Networks (8 h)			
10	History of copyright	Lecture with the elements of discussion	Formation of an author's contract
11	The fourth chapter of Civil code of the Russian Federation	Group work, mind game, work with the fourth chapter of Civil code of the Russian Federation	Test
12	The Internet in daily life: moral statutes and legal acts	Lecture with the elements of discussion, "brainstorm"	Mini-composition "How I understand information ethics"
13	The role of World Intellectual Property Organization in solving problems of using the Internet	Lecture with the elements of discussion, searching information on the Internet	Recitation
14	Intellectual property items on the Internet	Lecture with the elements of discussion	Test. Making a table "Intellectual property items on the Internet"
15	Ways of protection of net publications	Lecture with the elements of discussion, "brainstorm"	Participation in work
16	Measures of protection of net publications. What is Internet-law?	Lecture with the elements of discussion	Legal task solution
17	Final lesson	Round table discussion "Respect of human rights and intellectual property protection in modern society"	Speech with reports

6 Future Work

Development and implementation of innovative forms of organization of the process of development of information and legal culture of a pupil in general school as part of integrated learning.

7 Conclusion

This article contains the analysis of the modern situation of the problem of legal education of youth in the sphere of using of information intellectual products, the investigation of the becoming of the notion "intellectual property". There is a brief review of the state of the problem of intellectual property protection in Russia. The results of social research of the state of legal culture of youth are summarized. The notion of information and legal culture in relation to the notion of information culture of pupil is determined. Also you can see methodical system of law education of pupils in terms of using ICT, which is directed to development of information and legal culture of a pupil.

References

1. Guan, W.: Intellectual Property Theory and Practice. Springer, Heidelberg (2014). https://doi.org/10.1007/978-3-642-55265-6
2. World Intellectual Property Organization. http://www.wipo.int/wipolex/en/treaties/text.jsp?file_id=283833
3. Bell, D.: The Coming of Post-Industrial Society: A Venture in Social Forecasting. Basic Books, New York (1999)
4. Toffler, A.: The Third Wave. Pan Books Ltd., London (1981)
5. Toffler, A.: Future Shock. Random House, New York (1970)
6. Toffler, A.: Power Shift: Knowledge, Wealth, and Violence at the Edge of the 21st Century. Bantam Books (1991)
7. Castells M.: The Information Age: Economy, Society and Culture, vol. 3. Blackwell, Oxford (1996–1998)
8. Shiller, H.: Information Inequality: The Deepening Social Crisis in America. Routledge, New York (1996)
9. BSA. The Software Alliance. http://globalstudy.bsa.org/2016/downloads/press/pr_russia.pdf
10. Starkey, L., Corbett, S., Bondy, A., et al.: Intellectual property: what do teachers and students know? Int. J. Technol. Des. Educ. **20**(3), 333–344 (2010). https://doi.org/10.1007/s10798-009-9088-6
11. Gusel'nikova, E.V.: The internet and information culture of pupils. Pedagog. Inform. (3), 3–5 (2001) (in Russian)
12. Nepobednyj, M.V.: On opportunities of the development of legal culture of pupils within the technological education. Law Educ. **6**, 251–256 (2006). (in Russian)
13. Musinov, P.A., Musinov, E.P.: Legal norms and ethical code as structural components of moral and legal culture. Law Educ. **1**, 76–88 (2006). (in Russian)

14. Balakleets, I.I., Sokolov, A.N.: Legal culture: genesis, essence, state, problems and perspectives of development. Kaliningrad Institute of Law MIA of the Russian Federation, Kaliningrad (2012). (in Russian)
15. Cotterell, R.: The Concept of legal culture. In: Nelken, D. (ed.) Comparing Legal Cultures, pp. 13–31. Dartmouth Publishing Company, Aldershot (1997)
16. Gendina, N.I.: Information culture of individual: diagnostics, technology of development: study guide. P.2. Kemerovo (1999). (in Russian)
17. Babanskij, Yu.K.: Optimization of teaching process. General education aspect. Prosveshche-nie, Moscow (1977). (in Russian)

E-City: Smart Cities & Urban Planning

The Post in the Smart City

Maria Pavlovskaya[1,2] and Olga Kononova[1,3(✉)]

[1] St. Petersburg National Research University of Information Technologies,
Mechanics and Optics (ITMO University), 199034 St. Petersburg, Russia
pavlovskayamaria@gmail.com, kononolg@yandex.ru
[2] Department of Service Architecture, Russian Post, 190000 St. Petersburg, Russia
[3] The Sociological Institute of the RAS, 199034 St. Petersburg, Russia

Abstract. The paper substantiates the possibility of the Russian Post's participation in the Smart City projects due to the integration of a smart city's information systems and the postal services' assets for the collection of the urban data
and support of the information processes inherent in the city economy in the
information society stage. Integration will improve the results of a smart city's
management and the provision of municipal services to citizens through the use
of the technologies underlying the digital economy by the postal services. The
transition of the postal authorities from the different countries and the Russian
Post to the provision of digital services determines their willingness to become
full participants in the Smart City projects launched around the world. The authors
present the results of an analysis of international sources and an online survey of
the Russian citizens in order to justify the relevance of the research, identify the
opinions of the citizens to the Smart City projects, the participation of the Russian
Post in the similar projects. The survey reveals the respondents' attitude to the
use of the digital technologies, IoT in the city initiatives, assessment of the potential of the Russian Post in implementing the Smart City projects.

Keywords: Big data · Data-Driven city · IoT · Internet-of-Postal-Things
Postal assets · Postal electronic services · Smart city · Smart technology

1 Introduction

Smart City – a set of technical solutions and organizational activities aimed at achieving
the highest possible quality of the urban management. Technologies of the Smart City
reveal wide opportunities for the development of the urban environment. The urban
environment becomes smarter when the infrastructure of the city's information and
communication technologies providing most of the city's functional needs. Currently
the Russian federal and city authorities, primarily in Moscow and St. Petersburg,
demonstrate an increased interest in the Smart City projects, IoT, digital technologies
that contribute to the intellectualization of the urban environment. Most initiatives are
in the early stages. This is due, in addition to the lack of sufficient funding and incompleteness of the regulatory framework, to the complexity of the processes of collecting,
storing and processing of the data on the region economy and infrastructure generated
by all the participants of the urban environment. The city authorities build relationships

© Springer Nature Switzerland AG 2018
D. A. Alexandrov et al. (Eds.): DTGS 2018, CCIS 858, pp. 227–242, 2018.
https://doi.org/10.1007/978-3-030-02843-5_18

with the key organizations that provide the necessary information, but such interactions are not developed enough.

The collection of data on the state of urban infrastructure in the concepts of smart cities entrusted in most cases, including Russia, to the enterprises of the transport sphere or specialized state organizations and services. State postal services as a rule remain outside the concepts and models of Smart Cities. Meanwhile, the material and technical basis of postal services in the most countries is a serious material asset used in the urban smart projects by the Universal Postal Union (UPU), consulting and IT companies, and by the postal operators themselves [10, 14].

The complexity of the urban systems, embodied in the architecture of a smart city, is a significant factor in the actualization of the concept and model of a smart city, taking into account the inclusion of postal departments in them. A large number of urban participants can act as data sources:

- federal and municipal authorities;
- government agencies;
- housing and communal services;
- telecommunication organizations;
- Internet resources;
- other commercial companies and public associations;
- individuals.

To organize the data collection, city authorities must build partnerships with the key organizations that provide information in the city. State and local government authorities should also enlist the support of the population in implementing the initiatives based on the data. The support of the population will significantly increase the effectiveness of the managerial and organizational decisions, give the legitimacy to the solutions and the image of a modern and convenient place to live for the city. Technological decisions chosen by the city should improve the information interaction of all the stakeholders in the best possible way.

Working with the urban data requires the allocation of the information flows and the formalization of the necessary information for the authoritative urban structures to enhance the effectiveness of the management decision-making. Currently, there is no unified list of the urban data sources, fixed normatively, adopted at the national or international level, recommended as a set of the best world practices. The sources of the city data mentioned in the scientific literature and regulatory documentation are, as a rule, not equivalent in the composition, quality and volume of the data processed. The state postal services and their assets were not mentioned until recently in the similar documents. In this way, the Post is kept away from the involvement in the city initiatives and projects such as Smart City. Although the relevance of the participation of postal services in such projects is confirmed by the studies conducted in the world. One of the important factors explaining this position is the high density of presence and significant material assets of the state postal services.

The dynamics of the Russian Post development in recent years leads to the conclusion about the possibility of changing the role of Russian postal service in society. According to the conclusion of the Russian Post prepared for the Universal Postal Union, among the technological trends that will affect the provision of electronic services in the coming years, particularly emphasized are Big Data and Internet-of-Postal-Things. By analogy with the Internet of things technology the described approach could be named the Internet of Postal Things (IoPT), instrumenting the postal infrastructure with low-cost sensors to enable them to collect, communicate and act upon a broad variety of data. It could help the Postal Service generate operational efficiencies, improve the customer experience, and develop new services and business models.

2   The Use of Up-to-date High Technologies by Postal Operators

2.1   Postal Services and Technologies Used in the Smart City Projects

Postal operators around the world already actively participate in the providing of public services to citizens and in the development of socially significant initiatives.

For many international postal operators the services provided by e-government are an integral part of their products and services portfolio. In the industrialized countries, postal services play a crucial role in the organization of interaction between all levels of the government and citizens in both the physical and digital spheres. The traditional intermediary function of postal operators, the geographic density of their retail networks and their growing technological potential are the assets that governments rely on to provide more efficient, safe and easily accessible services. In addition to supporting their citizens, some international postal operators view e-government services as a strategic opportunity to generate new revenues, maintain their postal networks and expand their natural intermediary role in the digital field.

The most advanced postal services try to turn the social responsibility of the enter-prise into one of the most important components of its effective work and innovations. Relative to the sustainable development objectives set by the United Nations, the postal sector is to become one of the major players and over the time contributes to the imple-mentation of many initiatives. Introducing innovations, the postal sector constantly mobilizes its resources and undertakes obligations to support social, societal and envi-ronmental changes, and also expresses its readiness to place its experience and qualifi-cations in the service of society.

E-government services offered by international postal services range from digital and hybrid communications management for citizens to electronic payments, authenti-cation, verification, front-office functions. Many postal administrations provide local government services through the windows at the post office [13]. For example, Poste Italiane offers the "Sportello Amico" window where the residents could conduct a variety of transactions, including different kind of local payments [20]. The Russian Post also provides the opportunities for receiving state and municipal services, making payments, issuing identifiers for accessing electronic services in the post offices.

Furthermore, many posts, for example in Norway and Portugal, helping cities promote efficient transportation by using fuel-efficient vehicles, such as electric vehicles or bicycle couriers [16, 17]. Swiss Post is directly involved in the improving of the mobility in the cities through its PostBus service (public transportation system provided by Swiss Post which uses buses to carry passengers to and from different cities in

Switzerland, France, and Liechtenstein), which is now testing autonomous (driverless) buses [18]. Swiss Post also offers a bikeshare program called PubliBike [26].

It is obvious that big data guarantees the good result from administrative decisions adoption. A data-driven city is characterized by the ability of municipal authorities to use data collection, processing and analysis technologies to improve the social, economic, environmental situation and improve the living standards of residents [3, 8, 9, 11, 23, 31].

That's why some of the Postal services are already beginning to explore sensor-based data collection. As early as 2014, Spanish post Correos was involved in developing air quality monitoring sensors for placement on postal vehicles [4]. Finnish Postal service Posti is beginning to conduct experiments on how sensor-based collected data (for example, road conditions, traffic flow, and signal strength data) could be used [21]. French postal operator La Poste, through its subsidiary Docapost, is taking a different tack, aiming to be a platform where sensor-based data from variety sources can be housed together securely for easy access. Under this model, La Poste plays the of data broker, offering storage and analytics services [4].

Smart mailboxes are becoming more and more popular. They are equipped with Wi-Fi, work on solar panels, inform the recipient at the time when the shipment was delivered to his mailbox, use an intelligent locking system, are connected to the mail processing center and receive data on the mailman's schedule and send information about empty boxes for optimization daily routes for collecting items. A user with a mobile application can remotely monitor what happens with the mailbox – incoming mail is delivered, outbound – received by the postman, an unauthorized opening of the box occurs, the door remains open, other.

Mobile technology has already helped redefine the role of carriers, expanding the variety of tasks they can perform. USPS has equipped carriers with mobile delivery devices to facilitate scanning packages at delivery and communicating with the post office. Carrier handheld devices could also become a platform for a variety of other activities, such as collecting sensor data and interacting with citizens in support of new services [27].

Postal operators also implement various monitoring services. One example of such a service is the "lost and found" service implemented in Denmark, where postal vehicles help identify stolen bicycles. A sensor embedded in the bicycle automatically registers its location through the closest postal connected device in the vicinity (up to 200 yards) [12]. This approach could be extended to monitoring the status of components of the city infrastructure such as road conditions or street lights.

Several posts have created passive and active "check on" services, whereby carriers regularly visit elderly or disabled people. As part of a new Japan Post/IBM/Apple partnership, these clients will receive iPads with apps to connect them with services, health care, community, and their families [5]. The interconnection of sensor data from the elderly citizen's and the carrier's smart devices could be key to the effective provision of innovative check on services. For instance, the system schedules the visits, alerts the client that the carrier is on his way, enables the timely delivery of medication, or reports back to family members or local healthcare authorities. Table 1 presents a general view of the world experience of the postal service's involvement in socially significant initiatives.

Table 1. World experience of the postal service's involvement in socially significant initiatives

Initiatives of the Postal administrations

The Postal operator	The operator of the electronic government: identification, state services, acceptance of payments, etc.	Environmentally friendly transport	Data collection	Data storage and analysis	Monitoring services
Italy	+	+			
Switz.	+	+			
Spain	+	+	+		
Finland	+	+	+	+	
France	+	+	+	+	
Norway	+	+			
Germany	+	+	+	+	
Denmark	+	+	+		+
USA	+	+	+	+	+
Japan	+	+			+
India	+				
Russia	+				

The data indicates high levels of the post involvement in the government and municipal services provision, acceptance of payments, issuing identifiers for accessing to electronic services through the post offices [13, 20]. Among environmental initiatives of cities, where the postal services participate one of the most important is efficient transportation by using fuel efficient vehicles, such as electric vehicles or bicycle couriers, public transportation system that uses autonomous (driverless) buses to carry passengers, bike share programs and others [2, 6, 16, 17, 19, 26].

The whole range of socially significant initiatives has not been implemented even in the USA, which Postal Service is recognized as the best postal service in the top 20 largest economies in the world [17]. At the same time, the least attention is paid to the collection, storage and analysis of data on both the various spheres of the city economy and the main activity of the postal service.

2.2 The Russian Post Assets

The postal assets can be broadly divided into three main categories, such as stationary assets, transport fleet and carriers. In Russia, the category of stationary objects includes post offices, collection boxes and home mailboxes which have been installed throughout the country. The transport fleet of the Russian Post presented by various vehicles including automobiles, trains, plains, and others. The total length of main and internode mail routes exceeds 2.8 million km. The structure of the Russian Post assets is shown in Table 2.

Table 2. The Russian Post assets

Categories	Postal assets	Number of objects
Stationary objects of the Russian Post	Post offices	42.000
	Collection boxes	over 140.000
	Home mailboxes in the residential sector	Moscow – 3.5 million Moscow region– 1.3 million, Nizhny Novgorod – 0.5 million Samara – 0.4 million Saratov – 0.3 million Voronezh – 0.3 million
The Russian Post transport fleet	Automobiles	14.000
	Other vehicles	3.000
Couriers' service	Couriers and postmen	about 100.000 [19]

The important postal network characteristics are frequency and consistency which are more relevant for dynamic types of the assets. Since the Postal Service is considered as a universal service in the most countries, Post offices are situated in every community including remote and sparsely populated; their vehicles pass through almost every road, including the roads that bus routes may not cover. Such wide coverage by one enterprise allows Smart City projects a degree of flexibility in their scope. Data could be collected nationally, locally or even just along specific areas [22]. Accordingly, the data collection potential of a large number of vehicles overcoming significant distances is enormous and create a powerful information network.

Postal transport assets have several advantages over other potential service providers associated with the data collection. The indicators characterizing these advantages are considered in the Table 3.

Table 3. Characteristics of the main providers of the urban data collection services

Type of transport	Characteristics				
	Unified state owner	Regular routes	Travel time	Geographic coverage of the route	Centralized service
Taxi			+		
Police cars	+		+		+
Public transport		+	+	+	
Utilities transport		+			
Postal transport	+	+	+	+	+

The Russian Post strategy implies digital transformations that will make the Russian Post a profitable, customer-oriented, efficient and technologically advanced company. Digitalization of Postal Services, the existence of a strategic goal allows to conclude that the company is ready to use the results of world experience in applying modern technologies to expand the spectrum of the provided products [15].

2.3   The Russian Post Readiness Level to Use the Smart Technology

The practice of the Russian Post enterprise architecture management is based on the product-service model, where the modeling of the current and target architecture is performed in the context of products (the activity of the enterprise in providing products to customers) and services (the internal activity of the enterprise). The product landscape of the Russian Post on a conceptual level includes Postal Services, Financial Services, Commercial Services, Provision of State and Municipal Services, Services of Property complex.

The enterprise's revenue structure is shown in Fig. 1. The revenue structure of the enterprise shows that the most profitable issues are the postal (domestic and international written correspondence, parcels and EMS) and financial products as well as commercial services (sale of goods and subscription services). Internal activity of the enterprise is also extremely important primarily because of the activities related to production and logistics. These types of activities represent the main activity of the Post, they spend the main production capacities and resources of the enterprise, the productivity of the Postal Service as a whole depends on the quality of their provision [28, 29].

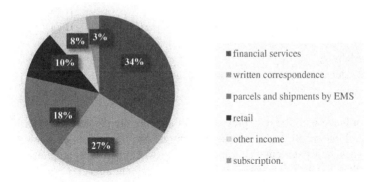

Fig. 1. Revenue structure of the Russian Post

Currently, the data architecture of the Russian Post is under development. At the same time, both scattered descriptions of data generated and received by some information systems or organizational units of the enterprise and data flows identified as a result of modeling products and services of the enterprise are available. An album of data formats and data models of subject domains is created. The data identified during the implementation of information systems and collected in the corporate data warehouse is classified.

2.4 Technological Trends that Will Affect the Provision of Electronic Services in the Russian Post

While basing on the information about the current state of the Russian Post is impossible to give an unambiguous assessment about the impossibility of significant changes in the status and the role of the enterprise in the society. Table 4 presents the conclusion of the Department of Enterprise Architecture of the Russian Post in terms of technological trends that will influence on the provision of electronic services in the Russian Post, prepared as a part of the Universal Postal Union report. For each factor, the level of influence from the critical to average is given.

Table 4. Technological trends that will affect the Russian Post digital services

Technological trends	Level of influence
Big data, data analytics and cloud computing technologies	Critical
Sensors for postal infrastructure (postal vehicles, mailboxes) – Internet of Things	Critical
The new generation of portable terminals for postmen	Significant
New payment technologies	Significant
Security standards and technologies in cyberspace	Significant
Augmented reality or virtual reality	Significant
New improvements in e-health and services for the elderly	High
3D Printing Technologies	High
Blockchain technology (identification information, logistics, virtual currency)	High
Drones for delivery	Average
Unmanned vehicles or autonomous robots for delivery	Average
Crowdshipping	Average

In accordance with the data presented in the table, the greatest prospects for use in the Russian Post are Big data, Internet of Things, mobile devices of a new generation for employees, new payment technologies, security in cyberspace, augmented reality or virtual reality. The Russian Post and various government agencies are also constantly announcing the launch of new Postal Services that support intellectual technologies. At the moment, the Russian Post is working on a technology for identifying customers by the face at the entrance of the post office.

3 "Smart City and the Russian Post" Survey

3.1 Purposes and Issues

The influence of public opinion on the government activities is constantly increasing, and the need to adopt socially-oriented management decisions, taking into account the interests of various social groups, is beyond doubt. Sociological analysis of public opinion contributes to raising the level of conceptual interpretation and justification of socio-economic reforms, optimizing the activities of power structures [33, 35].

One of the most important components of Smart City is Smart Citizens [25] and only they can make the existence of such cities possible [1]. Also, the problem of the need to change the mentality of people living in cities claiming to be 'smart' is also topical. Citizens are required as a willingness to use the initiatives introduced by the city authorities, as well as active participation in the formation of needs for the introduction of such initiatives, the participation of citizens in management [34]. This challenge, facing cities, pushes to the background the problems of choosing and implementing technologies. Initiatives should also have upward character, because the approach of the 'ideal' Smart City with a downward orientation, which is ubiquitous today, destroys democracy and often minimizes the involvement of citizens [1].

Thus, public opinion is an important factor in the decision making by city authorities. The study of its influence should be one of the first stages of research on the development of proposals for involving the Russian Post in the Smart City projects.

The purpose of the study is to identify trends in relation to the Smart City projects, to the participation of the Russian Post in such projects of citizens of different regions and age groups. At the same time, special attention is paid to identifying the relationship, assessing the potential of the Russian Post in the implementation of Smart City and Smart Technology projects from the staff of the Russian Post. The study can be considered as exploratory and aimed the confirmation or refutation of hypotheses and propositions. Based on the results, priorities and strategies for the further development of ongoing research will be determined.

Within the framework of the research, an online interviewing of Russian citizens was conducted (including employees of public authorities and subordinate organizations, representatives of the scientific and business communities), as well as an interviewing of the employees of the Russian Post. The purpose of the study is both to identify trends in the relation of the citizens from different regions and age groups to the Smart city projects and to the participation of the Russian Post in them and to identify the relation, assessment of the Russian Post potential in the implementation of Smart cities and Smart Technology projects of the Russian Post staff.

The research tools (method of the survey) was the online questionnaire that contains 30 questions and consists of 4 parts, which was developed in accordance with the purpose and objectives of the study.

The rationale for the sample is based on the ideas of the approach formulated by Everett Rogers [24]. The general population is hyper-digital users [30] – students, employees of the Russian universities, employees of IT companies (IT divisions of the various companies). Also, an important role is given to the views study of the transport/ logistics employees, in particular employees of the Russian Post and respondents who are the most competent in making managerial decisions, that is, representatives of the public administration and managers at different levels. Quotas were maintained by sex, age, level of position and profession. The sample was purposive and formed by the snowball method through the social connections of the researcher.

3.2 Survey Results

Among the respondents prevailed the age categories up to 35 years, which is determined by the specificity of the target group. To the age categories 35–44 and 45–54 are 15% of respondents. 30% of respondents classified themselves into the age categories 35-44 and 45–54. 21% of respondents refer the organization in which they work/study to the professional field of postal activity, 20% – to the IT field, 19% – to the science and education, 10% – to the public service. The overwhelming majority of respondents (69%) highly assessed their skills in using information technology in their daily and professional activities, and only 5% identified themselves as inexperienced users.

The results of respondent's assessment of their level of the awareness of the global trends in the field of digital technologies, Russia's digital technology, the use of digital technologies in various sectors of the Russian economy as well as the use of digital technologies in the urban economy of regions and settlements indicate an average level of citizens' awareness of those areas.

The respondents suppose that the implementation of the Smart City project in their region will improve the quality of their family life, and rather noticeably (Fig. 2). The evaluation was carried out on a scale of 1 to 5, where 5 – the quality of life will be noticeably improved, and 1 – will not affect in any way.

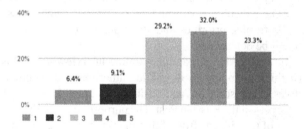

Fig. 2. How the implementation of the Smart City project will the lives of families?

Slightly less than a half of the respondents (46%) refer the organization in which they are working or study to the participates of the city socially significant projects based on digital technologies, and 20% of respondents stated that their organization is a direct participant in the projects "Smart City". 23% of respondents say that their organization uses modern technologies, but there is no interaction with participants in urban life.

The respondents primarily see the government bodies and their subordinate structures as the main participants in the "Smart City" projects (84%); the next three positions are occupied by business, scientific, public and non-profit organizations with a small difference (see Fig. 3). It should also be noted that the missed position in the questionnaire - the "Citizens" option, which should certainly be presented, is the most mentioned among the respondents who chose the "Other" option.

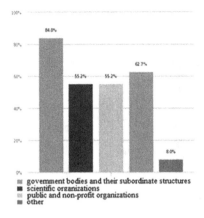

Fig. 3. The main participants of the Smart City projects

The leading position among the new technologies that can serve as the basis for the services provided by the Russian Post is occupied by new payment technologies (57%), followed by the analysis of big data (45%), augmented reality (35%), Internet of Things (35%), face recognition technologies (35%), autonomous robots (28%), unmanned vehicles (27%) and drones (22%) for delivery of mail items. It is important to note that most of the mentioned technologies are currently considered by the Russian Post as promising, and new payment technologies, big data analytics, augmented reality technologies and face recognition technologies are already being used in the projects developed by the Post. Moreover, the opinion of the Russian Post regarding the distribution of the importance of the technologies listed in the questions corresponds to the respondent's assessment.

The majority of the respondents agree that the involvement of the Post in the Smart City projects is possible, but the opinion as to the appropriateness of such projects is equally divided.

Among the areas where the problems are most acute in the regions and localities, citizens identified primarily housing and utilities (67%), healthcare (65%), environment (49%), transport (48%), interaction of the urban authorities and the citizens (48%) and education (40%) (Fig. 4). Note that the problems in the field of postal activity are only on the 8th place.

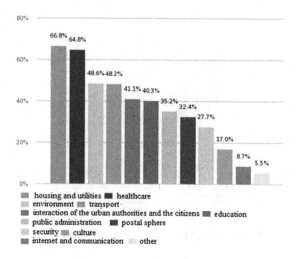

Fig. 4. Problem areas in the urban governance

According to respondents, the Russian Post should organize data collection during the implementation of the Smart City project primarily for the postal sphere. Close indicators are for transport and housing and utilities (Fig. 5).

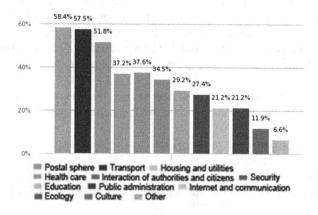

Fig. 5. The areas of the urban economy for which, first of all, it is necessary to implement data collection with the usage of the postal assets in the Smart City projects

Respondents who refer to the organization in which they work, to the professional field of postal activities, were asked several additional questions. 90% of respondents believe that participation in Smart City projects corresponds to the strategic goal of the Russian Post - to become a profitable, customer-oriented, efficient and technology company, a reliable and modern provider of postal, logistics and financial services for the whole country. At the same time, 83% of respondents are ready to take part in activities within the framework of the Smart City projects.

4 Conclusions and Recommendations

The revision of the urbanization opportunities provides updated information on city growth and global transformation processes. Recognizing the importance of information technologies, the revision expands the Smart City architecture, takes into consideration the postal assets and services. The study has showed the Russian Post mission corresponds the Smart City vision. The Russian Post also strives to match the trend of data-driven enterprises that allows considering it as a potential partner in the construction of data-driven cities.

It can be concluded that there are many opportunities to involve the Russian Post in the processes of building and managing Smart Cities, which are mainly related to the use of postal assets to collect large amounts of urban data. The Internet of Postal Things technology is able to provide the postal infrastructure with low-cost sensors to enable them to collect, communicate and act upon a broad variety of data. It could help the Postal Service, generate operational efficiencies, improve the customer experience and develop new services and business models. Smart City projects exist in the interests of cities and citizens. Having become involved in these projects, the Russian Post could translate this interaction into the cost savings of a city, improving its activity efficiency, promoting its sustainability plans, strengthening the role as a national public infrastructure and service provider. The Russian Post will accomplish its mission the best and achieve its goals.

It is also important to apply the architectural approach to the construction of urban agglomerations. It allows looking at the city as a complex system. Then the participation of new enterprises, such as the Postal Service, in the city projects will become easier and be in accordance with the interests of all stakeholders. At present, there is no need for significant changes in the Postal Services and its functional capabilities for taking part in smart urban initiatives. It is enough to add the capabilities of the Postal Service to the existing city architecture and to update the communication between the key city domains by connecting them to the Postal Services.

The relevance of the study is further conditioned by increased government activity in the Smart Cities development in Russia, which is caused by "Digital Economy of the Russian Federation" release, where the Smart City direction is allocated. In accordance with the document, the city authorities, scientific and business communities started "Smart Saint Petersburg" program, where the research results could be used [32].

Hypotheses of the study are confirmed. It has been revealed that the Smart City projects have ambiguous support from the population. The attitude of respondents to Smart Cities and technologies depends on their level of awareness about the latest technological trends, the level of competence of respondents in the field of information and communication technologies. The attitude of citizens towards the possibility of the Russian Post participation in innovative projects and initiatives varies from "restrained" to "critical". At the same time, a high level of interest of the expert group (employees of the Russian Post) is established to participate in large-scale, high-tech city initiatives. As the recommendations made on the results of the study, it is necessary to emphasize the importance of raising the awareness of the population and employees of the Russian Post about smart projects, concepts, trends and technologies. Employees of the Post should also be properly informed about the possibilities of the enterprise involving in Smart City projects in order to increase their efficiency.

Correctly selected recommendations on the involvement of the Russian Post in the Smart City projects, developed within the framework of the architectural approach, taking into account the opinions of citizens and employees of the enterprise, can facilitate the organization of the effective interaction between stakeholders.

The world experience in the creation of information systems in various spheres of human activity says that any initiative to create an Intelligent City must be accompanied with the set of basic documents, in particular the architecture of the Smart City. Involving the Russian Post in the Smart City projects leads to the change in the different levels of its architecture. The importance of architectural principles, which are one of the main components of the architecture, as well as the need to develop them at the initial stages of architecture creation, is confirmed by leading methodologies and standards. In connection with this, the important recommendation is the development of the principles of the Smart City projects with the participation of the Russian Post. It is planned to develop such principles, primarily affecting the business architecture and data architecture domains, as a part of the further study in accordance with the methodology of Griffhorst & Proper [7] and TOGAF.

For the Russian Post, there are many opportunities to expand the range of its products and services that support socially significant initiatives and initiatives of city authorities, following the example of world practice. It is necessary to understand the potential of the Post to meet the state interests and develop proposals for strengthening the role of the Post in the public administration system. As a direction for future research, we should highlight a more detailed study of the data required to collect in the framework of Smart City projects and the possibility of its collection and aggregation using the assets of the Russian Post.

References

1. Allessie, D.: Only smart citizens can enable true smart cities. In: KPMG Innovative Startups. https://home.kpmg.com/nl/en/home/social/2016/02/only-smart-citizens-can-enable-true-smart-cities.html
2. Chourabi, H., Nam, T., Walker, S., Gil-Garcia, J.R., Mellouli, S.: Understanding smart cities: an integrative framework. In: 45th Hawaii International Conference on System Sciences, pp. 2289–2297 (2012). https://doi.org/10.1109/hicss.2012.615, http://observgo.uquebec.ca/observgo/fichiers/78979_B.pdf
3. Data-Driven City: from the concept to application-oriented decisions (2016). (in Russian). https://www.pwc.ru/ru/government-and-public-sector/assets/ddc_rus.pdf
4. Docapost, "Digital Hub and IOT" (2016). http://en.docapost.com/solutions/digital-hub-iot
5. Etherington, D.: Apple and IBM team with Japan post to address the needs of an aging population. TechCrunch. http://techcrunch.com/2015/04/30/apple-ibm-japan-post/#.appdc9:DFfD
6. Giffinger, R., Pichler-Milanović, N.: Smart cities: ranking of European medium-sized cities (2007)

7. Greefhorst, D., Proper, E.: Architecture Principles. The Cornerstones of Enterprise Architecture. The Enterprise Engineering Series, vol. 4, 197 p. Springer, Heidelberg (2011). https://doi.org/10.1007/978-3-642-20279-7-6

8. Grupo Correos, "2014 Integrated Annual Report: Innovation and Technology, Our Present, Our Future", p. 36 (2014). http://www.correos.es

9. Kupriyanovsky, V., Martinov, B.: "Smart planet" – how to do it? ArcReview **1**(68) (2014). (in Russian). https://www.esri-cis.ru/news/arcreview/detail.php?ID=16987&SECTION_ID=1048

10. Measuring postal e-services development. Universal Postal Union. http://www.upu.int/uploads/tx_sbdownloader/studyPostalEservicesEn.pdf

11. Narmeen, Z.B., Jawwad, A.S.: Smart city architecture: vision and challenges. (IJACSA) Int. J. Adv. Comput. Sci. Appl. **6**(11) (2015). http://www.academia.edu/25414958/Smart_City_Architecture_Vision_and_Challenges

12. New Cheap Device to Track your Lost Bike. Cambridgeshire Business. https://cambsbusiness.wordpress.com/2013/02/13/new-cheap-device-to-track-your-lost-items/

13. OIG, "E-Government and the Postal Service: A Conduit to Help Government Meet Citizens' Needs" RARC-WP13-003 (2013). https://www.uspsoig.gov/sites/default/files/document-library-files/2015/rarc-wp-13-003_0.pdf

14. Oxford Strategic Consulting Report. Oxford Press (2017). http://www.oxfordstrategicconsulting.com/wp-content/uploads/2017/03/Delivering-the-future-16-03c.pdf

15. Pavlovskaya, M., Kononova, O.: The usage of the postal assets in the secure information space of a Smart city, regional informatics and information security. In: Proceedings of SPOISU 2017 Conference, pp. 22–24 (2017). (in Russian)

16. Post and Parcel "CTT Group Invests €5 m in Green Fleet" (2014). http://postandparcel.info/60290/uncategorized/ctt-group-invests-e5m-in-green-fleet/

17. Post and Parcel "Norway Post to add 330 Electric Vehicles to Fleet" (2015). http://postandparcel.info/65771/news/environment-news-2/norway-post-to-add-330-electric-vehicles-to-fleet/

18. Postal Services in the Digital Age. Global E-Governance Series (Vol. 6). IOS Press (2014)

19. Postbus website (2017). https://www.postauto.ch/en

20. Poste Italiane, "Sportello Amico" (2017). http://www.poste.it/ufficio-postale/sportello-amico.shtml

21. Posti, Annual Report 2015, p. 39 (2015). http://annualreport2015.posti.com/filebank/1229-POSTI_Annual_Report_2015.pdf

22. Ravnitzky, M.J.: Offering sensor network services using the postal delivery vehicle fleet. In: Crew, M.A., Kleindorfer, P.R. Reinventing the Postal Sector in an Electronic Age, Chapter 26. Edward Elgar (2011). https://doi.org/10.4337/9781849805964

23. Robinson, R.: The new architecture of Smart Cities (2012). https://theurbantechnologist.com/2012/09/26/the-new-architecture-of-smart-cities/

24. Rogers, E.M.: Diffusion of Innovations, 5th edn. Free Press, New York (2003). https://teddykw2.files.wordpress.com/2012/07/everett-m-rogers-diffusion-of-innovations.pdf

25. Smart Cities – A $1.5 Trillion Market Opportunity. Forbes. https://www.forbes.com/sites/sarwantsingh/2014/06/19/smart-cities-a-1-5-trillion-market-opportunity/#289b18576053

26. Swiss Post, The Pleasure of Simple Solutions: Annual Report (2015). http://annualreport.swisspost.ch/15/ar/downloads/geschaeftsbericht_konzern/en/E_Post_GB15_Geschaeftsbericht_WEB.pdf

27. The Internet of Postal Things. U.S. Postal Service Office of Inspector General. https://www.uspsoig.gov/sites/default/files/document-library-files/2015/rarc-wp-15-013_0.pdf

28. The Russian Post intends to introduce identity identification at the entrance of the offices. Vedomosti. https://www.vedomosti.ru/business/news/2017/10/25/739332-identifikatsiyu-lichnosti. Accessed 21 Feb 2018. (in Russian)
29. The Russian Post, the development strategy of the federal state unitary enterprise "The Russian Post" for the period until 2018 (2015). https://www.pochta.ru/about-documents. Accessed 21 Feb 2018. (in Russian)
30. U.K. Consumer Payment Study (2016). https://www.tsys.com/Assets/TSYS/downloads/rs_2016-uk-consumer-payment-study.pdf
31. U.S. Postal Service Office of Inspector General, "The Postal Service and Cities: A "Smart" Partnership", (2016). https://www.uspsoig.gov/sites/default/files/document-library-files/2016/RARC-WP-16-017.pdf
32. Urban development program "Smart Saint Petersburg" (2017). (in Russian). https://www.petersburgsmartcity.ru
33. Vezinicyna, S.V.: Vzaimodejstvie obshhestvennogo mnenija i organov municipal'-noj vlasti: mehanizmy, problemy, sovershenstvovanie. Izvestija Saratovskogo un-ta Ser. Sociologija. Politologija. (2013) №1. http://cyberleninka.ru/article/n/vzaimodeystvie-obschestvennogo-mneniya-i-organov-munitsipalnoy-vlasti-mehanizmy-problemy-sovershenstvovanie.   (in Russian)
34. Vidyasova L.A.: Conceptualization of the "smart city" concept: socio-technical approach. Int. J. Open Inf. Technol. (11) (2017). (in Russian). http://cyberleninka.ru/article/n/kontseptualizatsiya-ponyatiya-umnyy-gorod-sotsiotehnicheskiy-podhod
35. Vishanova, P.G.: Vlijanie obshhestvennogo mnenija na dejatel'nost' organov gosu-darstvennogo i municipal'nogo upravlenija v sub#ekte Federacii: dissertacija kandidata sociologicheskih nauk: 22.00.08. Moskva (2005). 171 s. (in Russian)
36. Respondents suppose that the postal offices, vehicles and employees are the most in demand assets of the Russian Post in the Smart City projects in Russia

The Smart City Agenda and the Citizens: Perceptions from the St. Petersburg Experience

Lyudmila Vidiasova[1]([⊠]), Felippe Cronemberger[2],
and Iaroslava Tensina[1]

[1] ITMO University, Saint Petersburg, Russia
bershadskaya.lyudmila@gmail.com,
tensina.yaroslava@mail.ru
[2] University at Albany, Albany 12205, USA
fcronemberger@alumni.albany.edu

Abstract. The paper contributes to literature on smart cities by focusing on the demand side of smart city projects. For this endeavor, the SCOT approach is used to describe the construction of the concept of Smart City from the perspective of the mass media agenda and, in particular, from citizens' needs and expectations in the city of Saint Petersburg, in Russia. Authors used an automated tool to perform content analysis on 589 articles that discuss smart cities in the Russian media from 2010 to 2017 as well as a survey of 421 citizens in the city. Findings suggest that the prevalence of technical descriptions involving the Smart City topic do not reduce citizens' interest in the phenomenon nor foster their willingness to participate in city management through ICT.

Keywords: Smart cities · Socio-technical approach · Citizens
Opinion poll · Semantic analysis

1 Introduction

The "smart city" topic is becoming increasingly popular among experts from different fields: IT, urban studies, public administration and the Internet of Things are only a few of the many realms where the topic has been discussed. However, providing a smart city is a socio-technical phenomenon, there is a risk to succumb to technological determinism. In face of the risk, taking an exclusively technological perspective on the phenomenon, research should not ignore that a city entails a community of people whose attitudes, feelings and expectations should be dutifully considered when any effort towards becoming "smart" or "smarter" takes place.

In 2017, the Saint Petersburg Administration launched the project "Smart Saint Petersburg". As a priority urban development program, it aimed at creating a city management system that improves the quality of life of the population and promotes the sustainable development of the city. Among the targets for the smart cities development, financial efficiency and calculated savings were expected. However, the concept of a smart city also implies the development of human capital as well as the creation of opportunities for a creative class and initiatives for the development of a

© Springer Nature Switzerland AG 2018
D. A. Alexandrov et al. (Eds.): DTGS 2018, CCIS 858, pp. 243–254, 2018.
https://doi.org/10.1007/978-3-030-02843-5_19

knowledge economy. In this regard, indicators of the social effectiveness of the projects being implemented should not be ignored.

This paper considers a specific initiative that takes place in St. Petersburg, Russia, to enhance understanding about the citizens' perspective on smart cities. Called *Foresight Trip* [7], this expert forecasting practice provides joint design of roadmaps for sectoral and territorial development, fosters the development of competences for strategic vision in the business environment and helps in the formation of personnel reserve for public administration and sectors of the economy. In the process of designing the priorities for the City program, it was important to look into the citizens' needs and attitudes toward the modern ICT inclusion across different fields. Recognizing citizens as a major stakeholder in Smart cities development, this paper aims to contribute to the literature by explaining how a smart city appears to citizens and by showcasing what they expect from such projects at the very beginning. It achieves its goal by examining smart city developments in Saint Petersburg in relation to the citizens' demand and expectations and it concludes with aspects that are worth investigating within the public value research agenda.

2   Literature Review

Research on "smart cities" has been growing steadily for the past decade and it has been quite interdisciplinary. Frequently, research is on the computer science and engineering realms and is concerned with addressing how particular technologies can be enabled to achieve smart cities' goals, but continues to be expanded in scope. Besides ongoing definitional efforts [8, 16] and the development of frameworks that help defining the problem [3, 19], research is also becoming more prominent at the empirical side of this socio-technical phenomenon. Endeavors now include not only conceptualizing smartness, but moving towards scrutinizing many of the underpinning components of smartness at the local government level, many of those already explored in literature [6, 14]. Those components may be more socio-technical technical, like underlying infrastructure and the ability to use data effectively [13] or essentially governance or managerial-related [21, 22].

Increasingly, though, the role of citizens and participation is being incorporated into discussions about smart cities [25]. Although citizens have been pointed as being relevant for the development towards smartness in cities [11], a citizen-centric city may not unfold automatically from the sum of technological projects in the public sector. Aside from the difficulty from measuring participation itself [20], factors may encompass technicalities inherent to the technologies being used [9] or the realization that citizens may perceive technology ubiquity differently and not engage with it prolifically [17, 29].

Research has found that, in the context of ICT use in smart cities' initiatives, participation may occur in different ways and require quite distinct types of citizen engagement [12, 18]. Part of the challenge remains in understanding and tentatively defining "what", "how", "where" and "why" citizens may "influence the governance of their cities" [2]. As research evolves, findings suggest that ICT may act as an enabler of governance through collaborative practices and participation [4], may be used as a tool to foster citizen's "co-production of public services" [5, 15] or by collecting citizens' opinion for urban design projects [23]. To Gabrys [12], citizenry does not invite a passive stance in smart cities development; rather, it needs to be "articulated" with the environment through urban data practices that include feedback collection, distribution and monitoring. Complementarily, understanding "city-specific" channels where "city-specific" content will be diffused is expected to have an effect on the extent to which citizens will be engaged with smart cities' initiatives [28].

According to Abella et al. [1], citizen engagement in smart cities' ecosystems may be fostered through three stages: (1) disclosing data to citizens in an appealing fashion; (2) walking citizens through of mechanisms that help creating new products and services; and (3) making citizens aware of how products and services have an effect in society. Those steps may suggest a more relativistic approach to the problem because it constitutes a shift from understanding citizen engagement issues as people-centric technologies issues [10] to public-value creation as a result of citizen's collaborative involvement with smart cities' initiatives [27]. Although this second instance can make an approximation with the smart cities' vision, perspectives on what a smart city is can or should be taken into consideration [32].

It is important to highlight, however, that research focused on the specifics of citizen involvement in smart cities' initiatives is not particularly abundant or has been done systematically. As a topic, citizens are either explored indirectly or as a self-evident goal for smart cities' initiatives. In contrast with studies that explore technologies as artifacts that gravitate around citizen needs, the topic "citizens" seems to be peripheral to discussions involving technologies and their use of it. In a generic search about most frequent keywords associated to "smart cities" in Scopus, for example, the word "citizen" (or variants like people) did not appear a single time among any of the 150 most frequent keywords across any article from 2009 to 2017. Direct references to terms like "population" or "community" were also markedly sporadic. Alternatively, using the same database for the same period of time, a search that combines "smart cities" or "smart city" and "citizen" found "citizen participation" to occur 37 times, while "citizen engagement(s)" occured 38 times. Within the results of the same query, the topic with the highest number of keywords was IoT (Internet of Things), with 158 keywords, more than two times the amount of keywords for all references made to "citizens" combined. In addition to what is already being developed in literature, that adds further justification for research that more carefully considers the citizens' perspective when advancing with the smart cities' research agenda.

3   Research Design

The study considered the theoretical lenses of the Social construction of technology (SCOT). This approach challenges linear scientific and technical development and the heterogeneous relationships of users in the process of rooted innovation by accounting for the flexibility of technology use and the unpredictability of possible social effects from its use [24]. According to SCOT, the impact of technology on society and the formation of technology by society are parallel processes, and their interdependence is reflected in the concept of socio-technical ensembles. Such framework helps avoiding the deterministic interpretation of computerization as a stage of objective progress of technology and helps discovering the features of acculturation of new technologies in various institutional spheres.

Through SCOT theoretical lenses, this study used two approaches: (a) content analysis on how the Smart city agenda was constructed by the Russian social media and news; (b) survey of Saint Petersburg citizens identifying their needs in "smart city" technologies (open data, electronic public services and the possibilities of involving citizens while attempting to solve issues of city life). The purpose is to determine how the concept of Smart City was framed content produced by the Russian media. In this study, the automated system for semantic analysis Humanitariana (TLibra full-text search system) has been selected as the main research tool because it provides the search of terms and its frequencies as well as it allows for clustering terms into semantic groups [30]. As a tool for analyzing the received data, the Analysis ToolPak and infographics of MS Excel were used. Data were collected from 2010 to 2017. The research team used CNews portal and search services (Google and Yandex) to quantify and analyze mass media reports that involve the Smart city concept. In searching procedures, terms such as «Smart city», «Smart governance», «Smart house» and variations were entered into the database.

Authors examined major media sources for those mentions between the referred dates. As a result, a sample of 589 articles was produced using the online sampling process with the following proportion: 2010- 87, 2011- 35, 2012- 46, 2013- 67, 2014- 62, 2015- 79, 2016- 94, 2017- 119.

Articles for each year were converted into eight text files in MS Word for further analysis. With the help of the TLibra full-text search system, lists of the most frequently used terms were constructed for each year. The aim of the semantic analysis was to identify the dynamics and the specifics of smart city topics. It should be noted that each term in the resulting list had two main characteristics: (1) the number (2) and the frequency of used terms. In this study, frequency was used to conduct the content analysis. TLibra calculates the frequency of terms by first discarding irrelevant words (for instance, "an" and "the"). It then calculates the frequency of each remaining word as the ratio of the occurrences of that word to the total number of remaining words associated to acts adopted in a particular year, expressed as a percent. Based on the output, an expert group clustered terms into thematic semantic groups. Subsequently, individual terms and groups were analyzed to understand trends and areas of emphasis.

The citizens' survey was focused on the three thematic sections: (1) citizens' IT usage to interact with authorities; (2) important urban issues; (3) expectations from Smart city project. The study was conducted in November, 2017 using an online questionnaire. The target group of respondents was active citizens - Internet users. The choice of this target group was determined by the purpose of the research, as well as by its membership to a group that could be considered "early adopters" of innovation [26].

To calculate the sample, data on the number of the general population of 3.36 million people were used (Internet users among the population of St. Petersburg aged 18 and older). For conducting the surveys, a minimum sample size of 384 people was considered (simple repetitive sampling, 95% accuracy, confidence interval 5%). The questionnaire and news about the survey were published at different official and non-government popular internet-resources and 421 respondents took part in the survey

(47,3% male, 52,7% female). Taking into account the specific nature of the target group, the age structure of the respondents was shifted to younger age groups, however, researchers managed to attract an older audience: 18–30 y.o - 51,3%; 31–45 y.o - 34%; 46–59 y.o. - 11,6%; and 60 and older - 3,1%.

In particular, the study considered the following characteristics: citizens' IT competences (Internet usage, Potential Readiness for E-communication); experience in Communication with Officials and the Preferences of Channels; influence of Opinions from Internet Portals on decision-making and city management; recognition of the Smart City concept (Awareness, Readiness, Expectations). By applying the research methods described, the study attempts to explain the construction of the Smart City concept by citizens from different kinds of media. The results could inform and perhaps help improving the design of the existing Smart City program as well as future initiatives.

4   Findings

The research findings covered the construction of a Smart City concept from the citizens' perspective and the developed Smart City agenda.

4.1   Semantic Analysis the Smart Cities Media Agenda

For the analysis, the research team gathered the expert meeting and identified terms that provide the greatest interest for the assessment. The identified terms were separated into 7 semantic groups: «Authorities», «Business», «Citizens», «Technologies», «Governance», «Services», «Processes». For the analysis of semantic groups, the authors used integral indicators for each group. The calculation of the integral indicator was based on the calculation of the sum by the formula $= \sum_{i=1}^{N} K_i W_i$, where K_i is an indicator of frequency and W_i is the weight of the indicator by the semantic group for each year. The final integral indicators were used to construct the graphs in Excel and the comparative analysis of the semantic groups presented on Figs. 1 and 2.

Sematic analysis showed that Smart City topics were mostly found in business and IT companies' texts that describe new technologies and gadgets. Articles addressing citizens' usage of such gadgets and their assessment on their experience appeared, on average, half as often.

According to the collected data, a smart city is presented in the Russian media predominantly as a technological phenomenon. In the early 2010s, there were more texts on administrative reform and the need to apply ICT solutions in this regard. In last 3 years, technical terms started to become more pronounced for the rest of the topics as well. It is important to make clear, however, that there is no single program or technological complex being presented, but a rather heterogeneous set of technological solutions. Also, the research agenda seems to increasingly involve authorities, as the developers of government programs and concepts, and investors, as stakeholders directly interested in the potential associated to the smart city phenomenon.

Despite of domination of technological terms, the peak in "Governance" semantic group in 2011 demonstrates increased attention to management issues of smart-city

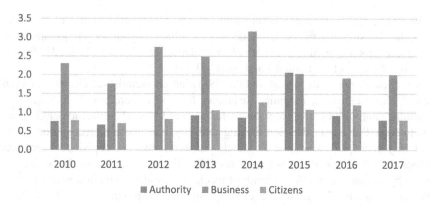

Fig. 1. Semantic groups «Authority», «Business» and «Citizens» by integral indicators, 2010–2017.

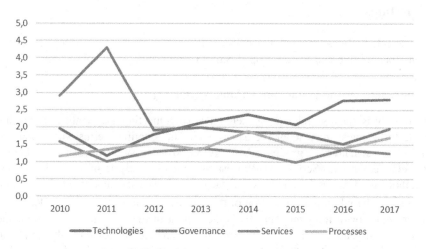

Fig. 2. Semantic groups «Technologies», «Governance», «Services» and «Processes» by integral indicators, 2010–2017.

technologies. Particularly, most of media messages this year were related to management of "smart house" and "smart building". It can be assumed that it allowed to close the gap between "Technologies" and "Governance" since both of those topics are essential parts of development of "Smart city" conception. Based on the results of the analysis, discussions around the concept of a Smart City in the articles analyzed are mainly directed to the expert community of IT companies and the public sector. The terms used in the texts are not addressed to the average citizen, and probably will not always be clear to the public. In comparison with other topics, such as digital economy, e-government services and usage of modern IT in social spheres, media does not provide enough examples of specific services that, in the context Smart Cities, can attract citizens' attention.

4.2   Survey of Citizens' Expectations from a Smart City

At the very beginning of the survey, respondents were asked about their experience in using information technology (IT), the frequency of its use and specific practices of interaction with the authorities via the Internet. Information technology is a part of everyday practice of respondents, with the majority of respondents feeling confident about using computers and the Internet. According to the survey results, 94% prefer to communicate with the authorities in full or in part in electronic format. Besides, more than 60% of the respondents consider themselves to be experienced users of IT, capable, henceforth, of studying new programs, applications and products. A little less than a third attributed themselves to the category of "rather experienced users" who easily manage a standard set of programs for personal needs and performance of work duties.

The active use of Internet technologies in everyday practices is also emphasized by respondents' preferences regarding communication channels for interaction with the authorities. According to the survey, almost half of the active citizens (47%) would prefer to communicate fully electronically, and as many as in a partially electronic form. At the same time, the assessment of the effects of electronic interaction between the authorities and citizens at the moment is quite restrained. Respondents were asked to assess the 5-point scale of achieving various goals in during IT-mediated interactions. The graph shows the average scores given by the respondents for achieving each goal (see Fig. 3). Residents of St. Petersburg tended to give not high marks (5 and 4 points). The collected data demonstrated that at this stage the current level of online interaction contributed to an improvement in social situation understanding by the authorities, as well as a quicker response to the hotbeds of social tension, and improving the image of government.

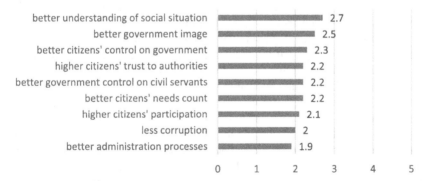

Fig. 3. Answers to the question: "In your opinion, to what extent does the level of interaction between citizens and authorities through electronic channels at this stage achieve the following objectives?", 5-point scale.

In order to find out how citizens are trying to solve their problems in practice, the questionnaire included the question "How do you react in most cases to urban problems?". According to the survey, one third of the citizens do not take any measures a problem is noticed because of time constraints (see Fig. 4). Among the specific solutions, the most popular was the use of Internet portals (22%).

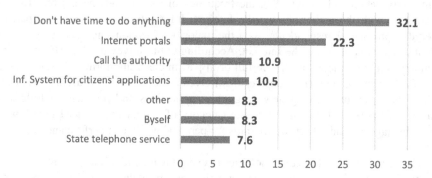

Fig. 4. Respondents' answers to the question: "How in most cases do you respond to city problems?", %.

At this stage and according to the citizens, the electronic interaction of government and society contributes to an improved understanding of the social situation and an accelerated response to emerging issues. In addition, 57% of respondents consider online portals to be the most effective way for solving urban problems. In contrast, only 11% prefers a personal visit to authorities, and 17% - paper application. To build an effective dialogue, it is necessary to increase the image of the authorities in the eyes of citizens and overcome the existing negative practices of using separate portals or ineffective appeals.

The level of awareness of the "Smart City" project reaches 74.6% among the respondents: 19,6% - exactly know how to build it, 23.7% - know what is it, and 31? 3% - have heard something about it. According to urban activists' opinion, a smart city is a comfortable environment for living with a developed infrastructure, where citizens participate in management, and the authorities, in turn, are set for a productive dialogue. Respondents also said that the most urgent urban problems are related to public transport, roads, parking, traffic jams, infrastructure, construction and improvement. It is advisable to introduce the technologies of the "smart city" to solve precisely these problems, which are of concern to the citizens.

For those respondents who showed their knowledge about smart cities projects, a transition to questions about the views and expectations from the project implementation was opened. In the opinion of the respondents, a smart city is, first of all, an effective system of urban management, which takes into account the opinions of citizens, and where a productive dialogue between the authorities and society is built (see Fig. 5).

Citizens considered the following priority areas for the "Smart St. Petersburg" project: openness of government and citizens' inclusion in city management (52.5%), solving environmental issues (44.2%) and improving the quality of life (33%), human capital building (26%).

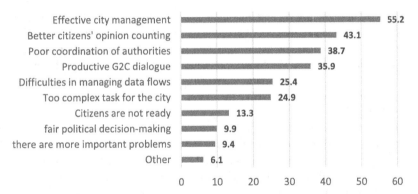

Fig. 5. Answers to the question: "Which of the following statements correspond to your expectations from "Smart St. Petersburg" project?", %.

Among the city residents, optimists prevailed, with 77% believing that the use of electronic portals will help to influence political decisions. Also, 91% of the respondents are ready to take part in the management of the city. It should be emphasized that the results of the survey do not apply to the entire population of St. Petersburg because data was collected through a survey of a separate target group of Internet users. At the same time, it is relevant to highlight that this group of respondents already has experience in e-communications and, at the same time, expresses readiness to continue using such channels and look forward to having their needs met by interacting with the authorities.

5   Conclusion

This research underlined the prevalence of the technical over the social side in the Smart City agenda constructed in media. Services for citizens were barely discussed in the majority of texts analyzed. At the same time, the citizens' survey revealed the rising interest in the Smart city project as well as a high level of readiness to participate in related activities.

In the light of previous practices, results contrast with experiences such as the Saint Petersburg portal for urban solutions development, which illustrates the high response of citizens who followed its start [31]. The popularity of such portal was explained through the importance of the topics published on the site, as well as the high level and efficiency of solutions proposed (more than 50%). This finding suggest that Saint Petersburg citizens' apparent readiness to participate online in the city life is not necessarily echoed in the media.

It could be speculated that positive expectations from the project "Smart St. Petersburg" relate to a genuine belief in building a comfortable environment. However, there are also conservative estimates of the project's prospects. Those estimates are often coupled with the translation of past negative experiences, corruption scandals and the presence of administrative barriers in the development of innovative projects. In this regard, when implementing the project "Smart St. Petersburg", it may be critical for citizens to remain active and maintain an optimistic mood towards less active comrades in city projects. That could be done by proactively disseminating information about positive experiences, breakthroughs and the usefulness of using new technologies to solve city problems. For Smart city development, in the eyes of the citizens of the city, quality growth is important so the city can become comfortable for the residents. It is hence important to involve the urban community and representatives of the creative class.

One major limitation of current research is linked with the sample used in the survey. At the same time, the research attempted to explain citizen's attitudes since the early stages of the Smart City project. From this perspective, the obtained data could be considered timely and indeed useful for Saint Petersburg Smart City project development. Research should continue to look for ways of collecting data that reflects citizen's perspectives as it may be a way of understanding expectations and directing governance efforts. Although findings in this research agenda remain modest, efforts to collect data from the media and from the perspective of the citizens should endure. Complementarily, fostering the use of creative technologies or creative uses of citizen inputs may be open important avenues for research.

Acknowledgements. The study was performed with financial support by the grant from the Russian Science Foundation (project № 17-78-10079): "Research on adaptation models of the Smart City Concept in the conditions of modern Russian Society".

References

1. Abella, A., Ortiz-de-Urbina-Criado, M., De-Pablos-Heredero, C.: A model for the analysis of data-driven innovation and value generation in smart cities' ecosystems. Cities **64**, 47–53 (2017). https://doi.org/10.1016/j.cities.2017.01.011
2. Batty, M., et al.: Smart cities of the future. Eur. Phys. J. Spec. Top. **214**(1), 481–518 (2012)
3. Bolívar, M.P.R.: Governance models and outcomes to foster public value creation in smart cities. In: Proceedings of the 18th Annual International Conference on Digital Government Research, pp. 521–530. ACM (2017)
4. Boukhris, I., Ayachi, R., Elouedi, Z., Mellouli, S., Amor, N.B.: Decision model for policy makers in the context of citizens engagement. Soc. Sci. Comput. Rev. **34**(6), 740–756 (2016). https://doi.org/10.1177/0894439315618882
5. Castelnovo, W., Misuraca, G., Savoldelli, A.: Citizen's engagement and value co-production in smart and sustainable cities. In: International Conference on Public Policy, Milan, pp. 1–16 (2015)
6. Chourabi, H., et al.: Understanding smart cities: an integrative framework. In: Proceedings of the 45th Hawaii International Conference on System Science (HICSS), pp. 2289–2297 (2012). https://doi.org/10.1109/hicss.2012.615
7. Creators of unique methods of working with the future are invited to participate in the design of the NTI University. Agency for Strategic Initiatives material, 12 October 2017 (2017). http://asi.ru/eng/news/84160/
8. Dameri, R.P.: Searching for smart city definition: a comprehensive proposal. Int J. Comput. Technol. **11**(5), 2544–2551 (2013)

9. Degbelo, A., Granell, C., Trilles, S., Bhattacharya, D., Casteleyn, S., Kray, C.: Opening up smart cities: citizen-centric challenges and opportunities from GIScience. ISPRS Int. J. Geo-Inf. **5**(2), 1–25 (2016). https://doi.org/10.3390/ijgi5020016

10. Delmastro, F., Arnaboldi, V., Conti, M.: People-centric computing and communications in smart cities. IEEE Commun. Mag. **54**(7), 122–128 (2016). https://doi.org/10.1109/MCOM. 2016.7509389

11. Dewalska–Opitek, A.: Smart city concept – the citizens' perspective. In: Mikulski, J., (ed.) Telematics - Support for Transport, TST 2014. Communications in Computer and Information Science, vol. 471, pp. 331–340. Springer, Heidelberg (2014). https://doi.org/ 10.1007/978-3-662-45317-9_35

12. Gabrys, J.: Programming environments: environmentality and citizen sensing in the smart city. Environ. Plan. D: Soc. Space **32**(1), 30–48 (2014). https://doi.org/10.1068/d16812

13. Gasco-Hernandez, M., Gil-Garcia, J.R.: Is it more than using data and technology in local governments: identifying opportunities and challenges for cities to become smarter. UMKC Law Rev. **4**, 915 (2016)

14. Gil-Garcia, J.R., Zhang, J., Puron-Cid, G.: Conceptualizing smartness in government: an integrative and multi-dimensional view. Govern. Inf. Q. **33**(3), 524–534 (2016). https://doi. org/10.1016/j.giq.2016.03.002

15. Granier, B., Kudo, H.: How are citizens involved in smart cities? analysing citizen participation in Japanese 'Smart Communities'. Inf. Polity **21**(1), 61–76 (2016). https://doi. org/10.3233/IP-150367

16. Höjer, M., Wangel, J.: Smart sustainable cities: definition and challenges. In: ICT Innovations for Sustainability, pp. 333–349. Springer (2015)

17. Hollands, R.G.: Critical interventions into the corporate smart city. Camb. J. Reg. Econ. Soc. **8**(1), 61–77 (2015). https://doi.org/10.1093/cjres/rsu011

18. Joss, S., Cook, M., Dayot, Y.: Smart cities: towards a new citizenship regime? a discourse analysis of the british smart city standard. J. Urban Technol. **24**(4), 29–49 (2017). https://doi. org/10.1080/10630732.2017.1336027

19. Li, F., Nucciarelli, A., Roden, S., Graham, G.: How smart cities transform operations models: a new research agenda for operations management in the digital economy. Prod. Plan. Control. **27**(6), 514–528 (2016)

20. Marsal-Llacuna, M.L.: Building universal socio-cultural indicators for standardizing the safeguarding of citizens' rights in smart cities. Soc. Indic. Res. **130**(2), 563–579 (2017). https://doi.org/10.1007/s11205-015-1192-2

21. Meijer, A., Bolívar, M.P.R.: Governing the smart city: a review of the literature on smart urban governance. Int. Rev. Adm. Sci. **82**(2), 392–408 (2016)

22. Michelucci, F.V., De Marco, A., Tanda, A.: Defining the role of the smart-city manager: an analysis of responsibilities and skills. J. Urban Technol. **23**(3), 23–42 (2016)

23. Mueller, J., Lu, H., Chirkin, A., Klein, B., Schmitt, G.: Citizen design science: a strategy for crowd-creative urban design. Cities **72**, 181–188 (2018). https://doi.org/10.1016/j.cities. 2017.08.018

24. Orlikowski, W.J.: Using technology and constituting structures: a practice lens for studying technology in organizations. Organ. Sci. **11**(4), 404–428 (2000)

25. Puron-Cid, G.: Interdisciplinary application of structuration theory for e-government: a case study of an IT-enabled budget reform. Gov. Inf. Q. **30**, S46–S58 (2013)

26. Rogers, E.M.: Diffusion of Innovations. Simon and Schuster, NY (2010). https://books. google.com/books?hl=en&lr=&id=v1ii4QsB7jIC&oi=fnd&pg=PR15&dq=rogers +diffusion&ots=DK_xvKQs5U&sig=fnbIYiB_VPURY8hc6dN0omqvOyA

27. Schlappa, H.: Co-producing the cities of tomorrow: fostering collaborative action to tackle decline in europe's shrinking cities. Eur. Urban Reg. Stud. **24**(2), 162–174 (2017). https://doi.org/10.1177/0969776415621962

28. Schumann, L., Stock, W.G.: Acceptance and use of ubiquitous cities' information services. Inf. Serv. Use **35**(3), 191–206 (2015). https://doi.org/10.3233/ISU-140759

29. Suopajärvi, T.: Knowledge-making on 'ageing in a smart city' as socio-material power dynamics of participatory action research. Action Res. **15**(4), 386–401 (2017). https://doi.org/10.1177/1476750316655385

30. Vidiasova, L., Dawes, S.S.: The influence of institutional factors on e-governance development and performance: an exploration in the Russian Federation. Inf. Polity **22**(4), 267–289 (2017). https://doi.org/10.3233/IP-170416

31. Vidiasova, L., Mikhaylova, E.V.: The comparison of governmental and non-governmental e-participation tools functioning at a city-level in Russia. Commun. Comput. Inf. Sci. **674**, 135–144 (2016)

32. Waal, M., Dignum, M.: The citizen in the smart city. how the smart city could transform citizenship. Inf. Technol. **59**(6), 263–273 (2017). https://doi.org/10.1515/itit-2017-0012

Crowd Sourced Monitoring in Smart Cities in the United Kingdom

Norbert Kersting and Yimei Zhu[✉]

Institute of Political Science, Westfälische Wilhelms-University Münster,
Scharnhorststr. 100, 48151 Münster, Germany
norbert.kersting@uni-muenster.de, yimeizhu1@yahoo.com

Abstract. Smart cities can be regarded as the latest administrative reform and digital innovation in most metropolitan cities globally. In smart cities as well as in former urban New Public Management modernization and Post Weberian reforms, the important role of the citizens in planning as well as monitoring has been highlighted. Online and offline participation along with feedback can reinvigorate town planning and policymaking as well as policy monitoring processes at the local level. The UK as many other countries reacted to this trend by offering new channels for online participation. The new participative innovations allowed for more participation and more influence by citizen. FixMyStreet is a crowdsourced monitoring instrument implemented in the UK. How it works, what the role of the state and civil society represent, and is crowd monitoring vote-centric or talk-centric will be discussed in the paper. It represents a successful bottom-up innovation approach that was used by numerous municipalities. It is a successful public private partnership and a mix between 'invented' and 'invited' space, where the role of the state is redefined.

Keywords: Crowd sourcing · Smart city · Participation

1 Introduction

In the process of digitalization, local governments try to find the best way to integrate the new technology into the public administration as well as into the local political process. Each political system or local government tries to pursue through political innovation or reform a good governance, in which the participatory element is the most accepted approach in reaching the goal [9]. 'Smart city' is an attempt, which is based on this context and elicits an increase in participation, which is one of its crucial functions. When building 'smart cities' most of the governments start firstly to integrate the multiple ICT solutions for the city services and secondly facilitating an increase in citizen's participation [17]. No matter if the strategy of 'Internet of things' followed by the European Union or the project of 'Internet Plus', which stems from China, the governments are looking for a balance in between the demands of citizens and the fast growing Internet technology. Building 'smart cities' has become a common approach among governments in maintaining the urban modernization process. E-governance should be the core project midst the entire 'smart city' building. Traditional institutions with only offline administration services and functions do not seem to be suitable any

© Springer Nature Switzerland AG 2018
D. A. Alexandrov et al. (Eds.): DTGS 2018, CCIS 858, pp. 255–265, 2018.
https://doi.org/10.1007/978-3-030-02843-5_20

more in modern local societies. A more transparent, flexible, intelligent and open government has been demanded and is becoming the trend. There is therefore a trend towards easier and cheaper online instruments. However, there seems to be a metamorphosis of participatory instruments when they go online [19]. The Internet has benefits as a memory of organizations and as an instrument for short-term mobilization. However, it seems to be less useful in the heart of deliberation [15]. With digitalization, participatory instruments became more numeric and voter oriented. However, are they enhancing the quality of democracy and are they sustainable? This paper argues that the future of planning lies in better participatory instruments (Offline and online) and in a blended democracy, which would combine the best of both worlds. For monitoring purposes, online participation seems adequate. The question arises, what the role of the state should be.

From the civic side, the government initiatives and activities from the Transformed Local Government strategy have not yet reached the goal as they had promised although many local governments have launched their own websites and contact centers to engage with the citizens. The process of 'shifting the power' to the citizens and people communities is still a difficult task lying in front of the society [10].

2   'Smart City', Participatory Rhombus and 'Crowd Sourced Monitoring'

In this research, the term 'smart city' only refers to the ICT innovated facilities that are used by a government for the purpose of improving the efficacy of the administration as well as enhancing the citizen's political engagement. The European Parliament defined smart city as a city seeking to address public issues via ICT-based solutions on the basis of a multi-stakeholder, which is a municipally based partnership. This concept has been used for promoting the efficiency of all the city services. These services not only include the city administrative managements, but also embrace the assets of local communities, energy supply networks, transportation systems, schools, libraries, waste management and so on [24]. The innovation of administrative management and the forms of participation are the foundation of the development of the crowdsourcing. The main difference between managing a 'smart city' and governing a traditional form of city, is by processing and analyzing the data from citizens and devices, which collected Big data by social media analysis along with the usage of sensors equipped with real-time online monitoring systems [30]. New information and communication technology (ICT) can be used as efficacy instruments to enhance quality, performance and interactivity of urban services, to reduce administration costs and resource consumption and to improve contact between government and citizens [31]. Here, crowd-sourced monitoring is regarded as an important participatory instrument. The participatory turn in the 1990s triggered a wave of democratic innovations [22, 28]. In the 2010s digitalization broadened the spectrum of new participatory instruments. These have to fulfill the function of planning and monitoring, which both give relevant feedback in all political systems.

Here, participation can be bottom-up, which is initiated in the invented space in form of protest or organized interest groups – conversely these participatory instruments can also be initiated by the state in the invited space to channel protest [19, 20].

A decline in voter turnout and an increase of political protest lead to a crisis of legitimacy [3, 6, 21]. Political participation is defined as an activity influencing political decision-making at the local, regional, and (supra-) national level. Governments are channeling protest through democratic innovation, which offers new instruments for participation. These instruments of political participation are part of the invited space. Invited space is defined as political participation, which is planned and organized in a top-down manner by local regional and national governments [19]. In contrast, invented space encompasses instruments that are initiated and organized to a certain extent autonomously by the citizenry in a bottom-up manner [19].

Political participation comes in many forms and can be presented as heterogeneous instruments [19, 20]. These diverse forms could be related to four different spheres of democratic participation, characterized by different intrinsic logics, more specifically in participatory online and offline instruments: representative democracy, direct democracy, deliberative democracy and demonstrative democracy [19, 20]. In the following, these areas will be presented briefly.

The first two spheres: representative participation and direct democratic are not talk-centric, but vote-centric. This means that they are focusing on large numbers and also representativeness. However, these spheres are also included in the legal framework with certain controlled procedures, rules, and regulations regarding democratic principles, like openness, transparency, control of power, as well as majority rules and minority rights.

Representative democracy is vote-centric and is based on elections. Representative participation, elections and contacts to politicians etc. are characteristics of modern liberal democracies. In modern, liberal democracies all other forms of direct democratic instruments, deliberative instruments as well as demonstrative participation are in this case however secondary for representative democracies. Online participation includes internet-voting or direct contact to politicians via e-mail or Facebook [2, 20]. Representative participation is a dominant form of liberal democracies. Legislative and executive branches, parliaments and the government are primarily based on the competition between political parties and political candidates. The institutions of representative democracy are formalized and enshrined in the constitution, local charters, and other legal frameworks. Representative democracy is characterized as a numerical democracy, where delegates and/or trustees are chosen by a majority on the one hand, while on the other hand, minorities' rights have to be protected. Representative participation encompasses other forms of participation, such as direct contact with the incumbents, membership in political parties, campaigning, and candidature for political mandates etc.

The sphere of direct democratic participation is the second area of democratic involvement, which is issue oriented and vote-centric. Direct democratic participation is mainly used in the form of referenda and citizen initiatives, which can produce binding decisions. There are other online and offline instruments that are vote- centric and issue oriented, such as opinion polls. In the direct democratic participation area

[15, 16] online petitions, but also other instruments, which is problem-oriented and numeric, such as online surveys, are included.

Deliberative participation is by nature talk-centric. It has its origins in the deliberative turn in the last decade of the 20th century [16, 19]. Offline deliberative arenas are generally small by nature. In online participatory budgeting processes there are a couple of hundred participants. For example, in bigger cities there are up to 10,000 participants in the online participatory budgeting process [18].

The last sphere of participation is called demonstrative democracy. Individualism, societal change of values and political disenchantment lead to new forms of expressive participation, inter alia, political demonstrations, and wearing campaign badges [4]. Online demonstrations comprise civil society protests like shit storm and flash mobs [11]. Protest can be conducted in a much bigger fashion via the Internet (see Arab spring). Online shit storms focus less on local politics but more on individual websites or companies. These can mobilize around 1 million participants globally [12] (Fig. 1).

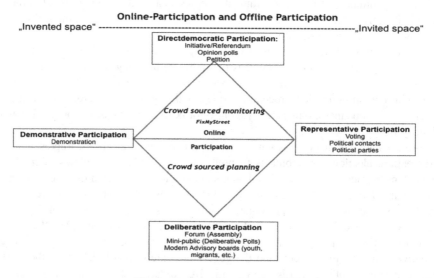

Fig. 1. Participatory rhombus [18]

Planning and Monitoring can be regarded as two main functions in political systems. In both areas the feedback of the citizen play an important role. Crowdsourcing and crowd sourced monitoring refers to an open online platform for anybody to participate [7, 14]. The "crowd" in this context refers to the undefined group of citizen who participate, it is initially used in the private and enterprises sectors to gather collective intelligence for a variety of purposes, then the government widely accepted it as an innovated application to promote democratic process [27]. In this regard citizen sourcing is a better but less recognized terminology. Crowdsourcing is the common method in collecting citizens' information as well as seeking for a variety options for societal services and has been constantly accepted by many governments. Jeffrey Howe was the first one, who used this term in his articles, which was published in Wired magazine (2006) and also in his subsequent book on the topic (2009). He named the rise of the countercurrent in response to the outsourcing of problem solving of firms in India and China, as crowdsourcing. Many scholars have extended the scope and definition of this term.

However, Chinese scholars Zhao and Zhu (2012) defined crowdsourcing as a "collective intelligence" system with three basic elements of the crowd, the beneficiary organization and an accessible hosting platform [32]. Seltzer and Mahmoudi set a more restrictive standard, which is: a diverse crowd, a well-defined problem, ideation, the Internet and solution selection [27]. Brabham [8] describes crowdsourcing as being more an online-based business model than having other functions. Most of the theorists have been emphasizing more the political functions of crowdsourcing, This is due to firstly, its potential in creating transparency, which increases trust in political institutions when the democracy system however falls into a recession [12] the decline of the citizens' trust in institutions seems to become obvious [5]. Secondly, it enhances citizens' participation. Brabham [7] and Seltzer and Mahmoudi [27] all agree that crowdsourcing defends citizens' right in decision-making and thus gives more voice to the citizen (crowd). Thirdly, it builds a value of common contribution. Brabham [7] argue that Individuals should be incorporated in a discussion to contribute individual solutions for common good.

With the outcomes of building a common contribution and empowering the citizens, the practical functions of crowdsourcing has exceeded its original setting in gathering collective intelligence to solve certain problems. It has evolved into the promotion of the democratic process by empowering citizens with new channels to present their desires and interests. In the process of New Public Management reforms as well as democratic innovations, crowdsourcing corresponds to the government strategy in highlighting the citizens' planning as well as monitoring functions. Therefore, it has been classified as a new form of a participatory instrument in the political field. Considering the participatory function of crowdsourcing, theorists hold different views about its actual effects. Some opinions insist that crowdsourcing can function well in combination with direct democracy, such as referendum, but may not be suitable in the context of representative and deliberative participation [26]. That is partially due to the nature of crowdsourcing as the method mainly focuses on participants' real-time reaction and singular shot of action.

In the crowdsourcing process, most of the practical crowdsourcing cases represent the gathering of the crowds' ideas and views directly, however it further on does not require neither the representatives to represent each person's idea nor a longer time of deliberation [1]. Co-creation is another form of open innovation, which instead, emphasizes more on building an open and long lasting discussion space for fully-fledged deliberation. Both crowdsourcing and co-creation are defined as the innovations for realizing and improving the participation in this digital age but with different specialties [25]. Moreover, one of the pioneer researchers of crowdsourcing, Brabham, indicates that the way of crowdsourced monitoring cannot replace any kind of original political participation instruments or innovations, since legitimacy and fairness has been questioned in this instrument. He also indicates that crowdsourcing is a form of participation that can strengthen representative democracy, because it may be easily manipulated by the elites which act in favor of their interest groups [8]. On the other hand, a bottom-up approach often lacks effectiveness and thus good ideas are not implemented. From this, it appears that there is no unique conclusion about top-down crowd sourcing in the invited space and bottom-up crowdsourcing in the invented space, in terms of its political function. The actual effects or the practical performance should be discussed in the context of certain forms of participation that it is applied with. Otherwise, the role of the state as a reaction to bottom-up processes is crucial. The innovation of administration management and the forms of participation is the foundation of the development of crowdsourcing.

3 Crowdsourcing Instrument-FixMyStreet

According to our framework, all the participatory innovations should come either from the 'invited space' or from the 'invented space'. In most of the cases, the innovated participatory instruments are characterized by a variety of spheres of participation for the sake of achieving better effects. The modern society often only adopts one form of participation, either with 'invited' or 'invented' channels. This cannot fulfill the constantly increasing demands of the citizens, which will cause an unstable society. Therefore, implementing a mix of participation forms (or balance and check) is a common way adopted by most of the governments.

This study will introduce an important crowdsourcing case from the UK in describing this new form of a participation mode from the 'invented' space. The fast growing field of ICT pushes the UK in two ways. Firstly, the UK needs to find a path in combining this new technology with modern administration for the sake of enhancing the efficacy of government work and secondly, to promote the social democratic process. To introduce a crowdsourcing platform into the government administration system is the outcome of modern state governance and the deployment of ICT.

Fix My Street.com (FMS) is a web-based civic crowdsourcing platform, which enables citizens to report, view and discuss local problems, such as abandoned vehicles, fly posting, graffiti, fly tipping, unlit lampposts, potholes, litter, street cleaning, etc., as well as tracking resolutions by the relevant office. It is a online-complaint-management-system. When citizens report deficits in infrastructure or with services it is made public immediately, where and when this dysfunction happened. This puts an enormous pressure on the administration to react timely. The status of each post either has been fixed or remains unfixed. The proposed working period of each problem is four weeks, after this time the problem will be labeled as unfixed, either from the proposer or from the platform. FixMyStreet is a nongovernmental site that has been developed by the charity Mysociety in 2007 and received a £10,000 grant from the Department of Constitutional Affairs' Innovation as the initiative capital. As the nonprofit organization, FixMyStreet gets the financial support from the central government in starting its activities as well as in maintaining the normal operation. It does not possess the executive power to react to the reported issues directly, but it provides an open and professional platform to report and track the action. Therefor, citizens are enabled in having more power to influence their daily life [23].

3.1   The Working Principle of FixMyStreet

From the governmental side of the UK and in the background of the digital society, which is the same as in other countries the new form of administration innovation with the facilities of ICT has the purposes of improving the public services, transforming the governmental duties to a more transparent and efficient stage, so that the citizens 'engagement in the public affairs can be enabled. The strategy of a Transformed Local Government in the UK was set in this context of engaging with the community and its citizens, which is one of the leading pillar of this strategy and thus lays out the foundation for developing those 'invented' civic-centered social engagement instruments, such as FixMyStreet [10].

According to the official published data, 420 (accounts for 98% of them all) of the British Councils accept the cooperative service with FixMyStreet, which means nearly 65,16 million of the British population can report to their community, problems via FixMyStreet platform [29]. By the year 2017, the website can deliver 12,000 reports to different British Councils per month and has more than 50,000 platform visiting. By the time of March 2018, the FixMyStreet has received 1,204,699 problem reports, in which 484803 of them have been marked as fixed; the finished rate is about 40% (see Fig. 2). FixMyStreet has divided the reported problems into six main categories, which are Footpaths, Bus stops, Potholes, Street Lighting, Flytipping and Rubbish.

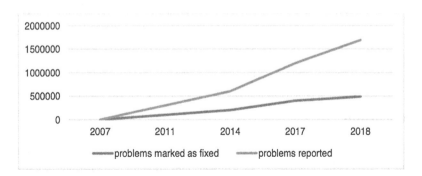

Fig. 2. Reported problems on FixMyStreet from 2007 to 2018

From the civic side, the government initiatives and activities from the Transformed Local Government strategy have not yet reached the goal as they had promised although many local governments have launched their own websites and contact centers to engage with the citizens. The process of 'shifting the power' to the citizens and people communities is still a difficult task lying in front of the society. It has been observed that, "[...] :, our staff and our partners much more [10].

3.2   The Effects of the FixMyStreet

An evaluation by FixMyStreet (2017) analyses the finish rate of the instrument by categories within a selected working week in 2016 (see Fig. 3). The average finished rate is 40%, and there are slightly different finished rates among categories. These findings indicate the effects of the FixMyStreet as an 'invented' participatory instrument in society. It shows a successful mode of combining the bottom-up initiative with government action so to solve certain social problems, which help the government improve its working efficiency. On the other side, the findings also show the weakness of the 'invented' instrument, which has limited executive power in pushing the implementation of the administrative work, 40% of the finished rate shows that less than half of all the requests can be properly fixed in time and that most of the problems only remain in the unfixed status. In addition, the finished rate has close relation with the facility value of the reported problems, some easy accessible problems such as rubbish cleaning or bus stop changing have a higher finished rate than those that require a higher administrative process.

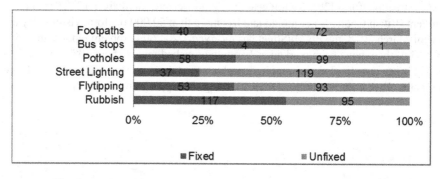

Fig. 3. FixMyStreet posted problems coding and solving situation [13]

4   Conclusion

Political systems, democracies as well as non-democracies require a kind of feedback function or oversight function so to evaluate and monitor policies and control the political incumbents. Here, smart cities offer crowdsourced monitoring in form of a highly transparent online complaint management system. This kind of feedback is sometimes also relevant for the planning process (see crowdsourcing or crowdsourced planning support systems). Without feedback, political leaders will fall into the trap of the dictator's dilemma. Political leaders misinterpreted the needs of the citizenry. This leads to miss-planning and false allocation of resources. Social welfare policies, such as physical infrastructure and housing policies do not deliver adequate and accepted goods and services even by a benevolent autocratic regime. On this background, crowdsourcing emerges when the times require it and brings new possibilities to the original political system. It cannot be defined as a specific form of participation, since it combines various features of different participation norms and presents different functions for case by case processing.

FixMyStreet shows the successful case of Public private partnership and a cooperation between the government and civic power; instead of staying in the absolute leading position, the government in this case is more likely to be a participator of social issues. In this mix between 'invented' and invited participation, the relationship between the government and the citizens seems to be more relaxed than in the 'invited' participation [19]. Based on the third party protocols, both of the two sides are releasing from the traditional social responsibility and limitation into a new form of administration order, which is developing. FixMyStreet seems to create a new promising participation mode, where the role of the government has been placed in a functional position.

However, it is notable that the mode of FixMyStreet cannot be adopted in every society since it has some requirements that are not easily fulfilled. For instance, it requires the citizens to have higher social qualities as well as political awareness. In democracies, citizens have developed their democratic virtues and skills in the long process of the democratization of society and they possess the ability of making a rational reaction when facing the innovation of participation methods. But in non-democratic countries, citizens are lacking influence as well as the experience of democratization. When facing those open innovation instruments, some of them may misuse and cause irrational actions. In addition to citizens 'political virtue, the modernization degree of the government is another crucial factor. This form of 'invented' participation may only be accepted when the government has implemented the open and democratization strategy (ready for the bottom-up innovation). In some of the autocratic governments, neither the government nor the citizens are ready for the power shifting as well as the social roles changing innovation; the unlimited online 'invented' participation such as FixMyStreet may play counterproductive effects in those societies. Nevertheless, as we have seen, in this process transparency seems to be crucial to put pressure on the administration to fulfill its duties. Finally yet importantly, those online 'invented' participation mode require high level of an Internet coverage rate as well as a limited digital divide.

Therefore, online 'invented' participation does not have universal applicability in every society. In general, the crowdsourcing instrument as one of the governmental open innovation has begun to receive attention from the public, and it shows the tendency of becoming a participation norm in many societies, even though these methods still represent new and exotic characteristics. Most of the citizens are willing to use these digital means to express their opinions and share their knowledge about matters around them.

It is notable that those online crowdsourcing methods cannot replace the traditional offline participatory means in the short time, but the changes they have brought to civil society and the political system will exert a far-reaching influence. According to Kersting [18, 19], crowdsourcing platforms with complaint crowd monitoring and complaint management systems can focus on online participation. However, crowd planning and deliberative participation will have to present an online and offline combination, or blended participation. So far, it remains unknown whether they will be fully accepted by the current political decision-making process or not, and how they will change the political ecosystem in the future. The goal of implementing these methods is in finding a better way to optimize the political system as well as promoting the democratic process; at the same time, citizens are empowered in having more chances to make declarations and thus influence the politics in the smart cities.

References

1. Aitamurto, T.: Crowdsourcing for Democracy: A New Era in Policy-Making. Publications of the Committee for the Future. Parliament of Finland 1/2012, Helsinki, Finland (2012)
2. Baldersheim, H., Kersting, N. (eds.): The Wired City: A New Face of Power?: A Citizen Perspective. In: Oxford Handbook of Urban Politics. Oxford University, Oxford, pp. 590–607 (2012)
3. Barber, B.: Strong Democracy: Participatory Politics for a New Age. California University Press, Berkeley (1984)
4. Baringhorst, S.: Internet und Protest. Zum Wandel von Organisationsformen und Handlungsrepertoires – ein Überblick. In: Voss, K. (Hrsg.) Internet & Partizipation. Bottom-up oder Top-down? Politische Beteiligungsmöglichkeiten im Internet. Springer VS, Wiesbaden, pp. 91–114 (2014)
5. Beck, U.: Living in the World Risk Society. Econ. Soc. **35**(3), 329–345 (2006). https://doi.org/10.1080/03085140600844902
6. Budge, I.: The New Challenge of Direct Democracy. Cambridge: Polity. 2001. 'Political Parties in Direct Democracy' (1996). In: Mendelson, M., Brabham, A., Daren, C. (eds.) Moving the Crowd at iStockphoto: The Composition of the Crowd and Motivations for Participation in a Crowdsourcing Application (2008)
7. Brabham, D.: Crowdsourcing the public participation process for planning projects. Plan. Theory **8**, 242–262 (2009). https://doi.org/10.1177/1473095209104824
8. Brabham, D.: Moving the crowd at threadless. Inf. Commun. Soc. **13**, 1122–1145 (2010). https://doi.org/10.1080/13691.181003624090
9. Chourabi, H., et al.: Understanding Smart cities. In: Hawaii International Conference (2012)
10. CIO Council. Homepage: Transformational Local Government: Discussion Paper. http://www.cio.gov.uk/documents/pdf/transgov/trans_local_gov060328.pdf. Accessed 28 Apr 2006
11. Della, P.: Clandestine Political Violence. Cambridge University Press, Cambridge (2013)
12. Diamond, L., Morlino L.: The quality of democracy. In: Diamond, L., (ed.) In Search of Democracy. Routledge, London (2016). https://doi.org/10.4236/ajc.2015.31003
13. FixMystreet Homepage: Free statistics for councils. www.fixmystreet.com. Accessed 12 Nov 2017
14. Howe, J.: Crowdsourcing: Why the Power of the Crowd Is Driving the Future of Business. Three Rivers Press, New York (2009). https://doi.org/10.1057/9780230523531
15. Kersting, N., Baldersheim, H.: Electronic Voting and Democracy: A Comparative Analysis. Palgrave Macmillan, UK (2004)
16. Kersting, N. (ed.): Politische Beteiligung: Einführung in dialogorientierte Instrumente politischer und gesellschaftlicher Partizipation. VS - Springer, Wiesbaden (2008)
17. Kersting, N., et al.: Local Governance Reform in Global Perspective. Springer VS, Wiesbaden (2009). https://doi.org/10.1007/978-3-531-91686-6_1
18. Kersting, N.: The Future of Electronic Democracy. In: Kersting, N. (ed.) 2012: Electronic Democracy, pp. 11–54. Barbara Budrich, Opladen (2012)
19. Kersting, N.: Online participation: from 'invited' to 'invented'spaces. Int. J. Electron. Governance **4**, 270–280 (2013). https://doi.org/10.1504/IJEG.2013.060650
20. Kersting, N.: Participatory turn? comparing citizens' and politicians' perspectives on online and offline local political participation. Lex Localis, J. Local Self-Gov. **14**(2), 225–246 (2015). https://doi.org/10.4335/14.2.249-263

21. Kersting, N.: Demokratische Innovation: Qualifizierung und Anreicherung der lokalen repräsentativen Demokratie. In: Kersting, N. (ed.) Urbane Innovation, pp. 81–120. Springer VS, Wiesbaden (2017). https://doi.org/10.1007/978-3-658-07321-3

22. Kersting, N., Caulfield, J., Nickson, A., Olowu, D., Wollmann, H.: Local Governance Reform in Global Perspective. VS Verlag. Wiesbaden, Germany (2009)

23. King, S., Brown, P.: Fix My street or else: using the internet to voice local public service concerns. In: Proceedings of the 1st International Conference on Theory and Practice of Electronic Governance (ICEGOV 2007), Macao, China, pp. 10–13 (2007)

24. Komninos, N.: What makes cities intelligent? In: Deakin, M. (ed.) Smart Cities: Governing: Modelling and Analysing the Transition. Taylor and Francis, London (2013)

25. Roussopoulos, D., Benello, G. (eds.): Participatory Democracy: Prospects for Democratizing Democracy. Black Rose Books, Portland (2005)

26. Schaal, G.: Die Theorie der e-democracy. In: Lembcke, O., Ritzi, C., Schaal, G. (ed.) Demokratietheorie. Band 2: Normative Demokratietheorien. VS-Verlag, Wiesbaden (2014)

27. Seltzer, E., Mahmoudi, D.: Citizen participation, open innovation and crowdsourcing: challenges and opportunities for planning. J. Plan. Lit. **28**(1), 3–18 (2013). https://doi.org/10.1177/0885412212469112

28. Smith, G.: Democratic Innovations: Designing Institutions for Citizen Participation. Cambridge University Press, Cambridge (2009)

29. Steiberg, T.: 98% of councils accept FixMyStreet reports. Here's how we cope with the rest. https://www.mysociety.org/2015/07/29/98-of-councils-accept-fixmystreet-reports-heres-how-we-cope-with-the-rest/. Accessed 12 Nov 2017

30. Musa, S.: Smart cities - a roadmap for development. J. Telecommun. Syst. Manag. **5**, 144 (2016)

31. New York City Government: Building a smart + Equitable City. http://www1.nyc.gov/assets/forward/documents/NYC-Smart-Equitable-City-Final.pdf. Accessed 12 Nov 2017

32. Zhao, Y.Z., Zhu, Q.H.: Evaluation on crowdsourcing research: current status and future direction. Inf. Syst. Front. **16**, 417–434 (2012)

General Concept of the Storage and Analytics System for Human Migration Data

Lada Rudikowa[1], Viktor Denilchik[1], Ilia Savenkov[2],
Alexandra Nenko[2], and Stanislav Sobolevsky[2,3(✉)]

[1] Yanka Kupala State University of Grodno, Grodno, Belarus
rudikowa@gmail.com, iesekiel@gmail.com
[2] Saint-Petersburg National Research University of Information Technology,
Mechanics and Optics (ITMO), St. Petersburg, Russia
savenkovilya93@gmail.com, al.nenko@gmail.com
sobolevsky@nyu.edu
[3] New York University, New York City, USA

Abstract. The population mobility, related to long-term and short-term migrations, happens on an increasing pace, affecting various fields of activity in a single country and the world community as a whole. Large amounts of diverse migration-related data are recorded by different entities all over the world, making it important to develop and implement a system for storing and analyzing such data. The proposed article describes the subject area associated with socio-economic displacements of people, the key features of internal and external migrations are noted. Based on that, the general architecture of the universal system of data storage and processing is proposed leveraging the client-server architecture. A fragment of the data model, associated with the accumulation of data from external sources, is provided. General approaches for algorithms and data structure usage are proposed. The system architecture is scalable, both vertically and horizontally. The proposed system organizes the process of searching for data and filling the database from third-party sources.

A module for collecting and converting information from third-party Internet sources and sending them to the database is developed. The features of the client application, providing a convenient visual interface for analyzing data in the form of diagrams, graphs, maps, etc. are specified. The system is intended to instrument various users interested in analyzing economic and social transfers, for example, touristic sector organizations wishing to obtain statistics for a certain timeframe, airlines planning flight logistics, as well as for state authorities analyzing the migration flows to develop appropriate regulations.

Keywords: OLTP-system · Socio-economic migration · Data model
General architecture · Boyer-Moore algorithm · Client-server
Analysis subsystem

1 Introduction

Today increasingly many practitioners and researchers are leveraging big data measurements of various aspects of human activity, including human mobility. For example, such datasets are being used for regional delineation at various scales [1],

© Springer Nature Switzerland AG 2018
D. A. Alexandrov et al. (Eds.): DTGS 2018, CCIS 858, pp. 266–276, 2018.
https://doi.org/10.1007/978-3-030-02843-5_21

land use classification [2], transportation optimization [3] and transportation research [4], scoring of socio-economic performance of urban neighborhoods [5], study of touristic behavior [6] and many other social science, urban planning and policy-making applications. Human migration data in particular saw such applications as well [7–9].

Huge amounts of information are accumulated all over the world, but are often highly disjointed and is far from providing general picture of the life of society. Various methods, algorithms and methodologies for data analysis have been developed [e.g. 10–12], which can be used for a specific sample or a set of the researched data. There is a sufficient number of necessary software, technologies and methods for formalizing data arrays, which allow us to structure the data of particular subjects. On the other hand, in a unified information space, the data are practically interrelated, are generated by various types of society activities and we should consider them in the context of whole view, considering a certain type of activity or interactions (for example: development of a worldwide network).

This motivate creating a concept and implementation of a system for storing and processing data related to various types of people's activities. This system can be considered as a way of creating some federal data repository [13, 14]. The study and generalization of various subject areas are in demand in different research directions [7, 15].

Here we consider the main aspects of the subject area associated with socio-economic displacements of people. The displacement of the population or migration is understood as its "mechanical movement" across the globe. Migrations can be external and internal. The internal migration is associated with the movement of people from one region of the country to another in order to find a new place of residence and or work. The internal migration is observed within the territory of the country (for example, migration from rural to urban areas).

External migrations consider the movement of people outside their country, moreover, we can distinguish the following types of external migration:

- emigration is the departure of citizens from their country to another (for permanent residence or a sufficiently long period);
- immigration is the entry of citizens into another country (for permanent residence or a sufficiently long period).

Besides, migration can be both short-term (for example: for tourism purposes), both long-term (work, study, etc.). The data on economic and social displacements in our work are meant as the number of people who have moved from one geographic region to another. Also we include various parameters related to social, financial, economic, cultural, etc. status of people.

The study of economic and social movements of people will allow to the most favorable geographical objects for people identify with the highest degree of reliability in accordance with certain criteria of their life and internal attitudes. Besides, it is possible to track global trends both in terms of economic and social development, both in terms of the region's attractiveness for tourism in specific periods of time.

Generally, the movement of population is growing. This is facilitated by the processes of globalization in the modern world, simplification of the visa regime between countries, the growth of political migration and other factors. The general statistics do not take into account the causes of the emergence of certain trends, there are no specific demographic, political, social factors, which are the primary cause of the emergence of various migration flows. The collection of statistical information, mainly, has an isolated nature and represents only numerical indicators of the selected metrics. The received data is accepted as a display of the current position. Sources of data from government agencies are not always easy to process because of the lack of a software interface and specific storage formats, but they are publicly available. As a rule, such restrictions make them (data) harder to use during the analysis. There is also a question of displaying data in an accessible form, in particular, in the form of various graphic visualizations. Based on statistical data on migrations and analysis of related data, it is possible to create a forecasting apparatus, which allow us to predict, for example, the pace of migration to a particular region.

Thus, the proposed development uses data on socio-economic displacements of people. What is more, the United Nations web resource was chosen as the main source of demographic and migration data [16], which has a huge amount of information about migration indicators in various countries all over the world. Data can be obtained as a file. This resource is the main source of data for the application is being developed.

To study the internal migration in specific countries, we can use national resources, for example, website of European statistics Eurostat [17] or the website of the National Statistical Committee of the Republic of Belarus [18].

2 General Architecture of the Application Associated with Data Connected to Migration

The system for processing socio-economic displacements uses client-server architecture and it is designed to provide users with the most up-to-date data on socio-economic displacements of people. Our application organizes the process of data searching and data filling for the database from third-party sources. To reach this, we developed the system with a module for collecting and converting information from third-party Internet sources and sending them to the database. The system provides an unauthorized user with the ability to log in to the system, and also the opportunity of filtering and viewing information. An authorized user can take one of three roles: Administrator, Editor or User.

The administrator must have the ability to edit the data of users, including creating the new ones, or changing their roles. Other features of the Administrator should be the same as the features of Editor. The Editor can add, edit and delete content. He must update information related to economic and social movements of people. The user is given the opportunity to set the filtration data of economic and social movements for further analysis and visualization. The overall architecture of the system implementation and the relationships between levels are shown on Fig. 1.

The system is implemented in three levels. These levels have minimal connections between each other: database level; level, including access to data; service level; level, including business logic; interaction level (with the user).

The database level is a separate server on which the database is deployed. The database level is associated with the service mapping of business models to relational

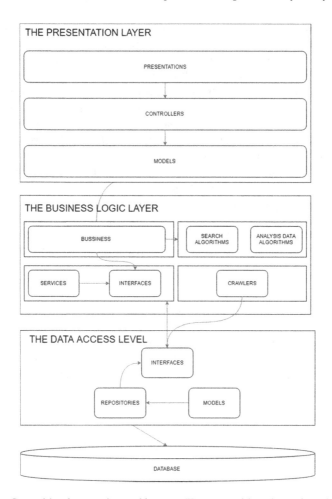

Fig. 1. General implementation architecture (Was created in Microsoft Visio 2016)

database objects using Repository (Repository component). Repository is also responsible for working with data (saving, updating, deleting, selecting). The basis of the Repository is the technology called ADO.NET Entity Framework. Entity Framework is powerful and free tool to work with Microsoft SQL Server – an enterprise database server that provides the most suitable data analysis services [19, 20]. The database of the system contains information about users of the system, content and statistics related to socio-economic displacements of people. The interaction database layer contains a set of classes representing data models from the domain field. Repository classes are also realized on this layer, which combine in itself a connection to the database and the formation of requests, presenting an interface for the client, through which opens the possibility of CRUD operations on the elements of the database. The architecture of the database filling system is highlighted separately. This component interacts with the database through the interaction layer and it was designed to generate consistent data. Classes that interact with external data sources must be implemented at this module level. These classes are used to download the specific data to the server, their conversion, taking into account the structure of the source files, and also to record this data into database. A layer of services is situated in parallel with the database filling layer. This layer consists of modules of search and cluster analysis of statistical data of socio-economic displacements of people. The search module implements the Boyer-Moore algorithm, and use it together with the cluster analysis module when generating relevant search results. The cluster analysis module implements the unweighted pairwise mean method to allocate clusters on the basis of statistical data. Both modules are encapsulated by a special layer of services, which is designed to provide data to external clients.

A web application is an external client that is represented by a layer of business logic and a presentation layer. A business logic layer interacts with a layer of services to obtain data related to socio-economic displacements of people and the results of their analysis. The rendering layer is intended for visualization of the received data as diagrams, schedules and tables.

3   Conceptual Modeling of System Data

We used Power Designer to construct the data model of the system [10, 14]. Power Designer is a structural methodology and also an automated design tool. On Fig. 2 are shown system entities, their relationships, data restrictions, integrity constraints, and user restrictions.

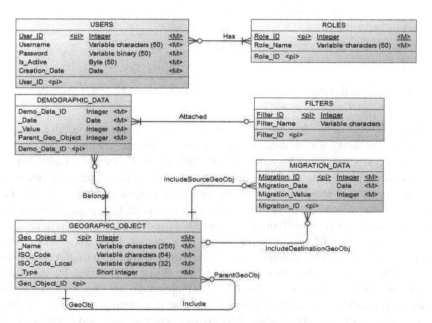

Fig. 2. A fragment of the conceptual data model associated with demographic and migration indicators (Conceptual data model was created in Power Designer based on migration data)

The specified fragment of the data model is used to analyze the data that is loaded into the system through an automated search. To create a system, we used the following software technologies: .NetFramework Microsoft, C# language, MS SQL SERVER, and various software tools (for example: Entity Framework, jQuery, amCharts), which admit to solve the tasks in the most effective way.

4 Data Search and Analytic Approaches

To fill the database we will create special source-based subprograms. These crawlers will be adapted for various heterogeneous data origins, like excel and xml files or open API's. We used a search algorithm for the Boyer-Moore substring [21] in crawlers to search the data needed (Fig. 3) at sources, based on its features.

The algorithm compares the symbols of the template x from right to left one after the other with the characters of the original string y. It starts with the rightmost one.

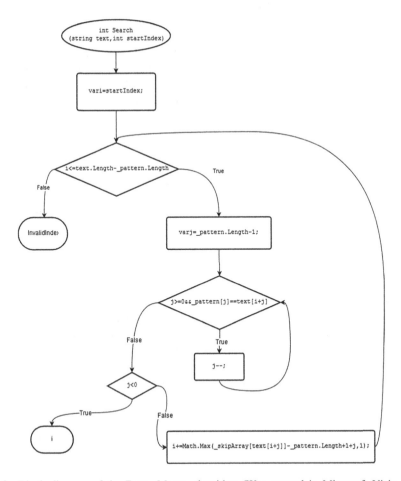

Fig. 3. Block diagram of the Boyer-Moore algorithm (Was created in Microsoft Visio 2016 based on Boyer-Moore algorithm data)

If all the symbols of the pattern match the superimposed characters of the string, the search is cancelled, because substring was found. In case of mismatch of some symbol (or full match of the whole template) the algorithm uses two precomputed heuristic functions – shifting the position to the right to start comparison. Thus, the Boyer-Moore algorithm selects between two functions in order to shift the comparison start position. These functions are called: heuristics of a good suffix and bad symbol (another name is: heuristics of the matched suffix and stop symbol). Given the fact that the functions are heuristic, the choice between them is carried out by the final value.

We denote the alphabet by $\sum$. Let $|y| = |n|$, $|x| = m$, $|\sum| = \sigma$. Suppose that we have a mismatch between character of template $x[i] = a$ and character of the original text $y[i + j] = b$ while checking position j. Then $x[i = 1 \ldots m - 1] = y[i = j = 1 \ldots j = m - 1] = u$, $x[i] = y[i = j]$ and $m - i - 1$ characters of template are coincided.

Unweighted pairwise mean method. We chosen the unweighted pairwise mean to determine clusters. We need it to analyze the data of socio-economic displacements of people.

Thus we need to classify a given set of objects using the unweighted pairwise mean method. We compute the matrix of distances between objects before the algorithm starts: at each step in the distance matrix there is a minimum value that corresponds to the distance between the two closest clusters. We form a new cluster k using the clusters u and v (they were found previously). We made it in the following way: the rows and columns corresponding to the u and v clusters are ejected from the distance matrix, and a new row and a new column are added to the cluster k. As a result, the matrix is reduced by one row and one column. This procedure is repeated until all clusters are combined.

Let clusters u, v and k contains T_u, T_v and T_k objects. The cluster k is formed by combining clusters u and v, we have:

$$T_k = T_u + T_v \tag{1}$$

Then it is necessary to calculate the remoteness of the cluster k from a certain cluster ω. The distance between these clusters is determined according to formula:

$$D((u,v), \omega) = \frac{T_u D_{u,\,\omega} + T_v D_{v,\,\omega}}{T_u + T_v} \tag{2}$$

In the sphere of economic and social movements of people we should use trend lines, moreover, exponential dependence is often used for forecasting certain trends.

As a rule exponential approximation is used due to the fact that the input data rate of increase in input data is large enough. However, there are restrictions on the use of such an approximation (for example: input data can not contain zero or negative characteristics). In general, the equation for exponential regression has the following form:

$$y = ae^{\beta x} \tag{3}$$

where y – function value, x – function definition area, a and β – constants.

5   Web Client Application

The main task of a web client is to display demographic and migration data on an interactive map, build trends, display other diagrams and visualizations (Figs. 4 and 5).

If we analyze the trend lines for certain clusters, we can make some predictions, for example: the limit of the number of people entering a certain region. Figure 5 presents a map of those entering the French Republic. The trend lines shows that a cluster of countries consisting of North African countries, such as Morocco and Algeria, will be dominant in 2020–2025 by the number of people leaving.

The Web client also contains a module for the system administrator, allowing users to edit and to add new data for analysis. We can build the necessary schedules based on

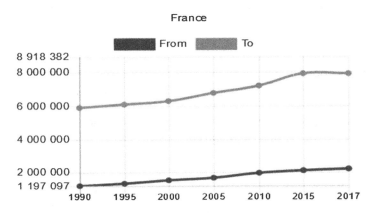

Fig. 4. The Trend Line of the French Republic (created in Microsoft Excel 2016 based on migration data for France)

Fig. 5. Map of immigrants to the French Republic (using amCharts framework)

clustered data using GoogleChartsApi. Listing 1 shows an example of visualizing data as a schedule based on clustered data.

Implementing a schedule based on clustered data:

```
// Load the Visualization API and the corechart pack-
age.
google.charts.load('current', {'packag-
es':['corechart']});

// Set a callback to run when the Google Visualization
API is loaded.
google.charts.setOnLoadCallback(drawChart);

// Callback that creates and populates a data table,
// instantiates the pie chart, passes in the data and
// draws it.
function drawChart() {

    var elements =
@Html.Raw(JsonConvert.SerializeObject(Model, Format-
ting.None));
    var array = elements.map(function(item) {
        return [item[0], parseInt(item[1])];
    });

    // Create the data table.
    var data = new google.visualization.DataTable();
    data.addColumn('string', 'Country Name');
    data.addColumn('number', 'Number of People');
    data.addRows(array);

    // Set chart options
    var options = {
        'title': 'How much people immigrate',
        'width': 400,
        'height': 300
    };
    // Instantiate and draw our chart, passing in some
options.
    var chart = new
google.visualization.PieChart(document.getElementById('@g
uid'));
    chart.draw(data, options);
}
```

We used the MVC design pattern, when implementing the client application. Its concept admits to split the data, presentation and processing of user actions into three separate components.

6 Conclusion

The paper proposes a concept the system for processing data related to socio-economic displacements of people. This system also serves as a background for a more general universal storage and analytics system for the big data on human activity.

Proposed system can be used not only as the first level of universal system based on data warehousing technology. It also can be claimed by a wide range of stakeholders interested in economic and social movements (for example: tourist organizations, logistic companies, urban planners, policy-makers and other governmental stakeholders) and leveraging the population migration flows to inform their decisions, strategy and regulations.

Acknowledgements. The results of the work were obtained during the implementation of the State Program Of Scientific Research «Development of methodology and tools for building universal systems for storage, processing and analysis of structured practice-oriented data».

References

1. Amini, A., Kung, K., Kang, C., Sobolevsky, S., Ratti, C.: The impact of social segregation on human mobility in developing and industrialized regions. EPJ Data Sci. 3(1), 6 (2014)
2. Pei, T., Sobolevsky, S., Ratti, C., Shaw, S.L., Li, T., Zhou, C.: A new insight into land use classification based on aggregated mobile phone data. Int. J. Geogr. Inf. Sci. 28(9), 1988–2007 (2014)
3. Santi, P., Resta, G., Szell, M., Sobolevsky, S., Strogatz, S.H., Ratti, C.: Quantifying the benefits of vehicle pooling with shareability networks. Proc. Nat. Acad. Sci. 111(37), 13290–13294 (2014)
4. Kung, K., Greco, K., Sobolevsky, S., Ratti, C.: Exploring universal patterns in human home/work commuting from mobile phone data. PLoS ONE 9(6), e96180 (2014)
5. Hashemian, B., Massaro, E., Bojic, I., Arias, J.M., Sobolevsky, S., Ratti, C.: Socioeconomic characterization of regions through the lens of individual financial transactions. PLoS ONE 12(11), e0187031 (2017)
6. Bojic, I., Belyi, A., Ratt, C., Sobolevsky, S.: Scaling of foreign attractiveness for countries and states. Appl. Geography 73, 47–52 (2016)
7. Belyi, A., Bojic, I., Sobolevsky, S., Sitko, I., Hawelka, B., Rudikova, L., Kurbatski, A., Carlo, R.: Global multi-layer network of human mobility. Int. J. Geogr. Inf. Sci. 31, 1381–1402 (2017)
8. Sabou, M., Hubmann-Haidvogel, A., Fischl, D., Scharl, A.: Visualizing statistical linked knowledge sources for decision support. Semantic Web. 1, 1–25 (2016)
9. Li, Q., Wu, Y., Wang, S., Lin, M., Feng, X., Wang, H.: VisTravel: visualizing tourism network opinion from the user generated content. J. Vis. 19, 489–502 (2016)
10. Rudikova, L.V.: On the development of a system for the support of laser rapid examination: monograph. LAP LAMBERT Academic Publishing, 134 p. (2014). (in Russian)

11. Barsegyan, A.A., Kupriyanov, M.S., Stepanenko, V.V., Kholod, I.I.: Methods and models of data analysis: OLAP and DataMining. "BHV- Petersburg", St. Petersburg, 336 p. (2009). (in Russian)
12. Paklin, N.B., Oreshkov, V.I.: Business analytics: from data to knowledge. "Piter", St. Petersburg, 624 p. (in Russian)
13. Rudikova, L.V.: About the general architecture of the universal data storage and processing system of practice-oriented orientation. System Analysis and Applied Informatics. "BNTU", Minsk, vol. 2, pp. 12–19 (2017). (in Russian)
14. Rudikova, L.V., Zhavnerko, E.V.: About the modeling of data subject-areas of practical orientation for a universal system of storage and data processing. In: System Analysis and Applied Informatics. "BNTU", Minsk, vol. 3, pp. 19–26 (2017). (in Russian)
15. Belyi, A.B., Rudikova, L.V., Sobolevsky, S.L., Kurbatsky, A.N.: Flickr data service and country communities structure. In: International Congress on Computer Science: Information Systems and Technologies: Materials of Internship Science of the Congress, "BSU", Minsk, pp. 851–855 (2016). (in Russian)
16. United Nations [Electronic resource]: Mode of access: http://www.tandfonline.com/doi/full/10.1080/13658816.2017.1301455. Accessed 14 May 2018
17. Eurostat [Electronic resource]: Mode of access: www.ec.europa.eu/eurostat. Accessed 14 May 2018
18. National Statistical Committee of the Republic of Belarus [Electronic resource]: – Mode of access: http://www.belstat.gov.by/. Accessed 14 May 2018. (in Russian)
19. Kurtz, J.J.: ASP.NET MVC 4 and the Web API. Apress, 140 p. (2013)
20. Using entity framework on new data platforms [Electronic resource]: Mode of access: http://blogs.msdn.com/b/adonet/archive/2014/05/19/ef7-new-platforms-new-data-stores.aspx. Accessed 14 May 2018
21. Algorithm Boyer-Moore University ITMO [Electronic resource]: Mode of access: https://neerc.ifmo.ru/wiki/index.php?title=%D0%90%D0%BB%D0%B3%D0%BE%D1%80%D0%B8%D1%82%D0%BC_%D0%91%D0%BE%D0%B9%D0%B5%D1%80%D0%B0-%D0%9C%D1%83%D1%80%D0%B0. Accessed 14 Feb 2018. (in Russian)

Digital and Smart Services - The Application of Enterprise Architecture

Markus Helfert$^{(\boxtimes)}$, Viviana Angely Bastidas Melo,
and Zohreh Pourzolfaghar

School of Computing, Dublin City University, Dublin, Ireland
{markus.helfert,zohreh.pourzolfaghar}@dcu.ie,
viviana.bastidasmelo2@mail.dcu.ie

Abstract. The digitalization of public administration presents significant challenge for many municipalities. At the same time, many larger cities have well progressed towards applying Information and Communication Technologies (ICT) to develop modern urban spaces, commonly referred to as Smart Cities. Smart Cities are complex systems whereby ICT plays an essential role to address the needs of many stakeholders. Obviously public services are key for the development. However many municipalities and cities face challenges to transform and digitalize these services. Although single projects are often successful, the coordination and coherence of services, the consideration of many stakeholders together with strategic alignment is complex. The concept of Enterprise Architectures is seen in many organizations suitable to manage the complexity of heterogeneous systems and technologies. Therefore in this paper we extend our earlier work, and present key concepts for Enterprise Architecture Management in Smart Cities that can assist cities and municipalities to digitalize and transform public services. We particular focus on the alignment and connection related to the service layer in the Architectural Framework, and present key concepts related to this layer.

Keywords: Digitalization · Public services · Enterprise architecture
Smart city · Service layer

1 Introduction

With the expected continuation of urbanization it has been estimated that the urban populations will increase by 84% to 6.3 billion by 2050 globally [1]. Commonly referred to as 'Smart City', major bases of recent urban planning include the implementation of information systems by adopting novel Information and Communication Technologies (ICT). Aiming to improve overall the quality of life, Smart Cities are described as innovative cities that are underpinned by advanced information technologies (IT). As a result, Smart Cities require the constant development of dynamic, advanced and novel services [2]. The importance of ICT has been emphasized in many publications, relating IT, processes and services and the associated business and information architectures. With a focus on various stakeholders [3], services are central in cities and municipalities. At the same time, the use of new and often disruptive ICT

© Springer Nature Switzerland AG 2018
D. A. Alexandrov et al. (Eds.): DTGS 2018, CCIS 858, pp. 277–288, 2018.
https://doi.org/10.1007/978-3-030-02843-5_22

(i.e. data analytics, Blockchain, Internet of Things, Sensors, and Machine Learning, Artificial Intelligence etc.) in the public sector is growing and is expected to increase efficiency and effectiveness of the sector. Yet, the application and adoption of these new technologies is challenging and best practices, implementation paths and associated risks are largely unknown. Implementations and projects depend often on experience from other sectors. As a result, deploying these innovative technologies in the public sector requires a coherent and structured approach for the digitalization and transformation of public services.

On tool for assisting the digital transformation in the public sector might be Enterprise Architecture (EA). Numerous researchers describe concepts and frameworks for EA, and emphasize its benefits. EA frameworks, concept and modelling approaches aim to support efficiency gains while ensuring business innovation and strategic alignment. Indeed alignment of various views and aspects is one of the key drivers for EA approaches. Organizations may use EA frameworks to manage system complexity and align business and ICT resources within an enterprise.

Thus, we argue that EA may be suitable and beneficial to support the digital transformation in the public sector. Indeed, EA assists to consider, organize and describe the various elements, stakeholders' views, goals, considerations, factors and components and IT applications as well as constraints by facilitating the transformation and digitalization of public services. The benefits of applying EA approaches are – among others– increase in organizational stability and support of managing complexity. This helps to manage constant change in complex (organizational) systems, better strategic agility, and improved alignment with business, strategy and IT. EA is suitable to manage the complexity of large enterprises where multiple stakeholders and heterogeneous systems and technologies coexist and interact. In the sense of a blueprint of the enterprise, EA impacts opportunities, capabilities, qualities and services of a City.

In this paper, we build on our previous work on applying EA to Smart Environments, in which we have broaden the traditional EA view of multi-layered frameworks by incorporating the elements of context and services [3–6]. In our opinion, the wider view is essential to capture the various stakeholders' views as well as providing a description for services in Smart Cities. Guided by a design oriented research approach [7] and collaboration with Cities in Ireland, in this paper we identify key concepts and discuss the framework application. In this paper, a focus is given to the service layer and its relation to the information layer. This helps to structure a layered design, allowing the consideration of various views and strategic aspects in transforming and digitalizing public services.

The remainder of the paper is organized as follows: Section introduces the background in relation to EA and Smart Cities. Section 3 presents our main contribution, key concepts related to the Service Layer within our EA reference framework for Smart Cities. Section 4 discusses an application of the framework and Sect. 5 concludes the paper and proposes future directions for this work.

2 Enterprise Architecture in Smart City

Many definitions and constructs associated with Smart Cities exist. Due to the emphasis on ICT we follow the International Telecommunications Union definition of a Smart City as: "An innovative city that uses ICTs and other means to improve quality of life, efficiency of urban operations and services, and competitiveness, while ensuring that it meets the needs of present and future generations with respect to economic, social, environmental as well as cultural aspects" [8]. Following this definition Smart Cities are characterized with a high level of innovation. Smart cities are underpinned by ICT solutions that help to increase efficiencies and improve service delivery in urban areas and thus overall to improve the quality of life of citizens. Smart Cities are also characterized by a high degree of complexity using many individual systems, involving many stakeholders and aiming to fulfil multiple aims and goals.

Smart Cities can be viewed as entities in form of enterprises, with organizational aspects, governance and innovation capabilities. Therefore, Smart Cities can be seen as enterprises with multi-layered and multidimensional issues [9]. How to integrate, plan, manage and maintain these various systems and aspects is yet an open challenge. At the same time, cities are rapidly moving to the adoption of ICT and thus transformation, digitalization and planning aspects are critical. The fundamental idea behind this scheme is that ICT is needed to build smart social and public systems, which help to achieve the goals within cities and help to improve urban life in a sustainable manner. However, many case studies show that Smart Cities and the digitalization of public services are difficult to realize.

EA assists in providing an integrated environment supporting continuous alignment of strategy, business and IT [10, 11]. Architectures may be defined as "the fundamental organization of a system embodied in its components, their relation-ships to each other, and to the environment, and the principles guiding its design and evolution" [12]. EA is viewed as an engineering approach to determine the required enterprise capabilities and subsequently designing organization structures, processes, services, information, and technologies to provide those capabilities [13]. Elements, views and layers of EA are specified in many publications. However, a common agreement concerning architecture layers, artefact types and dependencies has not been established yet, and there is ongoing discussion what constitute the essence of enterprise architecture [19]. [19] for example propose a hierarchical, multilevel system comprising aggregation hierarchies, architecture layers and views and interfacing requirements with other architecture models. The suggested approaches using a multi-layered architecture include for example [9, 14–17].

EA may help to address the complexity of Smart Cities [18]. Therefore, to manage complexity, many frameworks use the concept of views and layers to describe elements of architectural content. Core layers of EA models represent business architectures, application and information architectures, and technology architecture. General examples range from simple, three-layered frameworks to multi-layered EA frameworks [19, 20]. Each view illustrates a distinct perspective meaningful to specific stakeholder groups. Layering decomposes a system into distinct but interrelated components, key concerns and inter-related layers. Static relationships as well as behavioral aspects are considered in order to describe an architecture. For example, a technology layer supports an application layer which in turn provides application services to the business layer. The data flow and information exchange can be viewed as behavioral aspect of the system. With the concept of layers and views, EA assists to understand and manage the complexity of enterprises. However the complexity of Smart Cities with diverse interests and objectives from a range of stakeholders are hamper the use of EA concepts in this domain, although at the same time EA approaches are particular beneficial in such complex environments.

One example, the European project 'ESPRESSO', highlights the application of EA to Smart Cities. However, the use of EA concepts as overall approach to manage IT within Smart Cities and the wider public sector are still rare. The ESPRESSO project applies the Open Group Architecture Framework (TOGAF) as a foundation to describe a reference architecture for Smart Cities. Using a systems approach, the project focuses on the development of a conceptual Smart City Information Framework based on open standards. It consists of a Smart City platform and a set of data management services [14].

3   Key Concepts Related to the Service Layer

In our (earlier) work we have adopted the TOGAF architecture development method together with its modelling language Archimate [3–6]. This related work presents an initial version of a reference framework for designing and transforming smart services. The framework consists of four main layers, including: (1) contextual layer, (2) service layer, (3) information layer, and (4) technology layer. An example for layers 2–4 in Archimate is presented in Fig. 1. The approach helps to address the complexities associated with service systems in the public sector. It can be used to highlight open challenges of developing enterprise architecture in Smart Cities and to guide future work.

3.1   Extracting Architectural Concepts

The TOGAF content metamodel structures architectural information in an ordered way to meet stakeholder needs. Due to its definition of architectural concepts to support consistency, completeness, traceability, and relationship of components and layers [23], this study uses the TOGAF content metamodel as foundation. The metamodel is represented in the core content which contains the fundamental elements and the extension content which represents elements that enrich the core metamodel [22]. Table 1 presents the entities and the relationships extracted from [23], to connect the business architecture and the information systems architecture (data and application architectures) within the core and extension content. The definition of these entities is used by TOGAF as the basis for designing the content metamodel [23].

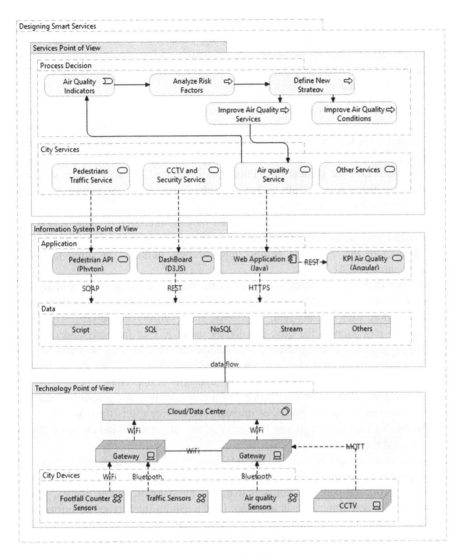

Fig. 1. Layered architecture

Table 1. Metamodel relationships, extracted from [23]

Source entity	Target entity	Name
Actor	Data entity	Supplies/Consumes
Business service	Data entity	Provides/Consumes
Business service	Information system service	Is realized through

These entities constitute a set of justifications regarding the architecture and they can be used as starting points for maintaining traceability links [22]. This paper analyses this list of concepts in Smart City contexts as a foundation for designing an effective Smart City reference architecture. We have identified the following four key concepts most relevant to the service layer:

- **Stakeholder.** A stakeholder typically relates to related group or organization unit that have similar interest in a particular matter [16]. Comerio et al. [24] define a procedural path for the life-cycle of the planning, design, production, sale, use, management and monitoring of services. They view this from the point of view of three main actors: the planner (e.g. Public administrator), the service provider (e.g. public administrator or private broker), and the consumer of the service (e.g. citizens, communities, retailers, etc.).
  Example. A citizen who changes the address may be interested in requesting several services, such as facilities for the use of public transport in the new municipality; the transfer of the telephone number into the new building; updating insurance policy contracts [24].

- **Smart Service.** Many researchers have stated, that one of the goal of utilizing ICT is to improve existing city services by digitizing these and thus making them more efficient, more user-friendly and, in general, more citizen-centric [25]. Therefore, Smart Services support the city, usually by using ICT to facilitate and optimize intelligent decision making. Smart Services can be described as Services that are used by and provide direct value to various stakeholders in a city by the use of ICT. The consideration of various stakeholders' concerns is important.
  Example. The noise-monitoring service of a city measures the amount of noise at any given hour in various places of interest. The service meets the concerns of the authorities and citizens regarding the safety of the city at night and the reliability of public establishment owners [26].

- **Information Service.** In order to include 'smartness' into a city, and to maintain interoperability among different systems [27], integration of various information services across different city domains (e.g. education, environment, energy, health, tourism, transportation, etc.) is required. [28] examine three types of information services: computational, adaptive, networking and collaborative processing capabilities. These types are mainly oriented on information exchange. In contrast, in [5] we have described various types of EA Services based on a lifecycle approach.
  Example. A smart parking service is provided to visitors of the mall. This service aims to help visitors find parking space near to their desired entrance. The smart service is supported by an information service which offers following example operations: Read Plate Number, Get User Profile, Allocate Parking Spot (based on disability and nearest entrance), Update Registry, Inform User (on his smartphone) [29].

- **Data Entity.** Data in various formats exists and are valuable in Smart Cities, and as such require particular attention. Therefore, data entities need to be governed, managed and maintained. Organizational concepts with clear responsibilities and processes as well as data ownerships and access rights are important. The identification of data entities facilitates the inter-change and operation of data, providing the application developers with the opportunity to design services efficiently [30].

Example. A footfall-counter sensor is installed in the city center. A service provider provides a data entity of the service with attributes such as zone name, sensor name, sensor type, site name, location name, registration date, the number of entries and exits. An Application Programming Interface (API) is developed based on these parameters and offered to the citizens. The city council defines the data entities regarding the location or end-point of the service in the network, to find and consume the service when necessary. An analysis of the collected data is used for making decisions about the performance of pedestrian mobility, the assessment of tourism strategies and the future planning of city environments.

4   Discussion

In the following, we present a conceptual example of a layered enterprise architecture as the first indication of the utility of the proposed architectural concepts and reference framework.

Conceptual Example

Figure 2 depicts a model representation of the architectural concepts and relationships among the service layer and information layer using Archimate. One of the most important layers is the Service Design and Architectural vision, in which several stakeholder views across various domains converge. This is analogous to a political layer, wherein various interests and constraints are balanced to define a suitable value proposition for the enterprise. The business oriented layer of EA concerns business processes and services and relates to organizational structures (including roles and responsibilities). This layer is closely related with value drivers that should be aligned to the business strategy and business models [31]. Following the classification presented in [32], in Table 2 we outline some examples services related to the business layer for the domains transport and health.

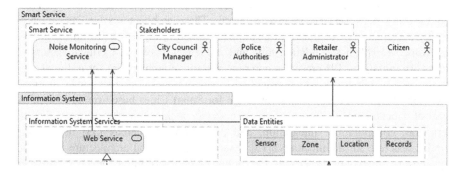

Fig. 2. Key concepts on service and information layer

Table 2. Examples in Traffic and Health, extracted from [5]

	Domain traffic	Domain health
Information services	Traffic flow; Environment Information; *Noise Monitoring Service*	Hospital Indicators
Interactive and Planning services	Pedestrian Flow for Infrastructure Planning	Capacity Planning for Emergency Services
Transaction services	Motor Tax and road charges	Prescription and Referrals

The selected *'noise monitoring service'* represents an example smart service which addresses concerns regarding the safety of the city. This service uses a web service to provide data about the amount of noise produced in various places of interest. The data is used by different stakeholders such as city council managers, police authorities, retailer administrators and citizens. The noise information service are represented by data entities such sensor, zone, location, and records. All the data collected by external services may be integrated via some API (i.e. such as REST). The relationships between smart service layer and information layer provide a way to connect the different architectural components resulting in coherent and integrated architecture to guide the design of Smart City services.

Overall Positioning of Contribution and Related Work

Smart Cities result in increased complexity resulting from connecting various, often heterogeneous systems to deliver advanced services. Many researches have proposed ways to address the complexity issues. In the follow, some selected existing architectures and frameworks are discussed in order to contrast those with our work.

Some research focus on *development methodologies*, such as in [34] presented. [34] propose a development methodology of a sample digital city, which can act as a general implementation model. The methodology includes multiple considerations and the investigation of parameters that influence a digital environment. [27] elaborated critical success factors in smart cities including, administration requirements, security (sensor security, transmission security, data vitalization security and application security), and standards. In [33] a Smart City infrastructure architecture development framework is proposed.

Many authors propose a range of *architectures and frameworks*, often open and modular following a service oriented concepts. These architectures facilitate interoperability and sharing of data as well as its management. [36] developed an integrative framework to explain the relationships and influences between 8 critical factors of Smart City initiatives. [9] present a common enterprise architecture for a digital city. [39] describe a framework which described foundation and principles for IT in Smart Cities. [35] propose a high level architecture for Smart Cities based on a hierarchical model of data storage. [37] propose an open service architecture that allows a flexible interaction, collaboration, integration, and participation, whereas [33] describes a modular structure for architectures. [15] describe a conceptual architecture for Smart City sensors interconnection with the organization, and interconnection between organizations. [27] propose a Smart City architecture from the perspective of data that underpins functionality of Smart Cities. [38] present an Event Driven Architecture that allows the management and cooperation of heterogeneous sensors for monitoring public spaces as a solution architecture.

Table 3. Overview of selected smart city architecture frameworks (Own source)

	Service	Info	IT
Open service architecture [37]	–	✓	–
Multi-tier architecture of digital city [9]	✓	✓	✓
Smart city Unites [33]	–	–	✓
A high level Smart City architecture [38]	✓	–	–
Hierarchical Model of interconnection [39]	–	–	✓
Smart City initiative framework [36]	–	–	–
Conceptual Architectural framework [15]	–	–	✓
Smart city architecture [27]	–	–	–
Service oriented architecture [35]	–	✓	✓

In Table 3 we present an overview of selected architectures and frameworks, highlighting the important architectural layers. Each of the examined architectures has their own perspective to address complexity issues. Relative few approaches address the interrelation between layers and in particular the relation to strategy and stakeholder views. Although some of the architectures have considered stakeholders as one of the architectural components, none of the selected frameworks examine or detail relationships between layers. In particular the incorporation of stakeholders concerns into the service layer is lacking.

5   Conclusion and Further Research

Smart Cities are complex systems that typically operate in a dynamic and uncertain environment. EA is suitable to manage the complexity of Smart Cities [14, 18]. A relative small number of existing EA developed for Smart Cities describe different components and layers. However, they mostly are derived from experience in the corporate and profit oriented sector, with limited consideration of specifics of the public sector. They often fall short in investigating specific architectural concepts and their relationships between different layers. Furthermore continuous strategic alignment in the public sector is challenging. This results in Smart City systems that often fail or do not provide desired level of services and innovativeness.

In order to address this problem, this paper provides a list of key concepts as references to assist the design and digitalization of Smart Services. The paper builds on a reference framework together with a first example for utilizing this framework within the context of Smart Cities. Our work allowed us to understand the wider challenges in developing EA in Smart Cities. Smart Cities should ensure that goals and objectives trace to services. Cities have many broad initiatives in different domains such as mobility, environment, sustainability, etc., and thus we believe the presented architecture reference framework can assist cities in this challenge.

Considering the challenges faced with the digitalization of public services, as part of the future work we need to identify other concepts, elements and relationships that should be considered between smart service layer and other architectural layers. We aim to continue with the evaluation of the proposed approach for its improvement and refinement. Future research will investigate the templates for Smart Service description as well as a deeper understanding of inter-layer relations. This will allow the design of coherent and integrated architectures in Smart Cities. It can help Smart City initiatives to design and offer desired services, and assist the digitalization and transformation of public services.

Acknowledgements. This work was supported by the Science Foundation Ireland grant "13/RC/2094" and co-funded under the European Regional Development Fund through the South-ern & Eastern Regional Operational Programme to Lero - the Irish Software Research Centre (www.lero.ie).

References

1. United Nations Department of Economic and Social Affairs: United Nations Population Division | Department of Economic and Social Affairs. http://www.un.org/en/development/desa/population/publications/urbanization/urban-rural.shtml
2. Piro, G., Cianci, I., Grieco, L.A., Boggia, G., Camarda, P.: Information centric services in smart cities. J. Syst. Softw. **88**, 169–188 (2014). https://doi.org/10.1016/j.jss.2013.10.029
3. Pourzolfaghar, Z., Helfert, M.: Taxonomy of smart elements for designing effective services. In: AMCIS, pp. 1–10 (2017)
4. Pourzolfaghar, Z., Helfert, M.: Investigating HCI challenges for designing smart environments (n.d.). https://doi.org/10.1007/978-3-319-39399-5_8
5. Helfert, M., Ge, M.: Developing an enterprise architecture framework and services for smart cities. In: Doucek, P., Chroust, G., Oškrdal, V. (eds.) IDIMT-2017 Digitalization in Management, Society and Economy, pp. 383–390. Czech Republic, Poděbrady (2017)
6. Bastidas, V., Bezbradica, M., Helfert, M.: Cities as enterprises: a comparison of smart city frameworks based on enterprise architecture requirements. In: Alba, E., Chicano, F., Luque, G. (eds.) Smart Cities. Smart-CT 2017. Lecture Notes in Computer Science, vol. 10268, pp. 20–28. Springer, Cham (2017). https://doi.org/10.1007/978-3-319-59513-9_3
7. Peffers, K., Tuunanen, T., Rothenberger, M.A., Chatterjee, S.: A design science research methodology for information systems research. J. Manag. Inf. Syst. **24**, 45–77 (2007)
8. ITU: Smart sustainable cities: An analysis of definitions, Focus Group Technical report. https://www.itu.int/en/ITU-T/focusgroups/ssc/Documents/Approved_Deliverables/TR-Definitions.docx
9. Anthopoulos, L., Fitsilis, P.: Exploring architectural and organizational features in smart cities. In: International Conference on Advanced Communication Technology, ICACT, pp. 190–195 (2014). https://doi.org/10.1109/ICACT.2014.6778947
10. Šaša, A., Krisper, M.: Enterprise architecture patterns for business process support analysis. J. Syst. Softw. **84**(9), 1480–1506 (2011). https://doi.org/10.1016/j.jss.2011.02.043

11. Clark, T., Barn, B.S., Oussena, S.: A Method for enterprise architecture alignment. In: Proper, E., Gaaloul, K., Harmsen, F., Wrycza, S. (eds.) Practice-Driven Research on Enterprise Transformation. PRET 2012. Lecture Notes in Business Information Processing, vol. 120, pp. 48–76. Springer, Heidelberg (2012). https://doi.org/10.1007/978-3-642-31134-5_3

12. IEEE 42010-2007 - ISO/IEC Standard for Systems and Software Engineering - Recommended Practice for Architectural Description of Software-Intensive Systems. https://standards.ieee.org/findstds/standard/42010-2007.html

13. Giachetti, R.E.: A flexible approach to realize an enterprise architecture. Procedia Comput. Sci. **8**, 147–152 (2012). https://doi.org/10.1016/J.PROCS.2012.01.031

14. Espresso Project D4.2 – Definition of Smart City Reference Architecture

15. Kakarontzas, G., Anthopoulos, L., Chatzakou, D., Vakali, A.: A conceptual enterprise architecture framework for smart cities: a survey based approach. In: 11th International Conference e-Business, ICE-B 2014 - Part 11th International Joint Conference on E-Business and Telecommunications, ICETE 2014, pp. 47–54 (2014)

16. Lnenicka, M., Machova, R., Komarkova, J., Pasler, M.: Government enterprise architecture for big and open linked data analytics in a smart city ecosystem. In: Uskov, V.L., Howlett, R.J., Jain, L.C. (eds.) SEEL 2017. SIST, vol. 75, pp. 475–485. Springer, Cham (2018). https://doi.org/10.1007/978-3-319-59451-4_47

17. Anthopoulos, L.: Defining smart city architecture for sustainability. In: Electronic Government and Electronic Participation: Joint Proceedings of Ongoing Research and Projects of IFIP WG 8.5 EGOV and ePart 2015, pp. 140–147 (2015). https://doi.org/10.3233/978-1-61499-570-8-140

18. Mamkaitis, A., Bezbradica, M., Helfert, M.: Urban enterprise principles development approach: a case from a european city. In: AIS Pre-ICIS Work. IoT Smart City Challenges and Applications, Dublin, Ireland, pp. 1–9 (2016)

19. Winter, R., Fischer, R.: Essential layers, artifacts, and dependencies of enterprise architecture. In: 2006 10th IEEE International Enterprise Distributed Object Computing Conference Workshops (EDOCW 2006), p. 30. IEEE (2006). https://doi.org/10.1109/EDOCW.2006.33

20. Meyer, M., Helfert, M.: Enterprise architecture. In: Computing Handbook Set – Information Systems and Information Technology. CRC Press (2014)

21. Czarnecki, A., Orłowski, C.: IT business standards as an ontology domain. In: Jędrzejowicz, P., Nguyen, N.T., Hoang, K. (eds.) Computational Collective Intelligence. Technologies and Applications. ICCCI 2011. Lecture Notes in Computer Science, vol. 6922, pp. 582–591. Springer, Heidelberg (2011). https://doi.org/10.1007/978-3-642-23935-9_57

22. Desfray, P., Raymond, G.: Modeling Enterprise Architecture with TOGAF: A Practical Guide Using UML and BPMN. Morgan Kaufmann (2014). https://doi.org/10.1016/B978-0-12-419984-2.00001-X

23. The Open Group: Open Group Standard TOGAF Version 9.1 (2011)

24. Comerio, M., Castelli, M., Cremaschi, M.: Towards the definition of value-added services for citizens: a new model for the description of public administration services. Int. J. Manag. Inf. Technol. **4**, 166–173 (2013)

25. Mohamed, N., Al-Jaroodi, J., Jawhar, I., Lazarova-Molnar, S., Mahmoud, S.: SmartCity-Ware: a service-oriented middleware for cloud and fog enabled Smart City services. IEEE Access **5**, 17576–17588 (2017). https://doi.org/10.1109/ACCESS.2017.2731382

26. Zanella, A., Bui, N., Castellani, A., Vangelista, L., Zorzi, M.: Internet of things for smart cities. IEEE Int. Things J. **1**(1), 22–32 (2014). https://doi.org/10.1109/JIOT.2014.2306328

27. Rong, W., Xiong, Z., Cooper, D., Li, C., Sheng, H.: Smart city architecture: a technology guide for implementation and design challenges. China Commun. **11**(3), 56–69 (2014). https://doi.org/10.1109/CC.2014.6825259

28. Mathiassen, L., Sørensen, C.: Towards a theory of organizational information services. J. Inf. Technol. **23**(4), 313–329 (2008). https://doi.org/10.1057/jit.2008.10

29. Hefnawy, A., Bouras, A., Cherifi, C.: IoT for smart city services. In: Proceedings of the International Conference on Internet of Things and Cloud Computing, pp. 1–9 (2016). https://doi.org/10.1145/2896387.2896440

30. Consoli, S., Presutti, V., Recupero, D.R., Nuzzolese, A.G., Peroni, S., Gangemi, A.: Producing linked data for smart cities: the case of catania. Big Data Res. **7**, 1–15 (2017)

31. Versteeg, G., Bouwman, H.: Business architecture: a new paradigm to relate business strategy to ICT. Inf. Syst. Front. **8**(2), 91–102 (2006). https://doi.org/10.1007/s10796-006-7973-z

32. Anttiroiko, A.-V., Valkama, P., Bailey, S.J.: Smart cities in the new service economy: building platforms for smart services. AI Soc. **29**(3), 323–334 (2014). https://doi.org/10.1007/s00146-013-0464-0

33. Al-Hader, M., Rodzi, A., Sharif, A.R., Ahmad, N.: Smart city components architicture. In: 2009 International Conference on Computational Intelligence, Modelling and Simulation, pp. 93–97. IEEE (2009). https://doi.org/10.1109/CSSim.2009.34

34. Anthopoulos, L.G., Siozos, P., Tsoukalas, I.A.: Applying participatory design and collaboration in digital public services for discovering and re-designing e-Government services. Gov. Inf. Q. **24**(2), 353–376 (2007). https://doi.org/10.1016/J.GIQ.2006.07.018

35. Zakaria, N., Shamsi, A.J.: Smart city architecture: vision and challenges. Int. J. Adv. Comput. Sci. Appl. **6**(11) (2015). https://doi.org/10.14569/IJACSA.2015.061132

36. Chourabi, H., et al.: Understanding smart cities: an integrative framework (2012). https://doi.org/10.1109/HICSS.2012.615

37. Ferguson, D., Sairamesh, J., Feldman, S.: Open frameworks for information cities. Commun. ACM **47**(2), 45 (2004). https://doi.org/10.1145/966389.966414

38. Filipponi, L., Vitaletti, A., Landi, G., Memeo, V., Laura, G., Pucci, P.: Smart city: an event driven architecture for monitoring public spaces with heterogeneous sensors. In: 2010 Fourth International Conference on Sensor Technologies and Applications, pp. 281–286. IEEE (2010). https://doi.org/10.1109/SENSORCOMM.2010.50

39. Harrison, C., et al.: Foundations for smarter cities. IBM J. Res. Dev. **54**(4), 1–16 (2010). https://doi.org/10.1147/JRD.2010.2048257

Analysis of Special Transport Behavior Using Computer Vision Analysis of Video from Traffic Cameras

Grigorev Artur$^{(\boxtimes)}$, Ivan Derevitskii, and Klavdiya Bochenina

ITMO University, Saint-Petersburg, Russian Federation
agsci2017@gmail.com, iderevitskiy@gmail.com,
k.bochenina@gmail.com

Abstract. Traffic analysis using computer vision methods becoming an important field in the traffic analysis research area. Despite this, common traffic models still rely on traffic planning methods, which treat all cars uniformly, meanwhile special vehicle can bypass traffic rules. Considering this, special vehicle can travel noticeably faster by avoiding traffic jams. This paper presents an analysis of special transport behavior case - movement by the opposite lane(MBOL). Our goal is to analyze under which conditions, such kind of specific traffic behavior happens and to present a regression model, which further can be used in special transport route planning systems or transport model simulations. The video from the traffic surveillance camera on the Nevsky Prospect (the central street of the city of Saint-Petersburg) have been used. To analyze traffic conditions (and detect MBOL-cases) we use well-established computer vision methods - Viola-Jones for vehicle detection and MedianFlow/KCF for vehicle tracking. Results show that MBOL happens under extreme main lane conditions (high traffic density and flow), with wide variety of parameters for the opposite lane.

Keywords: Special transport · Vehicle behavior model · Traffic analysis
Computer vision

1 Introduction

Arrival time of ambulances has a great impact on the health and life of a patient. Routing of special transport is a well-studied scientific field. Models of movement of special transport (as well as transport in general) can be divided into micromodels, macromodels and hybrid models. Macromodels are based on estimates of travel time along the edges of the road network using the history of previous travels [1], waiting time at intersections [2] and data on the current load of the transport network [3]. Micromodels use multi-agent modeling [4] and simulate the individual behavior of drivers. However, the majority of general-purpose transport models do not take into account special transport behavior such as ability to move by the opposite lane or exceeding the speed limit (see, e.g. [4–6]). MBOL pattern of special transport behavior is also considered in the literature [7]. In this work, the decision about the MBOL depends on the state of traffic on the main and the opposite lanes of the road. However, development of a full-fledged model of special

D. A. Alexandrov et al. (Eds.): DTGS 2018, CCIS 858, pp. 289–301, 2018.
https://doi.org/10.1007/978-3-030-02843-5_23

transport behavior is hampered with the lack of data on the real movement of special vehicles. In this study, we propose a framework to address this problem.

Traffic analysis with the use of video surveillance systems is gaining relevance because it is an affordable tool that allows to collect statistical data about road traffic [8]. Using this approach, the data related to special transport movement cases can be obtained [9]. The data then can be used to identify the parameters of special vehicle behavior model.

The contribution of this paper is two-fold. Firstly, we propose a method to collect data on the special behavior of special vehicles from video traffic cameras. Secondly, we develop a model capturing behavior of the driver of a special transport based on collected traffic statistics. For traffic analysis and model formulation, it was necessary to collect video data for a long time (at least a month) and collect the basic traffic statistics related to the MBOL cases. This model can further be used for planning and optimization of special transport movement.

In [7], a model is proposed that takes into account the possibility of going by the opposite lane, but the author needs real data on the movement of ambulances for validation of the model. Our study addresses this problem.

The rest of the paper is organized as follows. Section 2 justifies the actuality of the problem and the choice of approaches to its solution through the analysis of existing works. Section 3 describes the formation and structure of a data set. Section 4 describes in detail the method of data processing and the comparison of the efficiency of the recognition methods on our set. We describe the results of the experiment and the model of special behavior in Sect. 5. Finally, conclusions and a description of future research are presented.

2   Related Works

One of the main tasks in this article is to obtain data on the movement of special vehicles. The main methods of traffic estimation use cameras, GPS, radars and loops [10]. However, loops and radars are not suitable for the identification of certain types of vehicles. The disadvantage of GPS-data in the context of detecting the special behavior detection is the measurement error, which is up to several meters [11]. This error may lead to an inaccurate definition of the lane, that is, the impossibility of determining the movement by the opposite lane. In addition, GPS data on the movements of one car do not contain information about the state of the surrounding traffic. Thus, the appropriate method to tackle with our task is to analyze video from traffic cameras.

Analysis of the movement of individual vehicles using Computer Vision (CV) methods can be divided into two stages. The first stage is the recognition of the vehicles in the image. To detect vehicles, researchers use the Viola-Jones method [12], the background subtraction method [13], and HOG [14]. The task is complicated by the fact that the analysis of the movement of special transport is of interest primarily in an urban environment in which the application of CV methods is difficult due to the fact that the cameras are directed at a small angle to the horizon and, consequently, the large number of vehicle occlusions is observed [15]. In this study, we investigate the comparative efficiency of these methods on the data of open traffic cameras.

The second stage concerns tracking the trajectories of the detected vehicles. This can be done by methods such as Multiple Instance Learning [16] that analyzes the space in some area from the previous position of the object and its modification called Kernelized Correlation Filters (KCF) [17], "Tracking, Learning and Detection" [18] focusing on tracking one object, MedianFlow [19] tracking the object in both the forward and reverse directions. In this work, the MedianFlow method is used, because it is optimal for direct predictable motion.

There are several studies devoted to tracking special transport by video from traffic cameras. In [9], the method of detecting movement by the opposite lane based on video from the traffic cameras in St. Petersburg was proposed. However, the authors analyzed too short time interval to collect sufficient dataset to identify parameters of driver behavior model and did not compare the effectiveness of the applying various methods of CV. In [20], the system of acceleration of ambulances using cameras on crossroads is described. However, the system uses the distance between the ambulance and the cross-over without getting any data about vehicle movements.

Based on the above considerations, it can be concluded that the task of obtaining data on the movement of special vehicles (using video from traffic cameras and CV methods) and the task of analyzing the effectiveness of these methods are actual.

3 Dataset

To collect the data about movement by opposite lane, video from traffic camera should cover a road segment with traffic light and dense two-way movement. Selected camera (see Fig. 1) covers road segment (102 m long and 17.5 m wide) of Nevsky prospect between the Moika river and the street Bolshaya Konuyshennaya [21].

The video was collected during different months.

Fig. 1. View from the traffic camera

First dataset duration is 7 days in April 2017 with resolution of each video of 330 × 480 pixels (further mapped to 640 × 480 resolution to fit data processing algorithms).

The second dataset - video with a resolution of 960 × 720, was also collected in autumn and winter.

- 16 November–29 November (14 days);
- 17 December–22 December (6 days);
- 30 December–31 December (2 days);
- 2 January–7 January (6 days).

Video data with duration of 35 days was used in total. The dataset is organized in files of one hour each. The dataset is available by the link [22].

4 Method

Video analysis procedure is organized as follows (see Fig. 2).

1. **Opposite movement detection** using loop tracking (using KCF). On this step, list of video files in day-hour naming format is produced. Dataset and compilation of MBOL cases are available by the link [23].
2. **Traffic flow estimation** using detect-and-track approach (Viola-Jones (for object detection) and MedianFlow (for object tracking) methods for the MBOL hours.
3. **Traffic density estimation** using edge-detection (using Sobel operator) and binarization for the MBOL hours.

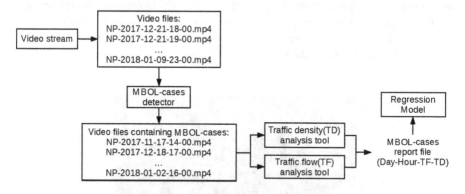

Fig. 2. Current video analysis dataflow scheme

Analysis and detection steps can be parallelized to process multiple files simultaneously. From statistical traffic measurements, only traffic flow and traffic density were analyzed. Precision of measurements is one hour.

Note that we use data from only one surveillance camera in this article. Thus, the received data on the behavior of a special transport cannot be applicable in all road network configurations.

4.1   Comparison of Vehicle Recognition Methods with Manual Markup

In this section, the choice of Viola-Jones method for detecting vehicles is justified. Considering requirements of different methods (Viola-Jones (using boosted cascade of Haar features) next referred as Haar, histogram of oriented gradients extraction and classification using support-vector machines, next referred as HOG) unified dataset was produced (800 positive and 310 negative images were collected), to derive reliable conclusions from methods comparison. Big dataset with increased number of samples was also produced (containing 3000 positives and 700 negative images).

Ten frames of test video were selected for markup comparison. Manual markup (representing total number of vehicles in frame) was done. Haar and HOG are related to small unified dataset, Haar2 and HOG2 are related to a big unified dataset. Background subtraction (next referred as BGS) does not depend on dataset (Fig. 3).

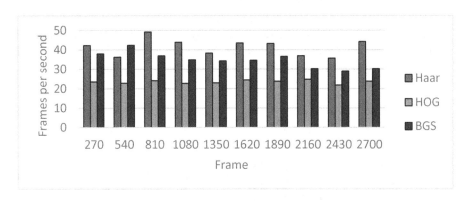

Fig. 3. Performance of recognition for the small dataset of samples

It can be concluded, that Haar surpasses BGS and HOG in terms of speed (see Fig. 4) and quality of recognition (see Fig. 5).

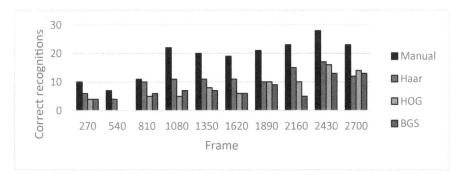

Fig. 4. Quality of recognition comparison for the small dataset of samples

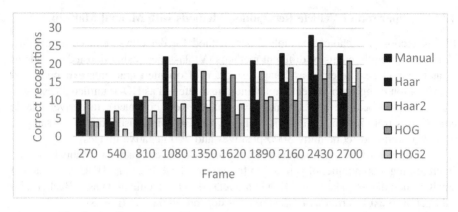

Fig. 5. Quality of recognition comparison for the big dataset of samples

Haar also shows significant increase in quality of recognition, when dataset of samples becomes larger (see Fig. 6). For the cases of high traffic density, car partial occlusion significantly reduces BGS quality of recognition.

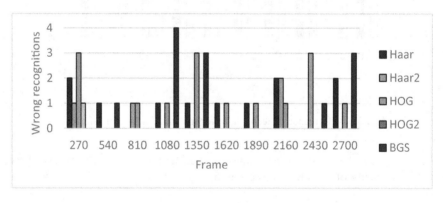

Fig. 6. False positives for small and big datasets of samples

HOG2 and Haar2 both have the least number of false positives (see Fig. 7). Size of a dataset plays the crucial role in quality of recognition improvement.

 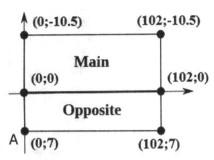

Fig. 7. Mapping of in-frame coordinates to a virtual rectangle

The main problem was a partial occlusion of vehicles, that happens frequently on a road with high traffic congestion, which results in a low recognition quality.

4.2 Design of the Detection Procedure for Oncoming Traffic

To detect oncoming traffic, a method was used that includes tracking rectangles located at certain points on the road (the corresponding tool, hereinafter referred to as the MBOL detector). Tracking rectangles are placed for a limited number of frames (for example, seven). Change in y-coordinate is then analyzed: if tracking rectangle traveled against lane movement three or four times in a row at a sufficient distance (at least a meter, to exclude tracking inaccuracies from camera trembling), then MBOL case is detected. The case is then written to a report file.

4.3 Design of Detect-and-Track Procedure

Detect-and-track procedure is organized as follows:

1. Frame is checked for vehicles using Viola-Jones method – rectangle regions (containing vehicles) are produced.
2. Detected vehicles are then tracked using MedianFlow algorithm.
3. Once the center of the vehicle's rectangle moves outside the bounding rectangle, number of vehicles that crossed the road incremented.

For the Viola-Jones method, trained cascade (using 3000 positives, 700 negatives with 17 stages training) was used.

Lane of movement is determined using projective transformation of vehicle's rectangle center coordinate. Projective transformation maps in-frame coordinates to a virtual rectangle (see Fig. 8) This kind of transformation allows to estimate physical measurements of movement (in meters) and speed (in km/h), but because of partial occlusion of vehicles, and therefore non-recognition of some vehicles, this measurement can't be estimated accurately.

Fig. 8. Video frame with application of edge detection algorithm and binarization

If the y-coordinate of the center of the vehicle's rectangle is below zero then it travels main road, otherwise – opposite road.

4.4 Design of Density Estimation Procedure

Density estimation procedure is organized as follows.

1. To estimate the main and the opposite road traffic densities, it is necessary to extract corresponding road areas. To get these areas, two masks are applied separately.
2. Edge detection algorithm (Sobel edge detection using kernel size of 3) with binarization (after the edge detection step, every pixel with intensity above 70 becomes black, otherwise – white) are applied (see Fig. 9).

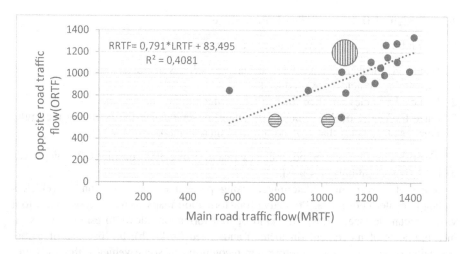

Fig. 9. Scatterplot for traffic flow. Marker with vertical lines represents 4 cases. Marker with horizontal lines represents 2 cases.

3. Counting of the number of black pixels in the extracted and processed areas. This number is then divided by the number of pixels in the area. Percentage of black pixels (relative to the lane segment area) is then considered as the traffic density of the lane [24].

5   Results

36 days of video were analyzed and 25 facts of movement to the opposite lane were detected. In all cases it was a special transport. With one-hour precision, statistical data (traffic flow and traffic density) was collected on the traffic conditions at the time of exit to the opposite lane.

First, data was collected from the camera. Then, a MBOL-detector was applied to the data and a collection of images of MBOL cases was produced with frame-day-hour naming. Image collection then was assessed for false positive cases. Then, corresponding video files were accumulated into one directory. Also, dataset of MBOL cases was produced.

Second, density and flow analysis tools were applied to the MBOL cases dataset. Files, containing traffic flow and average traffic density (for the main and the opposite lanes) were produced. Then it became possible to produce scatterplots for traffic flow and traffic density.

With a visual analysis of the traffic flow graph (see Fig. 10), a linear positive correlation is observed between the values of the main and opposite values of the traffic flow for the MBOL cases. The correlation coefficient between the main and the opposite road traffic flows is 0.64.

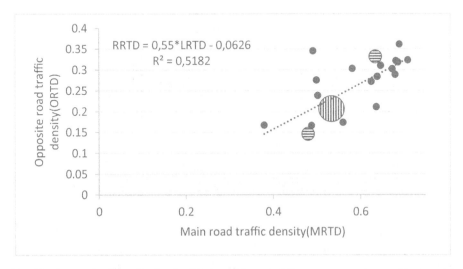

Fig. 10.   Scatterplot for traffic density. Marker with vertical lines represents 4 cases. Marker with horizontal lines represents 2 cases.

Most of the MBOL cases happened when traffic flow value for the main road was higher than 800 cars per hour, with a wide range of traffic flow (between 400 and 1300) for the opposite road.

From the traffic density scatterplot (see Fig. 11), it can be observed that most of the MBOL cases are related to the main lane density with value higher than 0.45. The correlation coefficient between the main and the opposite road traffic densities at the hours of MBOL cases is 0.724.

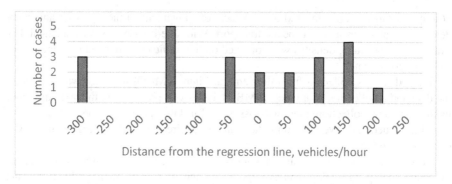

Fig. 11. The distribution of points by distance relative to the regression line for the traffic flow

For the traffic flow, a linear regression equation was obtained (see Fig. 10). Points (representing traffic flow related to an hour when the MBOL-case was observed) are placed at the distance between −300 and 250 from the regression line. Distance has a positive sign if a point is placed above the regression line (see Fig. 11).

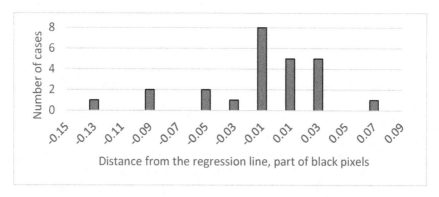

Fig. 12. The distribution of points by distance relative to the regression line for the traffic density

For the traffic density, a linear regression equation was also obtained (see Fig. 11). Points (representing traffic density related to an hour when the MBOL-case was observed) are placed at the distance between −0.15 and 0.07 from the regression line (see Fig. 12).

6 Conclusion

In this work, we detect movement by the opposite lane using video from traffic cameras. With the help of Viola-Jones and Median-Flow methods of computer vision, we obtained data on traffic conditions (traffic flow and traffic density) on the main and the opposite roads.

The contribution of this article is two-fold. First, a method was proposed to collect data on the special behavior from open traffic cameras. In addition, data was received on the movement by the opposite lane and a model for the special behavior of the special transport driver was constructed, depending on the state of the traffic. Using the model and the distribution of points relative to the regression line, it is possible to make assumptions about MBOL cases, based on the density and traffic flow values.

The Viola-Jones method showed the best quality and performance of recognition, as well as the peculiarity that the quality of recognition significantly increases with the growth of the sample data.

After traffic flow and traffic density analysis of MBOL hours, regression lines and distribution graphs with respect to the regression lines were obtained. Strong positive linear correlation between the main and the opposite road traffic densities at the hours of MBOL cases was observed.

The results of this study can be used to improve existing models of special transport traffic (for example, the model described in [7]), and also in navigation systems calculating the shortest route for a special vehicle. In addition, we compared the efficiency of different vehicle recognition methods for the data from open low-quality camera in St. Petersburg. These results can help to choose the vehicle detection method for traffic simulation problems with similar data available.

Future research will be conducted in two directions. First, we need to expand and refine the data set, by increasing the analyzed time interval, increasing the number of cameras, and identifying other types of special behavior (ignoring traffic lights, exceeding speed, etc.). Secondly, we will develop a micromodel for the movement of special vehicles using a model of special behavior, and we will explore the effectiveness of this micromodel in the tasks of ambulances routing.

Acknowledgements. This research is financially supported by The Russian Science Foundation, Agreement №17-71-30029 with co-financing of Bank Saint Petersburg.

We thank our colleagues from ITMO University for their support and encouragement which gave us an inspiration to complete our research.

References

1. López, B., Innocenti, B., Aciar, S., Cuevas, I.: A multi-agent system to support ambulance coordination in time-critical patient treatment. In: 7th Simposio Argentino de Intelligencia Artificial-ASAI2005 (2005)
2. Vlad, R.C., Morel, C., Morel, J.-Y., Vlad, S.: A learning real-time routing system for emergency vehicles. In: 2008 IEEE International Conference on Automation, Quality and Testing, Robotics, AQTR 2008, pp. 390–395 (2008)

3. Gayathri, N., Chandrakala, K.R.M.V.: A novel technique for optimal vehicle routing. In: 2014 International Conference on Electronics and Communication Systems (ICECS), pp. 1–5 (2014)
4. Ibri, S., Nourelfath, M., Drias, H.: A multi-agent approach for integrated emergency vehicle dispatching and covering problem. Eng. Appl. Artif. Intell. **25**, 554–565 (2012). https://doi.org/10.1016/j.engappai.2011.10.003
5. Créput, J.-C., Hajjam, A., Koukam, A., Kuhn, O.: Dynamic vehicle routing problem for medical emergency management. In: Self Organizing Maps-Applications and Novel Algorithm Design. InTech (2011)
6. Maxwell, M.S., Restrepo, M., Henderson, S.G., Topaloglu, H.: Approximate dynamic programming for ambulance redeployment. INFORMS J. Comput. **22**, 266–281 (2010). https://doi.org/10.1287/ijoc.1090.0345
7. Haas, O.C.: Ambulance response modeling using a modified speed-density exponential model. In: 2011 14th International IEEE Conference on Intelligent Transportation Systems (ITSC), pp. 943–948 (2011)
8. Liu, X., Nie, M., Jiang, S., et al.: Automatic traffic abnormality detection in traffic scenes: an overview. DEStech Trans. Eng. Technol. Res. (2017)
9. Derevitskii, I., Kurilkin, A., Bochenina, K.: Use of video data for analysis of special transport movement. Procedia Comput. Sci. **119**, 262–268 (2017). https://doi.org/10.1016/J.PROCS.2017.11.184
10. Zhang, J.-D., Xu, J., Liao, S.S.: Aggregating and sampling methods for processing GPS data streams for traffic state estimation. IEEE Trans. Intell. Transp. Syst. **14**, 1629–1641 (2013)
11. Wing, M.G., Eklund, A., Kellogg, L.D.: Consumer-grade Global Positioning System (GPS) accuracy and reliability. J For **103**, 169–173 (2005)
12. Viola, P., Jones, M.: Rapid object detection using a boosted cascade of simple features. In: Proceedings of the 2001 IEEE Computer Society Conference on Computer Vision and Pattern Recognition, CVPR 2001, p. I (2001)
13. Cheung, S.-C.S., Kamath, C.: Robust techniques for background subtraction in urban traffic video. In: Proceedings of SPIE, pp. 881–892 (2004)
14. McConnell, R.K.: Method of and apparatus for pattern recognition (1986)
15. Buch, N., Velastin, S.A., Orwell, J.: A review of computer vision techniques for the analysis of urban traffic. IEEE Trans. Intell. Transp. Syst. **12**, 920–939 (2011)
16. Chen, X., Zhang, C., Chen, S.-C., Rubin, S.: A human-centered multiple instance learning framework for semantic video retrieval. IEEE Trans. Syst. Man Cybern. Part C Applications Rev 39, 228–233 (2009)
17. Henriques, J.F., Caseiro, R., Martins, P., Batista, J.: High-speed tracking with kernelized correlation filters. IEEE Trans. Patt. Anal. Mach. Intell. **37**, 583–596 (2015)
18. Kalal, Z., Mikolajczyk, K., Matas, J.: Tracking-learning-detection. IEEE Trans. Pattern Anal. Mach. Intell. **34**, 1409–1422 (2012)
19. Kalal, Z., Mikolajczyk, K., Matas, J.: Forward-backward error: automatic detection of tracking failures. In: 2010 20th International Conference on Pattern Recognition (ICPR), pp. 2756–2759 (2010)
20. Nellore, K., Hancke, G.P.: Traffic management for emergency vehicle priority based on visual sensing. Sensors **16**, 1892 (2016)
21. Saint Petersburg TV Channel (2018) Nevsky Prospect Street Camera. https://topspb.ru/online-projects/46
22. Grigorev, A.: Nevsky prospect traffic surveillance video (2018). https://doi.org/10.6084/m9.figshare.5841846.v5

23. Grigorev, A.: Nevsky prospect traffic surveillance video(movement by the oncoming lane cases hours) (2018). https://doi.org/10.6084/m9.figshare.5841267.v3
24. Li, X., She, Y., Luo, D., Yu, Z.: A traffic state detection tool for freeway video surveillance system. Procedia – Soc. Behav. Sci. **96**, 2453–2461 (2013). https://doi.org/10.1016/j.sbspro.2013.08.274

Woody Plants Area Estimation Using Ordinary Satellite Images and Deep Learning

Alexey Golubev[1($\boxtimes$)], Natalia Sadovnikova[1], Danila Parygin[1],
Irina Glinyanova[1], Alexey Finogeev[2], and Maxim Shcherbakov[1]

[1] Volgograd State Technical University, 28, Lenina Ave., Volgograd 400005, Russia
ax.golubev@gmail.com,npsn1@yandex.ru,dparygin@gmail.com,
kaf_bgdvt@mail.ru,maxim.shcherbakov@gmail.com
[2] Penza State University, 40, Krasnaya Str., Penza 440026, Russia
alexeyfinogeev@gmail.com

Abstract. Modern solutions based on machine learning and map data are discussed in the paper. A convolutional neural network is proposed to use for urban spaces tree canopy evaluation. The developed method allowed to formulate a criterion for assessing the "green" infrastructure of a territory. The index, called Abin, is proposed to be used to estimate the area of woody plants. The process of preparing training datasets and carrying out search studies on the model of the neural network used are described. The results of training and testing of trained networks in arbitrary areas of the city are given. The analysis of the final results is carried out for the training errors revealed in the test cases, the prospects for the application of the trained models, the proposed method for estimating the "green" environmental conditions by the Abin index.

Keywords: Deep learning · Neural network · GIS
Tree canopy evaluation · Woody plant · Abin · Geospatial data
Urban area · Satellite imagery · Image processing · Computer vision
City ecology · Data mining · LandProber

1 Introduction

To date, provision of a city with green plantations is one of the key indicators of an urban environment comfort, affecting the development of urban spaces. In addition, this indicator significantly affects the value of real estate in one or another area. People are willing to pay for a quality of life.

Formation of a system of gardening is usually carried out in accordance with the territory improvement project, which is based on modern requirements. However, the state of a green spaces system does not change for the better during the operation of territories. For example, in Volgograd, Russia, one resident of the city is provided with an average of 10.0 "green" m^2 at a norm of 25.0 m^2 [1].

© Springer Nature Switzerland AG 2018
D. A. Alexandrov et al. (Eds.): DTGS 2018, CCIS 858, pp. 302–313, 2018.
https://doi.org/10.1007/978-3-030-02843-5_24

The real situation can be even worse, given that these figures are obtained on the basis of official sources, which lose relevance over time.

In this regard, there is a problem of an objective assessment of the territory greening on the basis of accessible information. Modern cartographic services allow you to obtain and analyze the spatial data needed to solve a variety of a town planning tasks. However, there is the problem of time and efficiency of data processing for decision making. Along with this, the development of machine learning technologies allows solving recognition problems faster and more efficiently.

In this paper, it is proposed to use a convolutional neural network and satellite map data to estimate an urban woody plants area. Based on this approach, it is proposed to develop a criterion for evaluation of a territory "green" infrastructure.

2   Background

Detailed analysis of major European cities to assess the degree of their greening was made in the Philipp Gartner paper [2]. The authors analyzed satellite images of Sentinel-2 using an analysis of the vegetation index (NVDI). They compiled the ratings of European cities for the presence of parks, forests and green plantations in relation to the population. The analysis was carried out for cities of more than 500 thousand people.

However, the example above is aimed at assessing the overall "green" level. A large localization for the assessment of environmental problems using machine learning is suggested in the paper [3]. In [4], the authors suggest a system that calculates the number and location of palm trees. They use a convolutional neural network, which they trained in two classes (pictures with palm trees and without) using the sliding window method. The system they trained achieved very good accuracy in more than 99% on a very small set of input data.

The authors of paper [5] describe the use of machine learning methods for the classification of urban environments. The study is mainly aimed at identifying some patterns in cities and cities among themselves.

Recently, the number of studies related to the analysis of spatial data to support decision-making in urban studies has increased [6]. A selection of examples of such descriptions is given in [7]. It includes an overview of computer vision and its impact on science in these aspects. So, for example, there is mentioned the article [8], in which the author defined by means of machine vision the types of urban development. The principle of training and research is based on the classification of satellite images in the tile grid [9].

Nevertheless, existing studies are inherently focused on solving special data processing tasks [10–13], object classification [14] and other knowledge extraction tasks [15]. However, there is no comprehensive methodology for assessing the quality of the urban environment based on such decisions. Existing methods are not invariant for solving various analysis problems. The emphasis is often placed on the implementation of models. At the same time, that the use of the original satellite images, which are subject to increased quality requirements, is implied.

3 Method for a Woody Plants Area Estimation by the Abin Index

3.1 Abin Index

The possibility of estimating the area and location of green spaces in the urban environment was decided to study on the basis of modern approaches and the practice of applying machine learning technology. The following hypothesis was proposed: the maximum level of greening of the territory used by a person for living corresponds to the placement of a residential object in the center of pedestrian diameter, the entire area of which is covered with woody plants such as trees and/or large perennial bushes. A pedestrian diameter means a distance that fits into a 10-min pedestrian isochron [16].

In addition, initially a decision was made, which is based on the experience of previous studies [17], to focus on common satellite images offered by the main publicly available mapping services from Google [18], Yandex [19], Bing [20], etc. As a reference area of pedestrian diameter, it is proposed to consider a $1\,km^2$ area in the interfluve of the rivers Abin and Michal (44.665527 N, 38.192211 E) in Abinsky district of the Krasnodar Territory, Russia, represented on satellite images provided by Yandex [21] according to "(c) 2012 DigitalGlobe, Inc., (c) SCANEX, (c) CNES 2013" (Fig. 3a). The greening of such a site, estimated by the method proposed below, is taken to be 1 Abin. At the same time, based on the norms of gardening established by the World Health Organization [22], the following values of the criterion of "green" quality of the urban territory, measured by the proposed index: poor conditions when less than 0.1 Abin, satisfactory is 0.1–0.4 Abin, good is 0.4–0.6 Abin, and excellent conditions is more than 0.6 Abin.

3.2 Method for Assessing the Greening of the Territory

1. Obtaining images of the investigated territory:
   (a) Binding to the average pedestrian diameter. The picture shows a square area with a side of 850–1020 m.
   (b) Satellite images are obtained at a single scale, corresponding to 1 m in 2.5–3 pixels, from any, distributed by reference, online maps.
   (c) Formation of the image size 2550 × 2550 pixels.
2. Training of the neural network:
   (a) Selecting of tile size (25–75 pixels).
   (b) Forming a training sample that includes groups of images with objects of interest. Among others, one or more groups should include plant-derived objects and/or covers.
   (c) Classifier training for recognizing the necessary classes.
3. Classification of the input image:
   (a) Using a neural network trained to recognize several classes (for example, "Trees", "Grass" and "Constructed").
   (b) Create a semi-transparent color mask for the found objects that belong to the class of interest (for example, "Trees").

4. Estimation of the greening level for the territory:
   (a) Determination of the number of area units covered with trees.
   (b) Calculation of the Abin index as a ratio of the number of greened area units to the area of the reference site.
   (c) Calculation of the absolute value of the area of green area in m^2.

4   A Deep Neural Architecture

4.1   Neural Network Model

In the conducted study it was decided to use a convolutional neural network (Fig. 1) to classify fragments of satellite images for determining the woody green plantations on them. The structure of the chosen network [8,9] consists of three convolutional layers.

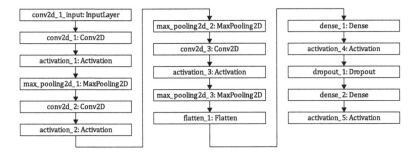

Fig. 1. Structure of neural network

4.2   Creating of Datasets

As initial data for the classification was decide to use fragments of satellite images obtained by creating screenshots. Under the terms of the Abin index valuation method, images must meet the following requirements:

– each fragment must contain objects that belong to only one class;
– screenshots should be taken from satellite images displayed on the screen in a single scale, corresponding to 1 m in 2.5–3 pixels;
– fragments of the same class should be obtained in equal numbers from photographs of different cities of Russia and adjacent territories;
– sample of cities should be formed from settlements that are evenly distributed throughout the country at different latitudes and longitudes;
– fragments of one class should include the maximum diversity of states represented on satellite imagery for natural classes and anthropogenic classes;
– same content of fragments of the same class should be equally represented in photographs of different periods and quality of the survey;
– data set of each class should not differ from any other set by more than 30%.

3789 screenshots corresponding to the requirements formulated above with sizes from 75×75 to 1290×704 pixels were made at all stages of the search studies on the selection of the number and content of classes for identification on images.

It was decided to use a grid with a cell size of 75×75 pixels. This decision was made based on the preliminary expert assessment. However, after obtaining the first results and additional literature review [4,5,23,24], it was decided to investigate the possibility of reducing the cell size to 25×25 pixels. Such a size at the scale used would give a more accurate indication of the location.

Table 1. Initial dataset

Tile size, pixels	Number of tiles per class		
	Trees	Grass	Constructed
75x75	18 642	14 160	13 245
25x25	191 282	140 284	139 332
Example fragment			

The original images were cut into the selected sizes using a written script in Python. Based on the total initial sample for the three classes, 46047 tiles with a size of 75×75 pixels and 470898 tiles with a size of 25×25 pixels were obtained (Table 1).

Also, a program was created to increase the original set of images. This program in automatic mode multiplies the original sample by 8 times due to rotations (3 turns $90°$) and reflection of images. Accordingly, the final models of classifiers were trained on cumulative samples: 368 376 unique tiles with size of 75×75 pixels and 3 767 184 unique tiles with size of 25×25 pixels.

4.3   Pilot Studies

The idea of the study was to create a classifier able to distinguish the territories covered by green spaces on satellite images. Initially, it was decided to allocate 4 classes of vegetation: "Trees", "Lawn", "Motley grass", and "Cropland".

These classes have sufficient visual distinctive features. In addition, almost all combinations of vegetation found in urban buildings can be referred to them. However, the results of training classifiers on the tests did not show the expected results of the quality of recognition of woody plants: moreover, in the derivation of classification results at once for 4 classes, all objects, including objects of anthropogenic origin, were assigned to one or another class (Fig. 2a).

It was decided to conduct training only for the 1st class "Trees" to exclude the classification of non-target objects. The results obtained were characterized by considerable noisiness of the classification by the objects of dense grass cover, elements of farming or soil irregularities (Fig. 2b).

In order to distinguish between woody and herbaceous plants, it was decided to conduct training for two classes of "Trees" and "Grass". The class "Grass" combined the following classes: "Lawn", "Motley grass" and "Cropland". The results of the test classification, based on the results of training, showed the principal overcoming of the problem of the erroneous classification of grassy areas. Nevertheless, the problem of noisy classification by objects of anthropogenic origin is still remains (Fig. 2c).

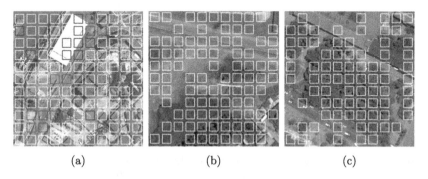

(a)   (b)   (c)

Fig. 2. Classification tests for exploratory studies (white squares – "Trees", different color – other classes): a – model trained in 4 plant classes; b – model trained in the "Trees" class; c – the model trained on classes "Trees" and "Grass"

4.4   Training with Tiles 75 × 75 Pixels

It was decided to use the 3 classes (Trees, Grass, Constructed) for the final training with tiles of 75 × 75 pixels ("LandProber 1.0.1") according to the results of the research study. And the Constructed class included all objects of anthropogenic origin (buildings, structures, artificial coverings, traces of human impact on the natural landscape). The results of the accuracy of training for different epochs are given in Table 2.

In total, the test program assumed the consistent creation of classifiers, trained for 1, 2, etc. up to 30 epochs. The training time for one epoch averaged 246 s. At the same time, a number of neural networks showed negative values of accuracy and the absence of recognized vegetation on the benchmark test. This situation as a whole is the subject of ongoing research.

In view of the current situation with the quality of the neural networks received, it was decided to interrupt the cycle of launching new training in 20 epochs. The neural network, which passed 11 epochs of training, showed an ideal result on the Abin index and the accuracy of the model itself and was applied at the next stage of the study.

Table 2. Epochs of learning a neural network on a grid of 75 × 75 pixels

Epochs	Model accuracy, %	Accuracy on the validation sample, %	Abin index
1	95.63	97.75	0.84
2	97.84	98.68	0.92
3	97.74	98.11	0.95
4	98.28	98.23	0.99
5	98.61	98.80	0.89
6	98.80	98.41	0.92
7	98.76	98.70	0.80
8	*42.86*	*32.99*	*0.00*
9	98.89	98.93	0.70
10	98.82	98.39	0.95
11	**98.92**	**98.53**	**1.00**

4.5   Training with Tiles 25 × 25 Pixels

Classifier training on tiles of 25 × 25 pixels ("LandProber 1.0.2") was originally implemented in 3 classes (Trees, Grass, Constructed). 20 cycles were prepared like in the experiment with training on tiles of a larger size. However, most of the models did not classify. Most models received NaN in the parameters "losses" and "accuracy" during the training. Only one classifier for three classes in two epochs was correctly trained: LandProber 1.0.2 with 2 epochs in 3 classes have 0.97 Abin index and LandProber 1.0.3 with 3 epochs in 2 classes have 0.64 Abin index. The model value of the Abin index is 0.97. The fragment of classification result is shown in the Fig. 3b.

In this regard, there was decide to combine the Grass and Constructed samples. Thus, training ("LandProber 1.0.3") was done for two classes (Trees, Miscellaneous). In general, the situation turned out to be similar to that for three classes. A correct result was obtained at three epochs of training. Average training time of the described networks was about 1500 s.

(a)   (b)

Fig. 3. Exemplary territory, real 1.0 Abin: a – screenshot; b – LandProber 1.0.2

5   Test Results on Trained Models

The CentOS Linux 7 (Core) operating system, Python 3.6.3, Keras 2.1.3, Tensorflow 1.4.1, Theano 1.0.1, CUDA 9.0.176 Toolkit and CuDNN 7 were used to implement the research. The research team of the UCLab laboratory had the following equipment for the experiment: Intel(R) Xeon(R) CPU E5-2660, 2.2 GHz, 16 core and Nvidia Tesla K20c, 4 Gb.

The trained model classifiers, which showed the highest results in the reference area, were used to study arbitrary parts of the territory with the Abin indices calculated in advance for them manually ("real"). The classification of arbitrary images was carried out as follows:

– input image is divided into tiles of the required size (25 × 25, 75 × 75 pixels);
– resulting tile grid is sequentially fed to the input of the trained classifier;
– if the tile is "Trees" type, then it painted with a transparent red mask;
– calculate Abin index.

Testing was carried out on four sections of the territory arbitrarily selected in the Central and Vasileostrovsky districts of St. Petersburg, Russia with the condition of compliance with the following criteria:

– site of mixed planning, including dense wood and shrub massifs (Fig. 4);
– site without woody plants (Fig. 5);
– two sites with a dense urban development and various in size small inclusions of woody plants (Figs. 6 and 7).

| (a) | (b) | (c) | (d) |

Fig. 4. Mixed urban landscape: a – screenshot; b – LandProber 1.0.2; c – LandProber 1.0.3 (enlarged fragment); d – LandProber 1.0.1

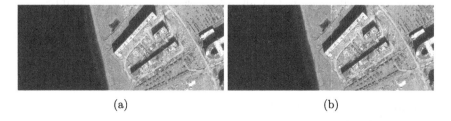

| (a) | (b) |

Fig. 5. The absence of woody plants: a – screenshot; b – LandProber 1.0.2

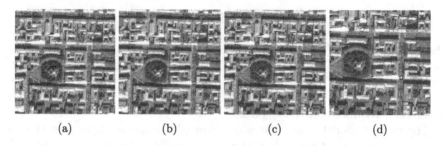

(a)   (b)   (c)   (d)

Fig. 6. Dense urban development: a – screenshot; b – LandProber 1.0.2; c – LandProber 1.0.3; d – LandProber 1.0.1 (enlarged fragment)

(a)   (b)   (c)   (d)

Fig. 7. Ultra dense urban development: a – screenshot; b – LandProber 1.0.2 (enlarged fragment); c – LandProber 1.0.3; d – LandProber 1.0.3

The test results of the conducted studies in full resolution are available by https://drive.google.com/drive/folders/1IWpkZlOXS-Q1T250NUomtq7QQBHehZ9w.

The results of the modeling, cited to the Abin index, are summarized in Table 3. The average error in the classification of woody plants in five test areas and separately in tests 2–4, respectively:

- 12.4% and 19.3% for LandProber 1.0.2 (tile size 25×25 pixels, number of classes is 3, 2 epochs of training);
- 22.3% and 15.2% for LandProber 1.0.3 (tile size 25×25 pixels, number of classes is 2, 3 epochs of training);
- 27.3% and 45.4% for LandProber 1.0.1 (tile size 75×75 pixels, number of classes is 3, 11 epochs of training).

However, it is necessary to give an explanation for the investigated test cases 2–4 in Table 3, obtained on LandProber versions 1.0.2 and 1.0.3. Most of the errors in the determination of woody plants at this stage are not related to the omission of significant arrays of green plantations. The main problems in the detection of woody plants in urban areas with an estimate of their contribution to the recognition error can be divided into the following groups:

- omissions of planted areas:
  - edges of tree crowns, 45%;
  - single regular alleine plantings of young/ornamental trees, 25%;

Table 3. Results of testing on a random site of the territory

Abin index for the territory								
#	LandProber 1.0.2		LandProber 1.0.3		Real, at 25 px	LandProber 1.0.1		Real, at 75 px
	Model	Error	Model	Error		Model	Error	
1	0.9700	−0.0300 +0.0	0.6404	−0.3596	1.0	1.0	−0.0 +0.0	1.0
2	0.2866	−0.0173 +0.0055	0.2912	−0.0120 +0.0048	0.2984	0.3993	−0.0476 +0.0035	0.4434
3	0.0518	−0.0376 +0.0067	0.0475	−0.0380 +0.0028	0.0827	0.0713	−0.1583 +0.0052	0.2244
4	0.0363	−0.0153 +0.0085	0.0300	−0.0162 +0.0031	0.0431	0.0446	−0.0623 +0.0	0.1069
5	0.0049	−0.0 +0.0049	0.0	−0.0 +0.0	0.0	0.0	−0.0 +0.0	0.0

– allocation of sites without plants:
  • small structural elements on the roofs of buildings, 15%;
  • edge glare and damaged areas of images, 6%;
  • watermarks on screenshots that included in the training sample, 1%.

6   Conclusion

A number of conclusions can be drawn from the results of the study. It is possible to say about the applicability of deep learning technology for recognizing objects of a certain class on ordinary satellite imagery, including in a complex structure of urban built-up area. Trained models of classifiers are already capable of recognizing woody plants with acceptable accuracy. In this case, each detected fragment of the image can be associated with a section of the real territory, tied to geographical coordinates.

Practical point of view shows that the geospatial linking of classified objects makes it possible to evaluate and compare different territories for their prestige. Considering that environmental problems are of particular importance today, a rapid and effective analysis provides an opportunity to choose well-grounded solutions for environmental protection, planting of greenery, estimating the cadastral value of land. Thus, the methodology followed in this study can be used for various spatial analyses and management capabilities of an urban decision support systems [25, 26].

The results obtained at this stage determined the direction of further research:

– It is necessary to improve the accuracy of the classification of the image. It is supposed to use the sliding window method, but our first implementation was not fast enough on large images.

– Satellite images on adjacent sites of the same locality can have different quality. This is due to the time of the creation of the images themselves, as well as the importance of the captured territories for image operators/suppliers. The poor quality of the images affects their color and depth of field. To overcome this problem, it is proposed to implement the method of auto-correction of contrast for parts of the original images.
– The obtained data testify to the expediency of differentiating the sizes of tiles in the grid for different tasks or different stages of the problem. It is necessary to continue testing to determine the optimal size of tiles.
– The results of training at different epochs are characterized by volatility, as well as obtaining the NaN value in the "losses" and "accuracy" parameters. It is necessary to study the behavior of neural networks in training.

In addition, it is planned to calculate Abin index for test territories in several cities. And it is also planned to develop a service for the evaluation of arbitrary sections of the territory with a query on the center of the site.

Acknowledgments. The reported study was funded by RFBR according to the research projects No. 17-37-50033_mol_nr, No. 16-07-00388_a, No. 16-07-00353_a, No. 16-37-60066_mol_dk, No. 18-07-00975.

References

1. Nechaeva, T.: State of the Green Fund of the City of Volgograd (2016). http://vgorodemira.ru/archives/193
2. Gartner, P.: European Capital Greenness Evaluation (2017). https://philippgaertner.github.io/2017/10/european-capital-greenness-evaluation/
3. Zhang, C., Yan, J., Li, C., Rui, X., Liu, L., Bie, R.: On estimating air pollution from photos using convolutional neural network. In: Proceedings of the 2016 ACM on Multimedia Conference, MM 2016, pp. 297–301. ACM, New York (2016)
4. Cheang, E.K., Cheang, T.K., Tay, Y.H.: Using convolutional neural networks to count palm trees in satellite images. arXiv preprint arXiv:1701.06462 (2017)
5. Albert, A., Kaur, J., Gonzalez, M.C.: Using convolutional networks and satellite imagery to identify patterns in urban environments at a large scale. In: Proceedings of the 23rd ACM SIGKDD International Conference on Knowledge Discovery and Data Mining, pp. 1357–1366. ACM (2017)
6. Salesses, P., Schechtner, K., Hidalgo, C.A.: The collaborative image of the city: mapping the inequality of urban perception. PloS one **8**(7), e68400 (2013)
7. L'vova, A.: Photo-Telling: Machine Vision Predicts the Future of Citizens (2017). https://strelka.com/ru/magazine/2017/06/15/machines-can-see
8. Kuchukov, R.: Cityclass Project: Analysis of Types of Urban Development Using a Neural Network (2017). https://medium.com/@romankuchukov/cityclass-project-37a9ebaa1df7
9. Kuchukov, R.: Cityclass Project #2: Conclusions and Plans for the Future (2017). https://medium.com/@romankuchukov/cityclass-project-2-13fe3aa35860
10. Korobkin, D., Fomenkov, S., Kolesnikov, S.: A function-based patent analysis for support of technical solutions synthesis. In: International Conference on Industrial Engineering, Applications and Manufacturing (ICIEAM), pp. 1–4. IEEE (2016)

11. Korobkin, D., Fomenkov, S., Kolesnikov, S., Kizim, A., Kamaev, V.: Processing of structured physical knowledge in the form of physical effects. In: Theory and Practice in Modern Computing 2015: Part of the Multi Conference on Computer Science and Information Systems 2015, pp. 173–177 (2015)

12. Barabanov, I., Barabanova, E., Maltseva, N., Kvyatkovskaya, I.: Data processing algorithm for parallel computing. In: Kravets, A., Shcherbakov, M., Kultsova, M., Iijima, T. (eds.) JCKBSE 2014. CCIS, vol. 466, pp. 61–69. Springer, Cham (2014). https://doi.org/10.1007/978-3-319-11854-3_6

13. Brust, C.A., Sickert, S., Simon, M., Rodner, E., Denzler, J.: Convolutional patch networks with spatial prior for road detection and urban scene understanding. arXiv preprint arXiv:1502.06344 (2015)

14. Castelluccio, M., Poggi, G., Sansone, C., Verdoliva, L.: Land use classification in remote sensing images by convolutional neural networks. arXiv preprint arXiv:1508.00092 (2015)

15. Finogeev, A.G., Parygin, D.S., Finogeev, A.A.: The convergence computing model for big sensor data mining and knowledge discovery. Hum. Centric Comput. Inf. Sci. **7**(1), 11 (2017)

16. Parygin, D.S., Sadovnikova, N., Schabalina, O.: Informational and analytical support of city management tasks (2017)

17. Golubev, A., Chechetkin, I., Parygin, D., Sokolov, A., Shcherbakov, M.: Geospatial data generation and preprocessing tools for urban computing system development. Procedia Comput. Sci. **101**, 217–226 (2016)

18. Google: Google Maps. https://www.google.ru/maps

19. Yandex: Yandex Maps. https://yandex.ru/maps/

20. Microsoft: Bing Maps. https://www.bing.com/maps

21. YandexMaps: Abinsky District of the Krasnodar Territory, Russia. https://yandex.ru/maps/?ll=38.192211

22. Narbut, N., Matushkina, L.: Selection and justification of environmental criteria for assessing the state of the urban environment. In: Vestnik TOGU (2009)

23. Das, N., Dilkina, B.: A Deep Learning Approach to Assessing Urban Tree Canopy Using Satellite Imagery in the City of Atlanta. http://nilakshdas.com/papers/nilakshdas-deep-learning-satellite-imagery.pdf

24. Vytovtov, K., Bulgakov, A.: Investigation of photonic crystals containing bianisotropic layers. In: 2005 European Microwave Conference, vol. 2, 4 pp. IEEE (2005)

25. Parygin, D., Sadovnikova, N., Kalinkina, M., Potapova, T., Finogeev, A.: Visualization of data about events in the urban environment for the decision support of the city services actions coordination. In: 2016 International Conference System Modeling Advancement in Research Trends (SMART), pp. 283–290, November 2016

26. Sadovnikova, N., Parygin, D., Gnedkova, E., Sanzhapov, B., Gidkova, N.: Evaluating the sustainability of volgograd. WIT Trans. Ecol. Environ. **179**, 279–290 (2013)

E-Economy: IT & New Markets

The Political Economy of the Blockchain Society

Boris Korneychuk[✉]

National Research University Higher School of Economics,
Saint Petersburg, Russia
bkorneychuk@hse.ru

Abstract. The review discusses the political-economic aspects of the concept of distributed capitalism allowed for by blockchain technology. As opposed to the first era of the Internet, where the industry of financial and information services was dominated by intermediaries, the blockchain era is characterized by development of a new institution of trust; disruption of financial intermediation; economic inclusion of hundreds of millions of citizens in developing countries; an increase in competition and a decrease in inequality. The paper focuses on the content of key political-economic categories being redefined in the blockchain era. First, labor value gives way to creative value which is manifesting itself in cryptocurrencies. Second, exploitation of workers is replaced by digital discrimination. The blockchain revolution is a solution to the problem of discrimination against intellectual property creators, who have to hand over a large part of the value created to intermediaries. Third, capitalism characterized by information monopoly gives place to free competition based on rivalry between cryptocurrencies. Fourth, class struggle is substituted by confrontation between agents of information monopoly system and those of distributed economy. The author considers the main opposition to distributed capitalism to stem from the feudal financial system which loses ground under new conditions, where economic agents may use alternative currencies and interact directly with one other without risk and high transaction costs.

Keywords: Political economy · Blockchain technology · Bitcoin
Financial intermediation · Discrimination · Distributed capitalism

1 Introduction

The current boom in blockchain technology and cryptocurrencies took economists by surprise, forcing them to reconsider the seemingly fully-developed theory of post-industrial (information) economy. The social practice shows that blockchain technology revolutionizes all aspects of economic life and generates a completely new economic order. Specifically, while until recently Hayek's [11] idea of competing private currencies has been seen as an odd example of a radical free-trade ideology, today it seriously claims to be the basic principle of the new financial arrangement. The challenge we are faced with is to create a basic economic paradigm that would be relevant to the realities of the blockchain society. In the meantime, the majority of works on blockchain economy are primary of descriptive or futurological nature and do

© Springer Nature Switzerland AG 2018
D. A. Alexandrov et al. (Eds.): DTGS 2018, CCIS 858, pp. 317–328, 2018.
https://doi.org/10.1007/978-3-030-02843-5_25

not claim to provide deep theoretical analysis of the occurring profound changes. The author is unaware of any studies that consider the impact of blockchain on society from the political-economic perspective. The aim of this paper is to develop the fundamentals of the political economy of society in the age of blockchain. It shows that with the formation of *distributed capitalism* [15, 30] or *peer-to-peer economy* [25] comes the changing of the content of such fundamental categories of political economy as labor value, productive labor, equivalent exchange, exploitation, and free competition. The paper does not address the issue of blockchain technology impact on the political system, which is covered in the article [24] and other works. We also do not discuss the questions related to "Blockchain Sociology" [23], bitcoin [6] and other particular aspects of the blockchain society.

The author's goal was specifically to answer the fundamental questions of political economy in reference to the new society: (1) Which mode of production dominates the economy and what is its impact on social development? (Sect. 3); (2) What becomes the main form of value? (Sect. 4); (3) What is the role of market mechanisms in creating the new value? (Sect. 5); (4) Will the new economy allow for a fairer distribution of value? (Sect. 6); (5) Is blockchain able to affect the trend of market monopolization and overcome the crisis of free competition philosophy? (Sect. 7); (6) Can we recognize the practical importance of the blockchain society political economy? In order to achieve the purpose of the study, the author used the methodology of classical political economy (A. Smith, K. Marx, K. Menger) to analyze the profound social change brought about by blockchain technology.

2 Related Works

As blockchain technology has gained all the more public importance only in recent years, by now there are few works offering theoretical analysis of economic implications of the new technology. Most authors come to a conclusion that blockchain usage generates a new type of economic order which requires analysis and thorough understanding. They agree that we may be at the dawn of a new revolution [17, 20, 30, 33]. Sharing the prevailing view, Swan [27] claims that blockchain is capable of dramatically changing most aspects of society's life, which brings into question the immutability of traditional components of the modern world, such as cash money, economy, trustful relations, value, and stock market mechanisms. MacDonald, Allen and Potts [17] consider blockchain as a technology for creation of new institutions. This is a political-economic rupture and bifurcation in which an incumbent institutional order precipitates a constitutional ordered catallaxy. Davidson, De Filippi and Potts [8] suggest two approaches to the economics of blockchain: innovation- and governance-centered. They view the governance-entered approach based on new institutional economics and public choice as the most promising.

Some economists reject the dominant opinion that blockchain plays a crucial role in modern society's development. L. Swartz sees blockchain projects as a form of utopian science fiction and characterizes the radical blockchain by three components: futurity; decentralization and disintegration; and autonomy and automation [28]. V. Kostakis and C. Giotitsas challenge the view on distributed capitalism as a more fair system than the present capitalism. According to them, distributed capitalism is not a Commons-oriented project aiming to satisfy the needs of society, because it creates a new aristocracy that has accumulated a great deal of bitcoins. Members of this aristocracy are those that got into the bitcoin game earlier on, when it was easy to create new units [15].

The book by D. Tapscott and A. Tapscott entitled "Blockchain Revolution" [30] stands out in that it provides a broader and deeper analysis of economic changes brought about by blockchain. The authors show that, with the rise of the blockchain, we are entering a whole new "economic" era of the Internet. The old Internet has enabled many positive changes, but it has serious limitations for business and economic activity. Whereas the Internet democratized information, the blockchain democratizes value and cuts to the core of traditional finance industry. The authors demonstrate that the institutional base of the blockchain revolution is shaped by a dramatic transformation of the institution of trust. While in the first era of the Internet trust between economic agents was provided by a hierarchical financial system of a feudal type, now it is provided globally by an autonomous distributed network of computers.

3 Theory of the Information Society

The creation of intellectual products plays a leading role in the information society, whereas in the industrial society the role belongs to the creation of material products. The evolution of the information economy theory can be divided into three phases. In the first phase, economists studied the process of simple labor dwindling and mental labor/creative work assuming a growing importance as a result of technical progress. Information technologies were overlooked back then, as they were in their infancy. The critical importance of creative activity for economic progress was first shown by Schumpeter [26], who described three families of entrepreneurial motives: the desire to get a sense of power, the will to succeed, and the joy of creation. He argued that profit is nothing but an indicator of triumph, while a determinant factor of business behavior is the joy of creating. He focused on creativity of entrepreneurs, whose social function is "to implement new combinations". The psychological foundation of the theory of the information society is given in the writings of Fromm [9], who identified two opposite character orientations—a marketing and a productive one, the former being determined by a striving for possession and the latter by a craving for creative activity, or a commitment to the "being" mode of existence. As he wrote, "there is also no strength in use and manipulation of objects; what we use is not ours simply because we use it. Ours is only that to which we are genuinely related by our creative activity, be it a person or an inanimate object". The first phase of the information economy theory development resulted in works by Beck [2], Bell [4], Galbraith [10], Schiller [25]. The review of these studies is given in Webster's book [34]. In the second phase, information technologies (primarily Internet) were seen as a key determinant of economic development. Castells [7] proposed a technical-economic paradigm defined by pervasiveness of new technologies; networking logic; institutional flexibility; and convergence of technologies. According to him, in an age of rapid technological change, networks rather than firms become efficient producing units. The works of Toffler [31] and Tapscott [29] include, along with economic analysis, some elements of futurology.

The third, modern, phase of the information economy theory development is associated with the emergence of blockchain technology [17, 27, 30, 33].

4 Blockchain Changes the Nature of Value

Gold currency is rare as its mining in the industrial age requires a great amount of energy in the form of simple labor work. Therefore, in the classical political economy, a simple labor unit becomes a measure of "labor value". In the information economy, the term "labor value" needs to be re-identified since it implies that value is created by any kind of labor. Actually, in the framework of classical theory, this concept denotes the exchange value produced by manual labor in the course of substance-processing. Mental work, or the process of information being processed by an individual, was not considered by the classics to be productive. This ethical position was first attacked by the representatives of the historical school headed by F. List, who took an important step towards creating the political economy of the information society. As he put it, "those who fatten pigs, make bagpipes or prepare pills are productive, but the instructors of youth and of adults, virtuosos, musicians, physicians, judges, and administrators, are productive in a much higher degree. The former produce *values of exchange*, and the latter *productive powers*" [16].

The labor theory of value and the creative one rest upon opposite ethical postulates, but are kindred methodologically. In both conceptions, human life time is assumed to be the underlying principle of value. The classic labor theory contends that value is formed in the process of expenditure of simple labor-power, which, on an average, apart from any special development, exists in the organism of every ordinary individual [19]. The creative theory, on the contrary, argues that value is formed by creative labor. H. Bergson even claimed that "time is invention or it is nothing at all" [5]. As long as the total existence of society members splits into simple and creative components, there is quite a lucid correlation between the labor and the creative value: the greater is one of them, the less is the other, and vice versa. Consequently, as the role of creative labor in economy rises, the domain of commodities exchange shrinks, and the place of exchange value is filled by creative value. The discrepancy between the basic assumptions of classical political economy and information economy theory is linked to differing ethical and empirical foundations. While the classical theory was developed when manual labor prevailed, the informational theory is taking shape in the period when the dominance of creative labor is becoming more and more evident. As long as in practice any labor can be divided into simple and creative elements, the representation of reality given by either of the two theories separately is highly schematic and can be easily, and justly, criticized by the opposing school of economics. For instance, orthodox followers of A. Smith are not likely to agree with the statement that in the future physical labor will be deprived of value and physical means of production won't be considered as capital. Yet, symmetrical objections could be raised to the classical theory: in its framework, creative labor, together with its products, is treated as devoid of value, and individual creative ability has allegedly nothing to do with capital [14].

In the information age, the second most important rare resource is information produced in the course of creative activity. The value creation now requires both simple labor and creative work, calling for introduction of a new unit of value. What becomes such a unit is bitcoin created as a reward for utilized electric energy and computing processing work. Incorporation of a multifaceted human dimension into the new concept of value implies multiple value measures, i.e. simultaneous circulation of different currencies.

5 Blockchain Creates a Market for Information

The exchange of information products plays in contemporary society a role as fundamental as the exchange of material products played in industrial society. Yet, owning to a number of specific properties of information, the mechanics of information exchange differ from that of commodities exchange. First, a buyer can get information prior to making a deal and free of charge—when learning about the essential characteristics of the purchased product, these representing the core value of information. In general, an information product can be used without its creator's permission more easily as compared to a physical good. Second, after the deal has been arranged, the information remains at the disposal of its creator and can be sold to other buyers [14]. Thanks to the specified attributes, information is freely distributed and is assuming all features of a public good, and information exchange is assuming a specifically social character. The information which is public is often considered valueless [18]. In general, the debate over whether information was essentially a public or a private good remained unresolved in the Internet society [1].

Prior to the emergence of blockchain technology, the markets of information products were diffuse and local, as the establishment of trust required personal acquaintance between the parties or engagement of a dedicated intermediary. Therefore, in the first era of the Internet, creators of intellectual property did not receive fair compensation for it. This old model is unsustainable as a means of supporting creative work of any kind, because with each new intermediary the creators get a smaller cut. The control of intellectual copyright is concentrated in the hands of few monopolists. This means getting a cut of all the revenues that a creator generates regardless of whether or not the intermediaries invested in the cultivation of those rights. As a result, the creator is the last to be paid. Finally, technology intermediaries like YouTube inserted themselves into the supply chain between creators and monopolies, slicing the creators' part of revenue even thinner. Banks centralized the system of trust and put themselves in the middle of it, becoming extremely powerful.

Blockchain technology enables the creation of a global market of intellectual products based on the institution of trust building. A new protocol for a peer-to-peer electronic cash system using a cryptocurrency, or the Trust Protocol [30], established a set of rules—in the form of distributed computations—that ensures the integrity of data without going through a trusted third party. The most important role of the Trust Protocol is eliminating centralized intermediaries and handing the ledger-keeping function to a network of autonomous computers, creating a decentralized system of trust. The Trust Protocol removes obstacles for a development of a full-blown market of intellectual products. First, smart contracts eliminate the need for a special type of trust between demander and supplier of intellectual products. Second, one of the first services to offer blockchain attestation is Proof of Existence, which demonstrates document ownership without revealing the information it contains. Third, a global blockchain-based reputational system tracks, posts and archives all cases of intellectual property infringement, which makes such violations disadvantageous and rare.

Blockchain technology provides a new platform for creators to transform intellectual property into a tradable asset and to receive proper compensation for it. This paper looks at ways that blockchain technologies are putting creators at the centre of the model so they can maximize the value of their moral and material interests in their intellectual property, with no greedy intermediaries and government censors. First, smart contracts on the blockchain can eliminate the magnitude of the complexity of the intellectual products market, replacing a critical role of information monopolies. The combination of blockchain-based platforms, smart contracts and intellectual community's standards of inclusion, integrity, and openness could enable creators and their consumers to form an efficient market of intellectual products. Second, creators could issue their own tokens to make a store of value, the valuation of which correlates to the creator's professional success. As the former rises, the value of the tokens rises, and the consumers of intellectual product could potentially benefit financially from supporting creators before they become famous.

The contemporary market for information products is notoriously exclusive and opaque. A small number of intermediaries represent an incredibly large share of the market, and there are few paths for emerging creators to enter this market. Such nature of the market encourages experimenting with new concepts, democratizing the market by the transformative and disruptive power of the bitcoin blockchain. For example, Artlery describes itself as a network of artists who have agreed to share some of their revenues with peers who engage socially with their works. Its goal is to mint an art-as-asset-backed currency on the blockchain by engaging fans as partial owners and stakeholders of the art with which they interact. To foster patronage and build reputation for an artist, Altlery stages IPOs of digital pieces of the artist's work. D. Tapscott and A. Tapscott also consider crowdfunding journalists on the blockchain. Journalists could try to use the distributed peer-to-peer platforms such as Koinify, which protects the identities of sender and recipient better than pure Internet systems. Another bitcoin tool is the app GetGems, which guards and monetizes instant messaging through bitcoin. Reporter could purchase entry credits—rights to create entries on Factom's ledger. As with the bitcoin ledger, every one would get the same copy, and anyone could add to it but no one could alter entries once they were filed [30]. In science, an author could publish a paper to a limited audience of peers and receive the credibility to publish to a larger audience, rather than assigning all intellectual rights to a journal. Journalcoin could be issued as the token system to reward creators, reviewers, editors and others involved in scientific publishing. With Journalcoin, reviewers can receive reputational and remunerative rewards [27].

6   Blockchain Eliminates Digital Discrimination

The theory of workers' exploitation is the major social element of K. Marx's political economy [19]. The equivalent of this theory in the blockchain era is a concept of digital discrimination. The fundamental difference between these theories is that exploitation concerns employed workers receiving wages at the minimum subsistence level, whereas digital discrimination affects employed and unemployed citizens of backward countries who have no opportunity to achieve proper living standards. In contemporary society, digital discrimination has a more important role to play as compared to exploitation. First, workers' wages in developed countries are by far higher than the minimum subsistence level set by the classical "iron law of wages". Second, the number of simple labor workers that can potentially be subject to exploitation is much less than the number of those who experience poverty due to forced exclusion from the economy.

In order to achieve prosperity in contemporary world, an individual must have access to basic financial services to connect to the economy. But even with the Internet, more than two billion people are excluded from the world financial system; thus, the economic benefits are asymmetrical. On the Internet, people haven't been able to transact or do business directly for the reason that money isn't like other information goods: you can send e-mail, but you can't send a dollar. As basic financial services in the informational economy are provided in electronic form, their inaccessibility for a person can be called digital discrimination, or digital divide [27, 32]. B. Wessels argues that key themes that Marx identified about inequality are still relevant in the contemporary, digitally enabled society. The digital divide needs to be considered in terms of the dynamics of inclusion and exclusion in global informational capitalism [35]. The concept of a "taste for discrimination" proposed by G. Becker at the dawn of the information age has features of both Marxian exploitation and digital discrimination. On the one hand, this type of discrimination concerns employed workers and is attributed to some "unfair" actions of an employer. On the other hand, it is to a great extent determined by lack of information: "Since a taste for discrimination incorporates both prejudice and ignorance, the amount of knowledge available must be included as a determinant of tastes" [3].

The inevitable elimination of digital discrimination, as well as of Marxian exploitation, is predetermined by the evolution of productive forces. It has become clear that concentrated powers in business have bent the democratic structure of the Internet to their will. The new aristocracy uses its insider advantages to exploit Internet and strengthen its influence over society. Such companies as Airbnb and Uber are successful because they aggregate data for commercial use, so the Internet economy is an aggregating economy. Now, with blockchain technology, billions of excluded people can do transactions, create and exchange value without powerful intermediaries. Rather than trying to solve the problem of inequality through the redistribution of gross product, we can change the way it is distributed—how it is produced in the first place. Whereas Internet tends to automate workers on the periphery doing menial tasks, blockchain automates away the center, and so "big disrupters are about to get disrupted" [30]. In other words, the development of blockchain inevitably leads to elimination of digital discrimination in the same way as the suppression of exploitation in K. Marx's theory is achieved—specifically, by the "expropriation of the expropriators".

D. Tapscott and A. Tapscott imagine instead of the centralized company Uber a distributed application—a cooperative owned by its members. Then "instead of putting the taxi driver out of a job, blockchain puts Uber out of a job and lets the taxi drivers work with the customer directly" [30]. Distributed ledger technology can liberate many financial services, and this shift could liberate and empower entrepreneurs everywhere, because no resource is too small to monetize on the blockchain. It drastically lowers the cost of transactions and the barrier to having a bank account and obtaining credit, it supports entrepreneurship in global economy. The result can be an economy without digital discrimination—distributed capitalism, not just a redistributed capitalism. The spread of inclusion as the foundation of prosperity, and elimination of digital dis-crimination will ensure growth of economic efficiency, since economy works best when it works for everyone. As distributed capitalism provides equal access to eco-nomic resources and fair distribution of the public product, it functions as an equivalent of socialism in Marxism.

The elimination of digital discrimination is achieved by development of a new type of markets, allowing previously excluded individuals to enter the economy [21]. Thanks to blockchain, hundreds of millions could become microshareholders in new corporations. Nseke [22] concludes that users in African countries benefit from usage of bitcoin. Blockchain enables the creation of a decentralized prediction market plat-form that rewards users for correctly predicting political, economic or sporting events. The users can purchase or sell shares in the outcome of a future event. The market relies on "wisdom of the crowd", the principle that a large group of people usually predicts the probability of a future event with greater accuracy than a small group of experts. On the Augur platform, anyone can post a prediction about anything; its arbiters are known as impartial referees and their legitimacy derives from their repu-tation points [30]. Blockchain creates a metering economy where everyone can rent out and meter the use of excess capacity for certain commodities—computing power, extra mobile minutes, garage, or power tools. Using existing blockchain technologies like EtherLock and Airlock owners can unlock and use a car for a certain amount of time. Because blockchain is transparent, the owners can track who is abiding by their commitments. Those who aren't take a reputational hit and lose access altogether [30]. Blockchain gives the opportunity to construct open networked enterprises that displace traditional centralized models. Peer producers are dispersed volunteers who bring about social innovative projects, such as Wikipedia. Social production means that goods and services are produced outside the private sector. Now, blockchain can improve the efficiency of volunteers and reward them for their work by creating a reputation system and other incentives. To discourage bad behavior, members could ante up a small amount of money that either increases or decreases based on contribution and repu-tation. Blockchain enables outside individuals to cocreate value with open enterprises. A new generation of consumer is prosumer, customer who produces. Blockchain creates ideagoras—emerging markets for ideas and uniquely qualified minds, which enable companies to tap global pools of talent. Talents can post their availability to the ledger so that firms can find them [30]. Blockchain creates an attention market—every user of a social network has a multifaceted wallet and can receive microcompensation for agreeing to view or interact with an advertisement. Blockchain enables building of a cap-and-trade system for people—personal carbon trade working through the Internet of Things. A home owner could earn credits by acting in a practical way: putting a solar panel on his roof, he would earn money for pumping excess electric energy back to the grid.

7 Blockchain Brings Back Free Competition

The transformational effect of the blockchain on the economic system consists in the elimination of two types of monopolism. The first type is the information monopolism of aggregators and other companies that use information asymmetry for commercial benefit. As illustrated above, the main reason of information asymmetry in the Internet era is underdevelopment of the institution of trust which undergoes revolutionary changes under the influence of blockchain technology. The second type of monopolism is the state's monopoly position in financial sector, which is primarily apparent in the state's monopoly on currency issue.

The financial system is antiquated and the most centralized industry governed by regulations dating back to the nineteenth century. Bankers gain competitive advantages from information asymmetry and so they don't like the idea of openness, decentralization, and new forms of currency. Because of their monopoly position, banks have no incentive to improve products and increase efficiency and therefore they reinforce the status quo and stymie disruptive innovation. Apprehensive about new companies, banks argue that blockchain businesses are "high-risk" investments. A. Moazed and N. Johnson argue that next decade could see a number of as-yet-unknown platforms disrupt the finance industry in new and surprising way. And big banks have little incentive to play nice and no reason not to press the existing regulatory regime to their advantage [21]. Visa and Mastercard face the risk that they become obsolete once cryptocurrencies and blockchain applications become more accepted [13]. In contrast, T. Hughes suggests that instead of being disruptive to major incumbent institutions, blockchain-based innovation will tend to strengthen existing market participants [12].

In 2015, the world's largest banks announced plans to start the R3 Consortium and Hyperledger projects to collaborate on common standards for blockchain. It demonstrates how reluctant the industry is to embrace fully open, decentralized blockchains like bitcoin. D. Tapscott and A. Tapscott argue that banks aim to reign supreme by deploying the blockchain without bitcoin, welding elements of distributed ledger technology to existing business models [30].

Blockchain is the evidence of the world transforming from closed systems to open systems. New technology will bring about profound changes in the industry, destroying the finance monopoly, and offering individuals a choice in how they create value. Now, two parties who neither know nor trust each other can do business. Anyone will be able to access loans from peers and to issue, trade, and settle traditional instruments directly. Blockchain also supports decentralized models of insurance based on a person's reputational attributes. New accounting methods using blockchain's distributed ledger will make financial reporting and audit transparent. Some authors argue that bitcoin technology itself functions as a regulator in the financial industry. Thus, blockchain raises an existential question for central banks, and we might expect them to oppose the new technology.

By eliminating the two aforementioned types of monopolism, blockchain technology busts the information monopolistic system of the Internet era. Along with that, it allows for the return of free competition of the age of barter, where multiple equally recognized and mutually competing highly marketable commodities were simultaneously used as money. Thus, in the blockchain era, the political-economic content of the term "free competition" proves to be far wider as compared to Smith's classical political economy. As F. Hayek wrote as far as half a century ago: "What we now need is a Free Money Movement comparable to the Free Trade Movement of the 19th century" [11].

8   Conclusion

The economy as a separate field of social life emerged only when strong states became capable of creating a centralized system of trust for ensuring fair exchange. At the present day, this infrastructure for the first time in history undergoes profound changes, because trust is now provided by new blockchain-based decentralized mechanisms, rather than by violence and law. Hence, the nature of economic relations and the paradigm of the whole economic science are changing dramatically. The paper shows that the political economy of society in the age of blockchain is based on new categories: labor value gives way to creative value; Marxian exploitation is replaced by digital discrimination; class struggle is substituted by economic and ideological confrontation between agents of information monopoly system and those of distributed economy; employment system is replaced by completely new blockchain-based types of economic activity. In order to create new bitcoins and other cryptocurrencies one has to expend both energy and intellectual efforts. This distinctive feature of cryptocurrencies reflects the creative nature of value in the information age, enabling the creation of full-blown markets of intellectual products and for the first time in history providing fair income to intellectual property creators.

The main focus of the paper is the transformation of the institution of trust, a process which exerts a revolutionary influence on the economy. Along with that, affected by blockchain technology, traditional institutions become decentralized and transform into new ones, such as direct democracy and distributed governance, peer-to-peer investing, etc. In the future, this global trend in general and its separate aspects are to become the key topics of political-economic studies of the blockchain economy.

The political-economic approach to the study of blockchain's transformational role enables a long-term prediction of society's development, which is erroneously confused by some authors with "Futurism". Marx's proletarian socialism theory is an example of such long-term prediction based on a political-economic concept. The application of this theory had a significant effect on the development of civilization, demonstrating the practical relevance of political-economic concepts. The study's main finding is that the progress of blockchain technology drives a social development trend counter to Soviet socialism and Post-Soviet oligarchic capitalism: a class-divided society gives way to a homogeneous peer-to-peer community; monopolists and information intermediaries losing economic power; and government regulation of economy is being replaced by self-regulation of distributed markets.

References

1. Bates, B.: Information as an economic good: a re-evaluation of theoretical approach. In: Ruben, B.D., Lievrouw, L.A. (eds.) Mediation, Information, and Communication. Information and Behavior, vol. 3, pp. 379–394. Transaction, New Brunswick (1990)
2. Beck, U.: Risk Society: Towards a New Modernity. Sage Publications, London (1992)
3. Becker, G.: The Economics of Discrimination. University of Chicago Press, Chicago (1971)
4. Bell, D.: The Coming of Post-Industrial Society: A Venture in Social Forecasting. Heinemann, London (1974)
5. Bergson, H.: Creative Evolution. Henry Holt and Company, New York (1911)
6. Bohme, R., Christin, N., Edelman, B., Moore, T.: Bitcoin: economics, technology, and governance. J. Econ. Perspect. **2**(2), 213–238 (2015). https://doi.org/10.1257/jep.29.2.213
7. Castells, M.: The Internet Gallaxy: Reflections on the Internet, Business and Society. Oxford University Press, Oxford (2001)
8. Davidson, S., De Filippi, P., Potts, J.: Economics of blockchain. In: Proceedings of Public Choice Conference. Fort Lauderdale (2016). https://doi.org/10.2139/ssrn.2744751
9. Fromm, E.: Escape from Freedom. Avon Books, New York (1966)
10. Galbraith, J.K.: The New Industrial State. Houghton Mifflin Company, Boston (1967)
11. Hayek, F.A.: Denationalization of Money: The Argument Refined. Institute of Economic Affaires, London (1976)
12. Hughes, T.: The global financial services industry and the bitcoin. J. Struct. Financ. **23**(4), 36–40 (2018). https://doi.org/10.3905/jsf.2018.23.4.036
13. Koeppl, T., Kronick, J.: Blockchain Technology—What's for Canada's Economy and Financial Markets? C.D. Howe Institute Commentary 468, 2 February 2017. https://doi.org/10.2139/ssrn.292781
14. Korneychuk, B.: The political economy of the informational society. Scienta and Societas **1**, 3–11 (2007). http://files.sets7.webnode.cz/200000120-bd893be81e/2007_01_sets.pdf
15. Kostakis, V., Giotitsas, C.: The (A) political economy of bitcoin. tripleC. J. Global Sustain. Inf. Soc. **2**, 431–440 (2014). https://doi.org/10.31269/triplec.v12i2.606
16. List, F.: The National System of Political Economy. JB Lappincott and Co., Philadelphia (1856)
17. MacDonald, T.J., Allen, D.W.E., Potts, J.: Blockchains and the boundaries of self-organized economies: predictions for the future of banking. In: Tasca, P., Aste, T., Pelizzon, L., Perony, N. (eds.) Banking Beyond Banks and Money. NEW, pp. 279–296. Springer, Cham (2016). https://doi.org/10.1007/978-3-319-42448-4_14
18. Marshall, J.M.: Private incentives and public information. Am. Econ. Rev. **64**(3), 373–390 (1974)
19. Marx, K.: Capital. Encyclopedia Britanica, Chicago (1994)
20. Morabito, V.: Business Innovation through Blockchain: The B3 Perspective. Springer, New York (2017)
21. Moazed, A., Johnson, N.: Modern Monopolies: What it Takes to Dominate the 21st Century Economy. St. Martin Press, New York (2016)

22. Nseke, P.: How crypto-currency can decrypt the global digital divide: bitcoins a means for African emergence. Int. J. Innov. Econ. Dev. **3**(6), 61–70 (2018). https://doi.org/10.18775/ijied.1849-7551-7020.2015.36.2005

23. Reijers, W., O'Brolchain, F., Haynes, P.: Governance in blockchain technologies & social contract theories. Ledger **1**, 134–151 (2016). https://doi.org/10.5915/LEDGER.2016.62

24. Sandstrom, G.: Who would live in a blockchain society? The rise of cryptographically-enabled ledger communities. Soc. Epistemol. Rev. Reply Collect. **6**(5), 27–41 (2017). http://wp.me/p1Bfg0-3A8

25. Schiller, H.I.: Information Inequality: The Deepening Social Crisis in America. Routledger, New York (1996)

26. Schumpeter, J.: The Theory of Economic Development. Transaction Publishers, Brunswick (1912)

27. Swan, M.: Blockchain: Blueprint for a New Economy. O'Reilly, Sebastopol (2015)

28. Swartz, L.: Blockchain dreams: imagining techno-economic alternatives after bitcoin. In: Castels, M. (ed.) Another Economy Is Possible: Culture and Economy in a Time of Crisis, pp. 82–105. Polity, Malden (2017)

29. Tapscott, D.: The Digital Economy: Promise and Peril in the Age of Networked Intelligence. McGraw-Hill, New York (1995)

30. Tapscott, D., Tapscott, A.: Blockchain Revolution. How the Technology behind Bitcoin is Changing Money, Business, and the World. Penguin Random House, New York (2016)

31. Toffler, A.: The Third Wave. William Morrow, New York (1980)

32. Van Dijk, J.: A theory of the digital divide. In: Ragnedda, M., Muschert, G. (eds.) The Digital Divide: The Internet and Social Inequility in International Perspectives, pp. 29–62. Routledge, New York (2013)

33. Vigna, P., Casey, M.J.: The Age of Cryptocurrency: How Bitcoin and the Blockchain Are Challenging the Global Economic Order. Picador St.Martin's Press, New York (2015)

34. Webster, F.: Theories of the Information Society. Routledge, London (1995)

35. Wessels, B.: The reproduction and reconfiguration of inequility. In: Ragnedda, M., Muschert, G. (eds.) The Digital Divide: The Internet and Social Inequility in International Perspectives, pp. 17–28. Routledge, New York (2013)

A Comparison of Linear and Digital Platform-Based Value Chains in the Retail Banking Sector of Russia

Julia Bilinkis[✉]

National Research University Higher School of Economics,
33 Kirpichnaya Str., Moscow, Russia
ybilinkis@hse.ru

Abstract. In recent years more and more participants of the retail segment of the banking sector of Russia are launching platform-based value chains along with traditional linear value chains. As a result, business organizations are transforming into a complex system within which customers, banks and retail chains enter into business relations with each other as well as the platform itself, the owner of which is one of the participants of this interaction. A new kind of value exchange is the result of this which has become possible due to the existence of the platform. Platforms complement and compete with linear value chains in order to attract customers. In this article a comparison of these two types of value chains is presented using the example of purchasing goods by installments in Russia, their peculiar workings are also distinguished.

Keywords: Platform · Value chain · Banking · Value

1 Introduction

For the last 15 years joint value chains have been the subject of scientific and business-related articles [1–5]. They are based on mutually beneficial long-term cooperation of value chain participants with the aim of achieving a competitive advantage from access to consumers, resources, competence, cost minimization, innovative products and services time to market acceleration, improvement of service operation, consideration of consumers' needs, etc.

Traditionally a joint value chain is viewed as a linear process (the concepts of "pipes" and "one-sided businesses" can also be found) in which the customer consuming goods and services is at the end of the chain. This approach is a dominant standard in industrial economies where firm's competitive advantage formation is explained by means of Porter's Five Forces, in other words, by means of building a positioning strategy and protecting the business from competitors. A supply chain strategy which is based on vertical integration for direct access to the customers can serve as a typical example of such kind of business model. The more complicated the transaction, the degree of the specificity of assets involved, the degree of uncertainty, the value of quasi-rent subject to appropriation, the complexity of quality support and the longer term during which the assets can be used is, the higher the probability of

© Springer Nature Switzerland AG 2018
D. A. Alexandrov et al. (Eds.): DTGS 2018, CCIS 858, pp. 329–342, 2018.
https://doi.org/10.1007/978-3-030-02843-5_26

making a decision to perform an internal transaction within a company is [6], i.e., the decision to produce goods or services independently or to have a vertical integration within the company. Competition between participants of the value chain is more common within the activities that are more related to customers and cooperation between them is stronger within the activities that are far from customers [7], since the customer base is the main specific intangible asset. The phenomenon of simultaneous cooperation for creating value and competition for appropriating a larger share of rent between value chain participants has been given the name of coopetition [8–11]. When considering traditional joint value chains from Porter's point of view and the positioning school the following known assumptions are accepted: (1) customers, competitors and suppliers are not interrelated, do not interact and do not come to any arrangements with each other (an industry is a set of unrelated firms), (2) price is determined by structural advantages of the company (the essence of the business strategy is in building high entrance barriers), (3) the level of instability in the market is quite low and allows market participants to plan their reaction to the actions of their competitors.

Since mid-1980s the nature and boundaries of competition have started to transform rapidly under the simultaneous influence of many factors, especially accessible innovations, business globalization, continuing technology renewal and the changing expectations of the customers. With the advent of "a new network economy" based on information, and information technologies penetrating joint value chains, these restrictions have ceased to be effective at all. The powerhouse of this kind of economy is information represented in a digital form and the technologies to manipulate it: Big data, Business Intelligence, etc. Information has one important economic property: it has zero marginal costs when replicating it [12]. Thus, companies are guided by the utility of a product but not the costs of its production in the process of price formation. As a result, a new wave of business strategies and models based on the principle of network usage for information creation and transfer which make the process of information transfer substantially easier due to their structure and horizontal bindings, is emerging. Network-based value chains are called two-sided or multi-sided ecosystems [13].

The most important thing is consideration of these business models in the context of highly competitive industries. This article researches the portfolio of business models applied by Russian companies functioning in the banking sector using the example of the retail lending sector where loans are provided to the customers for the purchase of goods by installments. The specific feature of these business models is the market presence of joint value chains realized whether in the form of a linear model or in the form of a platform in which the same companies participate but play different roles. Any business model is based on the interaction of three main participants: a bank, a retail chain and a client for the creation of value, however, the way a value proposition is implemented differs greatly in terms of content, structure and management, and in terms of the volume of the rent received. The following tasks have been formulated to reach the goal set:

1. Define the approach to the analysis of linear value chains and a platform-based one.
2. Highlight features of such value chains specific to the banking sector of Russia.
3. Create methodological recommendations for the study of value chains.

2 Theoretical Framework

2.1 Definition of the Approach to the Analysis of Value Chains

Within value chains different market participants (suppliers, business partners, and customers) cooperate with each other for the joint production of value. They perform operations that include exchange and transformation and combining resources and information. At the same time the efficiency of one action affects the efficiency of another action and the entire chain in general, in other words, the connection between different parts of the chain occurs in the case of interdependence of actions. This kind of interdependence should be managed by using coordination and control mechanism, especially, when it occurs at the intersection of functional areas [14]. Joint value chain management can be achieved by applying formal methods (agreements and contracts) which are defined by Dyer and Singh as third-party enforcement and informal methods, otherwise known as self-enforcing agreements. Informal methods are often based on trust, guarantees in the form financial integration (for instance, in the form of equity, joint investments in specific assets), logistic integration (resource flow control), media integration (brand promotion) and cultural integration as well as reputation and future business opportunities. A complex of various formal and informal methods is often used. The management setup process is accelerated and facilitated if participating parties represent the same overall corporate culture and standardize all processes in joint information systems.

Value chain strategic management is being studied from the point of view of different theories: economic (industrial organization, transaction costs economics, new institutional economics, agency theory), sociological and psychosocial (resource dependence theory, sociology of organizations, theory of social networks), biological ones (population ecology) [15]. In our research we will be using basic theories that are described below to analyze the characteristics of business models.

First, resource dependence analysis [16], i.e., the analysis of dependence in terms of the extent to which other firms need resources available to a certain firm and the degree this certain firm manages to concentrate control over these resources and reduce the level of its dependence from other market participants in terms of these resources. This theory is proved by several studies [17–19]. However, the availability of the best resources does not always guarantee the firm a sustainable competitive advantage. To obtain higher economic rents a firm needs to have a unique capability that will allow utilizing the available resources in the best possible way. Therefore, secondly, it is necessary to perform the analysis of managerial and dynamic capabilities that are defined as repetitive action patterns of using assets in order to create, produce and/or offer products in the market [20]. According to [20] these are managerial and dynamic capabilities that act as a foundation for the generation of economic rents that are hierarchal for individual companies, rather than market ones due to the complexity of their creation, their unique character in the case of determined by implicit knowledge embedded inside them and the complexity caused by these reasons or even impossibility of their copying or imitation. Teece distinguishes three main elements of dynamic capabilities: (1) the ability to discover and perceive opportunities and threats, (2) the ability to use discovered possibilities and (3) the ability to maintain competitive performance by increasing, combining, protecting, reconfiguring tangible and intangible assets of the firm, if necessary [20]. Thirdly, the analysis of transaction costs (Williamson 1985) also provides insight into the impact of new information and communication technologies and reasons for the conversion in economy. According to this theory an organization can organize its activity either as an internal hierarchic structure or by means of market relations with external firms, in other words, the connection of different types of transactions with different mechanisms of their management is not accidental.

2.2   Linear Value Chain or Value Network

A Linear value chain is a concept introduced by Porter for a traditional industry structure. It is a logically connected sequence of interdependent actions that have inputs and outputs in which client is at the end of the chain and value is delivered to him by means of companies` cooperation, within the chain and by means of management transfer from one company to another. A simple illustration of such kind of value chain is shown in the figure below (Fig. 1):

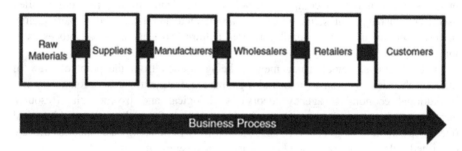

Fig. 1. The traditional one-sided value chain

This is the essence of Porter's strategic approach to supply-side economies of scale, the main powerhouse of which are investments into the production of goods and services and production costs. In the process of production firms bear huge fixed and low marginal costs which means that they must achieve a higher sales volume compared to their competitors in order to reduce average unit cost. Economies of scale allow them to reduce prices what in promotes increased output which in its turn again promotes greater price reductions, thereby, reproducing the cycle of monopolistic rent appropriation. According to Porter, monopolistic rents are the source of competitive advantages in industry thanks to which a firm exercising the most market power dominates the industry strategically. This firm has direct and indirect contacts with other companies within rigidly formed vertical structure (sometimes called supply focal network.

Focal networks are strategic and are intentionally formed by manufacturing companies exercising significant market power in their industries. At the same time legally independent suppliers that do not exercise market power are always subordinate to a strong manufacturing company in a network. This is because a company`s market power is determined by specific resources, tangible (factories, production equipment) and intangible (accumulated customer base, company's brand, its reputation) assets. Market power is the main criteria based on which a firm dominates in business relations [21], any cooperation with such firm is asymmetric; it leads to either a prolongation of dependence relations or the occurrence of dependence as a weaker business partner interested in shared usage of the brand as an intangible asset voluntarily delegates some of his rights to the owner of this asset. On the other hand, the dominant firm that owns the brand takes on the role of the coordinator in the value chain to keep up its reputation as the end-consumer identifies it as the one "responsible" for meeting customers' requirements in terms of this branded product. If the quality of goods or services does not conform to certain standards this will be a dominant firm that will be responsible for that [22].

If specific assets can give dominant firms a flying start over other participants of the value chain but they can lead to an inertia of investments into innovation due to the fear of cannibalization and conflict of interest due to the imbalance in the diffusion of profits from the implementation of the joint value chain. Contradictions between business partners may arise as a result of conflicting goals and the lack of agreement on common goals, the reluctance or inability to achieve results within agreed time frames [23]. These reasons can lead to the disruption and destruction of the joint value chain and either result in the creation of a new value chain with a change of the dominant firm or a change of the existing chain with a redistribution of the share of profit between the participants of the joint value chain.

The consolidation of business is a trend of recent years in Russia; value focal networks are gradually evolving toward integrated structures as management and scaling are implemented by means of vertical integration, mergers and acquisitions. This is the way the control over suppliers is intensified by the producers of goods and services and it is more likely to cause the uneven distribution of profit between producers and suppliers other than joint realization of profit. According to the theory of transactional costs such kind of decision on firm's boundaries is determined by cost saving.

Although this business model is the basic one in industrial and sale value chains there has recently been a paradigm shift from supply-side economies of scale to demand-side economies of scale. Customer involvement and the satisfaction of their needs is a source of value [24, 25] through balancing and coordination of the entire demand chain starting from the end – from end-consumers and following through the entire chain to the suppliers of suppliers. The result of the combination of marketing and logistics is the creation of a demand chain by which value is delivered to a consumer in the most effective way and consumers determine the type of a business model that will become the next dominant standard of the industry through its compliance with their value system.

2.3 Platforms

Either way markets that are also called two-sided networks are economic platforms that have two different user groups that provide each other with the advantages of the network. Platforms create appreciated value not by means of access to physical resources but by processing information needed for coordinating interactions in the ecosystem. As interaction occurs between two (or more) different types of users, such platforms are called multi-sided platforms (MSP) (Fig. 2).

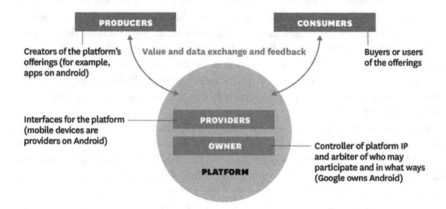

Fig. 2. Platform value chain

The foundation of a demand-based internet economy is in network effects [36], which are supported by such technologies as social media, internet communities, big data, Activity Feeds, the exchange of ideas. There are increasing returns to scale due to network effects – the scale-up of the user base leads to a greater increase in the number of users that are ready to pay more money for the access to a larger network. Thus, a feedback loop producing the appearance of digital monopolies is created. In traditional industries increasing return to scale may be replaced by decreasing return to scale from a certain moment due to the loss of control and decrease in the flexibility of their reactions to changes in the external environment, the build-up of in-house contradictions. Platforms in contrast are characterized by a lack of stability, a lack of internal competition and open access to the network, in other words, the expressed striving towards an increase of the aggregate size of the network and, thus, maintaining constant beneficial effects of scale.

To consider platform-based business models it is necessary to distinguish a central company who is the owner of the platform that coordinates the activity of value creation by means of establishing uniform rules and standards [32]. This company implements the innovation of the business model based on the following paradigms [13]:

1. De-linking assets from value.
2. Re-intermediation.
3. Market aggregation.

Innovations of a business model can be achieved only if a company has a platform stack. There are three different architectural layers had repeatedly emerged in all types of platforms [13]. Those three layers consisted of:

1. Community members (includes its members and their relationship as well, social media).
2. Infrastructure (includes tools, services and rules that make interaction possible).
3. Data (that allow a platform to determine the exact match between demand and supply).

Competition and differentiation between platforms is realized by means of domination in any of three layers or in all three layers at once. The first layer is the most important one – a platform cannot exist without its users, however both infrastructure and data affect the process of user involvement. Market leaders dominate in all three layers and reinforce their domination by using new technologies, such is AI.

2.4   Strategic Difference Between Platforms and Value Chains

According to the analysis considered above the following conceptual differences between strategies and business models based on value chains and business models based on platforms can be mentioned (Table 1).

Based on these differences the analysis of business models based on value chains and platforms for the Russian banking sector and their attractiveness for companies will be carried out further. Business model innovation is considered as the way of obtaining market power and consequently increasing the share of rent based on revenue sharing.

Table 1. Difference between platforms and value chains

Value chain	Platform
Market forces	
New substitute product emergence threat analysis; New player emergence threat analysis; Supplier market power analysis; Consumer market power analysis; Competition struggle analysis	The analysis of target audience, interactions and network effects by means of three-layer concept: community, infrastructure and data
Focus	
Specific resources (material and immaterial) and internal capabilities (routines and dynamic capabilities), their management and control over them	Ecosystems and network cooperation through the orchestration of the resources and capabilities of the community (users), the main resource is the network
Orientation	
Supply orientation, economies of scale by means of the volume of goods or services produced	Demand orientation, economies of scale by means of network effects

(continued)

Table 1. (*continued*)

Value chain	Platform
Strategy	
Cost leadership	Transaction costs reduction
Differentiation	Positive network effects
Focusing	Involvement
Optimization by means of lean production and balancing value chain	Optimization by means of encouraging interaction between external producers and consumers and platform management
Emphasis on consumer lifetime value	Emphasis on ecosystem (of suppliers and consumers) value

3 Research Design

We have used a multiple-case study approach based on interviewing and complemented it with a review of secondary data obtained from open sources.

Our research consists of three parts:

1. The review of secondary data.
2. Interviewing.
3. Conceptualization and expert estimation of conclusions.

Within the Framework of our research the review of secondary data has been carried out for information extraction and typical business models. For this purpose, semantic analysis of open sources – the biggest news portals of Russia for the last years - has been conducted. Within the Framework of our research more than 40,000 sources of information (TV, radio, printed media, information agencies, Internet media) on the federal, regional, industrial level have been analyzed in which the participants of joint value chains were mentioned in the leading role. The algorithm has been used for the review of secondary data. It consists of 3 consecutive steps described below.

1. News items aggregation
2. Automatic highlighting of the most prominent newsmakers (news events).
3. Expert estimation of newsmakers and their selection for further analysis. Upon completion of the process of clustering only those news events are manually sorted and selected that are related to the topic of research.
4. According to the selected news events from the first part we have studied transformations of the business model, interviews with industry experts were also conducted for the estimation of developed business models, having additional expert examination and making conclusions. These interviews have been conducted at different conferences and personal meetings with 15 industry experts – the employees of leading TOP-50 banks responsible for the development of processes and systems.

4   Discussion

4.1   Building Conceptual Scheme

The results of this study shed light on the contingencies in business environments in which linear or platform business models are used in banking sector. The aggregation of obtained information was carried out and a conceptual scheme was built that was also estimated by the experts. Clustering of characteristics inherent in different regulatory structures indicates the most important feature of institutional environment – its discreteness. Functioning organizational forms do not flow into each other smoothly; transitions between them have intermittent, spasmodic nature. According to terminology used by Williamson they represent "discrete institutional alternatives." As transactions tend to cluster around the limited number of transaction management mechanisms (market, hybrids, firms), then business models tend to generalize due to the nonviability of all the rest.

The results indicate, first, that with regard to market uncertainty and economic crisis a platform business models strategy is beneficial under high market uncertainty. Retail chains cooperate with banks to provide their clients with installment loans and consumer credits both in offline and online stores to support fixed demand for their goods (especially in household appliances and consumer electronics segment).

At the moment this market is mainly in the hands of major market players: banks and retail chains, which account for 90% from all loans provided. For banking sector this includes the following banks: "Home Credit" (with 54.3 billion rubles portfolio and a market share of 25.7%), "OTP Bank" (with 32.7 billion rubles portfolio and a market share of 15.5%) and "Renaissance Credit" (with 25.2 billion rubles portfolio and a market share of 11.9%). For retail trade it includes the following stores: "M. Video", "Eldorado", "Svyaznoy", "Media Markt", "RTK", "Yulmart" as well as the largest web-sites: Aliexpress.ru, Ozon.ru, Eldorado.ru, Dns-shop.ru. Installment loan is an opportunity to purchase goods when payment is made not in full but in parts (installments) on a monthly basis during the chosen installment term. After termination of payout period the amount of money paid is equal to the cost of a purchased product. In case of an installment plan trading organization gives his client a discount for the amount the interest on the loan provided, in other words, it compensates the loss of interest on the loan to banks in case of installment plan which price the bank interest in the retail price of the product or considers the discount as the marketing cost for customer acquisition. Business models will be considered in more detail in terms of joint value chain according to the order of their appearance in the market (see Table 2).

Linear value chains shown on the example of purchasing goods by installments are quite common and popular in retail sector. Large retail chains have a sufficient volume of sales and can go for offering discounts to their clients. Realizing that, they will cooperate with banks only in case of a tangible benefit. Innovative schemes can serve as the example of such kind of benefit, for instance, cash on delivery option – a bank finances a transaction instead of a client and the client pays for it in cash to a messenger of the bank on delivery and after that money are transferred to the bank (in fact, this is a factoring). In case when a trading organization represents a small retail chain, cooperation with it won't be profitable for banks as very often transaction costs are not

Table 2. Difference between platforms and value chains in retail banking sector

Linear value chain	Platforms	
	A retail chain or a broker is the owner of a platform	*A bank is the owner of a platform*
1. A customer comes to a store, chooses a product; 2. For purchasing the chosen product the client interacts with the loan officer who will draw an agreement for a loan (an installment) by using bank socialized software; 3. After loan approval the customer picks up the purchased product and the loan agreement; 4. The customer makes monthly payments to the bank that has provided the loan according to the terms of the loan agreement	1. A customer visits a store or a web-site or has an installment card, chooses a product according to the desired terms of price, delivery, etc., chooses the desired banking installment product according to the available banking offers. The customer himself chooses the comfortable size of monthly payment, specifying the amount of initial installment and the term of the loan, thus, choosing a bank to get the installment loan; 2. The customer picks up the purchased product and applies for the installment loan; 3. The customer makes monthly payments to the bank that has provided the loan according to the terms of the loan agreement	1. A customer visits a website, chooses a product according to the desired terms of price, delivery, etc. In other words, the competition among retail stores is created; 2. The customer signs a loan agreement online in a bank; 3. After that the customer meets a bank messenger for signing the loan agreement; 4. Upon signing the loan agreement retail store messenger comes to the customer Installment card use option is as follows: 1. Installment card can be ordered via Internet or mobile application; besides that, installment cards pick-up points are located at the places of mass gathering; 2. The bank approves customer's card cash limit; 3. The customer comes to the store, chooses a product; 4. The customer pays for the chosen product with his credit card

compensated by loan interest. Because of this in many cases banks had bargaining power receiving a commission from stores. Points of sales were ready to pay for the increase in sales intensely promoted by banks. In times of crisis when market is falling, retailers are interested in cooperation with banks and because of that they start lowering a commission fee for their presence in the points of sales and also give their clients a small discount to maintain installment programs.

Double-sided platforms exist because there is a demand for mediation to match both parts of a platform more effectively and minimize overall costs, for instance, by avoiding duplication or minimizing transactional costs and making market exchange possible. The involvement of an intermediary, affiliated with a bank, or a retail chain or a third party (an arbitrator) can serve as the example of such kind of platform in the banking sector. Trading networks prefer to work with many banks and meanwhile banks prefer to work with a large number of trading networks, thus, members of one group can easily find their trading partners from another group. If a client is put at the head of a value network, then big retail chains will try to increase profitability by reducing bank rates and banks will try to indirectly minimize interest rates by offering discounts to their clients. Network effects show that user will pay more for the access to a larger network, that's why, profitability of both sides is increasing as the user base is growing. A retail chain enters into partnership with brokers to independently regulate the share of sales in banks and to increase the percentage of loan approval and the speed of loan application preparation. Brokers are integrated into scoring systems of many banks, in other words, one universal customer application form is sent straight to several banks to get a simultaneous answer from them. The trading organization itself chooses the best terms among those that have been offered to it by different banks by means of tenders on preliminary announced terms (depending on the amount of bank's commission). Loan or installment application is simultaneously sent to all partner banks (more than 10) what enhances the likelihood of receiving of the loan and gives an opportunity to choose a more convenient/profitable credit proposal. All the processes are fully automated; it allows making the process of receiving of the loan quick and easy. As a result, the probability the customer will take advantage of store's offer and the store will be able to attend to all its customers. The whole process from filling out the loan application form to the completion of documents for receiving the chosen credit option takes, in average, less than 30 min. Brokerage platform allows not only saving time required for submitting the application and loan approval. The retail chain pays a commission to a broker (usually as a percentage from the amount of loan (installment) provided to the customer). On average, our customers' sales efficiency is increased by 30%. Turnover is growing due to the increase in the number of credit purchases as well as the increase in the average price of a purchase.

Realizing that banks create their own platforms. Banks are trying to avoid the dependency from trading organization and brokerage companies, creating new sales channels. The creation of a marketplace of the bank itself by means of online trading or an installment card can serve as an example of such kind of business model. The creation of such platform requires creation and maintenance of an IT-platform and cooperation with partner stores. The main limitation of the given scheme is the legislation which does not support remote user identification so far. Installment cards is a new retail experience for the customers. They allow purchasing goods with no overpayment but only from companies who are the participants of the installment program. Customer's extra costs arise only in case when the customer violates undertaken obligations to the bank on monthly repayments. Trading organizations are interested in cooperation with banks. Interest rate for partners is ranging from 3% to 6% and depends on installment period as well as the parameters of a certain partner. In terms of the annual profitability of the loan portfolio, the payment cards are inferior to traditional credit cards and POS-loans.

The findings presented in this study are relevant to managers making decisions on actions and governance in innovative business models.

4.2   Linear Value Chain

Based on product specifications and terms of the loan agreement the bank transfers the money for the purchased product to the trading organization;

The trading organization can pay the bank a certain fee for each agreement drawn. This is typical for small retail chains or stores.

The trading organization can charge a certain commission from the bank for its presence in the point of sales. This is typical for larger retail chains cooperating with a larger number of banks.

The size of the commission is different depending on a trade segment; in average, according to the estimation of experts banks pay commission with the interest rate ranging from 2% to 6% from the size of loans.

4.3   Platforms

Based on product specifications and terms of the loan agreement the bank transfers money for the purchased product to the trading organization. Compared to the first scheme the trading organization/bank is getting the following benefits: it reduces its costs for the conclusion of agreements as well as for the technical integration and increases the volume of sales by making their customers more favorable offers.

5   Conclusions

The analysis of joint value chains in the retail segment of the banking sector shows that new platform-based value chains are emerging. Platform competitive advantage is expressed in mediation between a customer, a bank and a retail chain which is accompanied by a significant reduction of transaction costs for all parties due to the transfer of the main transaction to the platform and the exact match of supplier's and customer's needs. From technological point of view platform is a system nucleus to which the participants of a joint value chain can connect following certain interaction rules. From economic point of view platform is a value exchange mechanism including network effects and the management of interdependent relations within a network. Goods or services' value increases in proportion to the increase of a beneficial network effect that is created by them which finally results in the appearance of a dominant platform in the market; this is what happened to installment cards of the leading banks and aggregator companies (like Yandex market), that create competition both among stores and banks.

References

1. Amit, R., Zott, C.: Value creation in eBusiness. Strateg. Manag. J. 6–7(22), 493–520 (2001)
2. Shafer, S.M., Smith, H.J., Linder, J.: The power of business models. Bus. Horiz. 48(3), 199–207 (2005)
3. Osterwalder, A., Pigneur, Y., Tucci, C.L.: Clarifying business models: origins, present, and future of the concept. Commun. AIS 15(May), 2–40 (2005)

4. Allee, V.: The Future Of Knowledge: Increasing Prosperity Through Value Networks. Butterworth-Heinemann, Amsterdam (2003)
5. Bovet, D., Martha, J. Value Nets: Breaking The Supply Chain To Unlock Hidden Profits, Wiley, New York, NY (2000a). Bovet, D., Martha, J.: Value nets: reinventing the rusty supply chain for competitive advantage, Strategy Leadersh. **28**(4), 21–26 (2000b)
6. Lafontaine, F., Slade, M.: Vertical integration and firm boundaries: the evidence. J. Econ. Lit. **45**(3), 629–685 (2007)
7. Bengtsson, M., Kock, S.: Coopetition in business networks—to cooperate and compete simultaneously. Ind. Mark. Manage. **29**(5), 411–426 (2000)
8. Ritala, P., Hurmelinna-Laukkanen, P.: What's in it for me? Creating and appropriating value in innovation-related coopetition. Technovation **29**, 819–828 (2009)
9. Bengtsson, M., Kock, S.: "Coopetition" in business networks to cooperate and compete simultaneously. Ind. Mark. Manage. **29**, 411–426 (2000)
10. Gnyawali, D.R., Madhavan, R.: Cooperative networks and competitive dynamics: a structural embeddedness perspective. Acad. Manag. Rev. **26**, 431–445 (2001)
11. Ritala, P., Golnam, A., Wegmann, A.: Coopetition-based business models: The case of Amazon.com. Ind. Market. Manag. **43**(2), 236–249 (2014)
12. Rifkin, J.: The Zero Marginal Cost Society: The Internet of Things, the Collaborative Commons and the Eclipse of Capitalism. Palgrave Macmillan, Basingstoke (2014)
13. Choudary, S.P.: Platform Scale: How a New Breed of Startups is Building Large Empires with Minimum Investment. Platform Thinking Labs, Boston (2015)
14. Gulati, R., Singh, H.: The architecture of cooperation: managing coordination costs and appropriation concerns in strategic alliances. Adm. Sci. Quart. **43**, 781–814 (1998)
15. Tretyak, O.A., Rumyantseva, M.N.: Network forms of inter-firm cooperation: approaches to phenomenon explanation. Russ. Manag. Mag. **1**(2), 25–50 (2003)
16. Pfeffer, J., Salancik, G.: The External Control of Organizations. Stanford University Press, Stanford (1978)
17. Cox, A., Sanderson, J., Watson, G.: Power Regimes Mapping the DNA of Business and Supply Chain Relationships, pp. 51–63. Earlsgate Press, UK (2000)
18. Cox, A.: The power perspective in procurement and supply management. J. Supply Chain Manag. **37**(2), 4–7 (2001a)
19. Crook, T.R., Combs, J.G.: Sources and consequences of bargaining power in supply chains. J. Oper. Manag. **25**(2), 546–555 (2007)
20. Teece, D.J.: Explicating dynamic capabilities: the nature and microfoundations of (sustainable) enterprise performance. Strateg. Manag. J. **28**, 1319–1350 (2007)
21. Buchanan-Oliver, M., Young, A.: Strategic alliances or co-branded relationships on the internet—an examination of a partnership between two companies, unequal in size. In: Managing in Networks. Abstracts Proceedings from The 19th Annual IMP Conference, pp. 17–18, University of Lugano (2003)
22. Hanf, J., Dautzenberg, K.: A theoretical framework of chain management. J. Chain Netw. Sci. **6**(2), 79–94 (2006)
23. Das, T.K., Rahman, N.: Determinants of partner opportunism in strategic alliances: a conceptual framework. J. Bus. Psychol. **25**, 55–74 (2010)
24. Walter, A., Ritter, T., Gemünden, H.G.: Value creation in buyer-seller relationships. Ind. Mark. Manage. **30**, 365–377 (2001)
25. Baker, S.: New Customer Marketing. Wiley, Chicester (2003)
26. Simon, P.: The Age of the Platform: How Amazon, Apple, Facebook and Google Have Refined. Business. Motion Publishing, Las Vegas (2011)
27. Downes, L., Nunes, P.: Big bang disruption. Harv. Bus. Rev. **91**(3), 44–56 (2013)

28. Van Alstyne, M.W., Parker, G.G., Choudary, S.P.: Pipelines, platforms and the new rules of strategy. Harv. Bus. Rev. **94**(4), 54–62 (2016)
29. Gawer, A.: Platforms, Markets and Innovation, pp. 45–77. Edward Elgar, Cheltenham (2009)
30. Rochet, J.C., Tirole, J.: Platform competition in two-sided markets. J. Eur. Econ. Assoc. **1** (4), 990–1029 (2003)
31. Iansiti, M., Levien, R.: The Keystone Advantage: What the New Dynamics of Business Ecosystems Mean for Strategy, Innovation and Sustainability. Harvard Business School Press, Boston (MA) (2004)
32. Parker, G.G., Van Alstyne, M.W., Choudary, S.P.: Platform Revolution: How Networked Markets are Transforming the Economy and How to Make Them Paper for You. Norton, London (2016)

Product Competitiveness in the IT Market Based on Modeling Dynamics of Competitive Positions

Victoriya Grigoreva[1] and Iana Salikhova[2(✉)]

[1] National Research University Higher School of Economics,
Saint-Petersburg, Russia
victoria.grigoryeva@gmail.com
[2] Saint-Petersburg State University of Economics, Saint-Petersburg, Russia
yana.salichova@mail.ru

Abstract. This paper is about evaluating product competitiveness in the IT market. The developed model is explained on the integrated approach that takes into account the dynamics of competitive positions and market structure. It reveals the changes of structural features in the IT market based on the index of structural shifts. The dynamics of competitive positions are proposed to be evaluated with the vector model. The procedure consists of two stages. Firstly, competitive position is estimated by means of expectancy-value model. Secondly, the index of product profitability is evaluated. Finally, we can form a vector of competitive position based on these two indicators and model the dynamics of it. Thus the comprehensive model of product's competitiveness is offered and managerial implications to develop the IT products' competitiveness are provided.

Keywords: Competitiveness · Competitive position
Dynamics of competitive positions · eEconomy · IT product

1 Introduction

The concept of "competitiveness" has different interpretations depending on the applied object. Nowadays it is recommended to evaluate competitiveness of product by a comparison of its properties with the properties of a competitor or an ideal product. An obvious drawback of this approach is the lack of consumer evaluation of the product properties.

Another less obvious disadvantage is that any improvement of a good's properties does not lead to an automatic strengthening of its competitive position. At the same time, the method of integrated assessment raises serious complaints because it attempts to take into account all the properties of the goods, which are measured in different scales and have different consumer value. Besides, the product competitiveness can be evaluated by relating qualitative, technical, economic, aesthetic and other characteristics, either to standards, or to the characteristics of market competitors. However, this approach does not consider the value of these characteristics to the consumer.

© Springer Nature Switzerland AG 2018
D. A. Alexandrov et al. (Eds.): DTGS 2018, CCIS 858, pp. 343–352, 2018.
https://doi.org/10.1007/978-3-030-02843-5_27

According to the modern theory assessment, the product's competitiveness level is based on the methods of portfolio analysis, integral indices, and methods of competitive advantages development. As their analysis showed, each of them has advantages and disadvantages. Their main advantage is the simplicity of its calculation and interpretation. Unfortunately, these methods have a significant drawback. The value of the indicators is very low correlated with the level of product competitiveness on the market and the dynamics of the business environment.

In order to get more explicit assessment of product competitiveness, it is necessary to obtain a comprehensive evaluation - not only of the technical, economic and consumer properties of the product, but its market position and its dynamics as well.

Thus, the goal of the paper is to develop the model of IT product competitiveness based on the dynamics of its competitive position and market structure. The model has been tested under the example of IT startup.

2 Related Work

Information technology (IT) firms face a new competitive environment [9] caused by narrowing of the gap between Internet services, mobile telephony and personal computing [3, 8]. The new competitive environment is redefining the boundaries between software, hardware, and services [9].

According to Kenney and Pon (2011), "the nature of IT industry lends itself to analysis from a technology platform perspective" [9]. Thus the platform control may affect the firm's competitive advantage and has been identified as a key success factor of IT industry.

Recently, IT product development has been dominated by the concept of platform ecosystem. Ecosystem value creation is based on encouraging other organizations to use their products or to build on their products (Apple, Google, Facebook). The platform infrastructure is used by third parties, which in turn provide value distribution. However, that creates obvious limitations to platform provider and product developer in meeting people's needs.

IT products have been evolved to ecosystems. Michael Cusumano believes that strong competitive advantages are provided by "the best platform strategy and the best ecosystem to back it up" [1]. The interdependence is the main idea around ecosystems [4, 5]. The connection to the ecosystem provides to its elements the possibilities to survive or sustainable development. The number of elements evolved to ecosystem defines its chances to survive. The more elements it's involved the more likely chances to survive. The same situation is observed with products. A common characteristic of the platform is that they are all based on exploiting network effects [4, 6, 7].

The product interdependence add value to IT product developers and end-users. The interdependence makes alive a technological ecosystem which is based on integration and strategic exchange among developers and end-users. People use products of the ecosystem and get extra value, for example, a better user experience, more functional products, better network effects and so on. Building an ecosystem helps developers to keep users from switching to other products, which belong to another ecosystem. Also a launch of new product in ecosystem makes it more competitive compared with similar products outside the ecosystem [9, 11].

The competition in the IT market is considered as a competition "for the market", rather than "in the market". Consequently, companies have to enhance the competitiveness of their IT products and track their changes in order to retain their dominant position on the market.

The study of competitiveness involves different concepts, approaches and disciplines. According to Flanagan et al. (2007), there were three main schools of theories identified.

According to Porter's theory the competitive advantage occurs from the competitive strategy an organization develops to avoid threats or to take advantage of opportunities presented by the industry [2].

The RBV theory of competitiveness assumes that competitive advantages are based on the firm-specific internal resource and do not depend on external factors, like industry structure.

The third school of firms' competitiveness theory focuses on the strategic management approach [2]. Recent development of strategic management theory has included the theories of Porter and the RBV.

Despite of all advantages of each school in finding ways of competitiveness development none of them can be curative for explaining the IT product's competitiveness.

From Shumpeter's point of view, the main factor of desirable functioning of the market is not a static competition between acting producers of existing products but real or potential competition from new products or new producers using new technologies. Static market power can be a supposition for competition based on innovations that is why the society should decide which type of limited monopoly it should use to stimulate intellectual competition [10].

According to authors' opinion, the competitiveness of an IT product is the ability to occupy a competitive position in the market through the best combination of competitive advantages.

Thus, the process of developing of IT product competitiveness is considered as an integrated approach that takes into account the dynamics of competitive positions and the changes of market structure.

3 Model Development Procedure

In our model, competitive positions of IT product are the first classification attribute of competitiveness from the developer point of view. The most informative metric of that position is recommended to be "Profitability" metric.

$$P = \frac{\mathrm{Pr} - \mathrm{CP}}{\mathrm{CP}}. \tag{1}$$

P – profitability, Pr – producer price for one product, CP - cost price for the producer.

Metric «relative consumer preferences» is used as an indicator of customer position.

$$Fi = \sum_{i=1}^{n} b_i * e_i \qquad (2)$$

Fi - Consumers' preferences, e_i- significance coefficient of the ith attribute, b_i – degree of opinion that product has the ith attribute, n – amount of product attributes from the set of product attributes in case when product is attractive for consumers that belong to the target market segment.

Taking into account typology attributes make it possible to do cross-classification and create a matrix that significantly simplifies the determination of competitiveness positions for IT product at market segment. The most competitive product will have the biggest number of such attributes, that we will take for 100%. Values of another product attributes we will calculate according to the proportion to the values of the leading product. Matrix field can be divided into nine sectors. Product competitiveness will be increasing while moving from the lower left sector to the higher right one. Vector drawn from the origin of that matrix will be an indicator of competitive position and will be looking like:

$$K_i = \sqrt{Pr_{oni}^2 + P_{oni}^2} \qquad (3)$$

K_i – Level of competitive position of the ith product in a target market segment, P_{oni}- calculated profitability for a producer, Pr_{oni} – consumers preferences for the ith product. Meaningful interval is $0 \leq K_i \leq 2$, in order to increase usability we have improved this index:

$$MK_i = \frac{K_i}{\sqrt{2}} \qquad (4)$$

Competing products may occupy positions "two" and "three", "four" and "six", "seven" and "eight" that can be seen in Fig. 1. The metric will indicate same values. Those competitive positions have equal preference levels, but they are based on different competitive advantages of producer or consumer. Therefore, the following metric is calculated:

$$tg\alpha = \frac{P_{npi}}{Pr_{oni}} \qquad (5)$$

Metric (5) indicates which competitive advantages determine a competitive position. It is interesting to follow positions dynamics. In order to do it, we are going to consider metrics "Relative Profitability" and "Relative Consumers' preferences" for several consecutive periods (we are going to call them first and second periods) or moments of time. Every value of the first and second periods provides an opportunity to create appropriate vectors. A vector of the difference between two vectors will be a metric of dynamics of competitive positions:

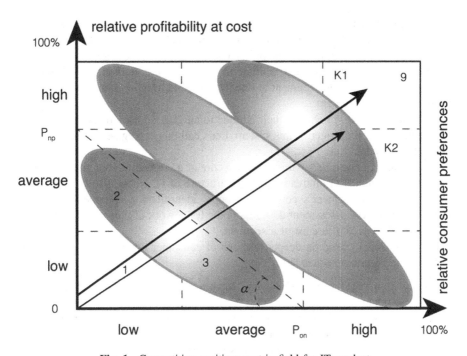

Fig. 1. Competitive positions matrix field for IT product

$$D_{k2-k1} = \sqrt{(P_{np2} - P_{np1})^2 + (Pr_{on2} - Pr_{on1})^2} \qquad (6)$$

Next, we have modified the metric to increase usability:

$$MD_{k2-k2} = \frac{D_{k2-k2}}{\sqrt{2}} \qquad (7)$$

During the competitiveness formation study from the digital surroundings, we have studied product competitiveness not for the whole market, but for the target market segment at the target period.

Study of the competitiveness formation process from the digital environment point of view assumes research of a product's competitiveness not in the general market, but in the market segment considered and for the certain period.

Authors offer a dynamic segment model, where segment is determined as a product developers' ecosystem. In other words, we can examine "market segment" as a model describing consumer market status in a certain period of time. The whole market can be presented only as a sum of clear segments and consumers that belong to some segment to some extent or that do not belong to any segment at all.

The largest part of a market is structured by segments. Each of these segments is the aggregate of consumers who react to the same IT-product ecosystem stably in the same way. Customers whose attitude to the product is changing join the segment. If we make an instantaneous cut of customers' attitude to a product in a market, we will see that they can be assigned to one segment at one moment and to other, but close to the first segment at another moment.

Customers, who don't change their attitude to an IT-product and stay a stable part of the segment, are the center of this system. Let's call this aggregate of customers as a "core" of a segment.

The quantity of customers who make up a core of a segment is changing over time. It allows the dynamics of innovative market structure of IT-products to be researched.

The method of segment's consumer groups' identification and methodology of consumer preferences assessment designed in the framework of this work are based on calculation of the size of a core of a segment.

The method is focused on deeper research of consumer preferences. Let's present our actions in a certain sequence:

1. Segmentation of IT-products' buyers. Identification of the closest rivals in the market segment researched.
2. Calculation of Fishbein index for preferences assessing of buyers of our IT-product and for buyers of rivals' IT-product.
3. Calculation of stability metric for groups of consumers.
4. Dividing consumers into three groups by each rival.

One of the stages of this method includes the methodology of consumer preferences assessment. It's aimed the identification of IT-products' set of attributes, which are attractive from the segment consumers' point of view, and at its following quantitative evaluation. This identifying process is implemented on three levels of a product, which were suggested and described in details by Philip Kotler. Secondly, consumers evaluate significance of product's attributes. It should be taken into account that consumers in a certain segment can be on different stages of acquaintance with the IT-product. Comparison of attributes' evaluations made by consumers, who are on different stages of acquaintance with the product, allows us to choose a set of products attributes which is preferable for consumers of a certain segment. Quantitative analysis of a set of product's attributes can be conducted using the multi-factor compensatory model of Fishbein. It allows us low evaluations to be compensated, given by the consumer to one attributes, with higher evaluations of another attributes.

Then we identify the groups of consumers in the researched segment. For this we use method of typological grouping and identify different types of situations as: "consumers without stable behavior", "consumers with preferences", and "the core".

Moreover, we choose grouping attributes describing the types of situations and establish boundaries of intervals. The structure of a consumer market segment depends on consumer preferences. The size of "consumer preferences" metric characterizes attitude of a consumer in a researched segment to the IT-product. Consumer preferences can be low, medium and high. Besides, when talking about stability or changing of segment's structure, it's important to pay attention to changes of consumer preferences in different periods. In order to apply the classification of segment consumers' groups, we use, firstly, the size of "consumer preferences metric" calculated under Fishbein model.

Secondly, the metric of "consumer preferences' stability" – the metric of absolute structural shifts based on the formula of the standard deviation:

$$S_{w1-w_0} = \sqrt{\frac{\sum_{i=1}^{k}(w_{1i} - W_{0i})}{k}} \tag{8}$$

Where $w1i$ and $w0i$ – shares of i-group in "0" and "1" periods, k – the number of groups. Accounting of these metrics, allows us to divide identified groups into three types.

After conduction of procedures it is recommended to sum the data about the sizes of "the core" groups by rivals. The ratio of quantity of customers in identified groups is changing over time reflecting thus the dynamics of a market's structures.

After studying the process of an IT-product competitiveness formation with taking into account specification of the IT-products' market, we move to the method of dynamic evaluation of IT-product competitiveness. The main result is the building of two-dimensional dynamic matrix, which helps to compare competitiveness by metrics characterizing trends in dynamics of the IT-product market. Metrics characterizing trends of dynamics are relative metrics of dynamics – chain growth rates.

The growth rate of the segment's core reflects its dynamics:

$$K_{i/i-1} = \frac{Y_i}{Y_{i-1}} \tag{9}$$

It characterizes the IT-market conditions. The growth rate of competitive position reflects the dynamics of developer's advantages.

$$KP_{i/i-1} = \frac{KR_i}{KR_{i-1}} \tag{10}$$

"Relative growth rate of 'the core'" – basic line, dividing segments with high and low growth rates, corresponds to the average growth rate of "the core" in the segment of IT-product researched:

$$\bar{K} = \sqrt[n]{\prod_{i=1}^{n} k_i} = \sqrt[n]{\frac{y_n}{y_{i-1}}} \tag{11}$$

For axis "Relative growth rate of competitive position" the basic line corresponds to the average growth rate of the IT-product's competitive position for the period researched:

$$\overline{KP} = \sqrt[n]{\prod_{i=1}^{n} kp_i} = \sqrt[n]{\frac{kp_n}{kp_{i-1}}} \tag{12}$$

Quadrants of matrix allow us to define the levels of competitiveness of the IT-product in the market, to describe competitive situations and to develop basic recommendations to improve competitive positions.

4 Data Analysis and Modeling Dynamics of Competitive Position

Current research is restricted with the Russian market. Our primary data source is Fund for the Development of Internet Initiatives database [12]. The Internet Initiatives Development Fund is Russian venture investment fund established by the Strategic Initiatives Agency. The Fund provides investments to technology companies at early stages of development, conducts accelerated programs and participates in the development of methods for legal regulation of the venture industry.

Further, we are going to present competitive position by modelling dynamics of the IT product under the example of "Step by step" mobile application. The position will be changed in comparison with competitive positions of "IT product developers" and positions of "consumers". The "IT product developers" group includes mobile app startups to measure physical activity of office staff. The "consumers" group includes office staff that use mobile application.

Next, we are going to calculate degrees of the competitive positions according to Table 1.

Table 1. Startup data to the competitive position matrix

Company	Profitability, % 2015	Relative Profitability, %, 2015	Profitability, % 2016	Relative Profitability, % 2016	Consumers' preferences % 2015	Relative consumers' preferences, % 2015	Consumers' preferences % 2016	Relative consumers' preferences, % 2016
Startup "Zdorovie"	18	100	18	100	41	69.49	37	61.6
Startup "Velness"	12	66.7	12	66.67	42	71.19	38	63.33
Startup "Fitness planet"	11	61.1	10	55.56	39	66.1	39	65
Startup "Skorohod"	8	44.4	9	50	39	66.1	40	66.67
Startup "Maraphonez"	10	55.5	15	83.33	53	89.83	52	86.67
Startup "step by step"	7	38.89	9	50	59	100	60	100

The value of "Step by step" startup competitive position in 2015 was equal to $\sqrt{\frac{0.555^2 + 0.898^2}{2}} = 0.746$. Specifying metric was equal to $tg\alpha = \frac{P_{npi}}{P_{oni}} = \frac{0.555^2}{0.898^2} = 0.618$ respectively. That metric indicates a big influence of startup's competitive advantages on consumer's preferences. The value of competitive position in 2015 is equal to $\sqrt{\frac{0.833^2 + 0.867^2}{2}} = 0.85$ and specifying metric was equal to $tg\alpha = \frac{P_{npi}}{P_{oni}} = \frac{0.833^2}{0.867^2} = 0.618$ respectively. It indicates that an influence of startup's competitive advantages on consumer's preferences was slightly smaller than the same figure in 2015.

Table 2. Data for building the matrix of the dynamic competitive position evaluation

	Growth rate, %	Average growth rate, %
"heart" of a segment	5.323	3.418
competitive position	14	9.2

Next, we focus on the competitive positions dynamics at 2015 and 2016. We can calculate it $\sqrt{\frac{(0.833 + 0.555)^2 + (0.867 + 0.898)^2}{2}} = 0.179$. It indicates a big value of competitive positions in 2015 as well as in 2016. There is a positive dynamics for the competitive position growth. Therefore, we would like to present a dynamic evaluation of competitive position taking into account the IT market development based on data from Table 2.

Therefore, "Step by step" startup occupies the forth quadrant – high growth area. It is determined by high value of "relative growth rate" and "relative growth rate of competitive position" metrics. In addition, it is characterized by high growth rate for "heart" of a segment, likewise high growth rate of the competitive position. The growth of the competitive position on rapidly growing segment indicates a leader position. Recommended actions are defense of your position and attack. Startup should not stop on current achievements. The probable areas of development are new services or new attributes introduction and performance enhancement of app promotion systems with costs reduction. Concerning competitors, recommended action is a combination of the competitive advantage defense and the attack of competitors' positions. The choice of the defense or the attack reaction types depends on competitive advantages and competitors' resource ration.

5 Conclusion and Future Work

At this work, metrics of evaluation of the IT product competitive position are developed and tested in practice. Dynamic models of competitive positions are created. Furthermore, we explained the correlation with the processes and methods of decision making management.

Acknowledgements. Work is performed with financial support of the Russian Fund for Fundamental Research, grant No 16-02-00172 "The development of multi-level competition theory, its methods and techniques".

References

1. Cusumano, M.: Technology strategy and management: the evolution of platform thinking. Commun. ACM **53**(1), 32–34 (2010). https://doi.org/10.1145/1629175.1629189
2. Flanagan, R., Lu, W., Shen, L., Jewell, C.: Competitiveness in construction: a critical review of research. Constr. Manag. Econ. **25**, 989–1000 (2007). https://doi.org/10.1080/01446190701258039
3. Funk, J.L.: The Mobile Internet: How Japan Dialed Up and the West Disconnected. ISI Publications, Pembroke (2001)
4. Gawer, A. (ed.): Platforms, Markets and Innovation. Edward Elgar, Cheltenham, UK, Northampton, MA, US (2009)
5. Gawer, A., Henderson, R.: Platform owner entry and innovation in complementary markets: evidence from Intel. J. Econ. Manag. Strategy **16**(1), 1–34 (2007). https://doi.org/10.1111/j.1530-9134.2007.00130.x
6. Hagiu, A., Yoffie, D.: What's your Google strategy? Harvard Bus. Rev. **87**(4), 74–81 (2009)
7. Hagiu, A., Wright, J.: Multi-Sided Platforms. Harvard Business School Working Paper, No. 12-024, October 2011
8. Ishii, K.: Internet use via mobile phone in Japan. Telecommun. Policy **28**(1), 3–58 (2004). https://doi.org/10.1016/j.telpol.2003.07.001
9. Kenney, M., Pon, B.: Structuring the smartphone industry: is the mobile internet OS platform the key? J. Ind. Compet. Trade **11**, 239 (2011). https://doi.org/10.1007/s10842-011-0105-6
10. Schumpeter, J.: The Theory of Economic Development. Transaction Publishers, New Brunswick (2005)
11. Tee, R., Gawer, A.: Industry architecture as a determinant of successful platform strategies: a case study of the I-Mode mobile internet service. Eur. Manag. Rev. **6**, 217–232 (2009). https://doi.org/10.1057/emr.2009.22
12. Internet Initiatives database fund. http://www.iidf.ru/

Assessing Similarity for Case-Based Web User Interface Design

Maxim Bakaev[(✉)] [iD]

Novosibirsk State Technical University, Novosibirsk, Russia
maxis81@gmail.com

Abstract. It has been said "all design is redesign", and it is particularly true for websites, whose number in the today's online environment has reached 1 billion. In our paper, we justify case-based approach (CBR) to designing web user interfaces (WUIs) and outline some currently unsolved problems with its application. In this research work, we focus on definition and measurement of similarity, which is essential for all the stages of the CBR process: Retrieve, Reuse, Revise, and Retain. We specify the structure of a case in the web design domain (corresponding to a web project) and outline the ways to measure similarity based on the feature values. Further, we construct artificial neural network model to predict target users' subjective similarity assessments of websites that relies on website metrics collected by our dedicated "human-computer vision" software. To train the model, we also ran experimental survey with 127 participants evaluating 21 university websites. The analysis of the factors' importance suggests that frequency-based entropy measure and the proposed index of difficulty for visual perception affected subjective similarity the most. We believe the described approach can facilitate design reuse on the web, contributing to efficient development of more usable websites crucial for the e-society advancement.

Keywords: Web engineering · User interfaces · Software reuse
Computer-aided design

1 Introduction

Given the significant amount of financial and human resources spent on creating new and re-designing existing websites, one should wonder if these expenses are entirely justified and valuable for the society. The number of existing websites that are operational and accessible on the World Wide Web is currently estimated as 100–250 millions. Reuse of such an extensive collection of solutions available to all should play more important role in today's web engineering for the needs of e-society. Nowadays, conventional websites are rarely created from scratch, as web design (front-end) and web development frameworks partially automate the process. The web frameworks provide libraries of pre-made functionality and user interface (UI) elements, but they are generally detached from the multitude of websites already existing on the Web.

Computer-aided design systems in architecture, mechanical engineering, etc. involve testing of existing solutions and evaluation of their performance in fulfilling the

© Springer Nature Switzerland AG 2018
D. A. Alexandrov et al. (Eds.): DTGS 2018, CCIS 858, pp. 353–365, 2018.
https://doi.org/10.1007/978-3-030-02843-5_28

requirements. But despite the emergence and development of web analytics and web design mining tools (such as [1]), there are currently no repositories of web design examples that would both allow finding existing solutions relevant to a new project's requirements and appraising their quality based on accumulated use statistics. As the result, neither a web designer choosing an appropriate web UI element in *Bootstrap* framework, nor a prospective business website owner browsing through an endless collection of pre-made web design templates [2], has any estimation of the solution's success chance with target users. Naturally, the existing website holders do mind sharing their use statistics to aid their prospective competitors succeed, while designs can be copyright-protected. But another impediment is that we currently don't have an integrated engineering approach or technical means to reuse solutions in the web design domain. For that end, we consider employing case-based reasoning (CBR), a reasonably mature AI method that has a record of fruitful practical use in various fields.

Case-based reasoning is arguably the AI method that best reflects the work of human memory and the role of experience. It continues to draw increased interest, particularly on account of the current rapid development of e-society and e-economy, with their Big Data and Knowledge Engineering technologies. CBR implies the following stages, classically identified as Retrieve, Reuse, Revise, and Retain [3]:

- describing a new problem and finding similar problems with known solutions in a CB;
- adapting the solutions of the retrieved problems to the current problem, in an assumption that similar problems have similar solutions;
- evaluating the new solution and possibly repeating the previous stages;
- storing the results as a new *case*.

So, each case consists of a *problem* and a *solution*, plus the latter can be supplemented with the description of its effect on the real world, i.e. the solution *quality*.

Overall, it's recognized that "...design task is especially appropriate for applying, integrating, exploring and pushing the boundaries of CBR" [4], but workability of the method depends of the design field's particularities. The attempts to use CBR in design were already prominent in the early 1990s [5], with AskJef (1992) seemingly being the first notable intelligent system in this regard, whose scalability however now seems doubtful, since it lacked a reliable knowledge-engineering foundation. Nowadays, with regard to web design, CBR appears to be better established in software engineering [6] and web services composition [7], compared to the user interaction aspect. A notable example of CBR application for web interaction personalization is [8], but the software operates on an already existing website and seems to be feasible mostly for projects in which repetitive visits of the same user are entailed.

The generally recognized advantages of CBR include its applicability to complex domains with unknown knowledge model that is not required for the method to work, ability to learn from both success and failure (since both can accumulate in the knowledge base), reliance on well-established database technologies, etc. However, the method depends heavily upon well-structured and extensive collection of cases, while adaptation of the end result from several relevant solutions can be problematic, as knowledge model have not been identified. In particular it means that a significantly large number of cases have to be collected before the method can start yielding any practically feasible results, and that feature engineering – that is, constructing the set of measurable properties to describe problems in CBR – is of crucial importance for the overall success. Web design appears suitable for the CBR approach since:

1. There are potentially a huge number of cases, given the 100–250 millions of websites currently openly available on the Internet. Today's web mining systems are capable of scraping their code, styling and content with reasonable efficiency.
2. The "lazy generalization" strategy of CBR is advantageous, since knowledge in web design is largely represented as qualitative principles and guidelines, while formal knowledge models or rules are relatively scarcely used.
3. The solutions can be promptly applied in the real world, their quality is not critical and they can be revised easily. That is, we consider rather conventional e-business or e-government websites, not e.g. a web-based interface of a nuclear plant management system.

At the same time, potential difficulties with CBR approach application in the web design domain include:

1. **Retrieve and Retain:** there's no yet an agreed structure of web design features that significantly influence the solutions usability, attractiveness for users, etc. Additionally, the case needs to accommodate quality attributes for several solutions, as different versions of websites can operate in different times, but basically solve the same problem (goal). The latest version is not necessarily the best solution – everyone probably has encountered a new design that is worse than an old one.
2. **Reuse and Revise:** to the extent of our knowledge, there are no established approaches for generating new web designs from several relevant solutions in the course of their adaptation to the initial problem. Actually, direct modification of existing solutions is very much restricted in the web design domain, and rather roundabout approaches have to be employed, where newly composed solutions are iteratively adjusted to match the retained ones (see in our other work [9]).
3. **Similarity measurements:** this missing link is actually required by both of the above items. The CBR algorithm for web design needs calculating similarity (a) between problems, to retain relevant cases, and (b) between solutions, to compose new solutions that are similar to the exemplar retained ones.

So, our current work is dedicated to the similarity measurements for the purposes of the CBR approach to web user interface design, which promises significant boost in conventional websites engineering. This paper is built upon several our previously published works (we provide references where appropriate) and integrates them into the unified case- and component-based approach to web design. Although the paper has a single author, "we" pronoun will be used throughout the text, to recognize the previous work of the collaborators. In Sect. 2 we consider the case structure in the web design domain and outline the ways to measure similarity based on the feature values. Further, we propose the metric-based technique and the software tool (the visual analyzer that we developed) to predict target users' subjective similarity assessments of websites using artificial neural network (ANN) model. In Sect. 3, we describe the experimental survey session where we collected the training data, and the construction and training of the actual ANN user behavior model. In Conclusions, we summarize our findings and outline prospects for further work.

2 Case-Based Approach in Web Design and Similarity Measures

2.1 Problem Features and Similarity

Different disciplines place distinct emphasis on the CBR-related activities of case storage, case indexing, case retrieval, and case adaptation (the Retrieve stage remains arguably the most popular). Still, there is a general consensus among researchers and practitioners about the crucial importance of devising an accurate form of problem description for the success of machine learning and automated reasoning in AI: e.g. "…a critical pain point in building (trained data) systems is feature engineering" [10]. Meanwhile, feature engineering appears to often remain a creative task performed "manually" by knowledge engineers, though the major stages of the conventional process can be identified as: forming the excessive list of potential features (e.g. through brainstorming session), implementing all or some of them in a prototype, and selecting relevant features by optimizing the considered subset.

First, it should be noted that there's a fair amount of research works that deal with feature selection for web pages, particularly for automated classification purposes [11]. Indeed a web page is a technically opportune object for analysis, as it is represented in easily processable code (HTML, CSS, etc.), but it's not self-contained, either content-wise or in terms of design resolutions, and can hardly be appropriate as a solution in a case. Clearly, such design- and goal-wise complete entity web project should correspond to case in CBR, while website is a solution, of which the case may have several. There are respective approaches aimed on selecting features for software or web projects, though focused rather on knowledge organization [6] or web service composition [7]. As we mentioned before, there seems to be no agreed structure of features in the web design domain, so we performed informal feature engineering for reuse and outlined their use in the cases' similarity calculation.

We founded ourselves upon the model-based approach to web UI development, which generally identifies three groups of models: (1) per se interface models – Abstract UI, Concrete UI, and Final UI, (2) functionality-oriented models – Tasks and Domain, and (3) context of use models – User, Platform, and Environment. Of these, we consider the Domain, Tasks, and User of higher relevance to web design reuse, while Platform and Environment models rather relate to website's back-office. Also, not all existing website designs are equally good (in contrast to e.g. re-usable programming code), so quality aspects must be reflected in the feature set.

Domain-Related Features. Reuse of design is considered domain-specific [12], and indeed a website from the same domain has a pretty much better chance to aid in solving the problem in CBR. Although the domain theoretically can be inferred from website content, this is complex and computationally expensive, so we propose using available website classifications by major web catalogues. For example, DMOZ claims to contain more than 1 million hierarchically-organized categories, while the number of included websites is about 4 million, which implies highly detailed classification. The domain similarity then can be defined as the minimal number of steps to get from one category item to another via hierarchical relations, divided by the "depth" of the item, to reduce potential bias for less specifically classified websites.

Task-Related Features. Although user activities on the web may be quite diverse, conventional websites within the same domain have fairly predictable functionality. For the purposes of CBR, there seems to be little need to employ full-scale task modeling notations, such as W3C's CTT or HAMSTERS [13], especially since by themselves they do not offer an established approach for evaluating similarity between two models. We believe that particulars of a reusable website's functionality can be adequately represented with the domain features plus the structured inventory of website chapters that reflect the tasks reasonably well. Then, the currently well-developed semantic distance methods (see e.g. [14]) can be used to retrieve the cases with similar problem specifications. A potential caveat here, notorious for folksonomies in general, is inventiveness (synonyms) or carelessness (typos) of some website owners – so, first the chapter labels would have to be verified against a domain-specific controlled vocabulary.

User-Related Features. User stereotype modeling in web interaction design employs a set of reasonably well established features to distinguish a group of users: age, gender, experience, education and income levels, etc. The corresponding personas or user profiles (usually no more than 3 different ones) are created by marketing specialists or interaction designers and are an important project artifact [8]. Evaluation of similarity between users is quite well supported by knowledge engineering methods and is routinely performed in recommender systems, search engines [15], social networks [16], etc. Thus, the real challenge is obtaining concrete values for the relevant features in the user model for someone else's website.

Quality-Related Features. The quality-related features won't be used for calculating similarity, but among the several potentially relevant cases (or among solutions in the same case – website versions) we would generally prefer solutions that have better quality. Website quality is a collection of attributes, some of them can belong to very different categories, e.g. Usability and Reliability, and their relative importance may vary depending of the project goals and context [12]. Correspondingly, today's techniques for assessing the quality attributes are very diverse: auto-validation of code, content or accessibility; load and stress tests; checklist of design guidelines, user testing, subjective impression surveys, etc. Thus, the set of quality-related features must remain customizable and open to be "fed" by diverse methods and tools – actually, the more quality attributes can be maintained, the better.

2.2   The Web Designs Similarity

After the cases are retrieved from the case base based on a certain similarity measure, the "classical" CBR prescribe adapting their solutions to the new problem. However, in web design domain this process (basically, the Reuse and Revise stages) can't be performed directly, as the solutions' back-office and server-side code is generally not available, while the designs are copyright-protected. The workaround (as we proposed in [9]) is to consider them as the reference solutions, generate new solutions from software and UI components, and iteratively make the new solutions similar to the reference ones. The problem, however, is that interactive evolutionary computation that involves human experts or even users to assess the similarity would make the adaptation process prohibitively slow. In resolving this, we propose relying on trained human behavior models – i.e. using pre-supplied human assessments to make predictions on the new solutions' similarity to the reference ones.

Classically, behavior models in human-computer interaction have interface design's characteristics and the context of use (primarily, users' characteristics) as the inputs, and they output an objective value relating to end users, preferably a design objective (usability, aesthetics, etc. [17]. In our study, we will fix the user characteristics by employing a relatively narrow target user group to provide the similarity assessments for a fixed web projects Domain. In representing website designs, we will rely on metric-based approach, i.e. describe the solutions with a set of auto-extracted feature values responsible for subjective website similarity perception in the target users.

There is plenty of existing research works studying the effect of website metrics on the way users perceive them and on the overall web projects' success (one of the founding examples is [18]). Particularly, both user's cognitive load and subjective perceptions are known to be greatly influenced by perceived visual complexity [19], which in turn depends of the number of objects in the image, their diversity, the regularity of their spatial allocation [20], etc.

In our study we employ the dedicated software tool that relies on computer vision techniques to extract the web interface metrics – the "visual analyzer", which we developed within the previously proposed "human-computer vision" approach. The visual analyzer takes visual representation (screenshot) of a web interface and outputs its semantic-spatial representation in machine-readable JSON format (see [21] for more detailed description of the analyzer's architecture, the involved computer vision and machine learning libraries, etc.). Based on the semantic-spatial representation, the analyzer is capable of calculating the following metrics relevant for the purposes of our current research:

1. The number of all identified elements in the analyzed webpage (UI elements, images, texts, etc.): N;
2. The number of different elements types: T;
3. Compression rate (as representation of spatial regularity), calculated as the area of the webpage (in pixels) divided by the file size (in bytes) of the image compressed using the JPEG-100 algorithm: C;
4. "Index of difficulty" for visual perception (see in [20]): IDM, calculated as:

$$IDM = \frac{N \log_2 T}{C} \tag{1}$$

5. Relative shares of the areas in the UI covered by the different types of UI elements:
6. Textual content, i.e. area under all elements recognized as textline: $Text$;
7. Whitespace, i.e. area without any recognized elements: $White$;

8. In addition to the metrics output by the analyzer, we also employed the standard Matlab's entropy(I) function (returns a scalar value E reflecting the entropy of grayscale image I) to measure frequency-based entropy of the website screenshot: *Entropy*.

The above metrics will act as the basic factors (F_i) for the ANN model we construct in the next chapter, in order to predict target users' similarity assessments of website designs. ANNs are gaining increased popularity recently, as they have very reasonable computational effectiveness compared to other AI or statistical methods and they don't require explicit knowledge of the model structure. The disadvantage is that they require a lot of diverse data for learning, and the results are hard to interpret in a conceptually meaningful way. ANNs are first trained and then tested on real data, attempting to generalize the obtained knowledge in classification, prediction, decision-making, etc. The available dataset is generally partitioned into training, testing, and holdout samples, where the latter is used to assess the constructed network – estimate the predictive ability of the model. The network performance (the model quality) is estimated via percentage of incorrect predictions (for categorical outputs) or relative error that is calculated as sum-of-squares relative to the mean model (the "null" hypothesis).

3   The Similarity Assessment

To obtain the subjective similarity evaluations for the ANN training, we ran experimental survey sessions with human evaluators. In the current research work, the input neurons are strictly the metrics that can be evaluated automatically for a webpage, without any subjective assessments. In one of our previous studies of subjective similarity, however, we relied on human evaluations for the "emotional" dimensions of websites, collected per the specially developed Kansei Engineering scales, to predict similarity of websites [22]. That ANN model had relative error of 0.559, which will act as the baseline for our current study, where the number of required evaluations is dramatically lower.

3.1   The Experimental Design

The research material was university websites (*Career and Education* domain in DMOZ), selected by hand with the requirements that: (1) the website has an English version that is not radically different from the native language version; (2) the website has information about a Master program in Computer Science; and (3) the university is not too well-known, so that its reputation doesn't bias the subjective impressions. In total there were 11 websites of German universities and 10 of Russian ones, so that their designs in terms of layout, colors, images, etc. were sufficiently diverse in each group. Correspondingly, the total number of distinct website pairs for the similarity assessments was $C_{21}^2 = 210$.

The assessments were collected from 127 participants (75 male, 52 female), aged 17–31 (mean = 20.9, SD = 2.45), who represented the target users. The subjects were university students (mostly majoring in Computer Science) or staff members: 100 from

Russia (Novosibirsk State Technical University) and 27 from Germany (Chemnitz Technical University). The participants used diverse equipment and environment: desktops with varying screen resolutions, mobile devices, web browsers, etc., to better represent the real context of use. Before the sessions, informed consent was obtained from each subject, and afterwards they could submit comments to their evaluations.

The participants used our specially developed survey software (currently available at http://ks.wuikb.tech/phase2.php). Each subject was asked to assess subjective similarity for 45 distinct website pairs composed from 10 randomly selected websites (see in Fig. 1). The participants were assigned no concrete tasks – they were presented the pair of screenshots linked to the actual websites and asked to open and browse the two homepages for a few seconds. The five possible similarity evaluations ranged from 0 (very dissimilar) to 4 (very similar).

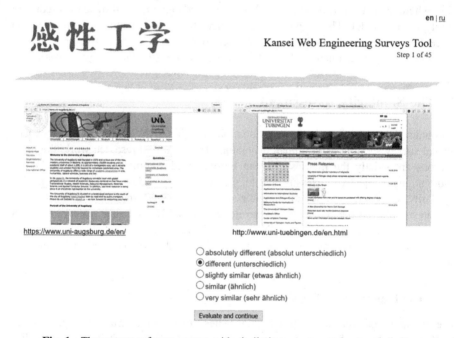

Fig. 1. The survey software screen with similarity assessment for two websites

3.2 Descriptive Statistics

In total, the 127 subjects provided 5715 similarity assessments, so for each of the 210 website pairs the average number of evaluations was 27.2. The resulting subjective similarity values averaged per website pair ranged from 0.296 to 2.909, mean = 1.524, SD = 0.448 (the similarity is in ordinal scale, so the values are given just for reference).

Further, we applied our visual analyzer to obtain the metrics for the experimental websites. Website #14 was excluded from the analysis due to technical difficulties with the screenshot (so, 90.5% of averaged similarity assessments were valid). The values for the 7 metrics extracted by the analyzer are presented in Table 1.

Table 1. The metrics for the website provided by the visual analyzer

Website ID	N	T	C	Text,%	White, %	Entropy	IDM
1	32	3	1.366	8.49	88.55	4.437	37.1
2	41	6	1.886	3.09	91.84	3.518	56.2
3	53	5	3.013	1.16	96.28	2.984	40.8
4	80	5	2.540	3.62	96.25	4.478	73.1
5	120	5	3.184	1.81	92.92	3.497	87.5
6	43	3	2.146	3.82	92.14	4.108	31.8
7	19	6	1.917	9.62	87.14	3.060	25.6
8	44	5	2.623	7.63	89.22	2.044	39.0
9	49	5	1.815	3.02	93.41	6.589	62.7
10	68	7	2.604	5.74	90.83	2.998	73.3
11	64	7	2.331	1.68	91.44	3.836	77.1
12	157	6	1.566	2.27	95.49	3.635	259.2
13	54	6	2.246	0.98	91.36	5.568	62.1
15	70	7	1.622	0.57	94.36	5.846	121.2
16	92	6	2.577	6.16	90.01	2.374	92.3
17	118	7	1.662	10.32	82.36	3.494	199.4
18	131	8	2.816	2.01	92.69	4.533	139.6
19	48	5	1.190	0.63	97.74	4.794	93.6
20	29	3	2.136	22.68	77.30	4.742	21.5
21	57	7	2.665	1.38	92.77	4.062	60.1
Mean (SD)	68.45 (28.89)	5.60 (1.14)	2.20 (0.46)	4.83 (3.68)	91.20 (3.30)	4.03 (0.89)	82.66 (41.42)

The distance measure between a pair of websites per each of the measured dimensions was introduced the ratio between the largest and the smallest value for the two websites (so 1 means no difference, larger values indicate greater difference):

$$Diff(F_i) = \frac{Max\{F_i(website_j), F_i(website_k)\}}{Min\{F_i(website_j), F_i(website_k)\}} \quad i = \overline{1,7}; j = \overline{1,21}; k = \overline{1,21} \quad (2)$$

Please note that the distance measure could be set this way since all the metrics were in rational scale, unlike in our previous work [22], where the human assessments of the factors' values were ordinal. The Shapiro-Wilk tests suggested that for all seven $Diff(F_i)$ factors the normality hypotheses had to be rejected (p < 0.001).

The analysis of correlations (non-parametrical Kendall's tau-b for ordinal scales) for the Similarity assessments found significant negative correlations with distances

Diff(Entropy) ($\tau = -0.146$, $p = 0.003$), *Diff(IDM)* ($\tau = -0.100$, $p = 0.04$), *Diff(Text)* ($\tau = -0.147$, $p = 0.003$), and *Diff(White)* ($\tau = -0.180$, $p < 0.001$).

3.3   The ANN Model for Assessing Web Designs Similarity

In the ANN model, the single output neuron was Similarity, averaged for each websites pair (website$_j$, website$_k$) per all the participants who assessed it, whereas the input neurons were the seven *Diff(Fi)* covariates for the websites. We employed Multilayer Perceptron method with *Scaled conjugate gradient* optimization algorithm in SPSS statistical software, hidden layer activation function was *Hyperbolic tangent*, output layer activation function was *Identity*. The partitions of the datasets (210 pair-wise similarity values) in each of the three models were specified as 70% (training) – 20% (testing) – 10% (holdout). The number of neurons in the single hidden layer was set to be selected automatically, and amounted to 4 neurons in the resulting model. The relative error in the best model was 0.597 for the holdout set. We also performed the factors importance analysis, whose results are presented in Table 2.

Table 2. The factors importance analysis

Factor	Importance	Normalized importance
Diff (Entropy)	0.283	100.0%
Diff(IDM)	0.223	78.8%
Diff(White)	0.155	54.6%
Diff(Text)	0.118	41.8%
Diff(T)	0.115	40.5%
Diff(C)	0.067	23.6%
Diff(N)	0.039	13.8%

Alternative ANN models that for the input neurons employed the factors values for the two websites separately, i.e. F_i(website$_j$) and F_i(website$_k$) instead of the differences, had notably lower predictive quality. The best model, with all the 14 F_i plus the categorical values of the website country (Russian or German), had relative error of 0.737 for the holdout set. The model seemingly suffered from overtraining, which may imply more training data would be required.

We also attempted ordinal regression to test whether the assessed similarity could be predicted by the seven *Diff(F$_i$)* factors. The resulting model was highly significant ($\chi^2(7) = 43.86$, $p < 0.001$), but had rather low Nagelkerke pseudo $R^2 = 0.206$. Moreover, the proportional odds assumption had to be rejected ($\chi^2(1155) = 1881$, $p < 0.001$), which suggests that the effects of the explanatory variables in the ordinal regression model are inconsistent.

4 Conclusions

The general idea of case-based design reuse has been around for quite a while, but its potential in web engineering is particularly appealing. In today's e-society, an archetypal web design company employs no more than 10 people, has no market share to speak of, and mostly works on fairly typical projects. Greater reuse of websites and automated composition of new solutions could significantly increase their efficiency, allowing to focus on e-marketing, content creation, usability refinement, etc.

In the current paper we focus on assessment of similarity, which is crucial within the CBR approach to WUI design, since retrieval of relevant cases and solutions is by and large based on similarity measure. We carried out informal feature engineering for web projects, inspired by the popular model-based approach to web interface development – thus the Domain, Task, and User dimensions – and outlined how similarity measures could be calculated for each of them. We also argue that CBR application in web design domain also requires measuring similarity between the new solution and the retrieved solutions, since direct adaptation of the latter is restricted by technical and legal considerations.

To predict similarity of web designs without actual users (as relying on human experts or users to assess all the similarities would make the adaptation process prohibitively slow), we proposed the approach based on auto-extracted website metrics. These values were extracted by our dedicated software, the web analyzer, and used as the basic factors in the predictive ANN model illustrating feasibility of the approach. Its relative error of 0.597 is rather appropriate compared to relative error of 0.559 in the baseline model relying on user assessments of emotional dimensions [22], while the other considered models showed lower performance. The analysis of the factors' importance suggests that frequency-based entropy measure was the most important for subjective similarity, in contrast to compression measure introduced in the analyzer to reflect spatial orderliness in WUI, which had considerably lower importance. The index of difficulty for visual perception that we previously devised [20] and that is based on the analyzer's measurements also had high importance, which implies significant effect of visual complexity on subjective similarity in websites. The aerial measures of shares under text and whitespace had moderate importance, while the number of elements in web interface was the least important factor – somehow unexpectedly, as our previous research suggests that the analyzer is rather accurate in this regard [21].

Our further research will be aimed on studying the dimensions of similarity and improving the model, particularly through: (a) getting more similarity-related website metrics to be assessed by the analyzer; (b) obtaining and utilizing more training data, as the extended ANN model suffered from their shortage.

Acknowledgement. The reported study was funded by RFBR according to the research project No. 16-37-60060 mol_a_dk. We also thank those who contributed to developing the visual analyzer software and collecting the human assessments: Sebastian Heil, Markus Keller, and Vladimir Khvorostov.

References

1. Kumar, R., et al.: Webzeitgeist: design mining the web. In: SIGCHI Conference on Human Factors in Computer Systems, pp. 3083–3092 (2013). https://doi.org/10.1145/2470654. 2466420
2. Norrie, M.C., Nebeling, M., Di Geronimo, L., Murolo, A.: X-Themes: Supporting Design-by-Example. In: Casteleyn, S., Rossi, G., Winckler, M. (eds.) ICWE 2014. LNCS, vol. 8541, pp. 480–489. Springer, Cham (2014). https://doi.org/10.1007/978-3-319-08245-5_33
3. De Mantaras, R.L., et al.: Retrieval, reuse, revision and retention in case-based reasoning. Knowl. Eng. Rev. **20**(3), 215–240 (2005). https://doi.org/10.1017/S0269888906000646
4. Goel, A.K., Craw, S.: Design, innovation and case-based reasoning. Knowl. Eng. Rev. **20** (3), 271–276 (2005). https://doi.org/10.1017/S0269888906000609
5. Schmitt, G.: Case-based design and creativity. Autom. Constr. **2**(1), 11–19 (1993)
6. Rocha, R.G., et al.: A case-based reasoning system to support the global software development. Procedia Comput. Sci. **35**, 194–202 (2014). https://doi.org/10.1016/j.procs. 2014.08.099
7. De Renzis, A., et al.: Case-based reasoning for web service discovery and selection. Electron. Notes Theor. Comput. Sci. **321**, 89–112 (2016). https://doi.org/10.1016/j.entcs. 2016.02.006
8. Marir, F.: Case-based reasoning for an adaptive web user interface. In: The International Conference on Computing, Networking and Digital Technologies (ICCNDT2012), pp. 306–315 (2012)
9. Bakaev, M., Khvorostov, V.: Component-based engineering of web user interface designs for evolutionary optimization. In: 19th IEEE/ACIS International Conference on Software Engineering, Artificial Intelligence, Networking and Parallel/Distributed Computing (SNPD 2018), pp. 335–340
10. Anderson, M.R., et al.: Brainwash: A Data System for Feature Engineering. In: CIDR (2013)
11. Mangai, J.A., Kumar, V.S., Balamurugan, S.A.: A novel feature selection framework for automatic web page classification. Int. J. Autom. Comput. **9**(4), 442–448 (2012). https://doi. org/10.1007/s11633-012-0665-x
12. Glass, R.L.: Facts and Fallacies of Software Engineering. Addison-Wesley Professional, Boston (2002)
13. Martinie, C., et al.: A generic tool-supported framework for coupling task models and interactive applications. In: Proceedings of the 7th ACM SIGCHI Symposium on Engineering Interactive Computing Systems, pp. 244–253 (2015). https://doi.org/10.1145/2774225.2774845
14. Park, J., Choi, B.C., Kim, K.: A vector space approach to tag cloud similarity ranking. Inf. Process. Lett. **110**(12–13), 489–496 (2010). https://doi.org/10.1016/j.ipl.2010.03.014
15. Sieg, A., Mobasher, B., Burke, R.: Web search personalization with ontological user profiles. In: Proceedings of the 16 ACM Conference on information and knowledge management, pp. 525–534 (2007). https://doi.org/10.1145/1321440.1321515
16. Kosinski, M., et al.: Manifestations of user personality in website choice and behaviour on online social networks. Mach. Learn. **95**(3), 357–380 (2014). https://doi.org/10.1007/s10994-013-5415-y
17. Oulasvirta, A.: User interface design with combinatorial optimization. Computer **50**(1), 40–47 (2017). https://doi.org/10.1109/MC.2017.6
18. Ivory, M.Y., Hearst, M.A.: Statistical profiles of highly-rated web sites. In: Proceedings of the ACM SIGCHI conference on Human factors in computing systems, pp. 367–374 (2002). https://doi.org/10.1145/503376.503442

19. Reinecke, K., et al.: Predicting users' first impressions of website aesthetics with a quantification of perceived visual complexity and colorfulness. In: Proceedings of the ACM SIGCHI Conference on Human Factors in Computing Systems, pp. 2049–2058 (2013). https://doi.org/10.1145/2470654.2481281

20. Bakaev, M., Razumnikova, O.: Opredeleine slozhnosti zadach dlya zritelno-prostranstvennoi pamyati i propustkoi spospobnosti cheloveka-operatora. Upravlenie bol'shimi sistemami=Large-Scale Systems Control **70**, 25–57 (2017). (In Russian)

21. Bakaev, M., Heil, S., Khvorostov, V., Gaedke, M.: HCI Vision for Automated Analysis and Mining of Web User Interfaces. In: Mikkonen, T., Klamma, R., Hernández, J. (eds.) ICWE 2018. LNCS, vol. 10845, pp. 136–144. Springer, Cham (2018). https://doi.org/10.1007/978-3-319-91662-0_10

22. Bakaev, M., et al.: Evaluation of user-subjective web interface similarity with Kansei engineering-based ANN. In: IEEE 25th International Requirements Engineering Conference, pp. 125–131 (2017). https://doi.org/10.1109/rew.2017.13

Multi-agent Framework for Supply Chain Dynamics Modelling with Information Sharing and Demand Forecast

Daria L. Belykh$^{(\boxtimes)}$ and Gennady A. Botvin

Saint Petersburg State University,
7-9 Universitetskaya Emb., 199034 St Petersburg, Russia
dariabelykh@gmail.com
http://spbu.ru

Abstract. Supply chain management is struggling with a bunch of issues that appear during supply chain members coordination. Raising of supply chain complexity leads to the necessity of developing new software applications, which can be used for analysis of supply chain dynamics, storing data about it's past and present states, predicting future behavior. This paper discusses current challenges in supply chain management and presents a model for the multi-agent framework in order to investigate supply chain dynamics.

Keywords: Supply chain performance · Supply chain management
Simulation · Multi-agent systems

1 Introduction

Huge number of companies are struggle for performance improvement in order to get competitive advantages on local or global markets. The problem become even more complex for companies, aimed on production of high-tech goods or services, because they have to unite with partners in supply chain and share their resources and knowledge with all partners for achieving common goals.

The supply chain management can be considered as a strategically important conception for achieving competitiveness in the business environment. It proposes an idea that supply chain companies don't have to compete with each other but supply chain needs to compete with other supply chains. It means that supply chain members should be concerned about improving the performance of the whole supply chain, not only improving their own performance. Supply chain performance depends on the continuous improvement of supply chain processes in order to decrease costs and increase profit.

Presented paper discussed supply chain management, its vital challenges and possible solutions for overcome this challenges. Moreover we discussed multi-agent systems and its application to supply chain management. We consider discrete-event modeling via agents and proposed model for supply chain simulation. We also explore opportunities of using forecast methods in order to achieve better supply chain management performance.

© Springer Nature Switzerland AG 2018
D. A. Alexandrov et al. (Eds.): DTGS 2018, CCIS 858, pp. 366–374, 2018.
https://doi.org/10.1007/978-3-030-02843-5_29

2   Research Field

Supply chain management [1] encompasses the planning and management of all activities involved in sourcing and procurement, conversion, and all logistics management activities. It integrates supply and demand management within and across companies.

Supply chain management is based on a term of the supply chain which is described by [12] as linked together companies starting with unprocessed raw materials and ending with the final customer using the finished goods. Supply chains can be found in any situation where numerous companies involved in a production process of some goods or services. Figure 1 illustrates example of the supply chain, which contains suppliers, producer, distributors, and retailers. Supply chain management drives coordination of processes and activities with and across marketing, sales, product design, finance and information technology. Importantly, it also includes coordination and collaboration with supply chain members.

In a context of supply chain management appears a bunch of issues that have to be handled. The most crucial one is a bullwhip effect. It means that small random variation in the demand of the downstream customers may cause very high variance in the procurement quantity of upstream suppliers [4]. Such variation makes demand unpredictable and amplified at each supply chain level. Bullwhip effect has less impact on a retailer. Bullwhip effect leads to increasing of inventory level of each supply chain member, decreasing supply chain flexibility and customer service because it is hard to determine when and what product would be in demand.

One of the possible and the most effective solution to this problem is an information sharing. An additional solution for decreasing bullwhip effect is a usage of more accurate forecasting methods and shared data. It is worth mentioning that bullwhip effect is also decreased if supply chain members from upstream nodes will order materials or goods more frequently and size of ordered units in a lot will be smaller.

Supply chain management assumes system approach to the supply chain. In practice, the optimization of the whole supply chain gives better results than isolated optimization of single partners. Some supply chain researchers [2,3] formalize supply chain as an optimization problem. They describe possible restrictions and propose objective functions for optimization. Even multi-objective optimization models cannot handle all restrictions of real-world scenarios. It leads us to the necessity of improving supply chain members information systems.

According to [10], among the seven principles of supply chain management, the six one is defined as developing supply chain wide technology strategy that supports multiple levels of decision making and gives a clear view of the flow of products, services, and information.

For the short term, the system must be able to handle day-to-day transactions across the supply chain and thus help align supply and demand by sharing information on orders and daily scheduling. For a mid-term perspective, the system must facilitate planning and decision making to allocate resources effi-

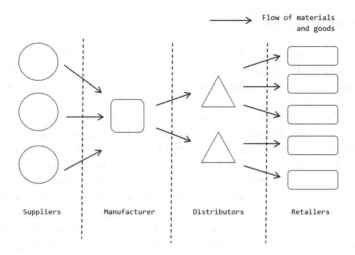

Fig. 1. Supply chain members

ciently. To add long-term value, the system must be enabled strategic analysis by providing tools, such as integrated network model, that synthesize data for use in high-level 'what-if' scenario planning to help managers evaluate plants, distribution centers, suppliers, and third-party service alternatives.

The additional crucial issue for systems that maintain supply chain management concerns data storing. It is necessary to monitor and record all demands and supplies as they occur [9]. Moreover, it is reasonable to storing all building forecasts of future demand and other characteristics. This data should be saved inside corporate systems in order to make reports of currents states. It also valuable for efficiency evaluation of implementing forecast methods.

3   Application of Multi-agent Systems in Supply Chain Researches

The presented paper focuses on the multi-agent system as a possible tool for using in supply chain technology strategy in order to develop a powerful tool for deep analysis of supply chain members behavior. Software system development based on the paradigm of intelligent agents [7] brings some crucial advantages over standard approaches. Large complex systems can be divided into smaller parts like autonomous agents. Design and implementation of such smaller parts much easier than design and implementation of the overall system. Moreover, if the number of agents in a system will increase significantly, the multi-agent system can be scaled with fewer labor expenditures. Multi-agent systems using in supply chain studies widely in order to solve NP-hard optimization problems [5] or implement discrete-event modeling.

Supply chain members ought to make decisions about production planning, inventory management, vehicle routing and so on continuously. Each supply chain member prefers to maximize their own profit than the profit of the supply chain. Decisions of supply chain members can positively or negatively effect the whole supply chain performance [6]. Supply chain management assumes that decision-making should support performance improvement for supply chain at all, not for single members. Supply chain optimization problems are NP-hard and they can be solved using natural inspired intelligence methods [8]. It assumes, that agents of multi-agent system solve its part of problem separately, and then the best solution selected among founded solutions.

There are two main approaches for modeling of supply chains: analytical approach and simulation [11]. The analytical approach relies on a mathematical formalization of the supply chains. Examples of analytical approaches are based on differential equations control theory and operational research optimization theories approach. Models for analytical modeling necessitate simplifying approximations, usually restrictive, and are limited to taking into account time.

Supply chain modeling and simulation was originally based on system dynamics. This was motivated by the fact that the structure of the supply chain and the flow control determine its performance. Nowadays discrete event simulation is preferable simulation method than continuous simulation for supply chain simulation. The emerging trend exploiting the agent approach builds on discrete event simulation. Modeling supply chain using intelligent agent paradigm has potential due to fact that agents are a natural metaphor for a set of independent companies.

Supply chain modeling used to be implemented in order to help decision-makers better understand behavior and performance of modeled supply chain. In recent time researchers make attempt to use simulation results for identifying the best decisions to take regarding structural, organizational, managerial and process transformations in order to achieve better performance. Agent-based simulation extends the capabilities of discrete event simulation for both descriptive and normative purposes in the context of complex knowledge intensive supply chains.

4 Model for Multi-agent Framework Implementation

The main goal of the presented research is to develop simulation tool, that enables to implement designed supply chain model, emulate the behavior of supply chain members and it's collective dynamics. In current paper we continue to improve our model for simulation assumes that each supply chain member implements as a separate software agent that has its own storage of data and knowledge about its environment. Agents that act on behalf suppliers, producer, distributors, and retailers make decisions about when and what number of raw materials or goods they want to buy from an upstream agent. Agents collect data about its own costs and profits, which is sums up after simulation execution in costs and profits of the whole supply chain.

$$I_k(t) = I_k(t-1) + \sum_{k'}^{n} q_{k',k}(t) - \sum_{k'}^{n} q_{k,k''}(t) \tag{1}$$

$$I_k(t) = I_k(t-1) + \sum_{k'}^{n} q_{k',k}(t) - q_k(t) \tag{2}$$

$$profit_k(t) = q_{k,k''}(t) * price_k - \sum_{k'}^{n} q_{k',k}(t) * costs_k - TC_k \tag{3}$$

$$\Delta q = |q_{k',k}(t) - q_{k',k}(t-1)| \tag{4}$$

$$I_k < I_k^{max} \tag{5}$$

In Eq. (1) $\forall k \in P, D$, in Eq. (2) $\forall k \in R$

According to presented model we investigate inventory level (1, 2) of supply chain members during one year in monthly periods. Agent can order more materials and goods than they can actually store (5). Supply chain performance in our case is measured by the profit (3) of the overall supply chain. Additionally we are calculating difference between size of orders in current period comparing to the previous period (4) in order to illustrate bullwhip effect (Table 1).

Table 1. Table of model variable description

S	supplier
P	producer
D	distributor
R	retailer
k	current node/agent
k'	upstream node/agent
k''	downstream node/agent
I_k	inventory level
I_k^{max}	max inventory level
$q_{k',k}$	quantity of qoods transported from k' to k
q_k	quantity of qoods transported to k
$profit_k$	profit of k node/agent
$price_k$	price of selling one good for k node/agent
$costs_k$	price of buying one good for k node/agent
TC_k	total costs of k node/agent

Simulations can be launched over and over under different conditions. We can analyze how one or another partner affect the whole supply chain and make management decisions about supply chain configuration, its processes, and performance.

In addition to presented model, this paper will discuss issues of information sharing and making forecasts about future demand. As it was described in Sect. 2, software for supply chain management should support information sharing, data storing, and building predictions. In order to meet this requirements agents exchange messages with information about current transactions and demand in order to decrease bullwhip effect. Additionally, each agent store all data about its transactions and demand and all shared data from other agents. Moreover storing data are using by agents for building forecasts about future demand.

In essence, each agent should be able to build forecasts of future demand using shared data. We are modeling supply chain in one year period hence we have not enough data building a neural network and training it. It is a reason why we implement exponential smoothing for making forecasts stored by agents and spread among supply chain members via messages.

$$F_{t+1} = \alpha D_t + (1 - \alpha) * F_t \tag{6}$$

$$F_{t+1}^D = 0.5 * F_{t+1}^D + 0.5 * F_{t+1}^R \tag{7}$$

$$F_{t+1}^P = 0.35 * F_{t+1}^D + 0.65 * F_{t+1}^R \tag{8}$$

$$F_{t+1}^S = 0.30 * F_{t+1}^P + 0.30 * F_{t+1}^D + 0.40 * F_{t+1}^R \tag{9}$$

Where F_{t+1} - next period forecast, D_t - actual demand in the present period, α - smoothing constant (=0.25).

Multi-agent framework based on the proposed model or another one can be implemented via various tools. JACK [13], JADE [14], AnyLogic [15] and some others supports agent development. Moreover, multi-agent systems can be constructed from agents implemented via different platforms, if all that platforms support a common standard of agent development, such as FIPA [16] or another one.

Table 2. Input data for modeling

Agent k	Costs per unit, $ $costs_k$	Price per unit, $ $price_k$	Transportation costs per order, $ TC_k	Max inventory level I_k^{max}
Suppliers	-	28	-	300
Producer	28	45	14	200
Distributors	45	74	18	300
Retailers	74	100	19	130

5 Analysis of Supply Chain Modeling Results

Multi-agent framework contains agents acting on behalf supply chain participants. Each agent has it's own storage of data about pricing, number of materials or goods he has got. We estimate supply chain performance via counting total costs and a total profit of supply chain based on simulation results.

Agents with roles "producer", "distributor" and "retailer" receives orders from upstream node, decides to execute the order or not, decides how much to order from agent in downstream node, makes orders if needed and makes reports to statistic agent. In our modeling propose that "supplier" agent has the same responsibilities, but without making orders. Agents interaction modelled by exchanging asynchronous messages.

Modeling was implementing with input data from Table 2. We run modeling three times: without forecast, with exponential smoothing forecast of distributor and retailer demand (6), with exponential smoothing forecast and information sharing (7–9).

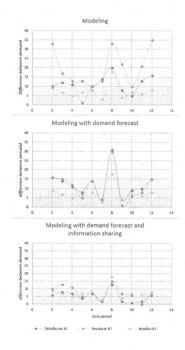

Fig. 2. Decreasing of bullwhip effect

According to modeling results, we can achieve increasing of supply chain performance due to building forecasts based on exponential smoothing and sharing information about demand and it's forecast between supply chain members. Figure 2 contains visual representation of demand Δq changes during simulation period. Figure 3 reveals profit increasing due to using demand forecast and information sharing.

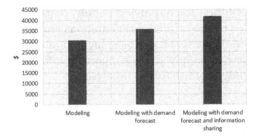

Fig. 3. Supply chain profit

6 Discussion

Supply chain coordination could be significantly increased by developing and implementing a modern software application. Such tools should support information sharing and data storing. Moreover, they should provide opportunities for accurate forecasting.

Raising of supply chain complexity imposes large restrictions on a variety of methods that can be used for supply chain modeling and simulation in order to investigate its dynamics. Supply chain dynamics analysis based on numerous simulation of real-world scenarios are vital for supply chain management because it can be used for making improvements in business strategies and operations.

The presented model is limited and cannot handle a large number of real-world scenarios. Model improving for investigating more complex operations in more wide supply chains can be selected as a further direction of research. Moreover, modeling of complex supply chains during a long-term period can give us enough data for neural network training in order to improve demand forecasting.

7 Conclusion

Supply chain management cover material flow from suppliers through producers, distributors, and retailers to end customers. Different companies unite their resources and knowledge in order to produce complex goods or services. The more complexity of produced goods, the more partners have to participate in process of their production.

Supply chains compete with another supply chains on local and global markets. In order to achieve better performance supply chain management considering issues of coordination. Coordination of supply chain members is a vital issue for supply chain performance. Effective coordination can result in (1) performance increase due to more accurate forecast about end-customers demand, (2) service quality increasing because of decreasing time for customer service, (3) increasing flexibility and reaction on high-speed changes, (4) usage of standard operations that make possible to get rid of duplicate actions and data sharing. A possible solution for improving supply chain performance is design and implementation of complex information systems aimed at information sharing, supporting day-to-day activities, processing and analyzing large volumes of data. Modeling as part of supply chain supporting information system reveals opportunities for supply chain dynamics analysis.

References

1. Oliver, R.K., Webber, M.D.: Supply-chain management: logistics catches up with strategy. Outlook **5**(1), 42–47 (1982)
2. Aqlan, F., Lam, S.: Supply chain optimization under risk and uncertainty: a case study for high-end server manufacturing. Comput. Ind. Eng. **93**, 78–87 (2016)
3. Tsai, J.F.: An optimization approach for supply chain management models with quantity discount policy. Eur. J. Oper. Res. **177**(2), 982–994 (2007). https://doi.org/10.1016/j.ejor.2006.01.034
4. Chaharsooghi, S.K., Heydari, J., Zegordi, S.H.: A reinforcement learning model for supply chain ordering management: an application to the beer game. Decis. Support. Syst. **45**(4), 949–959 (2008). https://doi.org/10.1016/j.dss.2008.03.007
5. Martin, S. et al.: A multi-agent based cooperative approach to scheduling and routing. Eur. J. Oper. Res. **254**(1), 169–178 (2016). https://doi.org/10.1016/j.ejor.2016.02.045
6. Belykh, D., Botvin, G.: Multi-agent based simulation of supply chain dynamics. J. Appl. Inform. **12**(4), 169–178 (2017)
7. Chaib-draa, B., Mller, J.: Multi-agent based Supply Chain Management (2006)
8. Minis, I. (ed.): Supply Chain Optimization, Design, and Management: Advances and Intelligent Methods. IGI Global, Hershey (2010)
9. Zipkin, P.H.: Foundations of inventory management (2000)
10. Anderson, D.L., Britt, F.F., Favre, D.J.: The 7 principles of supply chain management. Supply Chain. Manag. Rev. **11**(3), 41–46 (2007)
11. Labarthe, O., et al.: Toward a methodological framework for agent-based modelling and simulation of supply chains in a mass customization context. Simul. Model. Pract. Theory **15**(2), 113–136 (2007). https://doi.org/10.1016/j.simpat.2006.09.014
12. Council of Supply Chain Management Professionals. https://cscmp.org
13. JADE. Java Agent Development Framework. http://jade.tilab.com
14. JACK. Environment for building, running and integrating commercial-grade multi-agent systems. http://aosgrp.com/products/jack/
15. AnyLogic. Simulation Modeling Software Tools and Solutions for Business. https://www.anylogic.com
16. FIPA. Foundation of Intelligent Physical Agents. http://www.fipa.org/about/index.html

Application of Machine Analysis Algorithms to Automate Implementation of Tasks of Combating Criminal Money Laundering

Dmitry Dorofeev[1], Marina Khrestina[2], Timur Usubaliev[2],
Aleksey Dobrotvorskiy[1(✉)], and Saveliy Filatov[3]

[1] Moscow Institute of Physics and Technology (State University),
Moscow, Russia
dmitry@dorofeev.su, aleksey.dobrotvorskiy@gmail.com
[2] Quality Software Solutions LLC, Moscow, Russia
marina-khrestina@rambler.ru, ytr@kpr-it.com
[3] National Research University Higher School of Economics, Moscow, Russia
sava.colt@gmail.com

Abstract. The progress in IT gave people a bigger space for fraudulent activity. To help the analysis of criminal financial activity special software was invented. The problem is that the machine of money laundering becomes more sophisticated, but present ways of detecting such activities cannot match the level of fraud capabilities. The main objective in this case is finding methods to improve the available systems and designing new algorithms, understanding all principles that are used in money laundering. To accomplish this, all the steps in AML-systems should be revised or developed from the beginning, new tools should be included. This article gives an overview of the current situation with analysis of weaknesses in present AML-system versions and shows the examples of using machine learning.

Keywords: Antifraud · AML-systems · Machine learning · Financial crime
Digital economy · Analysis algorithms

1 Introduction

AML-systems, currently available on the market, work in accordance with static rules and usually consider only quantitative indices, such as: amount of transactions, period, and quantity. As a result, such systems frequently suffer from fake activations and errors. Analysis that is more detailed will require application of a wide range of various software tools, manual data collection from different sources.

Money laundering prevention systems become more important in digital economy, as more complicated organizational structures appear. Having a lot of members in business scheme gives more opportunities for obscure transactions that can be easily lost in array of operations. Present AML-systems cannot match the variety of gaps, so the fraud activity is still a great problem, in spite of that systems work. According to that fact we can conclude the necessity of developing such systems and paying attention to new ways of tracking dubious operations.

© Springer Nature Switzerland AG 2018
D. A. Alexandrov et al. (Eds.): DTGS 2018, CCIS 858, pp. 375–385, 2018.
https://doi.org/10.1007/978-3-030-02843-5_30

The objective of the current project is development and introduction of a new generation of specialized software complexes of AML-class to the market, which will help to detect suspicious financial operations and processes and estimate the state of their participants on the basis of the new developed and highly efficient, undemanding to resources, technology of analysis of unstructured data, categorization of investigated units, and detection of anomalies.

2   Related Work

There are a lot of articles in the subject area, including the articles on the theme of the use of artificial intelligence methods to solve the AML problem. The most active researchers are the researchers from the US, China and Australia [9, 11, 12, 14]. Apparently, this is due to the increased attention of the state to the problem, because in the United States and Australia, money laundering schemes are described at the legislative level. At the same time, the leading vendors of AML-systems do not publish any articles at all. Probably for the purpose of preserving the know-how. We also have to mention that researchers from European countries [6, 7] and India [4] are also active in this field.

A distinctive feature of the current work is the application, together with machine learning, of methods for detecting anomalies. Machine learning allows you to identify known laundering schemes that are present in the training sample. The detection of anomalies will provide a search and definition of new previously unknown illegal schemes. After verification, the detected anomalies are transferred to the input of machine learning, which increases the completeness of detection by the case of money laundering.

3   Methodology

The performed studies used the following methods of data analysis:

- machine learning;
- detection of anomalies.

Machine learning was applied to solve the problem of identifying known money-laundering schemes based on the accumulated retrospective of financial transactions. The use of machine learning methods to solve this problem will allow to fully automate the process of forming the criteria for selecting suspicious transactions, which should improve the effectiveness of combating money laundering in financial organizations.

In the framework of the study, the following methods were considered: Random Forest, SVM, logistic regression, and boosting.

The detection of anomalies was used to search for new previously unknown money laundering schemes, since this method allows determining anomalous suspicious transactions without the need for training on the training sample. The combination of the proposed methods should allow to effectively identify both known and new forms of money laundering without the need for manual analysis.

4 Development of Options of Possible Solutions for the Task, Selection and Substantiation of Optimal Solution Option

Finding a solution to counteract the laundering of criminal money requires development of a method (and, possibly, a set of new algorithm and methods), consisting of a number of algorithms able to solve the entire task. It would be reasonable to apply the basic approaches of the given field that have been applied globally in recent years – which is machine learning, anomalies detection, analysis the a graph of persons and transactions involved.

However, only a set of algorithms (with all the required modification and settings) can be applied in order to develop the given task. Limitation of amount of information in a bank will only hamper development of an efficient toolset.

These are the basic principles applied in fraud schemes which shall be taken into account as patterns for the algorithms developed:

- Application of 'layering' schemes, which causes a specific structure of a graph of persons and transactions to be detected by typical signs;
- Participation of suspicious persons in operations;
- Multiple and repeated funds transfers between accounts. This feature can also be detected through search of certain patterns in the graph;
- Employment of fake companies (or short-lived companies);
- Participation of foreign agents in operations.

Thus, we can extract a number of options to process the required information.

5 Legal Bodies Information Processing

The following legal bodies (banks' clients) data registering to analyze is planned. We analyze the following bodies presented in range of types:

- business entity, full title, abbreviated title, brand title, PSRN (Primary State Registration number), ITN (Identification Tax Number), IES (Industrial Enterprises Classifier), insurance policy holder's register number, type of authorized capital – in string type;
- basic activity and currency of authorized capital – in dictionaries (string);
- date of state registration – date;
- Amount of authorized capital – in fractional number;
- Foreign company – flag (number);
- Status of legal body – in dictionary (number).

Also for the analysis the following data on legal bodies (the list below is to serve as an example) shall be considered:

- card of legal body (full title, English title, actual address,
- address (location), phone number, e-mail, web, PSRN, ITN, OKOPF (All-Russian Classifier of Organizational Legal Form), Primary activity, CEO, Head company, scale of entity, personnel, authorized capital, sale proceeds, affiliated companies (RosStat));

- register Data (ITN, OKPO (All-Russian Classifier of Enterprises and Organizations), PSRN, IES, OKATO (All-Russian Classifier of Administrative-Territorial Division), OKTMO (All-Russian Classifier of Territories of Municipal Units), Code of Federal Service of financial Markets, OKFS (All-Russian Classifier of Forms of Ownership), OKOPF (All-Russian Classifier of Organizational Legal Form), OKOGU (All-Russian Classifier of State Authorities));
- financial data (for the last 5 years) (Balance, Report on financial results, Analytical report on financial results, Analysis of accounting balance (vertical and horizontal), Liquidity and efficiency indices).

6 Data Analysis Graph Development

6.1 Graph of Persons and Transactions Involved

A graph with a number of peaks – which is a multitude of various physical and legal bodies with relevant attributes – shall serve as an object of study to be manipulated with. The multitude of edges is various types of interconnections.

There are two graphs, logically independent – a graph of participated persons (similar to a social network) and a graph of transactions executed among the persons participated.

The peaks of graph are legal bodies. There is an edge between persons to be created in case if two persons, A and B, have:

1. Matching addresses (or similar, which is to be defined by a variable and adjusted),
2. Matching CEOs (or vaguely interconnected – this shall be formalized too),
3. Head company A = B or vice-versa,
4. B is in the list of affiliated companies of A or vice-versa.

In the first two cases the edges will have weight, and introduction of this variable will require additional investigation. Information on suspicious persons shall be introduced as persons' attributes, also it is required to specify whether a client is a foreign company or not. Within the process of development it is possible to introduce other edges. In order to develop a graph of transactions the edges of different type – the transactions – shall be added into the graph of participated persons. The period of history of transactions' analysis is a variable and an object of study.

6.2 Graph Development from Zero and Within System Operation

Taking into account the database containing all the required information on participated persons and transactions, the graph will be developed in accordance with the preset rules automatically. Then it will be required to develop a method of dynamic adjustment of the graph.

6.3   Analysis of Graph Properties

Extraction of Features to Analyze the Graph. All interconnections to be used to create an edge, which later can become a part of a criminal scheme, shall be analyzed and detected manually at the stage of task analysis. Either the edges of different types can be created or the weights can be introduced to the edges for various interconnections. For instance, in case of a several interconnections detected between two persons the weight of edge can be increased. However, it is supposed that at this stage it is better to preserve information and apply different types of edge for every type of interconnection. For instance, it is possible that two persons have similar, but not identical address, and in this case an edge can be created as well though with a reduced weight – comparing to the situation when the addresses fully match.

When a transaction is executed from A to B, a graph of connections will help build the following algorithms of graph processing:

(a) Communities detection on the basis of various signs;
(b) Building of all paths from A to B (existence of a path itself can be a sign of a suspicious transaction);
(c) Finding of linked components or tightly linked components (clicks) (studding of the literature have proved that, as a rule, transparent transactions are executed within a certain group of persons – components or clicks);
(d) Definition of betweenness centrality for every peak and possibly some other features;

The features that can be assigned to the each of objects:

(a) peaks degrees in the path graph (maximum, minimum and medium degree can applied);
(b) existence of paths, length of the paths in the graph;
(c) a property defining the extent of location of the peak in 'the center of graph' – i.e. the ratio of a number of paths in the graph passing through a given peak to the total number of paths (betweenness centrality property);
(d) number of connection components which a given peak belongs to;
(e) age of A and B accounts (for instance, when an account has been purposely created for a short period of time in order to provide money laundering);
(f) number of transactions (for different periods), volume (amounts of money to be transferred) operated between A and B both directly and indirectly;
(g) in-degree and out-degree for A and B (actually it is the same value as in the previous item, but not between A and B – this is to demonstrate the number of persons transferring money to A, its volumes etc.);
(h) the features can be collected not only from A and B, but from all the peaks on the paths connecting the peaks. However, there can be too many paths;
(i) the variables to connect the peaks in the paths, variety of these variables (their number), etc., can also be examined;
(j) confidence factor can be calculated for the each of objects on the basis of transactions graphs between different objects.

It is also required to mark all suspicious persons and everyone linked to them.

Patterns in the Graphs. Transactions history is an oriented graph. It is possible to extract AML-concerned patterns from the oriented graphs.

Figure 1 demonstrates an example of subgraph that is relevant to a total scheme of layering and integration [2] (initially the money have been placed in X). There are two more subgraphs typical for AML shown on the Fig. 2. There can be even more complex patterns which actually represent layering and integration—"volcanoes" and "black holes" respectively [16].

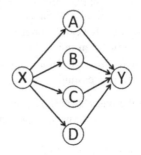

Fig. 1. Layering and integration: a simple example.

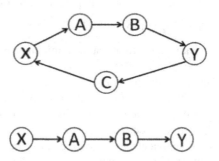

Fig. 2. Example of subgraphs frequently occurred in AML task.

We shall also note that the most works out of the amount of studies literature impose a search of clusters (or subgraphs) in accordance with some criteria as a main task to be solved at the level of graph. This subtask is to be resolved as early as possible. The clusters obtained can also serve as important features and be supplied at the input to the phase of machine learning.

7 Machine Learning Solution

The algorithms of classification task for machine learning work with a set of formalized features for the each of objects that would serve as a basis to make a decision whether an object is to be assigned as a member of the first or second class (i.e. whether a transaction is suspicious or not). Various algorithms of graphs processing can be applied to a developed graph in order to obtain a set of features for every object to be later used in the mechanisms of machine learning.

Then all these features shall be encoded and supplied at the input of various mechanisms of machine learning that would provide a response.

At the same time the following factors that can affect significantly the efficiency of machine learning application to solve the task shall be taken into account:

- Validity of the result will depend on the amount of information on different legal and physical bodies;
- This mechanism does not provide an automated adjustment in case when new attributes are added. It is possible to implement automated adding of new attributes, new interconnections (edges) into a graph, however, it can cause multiple calculations. It is also required in such case to introduce automated adding of new features;
- The list of features is not finite and requires extended studies. Probably, more data shall be used as features – including coding of a part of graph. However, it is necessary to reach compromise between a result obtained and an amount of calculations;
- The quality of system operation depends on the learning selection.

7.1   The Methods of Machine Learning

Support Vector Machine. Support Vector Machine, SVM, is one of the most popular methods of learning by incidents. The idea of method is shown on Fig. 3. It requires to build a hyperplane to divide data (multiple points within the space) on two classes. Among different hyperplanes the boundary planes are a matter of our specific interest – there are a certain number of points (out of learning selection) laying on these hyperplanes and these points are called support vectors (every point in the space can be shown as a vector). The method supposes that a hyperplane is to be selected, and the distance from it to the closest class will be maximally possible (i.e. a hyperplane equally-spaced from the boundary hyperplanes). There are some sources to state that SVM can be successfully applied for the task considered [8, 10].

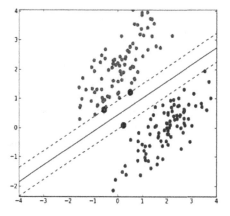

Fig. 3. The idea of the support vector machine method.

Logistic Regression. Logistic regression is a method of development of linear classifier enabling to estimate a posteriori probabilities of objects' belonging to classes. The space of initial values is divided with a linear boundary on two fields relevant to classes. The probability that a point belongs to one of the classes depends on the field of space where the point is located and on the distance from the point to the dividing boundary.

Boosting. Boosting is a procedure of sequential building of a composition of machine learning algorithms where every successive algorithm tends to compensate the defects of composition of all previous algorithms. Boosting is a selfish algorithm of building of algorithms composition. For the last 10 years, boosting has been remaining one of the most popular methods of machine learning – as well as neuron networks and support vector methods. Boosting over decision tree is considered one of the most effective methods in terms of the quality of classification.

Random Forest. Random forest is a machine learning algorithm requiring application of an ensemble of decision trees.

Decision trees reproduce the logical schemes that make possible to obtain final decision on object classification through responses to a system of questions arranged hierarchically. A question to be asked at the successive hierarchical level depends on an answer received at the previous level. The tree includes a root peak incidental only to initial edges; internal peaks incidental to an incoming edge and a number of outgoing; and the leaves – which are the end peaks incidental to only one incoming edge. Every peak of the tree, except for the leaves, corresponds with a question implying a few options to respond relevant to the outgoing edges. An answer selected defines the performance of the next step to the peak of the next level. The end peaks are tagged in order to assign an object under recognition to one of the classes.

Random forest algorithm builds a number of independent decision trees. The objects are classified by voting: the each of the trees of ensemble assigns ab object classified to one of the classes, and the class most voted for by the trees will win.

This list contains the machine learning methods that supposedly shall solve the problems of search of suspicious transactions most effectively in conditions of the task set. However, the matter shall be additionally examined at the stage of theoretical studies.

8 Detection of Abnormalities

As well as for the machine learning, it is required to extract features to serve to detect abnormalities for the algorithms of abnormalities detection. The features listed in the previous section can be applied too. We have to note that the vector of features (numbers) can be represented as a point in n-dimensional space (where n is a number of features). The purpose of the algorithm is to find abnormal points (emissions). The emissions can be searched with various algorithms – for instance, with K-nearest neighbors algorithm [3].

8.1   Software Implementation Technologies

As it is supposed to operate with huge amounts of data, the software technology Spark of Apache [1] is recommended to use. Spark is developing rapidly, it works above the distributed failing system HDFS with its calculating cluster. Spark performance is defined by the parallel data processing of the main memory of cluster. Spark includes the tools to work with GraphX graphs and MLlib implemented methods of machine learning.

8.2   Selection of Optimal Solution for the Task

On the basis of the analysis performed the optimal approach to solve the problem can be as follows:

The data arrow to analyze is to be structured into graphs of participated persons and graphs of transactions. Such approach will allow to apply the obtained experience of patterns of illegal transactions described in the form of graphs.

The next step is to detect different properties of the graph and clusters and filtration the most significant for the subject field investigated.

The basic tool of data analysis shall be the machine learning. It is supposed that the most efficient methods to solve this problem will be considered, including:

(a) SVM;
(b) Logistic regression;
(c) Boosting (for example, AdaBoost);
(d) Random Forest.

An auxiliary tool will be application of method of detection of abnormalities that, as expected, will help detect new schemes of illegal transactions that had no precedents earlier.

9   Development of Criteria of Assignation of Transactions to AML/CFT on the Basis of Current Legislation and Best Practices of Financial Agencies

9.1   The Criteria to Assign of Financial Transactions to Operations Subject to Mandatory Control

The list of operations subject to mandatory control - i.e. the information of which financial agencies must submit to the state authority - Rosfinmonitoring – is defined in the Federal Law "On Combating Legalization (Laundering) of Criminally Gained Income and Financing of Terrorism' of August 7, 2001 N 115-FZ [16] and the Provision of the Bank of Russia of August 2008 № 321-П 'On the disclosure procedure for credit agencies' in line with the Federal law 'On Combating Legalization (Laundering) of Criminally Gained Income and Financing of Terrorism".

As the list of financial operations is precisely defined and the data submitted to the above-mentioned authority marked with single-valued coding, it is not difficult to formulate the criteria of detection of given operations in the terminology of report coding submitted to the authority.

10   The Problem of Formalization of the Criteria Developed

It shall be notes that the formulated criteria to assign transactions to suspicious ones can hardly be represented as a set of formalized rules to serve as a guidance for financial agencies and authorities when conduct investigations. This is the cause of absence of the full list of transactions covered by the legislation in the normative documents. Criminals are consistently inventing new methods of money laundering; this is why it would not be efficient to formulate the criteria in the form of rules. Such rules will not be able to detect either new or non-described variations of financial schemes.

The selected approach to solve the problem supposes deviation from the method of examination in accordance with the rules and required analysis on the basis of principles which are the developed criteria as they are.

11   Conclusion

In the conditions of everyday progress, it is necessary to be ready to react to any kind of suspicious action in business sphere. In this article we made a research on different methods of detecting financial frauds.

Actual AML-systems cannot give an appropriate level of automatization – the main work is still done by people, who might make mistakes, because large companies perform millions of operations every day. That is why it is important for financial agencies to pay attention to the development of this kind of systems.

It should be noticed that the relevance of intellectualization of cities increases at the present time. The concept of smart cities implies widespread use of information and communication technologies in different spheres of city life for the stimulation of economic growth, effective use of resources and increase of the living standards. According to experts' opinion, the more widespread information technologies become, the more innovative protection is required for keeping data safe in digital space [15]. With the development of smart cities e-government gets more advanced, but the more operations are held in the electronic space, the easier it becomes for the state thieves to find occasions for committing economic crime. With the mass digitalization urgency of constant development in AML sphere is an obvious necessity for protection of Fintech industry.

We tried to cover main methods of money laundering detection and to analyze the key principals of their work in our project. Studying the question of AML-systems we learnt to use the main algorithms of machine learning, different softwares and method of detection of abnormalities. We also need to mention, that the project needs some improvements – learning period is required to make the results more accurate.

Acknowledgements. The research is being conducted with the finance support of the Ministry of Education and Science of the Russian Federation (Contract №14.578.21.0218) Unique ID for Applied Scientific Research (project) RFMEFI57816X0218. The data presented, the statements made, and the views expressed are solely the responsibility of the authors.

References

1. Apache Spark. http://www.spark.apache.org/
2. Kanhere, P., Khanuja, H.K.: A survey on outlier detection in financial transactions. Int. J. Comput. Appl. **17**(108), 23–25 (2014)
3. Keller, J.M., Gray, M.R., Givens, J.A.: A fuzzy k-nearest neighbor algorithm. IEEE Trans. Syst. Man Cybern. **4**(SMC-15), 580–585 (1985). https://doi.org/10.1109/tsmc.1985.6313426
4. Kharote, M., Kshirsagar, V.: Data mining model for money laundering detection in financial domain. Int. J. Comput. Appl. **85**(16), 61–64 (2014). https://doi.org/10.5120/14929-3337
5. Mazeev, A., Semenov, A., Doropheev, D., et al.: Early performance evaluation of supervised graph anomaly detection problem implemented in Apache Spark. In: 3rd Ural Workshop on Parallel, Distributed, and Cloud Computing for Young Scientists (Ural-PDC). CEUR Workshop Proceedings, vol. 1990, Aachen, pp. 84–91 (2017)
6. Michalak, K., Korczak, J.: Graph mining approach to suspicious transaction detection. In: The Federated Conference on Computer Science and Information Systems, Szczecin, Poland, 18–21 September 2011
7. Moll, L.: Anti money laundering under real world conditions—finding relevant patterns. University of Zurich, Department of Informatics, Student-ID: 00-916-932 (2009)
8. Molloy, I., et al.: Graph analytics for real-time scoring of cross-channel transactional fraud. In: Grossklags, J., Preneel, B. (eds.) FC 2016. LNCS, vol. 9603, pp. 22–40. Springer, Heidelberg (2017). https://doi.org/10.1007/978-3-662-54970-4_2
9. The Emergence of AI Regtech Solutions For AML And Sanctions Compliance. https://www.whitecase.com/sites/whitecase/files/files/download/publications/rc_apr17_reprint_white.pdf
10. Pozzolo, A.D., Caelen, O., Borgne, Y.-A.L., et al.: Learned lessons in credit card fraud detection from a practitioner perspective. Expert Syst. Appl. **41**(10), 4915–4928 (2014)
11. Another smart side of artificial intelligence. https://www.bai.org/banking-strategies/article-detail/another-smart-side-of-artificial-intelligence-quashing-the-compliance-crush
12. Artificial Intelligence in KYC-AML: Enabling the Next Level of Operational Efficiency. https://www.celent.com/insights/567701809
13. Semenov, A., Mazeev, A., Doropheev, D., et al.: Survey of common design approaches in AML software development. In: GraphHPC 2017 Conference (GraphHPC). CEUR Workshop Proceedings, vol. 1981, Aachen, pp. 1–9 (2017)
14. Machine Learning: Advancing AML Technology to Identify Enterprise Risk. http://files.acams.org/pdfs/AMLAdvisor/052015/Machine%20Learning%20-%20Advancing%20AML%20Technology%20to%20Identify%20Enterprise%20Risk.pdf
15. Vidiasova, L., Kachurina, P., Cronemberger, F.: Smart cities prospects from the results of the world practice expert benchmarking. In: 6th International Young Scientists Conference in HPC and Simulation, YSC 2017. Procedia Computer Science, Kotka, Finland, 1–3 November 2017
16. Li, Z., Xiong, H., Liu, Y.: Detecting blackholes and volcanoes in directed networks. In: 2010 IEEE International Conference on Data Mining (2010)

Do Russian Consumers Understand and Accept the Sharing Economy as a New Digital Business Model?

Vera Rebiazina[1]([✉]), Anastasia Shalaeva[1], and Maria Smirnova[2]

[1] National Research University Higher School of Economics, Moscow, Russia
{rebiazina, aashalaeva}@hse.ru
[2] Saint-Petersburg State University, Saint Petersburg, Russia
smirnova@gsom.pu.ru

Abstract. Increasing studies on sharing economy address a fast growing and spreading across the world phenomenon. Massive distribution of sharing economy applications contributes to co-evolution of consumer perceptions of the advantages, risks and opportunities of collaborative consumption. Future dynamics and transformation of sharing economy depends on both supply and demand sides of its diffusion as a digital business model. By diversifying the same concept (e.g. UBER) across the countries and contexts providers adapt to business environment, including existing regulation, protective measures, consumer perceptions and expectations. The current study is based on a large-scale survey of Russian consumers, evaluating their experience and expectations in the area of sharing economy in a context of an emerging market. As emerging markets face numerous market inefficiencies, they might be the most active and willing adepts of sharing economy practices. This adoption however is determined by the readiness and ability of both businesses and consumers in emerging market to deploy the full potential of collaborative consumption. Moreover, other determinants might be the differences in sharing economy consumer behavior, expectations and norms in emerging markets.

Keywords: Sharing economy · Digital economy · Collaborative economy
Business model · Consumer behavior

1 Introduction

Identifying the characteristics of consumers' behavior in the sharing (or collaborative) economy (hereafter – SE) remains an urgent issue among both academicians and practitioners due to the increasing importance of various sectors of the SE [57] and the ongoing development of effective SE business models. Despite the significant growth in the number of scientific publications (almost two-fold increase in the number of Scopus publications for the last 4 years), no generally accepted definitions of the terms «sharing economy» and «collaborative economy» exist in the academic literature. Theoretical gaps and the lack of systematization of numerous approaches that often contradict each other not only hinder the correct interpretation of these concepts, but also serve as obstacles to further research.

© Springer Nature Switzerland AG 2018
D. A. Alexandrov et al. (Eds.): DTGS 2018, CCIS 858, pp. 386–401, 2018.
https://doi.org/10.1007/978-3-030-02843-5_31

In addition, the features of consumer behavior in the SE vary significantly across countries and sectors. It is important to note that new digital business models are successfully growing in emerging economies, offering new opportunities for the consumers and changing their perceptions and behavior. The specifics of SE consumers in Russia in the context of emerging markets with just a few exceptions are still understudied. The few existing studies focus predominantly on electronic commerce, other forms of the collaborative economy such as short term/long term real estate renting, car/things sharing, food delivery, rental services are disregarded. Some researchers have addressed the issue of SE as a new business model in Russia, but unrepresentative samples (25 respondents and less) and lack of the methodology description make their findings fragmentary and calling for more substantial and systematic studies.

The purpose of this study is to address SE as a digital business model and its perception by the consumers in a context of the emerging Russian economy. In the course of the theoretical analysis, we systematize existing approaches to understanding the collaborative economy, identify its key components, develop a comprehensive definition of the collaborative economy as a new business model, and describe the factors that affect consumer behavior. The authors also reveal key trends in the global and Russian markets of the collaborative economy. Using online survey data, digital trends among services in the Russian market's sharing economy are highlighted.

2 Approaches to the Study and Definition of the Sharing Economy

The academia's interest in the collaborative economy has been confirmed by the significant growth of publications [24, 25, 31] over the past few decades. The economic model of SE involves sharing, bartering, and renting [3, 4, 9] to access necessary goods, services, and skills instead of owning them. The key idea of the model is that under certain conditions people prefer to have goods/services in temporary or joint use than to become their exclusive owners, thereby reducing the costs of ownership.

The phenomenon of SE, or collaborative consumption, has spread in tandem with the development and rapid growth of information technologies and information culture in various sectors of the world economy, including transport, real estate, finance, tourism, logistics, food delivery, clothing, furniture, rental of electronics equipment, software repositories security, online encyclopedias, crowdfunding platforms, microloans, and others. At the same time, the novelty of collaborative consumption as a socio-economic phenomenon is relative, since many of its elements, for example, public libraries, commission shops, taxis, and rental services for sports equipment, were in operation at the beginning of the last century. Moreover, economic crises in various countries have often served as an accelerator to save money and gain additional income by buying supported goods, reselling things, or offering their temporary use for a fee. The rapid growth of different services of the collaborative consumption in the emerging markets, for instance Russia, is a vivid example.

Due to the lack of a generally accepted definition of the term «sharing economy» in the literature, many concepts and their synonyms could be found (Table 1).

Table 1. Approaches to Define and Conceptualize SE. Source: Compiled by the authors

Approach	Source
Collaborative consumption	[9]
Sharing economy	[4, 27, 28]
Access-based economy	[3, 7, 64]
Peer-to-peer economy	[72]
On-demand economy	[14]
Commercial sharing systems	[39]
Co-production	[31]
Co-creation	[40, 55]
Product-service systems	[44]
Online volunteering	[54]
Anti-consumption	[52]

As Table 1 shows, generally SE can be understood as consumption, borrowing, reuse [42], donation [30, 63], the use of something that was in use, responsible consumption, and altruistic intentions [74]. «Collaborative consumption» focuses on earning money via economic exchange. «Access-based consumption» combines both elements of collaborative economy, sharing economy, and «anti-consumption» [2], where joint consumption stimulates decrease in the consumption rate of similar new products [50, 51, 62]. Since the terms «sharing economy» and «collaborative economy» are usually used as synonyms, here they are also considered as synonymous.

The need to introduce innovations and overcome the consequences of the unstable external environment, the shortcomings of the institutional environment, and growing competition, especially in the emerging economies, has served as an impulse to adopt business models, based on SE. Many goods and services used by consumers within the context of SE have the properties of innovative products; their appearance is associated mainly with the rapid growth of information technologies, especially the Internet. The large value contribution is made not through satisfying the basic need (e.g. transportation), but the way the value is co-created and delivered within the SE business models (e.g. UBER). Crowdsourcing, leasing, low-cost subscription models, and user communities are among the most common business models of the collaborative economy. In general, the organization of the SE by the criterion of market orientation can be divided into commercial and non-commercial, according to the business model – the «Consumer-to-Consumer» (Peer-to-Peer) and «Business-to-Consumer» (Business-to-Peer) models. The typical examples from the Russian market are in Table 2.

Table 2. Classification of the SE Organizations. Source: [61].

Market orientation	Business model	
	Peer-to-Peer	Business-to-Peer
Non profit	Example: 100friends, BashnaBash	Example: Charity projects
For profit	Example: Darenta, Repetitor.ru	Example: Delivery club, BelkaCar, Anytime

SE services in the Russian market demonstrate rapid growth in value and volume. For example, according to the information on the official web sites, the number of cars of Russian car sharing start-up "Belka car" has increased from 100 to 1000 since 2015, compared to 667 cars of Anytime, one of the first Russian car haring service, established in 2012. Both services are supported by the local government as a part of traffic congestion countermeasures in urban planning and development. The merge of local and international taxi service businesses (Yandex and Uber) in Russia in the middle of 2017 and the acquisition of local delivery service Foodfox by Yandex demonstrates the readiness to adapt new business models to develop a «win-win» strategy while entering the new markets. PwC report on emerging markets (2013) outlines that the development of emerging economies not only contributes to the global economic growth but also raise new risks. Lack of infrastructure, high corruption, restricted ownership of different types of assets, political instability and high inflation rates are major challenges of the emerging markets which could be combatted entering businesses by finding a local partner, according to Accenture (2013).

As a result of the generalization of the above approaches, a comprehensive definition of the SE as a new business model is "platform for co-creation of value by participants through consumption, borrowing, reuse, and the donation of goods and services". The proposed definition does not depreciate earlier approaches, but complements them, emphasizing the multifaceted nature of various aspects of consumer interaction in a digital economy. Based on the proposed definition of the SE we agree with one of the definitions of the digital sharing economy developed by the Dalberg Company [13]. Digital sharing is the collaborative consumption of assets through digital platforms by creating additional value without transferring ownership rights between two or more individuals. Crowdfunding is one of the examples of financial digital sharing. Digital sharing could solve such global problems of the emerging economies as illiteracy and a low level of education, poverty, limited access to finance, unemployment of young people, and agricultural productivity. As previous studies have predominantly focused on consumer behavior in the developed economies, understanding the factors of consumer behavior in emerging markets and highlighting disparities between markets is a remarkable area for SE research.

3   Features of Consumer Behavior of the Sharing Economy

Different stages of the purchasing decision-making process in the consumer market have been systematized and disclosed by such authors as Angel, Blackwell, Minard, Kotler, and Armstrong [37, 78]. The theory of planned behavior allows for the identification of the relationship between the beliefs, attitudes, intentions, and actions (behavior) of consumers (the founder is Aizen [1]). Factors behind the success of innovative products among consumers are described using diffusion of innovations theory by Rogers [58]. The issue of the so-called "attitude-behavior gap" [10, 36, 52, 68] (the discrepancy between the intentions and real actions of consumers) deserves special attention for further study of the characteristics of consumer behavior in the SE.

To identify the features and manage consumer behavior in a collaborative economy, it is necessary to consider the factors affecting consumption and correctly identify consumer roles and the social effects in different business models. Consumer motivations, income levels, attitudes and spending patterns vary significantly in emerging and developed markets. In general, the factors that influence consumer behavior in different business models of the SE can be divided into drivers and barriers (Table 3).

Table 3. Factors Affecting the Behavior of Consumers SE. Source: compiled by the authors

Type of factor	Factor	Source
Drivers	Enjoyment from participation	[26, 43, 53, 67]
	Benefits for the environment	
	Financial and economic advantages	[8, 28]
	Modern lifestyle	
	Trust in the service	
	Approval of the reference group (friends, family members, colleagues)	[34, 48, 73]
	Altruism	
	Being part of the community	[29]
	Communication with like-minded people	
	Sustainable development	[38]
	Flexibility and independence	[70]
	Development of social networks	[12]
	Development of information technologies and platforms, and wide access of mobile devices	[6]
Barriers	The need to make an effort to participate	[27]
	The risk of not getting the necessary goods/services at the right time	
	The belief that individuals with a lot of property have higher status in society	
	Lack of trust toward strangers	
	Lack of trust toward the service	
	Hygienic considerations	
	The inability to remain anonymous	[71]

Among the key drivers are: credibility and trust in the service, environmentally friendly approach, enjoyment and ease of use, the possibility to save and earn money, reflection of the modern lifestyle. Lack of trust, the need for additional efforts, access restrictions and hygienic issues are main impediments for participation. Such factors as recommendation of the reference group and preference of ownership are more typical for customers in the developing markets due to market failures and low trust.

Due to the asymmetry of information in the SE markets, such factors as trust should be mentioned with special attention. Numerous researches study trust as a key driver of consumer participation in different services of the collaborative economy [5, 21, 27, 66]. There is also a reverse effect: mistrust is a significant barrier to consumer participation in online transactions [11, 23]. The rapid growth of information technologies and Internet access has contributed to an increase in the degree of consumer confidence in services, reducing the time and financial costs of coordinating users in obtaining reliable information on the experience of using services [35, 59]. For the past decade, Eurostat [19] has been evaluating the 30% increase in the number of European households with Internet access (from 55% to 85%). For example, crowdsourcing of information from participants through Yelp (a service in which consumers leave a review of any purchased product/service) has triggered a decrease in consumer purchases in large retail chains and an increase in sales in small private shops [42]. The main tools for assessing the reputation and increasing consumer confidence in the services of the sharing economy include the system of quantitative assessments. Examples of such assessments are ratings (points, stars, and scales), verification of reviews (photo and video posting), profiles of participants, forums and discussions, and a system of recommendations [61]. Everyday use of social networks also increases the degree of confidence in the services of the sharing economy through the phenomenon of transitivity of trust [33].

Nowadays there is a consumer trust crisis around the world, modern consumers tend to trust other consumers' opinion and do not trust large brands and government bodies due to the recent financial crisis, increasing fees, and market failures. In 2017, the Edelman Trust Barometer (28 countries surveyed) indicated that since 2012 there has been an ongoing decrease in the number of people who trust major institutions such as government and non-governmental organizations, media, and business in the developing and developed economies. Edelman concluded that paying more attention to customer needs and opinions, enhancing product quality and being a human resources brand employer are integral parts of corporate strategy to build consumer trust [22]. There is positive correlation between the awareness of consumer protection and their online purchasing decisions [69].

The digital environment provides advantages and new opportunities for business and consumers. Modern consumers have a state of permanent connectivity (constant access to e-mail, chats, social media, and news.) In comparison to offline shopping, they are digitally empowered by quick and uncomplicated searching information, and are able to immediately compare offers and analyze reviews. According to Eurostat data, 70% of Europeans use the Internet daily [20], 34% of users check their mobile devices in the middle of the night. Approximately 80% of mobile device owners use their smartphones to communicate with friends [17]. Concerning the percentage of online shoppers, the gap between millennials and non-millennials is decreasing [16]. While purchasing goods and services online, consumers expect to get additional value in the form of inspiration, new experience, confidence, protection, simplicity, and ease of use. These intangible outcomes should be relevant to every individual, so almost half of consumers are interested in the customization of goods according to their needs, and two out of 10 consumers are willing to pay a 10% price increase for customization and individualization [15].

Consumer behavior in terms of values, attitudes and motivation is shifting both in emerging and developed economies, it is a well-known fact that every year globalization contributes to increasing similarities and decreasing differences in factors affecting consumer behavior. Euromonitor outlines that in 2018 consumers in European countries tend to prefer access, not ownership, save money, think about the ecology, and spend money on experience rather than things. Collaborative business models are becoming the mainstream. Despite the growing interest to consumer behavior in developing markets, studies on emerging economies are sufficiently present in the literature. Compared to developed countries, the question of such factors as environmental benefits, additional income, cost reduction, attitude of the reference group, trust, ownership status, affecting consumer participation in the collaborative services in developing countries still remains unclear.

4 Collaborative Consumption: International and Russian Perspective

Due to the lack of a unified approach to the definition of the sharing economy and its components, a comprehensive analysis of the market is limited because the values of the indicators vary significantly from source to source. For example, according to the PWC report [57, 58], in 2015, the total revenue of the SE sectors in the European region was €3.6 billion, while Deloitte estimates [18] only the car-sharing service amounted to more than $1 billion. Moreover, most studies have only focused on developed markets, emerging economies have been overlooked despite rapid growth of new SE business models, for instance, ride-sharing services «Didi Chuxing», «Ofo» in China, Indian thing sharing «Rentomojo».

According to the results of the Nielsen's global survey [45], every year the use of collaborative economy services around the world becomes faster, safer and easier for consumers. The cost of complex technologies has been reduced simultaneously with the constant improvement and customization of such technologies to match the growing needs of users. According to the company's estimates, in the framework of the project "Introducing the Connected Spender: The Digital Consumer of the Future" [46], modern consumers have, on average, up to five electronic devices in daily use. The results of the Deloitte 2016 digital influence survey [16] has demonstrated that the rate of retail sales in the world for different types of digital devices increased from 14% in 2013 to 56% in 2016. Under the conditions of digital transformation, a high degree of integration of communication channels into all spheres of consumer life forms an omnichannel environment in which electronic devices perform both basic functions and advanced ones.

In a survey of users of the sharing economy in 60 countries, Nielsen [49] found that the most active users of the collaborative economy are residents of the Asia-Pacific region (there is also the smallest gap between men and women in terms of the number of users); the least active are residents of North America. The most popular services of the collaborative economy in the world (top 5) include electronics rental, private lessons, the lease of tools and equipment, bicycle rental, and clothing rental. According to the report, the availability and wide spread of digital technologies have contributed to a steady increase in the number of users of services among older generations. At the same time, the Internet is the main tool for increasing trust in services all over the world: 69% of users leave feedback about their experience of participation, eight out of 10 users use a smartphone before buying to search for information on the Internet, and during the purchase itself. It is important to emphasize recommendations of the reference group (family members and friends) as another important way to increase the degree of confidence in the services of joint consumption, which was noted by more than half of the users.

The behavior of consumers in the Russian market of the collaborative economy deserves special attention. In 2016 Russia was recognized as one of ten countries with a rapidly developing digital economy [47]. At the same time, only a small number of studies highlight the specifics of consumer behavior in the Russian SE.

According to a 2017 survey by the Regional Center of Internet Technologies, a quarter of Russians actively use the services of the collaborative economy, the most popular of which are Uber, Airbnb, Blablacar, YouDo, and Delimobile. Most respondents emphasized their distrust of services as the main barrier to participation. A study by GFK [76] demonstrates a similar trend: strong brands in the sharing economy market "socialize," building relationships with consumers and increasing their trust. The communication strategies of Uber, Airbnb, Blablacar, YouDo, and Delimobile clearly confirm this.

In general, according to a report by GFK, "Global trends and the Russian consumer 2017," [77] factors affecting the behavior of consumers in Western countries are relevant for Russia. Among the key trends are globalization (unification of consumer behavior), urbanization, and migration (adaptation to new trends and the introduction of national characteristics), the aging of the population (the growth of the number of conservative and less mobile elderly consumers with higher requirements for quality and convenience), the predominance of nuclear families (relatively high income and the restriction of own consumption), the equal distribution of gender roles in purchasing decisions, and the rapid development of digital technologies.

Russia is among the countries that scored 5 on the Digital Sharing Readiness Score (115 countries were analyzed and scored from 1(least ready) to 7 (most ready)). Nevertheless, there is also a lack of quantitative studies devoted to Russia's digital sharing economy. Existing studies predominantly cover Moscow [60] (65% of Moscow's residents use sharing economy services via digital platforms). In 2017, the most popular services were taxi (45%), travelling (44%), and electronic tickets (40%). For the past two years (2015–2017), the total market volume (in rubles) of digital sharing economy services has grown almost fourfold. The main reasons for participation are convenience (8 out of 10 users), time saving (22%), and saving money (13%).

5 An Empirical Study of Consumer Behavior in the Russian Market of Sharing Economy

5.1 Design and Data

In order to identify factors affecting the consumer behavior in Russia as one of the developing market of SE, in autumn 2017 an online survey of 10,000 Russian consumers was conducted. The response rate was ~20%, and the sample includes 2,047 respondents. The structured questionnaire included about 30 questions using nominal and ordinal scales. Questions in the questionnaire, derived from existing literature, can be divided into the following groups: drivers, barriers, individual innovativeness, and socio-demographic characteristics of the respondent. Measurement of agreement or disagreement with specific judgments was carried out according to a Likert scale, ranging from 0 "completely disagree" to 7 "totally agree."

5.2 Findings

The majority of respondents in the survey were young people aged 18 to 35, with higher education, and middle-income individuals, mainly women (72%). Since the majority of respondents live in large Russian cities with a population of more than one million people, where different services of the collaborative economy are widely spread, it is assumed respondents had sufficient awareness and experience of interaction with services. The characteristics of the sample are presented in Table 4.

Young respondents (up to 35 years) and respondents living in large Russian cities tend to use the services based on digital SE business models several times a month, while the older generations (35–60 years) and residents of small towns use the services no more than once in a few months. Respondents with an above-average income do not use services more often than others; just several times a month. Every second respondent has already used rental services (46% of respondents), short-term renting/letting of apartments (44% of respondents), and buying things online (42% of respondents). The frequency of use of digital sharing economy services by type is presented in Table 5.

Taxi services and online shopping are of the greatest interest for future research, four out of 10 respondents have already used the services of Uber, GetTaxi, and Avito; approximately the same number are going to use these services in the future.

In recent decades, the accelerated pace of the digital economy has led to the development of new products and the generation of ideas that are embodied, among other things, indifferent digital services. The digital revolution helps to meet the diverse and increasing needs of people by improving the efficiency of processes and products. Six out of ten respondents in the survey agreed that participation in collaborative consumption is innovative and reflects the modern lifestyle. Three quarters of respondents consider joint consumption a trend that is keeping pace with the times.

However, despite the willingness to participate in digital sharing economy services in the future (60% of respondents are going to rent things in the future) and a relatively high degree of trust in services (60% of respondents), only 30% are ready to rent their own things. The low willingness to participate, according to respondents' answers, is related to the likelihood of risks, hygiene considerations, and personal safety. It is interesting that for a third of respondents to have different goods in ownership is a symbol of high social status; therefore, for this group of Russian consumers, this factor is a barrier to using sharing economy services. Similar results were obtained in a survey of Russian consumers conducted by the Analytical center of the National Agency for Financial Research (NAFI) in the spring of 2016: in spite of the general willingness and active participation in digital sharing economy services, only 17% of Russians are ready to lease their own things [78]. The prospect of savings and the possibility of additional earnings with the help of the services of the sharing economy are not attractive because of security issues and lack of trust in services and other users.

Table 4. Sample characteristics (N = 2047)

Criterion	Type of criterion	N	%
Gender	Male	561	28
	Female	1486	72
Age group	<18	5	0,2
	18–25	760	35,9
	26–30	562	26,6
	31–35	353	16,7
	36–40	177	8,4
	41–50	165	7,8
	51–60	28	1,3
	>60	5	0,2
Education	Primary education	8	,4
	Secondary education	38	1,8
	College degree	63	3,0
	Incomplete higher education	373	17,6
	Higher education (university degree)	1286	60,8
	Higher education in two or more fields	228	10,8
	PhD degree	61	2,9
Income level	Poverty level	67	3,2
	Low income	14	,7
	Lower middle	70	3,3
	Middle	976	46,1
	Upper middle class and high income	611	28,9
	High income	321	15,2
Marital status	Married/Civil marriage	974	46,0
	Divorced	121	5,7
	Not married	957	45,2
Settlement size	>1 million	1396	66,0
	500 000–1 million	256	12,1
	100 000–500 000	234	11,1
	50 000–100 000	62	2,9
	>50 000	51	2,4
	Difficulty answering	50	2,4

Factor analysis of the indicators influencing the behavior of the Russian SE users (n = 1,398) revealed four driver factors (explaining 61.2% of the variance) and three barrier factors (explaining 59.2% of the variance). Among drivers are the benefits associated with participation in the digitalSE; for example, interest, comfort, utility (1), approval by the reference group (family, friends) (2), ecological and environmental benefits (3), and ease of use (4). Barriers include risks associated with participation (hygienic risk, the likelihood of theft, etc.) (1), additional efforts for participation (time and financial costs) (2), and preference for ownership as a reflection of higher social status (3).

Table 5. Frequency of use of digital sharing economy services by type

Service	Respondents have already used the service		Respondents are familiar with the service and have already used the service		Respondents are familiar with the service but are not going to use it		Respondents are not familiar with the service	
	N	%	N	%	N	%	N	%
Car sharing	818	38,7	654	30,9	454	21,5	181	8,6
Things rental	975	46,1	337	15,9	430	20,3	361	17,1
Services rental	1072	50,7	524	24,8	393	18,6	119	5,6
Taxi	765	36,2	1229	58,1	103	4,9	8	0,4
Online shopping	885	41,8	1013	47,9	176	8,3	28	1,3
Intercity trips	886	41,9	452	21,4	452	21,4	314	14,8
Short-term flat rental	935	44,2	967	45,7	182	8,6	24	1,1

5.3 Discussion

The findings are consistent with the results of the literature review and are not country-specific. Re-evaluation of spending habits of modern smart consumers in developed and developing economies is driven by desire to benefit ecologically and environmentally, save time and money, getting more freedom and flexibility through safe and transparent transactions. At the same time, purchasing patterns are not shifting from ownership to experience for Russian consumers, compared to developed countries. Low level of trust in the society is highlighted by the increasing importance of approval by the reference groups in the decision making process to participate in sharing services. Credibility and hygienic risks associated with participation in sharing are still strong barriers for potential users.

6 Conclusion

As a result of theoretical review and systematization of key approaches, the authors developed a comprehensive definition of the SE as a new business model: "the creation of value by participants in interaction through consumption, borrowing, reuse, and donating goods and services that have the properties of innovative products'. The authors identified the most popular business models of the collaborative economy: crowdsourcing, leasing, low-cost, model from product to service, subscription model, and user community.

Based on the analysis of existing studies, key factors that influence consumer behavior in the collaborative consumption in developed and developing economies are categorized under the titles of drivers (high level of trust, environmental protection, cost reduction, additional income, modern lifestyle, and simplicity of use) and barriers (low level of trust, complexity of use, and different kinds of risks). Due to the lack of reliable customer data in emerging markets, most studies have only focused on developed markets, despite the fact that factors affecting consumer behavior in the developing markets every year attracting considerable interest of researchers.

Using online survey data, the authors identified the most popular services for Russian SE consumers. These services include renting services, renting things, renting out/renting apartments from private persons, and buying things online. Such drivers as recommendation of the reference group and preference of ownership as a reflection of higher social status are more typical for emerging markets because of market failures and low level of trust. As the results of empirical research on Russian consumers have shown, in order to build profitable long-term position in the emerging markets, companies in the sector of SE should pay special attention to consumer confidence (credibility and trust), since this factor is one of the most important barriers on the Russian market.

References

1. Ajzen, I.: The theory of planned behavior. Organ. Behav. Hum. Decis. Process. **50**(2), 179–211 (1991). https://doi.org/10.1016/0749-5978(91)90020-T
2. Albinsson, P.A., Yasanthi Perera, B.: Alternative marketplaces in the 21st century: building community through sharing events. J. Consum. Behav. **11**(4), 303–315 (2012). https://doi.org/10.1002/cb.1389
3. Bardhi, F., Eckhardt, G.M.: Access-based consumption: the case of car sharing. J. Consum. Res. **39**(4), 881–898 (2012). https://doi.org/10.1086/666376
4. Belk, R.: You are what you can access: sharing and collaborative consumption online. J. Bus. Res. **67**(8), 1595–1600 (2014). https://doi.org/10.1016/j.jbusres.2013.10.001
5. Bhattacherjee, A.: Individual trust in online firms: scale development and initial test. J. Manag. Inf. Syst. **19**(1), 211–241 (2002). https://doi.org/10.1080/07421222.2002.11045715
6. Black, S.E., Lynch, L.M.: What's driving the new economy? The benefits of workplace innovation. Econ. J. **114**(493), F97–F116 (2004). https://doi.org/10.1111/j.0013-0133.2004.00189.x
7. Böckmann, M. The shared economy: it is time to start caring about sharing; value creating factors in the shared economy. A Bachelor's dissertation at the University of Twente, Faculty of Management and Governance, The Netherlands (2014)
8. Bock, G.W., Zmud, R.W., Kim, Y.G., Lee, J.N.: Behavioral intention formation in knowledge sharing: examining the roles of extrinsic motivators, social-psychological forces, and organizational climate. MIS Q. **29**(1), 87–111 (2005). https://doi.org/10.2307/25148669
9. Botsman, R., Rogers, R.: What's Mine is Yours: How Collaborative Consumption is Changing the Way We Live. Collins, London (2011)
10. Burnett, L.: The Sharing Economy: Where We Go from Here. Leo Burnett Company, Inc. (2014)
11. Chang, M.K., Cheung, W., Tang, M.: Building trust online: interactions among trust building mechanisms. Inf. Manag. **50**(7), 439–445 (2013). https://doi.org/10.1016/j.im.2013.06.003
12. Constantinides, E., Fountain, S.J.: Web 2.0: conceptual foundations and marketing issues. J. Direct Data Digit. Mark. Pract. **9**(3), 231–244 (2008). https://doi.org/10.1057/palgrave.dddmp.4350098

13. Dalberg: Sharing resources, building economies. https://www.digitalsharingeconomy.com/#footnotes

14. De Stefano, V.: The rise of the 'just-in-time workforce': on-demand work, crowd work and labour protection in the gig-economy. Comp. Lab. Law Policy J. **37**(3), 461–471 (2016)

15. Deloitte: Consumer product trends. Navigating 2020. https://www2.deloitte.com/insights/us/en/industry/consumer-products/trends-2020.html

16. Deloitte: The new digital divide. The future of digital influence in retail. https://www2.deloitte.com/insights/us/en/industry/retail-distribution/digital-divide-changing-consumer-behavior.html

17. Deloitte: Global mobile consumer trends 2017. https://www2.deloitte.com/global/en/pages/technology-media-andtelecommunications/articles/gx-global-mobile-consumer-trends.html

18. Deloitte Perspectives: The sharing economy. How much can you earn? https://www2.deloitte.com/us/en/pages/strategy/articles/the-sharing-economy-how-much-can-you-earn.html

19. Eurostat Statistics Explained: Households with internet access and with broadband connection EU-28, 2007–2016. http://ec.europa.eu/eurostat/statistics-explained/index.php/File:Households_with_internet_access_and_with_broadband_connection_EU-28,_2007-2016_(as_%25_of_all_households).png

20. Eurostat Statistics Explained: Digital economy and society statistics – households and individuals. http://ec.europa.eu/eurostat/statistics-explained/index.php/Digital_economy_and_society_statistics_-_households_and_individuals

21. Finley, K.: Trust in the sharing economy: an exploratory study. Centre for Cultural Policy Studies, University of Warwick (2015). http://www2.warwick.ac.uk/fac/arts/theatre_s/cp/research/publications/madiss/ccps_a4_ma_gmc_kf_3.pdf. Accessed 2 2015

22. Forrester: Predictions 2018: the crisis of trust and how smart brands will shape CX in response (2018). https://www.forrester.com/report/Predictions+2018+The+Crisis+Of+Trust+And+How+Smart+Brands+Will+Shape+CX+In+Response/-/E-RES140084

23. Gefen, D., Straub, D.W.: Consumer trust in B2C e-Commerce and the importance of social presence: experiments in e-Products and e-Services. Omega **32**(6), 407–424 (2004). https://doi.org/10.1016/j.omega.2004.01.006

24. Gyimóthy, S.: Business models of the collaborative economy. In: Dredge, D., Gyimóthy, S. (eds.) Collaborative Economy and Tourism. TV, pp. 31–39. Springer, Cham (2017). https://doi.org/10.1007/978-3-319-51799-5_3

25. Gyimóthy, S., Dredge, D.: Definitions and mapping the landscape in the collaborative economy. In: Dredge, D., Gyimóthy, S. (eds.) Collaborative Economy and Tourism. TV, pp. 15–30. Springer, Cham (2017). https://doi.org/10.1007/978-3-319-51799-5_2

26. Hamari, J., Sjöklint, M., Ukkonen, A.: The sharing economy: why people participate in collaborative consumption. J. Assoc. Inf. Sci. Technol. **67**(9), 2047–2059 (2016)

27. Hartl, B., Hofmann, E., Kirchler, E.: Do we need rules for "what's mine is yours"? Governance in collaborative consumption communities. J. Bus. Res. **69**(8), 2756–2763 (2016). https://doi.org/10.1016/j.jbusres.2015.11.011

28. Hawlitschek, F., Teubner, T., Gimpel, H.: Understanding the sharing economy–drivers and impediments for participation in peer-to-peer rental. In: 49th Hawaii International Conference on System Sciences (HICSS), pp. 4782–4791 (2016)

29. Heinrichs, H.: Sharing economy: a potential new pathway to sustainability. Gaia **22**(4), 228–231 (2013). https://doi.org/10.14512/gaia.22.4.5

30. Hennig-Thurau, T., Henning, V., Sattler, H.: Consumer file sharing of motion pictures. J. Mark. **71**(4), 1–18 (2007). https://doi.org/10.1509/jmkg.71.4.1

31. Hibbert, S., Horne, S.: Giving to charity: questioning the donor decision process. J. Consum. Mark. **13**(2), 4–13 (1996). https://doi.org/10.1108/07363769610115366

32. Humphreys, A., Grayson, K.: The intersecting roles of consumer and producer: a critical perspective on co-production, co-creation and prosumption. Sociol. Compass **2**(3), 963–980 (2008). https://doi.org/10.1111/j.1751-9020.2008.00112.x
33. Hwang, J., Hwang, J., Griffiths, M.A., Griffiths, M.A.: Share more, drive less: millennials value perception and behavioral intent in using collaborative consumption services. J. Consum. Mark. **34**(2), 132–146 (2017). https://doi.org/10.1108/JCM-10-2015-1560
34. Josang, A., Ismail, R., Boyd, C.: A survey of trust and reputation systems for online service provision. Decis. Support Syst. **43**(2), 618–644 (2007). https://doi.org/10.1016/j.dss.2005.05.019
35. Kankanhalli, A., Tan, B.C., Wei, K.K.: Contributing knowledge to electronic knowledge repositories: an empirical investigation. MIS Q. 113–143 (2005). https://doi.org/10.2307/25148670
36. Keymolen, E.: Trust and technology in collaborative consumption. Why it is not just about you and me. In: Bridging Distances in Technology and Regulation, pp. 135–150 (2013)
37. Kollmuss, A., Agyeman, J.: Mind the gap: why do people act environmentally and what are the barriers to pro-environmental behavior? Environ. Educ. Res. **8**(3), 239–260 (2002)
38. Kotler, P., Armstrong, G.: Principles of Marketing. Pearson education (2010). https://doi.org/10.1080/13504620220145401
39. Kramer, M.R.: Creating shared value. Harv. Bus. Rev. (2011)
40. Lamberton, C.P., Rose, R.L.: When is ours better than mine? A framework for understanding and altering participation in commercial sharing systems. J. Mark. **76**(4), 109–125 (2012). https://doi.org/10.1509/jm.10.0368
41. Lanier, C.D., Schau, H.J., Muniz, A.M.: Write and wrong: ownership, access and value in consumer co-created online fan fiction. In: Advances in Consumer Research–North American Conference Proceedings, pp. 697–698 (2007)
42. Lessig, L.: Remix: Making Art and Commerce Thrive in the Hybrid Economy. Penguin (2015). https://doi.org/10.5040/9781849662505
43. Luca, M.: Reviews, reputation, and revenue: the case of Yelp.com. Harvard Business School NOM Unit Working Paper 12-016, 1-40 (2011). https://doi.org/10.2139/ssrn.1928601
44. Moeller, S., Wittkowski, K.: The burdens of ownership: reasons for preferring renting. Manag. Serv. Qual.: Int. J. **20**(2), 176–191 (2010). https://doi.org/10.1108/09604521011027598
45. Mont, O.K.: Clarifying the concept of product–service system. J. Clean. Prod. **10**(3), 237–245 (2002). https://doi.org/10.1016/S0959-6526(01)00039-7
46. Nielsen: What's next in tech? http://www.nielsen.com/content/dam/nielsenglobal/apac/docs/reports/2017/nielsen_whats_next_in_tech_report.pdf
47. Nielsen: Webinar: introducing the connected spender. http://www.nielsen.com/us/en/insights/webinars/2017/webinar-introducing-the-connected-spender.html
48. Nielsen: Global connected commerce. Report January 2016. https://www.nielsen.com/content/dam/nielsenglobal/jp/docs/report/2016/Nielsen-Global-Connected-Commerce-Report-January-2016
49. Nielsen: Global trust in advertising report, September 2015. https://www.nielsen.com/content/dam/nielsenglobal/apac/docs/reports/2015/nielsen-global-trust-in-advertising-report-september-2015.pdf
50. Nielsen: Is sharing the new buying? Report May 2014. http://www.nielsen.com/content/dam/nielsenglobal/apac/docs/reports/2014/Nielsen-Global-Share-Community-Report.pdf
51. Ozanne, L.K., Ballantine, P.W.: Sharing as a form of anti-consumption? An examination of toy library users. J. Consum. Behav. **9**(6), 485–498 (2010). https://doi.org/10.1002/cb.334

52. Ozanne, L.K., Ozanne, J.L.: A child's right to play: the social construction of civic virtues in toy libraries. J. Public Policy Mark. **30**(2), 264–278 (2011). https://doi.org/10.1509/jppm.30.2.264

53. Phipps, M., et al.: Understanding the inherent complexity of sustainable consumption: a social cognitive framework. J. Bus. Res. **66**(8), 1227–1234 (2013). https://doi.org/10.1016/j.jbusres.2012.08.016

54. Piscicelli, L., Cooper, T., Fisher, T.: The role of values in collaborative consumption: insights from a product-service system for lending and borrowing in the UK. J. Clean. Prod. **97**, 21–29 (2015). https://doi.org/10.1016/j.jclepro.2014.07.032

55. Postigo, H.: Emerging sources of labor on the internet: the case of America online volunteers. Int. Rev. Soc. Hist. **48**(S11), 205–223 (2003). https://doi.org/10.1017/S0020859003001329

56. Prahalad, C.K., Ramaswamy, V.: Co-creation experiences: the next practice in value creation. J. Interact. Mark. **18**(3), 5–14 (2004). https://doi.org/10.1002/dir.20015

57. PWC: Assessing the size and presence of the collaborative economy in Europe, April 2016. http://ec.europa.eu/DocsRoom/documents/16952/attachments/1/translations/en/renditions/native

58. PWC: Future of the sharing economy in Europe (2016). https://www.pwc.co.uk/issues/megatrends/collisions/sharingeconomy/future-of-the-sharing-economy-in-europe-2016.html

59. Rogers, E.M.: Diffusion of innovations. The Free (1995)

60. Sharing economy in Russia 2017 Workshop. https://runet-id.com/event/sharingeconomy17/

61. Schifferes, J.: Shopping for Shared Value. RSA, London (2014)

62. Schor, J.B., Fitzmaurice, C.J.: Collaborating and connecting: the emergence of the sharing economy. In: Handbook of Research on Sustainable Consumption, vol. 410 (2015)

63. Shaw, D., Newholm, T.: Voluntary simplicity and the ethics of consumption. Psychol. Mark. **19**(2), 167–185 (2002). https://doi.org/10.1002/mar.10008

64. Strahilevitz, M., Myers, J.G.: Donations to charity as purchase incentives: how well they work may depend on what you are trying to sell. J. Consum. Res. **24**(4), 434–446 (1998). https://doi.org/10.1086/209519

65. Stokes, K., Clarence, E., Anderson, L., Rinne, A.: Making sense of the UK collaborative economy, pp. 1–47. Nesta (2014). http://www.collaboriamo.org/media/2014/10/making_sense_of_the_uk_collaborative_economy_14.pdf

66. Think With Google: Digital Impact on In-Store Shopping: Research Debunks Common Myths. https://www.thinkwithgoogle.com/consumer-insights/digital-impact-on-in-store-shopping/

67. Tussyadiah, I.P.: An exploratory study on drivers and deterrents of collaborative consumption in travel. In: Tussyadiah, I., Inversini, A. (eds.) Information and Communication Technologies in Tourism 2015, pp. 817–830. Springer, Cham (2015). https://doi.org/10.1007/978-3-319-14343-9_59

68. Van der Heijden, H.: User acceptance of hedonic information systems. MIS Q. 695–704 (2004). https://doi.org/10.2307/25148660

69. Vătămănescu, E.M., Nistoreanu, B.G., Mitan, A.: Competition and consumer behavior in the context of the digital economy. Amfiteatru Econ. **19**, 354–366 (2017)

70. Vermeir, I., Verbeke, W.: Sustainable food consumption: exploring the consumer "attitude–behavioral intention" gap. J. Agric. Environ. Ethics **19**(2), 169–194 (2006). https://doi.org/10.1007/s10806-005-5485-3

71. Venkatesh, V., Morris, M.G., Davis, G.B., Davis, F.D.: User acceptance of information technology: toward a unified view. MIS Q. 425–478 (2003). https://doi.org/10.2307/30036540

72. Venkatesh, V., Thong, J., Xu, X.: Consumer acceptance and use of information technology: extending the unified theory of acceptance and use of technology. MIS Q. **36**(1), 157–178 (2012)

73. Vishnumurthy, V., Chandrakumar, S., Sirer, E.G.: KARMA: a secure economic framework for peer-to-peer resource sharing. In: Workshop on Economics of Peer-to-Peer Systems, vol. 35, no. 6 (2003)

74. Wasko, M.M., Faraj, S.: Why should I share? Examining social capital and knowledge contribution in electronic networks of practice. MIS Q. 35–57 (2005). https://doi.org/10.2307/25148667

75. Young, W., Hwang, K., McDonald, S., Oates, C.J.: Sustainable consumption: green consumer behaviour when purchasing products. Sustain. Dev. **18**(1), 20–31 (2010)

76. GFK Rus: Obzor dokladov yezhegodnoy konferentsii 13 oktyabrya 2017 goda. http://www.gfk.com/en/insaity/news/obzor-dokladov-ezhegodnoi-konferencii-gfk/

77. GFK Rus: Global'nyye tendentsii i rossiyskiy potrebitel' (2017). https://www.r-trends.ru/netcat_files/526/459/Gfk_Global_Russian_Trends_Sep_2017_Report.pdf

78. NAFI: Internet-uslugi dlya puteshestviy. 14 iyulya 2016 goda. https://nafi.ru/analytics/internet-servisy-dlya-puteshestviy/

Import Countries Ranking with Econometric and Artificial Intelligence Methods

Alexander Raikov[1]([✉]) [iD] and Viacheslav Abrosimov[2] [iD]

[1] Institute of Control Sciences, Russian Academy of Sciences,
Profsoyuznaya St., 65, Moscow 117997, Russia
Alexander.N.Raikov@gmail.com
[2] Smart Solutions Samara, 17, Moskovskoe sh, 12th floor,
Samara 443013, Russia

Abstract. This paper addresses the issue of creating the methodology that could help to answer the question about assessing the effects of a given export policy. The new approach for constructing and calculating the import countries ranking is proposed. The peculiarity of such problems lies in the weakly formalised set of factors that define the import rank of every country. The question is also complicated by the excessive flow of information which may be unreliable and contradictory. Therefore, the possibilities of statistical methods to support the solution of such a problem are limited. To forecast and support export solutions for the short and medium term, the concept of "Rank of the country's import priority" (Priority Index, PI) is introduced. It is built on historical data with applying the econometric methods. For the medium and long-term perspective and for taking into account non-quantitative factors, it is suggested using the methods of networked expertise (e-expertise), cognitive modelling, artificial intelligence (AI), inverse problems solving on cognitive model with genetic algorithms, and Deep Learning.

Keywords: Artificial intelligence · Cognitive modelling · Deep learning
Import prioritisation · Econometric methods

1 Introduction

In recent years, detailed export policy analysis has become increasingly demanding. During the early stages of the export planning, it is required to assess the effects of various action scenarios and to create proposals. A careful examination of the proposals with computer modelling is necessary to assess the effects of different decisions about tariff commitments.

The key question of the paper is to assess the effects of a given export policy and which methodology is best suited to answer this question. The suitable methodology has to be built or selected. The selection process involves choosing between statistics and modelling approaches, econometric methods and cognitive simulation, between ex-ante and ex-post assessments, general (including stochastic) [1, 2] and partial equilibrium [3]. The modelling approaches are typically used to answer "what if" and "what

© Springer Nature Switzerland AG 2018
D. A. Alexandrov et al. (Eds.): DTGS 2018, CCIS 858, pp. 402–414, 2018.
https://doi.org/10.1007/978-3-030-02843-5_32

needs to be done" questions. Ex-post approaches, wherein, can also answer these questions when past relations continue to be relevant.

Partial equilibrium modelling focuses on specific markets or products, ignoring the connection between the incomes and expenditures factor. General equilibrium modelling takes into account all links between different sectors of an economy: government, business, households, and global world.

Various factors are taken into account during modelling, like, for example, the factor of non-tariff regulation. This factor is taken into account in various modifications of the classical gravitational model. For example, as an additional variable in the gravitational equation, multilateral resistance (neighboring countries with the importing country) is introduced, varying in time [4], and a modification of the model for panel data is proposed in [5, 6].

There are as large a number of countries and industry products, as there are large amounts of open statistical information, and the question of automating the process of identifying the priorities of foreign trade stands by itself. However, traditional econometric models use statistical instruments, and sometimes they come without confidence information and intervals. Simulation modelling, as usual, is based on drawing information from different sources and has to be calibrated with the data of a reference years. But the sources could be discredited, as some parts of the model's parameters have to be estimated with networked expertise technology [7].

The urgency of resolving this issue does not subside. The reason is the need for constant rechecking of econometric models, as well as searching for non-standard solutions in the strategic planning of foreign trade, usually characterised by the need to achieve ambitious goals with finding inverse problem solutions that are unstable and may give many different local decisions.

This paper addresses the issue of forecasting and determining priority foreign markets for the export of products, taking different modelling features and restrictions into account. Priority foreign markets are understood as the markets of the highest export interest, characterised by high growth rates (more than 10% per year) of demand for industrial products. The paper proposes a comprehensive scientific and methodical approach to planning foreign trade, considering the strategic nature of the plans and the participation of expert groups in the strategic processes.

2 Basic Provisions

The priority country for export (the importing country) must have a set of positive political, economic and ideological features that create the most favourable conditions for ensuring the effective and efficient export of industrial products to this country. The following are the defining factors for choosing the importing country:

- In the field of politics:
  - (a) The positive relations between countries (conclusion of agreements, tourist activities, interaction of business, mutual exchange of opinions, visits, and etc.);
  - (b) Domestic policy predictability;

(c) Confirmation of the high accuracy of earlier made forecasts of the development of international relations;

- In the field of economy - significant demand for imports of a certain type of products, a dynamic increase in imports;
- In the field of geography - its territorial proximity to the Russian Federation (reducing transport costs, convenient and predictable logistics);
- In the methodological field - the possibility of constructing comprehensive (holistic) computer models to support the adoption of both tactical and strategic solutions with relatively low indicators of political and financial-economic risks.

The first three of these features are mainly determined by the presence of representative and reliable information – the latter, by building a proper methodological approach to modelling. Concerning the availability of raw data, it should be noted that, despite the external availability and openness of information about the world's countries, many of the necessary data are either specified indirectly (as part of more general characteristics) or absent, even in paid databases. For example, it is difficult to consider the full range of issues related to the semantic content of agreements between organisations involved in transport (sea, rail, etc.).

It is necessary to distinguish the classical scientific approach and real practice. For classical scientific calculations, it is permissible not to include in the analysis the indicators that differ in the low reliability of the values. On the other hand, it is possible to make certain assumptions that simplify or make the various calculations more vivid. For example, for small samples of data, it can be assumed that there is an a priori probability distribution of the parameter values; a symmetric form of external disturbances is given when performing a linear regression. With the so-called "noisy" observational data, statistical methods for minimising the average risk can be used. But their validity in theory is largely based on the use of a large set of observations (representative sampling).

In actual practice, with a small sample of observations and the presence of non-quantitative parameters, the use of traditional statistical methods is rather limited. The use of a purely classical approach in real practice can lead to large errors. To ensure the integrity of the methodology, to exclude cases of omission of the influence of important parameters, it is necessary to appeal to the system approach, which involves the use of a comprehensive set of approaches and methods. Therefore, in this paper, the following requirements were formulated.

It is necessary to apply both fundamental and technical analysis of the market. Moreover, if the former is used more effectively for building a long-term forecast and making a strategic decision, the latter is used to assess the dynamics of the current situation and to make short- and medium-term decisions. At the same time, technical analysis of the market can be used to build a strategic forecast – through a step-by-step recalculation of parameters; but such a forecast will be only extrapolating.

The fundamental parameters of the market can be taken into account, for example, using the macroeconomic theory and the approach of dynamic stochastic general equilibrium [1] with the final decision-making based on expert procedures and cognitive modelling (see Sect. 5).

Technical parameters of the market should be taken into account on the basis of the construction of the corresponding "Rank of the country's import priority" or *Priority Index* (PI) with using the econometric theory focused on the theoretical-quantitative and empirical-quantitative approaches, an application of statistics, a set of regression tools (for example, linear regression), along with various modifications of the gravitational approach, and so forth.

Currently, econometrics increases its capabilities by using methods of artificial intelligence (AI), big data analysis, data mining and neural-like deep learning models. In AI approaches, the knowledge is formulated, first of all, as: (a) the need of the importing country in the products of the exporting country; (b) willingness to enter into relevant international contracts. Such information is able to be extracted from accessible sources with AI. Reducing the problem of extracting knowledge to traditional statistical data processing and forming the corresponding long-term trends only turned out to be incorrect due to the high dynamics of political, economic and trade processes. The solution to the problem requires the development of algorithms for accounting of various and constantly changing factors, most of which are difficult to formalise.

The PI construction was carried out by considering the following features of the problem:

- Representative statistical information is periodically updated and the time series may have relatively small data heterogeneities (allowing piecewise linear approximation in the implementation of regression analysis);
- The model can be trained both by classical and heuristic methods on the available training data;
- The final (optimal) list of parameters for inclusion in the priority index is forming on the basis of the correlation analysis and estimation of data variability;
- The model has to be regular testing with possible re-training and correction of factors and parameters;
- The final decision on market prioritisation is carried out with the connection of cognitive modelling and experts' procedures (see Sect. 5);
- Methods of technical analysis have to be developed by the use of AI, Big Data analysis, and Deep Learning technologies.

3 PI Components

The creation of PI can take into account the maximum possible number of orthogonal factors. The number of factors is reduced by standard procedures of correlation and factor analysis. It is well-known that it is difficult to make semantic interpretation of a large number of factors. Excessive complication of PI is inexpedient. It is important to emphasise that not all factors are decisive. The main factors can be identified using the method of principal components and factor analysis, the construction of eigenvectors, and so forth.

It is also necessary to face the possibility of a high level of data fluctuation, when the parameters of the consumer characteristics of a certain market segment can change significantly and quickly. For example, the value of a number of parameters may change by more than 30% within a few months. Then, in the case of a fairly representative sample of data, a randomised algorithm of the stochastic approximation will be required, taking into account input perturbations to solve the problem of clustering data generated by a mixture of different probability distributions for unknown but limited interference. Such an algorithm, in addition to its resistance to external disturbances, should allow processing of streaming data practically "in real time" and have a high rate of convergence of the values of the model parameters during training. In the future, it will be possible to envisage the use of such an algorithm for tuning neural networks of deep learning through the possible replacement of this algorithm with a deep neural network.

It is also necessary to consider the possibility of influencing the development of the market situation of non-quantitative factors:

- Predictability of the importing country's economy;
- Political preferences of the leaders of industries;
- The religious affiliation of project managers;
- Ethical characteristics of countries;
- Level of development of expert activity, etc.

These factors can be taken into account with the use of cognitive modelling. The main provisions of this method - see Sect. 5.3. In this paper, use of the method of cognitive modelling with the solution of the inverse problem on the cognitive graph was proposed. In the cognitive model, the number of factors should not exceed 10–12 factors. A greater number of factors would be inappropriate, since in cognitive modelling, the mutual influence of factors has to be taken into account, and, consequently, the complexity of the model grows in a quadratic dependence on the number of factors.

During PI constructing, the following methodological features was considering:

- Different types of variables;
- Normalisation of variables;
- Comparison of variables of the same nature;
- Inadmissibility of the some mathematical operations;
- The need to determine the part, the fraction of the quantities;
- Proportionality accounting of changing the values of indicators trends;
- Introduction of weighting coefficients.

As a result, it is possible and appropriate to use a combination of available and weakly-correlated (orthogonal) variables, reduced to conventional units and a single domain of definition in the PI formula. This makes it possible to automate the process of preparing information for making a final decision on the basis of a comparative choice between the alternatives' scenarios.

For constructing PI, selection requirements included countries' parameters that are available for analysis, are isolated and are not a subject for significant influence of short-term and random fluctuations of the market. This problem is solved by eliminating less significant parameters. These parameters also include characteristics related to the political structure of the country, confessional preferences, ethical systems, and so forth. These parameters can be taken into account in the final decision-making, as above mentioned, using expert procedures and cognitive modelling (see Sect. 5).

4 Initial PI Formula

To assess the priority of import countries and products on the market, an initial formula for calculating the PI was created. At the same time, it was taken into account that during this formula, operating it may be regular and permanent modernising for growing the quality of forecasting and decision-making. The following initial formula for the PI was proposed:

$$
PI_n^m = \frac{V_{pot}^{n,m}}{\max\limits_{n,m}\left(V_{pot}^{n,m}\right)} \times \frac{\left(1 + \dfrac{\delta V_n^m - \overline{\delta V_n^m}}{\max\limits_{n,m}\left(\delta V_n^m\right) - \min\limits_{n,m}\left(\delta V_n^m\right)}\right)}{2}
$$

$$
\times \left(1 - \frac{Dist^m}{\max\limits_{m}(Dist^m)}\right) \times \frac{\sum_{k=1}^{K} k^m}{K} \times \frac{1}{EH^m},
$$

where m = {1, M}, *M* is the number of countries, n = {1, N}, *N* is the quantity of goods. It takes into account several key factors.

The *Export potential reserve* describes the first significantly influencing factor and is defined as the $\delta V_n^m = V_{pot}^{n,m} - V_{fact}^{n,m}$, where $V_{pot}^{n,m}$ - is the export potential, $V_{fact}^{n,m}$ - the actual volume of exports expressed in absolute monetary terms for the goods *n* of the country *m*. The difference in the export potential and the actual volume of exports is an indicator that characterises the potential possibility of increasing the export of the product for the selected country. The export potential reserve is presented in a standardised form in the formula, for which its value is divided into the maximum possible value of the export potential reserves for various goods in different countries. Thus, the first factor can take a value at the half-interval (0; 1]. The indicator actually means the interest of the potential country importer to the commodity *n*: The more the reserve potential of the commodity export *n* in the country *m*, the more the factor is closer to 1.

The second factor $\dfrac{\left(1 + \dfrac{\delta V_n^m - \overline{\delta V_n^m}}{\max\limits_{n,m}\left(\delta V_n^m\right) - \min\limits_{n,m}\left(\delta V_n^m\right)}\right)}{2}$ shows *Degree of deviation of the Export potential reserve of the country's N goods*. The semantic interpretation of this factor consists in reflecting the possible originality of the goods for the country market, the appropriateness of paying more attention to it when making an export decision. This factor also takes a value at the half-interval (0; 1]. The numerator of the fraction enclosed in brackets determines the magnitude of the possible deviation of the Export potential reserve of commodity *n* of country *m* from its average value made for all goods and countries. The denominator of the fraction specifies the possible maximum difference of the export potential for all goods and countries, and, thus, ensures the normalisation of the possible magnitude of the deviation of the export potential of commodity *n* of country *m* from the average value. This fraction can be a negative or a positive value. However, the addition of the fraction in the brackets with 1 and then dividing into 2 always leaves a positive value of this factor.

The third factor $\left(1 - \dfrac{\text{Dist}^m}{\max_m(\text{Dist}^m)}\right)$ characterises *the remoteness of the country m for exports*. This factor is also normalised and takes values on the half-open interval (0;1] - the closer the market, the closer the factor to 1. Indeed, with the maximum distance of the market, the fraction approaches the maximum value, and the value of the whole factor approaches 0. The value of this factor characterises the complication logistics, the cost of delivering the export goods to the country of the potential importer. The parameter Dist^m is the distance to the importing country. The factor takes into account both the transport costs of moving the goods, export barriers [8] and implicitly external process duration of delivery. This parameter is generated according to the orientation of reliable information.

The fourth factor $\dfrac{\sum_{k=1}^{K} k^m}{K}$ characterises the *Level of development of economic relations* with the importing country m, which is determined by the availability of relevant agreements with that country. Such statistical information is available. In this paper, K is the total number of possible trade agreements between organisations of the countries. Proceeding from the fact that the value of this factor is at the half-interval (0; 1], the highest priority is given to the country actively cooperating with the importing country (the more agreements, the closer the parameter is closer to 1).

The fifth factor - $\dfrac{1}{\text{EH}^m}$ determines the *Work Risk* in the market of the selected country. It is determined by the version of the country risk indicator of Euler Hermes [9]. It is generally recognised that the Euler Hermes indicator fairly faithfully at the international level reflects the so-called "commercial risks" of working with a potential country for interaction. This indicator takes into account the history of export credits, their careful execution, bankruptcy of countries and buyers. The risk was estimated in the range from 1 to 4. Using the reverse fraction and placing the indicator Euler Hermes in the denominator, it is possible to assess the risks of exports to a given country of any kind of goods. The value of this factor is also in the half-interval (0; 1].

Thus, all the considered factors, represented by the corresponding factors, have different dimensions and are essentially different. Therefore, they are all normalised to bring the values to the half-interval (0; 1]. The obtained formula makes it possible to compare and rank the priority of products and countries in the international product market automatically. However, in the PI applying process, it should be provided with its permanent assessment and, if necessary, modification ensuring the quality of the estimates. For example, import ranking of the countries for a certain market segment could be ranked (see Table 1).

Table 1. Import ranking of the countries

Name of the country	PI	Export potential *(US$)*	Growth rate *(US$ per year)*
Country 1	0.42	6,115,791,215	314,442
Country 2	0.31	4,451,907,114	177,330
...			

The decision of determining the ranks of the importing countries according to the degree of their prioritisation in the export of products with the PI-formula is new. No country in the world discloses the specifics of the national approach of determining its priorities, referring only to well-known and generally accepted models of world trade and the model of export-import. The methods previously used and known were mainly oriented on the analysis of statistical data, corrected according to information provided through official channels by representatives of the exporting country in the importing countries. The errors in the estimates using these methods were significant. Experience shows that experts working in potential importing countries evaluate the logistics component, transport difficulties, the impact of non-tariff measures very roughly because these parameters are formed outside of the experts' field of activity. The proposed PI-formula generalises the influence of various factors, including hidden ones. In addition, during calculating the formula, it is possible to avoid the subjectivity of the view on the country's export potential, so the situation is taken into account in many countries at once.

The expert approach to such a characteristic as *Work risk* is not always correct; here the spread of estimates can reach 50 percent (50%) or more. That's why the authors came to the conclusion about the possibility of using the world-recognised indicator Euler Hermes. In the future it is planned to replace it with coefficients reflecting the dependencies of this risk on time, obtained as a result of modeling international relations using methods of big data analysis and deep learning.

5   PI Adjustment and Modification

The proposed methodology allowed firstly reducing the problem to simple formula (see Sect. 4). The analysis of the practice of concluding international agreements over the last 7 years has shown that the adequacy of the choice of priority countries is rather high (the error was less than 20%), and it varies significantly by years due to the sharp variability of political factors. Forecast jumps remind candlestick patterns in Forex trading. Further development of the methodology in the direction of using AI approaches, such as: network expertise, cognitive modelling, fuzzy and genetic algorithms, soft computing, hierarchy analysis, as shown in the paper, will significantly reduce the error of assessing the prioritisation of countries.

The most important sign of the expediency of using AI methods was also the need to analyse unstructured data. In solving traditional assessment problems of the country's export potential the following problems arose: (a) significant information noise (media information, social networks, independent and engaged experts, etc.); (b) the lack of national information due to the weak attention of the government services of the exporting countries to the formation and updating of relevant databases containing statistics and necessary classifications; (c) orientation of existing methods of data analysis for the processing of primarily numerical information. This observation allowed to formulate promising directions for the development of the topic with using of AI method, including networked expertise (e-expertise), neural networks, deep learning, cognitive modelling, genetic algorithm, and the analytic hierarchy methods.

5.1 Networked Expertise

The PI formula could be modified during the exploitation process and additional factors could be included in the formula. For example, in the fourth factor it may be possible to include the parameter of the rate of change of the number of agreements during a year.

It is advisable to conduct appropriate expert procedures technology [9]. Various export potential experts can interpret differently: on resources, dynamically, on the performance of export activities. The final assessment of the export potential and the decision-making on the basis of experts' estimations makes the industry leadership. The experts include:

- Heads and leadership of public authorities;
- Leading experts of the industry;
- Experienced professionals in foreign trade;
- Foreign consumers of products.

The networked expert technologies for decision-making are illustrated with Fig. 1.

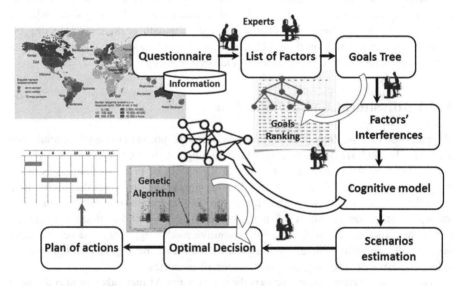

Fig. 1. The networked expert technology for decision-making support.

The following expert-analytical technologies could be recommended:

- Questionnaires with an assignment for each issue or individual questions of assessment (semantic, fuzzy, graded, etc.) scales and subsequent conceptual modeling of the situation;
- Networked expert meetings. The participants of the meeting are exchanging multimedia messages; formulate goals and ways of achieving them.

The networked expert technology for decision-making support uses the following methods:

- Neural networks (NN) and Deep Learning (DL);
- Cognitive modelling;
- Genetic algorithm;
- Analytic hierarchy method.

5.2   NN and DL

The basic idea of PI improving is to use NN for constructing semantic interpretation of the integrated set of parameters, characteristics, countries, factors, events, situations, precedents, solutions and other concepts [10]. Connections between neurons and neural ensembles can be changed with DL methods. The tools for DL based on Big Data analysis and multilayered NN methods are described in detail in [11].

During the formation of this recommendation such features of collective decision making as the possibility of temporary disruption of training data, the uniqueness of the forecasted situation, the incorrectness (inverse nature) of solved problems, the uncertainty of the situations and the qualitative nature of the factors (which necessitates the use of methods of cognitive modelling), interactive and expert character of the final decision on export of products. At the same time, data sets (documents, messages, photographs, records of negotiations, etc.), which describe different market situations descriptively, can differ greatly from each other.

The approach with a *Recurrent Neural Network* (RNN) was chosen as the basis of the deep neural network. This is a type of NN with feedback, which implies the connection between the elements of NN, located at different distances from the exit. It specifies the network topology and the activation function; but the weights of the bonds and the displacement of the neurons are learned. In a RNN neurons can be supplied with a gate system and long-term memory. Gates distribute the information in the neural structure; indicate the rules of mashing and the requirements for the formation of the result for the delivery of RNN at each step. A RNN provides work with different language models and an assessment of the context and word associations in the texts. In RNN special attention is paid to the aspects of dynamic management of time scales and behaviour of forgetting state blocks, optimisation in a context of long-term dependencies, quality indicators, debugging, training strategies, and etc. special issues.

For decision-making support in the field of export activities it is possible to recommend the LSTM-network (*long short-term method*). The LSTM-network is well-suited for tasks of classifying, processing and forecasting time series in cases where important events are separated by time lags with uncertain duration and boundaries. LSTM-network is well-integrated with cognitive models, allowing their verification and automated synthesis.

The choice of the LSTM network is also supported by the fact that leading technology companies, including Google, Apple, Microsoft, and others use the LSTM-network as a fundamental component of new products. Thus, the choice of such a network will ensure its appropriate semantic interoperability with other components of the digital tools that support foreign economic activity.

5.3   Cognitive Modelling

To optimise export activities, the creation of formal quantitative models based on methods of econometrics and analysis of quantitative data from historical databases may not be sufficient. This can happen if there is a need for a drastic change in the sales development strategy, when unexpected steps are taken into account in the process of diversification, shocks in the markets, in the absence of necessary statistical information, etc. For situations of this type, latency, chaotic, uncertainty, description of the situation on the qualitative level, ambiguity of consequences of these or those decisions.

In this case cognitive modelling methods can be used, which are based on the development of models for the situations that take into account not only the previous statistical experience and the uncertainty of the real situation, but also the qualitative specificity of the processes occurring in it in conditions of instability of the environment [12]. Cognitive modelling provides:

- Representation of the problem situation in the form of a structured set of up to several concepts (factors) and their mutual influences;
- Formation of cause-effect diagrams to reflect the dynamics of behaviour of inter-related factors;
- Assessment of management impacts on events, indicating the results of the evaluation on the time schedule.

5.4   Genetic Algorithm

The software for genetic modelling is designed to solve inverse problems, eliminating the repeated manual repetition of the procedure for evaluating control actions on the cognitive model [12]. Genetic modelling should allow in uncertain situations quickly and systematically justify the current situation and at a qualitative level helps suggesting the best options for influencing factors to solve the problem. Genetic modelling can be implemented in the following order:

- The cognitive model is constructed (see Sect. 5.3);
- Genetic optimisation of the model (operations of crossing, reproduction, mutation) by determining the change in the values of factors that provide the least cost to achieve the goals;
- Dynamics of optimisation is traced, the functional of quality is calculated (fitness function);
- The results and dynamics of the simulation are reduced to a table;
- From the results of optimisation modelling a relevant and meaningful conclusion is made.

5.5   The Analytic Hierarchy Method

During building a tree of goals or solutions for the development of export activities, for example, in a single country, and to determine the consistency of expert assessments the well-known Analytic hierarchy method and paired comparisons may be required.

This method is effective for expert evaluation of the result of the automatic construction of the "Decision tree" using the regression model. The regression method can have such restrictive features as:

- Low quality of the forecast during real problems solving - the model often converges on a local solution;
- Inability to build a forecast where the value of the target variable is outside the scope of the training set.

In order to neutralise these limitations of automatic work, it is expedient to evaluate its result with expert technology using the Analytic Hierarchy Process (AHP) method. The number of hierarchy levels in the target tree usually does not exceed 7 levels; the number of subordinate and compared positions in each level does not exceed 10 levels. The presentation of the toolkit can be in the form of a hierarchically-visualised graph or matrix.

The main element for representing the intensity of the interaction of objects in the AHP method is the matrix of paired comparisons. Objects that are on the same level have the same sets of indicators. The values of these indicators for each object are different.

The goal of comparing objects is to find out their rating among the set under consideration, and the rating is obtained in the form of a quantitative individual assessment. While comparing a pair of objects, the expert seeks to establish how much one object is better (worse) than the other, which is expressed by the establishment of a quantitative estimate. After viewing and estimating all combinations of possible pairs of objects, the experts receive a matrix of paired comparisons. The matrix shows to what extent the objects of the lower level affect the achievement of the goal.

6   Conclusion

This paper is an attempt to present the approach for creating the methodology that could answer the question about assessing the effects of a given export policy on the short-, medium- and long-term perspective. The Priority Index (PI) is proposed and justified by using the econometric theory, application of statistics' methods, a set of regression tools, and the gravitational approach.

It is shown that PI has to be proved during its exploitation and non-quantitative factors are to be taken into account. For this purpose, it was suggested that the AI methods, including cognitive modelling, inverse problems solving on cognitive models with genetic algorithms, and deep learning methods be used.

The paper proposes new scientific elements in the decision-making system. The main point is the networked expertise (e-expertise) introducing. Networked expertise becomes decisive in the decision-making process because, for a number of factors affecting the situation, there is no statistical or textual information.

The efficiency of the PI for calculating the rank of the country's import priority has to be experimentally approved in real practice.

Acknowledgment. This work is partially funded by the Russian Ministry of Agriculture, the State contract 497/12-SK of 07.12.2017; Russian Science Foundation, Grant 17-18-01326; Russian Foundation for Basic Research, grant 18-29-03086.

References

1. Wickens, M.: Macroeconomic Theory: A Dynamic General Equilibrium Approach. Princeton University Press, New Jersey (2012)
2. Lofgren, H., Harris, R.L., Robinson, S.: A Standard Computable General Equilibrium (CGE) Model in GAMS. International Food Policy Research Institute (IFPRI), Washington, D.C (2002)
3. Francois, J., Hall, K.: Partial equilibrium modelling. In: Francois, J., Reinert, K. (eds.) Applied Methods for Trade Policy Analysis: A Handbook. Cambridge University Press, Cambridge, UK (1997)
4. Chen, N., Novy, D.: International trade integration: a disaggregated approach. CEP Discussion Papers dp0908. Centre for Economic Performance, LSE (2009)
5. Novy, D.: Gravity redux: measuring international trade costs with panel data. Econ. Inq. **51** (1), 101–121 (2013)
6. Anderson, J.E., van Wincoop, E.: Gravity with gravitas: a solution to the border puzzle. Am. Econ. Rev. **93**(1), 170–192 (2003)
7. Gubanov, D., Korgin, N., Novikov, D., Raikov, A.: E-Expertise: modern collective intelligence. Springer Series Stud. Comput. Intell. **558**(18), 112 (2014). https://doi.org/10.1007/978-3-319-06770-4
8. Porto, G.: Informal export barriers and poverty, Policy Research Working Paper 3354, The World Bank, Washington, D.C. J. Int. Econ. **66**(2), 447–470 (2006)
9. Euler Hermes: http://www.eulerhermes.com/Pages/default.aspx. Accessed 24 Apr 2018
10. Abrosimov, V.: Swarm of intelligent control objects in network-centric environment. In: Proceedings of the World Congress on Engineering 2014, WCE 2014, 2–4 July, London, UK, LNECS, pp. 76–79 (2014)
11. Goodfellow, I., Bengio, Y., Courville, A.: Deep Learning. The MIT Press, Cambridge, MA (2016)
12. Raikov, A., Panfilov, S.: Convergent decision support system with genetic algorithms and cognitive simulation. In: Proceedings of the IFAC Conference on Manufacturing Modelling, Management and Control, MIM 2013, Saint Petersburg, Russia, June 19–21, pp. 1142–1147 (2013)

E-Society: Social Informatics

School Choice: Digital Prints and Network Analysis

Valeria Ivaniushina[1]([⊠]) and Elena Williams[2]

[1] National Research University Higher School of Economics,
Saint-Petersburg, Russia
ivaniushina@hse.ru
[2] Hamburg, Germany

Abstract. We apply social network analysis to examine school choice in the second-largest Russian city Saint-Petersburg. We use online data ("digital footprints") of between-schools comparisons on a large school information resource shkola-spb.ru. This resource allows to identify clusters of city schools that have been compared to each other more often and thus reflect choice preferences of students and parents looking for a school.

Network analysis is conducted in R ('igraph' package). For community detection, we employed fast-greedy clustering algorithm (Good et al. 2010). The resulting communities (school clusters) have been placed on a city map to identify territorial patterns formed according to choice preferences.

Network analysis of the district school networks based on between-schools online comparisons reveals two main factors for community formation. The first factor is territorial proximity: users compare schools that are relatively close to each other and not separated by wide streets, parks, industrial areas, rivers, etc. The second grouping principle is the type of school: private schools always form a separate cluster which shows that they are not being compared with public schools. In one district there was also a cluster of elite or academically challenging public schools grouped together.

Keywords: School choice · Digital prints · Network analysis

1 Introduction

In the last decades many countries introduced policies of school choice. Advocates of school choice argue that market-style mechanisms of consumer choice and competition between schools promote diverse and inventive approaches to school organization, curricula, teaching, and learning (Betts and Loveless 2005; Gibbons et al. 2008).

School choice is considered to empower parents by giving them more control over education and opportunity to find a more suitable learning environment for their child. Politics of free educational markets enforce schools to improve because unpopular schools are losing students (Hoxby 2003).

E. Williams—Independent Researcher.

Until recently school choice has been studies by traditional methods of sociology (surveys and interviews). Though spatial aspect of school choice is very important, it has not been studied much. Lately there were calls for "spatial turn" in education studies (Gulson and Symes 2007; Lubienski and Lee 2017), but there is still very little research using geo-information systems and trying to discover how city space, school location, and parental choice are interrelated. In this paper we attempt to bridge this gap.

2   Background Review

The term "school choice" refers to a variety of options to choose a school for children. School choice options may include magnet schools, charter schools, vouchers, tuition tax credits, homeschooling, and supplemental educational services (Berends 2015). In Russia the prevailing option is open enrollment law that allows to apply to schools outside of the student's area of residence, and many families use this option enrolling children not in the nearest school. The rules of school enrollment are under regulation of local government offices of education. 'School choice' in Saint-Petersburg means intra-district open enrollment plan: parents can nominate five schools[1] of their choice, in order of preference, in the city of Saint-Petersburg. The local law gives families an ample opportunity to select a school for their child among almost 800 city schools.

Historically, in the United States and many Western European countries residential segregation was inextricably intertwined with segregation of schools (Alba et al. 1999; Charles 2003). Public schools quality is strongly related to the affluence of neighborhoods, and property values are sensitive to school performance and demographic composition (Clapp et al. 2008; Gibbons and Machin 2008).

The situation in Russia is different. It is important to mention that unlike many European and American cities, cities in Russia are not segregated. Families of very unequal income and educational level often live in the same neighborhood; areas of concentrated poverty or very affluent districts are rare (Demintseva 2017). On the other hand, city schools are not very large and situated not far from each other. Schools differ by their types and curriculum. The majority of schools offer standard curriculum; there are also gymnasiums, lyceums, and specialized schools with enhanced curriculum in one or several school subjects. The diverse school system, absence of residential segregation, and open enrollment law makes Russia an interesting case for studying school choice.

When choosing a prospective school, students and parents often consider and compare several schools. Urban environment – school location and transportation options – is an important factor in the process of school selection; distance from home to school is a natural constraint to the parental choice (Alexandrov et al. 2018), especially for elementary school children, because children of this age are not independent travellers. Another important factor in school choice is school performance – Unified State Exam results, participation and prizes in various academic Olympiads.

---

[1] In 2015 and 2016 the limit for nominations was 5 schools, in 2017 - 3 schools.

This information is often displayed on school websites. Academic results are strongly related to school type – gymnasiums, lyceums, specialized schools score much higher on standardized tests and state exams (Yastrebov et al. 2015).

Hastings and Weinstein (2008), using experimental approach, demonstrated that when parents were provided with easily understandable information comparing performance of available schools, they used their right to choose schools outside of their neighborhood more often. This is a strong proof that a key issue when choosing a school is availability of information about school composition, performance, teachers' quality, sports teams, extracurricular activities and other characteristics.

The information about which schools are "good" is often spread through word of mouth: people simply "know" which schools are better. Besides information that parents and pupils can find directly on school websites, there are numerous groups in Facebook and other social networking sites, as well as forums and portals on other resources where parents exchange information about schools. In recent years in many countries emerge specialized web resources collecting and combining information about schools: administrative data, official test records, parents' reviews etc. Since it is a relatively new phenomenon, we were able to find only two articles based on the online search of schools.

Schneider and Buckley (2002) used an online schools database in Washington, DC to monitor search behavior of parents looking for schools as an indicator of parent preferences. The authors compared parental preferences revealed through search patterns with results obtained through traditional data collection methods (surveys via telephone interviews). They found that all parents, irrespective of their education level, were most interested in school location and demographic composition. School academic program and test scores were accessed less often. Schneider and Buckley argue that monitoring search behavior gives more "objective" results because it is free from social desirability bias.

The second article about online school search is based on data from GreatSchools Inc., a nonprofit organization whose website provides information and reviews on all grade schools in the United States (Lovenheim and Walsh 2018). The goal of the paper was to link parents' online search behavior with local (county or city) school choice policy. The authors demonstrated that changes in the local school choice policies and expanding choice options leads to considerable increase in the frequency of online searches about that locality. In other words, parents respond to increasing school choice options by collecting more information about local school quality.

In Saint-Petersburg a group of citizens has established and keeps updating a website www.shkola-spb.ru where they collect and present in a systematical manner all available information about schools: type and specialization, location, catchment area, school sores in Unifies State Exams for several years, participation in academic Olympiads and rewards, informal reviews of students and parents about their schools. This website provides rich information for parents and students choosing schools. Most interesting for our analysis is a special option for comparing schools to each other. It is designed in such a way that it saves requests and shows most frequent comparisons ("most often this school has been compared to the following schools:…"). We used the data from this website to analyze "digital prints" that were left by parents comparing schools.

3 Data and Method

This paper studies parental information-gathering behavior using a new source of data: special online resource Школа.спб (www.shkola-spb.ru). This website, which is free to use and does not require registration, provides detailed information on the all of public and private schools in the city of Saint-Petersburg, more than 700 schools in total. Featured prominently is information on school academic performance that may be of particular interest for school choosing parents. Specifically, it is average school results in standardized graduation exams (Unified State Exams in Math, Russian and other academic subjects) for the last 5 years. This information is presented in a convenient and easily comprehendible form: schools are ranked within city district and color-coded. The website makes it very easy to understand information and compare it between schools. There is also "people rating" of schools based on testimonials and reviews from students and parents, both current and former. Schools are rated from 1 star to 10 stars based on general impression of reviewers; number of reviews is indicated, and the actual reviews are also available.

Data for analysis was downloaded from the website www.shkola-spb.ru in September 2016. Results of between-school comparisons were presented on the website in the form "This school (Number A) most often has been compared to schools (Number B, Number C, Number D, Number E, Number F)". Thus, it gives us information about pairs of school that users – parents and students – compared to each other. In the terminology of network analysis the school Number A is sender, and the schools Number B - F are receivers.

Since the website www.shkola-spb.ru does not keep information about how often the webpage of a specific school has been visited, the frequency of visits can't be used as a measure of attractiveness or interest in this school. However, the website keeps the information about how often a particular school has been compared to other schools. The number of comparisons can be considered as school popularity among prospective choosers.

Analysis consisted of two parts. First, for analysis of factors predicting school online popularity we used multiple linear regression, with popularity as dependent variable and a number of school characteristics (school average results for Unified State Exams for 5 years, school type, school size, % of children with non-native Russian language, teachers qualification) as explanatory variables. School type was dummy-coded; all other variables were metric.

Second, we conducted network analysis of school online comparisons with dyads of schools compared to each other. For community detection in networks, we employed fast-greedy clustering algorithm based on modularity optimization (Good et al. 2010) realized in R ('igraph' package). The resulting communities (school clusters) have been placed on a city map to identify territorial patterns formed according to choice preferences. Geo-coding and spatial data visualizing have been done in R package 'ggmap'.

4   Results

4.1   Online Popularity

First stage of the analysis was evaluating school online popularity. Popularity was operationalized as a number of comparisons on the website shkola-spb.ru, that is how often a certain school has been compared to other Saint-Petersburg school. The number of comparisons is a measure reflecting the interest of parents and/or prospective students in a particular school.

Because of space limit of the article we do not show a regression table and instead report the model results. Only three variables appeared to be significantly related to school online popularity. The variable with largest effect was school type = Gymnasium/Lyceum; such schools have been chosen for comparison much more often than schools with standard curriculum or specialized school (these two types do not differ in popularity). The second variable predicting popularity was school academic standing reflected in its results on Unified State Exams; schools with better exam scores were more popular. The third variable positively related to popularity was percentage of school students from other city districts (that is not the same district the school is located in).

The interpretation of results is clear: users browsing the website shkola-spb.ru are mostly interested in prestigious, well-known schools with high academic results. All other school characteristics included in the model – school size, % migrant (non-Russian) students, average work experience of teachers – turned out to be statistically insignificant and thus not related to the online school popularity.

4.2   Nevskii District

On the next stage of our analysis we visualized the network of between-school comparisons and placed it on the city map using school coordinates. The mapping result for Nevskii district is shown below on Fig. 1. Nevskii district is situated on two sides of the Neva river, and one can see that most comparisons are between schools located on the same side.

For further analysis we conducted community analysis (cluster analysis) of the network. This type of analysis identifies densely connected parts of the network, or clusters of nodes that have more ties between them that outside of these clusters.

Results of community analysis for Nevskii district are shown on Fig. 2. Division of schools by clusters is founded on their location: school within one cluster are located closer to each other on the city map than to school from other clusters. On the right side of the Neva river there are blue cluster (north) and green cluster (south). On the left bank there are orange cluster (in the south part, in Rybatskoe) and yellow cluster that goes all along the Neva bank.

Two schools forming the red cluster are private schools. Even though they are located close to schools from the yellow cluster, they form a separate cluster by their own.

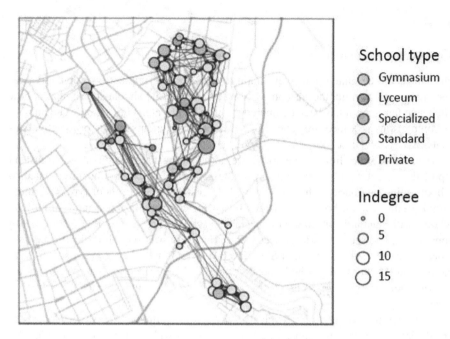

Fig. 1. Network of between-school comparisons in the Nevskii district. Color of circles reflects school type; size of circles reflect frequency of comparisons. (Color figure online)

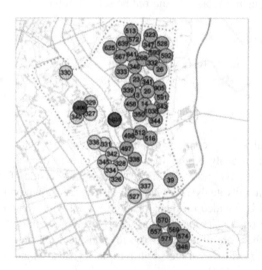

Fig. 2. Clusters of schools in Nevskii District detected by fast-greedy clustering algorithm. Colors of nodes identify clusters. (Color figure online)

4.3   Petrogradskii District

In Petrogradskii district the clustering algorithm identified 4 groups. Yellow cluster is presented by a single school – Nakhimov's Naval school (1201). Blue cluster is located along the Kamenoostrovskii prospect, green cluster is comprised of schools located between Chkalovskaya and Sportivnaya metro stations. Here we see the same pattern of spatial proximity as we already saw in the Nevskii district.

More interesting is the case of orange cluster. Schools from this cluster are located all over the Petrogradskii island. What do they have in common? The schools forming this cluster attract students from all over the city. Classical gymnasium #610 takes students into the 5th grade, and it doesn't have a catchment area since students living anywhere are eligible for entrance competition. Gymnasium #56 is a very large and well-known school that attracts students from all city districts. Goethe Shule (1020) and Shamir (224) are private schools. The remaining schools from the orange cluster are gymnasiums (67 and 70) and specialized school with a German language (75). We can say that these are prestigious schools, or schools of a very high academic standing. Evidently, for parents who compare these schools to each other their location in unimportant – or at least less important – that other school characteristics (Fig. 3).

Fig. 3. Clusters of schools in Petrigradskii District detected by fast-greedy clustering algorithm. Colors of nodes identify clusters (Color figure online)

4.4   Other Districts of Saint-Petersburg

We applies the same method of analysis for analyzing between-school comparisons in other districts of Saint-Petersburg. We took for analysis four central districts (Central, Admiralteiskii, Vasileostrovskii, Petrogradskii) and three peripheral districts (Nevskii, Krasnoselskii, Primorskii). Since between Central and Admiralteiskii districts there is no physical division in the form of industrial zone, river, railways etc., we assumed that parent may consider these two districts as one area for school choice, and accordingly we analyzed these two district networks together.

Summing up our results, we can say that in every district we have identified clusters of school that were located not far from each other. Private schools always formed a separate cluster.

5 Discussion

The internet has increasingly become the preferred means of information exchange and communication. Online school quality information tools can help overcome the information asymmetries that exist in the education market. One of such information tool is a website shkola-spb.ru. The type of information available on this website facilitates easy comparisons across local schools, and prior work has shown that providing parents with this type of information, when combined with school choice, leads parents to choose schools for their children that increase their measured academic achievement (Hastings and Weinstein 2008).

Our analysis of online search behavior corroborates earlier findings from survey data that parents choosing schools for their children care about the academic quality and the distance from home (Alexandrov et al. 2018; Burgess et al. 2015; Gibbons et al. 2008).

Cluster analysis of the network of online school comparisons revealed two main principles for school grouping. The first principle is school location: schools situated not far from each other are always grouped together. The meaning of "not far from each other" is different for central and peripheral districts and depends on the structure of the district. While comparing schools, user take into account and the development of transport infrastructure and obstacles in the form of industrial zones, rivers, wide avenues, park areas.

The second principle is school type. Our analysis have demonstrated that in every city district private schools form a separate cluster. Sometimes high-end prestigious schools of high academic standing also form a separate cluster (Petrogradskii district).

Summing up, our results demonstrate that "digital prints" of users' behavior in the Internet can be used by researchers as valuable sources of information – in our case, information about school choice. Online search tools such as shkola-spb.ru can be powerful mechanisms providing families with the information they need to take advantage of school choice programs.

In this paper we provide the first approach to analyzing spatial aspects of school choice in a Russian megapolis. Taylor (2007) calls for using geo-information services for analyzing school choice, school segregation and educational marketization because it gives the "living contexts" in which school choice occurs. At the same time he points out that families of different socio-economic status may have quite different approach to availability of school and residential geography. While there is no residential segregation in Russian cities yet, between-school differentiation by socio-economic composition provides an interesting study case. Russia's peculiar properties make it an interesting example for studying of school choice and school differentiation.

Our further plans include analyzing school choices of families of different socio-economic status, which requires other approaches for data collection. Another direction of research is studying of movements of students between schools and comparing "real" school clusters with online choice school clusters.

References

Alba, R.D., Logan, J.R., Stults, B.J., Marzan, G., Zhang, W.: Immigrant groups in the suburbs: a reexamination of suburbanization and spatial assimilation. Am. Sociol. Rev. 446–460 (1999). https://doi.org/10.2307/2657495

Alexandrov, D., Tenisheva, K., Savelieva, S.: Differentiation of school choice: case of two districts of St. Petersburg. Educational Studies (Moscow) (2018, in press)

Berends, M.: Sociology and school choice: what we know after two decades of charter schools. Ann. Rev. Sociol. **41**, 159–180 (2015). https://doi.org/10.1146/annurev-soc-073014-112340

Betts, J.R., Loveless, T. (eds.) Getting Choice Right: Ensuring Equity and Efficiency in Education Policy. Brookings Institute, Washington, DC (2005)

Burgess, S., Greaves, E., Vignoles, A., Wilson, D.: What parents want: school preferences and school choice. Econ. J. **125**(587), 1262–1289 (2015). https://doi.org/10.1111/ecoj.12153

Charles, C.Z.: The dynamics of racial residential segregation. Ann. Rev. Sociol. **29**(1), 167–207 (2003). https://doi.org/10.1146/annurev.soc.29.010202.100002

Clapp, J.M., Nanda, A., Ross, S.L.: Which school attributes matter? The influence of school district performance and demographic composition on property values. J. Urban Econ. **63**(2), 451–466 (2008). https://doi.org/10.1016/j.jue.2007.03.004

Demintseva, E.: Labour migrants in post-Soviet Moscow: patterns of settlement. J. Ethnic Migr. Stud. **43**(15), 2556–2572 (2017). https://doi.org/10.1080/1369183X.2017.1294053

Gibbons, S., Machin, S.: Valuing school quality, better transport, and lower crime: evidence from house prices. Oxford Rev. Econ. Policy **24**(1), 99–119 (2008). https://doi.org/10.1093/oxrep/grn008

Gibbons, S., Machin, S., Silva, O.: Choice, competition, and pupil achievement. J. Eur. Econ. Assoc. **6**(4), 912–947 (2008). https://doi.org/10.1162/JEEA.2008.6.4.912

Good, B.H., de Montjoye, Y.A., Clauset, A.: Performance of modularity maximization in practical contexts. Phys. Rev. E **81**(4), 046106 (2010). https://doi.org/10.1103/PhysRevE.81.046106

Gulson, K.N., Symes, C.: Spatial Theories of Education: Policy and Geography Matters. Routledge, New York (2007)

Hastings, J.S., Weinstein, J.M.: Information, school choice, and academic achievement: evidence from two experiments. Q. J. Econ. **123**(4), 1373–1414 (2008). https://doi.org/10.1162/qjec.2008.123.4.1373

Hoxby, C.M.: School choice and school productivity. Could school choice be a tide that lifts all boats? In: The Economics of School Choice. University of Chicago Press (2003)

Lovenheim, M.F., Walsh, P.: Does choice increase information? Evidence from online school search behavior. Econ. Educ. Rev. **62**, 91–103 (2018). https://doi.org/10.1016/j.econedurev.2017.11.002

Lubienski, C., Lee, J.: Geo-spatial analyses in education research: the critical challenge and methodological possibilities. Geogr. Res. **55**(1), 89–99 (2017). https://doi.org/10.1111/1745-5871.12188

Schneider, M., Buckley, J.: What do parents want from schools? Evidence from the Internet. Educ. Eval. Policy Anal. **24**(2), 133–144 (2002). https://doi.org/10.3102/01623737024002133

Taylor, Ch.: Geographical information systems (GIS) and school choice: the use of spatial research tools in studying educational policy. In: Gulson, K.N., Symes, C. (eds.) Spatial Theories of Education: Policy and Geography Matters. Routledge, New York (2007)

Website http://www.shkola-spb.ru/. Accessed 30 Jan 2018

Yastrebov, G., Pinskaya, M., Kosaretsky, S.: Using contextual data for education quality assessment. Russ. Educ. Soc. **57**, 483–518 (2015). https://doi.org/10.1080/10609393.2015.1096140

Collaboration of Russian Universities and Businesses in Northwestern Region

Anaastasiya Kuznetsova[(✉)]

National Research University Higher School of Economics, St. Petersburg, Russia
adkuznetsova13@gmail.com

Abstract. The main focus of this paper is the analysis of universities' embeddedness into industrial sector of the Russian Northwestern region. We use webometric approach to evaluate the collaboration of universities with the use of Social Networks Analysis, as well as the examination of co-authorship network among universities and other agents. We develop our research within the framework of Triple Helix concept, taking only two agents from there: universities and companies. As a result, we found two groups of universities: which have a lot of connections with a variety of industrial and business companies and behave as key agents for the whole network as well as some with more narrowly focused types of collaboration, having fewer links with companies.

Keywords: Russian universities · Business companies · Webometrics
SNA · Networks · Triple Helix concept

1 Introduction and Related Work

One of the main characteristics of universities is that they constitute the most significant part of all educational systems. Being a principal agent in the market, they behave in the same way as firms and industrial companies. Practices of promotion and self-positioning of universities in the market are very similar to other business agents. Hence, there is a need to study universities not only as producers of scientific knowledge but also as partners of companies. They all could collaborate in knowledge-sharing, internship possibilities, exchange of personnel and this could show universities embeddedness into the business area.

Universities embeddedness could help to analyze their behavior according to their place in the network. Moreover, universities' embeddedness into the local economics and culture reflects their orientation [7]. The concept of embeddedness includes the idea that agents behave within social context around them [2]. Even corruption activity and its spread could be analyzed through the concept of embeddedness into universities' collaboration network [15]. However, knowledge transfer analysis and universities cooperation are more common here. Regarding universities-companies' cooperation, universities embeddedness into business area improves industrial development and innovations' emergence [10]. Universities are producers and custodians of knowledge and experience, which they partially transfer to firms [5]. Moreover, new research made by universities about

© Springer Nature Switzerland AG 2018
D. A. Alexandrov et al. (Eds.): DTGS 2018, CCIS 858, pp. 427–435, 2018.
https://doi.org/10.1007/978-3-030-02843-5_34

firms and organizations increases the incentive for universities to work together with firms. Also, business companies could improve their innovative ability and creative potential by interacting with universities. As a result, their competitiveness, ensuring a stable position in the market niche as well [14].

The analysis of universities' performance was always a complicated process with the desire of ranking methodologies to include all possible measurements. A study of universities in the field of their collaboration and partnership could be made with the webometric approach. The idea of webometric analysis was designed by Ingwersen [3] and it focuses on assessing things through counting links of them on other web pages. In this paper, we do analyze links of universities on companies websites with the idea of revealing collaboration among them. Smith and Thelwall [11] found that the number of references to universities on the Web correlate with their off-line activity. That gives us enough degrees of freedom to consider that webometrics of universities performance, based on the business companies websites, would also reflect their off-line activity in industry and business.

Webometric analysis of companies and, what is more important for us, methodological approach, was described in Googling Companies - a Webometric Approach to Business Studies [9]. Authors examined co-links of companies, which were referenced on the same websites for detecting competitive companies. The idea is that if companies are referenced by the same web-pages, we could assume them as structurally similar. Taking into account this research, we applied Social Networks Analysis to universities-companies networks for revealing structurally identical universities and partly analyze their roles with text mining. As Thelwall and Wilkinson say [13], direct links to websites could be a measure of their similarity. And this also could be a measure of structure detection of the area [16]. In this way, the webometric analysis of links to the universities from the same companies could reveal their structural similarity.

As our methodological idea is clear now, our theoretical framework is concentrated around the Triple Helix concept, initiated by Etzkowitz and Leydesdorff [8]. The main idea is in the collaboration between universities, companies, and government for producing new knowledge and developing our life quality. Authors saw the potential for innovation and economic development in today's knowledge-oriented society in the more prominent role of universities and the close interaction of the university, industry, and government. These interactions should bring to the creation of new institutional and social forms of production, transfer and knowledge application. Universities in this Triple Helix concept take specific features of business and governmental structures and become the basis for innovations, scientific and practical developments and entrepreneurial projects.

This concept was partly researched by Stuart and Thelwall [12] in 2006. They used URL citation from universities, industrial and governmental agents for the analyses of their relationships. Authors found that links do not show the whole image of their types of collaboration because of different purposes of websites (like educational or marketing). However, it still could be used as a complementary indicator of cooperation.

In this way, we assume that analysis of universities through the references on business companies websites and co-authorship network could give us an understanding of collaboration processes in the field. Analysis of universities strategies through bibliometric analysis and their references on Mass Media was made in our previous work [6]. However, in this paper, we focus on business ties and embeddedness of universities into an organizational network of top regional companies, paying more attention to network analysis.

2   Data and Methods

Our same sample is the same as we used in our previous study [6] - 51 Northwestern universities, which have specializations in the fields of Economics, Management, Business, and Finance. Here this choice is becoming more evident because of the similarity between economically oriented companies and universities. Since in the West most of these universities create separate economic schools, in Russia this institutionalization is only in the beginning. Universities which are at least partly in the field of Economics and Management, have the knowledge and experience of partnership with companies, even if their primary specificity is in STEM sciences.

Firstly, we downloaded all publications of these universities from 2012 to 2016 in fields of Economics, Management and Business from Web of Science. This is a big assumption not to take other databases; however, that should be enough for getting the overall picture.

We also took TOP 50 companies from the EXPERT rating, based on their revenue [1]. Universities' references on these websites were taken as webometric indicators as well as the context of these references. Taking into account possibility of strong ties among universities and companies, we used penalties for counting weights of links among universities and companies:

$weight_i = x_i$, where x_i - number of references of all universities by i company

$$penalty_i = weight_i / ln(weight_i + 1)$$

Our methodological part includes bibliometric and webometric approaches. Being more precise - co-authorship network of universities from Web of Science Core Collection and references of them on the websites of TOP 50 Companies according to the EXPERT rating. Using Social Networks Analysis (SNA), we managed to found key universities and companies through centrality measures. The bibliographical network gives a representation of scientific collaboration while webometrics represent business connections and embeddedness of universities into industrial sector. Next, we used hierarchical clusterization from linkcomm R package [4] to extract groups of universities based on their references on companies websites. This method produces clusters based on similarity of links with Jaccard coefficient and subsequent hierarchical clusterization (Fig. 1).

3   Analysis and Results

Firstly we have decided to have a look at scientific collaboration among universities, companies and governmental centers. As this is Web of Science data, not all universities from our sample are presented - only 15 of them have publications in fields of Economics, Management, and Business indexed in WoS. We highlighted universities from our sample with colour and divided different types of agents manually. For example, different commercial banks or companies such as "Sberbank" or "McKinsey and Co Inc" were marked as "Companies", laboratories like "CEFIR" or "ISIS Laboratory" as "Research Centers" and Ministries or state organizations as "Governmental Centers". We got a wide variety of companies and governmental centers in co-authorship network around universities from our sample. These ties could represent their strong collaboration in common scientific production, knowledge and innovations. There is a possibility to examine collaboration with the government as well, but this is not the main focus of our research. However, we could still state that universities, companies and government work within the Triple Helix concept. As here are not only Russian agents

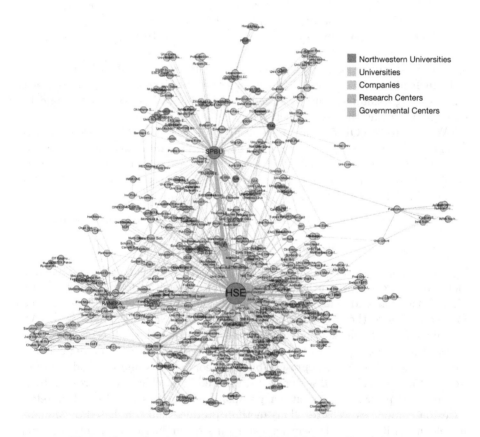

Fig. 1. Co-authorship network from Web of Science. Size - degree

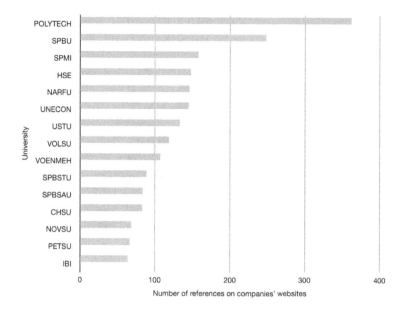

Fig. 2. The most referenced universities by companies

but also foreign ones, this bibliographical network is only the additional part of the analysis of universities-companies relationships. Though even here we could name HSE, SPBU, RANEPA as active scientific producers and partners for the industry. Moreover, these universities are embedded into the collaboration network of universities, governmental and research centers.

Next, we counted how often universities are mentioned on companies websites (Fig. 2). There are as highly popular and prominent Saint Petersburg universities - POLYTECH, SPBU, SPMI, HSE, as a variety of regional universities such as NARFU or USTU. This diversity could be explained by the different specificity of universities and companies. Some of them could be referenced as partners or providers of the labour force, while others as co-inventors of innovations.

The bipartite network of universities and companies helped us to examine key agents in the network and, respectively, in the field (Fig. 3). Technologically oriented companies like Rosseti, Lenenergo, Severstal are represented as good as different banks (Bank SPb) and industrial companies (ZAO VAD). There is no obligation for universities and companies to have the same specifications for having a collaboration because we can see these diverse ties. There are prominent universities which have connections with almost all universities, but we could also track the local industrial relationships. For example, relations among IKBFU (Immanuel Kant Baltic Federal University) and Avtotor (automobile manufacturing company located in Kaliningrad Oblast) or USTU (Ukhta State Technical University) and Ukhta Gazprom) reflects their partnership for solving regional problems and developing regional industry. Each university has its role in industrial development.

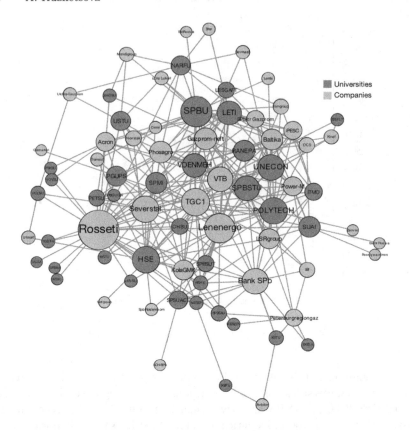

Fig. 3. Bipartite network of universities and companies. Size - degree

After hierarchical clusterization of links in the network of universities and companies projection, we got different groups of universities based on their mentions on companies' websites (Fig. 4). Hierarchical clusterization was made not only on the existence of the link but also the weight of these links - the intensity of the connection. We got 4 clusters of universities, but these communities were very nested, so here only 3 of them are visualized and analyzed. For example, there are some universities which have connections with almost all others and fall into 3 clusters - they are referenced by the same companies - these are HSE and UNECON. Both of them are considered to be the Saint Petersburg universities specialized in Economics and do have a lot in common.

Next, there are some universities which are included in 2 clusters, such as POLYTECH, SPBSAU, and SPSUACE. We could describe them as STEM universities, and they probably collaborate with companies in student internships or act as technical advisors. We assume that there are the same types of mentions with other "double-clustered" universities. However, while previously mentioned universities have a lot of companies in common, universities on the edges have more specific relationships with them. They are mentioned by a more limited

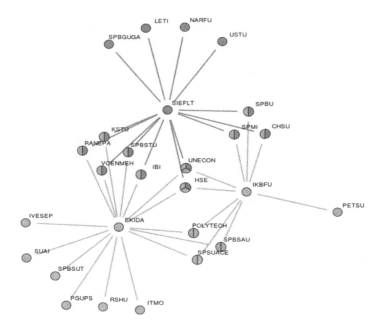

Fig. 4. Clusterization based on links of bipartite projection

number of companies, so their connections are more specific and more oriented to their common industrial or regional activity.

This part could provide us with the understanding of structural similarity of universities. As well as reflect the strong collaboration between universities and companies, corresponding to Triple Helix concept. Universities have a different level of embeddedness into the industrial sector but almost all of them cooperate with companies. This reflects mutual industrial development and emergence of innovations and new products, meeting the conditions of Triple Helix Concept. However, the governmental side is poorly illuminated, and we could not conclude that the concept works in Russian higher education completely.

4   Conclusion

In this paper, we have analyzed universities embeddedness into business ties. Relying on Triple Helix concept of university-industry-government collaboration for innovations development, we applied bibliometric and webometric analysis for universities scientific and business activity. We found that Russian Northwestern universities diverse by the level of collaboration with companies. We also got a variety of universities, which mostly contribute to industrial development, but are not oriented on knowledge production. Narrowly specialized and regional universities show collaboration with fewer companies, but they probably have stronger ties with them: for instance, among regional industrial companies and regional head universities (NARFU and SZNP Lukoil) or narrowly oriented ones (SUAI and Russian Airlines).

The focus is on structural similarity of universities: their large and spread ties with a wide variety of companies or narrowly specialized and regional universities with fewer but stronger connections. First ones are usually big and popular universities, and others are more thematically or regionally specialized ones. We believe that they have different types of collaboration and this would be checked in our next study. For example, partnership relationships, educational services for employees, internships or the development of the city. Preliminary results show us that Northwestern universities and, more likely, all Russian universities partly behave within the framework of Triple Helix concept and are embedded into the industrial area, producing common knowledge and innovations.

Acknowledgements. The article was prepared within the framework of the Academic Fund Program at the National Research University Higher School of Economics (HSE) in 2017 2018 (grant No. 17-05-0024) and by the Russian Academic Excellence Project "5-100".

References

1. Expert: Rating of the largest northwestern companies by revenue (2015). http://expert.ru
2. Granovetter, M.: Economic action and social structure: the problem of embeddedness. Am. J. Sociol. **91**(3), 481–510 (1985)
3. Ingwersen, P.: The calculation of web impact factors. J. Doc. **54**(2), 236–243 (1998)
4. Kalinka, A.T.: The generation, visualization, and analysis of link communities in arbitrary networks with the R package linkcomm. In: Dresden: Max Planck Institute of Molecular Cell Biology and Genetics, pp. 1–16 (2014)
5. Kim, E.H., Zhu, M.: Universities as firms: the case of us overseas programs. American universities in a global market, pp. 163–201. University of Chicago Press (2010)
6. Kuznetsova, A., Pozdniakov, S., Musabirov, I.: Analyzing web presence of russian universities in a scientometric context. In: Alexandrov, D.A., Boukhanovsky, A.V., Chugunov, A.V., Kabanov, Y., Koltsova, O. (eds.) DTGS 2017. CCIS, vol. 745, pp. 113–119. Springer, Cham (2017). https://doi.org/10.1007/978-3-319-69784-0_9
7. Lebeau, Y., Bennion, A.: Forms of embeddedness and discourses of engagement: a case study of universities in their local environment. Stud. High. Educ. **39**(2), 278–293 (2014)
8. Leydesdorff, L., Etzkowitz, H.: Emergence of a triple helix of university-industry-government relations. Sci. Public Policy **23**(5), 279–286 (1996)
9. Romero Frias, E.: Googling companies-a webometric approach to business studies. Electron. J. Bus. Res. Methods **7**, 93–106 (2009)
10. Schartinger, D., Rammer, C., Fischer, M.M., Fröhlich, J.: Knowledge interactions between universities and industry in Austria: sectoral patterns and determinants. Res. Policy **31**(3), 303–328 (2002)
11. Smith, A., Thelwall, M.: Web impact factors for Australasian universities. Scientometrics **54**(3), 363–380 (2002)
12. Stuart, D., Thelwall, M.: Investigating triple helix relationships using URL citations: a case study of the UK west midlands automobile industry. Res. Eval. **15**(2), 97–106 (2006)

13. Thelwall, M., Wilkinson, D.: Finding similar academic web sites with links, biblio-metric couplings and colinks. Inf. Process. Manag. **40**(3), 515–526 (2004)
14. Vedovello, C.: Firms' R&D activity and intensity and the university-enterprise partnerships. Technol. Forecast. Soc. Chang. **58**(3), 215–226 (1998)
15. Zhang, Q.F.: Political embeddedness and academic corruption in Chinese univer-sities. All Academic Incorporated (2007)
16. Zuccala, A.: Author cocitation analysis is to intellectual structure as web colink analysis is to...? J. Assoc. Inf. Sci. Technol. **57**(11), 1487–1502 (2006)

Social Profiles - Methods of Solving Socio-Economic Problems Using Digital Technologies and Big Data

Alexey Y. Timonin$^{(\boxtimes)}$ (ID), Alexander M. Bershadsky,
Alexander S. Bozhday (ID), and Oleg S. Koshevoy

Penza State University, Krasnaya Street, 40, 440026 Penza, Russia
c013s017b301f018@mail.ru, bam@pnzgu.ru,
bozhday@yandex.ru, olaal@yandex.ru

Abstract. One of the research directions of Internet public data is the social profiling task. Various analytical tools and technologies are used to quickly process large arrays of heterogeneous data within this task. The result is a social profile or a set of profiles. It represents value in various socio-economic spheres.

This article offers practical examples of social profiles application in various socio-economic tasks. A survey of existing works on social profiling task has been reviewed. There are suggestions of using social profiles built by Big Data technologies in the future of Russia and the world.

This work is carried out with the support of RFBR grant №18-07-00408 in a research project named "Fundamental theoretical bases development for self-adaptation of applied software systems".

Keywords: Big Data · Data analysis · Personal social profile
Public data sources · Social media · Unstructured data

1 Introduction

The heterogeneous Internet data processing is involved into a wide range of human activity applied problems. One of them is the social profile construction. A social profile (SP) is a data set that characterizes people in some way. This information should be grouped for the convenience of human perception. The social profiling task refers to the theoretical concept of analyzing social networks. Also, it uses similar mechanisms. Initially, a mathematical model is developed to take into account all connections between its elements. Then a social graph is constructed. The nodes are represented by social objects. The edges are shown by social connections between them. An example of such a graph is shown in Fig. 1.

Two main data types are used as raw for generated social profile. These types are personal and public information from Internet sources. By its nature, SP information can be divided into text, multimedia, geospatial and statistical data. Each data type requires a separate approach to processing. They are need prepared specialized data storage. It possible to increase the accuracy of the semantic content determining by means complex usage of Big Data technologies and neural networks in the process of analysis.

D. A. Alexandrov et al. (Eds.): DTGS 2018, CCIS 858, pp. 436–445, 2018.
https://doi.org/10.1007/978-3-030-02843-5_35

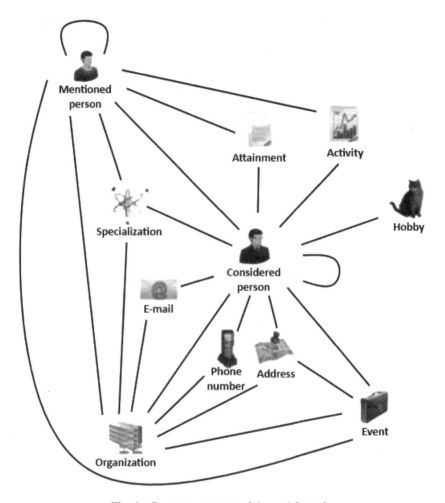

Fig. 1. Common structure of the social graph.

The task of a social profile building is divided into a sequence of steps [20–22]:

1. Raw information gathering from different sources for greater completeness of the final SP.
2. Filtering data from meaningless, contradictory and confidential information.
3. Separating unique key entities from the set of collected data. They will become the central nodes of the network. Structured information card [22] is created on their basis.
4. Distribution of dynamic content by its type into the corresponding data storage.
5. Further search for social objects in both text and multimedia data.
6. Allocating links between nodes (both unidirectional and two-way connections).

7. Expansion of the network to a state acceptable for the subsequent analysis, due to the objects not yet connected.
8. Search for existing multiple links;
9. Searching for analogies in unexamined dynamic data and including them in the description of the created network objects. It helps to avoid data inconsistency.
10. Construction of a social graph based on the resulting information.

Typical implementation of social profiling process represents in Fig. 2.

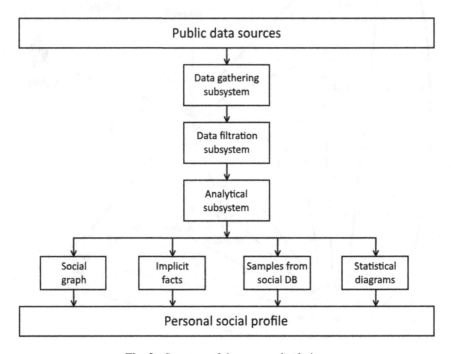

Fig. 2. Structure of the proposed solution.

The obtained results are sent for consideration to specialists after the creation of a separate social profile or their groups is complete. They deal with applied problems, in which the SP acts as input. This work is devoted to consideration both of already existing similar and potentially possible in the near future types of activities. This is due to the rapid spread of Internet communication services and Open data in the modern society.

2   Background

A lot of research works have been written on the social profiling topic at recent years. These papers are both technical and socio-economic orientation. Let's consider some of them.

Paper named "The sociability score: App-based social profiling from a healthcare perspective" of Eskes, Spruit, Brinkkemper, Vorstman and Kas [8] offers the method of using smartphone data for the diagnostic social deficits evaluation. Their study ensured an understanding of social significance assessments applicability to ensure objective indicators of a person's social characteristics in a natural environment.

Rossi, Ferland and Tapus consider the process of users profiling for the human-robot interaction task in their work called "User profiling and behavioral adaptation for HRI: A survey" [19]. It can be very productive in development purposes of augmented reality or human-like mechanisms such an autopilots and digital assistants.

Kristjansson, Mann, Smith, Inga Dora Sigfusdottir investigate teenage smoking phenomenon in work "Social Profile of Middle School-Aged Adolescents Who Use Electronic Cigarettes: Implications for Primary Prevention" [11]. Kaczmarek, Behnke, Kashdan and others in their paper called "Smile intensity in social networking profile photographs is related to greater scientific achievements" published a conclusion about the correlation between the success of scientists and the smiles frequency in their images from various public sources [10]. Social profiles usage improves answers quality on surveys.

A significant part of the SP-based works is related to the field of medicine. Chris Poulin and Brian Shiner investigated unstructured clinical records taken from medical reports U.S. Veterans Administration (VA). "Predicting the Risk of Suicide by Analyzing the Text of Clinical Notes" [15] dedicated to the development of a machine prediction algorithm for assessing the mental health of the individual and preventing the risk of suicide.

The publication called "A social LCA framework to assess the corporate social profile of companies: Insights from a case study" [23] proposes a new methodological framework to facilitate managers. It helps in assessing the social impacts which accrue from a company's daily activities and assists in building of a strong corporate social profile.

The purpose of Mustafa, Anwer and Ali "Measuring the Correlation between Social Profile and Voting Habit and the moderation effect of Political Contribution for this Relationship" [14] research study is to investigate whether there exists a strong correlation between social profile and voting habit.

There are a number of works devoted to the study different aspects in the social profile building process. Mitrou, Kandias, Stavrou and Gritzalis raise the problems of private life invasion and a specific person discrimination by society in the SP-building process. This work called "Social Media Profiling: A Panopticon or Omniopticon Tool?" [13]. Article named "On the Multilingual and Genre Robustness of EmoGraphs for Author Profiling in Social Media" of Rangel and Rosso describes novel graph-based approach for identifying different traits such as an author's age and gender on the basis of her writings [17]. Chin and Wright [7] consider the peculiarities of social media analysis in the social profiling purpose in their research called "Social Media Sources for Personality Profiling".

An analysis of the above works, it can be concluded that where social profiles are used now. Mainly this is a medicine and healthcare field, where SP is used to improve the quality of diagnosis. Also, it is various social researches in the political science, psychology, sociology and management areas, where the raw data gathering is produced in natural conditions. Another application area is the creation of flexible human-machine interface. In addition, there are problems of the accurate social profiles interpretation and privacy in circumstances when personal data are readily available. Topical questions are being raised in order to avoid exclusion of persons by society.

A more detailed analysis of these works allows to conclude demand social profiling in modern human activity. Also, it becomes clear that using social profiles in the above activities can enhance their effectiveness without the need for additional labor costs. There is a visible interest of the scientific community in social profiles creation and study. However, there is question of the need to develop personal social profiles based on Big Data technology. Raw SP data is taken from public Internet sources. Also, a description of specific applications must be considered. Number of similar research works is not enough.

3 Applicability Areas of Social Profiles

The analysis of literary sources revealed a number of areas using social profiling methods. The scope of possible application of social profile based on open sources of information is rather extensive. Now most popular areas are obvious tasks of collaborative filtration [16] and counteraction to crime (OSINT) [18].

Classical information systems include a server with a relational DBMS and a web interface. They are ineffective in terms of productivity and economics. Data processing can take a very long time, and the results will lose their relevance before they are received. The costs of electricity, maintenance and hardware upgrade are also prohibitively high. The Big Data technology implementation can solve these problems by making more efficient usage of existing hardware resources. This is achieved by paralleling information flows between clusters and using NoSQL- or NewSQL-based data warehouses.

The social data utilization is quite promising in the tasks of creating artificial intelligence and machine learning at the present time. Examples are the development of a car autopilot [12] and IBM Watson mainframe usage to diagnose human diseases [6]. In the first case, the driver profiles set will be a source of geodata and traffic violations information. These data are used to train the neural network of autopilot. In the second case, the data about patient disease histories, getting from files medical institutions. Also, information about their activity, hobbies and other implicit factors are analyzed from various public information sources. Such data may affect the accuracy of diagnosis and further effective treatment.

Next, it's need to review the application spheres that are already interested in the processing of social data. These areas can become the main consumers of social profiling systems in the near future. When developing a system for a social profile building, it will be necessary to focus on the possibility of using the final SP results in these spheres. This is particularly true for data gathering and representation subsystems.

Areas of legal and banking services directly work with people. The assessment of possible risks in cooperation for them is very important and affects both income and reputation. Social profiles in the activities of such companies will serve as a summary and document-characteristics of customers. On its basis the organization can make decisions: to allow or refuse a person in the services, to choose the most suitable package of services, for example, a type of bank deposit and its optimum term.

Another possible area for social profiles application is the administration of the large socio-economic systems. These systems are primarily "smart city" approaches. This approach integrates information and communication technologies with the Internet of Things (IoT) solution, to manage urban property and improve the quality of population life through urban processes optimization. In April 2018, the Russian Ministry of Construction announced preparations for the launch of the "Smart City" project in 18 cities of the country. "Smart City" is included in the state program named "Digital Economy". Social profiles can be used in electronic means of non-stop travel payment, security services or formation of urban processes advanced analytical reporting. This also applies to individual adjustment of the environment for a particular person by means the 'Internet of Things', such as adjustment of the room temperature by time, distribution of the communication load, products selection taking into diet account, etc.

On the other hand, the social profiles applying can simplify the procedure of employment and increase the team efficiency in the Human Resources services. The HR algorithm of SP processing is the following:

1. The improper candidates are discarded.
2. There is a distribution of candidates based on summary characteristics and preferences from the profiles.
3. The lists for the final interview are formed.

In educational institutions, the compilation of SP-groups will increase the educational work effectiveness. On their basis, the teacher can make adjustments to the curriculum, in order to introduce an individual educational approach to each student. Also, social profiles will help to more effectively prevent and resolve conflict situations in the student communities.

For the scientific purposes, it is possible to model social processes based on a SP variety and to develop more flexible social policy mechanisms. This includes researching and predicting the people behavior in various non-standard situations, simplification of the public surveys conduct. Example is comparison of social profiles of many people from one social group for revealing their needs, satisfaction degree and subsequent adjustment of regulatory state functions in order to improve the quality of life. Another example of open source SP variety usage: revealing the mood, welfare of the society and its tolerance in order to pursue an effective migration policy.

Profiles can be used to write biographies or to assess historical events. For example, to show the attitude of contemporaries, to make a comparative assessment on such criteria as the life standard of people from one social group in different historical periods.

There is a list of the more common tasks directly related to the social profile data processing [3]:

– User identification. Discovery of accounts belonging to some person in order to clarify the social profile picture and use in other tasks.
– Social search. Search for social objects based on the analysis of the relationships sequence that the search entities depend on.

- Identification of true relationships. The use of an open source exploration approach to identify interactions between network users (i.e. real friends, relatives etc.). Technique is being actively used by law enforcement agencies to combat terrorism around the world.
- Generation of recommendations. There are distinguish the content selection and recommendations of 'acquaintances'. It used to build a graph of interests based on the social graph. A graph of interests is a person's concerns representation, obtained on the basis of his internet activity.
- The interest graph usage. It is used to determine the text tonality and to establish links between users in social networks or the real life. The interest graph actively used in marketing to analyze a product target audience and to create targeted advertising. The interest graph has many other use cases, including content search and filtering. The purpose is to provide recommendations for content templates.

After all of the above it should be noted that all the variety of social profile data is required in most cases for solving a specific problem. Therefore, analysts are faced with the challenge of providing a flexible presentation of the SP results (see Fig. 3).

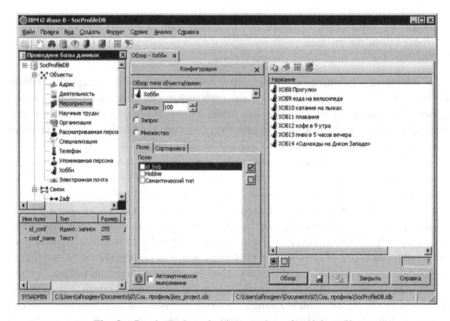

Fig. 3. Graph database implementation of social profile.

Various organizations such as Google [2], Microsoft [4], Usalytics [5] carry out work related to the creation and practical use of social profiles. But number of the completed software decisions and results in the public domain are not sufficient for an objective assessment. Therefore, current work is important for forecasting practical application options of the social profiling results. As noted above, the scope of existing solutions is limited. FindFace [1] is a project for finding people by reference image.

Wobot, Simply Measured, IQBuzz – solutions [9] for e-marketing and social relations analysis. Most of similar products cover only popular social networks. Also, they ineffective in the task of a person identification inside the network. These limitations lead to the fact that you have to handle large amounts of data manually [22]. It is necessary to introduce decisions based on the Big Data implementations, such as advanced methods of automated search and distributed storage for collected data.

Thus, it is possible to allocate the most obvious potential consumers of the developed system:

- Commercial organizations – for personalized promotion of goods and services, and to provide a better interaction with the consumers;
- Municipalities – for urban infrastructure construction and optimization, ensuring dialogue between citizens and the authorities, a fairly accurate identification of the people preferences;
- Law enforcement agencies – to identify criminals and draw up maps of social tension in order to prevent possible offences;
- Human Resources – to simplify and improve efficiency of employees search and hiring. Social profile groups can give invaluable help in organization of various public corporate events, such as conferences, forums, seminars etc.;
- Research institutes and organizations involved to investigation the behavior of society – various applied researches, such as: analysis of elective activity, definition of social tolerance value, medical statistics (diagnostics, epidemics forecasting, detection of new treatment methods), mental processes scrutiny of the person, automation processes of machine learning (development of human-like mechanisms, translators), etc.

Closure of social networks negatively affects the necessary information gathering for social graph building. Many Internet resources use Single Page Application, Ajax and DHTML for dynamic information output, which causes problems with parsers and search robots. European Union's General Data Protection Regulation (GDPR) become effective on 25 May 2018 and substantially change the collection of personal data of internet users. Personal data is allowed to use only with the consent of their owner even it located on public sources. Developed SP building system has filtering module and feedback means [21] for purposes of interaction with researched persons. That feature solves most privacy problems.

The main problem of generating recommendations is the "cold start" trouble – the recommendations calculation for new social facilities. There is another problem of the social profiling process that prevents its mass distribution. It is the difference between social networks: the general role is played by the connection semantics among social objects and social graphs with different topologies.

4   Conclusion

The final results of the social profiling process are the SP database and the graphical representation (a social graph). The graph is relatively simple for visual analysis and quite obvious. The social database is a base for further applied researches. It is possible to build statistical diagrams, get samples on specific issues by applying NoSQL queries.

It can be concluded that the possible application area of social profiles is wide, but not yet sufficiently mastered. It is expected that they will be actively used in business to assess customer demands and to build a successful dialogue with clients. Law enforcement agencies can use SP-groups to prevent offenses. Human resources departments can embed results of social profiling for more flexible interaction with the working team and staff recruitment. Also, it can be used in various scientific researches. Important problem of SP usage is a data privacy, that can be solve by usage filtering of restricted information.

The material presented above makes it possible to better understand the purposes of the social profile building system. Also, it determines requirements to developing a data presentation module. The results of a social profile building should be presented in a structured form, with the possibility of representing them in the graph or tables to facilitate their further processing by applied specialists, not related to programming.

References

1. Findface – Innovative service for people search by photo (2018). https://findface.ru
2. Google Analytics Solutions - Marketing Analytics & Measurement (2018). https://www.google.com/analytics/
3. Graph theory and social networks. Eggheado: Science (2014). https://medium.com/eggheado-science/778c92d20cea
4. Social Computing - Microsoft Research (2018). https://www.microsoft.com/en-us/research/group/social-computing/
5. Usalytics Careers, Funding, and Management Team | AngelList (2014). https://angel.co/usalytics
6. Bakkar, N., Kovalik, T., Lorenzini, I.: Artificial intelligence in neurodegenerative disease research: use of IBM Watson to identify additional RNA-binding proteins altered in amyotrophic lateral sclerosis. Acta Neuropathol. **135**(2), 227–247 (2018). https://doi.org/10.1007/s00401-017-1785-8
7. Chin D., Wright W.: Social media sources for personality profiling. In: UMAP 2014 Extended Proceedings, EMPIRE 2014: Emotions and Personality in Personalized Services, pp. 79–85 (2014). http://ceur-ws.org/Vol-1181/empire2014_proceedings.pdf
8. Eskes, P., Spruit, M., Brinkkemper, S., Vorstman, J., Kas, M.J.: The sociability score: app-based social profiling from a healthcare perspective. Comput. Hum. Behav. **59**, 39–48 (2016). https://doi.org/10.1016/j.chb.2016.01.024
9. Izmestyeva, E.: 12 tools for social media monitoring and analytics (2014). https://te-st.ru/tools/tools-monitoring-and-analysis-of-social-media/
10. Kaczmarek, L., et al.: Smile intensity in social networking profile photographs is related to greater scientific achievements. J. Posit. Psychol. **13**, 435–439 (2017). https://doi.org/10.1080/17439760.2017.1326519
11. Kristjansson, A.L., Mann, M.J., Smith, M.L.: Social profile of middle school-aged adolescents who use electronic cigarettes: implications for primary prevention. Prev. Sci. **19**, 1–8 (2017). https://doi.org/10.1007/s11121-017-0825-x

12. Kwon, D., Park, S., Ryu, J.-T.: A study on big data thinking of the internet of things-based smart-connected car in conjunction with controller area network bus and 4G-long term evolution. Symmetry **9**, 152. (2017). https://doi.org/10.3390/sym9080152
13. Mitrou L., Kandias M., Stavrou V., Gritzalis D.: Social media profiling: a Panopticon or Omniopticon tool? In: Proceedings of the 6th Conference of the Surveillance Studies Network (2014). https://www.infosec.aueb.gr/Publications/2014-SSN-Privacy%20Social%20Media.pdf
14. Mustafa, H., Anwer, M.J., Ali, S.S.: Measuring the correlation between social profile and voting habit and the moderation effect of political contribution for this relationship. Int. J. Manag. Organ. Stud. **5**(1), 44–57 (2016). http://www.ijmos.net/wp-content/uploads/2016/05/Haseeb-et.-al.pdf
15. Poulin, C., et al.: Predicting the risk of suicide by analyzing the text of clinical notes. PLoS ONE. **9**(1), e85733 (2014). https://doi.org/10.1371/journal.pone.0085733
16. Rajeswari, M.: Collaborative filtering approach for big data applications in social networks. Int. J. Comput. Sci. Inf. Technol. **6**(3), 2888–2892 (2015). https://www.scribd.com/document/289535998/Collaborative-Filtering-Approach-for-Big-Data-Applications-Based-on-Clustering-330-pdf
17. Rangel, F., Rosso, P.: On the multilingual and genre robustness of EmoGraphs for author profiling in social media. In: Mothe, J., et al. (eds.) CLEF 2015. LNCS, vol. 9283, pp. 274–280. Springer, Cham (2015). https://doi.org/10.1007/978-3-319-24027-5_28
18. Richelson, J.T.: The U.S. Intelligence Community, 7th edn. Routledge, 650 pages, London (2015)
19. Rossi, S., Ferland, F., Tapus, A.: User profiling and behavioral adaptation for HRI: a survey. Pattern Recognit. Lett. **99**, 3–12 (2017). https://doi.org/10.1016/j.patrec.2017.06.002
20. Timonin, A.Y., Bozhday, A.S., Bershadsky, A.M.: Analysis of unstructured text data for a person social profile. In: Proceedings of the International Conference on Electronic Governance and Open Society: Challenges in Eurasia, eGose 2017, St. Petersburg, Russia, pp. 1–5. ACM New York (2017). https://doi.org/10.1145/3129757.3129758
21. Timonin, A.Y., Bozhday, A.S., Bershadsky, A.M.: Research of filtration methods for reference social profile data. In: Proceedings of the International Conference on Electronic Governance and Open Society: Challenges in Eurasia, EGOSE 2016, pp. 189–193. ACM, New York (2016). https://doi.org/10.1145/3014087.3014090
22. Timonin, A.Y., Bozhday, A.S., Bershadsky, A.M.: The process of personal identification and data gathering based on big data technologies for social profiles. In: Chugunov, A.V., Bolgov, R., Kabanov, Y., Kampis, G., Wimmer, M. (eds.) DTGS 2016. CCIS, vol. 674, pp. 576–584. Springer, Cham (2016). https://doi.org/10.1007/978-3-319-49700-6_57
23. Tsalis, T., Avramidou, A., Nikolaou, I.E.: A social LCA framework to assess the corporate social profile of companies: Insights from a case study. J. Clean. Prod. **164**, 1665–1676 (2017). https://doi.org/10.1016/j.jclepro.2017.07.003

Methods to Identify Fake News in Social Media Using Artificial Intelligence Technologies

Denis Zhuk, Arsenii Tretiakov[✉], Andrey Gordeichuk,
and Antonina Puchkovskaia

ITMO University, 197101 St. Petersburg, Russia
ars.tretyakov@gmail.com

Abstract. Fake news (fake-news) existed long before the advent of the Internet and spread rather quickly via all possible means of communication as it is an effective tool for influencing public opinion. Currently, there are many definitions of fake news, but the professional community cannot fully agree on a single definition, which creates a big problem for its detection. Many large IT companies, such as Google and Facebook, are developing their own algorithms to protect the public from the falsification of information. At the same time, the lack of a common understanding regarding the essence of fake news makes the solution to this issue ideologically impossible. Consequently, experts and digital humanists specializing in different fields must study this problem intensively. This research analyzes the mechanisms for publishing and distributing fake-news according to the classification, structure and algorithm of the construction. Conclusions are then made on the methods for identifying this type of news in social media using systems with elements of artificial intelligence and machine learning.

Keywords: Fake news · Fake-news · Information falsification
Social media · Digital humanities · Artificial intelligence · Machine learning

1 Introduction

In 2016, a great public response occurred as a result of the assumption that fake-news strongly influenced the outcome of the presidential election in the United States. Some sources provide information that fake news about the US elections on Facebook was more popular among users than the articles belonging to the largest traditional news sources. However, the scope of active fake news usage is not limited to politics. For example, the 2016 news story reporting that Canadian, Japanese, and Chinese laboratory scientists were studying the effectiveness of ordinary dandelion roots on the treatment of blood cancer was shared user-to-user more than 1.4 million times.

False news is a concern because it can affect the minds of millions of people every day. Such coverage puts them in line with both traditional methods of influence, such as advertising, and the latest ones, such as search engine manipulation (the Search Engine Manipulation Effect) and affecting search options (the Search Suggestion Effect).

© Springer Nature Switzerland AG 2018
D. A. Alexandrov et al. (Eds.): DTGS 2018, CCIS 858, pp. 446–454, 2018.
https://doi.org/10.1007/978-3-030-02843-5_36

Currently, the popularity of a message matters more than its reliability. In the article "How technology disrupted the truth", The Guardian's editor-in-chief Katharine Viner mentions the problem of intensified dissemination of fake information through social networks. When people share news with each other in order to show some semblance of knowing the truth, they do not even verify the veracity of the information that they are sharing [13]. As the legal scholar and online-harassment expert Danielle Citron describes it, "people forward on what others think, even if the information is false, misleading or incomplete, because they think they have learned something valuable." All of this has led to emergence of the term post-truth, which in 2016 became the word of the year by the Oxford Dictionaries [11]. Thus fake news is defined as a piece of news that is written stylistically as real news but is completely or partially false [15].

Another problem that prevents users from getting the full news image of the day is so-called "informational separation" caused by filtration of information through news aggregators and social networks. In her article, Katharine Viner also proposes the term "filter bubble". This term describes a situation when two users google the same search query, but receive different results [16]. The same thing happens when Facebook is used [5]. For example, if certain users do not support Brexit, their news feeds are likely to contain posts from their friends who have the same attitude towards Brexit. Consequently, the users do not have any access to the opposing point of view, even if they intentionally seek it out.

In social media, people decide whose posts they want to read. There are "friends" or "followers", and people are apt to follow others whose opinions are more alike. As a result, users no longer select the *topics* to read but rather the *slant* in how news is presented. Thus users effectively construct their own "echo chamber" [13]. Zubiaga et al. [17] studied how users handle untried information in social media. Persons with higher reputation are more trusted, so they could spread false news amid other people without raising distrust about the reliability of the news or of its source.

As a solution to it, their employees began to mark each item of news depending on whether this news is truthful or not. Facebook marks some posts as "disputed" and gives a list of websites that consider this information fake [5]. Mark Zuckerberg estimates the volume of such news at Facebook to be 1% [1]. In 2016 "Google News", a news aggregator, began to mark news about the USA and the United Kingdom. Then the company started checking news about Germany and France, and since February 2017, this feature is available in Mexico, Brazil and Argentina [2]. The Russian government also paid attention to this problem. In February 2017, the Russian Ministry of Foreign Affairs started publishing examples of fake news by foreign mass-media companies [12]. Moreover, in August 2017 President of USA Donald Trump offered his own decision about spreading fake news items. He launched his own news program on his Facebook page "Real News" for posting only reliable news facts [6].

In November of 2017 the European Commission launched a public consultation on fake news and online disinformation as well as established a High-Level Expert Group representing academics, online platforms, mass media and NGOs [10]. The Expert Group includes citizens, social media platforms, news organizations, researchers and public authorities. Moreover, the International Federation of Library Associations and Institutions (IFLA) published instructions about fake news [4], which eight suggestions to help to define which information is false. Among other things, the authors recommend paying attention to news' headers, the placement, date and formatting. Infographics can be downloaded in the PDF format in different languages and to unpack. Besides in 2017 a group of journalists in the Ukraine started "StopFake News" with the goal of debunking. Started by professors and journalists from Kiev Mohyla University, "StopFake News" considers itself to be a media institution for providing public service journalism [7].

2   Classification of Fake News

Researching features of face news by aims and content is of great importance, thus issues such as, firstly, the "news" created and extended for Internet traffic. Users of social networks and messengers constantly face numerous examples of similar "news". For instance there is information about issues such as lost children, missing pets, and the necessity of blood donations from rare blood types, which spread throughout social networks like a virus, repeatedly multiplying revenues of mobile operators due to increase in Internet traffic.

Second is the "news" that is created and distributed to draw attention to the individual, company, project or movement.

Third is the "news" crafted and extended for manipulation with the market or obtaining certain advantages in economic activity.

Finally the "news" created and disseminated to manipulate the market, obtain certain advantages in economic activity, and discriminate persons on the basis of sex, race, nationality, language, origin, property and official capacity, the residence, the relation to religion, beliefs, are belonging to public associations and also other circumstances [15].

Moreover, additional classifications depend on the type of action. They include:

- Satire or parody – no motive to cause abuse but has probable to fool
- False connection – when headlines, visuals or captions do not match the content
- Misleading content – misleading use of information to fabricate an issue or individual
- False context – when honest content is divided with false contextual information
- Imposter content – when honest sources are impersonated
- Manipulated Content – when honest information or imagery is manipulated to trick
- Fabricated content – new content is 100% false, created to trick and do abuse [8]

3   Related Work

The general approaches for the detection of fake news, determining their classification and structure, and constructing the algorithm are described below.

3.1 A Subsection Sample

In the paper "Credibility Assessment of Textual Claims on the Web" [14], authors offered a familiar approach for credibility analysis of unstructured textual claims in an open domain setting. They used the language style and source credibility (or accuracy) of researches reporting a claim to assess its credibility in experiments on analyzing the credibility of real-world claims. The authors (see Fig. 1) considered a set of textual claims C in the form of textual frames, and a set of web-sources WS containing articles (or texts) A that release the claims. Allowing that $a_{ij} \in A$ denotes an article of web-source $ws_j \in WS$ about request $ci \in C$. Each claim o request c_i is combine with a double random variable y_i that details its credibility label, where $y_i \in \{T, F\}$ (T is for True, whereas F is for Fake). Every one a_{ij} is correlate with a random variable y_{ij} that represent the accuracy opinion (True or Fake) of the a_{ij} (from ws_j) in regard to c_i – when examining only this articles. Given the labels of a group of the claims (e.g., y_1 for c_1, and y_3 for c_3), the objective is to conclude the credibility label of the remaining claims (e.g., y2 for c2). To learn the criterions in the accuracy assessment model, Distant Supervision is used to attach detected true/fake labels of claims to matching reporting articles, and teach a Credibility Classifier. In this process, there is a need to (a) understand the language of the article, and (b) consider the reliability of the basic web sources reporting the articles. Thereafter, (c) the accuracy opinion scores of individual articles are computed, and finally, (d) these scores are aggregated from all articles to get the comprehensive credibility label of target claims.

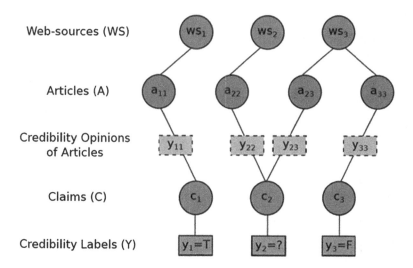

Fig. 1. The model of considering a set of textual claims.

3.2   The Reliability of Web-Sources

Then in Source Reliability, the web-source that hosts the article also has a significant impact on the claim's credibility [14]. It means one should not trust a claim reported in an article from one media source, as opposed to a claim on another website. To avoid modeling from infrequent observations, authors using this approach combine all web-sources that possess fewer than 10 articles into the dataset as a single web-source.

Moreover in this approach for credibility aggregation from multiple sources using Distant Supervision for training. Attaching the label y_i of each claim c_i to each article a_{ij} informing the claim (i.e., setting labels $y_{ij} = y_i$) like in Fig. 1 where $y_{11} = y_1 = T, y_{33} = y_3 = F$. Using these y_{ij} as the corresponding training labels for a_{ij}, with the corresponding feature vectors $F^L(a_{ij}) \cup F^{SR}(a_{ij})$, we train an L_1 - regularized logistic regression model on the training data.

In addition, there is a misinformation detection model (MDM) that combines graph-based knowledge representation with algorithms for comparing text-derived graphs to each other, fuse documents to construct aggregated multi-source knowledge graph, detect conflicts between documents, and classify knowledge fragments as misinformation [9]. This model (see Fig. 2) includes using probabilistic matching exploiting semantic and syntactic information contained in the knowledge graphs, and inferring misinformation labels from reliability-credibility scores of corresponding documents and sources. Preliminary validation work shows the feasibility of the MDM in detecting conflicting and false storylines in text sources.

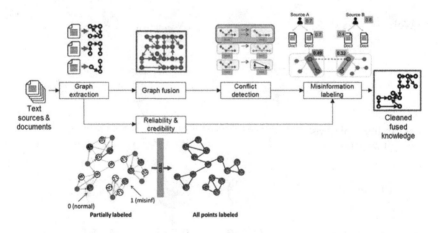

Fig. 2. Components of the misinformation detection model.

3.3   Language-Independent Approach

This approach of automatically distinguishing credible from fake news is based on a rich feature set using linguistic (n-gram), credibility-related (capitalization, punctuation, pronoun use, attitude polarity), and semantic (embeddings and DBPedia data) features. The result was described in the research "In Search of Credible News" [3].

Experimentation was conducted using the following linguistic features where n-grams is the existence of individual uni- and bi-grams. The explanation is that some n-grams are more typical of credible against false news. tf-idf is the same n-grams but weighted using tf-idf. Vocabulary richness is the number of exclusive word types used in the article, probably ordered by the sum of word tokens [3].

In addition, this approach uses embedding vectors to model the semantics of documents. In order to model implicitly some general world knowledge, word2vec vectors were trained using the text of long abstracts prior to building vectors for a document.

4 Using Artificial Intelligence Technologies (Machine Learning) to Identify Fake News

In the framework of this study, the task of creating a system model capable of detecting news content with inaccurate information (fake news) with high reliability (more than 90%) and dividing it into the appropriate categories was also completed. To solve this problem, the module of analysis and preprocessing of facts Akil.io was designed to accomplish tasks that automatically execute software and technical complexes through problem recognition and analysis. Those problems had been presented in the form of a system of facts formatted into text, and the subsequent transformation into a ready solution according to the input data (see Fig. 3). This module provides the following functions:

- Input and recognition of the input system of facts
- Analysis of data relationships in the graph
- Identify the sufficiency/inadequacy of data
- Formation of a request for additional data in case of their insufficiency
- Formation of the algorithm for solving the problem
- Formation of the execution plan for the solution
- Ensure interactive execution of the plan
- Representation of a ready solution in the form determined by the task manager

Since the training was done using the ready-made module for analyzing and pre-processing the facts of the system with elements of the artificial intelligence Akil.io, the most important stages were the collection of data for training and the subsequent verification of the reliability of learning outcomes.

To identify the categories of fake news, a large number of examples were needed from different categories of texts that the model would be able to recognize. As a result of the preliminary analysis, an average classification of fake news was compiled and used (misinterpretation of facts, pseudoscientific, author's opinions, humor and others). For the distribution of news by category, two approaches are tested: automatic collection of data from a list of sources with a pre-determined category of all news on this source and manual collection and subsequent sorting by category.

To collect data from a list of sources with a predetermined category of all news on this source, a crawler was used, which allows information to be collected automatically. With the use of this tool, 35,000 articles were collected, which is sufficient for teaching

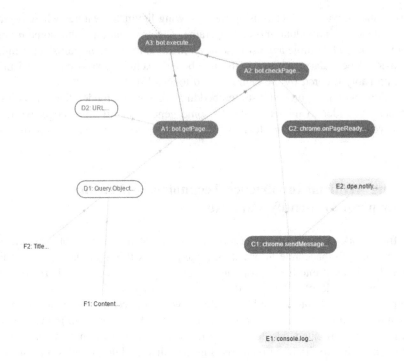

Fig. 3. The module of analysis and preprocessing of facts by Akil.io.

the model, but subsequent manual verification of the results of testing this method showed its unreliability (60% reliability). The reason for this is the heterogeneity of the data, combinations of fake and true news within a single resource and a short text length.

As part of the approbation of the manual collection approach and subsequent sorting by categories, a manual step-by-step review of each article, its category definition and subsequent entry into the database for analysis was performed. Based on the results of the training and the subsequent verification of the model, 70% accuracy was achieved.

Since approaches with the distribution of fake news in categories show low reliability, the approach with revealing non-fake news is tested, because there is much more information, generally accepted rules, classifications and other attributes for them. Reliable news is much easier to reduce to a single category. They are based on facts, set out briefly and clearly, and contain a minimal amount of subjective interpretation, and such reliable resources are plentiful.

The materials were distributed only in two groups: true and untrue. To the untrue belonged all possible categories of fake news and everything else that did not contain strictly factual information and did not fit into the standards of journalistic ethics developed back in the last century with the direct participation of UNESCO. The final sample was 14,300 fake articles and another 25,000 reliable ones. As a result of manual verification of this approach, the accuracy in 92% was attained. The high accuracy of the approach is due to the ability to provide a large array of reliable information for analysis, which is represented in the stylistics and language typical for a reliable news article.

5   Conclusion

For the purposes of building an information system, the main distinguishing features of the news were identified, and then applied singly or jointly with each other.

- False numbers
- Part of the truth (incomplete context)
- Non-authoritative experts in this field
- Average values
- Unrelated correlations of facts
- Incorrect selection
- Uncovered reasons for the phenomenon or event described

Ultimately, the model has learned to analyze how the text is written, and to determine whether it has evaluative vocabulary, author's judgments, words with strong connotations or obscene expressions. If it gives a very low score, it means that the text is not a fact-based news item in its classic form. It can be misinformation, satire, or subjective opinion of the author or something else. This method is quite effective.

Naturally, this method does not solve the problem of fake news definitively, but it helps with high confidence to determine the non-news news in the style of writing that in combination with other available methods (crowdsourcing, classification of sources and authors, fact checking, numerical analysis, etc.) increase the accuracy to as close to 100% as possible.

Acknowledgements. The reported study was funded by RFBR according to the research project № 18-311-00-125.

References

1. Fiveash, K.: Zuckerberg claims just 1% of Facebook posts carry fake news. Arstechnika (2016). https://arstechnica.com/information-technology/2016/11/zuckerberg-claims-1-percent-facebook-posts-fake-news-trump-election/
2. Gingras, R.: Expanding Fact Checking at Google. VP NEWS GOOGLE (2017). https://blog.google/topics/journalism-news/expanding-fact-checking-google/
3. Hardalov, M., Koychev, I., Nakov, P.: In search of credible news. In: Dichev, C., Agre, G. (eds.) AIMSA 2016. LNCS (LNAI), vol. 9883, pp. 172–180. Springer, Cham (2016). https://doi.org/10.1007/978-3-319-44748-3_17
4. How to Spot Fake News, IFLA (2018). https://www.ifla.org/publications/node/11174
5. Kafka, P.: Facebook has started to flag fake news stories. ReCode (2017). http://www.recode.net/2017/3/4/14816254/facebook-fake-news-disputed-trump-snopespolitifact-seattle-tribune

6. Koerner, C.: Trump Has Launched A "Real News" Program On His Facebook, Hosted By His Daughter-In-Law. BuzzFeed News (2017). https://www.buzzfeed.com/claudiakoerner/trumps-daughter-in-law-hosting-real-news-videos-for-the

7. Kramer, A.E.: To Battle Fake News, Ukrainian Show Features Nothing but Lies. New York Times (2017). http://nyti.ms/2mvR8m9

8. Lardizabal-Dado, N.: Fake news: 7 types of mis- and disinformation (Part 1). BlogWatch (2017). https://blogwatch.tv/2017/10/fake-news-types/

9. Levchuk, G., Shabarekh, C.: Using soft-hard fusion for misinformation detection and pattern of life analysis in OSINT. In: Proceedings of SPIE, 10207, Next-Generation Analyst V (2016). https://doi.org/10.1117/12.2263546

10. Next steps against fake news: Commission sets up High-Level Expert Group and launches public consultation. European Commission (2017). http://europa.eu/rapid/press-release_IP-17-4481_en.htm

11. Norman, M.: Whoever wins the US presidential election, we've entered a post-truth world – there's no going back now. The Independent (2016). https://www.independent.co.uk/voices/us-election-2016-donald-trump-hillary-clinton-who-wins-post-truth-world-no-going-back-a7404826.html

12. Ministry of Foreign Affairs will publish fake news and their disclosures, RIA Novosti (2016, in Russian). https://ria.ru/mediawars/20170215/1488012741.html

13. Pogue, D.: How to Stamp Out Fake News. Scientific American (2017). https://www.nature.com/scientificamerican/journal/v316/n2/full/scientificamerican0217-24.html, https://doi.org/10.1038/scientificamerican0217-24

14. Popat, K., Mukherjee, S., Strötgen, J., Weikum, G.: Credibility assessment of textual claims on the web. In: Proceedings of the 25th ACM International on Conference on Information and Knowledge Management, pp. 2173–2178, Indianapolis, Indiana, USA (2016). https://doi.org/10.1145/2983323.2983661

15. Sukhodolov, A.P.: The Phenomenon of "Fake News" in the Modern Media Space, pp. 87–106. gumanitarnye aspekty, Evroaziatskoe sotrudnichestvo (2017, in Russian)

16. Viner, K.: How technology disrupted the truth. The Guardian (2016). https://www.theguardian.com/media/2016/jul/12/how-technology-disrupted-the-truth

17. Zubiaga, A., Hoi, G.W.S., Liakata, M., Procter, R., Tolmie, P.: Analysing how people orient to and spread rumours in social media by looking at conversational threads. PLoS ONE **11**(3) (2015). https://doi.org/10.1371/journal.pone.0150989

A Big-Data Analysis of Disaster Information Dissemination in South Korea

Yongsuk Hwang⬛, Jaekwan Jeong$^{(\boxtimes)}$⬛, Eun-Hyeong Jin,
Hee Ra Yu, and Dawoon Jung⬛

Konkuk University, Seoul, South Korea
dbcjjk@gmail.com

Abstract. During the disaster periods, a large amount of information is created and distributed online through news media sites and other Web 2.0 tools including Twitter, discussion boards, online community, and blogs. As scholars actively debate on information dissemination patterns during the disasters, this study examined how individuals utilized the different forms of the Internet in order to generate relevant information. Using a big-data analysis of 3,578,877 online documents collected during 50 days periods each about the Gyeongju earthquake, and MERS, our results found that 1. The amount of information and its distribution by online platforms is significantly different between two disaster cases, 2. The proportion of daily generated documents during the disaster periods showed different patterns during each disaster case, 3. While the amount of daily generated information was gradually decreasing during the Gyeongju earthquake case, the information collected from non-media sites was increasing during the MERS period. The results highlight that individuals may utilize the Internet differently to deal with disaster-related information based on type of disaster. Therefore, a simple model would not accurately predict the online information dissemination pattern during the disaster.

Keywords: Information dissemination · Exponential curve
Online communication · Disaster information

1 Introduction

In the past two years, 2015 and 2016, South Korea was hit by two big disasters. The first was the Gyeongju earthquake, the strongest ever in South Korea since the first measurement of earthquakes was recorded in 1974 [1], and the second was the outbreak of Middle East Respiratory Syndrome (MERS), one of the biggest medical disasters in Korean history, which claimed 186 lives. During of these two disasters, people in South Korea used the Internet as a major source of information [2]. The Internet plays a critical role during a disaster by disseminating relevant information to audiences with concerns [3, 4]. While scholars generally agree that the Internet serves as an informative tool for disasters, there are debates on how people use information channels on the Internet and how information is disseminated over the disaster periods.

One of the issues of the debates is about the specific channels or media on the Internet that become the mainstream source of information. Some scholars argue that

D. A. Alexandrov et al. (Eds.): DTGS 2018, CCIS 858, pp. 455–467, 2018.
https://doi.org/10.1007/978-3-030-02843-5_37

online news media play a key role in generating and disseminating information during a disaster (e.g. [5]), while others suggest that social networking sites (SNSs) and other Web 2.0 tools are used more during the period [6].

Another point argued about is the manner in which the entire information is distributed over the disaster period. For instance, Downe [7] suggested that information generated about a disaster would gradually increase initially and then decrease after it reaches a peak. Another group of scholars proposed that daily informative documents would gradually increase as the disaster situation develops [8]. However, others argue that since disasters occur suddenly and without any warning, information is rapidly created, disseminated, and gradually decreased afterword. The goal of this study, therefore, is twofold. It examines (1) information distribution among the different types of online media during the two disasters and (2) the proportion of information changes over time in both cases.

2   Review of Literature

2.1   Internet as an Information Dissemination Tool

Online networks are structured to share information. These networks consist of platforms such as online news sites, social networking sites, or microblogs, each performing different functions [9]. In this networked cyberspace, Internet users send, receive, incorporate, and interact with various types of information on a daily basis [10]. While scholars generally agree that traditional news media and their online platforms are major sources of information (e.g. [11]), information dissemination occurs on different platforms, such as via e-mails [12], blogs [13], and other social networking sites [8, 14].

On the other hand, user-oriented online platforms provide much more control to participants to generate their own information environment. For instance, users from different sites interact with each other via posts, feeds, comments, messaging, photos, videos, and blogs [15]. With the ease of accessing and adding information to the site, Web 2.0 tools such as SNSs, blogs, microblogs, and online bulletin boards are an alternative source of information [16].

2.2   Online Information Dissemination During a Disaster

During a disaster, people require extensive amount and range of information in order to prevent possible threats that could break out. In addition, information needs to be provided persistently as the conditions change rapidly over time [17]. Palen [3] suggests that information created and disseminated online plays a critical role in disaster situations as information under Web 2.0 has "significant implications for emergency management practice and policy" (pp. 76). During disasters, individuals rely heavily on relative information by playing different roles in information circulation. First, they participate to provide appropriate feedback for immediate needs [18]. Second, individuals serve as important information producers and disseminators. The types of information they disseminate include reliable health information generated by media outlets or government officials that need to be spread quickly [19]. Third, individuals can serve as initial disaster reporters. For instance, students from universities in China were the first to report the outbreak of H1N1 flu on the Internet [20].Furthermore, Twitter was the first medium to report the US Airway 1549 airplane crash-land on the Hudson River [21].

While scholars have been arguing about the effects of news media and social media on disaster information dissemination, Chan [22] suggested that the role of social media in disaster information dissemination could be analyzed by its key characteristics: collectivity, connectedness, completeness, clarity, and collaboration. He insists that these characteristics help in supporting disaster management functions. In this process, individuals use social media in a pattern for the following four purposes: 1. information dissemination, 2. disaster planning and training, 3. collaborative problem solving and decision making, and 4. information gathering. The mediating role between traditional and social media is explained in Fig. 1.

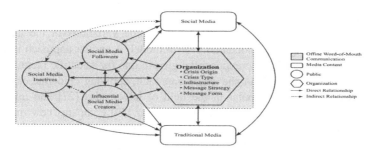

Fig. 1. Social-mediated disaster communication model. Adapted from [6, p. 192]

2.3   Dissemination of Disaster Information on the Internet

Shortly after a disaster occurs, related information quickly spreads over internet and this information is reinforced until the disaster is officially over [18]. In order to track the amount of information created regarding certain issues and to suggest appropriate models, a number of scholars have invested various efforts. For instance, Anthony Downe [7] suggests that disaster coverage by news media should be divided into five stages during the duration of a disaster as illustrated in Fig. 2.

The "pre-problem stage" refers to the period when an alert is raised about an impending disaster by an interest group or experts, and yet, it fails to gather mass attention. The second stage, "alarmed discovery and euphoric enthusiasm stage," is when the public suddenly realizes the magnitude of the issue and begins to pay attention. The next stage is "realizing the cost of significant progress." In this stage, public attention on the issue reaches a peak and people start considering the cost of resolving the issue. In the fourth stage, there is a gradual decline of intense public interest, people's attention to the issue declines, and another issue gains more prominence. The last stage, the post-problem stage, is when people no longer think about the issue. While this model has been used to test the attention life cycle of various issues,

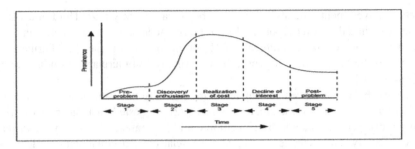

Fig. 2. Issue attention cycle. Adapted from [47, p. 20]

Kim and Choi [23] suggest that the model does not fit well for disaster analysis because pre-problem and alarmed discovery and euphoric enthusiasm stages rarely exist in unexpected disaster cases.

Another approach to tracking the amount of information disseminated during disasters was developed by Goffman [24]. He applied the epidemic model to estimate the diffusion of ideas. Later, Goffman [25] explained the variations in the amount of information by applying the exponential growth model. A similar approach is adopted by Price [26] as he finds that the exponential growth rate for scientific literature is 5% over the past two decades. After the initial approach, applying epidemic exponential growth model has become popular in the field of informatics [27] and information dissemination studies [28]. For example, Funkhouser [29] compares new media coverage and public perception of the past 10 years. The most widely used formula for exponential growth was developed by Egghe and Rao [30]. According to them, the exponential function is best calculated by $X(t) = a * \exp(bt)$, where $X(t)$ represents the size at time t, a is a constant, and $\exp(bt)$ is the constant growth rate.

This formula is widely used in the field of communication when observing information dissemination patterns. Forkosh-Baruch and Hershkovitz [31] analyzed 47 Facebook and 26 Twitter accounts of universities in Israel and suggested that SNS promotes information sharing by facilitating learning in the community. Scanfeld and Scanfeld [8] searched health-related data on Twitter and concluded that an increasing amount of health data serve Twitter as an important venue for health information. Yang and Counts [32] compared information dissemination patterns on Twitter and Blog. The results suggest that the distribution patterns are systematically different between the two channels. Analyzing epidemic information dissemination in mobile social networks showed that the amount of information over time is either gradually increasing or decaying [28].

However, research investigating disaster information diffusion showed slightly different results. When a disaster occurs, initially, information disseminates rapidly [33]. After a certain period, the amount of disaster information gradually wanes and then disappears [34]. A similar study was conducted by Greer and Moreland [35], who analyzed United Airlines' and American Airlines' Web sites after September 11, 2001. A one-month analysis revealed that the number of messages posted on the Web sites was consistent throughout September; then, it gradually decreased after October. Due to the characteristic of disaster information that it peaks initially and then decreases, the exponential decay model is more suitable to measure disaster information dissemination patterns [36].

2.4 Disaster Outline: Gyeongju Earthquake

Gyeongju earthquake occurred on September 12, 2016. The initial earthquake was recorded at 7:44 p.m., measuring 5.1 on the moment magnitude scale. Then, the main earthquake followed at 8:03 p.m., measuring 5.8. This was the strongest recorded earthquake in South Korea since measurement began in 1978 [1]. Immediately after the earthquake, Internet and smartphone messenger services were temporarily disrupted and the subway service in Pusan stopped. The next day, a few schools were closed in the area and the nuclear power plants in Wolsung were shut down.

2.5 Disaster Outline: Middle East Respiratory Syndrome (MERS) in South Korea

May 2015 saw the outbreak of the Middle East Respiratory Syndrome (MERS) infection in South Korea. The outbreak was triggered by a virus transmitted via import from overseas. After the first case infected by MERS was confirmed on May 20, 2016, 186 people were found to be infected, of whom 38 died, and 16,693 were quarantined to prevent further spread of the virus [37]. Until the Korean Ministry of Health and Welfare officially declared the end of MERS spread on July 4, 2015, people were seriously concerned about preventing infection by closing schools or canceling large events [38, 39].

3 Methods

3.1 Research Questions

> RQ1. How does the amount of information differ between the two the disaster cases?
>
> RQ2. How does the distribution pattern of disaster information change over the period of the disaster?
>
> RQ3. How do the exponential curves appear on each channel?

3.2 Data Collection

For this study, we collected online Buzz from Korean online news sites, blogs, online community sites, discussion boards, and Twitter. These media include 257 online news sites, 4 individual blog platforms, 2 community site platforms, 18 discussion boards, and Twitter. Each site is mentioned in Appendix 1. The Gyeongju earthquake Buzz data were collected using related keywords during the 50-day period from September 12, 2016 (the day when the first earthquake was recorded) to October 31, 2016. The MERS-related online documents were collected for the same number of days, that is, a 50-day period from May 20, 2015 (the day the first confirmed infection case was reported) to July 8, 2015. The 50-day data collection period is suitable for both disaster cases because, first, previous studies have shown that information dissemination duration usually ends within a 50-day timeframe [34, 36]. Second, the two disasters also ended within this term (the last aftershock was recorded on May 25, 2016, and the Korean government officially declared the end of MERS on July 4, 2015).

One of top three telecommunication companies in South Korea, SK Telecom, was contacted to conduct data collection and treatment. Like Tweetping (https://tweetping. net), Smart-Insight (http://www.smartinsight.co.kr/) by SK Telecom developed a system in which a file-system discovery crawler collected documents from different channels [40, 41].

3.3   Data Analysis

Using the Smart-Insight system, 40,606 categorized cleaned unstructured documents for the Gyeongju Earthquake case and 3,538,271 documents for MERS case were collected during the 50-day period. The documents were broken down into 3,014 news articles, 31,655 Twitter feeds, 740 discussion board posts, 2,532 blog pages, and 2,665 online community posts (for the Gyeongju earthquake); 70,122 news articles, 3,224,270 Twitter feeds, 138,767 discussion board posts, 34,249 blog pages, and 70,863 online community posts (for the MERS epidemic).

While the frequency and percentage of collected documents were analyzed and reported to understand the amount of information dissemination in the two disaster cases, which RQ1 aims to find, the numbers were converted using natural logarithm in order to see the dissemination patterns more clearly (Refer to RQ2). The natural logarithm conversion is useful when trying to find if complexly changing numbers show certain patterns or tendencies [42]. The natural logarithm used in this study is as shown in formulae (1)–(3).

$$\ln x = \int_0^x \frac{1}{t} dt \tag{1}$$

$$\ln x = \log ex \tag{2}$$

$$(\ln x)' = \frac{1}{x} \tag{3}$$

In order to answer research question 3, the patterns were further processed to find if the information dissemination in two disaster cases were gradually growing or decaying. Applying the exponential decay formula, we were able to find (1) an average number of documents per observation and (2) the exponential decay constant ratio. The widely accepted exponential decay formula is written as shown in formula (4) where N represents an average amount of information per observation and λ represents the exponential decay constant [43].

$$Y = Ne^{\lambda t} \tag{4}$$

4 Result

As summarized in Table 1, among the 3,578,877 online documents collected from 282 channels, the most prevalently used medium was Twitter with 3,255,925 (90%) online documents created for both disaster cases, followed by discussion boards (3.9%), online community (2%), news (2%), and blog (1%). During the disasters, Twitter served as the major source of information dissemination. This result is reasonable, as one of the main functions of the Twitter is to deliver breaking news while Blog deals more with analytical opinions [44]. Another finding from this analysis shows that 87 times more documents were created and distributed during the MERS period as compared to the earthquake period.

Table 1. Proportion of disaster buzz by online channels, N (%)

	News	Twitter	Discussion board	Blog	Online community	Total	χ^2 (p)
Earthquake	3014	31655	740	2532	2665	40606	392,424
	(7.5)	(78)	(1.8)	(6.2)	(6.5)	(100)	(<0.001)
MERS	70122	3224270	138767	34249	70863	3538271	
	(2)	(91)	(4%)	(1)	(2)	(100)	

An interesting difference between the two disaster cases is the proportion of online news articles in the two different periods. Online news provided the second largest amount of information during the Gyeongju earthquake. However, the proportion decreased to the second least medium when covering the MERS issue. This indicates that individuals relied heavily on Twitter and discussion boards in order to find the information needed while online news failed to be a source of information. All the findings were statistically significant ($\chi^2 = 392,424$, p < .001).

The distribution of online documents by date shows contrasting results as can be seen in Fig. 3. During the earthquake period, online Buzz increased at the beginning of the disaster. The amount of information quickly decreased from day 3 until the end of the disaster. The graph sporadically shows selective peaks whenever aftershocks occurred, which quickly goes down after that. On the other hand, during the MERS period, online Buzz stays calm during the initial stage. Then, it quickly rises from around day 13 to day 15. This was an important period for the MERS epidemic spread. The definite diagnosis cases reached 30 and the number of those quarantined touched 1000 on the same day, which was the 13th day of the observation. The next day, the first doctor who had made contact with patients in an emergency room was diagnosed with the infection. On June 15, 2015, day 15, the doctor insisted that he had made contact with more than 1,500 people in a large shopping mall. The increasing possibility of infection and fear prompted people to consume and disseminate more information about MERS.

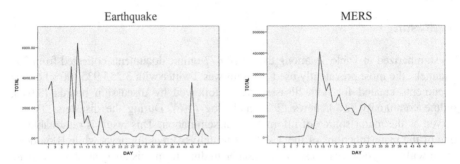

Fig. 3. Disaster Buzz distribution during the 50-day period

Figure 4 presents a clearer comparison between the two cases. Based on the natural logarithm conversion graphs, while the amount of Buzz for the earthquake data gradually decreases over time, the MERS information dissemination pattern shows a somewhat different direction. After the initial increase on day 13, the graph remained at the peak for more than 20 days before it started to show a drop. This pattern was observed in all types of media, supporting Dawne's [7] issue attention cycle model. One of the interesting differences in this graph is that on the cessation side of MERS, the downside slope of information on Twitter is much more gentle when compared to that of other media. This different pattern may suggest that individuals were still looking for the information in order to ensure that the disaster was definitely reaching its end.

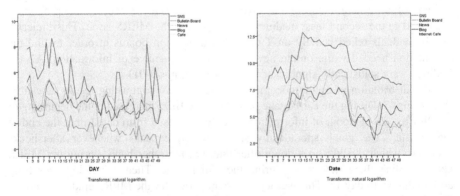

Fig. 4. Disaster Buzz distribution by online channels based on natural logarithm conversion

Tables 2 and 3 summarize the exponential decay constant values of each medium during the disaster. During the earthquake period, although the average number of observations varied by medium, information dissemination decreased among all five types of Internet media. The medium that showed the fastest decrease in the amount of information was the discussion board (λ = –0.1978, N = 153.38), while online news media recorded the slowest decrease (λ = –0.02832, N = 121.45). This suggests that news media were constantly putting out information regarding the earthquake during the period under observation, while Twitter (λ = –0.0681, N = 2445.43) and the discussion board (λ = –0.1978, N = 153.38) were losing attention.

Table 2. Exponential decay constant by online channels - Gyeongju Earthquake

Channel	Model	N	λ : Decay Constant
Twitter	$2445.4390 \times e^{-0.0681 \times t}$	2445.4390	–0.0681
Board	$153.3805 \times e^{-0.1978 \times t}$	153.3805	–0.1978
News	$121.45087 \times e^{-0.02832 \times t}$	121.45087	–0.02832
Blog	$162.78365 \times e^{-0.05339 \times t}$	162.78365	–0.05339
Community	$198.5266 \times e^{-0.06624 \times t}$	198.5266	–0.06624

Meanwhile, it is noticeable that the decay constant values of all non-news media were increasing during the MERS disaster: Twitter (λ = 0.0483, N = 10201), discussion board (λ = 0.058, N = 306.82), blog (λ = 0.043, N = 139.45), and Internet community (λ = 0.032, N = 406.67), while constant value for the news media was decaying (λ = –0.016, N = 546.86). The contrast in the exponential decay constant values between news sites and non-news sites suggests that while the amount of information gradually decreased from the online news media, individuals were using other channels of information as an alternative source.

5 Discussion

When observing information distribution among online medium (news, Twitter, discussion board, blog, online community) regarding two disaster cases, we were able to find a few interesting differences. First, the total amount of Buzz covering the MERS case was 87 times higher than that covering the Gyeongju earthquake. Second, while online news media played the second-largest role in disseminating information during the Gyeongju earthquake, the amount of information on the online new media was the second lowest for the MERS outbreak. Finally, Twitter served as the major channel of information circulation during both disasters.

The dominant amount of information on Twitter (Earthquake: 78%, MERS: 91%) indicates that people might consider SNS as a major channel of information when a disaster occurs. Previous studies found that individuals prefer SNSs over mainstream media because the types of information produced from the media sites are different from their expectation, and people seek information that news media sites do not cover such as family/friend-related information or insider facts [6]. Considering the different proportions of new media-generated information, it is recommended that future

Table 3. Exponential decay constant by online channels – MERS

Channel	Model	N	λ : Decay Constant
Twitter	$10201 \times e^{0.048 \times t}$	10201	0.0483
Board	$306.82 \times e^{0.058 \times t}$	306.82	0.058
News	$546.86 \times e^{-0.016 \times t}$	546.86	–0.016
Blog	$139.45 \times e^{0.043 \times t}$	139.45	0.043
Community	$198.5266 \times e^{0.0329 \times t}$	406.67	0.032

research focus on how news media agenda and other media agenda were different in covering each disaster case from the traditional agenda-setting perspectives.

In addition, although data for each disaster information were collected for the same period (50 days) using the same procedures, the big difference (87 times) in the amount of data amount suggests that there may be factors influencing people's motivation to collect and spread information to manage each disaster. Besides the fact that one is a natural disaster and the other one is a medical disaster, other differences, such as physical and emotional distance, influence people required more information for the MERS case. For instance, based on the Twitter feed analysis covering four disasters from 2010 to 2013, Simon, Goldberg, and Adini [45] found that the total number of tweets was significantly different and that this difference might be due to users' perceived relevance to each disaster. Future studies are suggested to investigate people's motivation or "need for orientation."

The amount of daily information in the graphs presented in Figs. 3 and 4 clearly show the different information distribution patterns during the disaster period in each case. Graphs after the natural logarithm conversion (Fig. 3) indicate that in the case of the earthquake, most of the information had been created during the first few days and then, the amount of information had decreased gradually. On the other hand, the amount of information distributed on the Internet during the initial stage of MERS had been consistently low until the definite diagnosis explosively increased the information in the intermediate stage. The daily information distribution pattern of the Gyeongju earthquake case is best explained by the exponential decay model as supported by Barton [33], Duggan and Banwell [34], and Greer and Moreland [35]. Meanwhile, the issue of the attention cycle can best predict the information distribution pattern in the MERS case. This finding suggests that the best available model to predict information dissemination during a disaster would be different depending on the type of disaster, such as natural disasters, medical disasters, or terror attacks.

Finally, this research reveals that information from all non-news media channels recorded positive decay constant values for the earthquake case, while it recorded negative values for MERS. This is an example of Freimuth [46] 's suggestion that if individuals' expectations are not met by media contents, they may seek for it from unofficial channels. It will be important to compare how public agenda and media agenda are correlated during a disaster and how the result of correlation can influence individuals' decision to select any major channel of information consumption and dissemination.

References

1. Park, S., Kim, R.: Strongest-ever earthquake hits Korea, tremors felt nationwide. The Korea Times, 12 September 2016. http://www.koreatimes.co.kr/www/news/nation/2016/09/116_214014.html
2. Park, H.W.: YouTubers' networking activities during the 2016 South Korea earthquake. Qual. Quant. 1–12. https://doi.org/10.1007/s11135-017-0503-x
3. Palen, L.: Online social media in crisis events. Educause Q. **31**(3), 76–78 (2008)
4. Perry, D.C., Taylor, M., Doerfel, M.L.: Internet-based communication in crisis management. Manage. Commun. Q. **17**(2), 206–232 (2003). https://doi.org/10.1177/0893318903256227
5. An, S.K., Gower, K.K.: How do the news media frame disaster? a content analysis of disaster news coverage. Publ. Relat. Rev. **35**(2), 107–112 (2009). https://doi.org/10.1016/j.pubrev.2009.01.010
6. Austin, L., Fisher Liu, B., Jin, Y.: How audiences seek out crisis information: exploring the social-mediated crisis communication model. J. Appl. Commun. Res. **40**(2), 188–207 (2012). https://doi.org/10.1080/00909882.2012.654498
7. Downs, A.: Up and down with ecology: the "issue-attention cycle". The public (1972). https://doi.org/10.1093/oxfordhb/9780199646135.013.34
8. Scanfeld, D., Scanfeld, V., Larson, E.L.: Dissemination of health information through social networks: Twitter and antibiotics. Am. J. Inf. Control **38**(3), 182–188 (2010). https://doi.org/10.1016/j.ajic.2009.11.004
9. Hamburger, Y.A., Ben-Artzi, E.: The relationship between extraversion and neuroticism and the different uses of the Internet. Comput. Hum. Behav. **16**(4), 441–449 (2000). https://doi.org/10.1016/S0747-5632(00)00017-0
10. Ellison, N.B., Boyd, D.M.: Sociality through social network sites. In: The Oxford Handbook of Internet Studies (2013). https://doi.org/10.1093/oxfordhb/9780199589074.013.0008
11. Lee, B., Kim, J., Scheufele, D.A.: Agenda setting in the internet age: the reciprocity between online searches and issue salience. Int. J. Publ. Opin. Res. **28**(3), 440–455 (2015). https://doi.org/10.1093/ijpor/edv026
12. Liben-Nowell, D., Kleinberg, J.: Tracing information flow on a global scale using internet chain-letter data. Proc. Nat. Acad. Sci. **105**(12), 4633–4638 (2008). https://doi.org/10.1073/pnas.0708471105
13. Gruhl, D., Guha, R., Liben-Nowell, D., Tomkins, A.: Information diffusion through blogspace. In: Proceedings of the 13th International Conference on World Wide Web, pp. 491–501). ACM, May 2004. https://doi.org/10.1145/988672.988739
14. Muralidharan, S., Rasmussen, L., Patterson, D., Shin, J.H.: Hope for haiti: an analysis of facebook and twitter usage during the earthquake relief efforts. Publ. Relat. Rev. **37**(2), 175–177 (2011). https://doi.org/10.1016/j.pubrev.2011.01.010
15. Zhao, S., Grasmuck, S., Martin, J.: Identity construction on facebook: digital empowerment in anchored relationships. Comput. Hum. Behav. **24**(5), 1816–1836 (2008). https://doi.org/10.1016/j.chb.2008.02.012
16. Mortensen, M.: When citizen photojournalism sets the news agenda: Neda Agha Soltan as a Web 2.0 icon of post-election unrest in Iran. Glob. Media Commun. **7**(1), 4–16 (2011). https://doi.org/10.1177/1742766510397936
17. Mileti, D.S., Darlington, J.D.: The role of searching in shaping reactions to earthquake risk information. Soc. Probl. **44**(1), 89–103 (1997). https://doi.org/10.2307/3096875
18. Wachtendorf, T., Kendra, J.M.: Improvising disaster in the city of jazz: organizational response to Hurricane Katrina. In: Understanding Katrina: Perspectives from the Social Sciences (2005)

19. Yang, Y.T., Horneffer, M., DiLisio, N.: Mining social media and web searches for disease detection. J. Publ. Health Res. 2(1), 17 (2013). https://doi.org/10.4081/jphr.2013.e4

20. Ding, H., Zhang, J.: Social media and participatory risk communication during the H1N1 flu epidemic: a comparative study of the United States and China. China Media Res. 6(4), 80–91 (2010)

21. Beaumont, C.: New York plane crash: Twitter breaks the news, again. The Telegraph, 16 January 2009. http://www.telegraph.co.uk/technology/twitter/4269765/New-York-plane-crash-Twitter-breaks-the-news-again.html

22. Chan, N.W.: Impacts of disasters and disaster risk management in Malaysia: the case of floods. In: Aldrich, D.P., Oum, S., Sawada, Y. (eds.) Resilience and Recovery in Asian Disasters. RGS, vol. 18, pp. 239–265. Springer, Tokyo (2015). https://doi.org/10.1007/978-4-431-55022-8_12

23. Choi, S., Bae, B.: The real-time monitoring system of social big data for disaster management. In: Park, J., Stojmenovic, I., Jeong, H., Yi, G. (eds.) Computer Science and its Applications. Lecture Notes in Electrical Engineering, vol. 330. Springer, Heidelberg (2015). https://doi.org/10.1007/978-3-662-45402-2_115

24. Goffman, W.: Mathematical approach to the spread of scientific ideas – the history of mastcell research. Nature 212(5061), 449–452 (1966). https://doi.org/10.1038/212449a0

25. Goffman, W.: A mathematical method for analyzing the growth of a scientific discipline. J. Assoc. Comput. Mach. 18(2), 173–185 (1971). https://doi.org/10.1145/321637.321640

26. Price, D.D.S.: A general theory of bibliometric and other cumulative advantage processes. J. Am. Soc. Inf. Sci. 27(5), 292–306 (1976). https://doi.org/10.1002/asi.4630270505

27. Yitzhaki, M., Shahar, T.: The emergence of alternative medicine as a new field: a bibliometric study of a rapidly-growing field. In: Proceedings of the 66th IFLA Council and General Conference (2000). http://archive.ifla.org/IV/ifla66/papers/055-127e.htm, https://doi.org/10.3389/fphar.2018.00215

28. Xu, Q., Su, Z., Zhang, K., Ren, P., Shen, X.S.: Epidemic information dissemination in mobile social networks with opportunistic links. IEEE Trans. Emerg. Topics Comput. 3(3), 399–409 (2015). https://doi.org/10.1109/TETC.2015.2414792

29. Funkhouser, G.R.: The issues of the sixties: an exploratory study in the dynamics of public opinion. Publ. Opin. Q. 37(1), 62–75 (1973). https://doi.org/10.1086/268060

30. Egghe, L., Rao, I.R.: Classification of growth models based on growth rates and its applications. Scientometrics 25(1), 5–46 (1992). https://doi.org/10.1007/BF02016845

31. Forkosh-Baruch, A., Hershkovitz, A.: A case study of Israeli higher-education institutes sharing scholarly information with the community via social networks. Internet High. Educ. 15(1), 58–68 (2012)

32. Yang, J., Counts, S.: Predicting the speed, scale, and range of information diffusion in twitter. Icwsm 10, 355–358 (2010). doi: 10.1.1.163.5416

33. Barton, A.H.: Communities in Disaster: A Sociological Analysis of Collective Stress Situations, vol. 721. Doubleday, Garden City (1969)

34. Duggan, F., Banwell, L.: Constructing a model of effective information dissemination in a crisis. Inf. Res. 5(3), 178–184 (2004)

35. Greer, C.F., Moreland, K.D.: United Airlines' and American Airlines' online crisis communication following the September 11 terrorist attacks. Publ. Relat. Rev. 29(4), 427–441 (2003). https://doi.org/10.1016/j.pubrev.2003.08.005

36. Matsumura, N., Ohsawa, Y., Ishizuka, M.: Influence diffusion model in text-based communication. Trans. Jpn. Soc. Artif. Intell. 17, 259–267 (2002). https://doi.org/10.1527/tjsai.17.259

37. Korea Centers for Disease Control and Prevention. MERS statistics_October 2 (2015). http://mers.go.kr/mers/html/jsp/Menu_C/list_C4.jsp?menuIds=&fid=5767&q_type=&q_value=&cid=65812&pageNum=

38. Byun, D.K.: S. Korea reports three more MERTS deaths, 4 new cases. Yonhap News Agency 16 June 2015. http://english.yonhapnews.co.kr/news/2015/06/16/0200000000AEN201506 16001352320.html?input=www.tweeter.com

39. Yong, Y.: S. Korea's last-remaining MERS patient dies. Yonhap News Agency, 25 November 2015. http://english.yonhapnews.co.kr/search1/2603000000.html?cid=AEN20 151125001500320

40. Chung, J.: SKT launches IT platform to enter 'big data' market. The Korea Herald, 14 October 2012. http://www.koreaherald.com/view.php?ud=20121014000268&ACE_SEARCH=1

41. Telecompaper. SK Telecom launches new IT platform Smart Insight 2.0, 15 October 2012. https://www.telecompaper.com/news/sk-telecom-launches-new-it-platform-smart-insight-20–901880

42. Grover, F.W.: Inductance calculations: working formulas and tables. Courier Corporation (2004)

43. Bouchaud, J.P.: Disaster and collective socio-economic phenomena: simple models and challenges. J. Statis. Phy. **151**(3–4), 567–606 (2013). https://doi.org/10.1007/s10955-012-0687-3

44. Bruns, A., Highfield, T., Lind, R.A.: Blogs, twitter, and breaking news: the produsage of citizen journalism. In: Producing Theory in a Digital World: The Intersection of Audiences and Production in Contemporary Theory, vol. 80, pp. 15–32 (2012)

45. Simon, T., Goldberg, A., Adini, B.: Socializing in emergencies—a review of the use of social media in emergency situations. Int. J. Inf. Manage. **35**(5), 609–619 (2015). https://doi.org/10.1016/j.ijinfomgt.2015.07.001

46. Freimuth, V.S.: Order out of chaos: the self-organization of communication following the anthrax attacks. Health Commun. **20**(2), 141–148 (2006). https://doi.org/10.1207/s15327027hc2002_5

47. Sidney Kirkwood, A.: Why do we worry when scientists say there is no risk? Disaster Prev. Manage. Int. J. **3**(2), 15–22 (1994). https://doi.org/10.1108/09653569410053905

Network Analysis of Players Transfers in eSports: The Case of Dota 2

Vsevolod Suschevskiy and Ekaterina Marchenko[✉]

National Research University Higher School of Economics, Soyuza Pechatnikov 16,
Saint Petersburg, Russia
vsuschewskiy@edu.hse.ru, eyumarchenko@gmail.com

Abstract. In this work, we analyse the structure of local and regional market of player transfers in popular eSports discipline Dota 2. Together with team performance metrics, these data provide us with an opportunity to model network of transfers between teams. In turn, the transfers show the actual structure of mobility in the industry. We collected the data on players' transfers for the top professional teams and their transfer partners, based on transactions between two world tournaments: The International 16 to The International 17. We built a directed network of transfers and analysed centralities, assortative mixing, and link formation.

The global transfer market structure is organised around continental regions. At the same time, teams with the same level of performance rarely have transfers. This can be a reliable indicator of the presence of mobility lifts, in this case, mastodons of the tournament accept in their ranks natives of the less rated teams. On the other hand, some successful players may leave the best teams to establish their own, in the same way as top managers leave the large corporations to launch startups.

Keywords: eSports · Transfer networks · Social network analysis

1 Introduction

Transfers widespread in diverse spheres, such as the labour market, in which employers are interested in foremost staff, or education, where universities want to enrol surpassing students, or sports/eSports, within which team performance depends on combinations of the most talented players. In all these domains, the ability to expose the superlative set of teammates cannot be overestimated.

Only the investment of money and time can make the existence of organisational mobility possible. However, it is not just about them because this concept is quite specific and does depend on factors specific to the certain area. For example, the Japanese model of the labour market presupposes lifelong contracts. Even so, such career longevity is not accustomed to eSports where one player can change several teams within the season.

Nevertheless, sports teams are perfectly suitable for the social network analysis as far as they consist of bounded, well-defined groups of individuals, or,

© Springer Nature Switzerland AG 2018
D. A. Alexandrov et al. (Eds.): DTGS 2018, CCIS 858, pp. 468–473, 2018.
https://doi.org/10.1007/978-3-030-02843-5_38

according to the social network terms, they do represent a full network. Furthermore, in our case, we can analyse it by taking into account geographical segments. They not only show homophily but possess unique structure. One outstanding example is the Chinese eSports ecosystem where the unique structure of organisations exists with several teams under the auspices of one brand, and recruitment to high-profile teams goes through these channels. There is no such structure in any other region.

Fig. 1. Example of transfer news. https://cybersport.com/post/aui_2000-officially-joins-fnatic

The transfer is an important event which is covered not only by media but also by official sources (Fig. 1) where organisations introduce new players to their audience.

Transfers can be used to explore intertwined connections between the personal and team's brands. The audience can find information about a player they are interested in official sources (e.g. website), and on personal players accounts (e.g. Twitter and Twitch.tv).

Team brand is supported by publishing interviews and stories about teams life and allows to establish closer relationships between players and audience.

2 Literature

Game industry raised a few years ago and from the year 2015 total industry revenue estimated two times more than film production. And this led to the emergence of special competitive games, also known as esports. Some types of eSport games are sport-related, for example, FIFA takes the name of a consonant, and it is a football simulator. On the other hand, some games create they own world, for example, DOTA 2 [7].

One of the areas of traditional sports management is the creation of a global transfer network, both within a single league and in the discipline in general. The transfer fees are the most precise assessment of the player's performance and their importance for the team, in comparison with the salary [3]. Thus, at the level of players, an important factor is the centrality of the position and activity in the game that influences managerial recruitment [4]. Considering the importance of individual players for the success of the team, it is necessary to assess the stability of the composition, the medium or small level of national diversity [3]. At the macro level, the study of transfers networks is used to assess the strength of the team to detect the most talented players [6].

For example, Liu et al. [6] analysed transfer network between 400 football clubs in 24 leagues in the period between 2011 and 2015. The main aim was to find a relation between a club's success and their actions on the transfer market. For that purpose, they created a network where elite clubs were considered as nodes and player transfers and loans as directed graphs. For the network, the authors identify two main node properties: coreness and brokerage of the nodes. For the former, they used eigenvector centrality and PageRank centrality, and for the latter – effective size, closeness centrality and betweenness centrality. The authors consider that clubs with large brokerage can control part of the transfer resources. Therefore, they become mediators of the market and, as a consequence, have the most beneficial position. There is a positive correlation between match performance and brokerage metrics, especially for international transfers.

Finally, several sports clubs with high rich-club coefficient were found in the network. This metric shows how well nodes with high degree are connected with other similar nodes. In this papers, authors show an interaction between such clubs which create a coalition. They do control resources spread within the network. Also, transfers between clubs are less frequent to lean toward an exchange of players if these players have a large number of peer clubs [6].

3 Data and Methods

For our study, we gathered data about Dota 2 players transfers conducted between The International 2016 and The International 2017. We have records about transfers between team-participants of TI, transfers from non-participants to participants, and vice versa. As a source of data which consists of 1007 transfers, we have chosen Liquipedia – the most significant community about eSport disciplines including Dota 2, its mechanics and the whole industry which content is produced by the players.

For each transfer observation, we have the following variables: date, players name, titles of former and current teams, and countries, in which those teams are located. We build a unimodal directed network, where nodes were teams and edges were transfer. Weight represents a number of transfers between two teams.

4   Analysis and Results

Transfers between teams in Dota 2 are visualised by employing a directed network. Network nodes are teams, and directed edges between them are players' transfers; the colour of the node stands for the affiliation region.

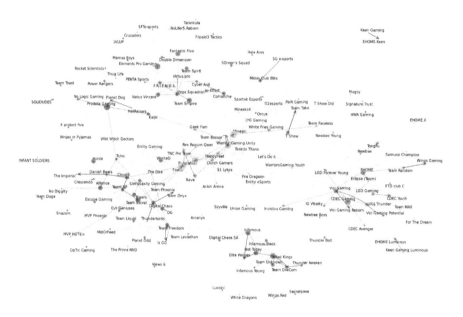

Fig. 2. Transfers of players between teams clustered by region

Figure 2 clearly shows that the number of transfers between teams is small, so the network is not saturated, and the teams that belong to the same region are grouped, furthermore in the centre, there is the core of the European teams.

For our research we propose the following hypotheses which will help to reveal the structure of the transfer network in eSport:

- Transfers between teams which are located in the same region are more frequent.

– Participation in TI is positively correlated with the probability of transfer.
– Belonging to the one organisation is significant for the probability of transfer.
– Difference in Elo rating decreases the probability of transfer.

As a measure of the homogeneity of the transfers, we found the assortativeness. Assortativity exists in the range of −1 – disassortativity, up to 1 –
maximal assortativeness and was calculated with the help of igraph package. It
is an external module for the R programming language [1]. By using random
permutation test with 3500 random reshuffles, we collect coefficient to compare
with the distribution of null hypothesis, in this way p-value was calculated.

Elo rating [2] measures the performance of a team and based on wins, draws,
and loses. The rating shows the relative superiority of the player over others and
the difference in ratings is responsible for the result of the match, namely for
scores. By dint of EloRating package in R [5] and data from dotabuff, by Elo
Entertainment LLC, contains data about the professional and the amateurs as
well, the rating for teams was calculated based on data for three months before
the transfer period. For teams that did not play at that time, the value 1000 was
set as the default.

These hypotheses were tested with the help of assortativity (Fig. 3) which
shows the number of transfers between residents of one region, relative to all.
For our first hypothesis, we get the value of 0.669 $p < .001$ which demonstrates
the high probability of transfers within the region. Thus, despite the declared
internationality of sports discipline, the mobility of players is more interregional.
In the second case, the assortativity coefficient is not significant – 0.052. Therefore, we can say there is no relation between players choice of the team they go,
and the teams of the TI remain open to players from weaker teams. Also, the

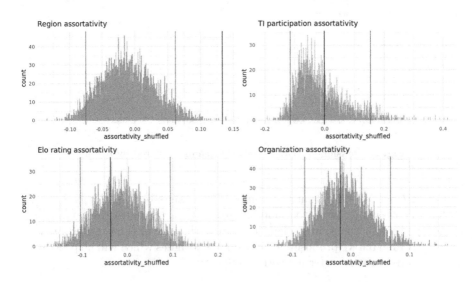

Fig. 3. Assortativity. Permutation tests.

role of the organisation is insignificant with coefficient 0.046. We can not consider that as a special channel of recruiting. For an assortativity by Elo rating of teams p-value, more than 0.517 was got, which is a strong indicator of the lack of connection between the rating and the transfer.

5   Conclusion

With the help of the Dota 2 data, one of the most popular cybersport disciplines, we show some unique features of transfers in eSports such as the importance of the country, and its absence if we speak about participation in the primary Dota 2 championship.

Teams in Dota 2, unlike the traditional sport, show more consistency, because when transferring only two players it almost breaks the team down, and three players are more than half, after all, there are only five members.

Our plans for developing this research project are following on conducting the QAP regression analysis to estimate the significance of attributes. We are going to use methods of relational event models to estimate the importance of the dynamics of the professional scene and to consider the factors specific to particular regions. Second, we will make an ERGM-model for adding new variables such as year of team formation and structural factors (e.g. istar or outgoing shared partner) to estimate the importance of unique patterns like a structure of organisations in China.

Acknowledgements. The article was prepared within the framework of the Academic Fund Program at the National Research University Higher School of Economics (HSE) in 2017 2018 (grant No. 17-05-0024) and by the Russian Academic Excellence Project 5-100.

We wish to thank Ilya Musabirov, Denis Bulygin, and Alina Bakhitova for their help.

References

1. Csardi, G., Nepusz, T.: The igraph software package for complex network research. Int. J. Complex Syst. **169**(5), 1–9 (2006). http://igraph.org
2. Elo, A.E.: The Rating of Chessplayers, Past and Present. Arco Pub., New York (1978)
3. Gerhards, J., Mutz, M.: Who wins the championship? Market value and team composition as predictors of success in the top European football leagues. Eur. Soc. **19**(3), 223–242 (2017)
4. Grusky, O.: Managerial succession and organizational effectiveness. Am. J. Sociol. **69**(1), 21–31 (1963)
5. Heinzen, E.: Elo: Elo Ratings, December 2017. https://CRAN.R-project.org/package=elo
6. Liu, X.F., Liu, Y.L., Lu, X.H., Wang, Q.X., Wang, T.X.: The anatomy of the global football player transfer network: club functionalities versus network properties. PloS One **11**(6), e0156504 (2016)
7. Miah, A.: Sport 2.0: Transforming Sports for a Digital World. MIT Press, Cambridge (2017)

Self-presentation Strategies Among Tinder Users: Gender Differences in Russia

Olga Solovyeva$^{(\boxtimes)}$ and Olga Logunova

National Research University Higher School of Economics,
Myasnitskaya 20, 101000 Moscow, Russia
osolovyeva@hse.ru

Abstract. The research outlines major self-presentation strategies and gender patterns of the online dating application Tinder users in Moscow. Authors conducted the case study and analysed 400 profiles of 20–40 years old female and male app users. Upon the content analysis, few patterns of gendered self-presentation were depicted, explained further through the prism of gender roles theory with the focus on the dominant cultural traits in modern Russia.

Keywords: Online dating · Self-presentation · Tinder

1 Introduction

In the past, the cyberspace has been intensely stigmatized for the lack of emotional, trustful and natural communication within the process of relationship building and maintenance. Such a stigma had been applied to online dating as well as computer mediated romantic relationships in general [1]. As in the early 80's the practice of exposing your desire to find a mate through the advertisement in printed media was associated with embarrassment and desperation, the situation nowadays is changing [2]. With the wide spread of Internet and online dating websites launch another major drive for the engagement in computer-mediated relationship (CMR) turned into the opportunity - to find a romantic partner without being exposed, known or humiliated by the society [3]. Nowadays the attitude to online dating is changing, as a positive image of such practice appears in various media. CMR becomes more popular as the benefits of such approach to search for a partner and selection tend to be settled as a common norm for the modern community. While research on online relationship development and online dating as a part of this process is well established, the new forms and types of media evolve to fit the changing demand of people. Online dating websites become old-fashioned and new forms of matchmaking have appeared - web applications for smartphones that provide users with an opportunity for easier partner search. Presented inquiry discloses the limitations for relationship formation within such means of communication as in online dating application (Tinder) focusing on the very first step - self-presentation as a part of the strategic impression management and outlining the gender differences presented within users.

The main purpose of this paper is to analyze the presence of different self-presentation strategies on Tinder and how such strategies vary due to gender

D. A. Alexandrov et al. (Eds.): DTGS 2018, CCIS 858, pp. 474–482, 2018.
https://doi.org/10.1007/978-3-030-02843-5_39

differences. This exploratory analysis is aimed to glance whether cultural patterns existing in the society would define the self-presentation strategies of individuals, which thus would be indicated thorough their profile analysis. Authors suggest that Tinder in Russia introduces gendered cultural context that reflects current online social practices of users and will be relevant for their self-presentation strategies.

2   Literature Review

While conceptualizing digital dating, Merkle and Richardson [4] focus on essential differences that draw the gap between face-to-face and computer-mediated relationships: the process of formation, nature of self-disclosure, methods of conflict management and the meaning of infidelity. Recent research highlights the essence of CMR as being more thoughtful and strategic in many ways while both partners can appeal to the advantages of the mediated environment: e.g., extended time for message formation, increased self-disclosure, driven by raised self-investment time [4] and a comprehensive approach to getting to know a prospective partner. Thus, online dating sites vary in their focus, goals and affordances. Finkel at.al [2] present a solid classification and distinguishes 14 types of romantic matchmaking services available based on their distinctive features. Apart from mobile apps, scholars identify general and niche self-selection sites, where a number of profiles of prospective partners are available for surfing and approaching. The other option is matching sites, applying specific algorithms to create matches e.g. self-reporting, matching interests, etc. The arousal of online dating applications and their widespread usage can be seen as a response to changing patterns in the instant gratification era, around 2000's [5]. Revolutionary for the market, Tinder, follows a similar application focused on same-gender partner search smartphone app Grindr, offered a simplified version of a communication tool, based on the "like or not" principal in 2012. The distinguishing features are: location-based search option and the order of prospective partners' profile appearing. The application interface includes 4 major parts: user profile, settings section, prospective partners profiles displaying one by one and chatroom. Tinder allows users to login with their Facebook profile and then upload up to 6 photos and fill a description text up to 500 symbols where users are encouraged to put any relevant information. The option to connect an Instagram profile is available for users along with the possibility to show favourite music and "life anthem" from Spotify. Settings allow to choose the distance for your search (limited to 180 km in its free version), gender and age range of a desirable match. The application streams user profiles compatible through geo-location, interests and mutual Facebook friends. At this point user carries on a decision: to like (swipe right) or stay not interested (swipe left). In case both users have liked each other, they will be able to start a conversation in a chatroom to exchange information or arrange a meeting offline. Tinder hits its popularity in 2016 with approximate number of users reaching up to 50 million which is still increasing. Such interest is presented in the academic research as well. Tyson et al. [6] distinguished the gender differences between female and male user experiences of application. Timmermans and De Caluwe [7] identified 13 motives most frequently appearing among the users. Apart from socializing, relationship seeking and sexual experience, researchers identified that

Tinder fulfils the psychological need of users in belonging and social approval, works as a distraction and a procrastination tool. It is also used by travellers to meet up with locals and as psychological support for people who went recently through break ups, as the number of matches helps to upgrade self-esteem to continue searching for a partner. Curiosity and peer pressure were distinguished among other motives. Another study conducted among Dutch emerging adults identified few similar motives: love, casual sex, ease of communication, self-worth validation and thrill of excitement [8]. Therefore, profile structure may highlight or hide users' intentions, which defines the communication pattern and is usually driven by the individuals' motives.

Still, self-presentation appears to be one of the drivers in social media usage. Self-presentation is generally motivated by user's intent to make a favourable impression on others. Combined with the approach to online dating as a 'market' where such profiles are shopped, authors assume that a certain strategy is picked by a user consciously or unconsciously to create a profile which would fit to the search criteria of a desired partner: e.g. Heino, Elisson and Gibbs [9] provide such definition: 'marketplace where individuals shop each other's profiles'. The user's profile can be perceived as 'a promise', constructed and an adapted form of a person which aims to be attractive to the prospective mate [10]. According to Myers [4], individuals tend to engage in a relationship that is rewarding or can be associated with a reward. Therefore, the significant body of research, devoted to the issue of deception in online dating, point out the problem of strategic image formation while providing untrue information about self. Users are balancing between the honest information and the idealised version of themselves they want to use to attract the prospective partner [11]. Focusing on Tinder, Ranzini, Lutz and Gouderjaan [12] revealed the correlation between individuals' psychological traits and the self-presentation patterns, claiming that ought-to self-presentation is most common self-presentation strategy, which is followed by actual and ideal ones. Such findings point to the fact, that individuals are strategic in their experience with application and the information provided is dependent on their psychological traits and usage purposes, which most likely reflects in the patterns possibly traced through the profile analysis.

The research on gendered self-presentation in social media refers to multiple studies underlying the differences across different media outlets. A recent study suggests that young females tend to limit visibility and extend privacy settings, facilitate social interaction through textual self-presentation and upload photos that 'appear attractive and sexually appealing' while boys were not that cautious about privacy, tend to provide false information and their 'linguistic choices reflect assertiveness in both style and tone' [13]. The research conducted by Tifferets and Vilnai-Yavetz [14] on gender differences in Facebook self-presentation focused on the visual aspect, considering photos uploaded by users. As hypothesized by scholars, male's photos were mostly reflecting the status of individual and risk-taking attitude while females uploaded pictures that showed family relations and emotional expression. The rhetorical analysis on self-presentation in dating media identifies that individuals even when searching for a partner (match) with specific characteristics tend to put in more socially desirable ones, which violates the strategic approach in matchmaking [15]. Another inquiry points out that the physical attractiveness appears to be more important for the women, contrary to the men, which results in the strategic choice of the profile pictures [16].

Focusing on the patterns of gendered self-presentation in online dating, Buss [17] comes to the conclusion that physical attractiveness appears to be one of the main drivers for the decision-making process among male individuals and thus, women tend to adapt their self-presentation strategies to the demands of prospective partners. Nevertheless, in the modern Russian society, social relationships are still engaging the dominant gender roles and traditional relational patterns between male and female heterosexual individuals. The explicit characteristic of online dating is that communication occurs in a reduced cue environment as non-verbal cues are excluded from this process as well as you have constant control over your profile and can provide changes any moment [18]. As communication appears in the reduced nonverbal cues environment, the means by which individuals can present their personal identity are limited. Thus, the impressive body of research supports our idea of finding certain patterns in self-presentation, which can be explained through the gendered approach to communication [19, 20]. Russian society is claimed to be mostly navigated by the patriarchal discourses and embedded gender roles [21]. With the changes occurring, women still are expected to be responsible for home and make a preference towards family on the contrary to the carrier. Outlining the preferred qualities for the ideal women, Russian man point at such characteristics as physical attractiveness and sexuality, while desired image of wife most often refers to thrift and love to children. At the same time, women express the need in a man, who is physically strong and has no pernicious habits for the ideal image, while the perfect husband is expected to be loyal and be a bread winner [22]. Thus, the hypothesis of this research is supported by the mainstream representation of citizens values in the search of prospective partner and expected to be reflected in the general self-presentation patterns.

3   Method and Data

3.1   Sampling Strategy

The data reported in this article comes from a quantitative content analysis of Tinder profiles. The data was collected in December 2016 using the focused method, a quota sampling of each gender was selected per two groups of age, constructing subsequently four mini-samples. The total number of profiles collected for the research was 400: 100 of male profiles aged 20–30, 100 profiles of females, aged 20–30, 100 profiles of male aged 30–40 and 100 profiles of females aged 30–40 respectively. The age distribution within mini-samples was random. Authors created neutral profiles (male and female) to collect these profiles, launched the search and took first 100 profiles for each sub-category that fit the limitations. The unit of analysis for this research is a Tinder profile item. The profile item is conceptualized as the mix of textual information about a user (maximum 500 symbols) along with visual information - users' photos (maximum of 6). For our research, authors choose only «complete profiles», containing at least one sentence of text and one photo. Moreover, the geography was limited to the centre of Moscow (10 km in diameter around the location point).

3.2   Coding Procedures and Measures

Five independent coders were trained in the application of a common codebook. Coder training included detailed discussions of key concepts as well as different examples of individual profiles. Prior to the beginning of the coding process, different coder-trainer tests were performed to ensure that they had a similar understanding of the codebook. The coding was done manually between February and April 2017. Based on Krippendorf's alpha formula, overall intercoder reliability was 0.74. Reliability scores ranged from 0.72 (interpretation) to 0.96 (for emotions).

The coding of the profile items was divided into four sections:

1. Metadata. In the first section, basic information of each profile item should be identified (time, date, source, author etc.).
2. General information. The second section of this codebook refers to basic characteristics of the profiles (number of photos and text; emoji; language; links to social media).
3. Users information. The third section of the codebook analysed personal information in the profiles (work/university; social networks; style of narration; motives for registration; information about self; descriptions (appearance and character); requirements for prospective partner; description of prospective partners).
4. Visual information. Users often tell us about themselves using images. Therefore, picture becomes a part of everyday communication and representation of usual practices. The last section analysed the models of visual representation such as type (selfie/not selfie); shot (long shot/full shot/medium shot); photos quality; number of people; location; other objects, etc. Collectively, 25 variables proposed by authors have been used. Each indicator was coded on the presence-absence basis.

4   Results

4.1   General Information

First of all, authors identified general characteristics of the profiles. The average text length composed by males is 7.1 lines, contrary to 5.45 among female profiles. Content analysis identifies that men communicate more about themselves and try to explain who they are and what they want. This fact is confirmed by the next indicator – the number of photos. Men, on average, upload 4.89 pictures, whereas women demonstrate themselves carefully – with only 3.47 photos, the full analysis could be found in Table 1. The majority of women tend to upload only one photo in the profile, as this trend occurs in approximately 40% of the cases.

Moreover, an analysis of self-presentation in the description text, below the set of profile pictures was conducted. It showed that man tend to provide more textual information as well, while women use more emoji's in their texts (38% against 24% in male profiles). Moreover, younger group uses emoji often, but this difference is minor, and is found in about 3% of all cases. Considering the relationship between the text length and emoji presence, an interesting pattern can be traced. Among women, in

Table 1. Distribution of photos according to genders

Male		Female	
1 photo	4.1%	1 photo	39.0%
2 photos	1.0%	2 photos	1.5%
3 photos	10.2%	3 photos	5.5%
4 photos	18.3%	4 photos	10.0%
5 photos	18.8%	5 photos	14.5%
6 photos	47.2%	6 photos	29.5%

cases of emoji presence - the average text length is 6.59, and in case of their absence – text is only 4.77. Another characteristic was the language of profile description, which is presented in the Table 2. Male profile is often written in English, which is a significant share of 35.5%, while only 22% percent of women use English instead of Russian. It is noteworthy that some profiles had descriptions both in English and in Russian.

Table 2. Language of the description text

Language	Male	Female
English	35.5%	22.0%
Russian	50.8%	61.0%
Russian, English	11.2%	12.5%
Other	2.5%	4.5%

Users also keep the tendency of uploading links to the social media in their profiles. The most popular social media used as an additional source is Instagram. The link to Instagram profile appears in 13% of female profiles and in of 9.6% men's profiles. Older groups of the sample often use visual reinforcement, as the link to the Instagram appears in 13.5% of the cases for both men and women. Thus, the general information section shows a more open men's attitude, which is reflected in their complete profiles and the broader range of data about themselves. Women, however, limit the potential scope of the proposed profile - write less, post fewer pictures and limit the textual self-expression, substituting with universal emoji language.

4.2   Visual Information

Authors tried to identify the patterns for photos uploaded by individuals to be in the focus of their profiles. First characteristic was the type and quality of the photographs. Selfie appeared to be most popular among women - 42% versus 27% among men. This explains the popularity of the full shot for the female part of the sample (54%), while men prefer the medium shot. It is also noteworthy, that among male images, group photos with two or more people are seen more often, which complicates the process of recognizing the account owner. Thus, men tend to encrypt themselves. Such images appear in 10% of the cases in the sample, which is four times less compared to female profiles sample. In addition, women tend to upload professional photographs. Popular locations for the main profile picture differ. Still, overall women tend to pick the locations creating an association with home and cosiness. The top five locations for men and women are shown in Table 3.

Table 3. Top-5 photo locations

	Male	Female
1	Urban view 16.8%	Home 21.0%
2	Home 13.7%	Urban view 12.1%
3	Nature view 12.7%	Nature view 9%
4	Beach 7.6%	Restaurant 8%
5	Club, bar 7.1%	Beach 7%

Summarizing, women emphasize homely atmosphere, nature and cosy restaurants. Men emphasize a more urban lifestyle with clubs, bars and the ability to relax, and travelling as a symbol of adventurous lifestyle and character.

4.3   Users Information

There is also a description of appearance - 7.5% of male profiles and 4.5% of female. The description or other information about the desired, prospective partner was not found often in the profiles. Users tend to hide their job and workplace as well. In particular, this information is absenting in 67% of the profiles. The remaining part more often indicates both the company and the position - 13%. Men tend to focus on their professional status (25% versus 15% among women), which emphasizes the role of their social status in this practice of strategic self-presentation.

Authors analysed the style of narration in such descriptions and for the given sample, presented in the Table 4. It appeared that the majority writes about themselves in a serious way: 67% of female and 59% of male profiles in such manner. For instance, users outline their intentions: "...in search of a serious relationship with the prospect of a family" or "looking for a husband". As for the differences – men more often write about themselves with humour (10%) and women are more self-ironical (10%).

Table 4. Distribution of attitudes in the description text

Language	Male	Female
Seriousness	58.9%	66.5%
Humor	10.2%	3.5%
Self-irony	6.1%	9.5%
Provocation	2.5%	5.0%
Other	22.3%	15.5%

Unfortunately, 72% of the database contains no significant self-description, despite the fact that only profiles that contain at least a minimal text description go to the sample. The remaining profiles most often describe character traits through positive identification (15%), this figure does not differ between the gender groups.

5 Conclusion

The research conducted on online dating self-presentation patterns in Tinder showed that there are some major differences between men and women strategies. Male users tend to provide more information, create a complete image of adventurous individuals, sharing their hobbies through the usage of related profile pictures, interests and personal data. Therefore, female users are more cautious while sharing their personal data, yet women tend to use more emoji's in their self-descriptions. Some of the traits were distinguished among different age groups: mature users tend to be more straightforward in their profiles, identifying direct search aspects and expectations towards the prospective partner. Younger individuals, on the contrary, use more flexible descriptions and focus on their own personalities. Authors thus can assume that patterns of self-presentation appear to be just the part of an overall cultural trait, and can be distinctly related to the gender roles existing in modern Russia society. As for methodological aspects - case study tactic suits for this research questions - four user groups were considered by content-analyses. Still, a number of limitations is embedded. First of all, the sample of profiles is reduced to the active users, located within the city centre of Moscow. Secondly, the algorithm for issuing potential partners is unknown, which does not allow us to talk about diversity or further generalizations to all Tinder users in Russia.

The research is supported by the Russian Science Foundation grant (RSF No17-78-20164) 'Sociotechnical barriers of the implementation and use of information technologies in Russia: sociological analysis'.

References

1. Wildermuth, S.M.: The effects of stigmatizing discourse on the quality of on-line relationships. Cyberpsychol. Behav. **7**, 73–84 (2004)
2. Finkel, E.J., Eastwick, P.W., Karney, B.R., Reis, H.T., Sprecher, S.: Online dating: a critical analysis from the perspective of psychological science. Psychol. Sci. Public Interes. Suppl. **13**(1), 3–66 (2012). https://doi.org/10.1177/1529100612436522
3. Schnarch, D.: Sex, intimacy, and the internet. J. Sex Educ. Ther. **22**, 15–20 (1997)
4. Merkle, E.R., Richardson, R.A.: Digital dating and virtual relating: conceptualizing computer mediated romantic relationships. Fam. Relations **49**, 187–192 (2000). https://doi.org/10.1111/j.1741-3729.2000.00187.x
5. Homnack, A.: Online dating technology effects on interpersonal relationships. Advanced Writing: Pop Culture Intersections, paper 4 (2015)
6. Tyson, G., Perta, V.C., Haddadi, H., Seto, M.C.: A first look at user activity on tinder. In: IEEE/ACM International Conference on Advances in Social Networks Analysis and Mining (ASONAM), pp. 461–466. IEEE (2016)

7. Timmermans, E., De Caluwé, E.: Development and validation of the tinder motives scale (TMS). Comput. Hum. Behav. (2017). https://doi.org/10.1016/j.chb.2017.01.028

8. Sumter, S.R., Vandenbosch, L., Ligtenberg, L.: Love me tinder: untangling emerging adults' motivations for using the dating application Tinder. Telemat. Inform. **34**, 67–78 (2017). https://doi.org/10.1016/j.tele.2016.04.009

9. Heino, R.D., Ellison, N.B., Gibbs, J.L.: Relation shopping: investigating the market metaphor in online dating. J. Soc. Pers. Relationships **27**(4), 427–447 (2010)

10. Ellison, N.B., Hancock, J.T., Toma, C.L.: Profile as promise: a framework for conceptualizing veracity in online dating self-presentations. New Media Soc. **14**(1), 45–62 (2012)

11. Hancock, J.T., Toma, C., Ellison, N.: The truth about lying in online dating profiles. In: SIGCHI Conference on Human Factors in Computing Systems, pp. 449–452. ACM (2007)

12. Ranzini, G., Lutz, C., Gouderjaan, M.: Swipe right: an exploration of self-presentation and impression management on Tinder. In: 66th Annual Conference of the International Communication Association (ICA) 2016, Washington DC (2016)

13. Herring, S., Kapidzic, S.: Teens, gender, and self-presentation in social media. In: Wright, J.D. (ed.) International Encyclopedia of Social and Behavioural Sciences, 2nd edn. Elsevier, Oxford (2015)

14. Tifferet, S., Vilnai-Yavetz, I.: Gender differences in Facebook self-presentation: an international randomized study. Comput. Hum. Behav. **35**, 388–399 (2014). https://doi.org/10.1016/j.chb.2014.03.016

15. Hancock, J.T., Toma, C.L.: Putting your best face forward: the accuracy of online dating photographs. J. Commun. **59**, 367–386 (2009)

16. Toma, C.L., Hancock, J.T.: Looks and lies: the role of physical attractiveness in online dating self-presentation and deception. Commun. Res. **37**(3), 335–351 (2010)

17. Buss, D.M.: The evolution of human intrasexual competition: tactics of mate attraction. J. Pers. Soc. Psychol. **54**, 616–628 (1988)

18. Ward, J.: What are you doing on Tinder? Impression management on a matchmaking mobile app. Inf. Commun. Soc. **20**(11), 1644–1659 (2017)

19. Lance, L.: Gender differences in heterosexual dating: a content analysis of personal ads. J. Men's Stud. **6**, 297–305 (1998)

20. Eisenchlas, S.A.: Gender roles and expectations. SAGE Open **3**(4) (2013). https://doi.org/10.1177/2158244013506446

21. White, A.: Gender roles in contemporary Russia: attitudes and expectations among women students. Eur. Asia Stud. **57**(3), 429–455 (2005)

22. Lezhnina, I.P.: The transformation of gender roles in today's Russia. Sociol. Res. **53**(5), 13–31 (2014). https://doi.org/10.2753/SOR1061-0154530502

Evaluation of Expertise in a Virtual Community of Practice: The Case of Stack Overflow

Anastasiia Menshikova[✉]

Higher School of Economics, St. Petersburg, Russia
anastasia1713@gmail.com

Abstract. Virtual communities of practice are becoming more and more efficient for professional knowledge sharing. Thus, most active internet platforms where professionals exchange their experience could be considered as the representation of current professional knowledge state. In this work in progress we analyse the structure of professional knowledge in IT sphere through the investigation of Stack Overflow. An analysis of bipartite network which connects question tags and IDs of users with the help of overlapping community detection algorithm allows to identify the intersections of different skill areas. Meaning the user reputation, we examine whether having the competencies in several areas at the same time (e.g., several programming languages) is more profitable for professionals than specific skills in the narrow field or not. The long-term goal of our study is to develop a metrics for the evaluation of user's professional expertise and professional knowledge complexity based on the skills overlap.

Keywords: Online community of practice · Overlapping community
User expertise

1 Introduction

Stack Overflow is one of the largest international platforms which provides programmers with the support of colleagues from all over the world in specific or day-to-day professional tasks. An opportunity to call for advice by posting a question on the international QA site and get the several possible solutions in ten minutes has been attracted almost 8 millions of users from the moment of the website launching until today. Stack Overflow has existed for 9.5 years, that is why it is not only the platform to consult with colleagues online but also a professional knowledge database where someone can find the answer for the question community has already provided an answer. Consequently, the QA site can represent the current state of professional knowledge in IT sphere.

Obviously, most of IT professionals have the competencies in several areas at the same time, or more precise to say, can perform the working tasks with the help of different tools. We suppose that if a professional skill of one specialist

© Springer Nature Switzerland AG 2018
D. A. Alexandrov et al. (Eds.): DTGS 2018, CCIS 858, pp. 483–491, 2018.
https://doi.org/10.1007/978-3-030-02843-5_40

frequently accompanied by several others, this skill is rather easy to learn and to use. At the same time, if a particular tool appears to be the only competence or one of the few, we guess that such knowledge is hard to gain and implement in day-to-day work. Of course, we should take into account that the older the specialist, the greater knowledge and experience he or she has. Additionally, in the case when the specialist is acquainted with a few tools, he or she can be incompetent at all. That is why we use the aggregated dataset from Stack Overflow, which allows us to avoid these kinds of bias.

On this step of our work we detect overlapping skills and try to compare the level of overlap with the different additional characteristics of skills (or tags, regarding Stack Overflow), such as overall incidence, the time it takes to answer, distribution of answers reputation. Since we are going to develop the complexity metric, we check the meaningful trend and correlations to find the relevant ones for our task.

Firstly, in this work we refer to the previous findings of the authors, who studied the expertise in a virtual community of practice, as well as advantages and disadvantages of overlapping communities. Secondly, we present the detailed description of the data gathering process and analysis tools. Thirdly, we show the preliminary results of our study. Finally, we provide the short discussion of the results and plans.

2   Related Papers

2.1   Expertise in Online Communities

Detection of expertise in knowledge-sharing communities is the common task for the researchers. The most well-versed participants can efficiently enrich a community knowledge and render the solutions for the intricate issues; consequently, they support and increase the level of community expertise. Moreover, an expertise in professional communities of practice, both online and offline, could be used by employers as a tool for the prospective workers assessment (e.g., user's profiles at GitHub or Stack Exchange have been used in a selection of programming specialists together with a resume and an interview for a long time already).

Previous studies explored the expertise in a virtual community of practice in a variety of ways. Hanrahan and colleagues [4] investigated Stack Overflow QA site to calculate the expertise of different roles of those who involved in the question discussion. Based on the time between the question post and the answer, comment, or accepted answer, the authors examined patterns of participation in the activity around the question in order to find different strategies of the best-reputed users.

In another study the authors [8] identified not only current experts but also users who have a potential to become an expert. Using the data from TurboTax Live Community and Stackoverflow QA services, they built a model which classified the users as experts or non-experts according to their question selection preferences. One of the main conclusions the authors made is that experts tend to choose the questions with the lower existed value (e.g., with the small amount of upvoted answers).

Japanese researchers [10] offered to assess a status of an expert by reviewing user's award achievement history. The authors build sequences of various badge earning, clustered these sequences and defined the key activities of the most successful users.

Zhang and colleagues [12] were one of the first who applied social network analysis to examine user expertise. They constructed the directed network of users, who posted and replied on Java Forum, claiming that it reflects shared interests of community members. The authors used PageRank and HIST ranking algorithms for the detection of the most competent users: the first one identifies those who can answer the question of participants who answer lot of questions themselves; the second one searching for people who both get the help from the other expert users and provide the community with the excellent answers himself.

2.2   Overlapping Communities

In this paper we investigate the expertise of users and the complexity of professional knowledge from the perspective of overlapping community. Scholars have not reached a consensus yet if the community intersection causes more benefits or losses for participants and communities.

On the one hand, there are several reasons why it appears to be profitable. First of all, organisation studies [7] underly that multiple team membership increases both a team and personal productivity. Overlapping members may obtain a range of skills and knowledge from the several communities at the same time. Furthermore, a person who involved in the activity of more than one community can transfer experience and information to the others, thereby providing a crossing enrichment and diverse perspectives.

The study of Burt [2] also demonstrates positive aspects of community intersection based on the example of technological innovation diffusion in medicine. He claims that overlapping members connect disconnected groups and bring invaluable resources and information to the community they are involved in, hastening the technology proliferation.

Zhu and colleagues [13] argue that the same principles are applicable to the large-scale online communities. Hall and Shaw [5] worked with the data from Wikipedia and found out that parallel participation of users in similar communities (Wiki topics) causes the competition which provides more active contributions to Wiki pages.

Another study of Wikipedia community [3] shows that moderate membership overlap may encourage a community survival. An intersection of communities with the different focuses results in a certain level of diversity, which increases the productivity and decreases participants turnover. Because of the diversity, a community does not break down into smaller ones devoted to the narrow topics and a content generation becomes more efficient.

On the other hand, in some cases belonging to members of several communities at the same time could have a negative impact on community functioning. Wang and colleagues based on Usenet groups investigation [11] state that despite the fact competition between the overlapping communities leads to the growth of productivity, it also puts competitive pressure on the participants and may harm a community.

Hill and Shaw [5] also argue that participation in several communities simultaneously requires an immeasurable amount of time and effort. When the overlapping members spend a considerable amount of their resources for the activity in one community, it, obviously, causes the harming of others. Allocation of time and efforts among many communities reduces both personal and community effectiveness.

Another important point scholars take into account is the matter of identity [9]. Common identity supports a stable membership and loyalty of community participants. However, in the situation of high membership overlap people do not to contrast themselves with members of the other communities; thus, it may weaken individual's ties to the community.

The last but not the least, the diversity overlapping members bring in the community functioning not only contributes to an increase in productivity but also may give rise to conflicts between the participants [3].

3   Data and Methods

3.1   Dataset

For the investigation of user expertise we gathered the data from Stack Overflow platform for 2017. It was decided to work on the data for one year because the primary insights into the data had shown that body of knowledge on the site is increasing gradually year by year. Once the new technologies are emerging, the users ask new questions related to them. Additionally, as we consider the knowledge complexity in IT sphere, it should correspond to the current level of technologies development.

Since the study aims at the examination of the indicators for the expertise evaluation, our interest was to capture both the users with some of their characteristics and the skills they have. Thus, all of the questions which were posted in 2017 were gathered, with the tags specifying them, as well as the answers user gave to the question, and such user's profiles characteristics as the reputation, location, age and registration date (however, in this paper we work only with the reputation parameter for users). Finally, we got the dataset which contains 1527584 questions, 2357920 answers, 8662 tags and 374160 users.

3.2   Network Construction and Attributes

Network analysis tools were chosen for the examination of the intersection of skill areas because it allows to link the skills and users at the same time. The author built the bipartite network, which connects question tags and users, who answered the questions. Firstly, it was agreed to take the user's answers, not questions, since the ability to reply reflects more sustainable knowledge in the field. Secondly, the author took the tags and will interpret them as skills below, because it is the mandatory element for each question on the Stack Overflow, which is supposed to be used as the question summary and helps users to navigate through the question topics. Then we constructed the unimodal projection, where question tags are linked if the user answered the questions with different tags. Therefore, weights, attached to the ties between the nodes, represent the number of cases users gave the answers for both tags in the pair.

Since the author considers the expertise as the competence of professional in one or several skill areas, it was decided to use an overlapping community detection algorithm to identify the intersection. There are several methods for detection overlapping communities in networks, here the link partitioning algorithm, which is developed by Ahn and colleagues, is applied [1]. According to this method, the node in the initial graph is defined as overlapping if the connected links belong to several clusters. For the clustering of links, hierarchical clustering is applied.

Fig. 1. Linkcomm algorithm visualisation

Then, for evaluation the user's expertise of skill areas the graph nodes were attributed with the user reputation. In general, reputation score measures how much the Stack Overflow community trusts a user. For every tag in the network the reputation of users who gave the answers to the questions with this tag was aggregated. Due to the uneven distribution of the reputation per tag (as a rule, it follows the long-tail distribution) the reputation was divided into deciles and the Gini coefficient to estimate the inequality among users was calculated.

4   Preliminary Results

First of all, the author ran the overlapping community detection algorithm on the unimodal projection of tags. The author got 1291 community based on the network which contained 2345 tags. Only those pairs of tags, which has a tie with the weight more than 100, were selected. Figure 1 shows the illustration of the overlapping community visualization, constructed with the help of Linkcomm package for R [6]. The color of links relates to the certain community. When the node looks like a pie, it belongs to the several communities, according to the number of pie slices. Single-colored nodes belong to one community. For instance, the graph shows that html tag is much more frequently accompanied by the other skills than javascript.

Then the author tried to check the whether the level of tag overlap correlates with the other characteristics or not. Spearman correlation was used, as the distribution of the overlap does not follow the normal distribution (Fig. 2).

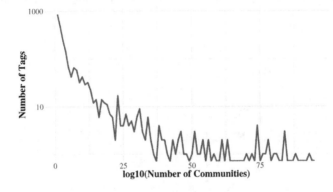

Fig. 2. The distribution of tag count per community

As a result, percent of the overlapping community the tag participates in negatively correlates with the time interval between question and answer ($r = -.223$, $p < 0$). Since the time before the first answer demonstrates the difficulty of the question (and, accordingly, the difficulty of the tag), this result approves the primary assumption about the inverse relationship between the overlapping level and competence complexity. Next, the author checked if the overall number of answers per tag correlates with the overlapping value. We found the strong significant correlation ($r = .601$, $p < 0$) between the tag popularity and the percent of the communities it belongs to. Finally, Gini coefficient of the reputation distribution does not correlate with the overlapping level significantly. It needs to be reminded, when the Gini coefficient close to 1, it means that the top of the sample is much richer than the bottom part and vice versa. In case of the user reputation on Stack Overflow, Gini coefficient for the tag is higher when there is a few high-reputed users and a huge amount of low-reputed. To make it clear,

Tag	Belongs to x% of all communities	N of answers	Gini index score	Median time until the first answer
php	2.6	147123	0.887	24
javascript	2.6	315950	0.880	21
html	6.8	62651	0.8781474	14
c++	1.8	73163	0.8775684	22
python	2.9	226229	0.878	25
c#	2.5	143962	0.864	35
objective-c	1.8	2920	0.8401435	59
swift	1.0	16545	0.839	40
sql	1.8	55654	0.834	13
r	5.7	51794	0.826	36
java	2.7	204052	0.823	34
scala	0.7	12921	0.757	67
ruby	1.2	8537	0.728	31
haskell	5.4	5042	0.627	41

the diagram which shows the distribution of the reputation deciles per programming languages tags was included (Fig. 3). Above the author also included the table to show the analysed characteristics for the most popular programming languages.

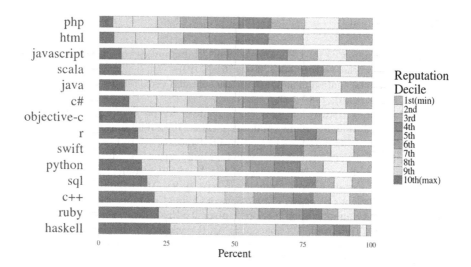

Fig. 3. The distribution of reputation deciles per tag

5 Conclusion

Based on the results received after the pilot analysis, following conclusions can be drawn. First of all, the time between the question posting and the first reply universally considered as the indicator of user expertise, and it negatively correlates with the proportion of overlapping community it belongs. It shows that the central assumption about the harm of high skills overlap is significantly confirmed, supported by the ideas and findings of Hill and Shaw [5]. However, as the correlation is significant but low, the relations between time and overlap should be examined in details. Secondly, the author discovered that the overlapping proportion strongly correlates with the count of answers given to the questions tagged by a particular skill. It corresponds to the findings of O'learly and colleagues, who state that participation in the several communities at the same time increase the productivity [7]. The author did not found a significant correlation between reputation distribution inequality and the overlap, however, we will examine these relations with the help of other inequality metrics later. All in all, the main trends were discovered and the analysis will be continued to construct the clear measure of user expertise and knowledge complexity. As the IT market could be characterised as the fluent one, measuring of expertise based on the set of skills professional has, seems to be an efficient way to evaluate the technology location on the map of IT market.

References

1. Ahn, Y.Y., Bagrow, J.P., Lehmann, S.: Link communities reveal multiscale complexity in networks. Nature **466**(7307), 761 (2010)
2. Burt, R.S.: Social contagion and innovation: cohesion versus structural equivalence. Am. J. Sociol. **92**(6), 1287–1335 (1987)
3. Chen, J., Ren, Y., Riedl, J.: The effects of diversity on group productivity and member withdrawal in online volunteer groups. In: Proceedings of the SIGCHI Conference on Human Factors in Computing Systems, pp. 821–830. ACM (2010)
4. Hanrahan, B.V., Convertino, G., Nelson, L.: Modeling problem difficulty and expertise in stackoverflow. In: Proceedings of the ACM 2012 Conference on Computer Supported Cooperative Work Companion, pp. 91–94. ACM (2012)
5. Hill, B.M., Shaw, A.: Studying Populations of Online Communities. The Handbook of Networked Communication. Oxford University Press, New York, NY (2017)
6. Kalinka, A.T., Tomancak, P.: linkcomm: An R package for the generation, visualization, and analysis of link communities in networks of arbitrary size and type. Bioinformatics **27**(14), 2011–2012 (2011)
7. O'leary, M.B., Mortensen, M., Woolley, A.W.: Multiple team membership: a theoretical model of its effects on productivity and learning for individuals and teams. Acad. Manag. Rev. **36**(3), 461–478 (2011)
8. Pal, A., Harper, F.M., Konstan, J.A.: Exploring question selection bias to identify experts and potential experts in community question answering. ACM Trans. Inf. Syst. (TOIS) **30**(2), 10 (2012)
9. Ren, Y., Kraut, R., Kiesler, S.: Applying common identity and bond theory to design of online communities. Organ. Stud. **28**(3), 377–408 (2007)

10. Thongtanunam, P., Kula, R.G., Cruz, A.E., Yoshida, N., Ichikawa, K., Iida, H.: Mining history of gamification towards finding expertise in question and answering communities: experience and practice with stack exchange. Rev. Socionetw. Strat. **7**(2), 115–130 (2013)
11. Wang, X., Butler, B.S., Ren, Y.: The impact of membership overlap on growth: an ecological competition view of online groups. Organ. Sci. **24**(2), 414–431 (2013)
12. Zhang, J., Ackerman, M.S., Adamic, L.: Expertise networks in online communities: structure and algorithms. In: Proceedings of the 16th International Conference on World Wide Web, pp. 221–230. ACM (2007)
13. Zhu, H., Kraut, R.E., Kittur, A.: The impact of membership overlap on the survival of online communities. In: Proceedings of the SIGCHI Conference on Human Factors in Computing Systems, pp. 281–290. ACM (2014)

How "VKontakte" Fake Accounts Influence the Social Network of Users

Adelia Kaveeva[1]([⊠]) [ID], Konstantin Gurin[2] [ID],
and Valery Solovyev[1] [ID]

[1] Kazan Federal University, Kazan, Russia
adele.kaveeva@mail.ru, maki.solovyev@mail.ru
[2] Udmurt State University, Izhevsk, Russia
rekonchik@mail.ru

Abstract. In this paper, the problem of fake accounts in online social networks is addressed through the lens of resulting misstatements of the structure of network interactions between users. The study of a network as a social space becomes difficult because of additional noise created by fakes.

The aim of the present paper is to assess the impact of fake accounts on the characteristics of local friendship networks between users of VKontakte website in Izhevsk (Russia). The authors highlight key characteristics recognizing a fake account and present experience of the design of classifier (based on random forest algorithm) to determine the authenticity of an account. Comparison of the VKontakte network topology before and after removing the fake accounts from it shows what specific network metrics are affected by the presence of fake profiles. It was found that as the fakes are being excluded the less integrated members lose contact with most part of the network while the number of its components increases. "Fakes" serve as strong link concentrators distributed throughout the network and these fakes overestimate observed levels of assortativity and transitivity.

Keywords: Social network analysis · VKontakte · Data analysis using R
Fake accounts · Online communities

1 Introduction

Recently, online social networks have been experiencing exponential growth in both profile page registrations and social interactions. These networks allow people to share information - news, photos, videos, opinions and other personal information. However, such rapid growth is accompanied with a sharp increase of malicious actions, such as spamming, fake accounts creation, phishing and distribution of malicious software [1]. According to Facebook estimations, 8.7% of the accounts registered in this social network (i.e. 83.09 million) don't belong to real users, and about 1.5% (14.32 million) belong to users who are able to distribute malicious content [12]. Notwithstanding, the development of an effective detection system that can identify malicious accounts as well as their suspicious behavior in social networks remains a difficult task.

© Springer Nature Switzerland AG 2018
D. A. Alexandrov et al. (Eds.): DTGS 2018, CCIS 858, pp. 492–502, 2018.
https://doi.org/10.1007/978-3-030-02843-5_41

Fake accounts can be used to suppress real users and undermine confident relationships in a social network by their use of various malicious activities such as spamming, private data collection, etc. [5]. By adding personal information such as photos and personal profile information into fake accounts, their creators aim to make these fake accounts look like real users. This imitation is initially based on the greater trust users have on similar "ordinary people" as themselves, as opposed to trust to the public media and other institutional agents that may be engaged by certain social and political forces in favor of certain opinions, goods and services.

Cresci and co-authors noted that the sale of fake accounts to those who want to build a reputation of their accounts has become a multimillion dollar business. Their research demonstrates that profiles of celebrities, politicians and popular organizations are expressing a suspicious increase in the number of subscribers attributed to fake accounts [8]. Such actions can often harm reputation and have far-reaching consequences and risks on social network. Examples of fakes used in political campaigns and creation of a political image (including "black PR" of competitors) are described in the work of Davydov [9].

Ferrara and co-authors integrate the problems of artificial social networks into an even broader social context. The authors consider the detection of such users ("social bots") as an important research task, because fakes can penetrate political discourse, manipulate the stock market, foment panic in emergency situations and spread disinformation, entailing the confidence erosion in social networks [11]. "Social bots" can also hinder promotion of public and state politics, presenting itself in the form of grassroot movements or contributing to a strong polarization of political debate on the Internet [6].

2 Identification of Fakes in Social Networks

The increase in the number of artificial accounts and their interfering effects do not go unnoticed at a level of topology of the social network that users form. This has led to a distortion of the picture of the interactions of real users, which may have led to incorrect conclusions on network characteristics drawn from basis of network analysis by researchers.

For example, the network visualization of Ferrara et al. [11] demonstrated the results of "social bots" intervention in online debates about the vaccination policy in California, USA, on Twitter. The fake node size of the retweet network graph is much larger than the size of the nodes (reflecting user's influence - the number of post retweets) from authentic accounts. Obviously, excluding artificial accounts from this network would significantly change its structure, giving the researcher more correct information about the distribution of the topic among only the real agents. However, identifying fakes is a difficult problem could be solved by means of various approaches: behavioral analysis, graph theory, machine learning [13]; as well as different algorithms are proposed (for example, [1, 3, 4, 16, 18]).

The behavioral approach is based on monitoring of users' behavior. There is the confidence that people behave different from the fakes, therefore detection of the artificial behavior will result in the identification of the fakes [10]. Alymov et al. had analyzed the possibilities of detecting fake accounts in Russian VKontakte network and distinguished two types of indicators for detecting them: static and behavioral. Static features include the completeness of the profile, the amount of friends (fakes have more friends than an average user), the number of comments from friends (fakes practically do not have these), the presence of advertising content, and others. Behavioral features reflect different forms of activity, for instance, the speed of commenting, which is much higher for artificial accounts [2]. The weakness of the behavioral approach is in the following: the spammer, who does not abuse various platforms using basic profile information, is difficult to detect.

The graph theory is known to be perspective in investigation of the fakes. For instance, Conti et al. [7] have analyzed social network graphs in dynamics to detect the persons creating the fake accounts and imitating real people, and then interacting with the real peoples' friends. Many researchers use the machine learning algorithms to detect the spam in the social networks. For example, Fire et al. [13] have used topology anomalies, decision trees, and naive Bayes classifiers to identify spammers and fake accounts in various social networks.

Some studies in this area are based on the fact the fakes are grouped into clusters, and there is a possibility to detect such groups of interrelated artificial accounts (e.g., [16]). However, a contrary picture is often being observed. A case study carried out on a Chinese social network "Renren" showed that fake accounts are often surrounded by real users. In other words, fakes do not form a cluster rather, they are well integrated into a wider social network [18]. These studies also showed that fake accounts have an ability to add friends using a principle similar to snowballing: starting with popular users, then gradually adding more and more ordinary users, with time becoming integrated into the social network and difficult to differentiate from ordinary members [17].

The work of Xiao et al. [16] was chosen as a base for the present research. To train the classifier to detect the fakes in LinkedIn the authors have used and compared the algorithms of random forest, logistic regression, and support vector machine classifiers. The random forest algorithm has shown the best results for all metrics (AUC value of a test set was 0.98). Therefore we used the random forest algorithm to create fakes' classifier in "VKontakte" Russian social network.

3   Fake Accounts in "VKontakte" Website

3.1   Research Questions, Data and Methods

In this work we develop a classifier to detect the fake accounts in online social network "VKontakte" using random forest algorithm. "VKontakte", the most popular Russian website [15], represents a social field for communication, maintaining social relations and forming social capital. The popularity of the platform is the reason agents enter the network. By creating a network of fake profiles they seek to use it as an economic tool for other purposes. The research interest of authors of the present paper is focused on how such penetration affects the topology and properties of "VKontakte" users' network. We propose an approach to identify artificial accounts using the friendship link network of

Izhevsk city as an example. Determination and exclusion of fakes allows adjusting the network of users and assessing the impact artificial accounts have on the network. The research questions of the paper in the following:

1. Does removing of the detected fake accounts affect the network cohesion (modularity)?
2. What role does the fake play in the integration of the weakly involved users in the network?
3. What effect does the removing of fakes have in the distribution of friendship links in the network (in other words, how do the indicators of assortativity and transitivity in the network change after removing fakes)?

The proposed classifier determines whether an account is artificial or not. We expect the removal of highly probable fake accounts from the network of accounts would influence the observable network metrics. Metrics calculated for networks of users is an indicator of cohesiveness of the community. It allows us to know if it contains subgroups, to know which nodes (i.e. users) have the greatest weight and importance and to know how and due to which participants network expansion and information distribution arise. Obviously, the presence of fakes in a network and their amount can significantly distort the accuracy of conclusions on network characteristics.

We consider the following metrics of network analysis as significant in the present work: network size, average path length, distribution of node degrees, assortativity, transitivity, modularity, etc.

Izhevsk city residents were used as a sample platform to create and apply a classifier of a local network. Izhevsk was chosen because of the relative simplicity of data collection due to the small size of the network (there are 507748 Izhevsk accounts registered in "VKontakte" website). User base of Izhevsk residents was collected from "VKontakte" using residents search algorithm. This includes users not indicating their city of residence. The network included 600315 users and 23113 thousand friendship links in total.

The object of the present research is the local friendship link network in "VKontakte" online social network of Izhevsk, and the subject is the topology of the network influenced by the artificial accounts. Therefore the aim of the research is to reveal the changes in network characteristics when users, much likely to be fakes, are excluded. To achieve the research aim following tasks were assigned and realized:

1. To define characteristics recognizing fake accounts;
2. To design a classifier based on user characteristics to determine whether user account is fake or not;
3. To assess impact on the local network topology and its characteristics after excluding the most likely fake accounts.

3.2 Design of Classifier to Recognize Fakes

First of all, to create a classifier it was necessary to form a training set. To do this, the authors collected information from 37 Izhevsk residing users. They had to specify which of their friends and subscribers they knew personally, which of them added or tried to add friends they have not met and/or if any of those added is a seller of some goods or services by "VKontakte" website. Thus, a set of Izhevsk residents was obtained to construct the classifier, containing after excluding duplicates and intersections 6252 real accounts and 2293 fakes.

Data collection of these users was carried out by R programming language and "VKR" open access library, developed by Sorokin [14]. "VKR" package contains a set of functions to access "VKontakte" website after a special application key is received to upload and analyze data about users and communities.

The information used to complete certain fields of the profiles of the selected sample of users (residence, sex, date of birth, school and university of study, political and religious views, presence of partner, maiden name) and the information on the type of device used for the last time to go online were collected. The network and behavioral metrics of users were also calculated: level of transitivity, number of friends and subscribers online, total amount of friends and subscribers, proportion of friends and subscribers of the user who are Izhevsk residents, eigenvector centrality, number of not confirmed friend requests sent to a user, number of groups user belongs to and groups popular among Izhevsk residents (with more than 500 Izhevsk residents). It was also defined at what size network segment a user is (the rank of the size of its cluster obtained as a result of graph partition). As it can be seen from the list of collected characteristics, they contain both static and behavioral features.

To create a model identifying whether a user is fake or not random forest algorithm was employed. Random forest draws a tree set, extracting from the training data random subsets and calculating what class for each observation was voted by the most trees. Random forest does not require transformation and assumptions about characteristics distribution, it is not sensitive to excess variables. However, as other methods of statistical training, random trees are inclined to be retrained. This requires a researcher to separate the sample set into training and test subsets. The resulting algorithm of 1000 trees was constructed on the base of two thirds of the database, and a third was used to check for retraining.

The algorithm correctly recognized 92% of users (15.2% of fakes were recognized as real users, 5.7% of real users were falsely recognized as fakes) on the test set. AUC value, estimated on the test set, is equal to 0.954, indicating high quality recognition of real as well as artificial accounts. Construction of models based on the XGBoost algorithm and logistic regression with regularization showed similar results.

3.3   Applying the Classifier to the Local Friendship Network of Izhevsk Residents

A developed classifier was applied to the friendship link network of "VKontakte" users, residing in Izhevsk. The following network features were investigated: graph size, number of connected components without removing fakes this was the only one connecting component as the classifier was compiled by graph walking algorithm), assortativity, that is the property to make friends with the same popular accounts in the network, transitivity, modularity, used in the present study as a level of heterogeneity of the network, and number of subgroups in the largest connected component. Correlation between centrality in the network before and after fakes are removed was also verified. The centrality includes centrality by the number of friends (degree centrality) and by eigenvector. In addition, as friendship network connected, changes in distribution of number of friendship links of users (mean, median, first and third quartiles, first and last quantiles) were monitored.

To determine which class the fakes belong to, a number of measurements at different threshold level of the proportion of trees identifying a member as fake were carried out. This was necessary since there was an error of the classifier and this error differed at various threshold levels. The values from 1 (i.e., including the entire graph) to 0.7 (i.e., excluding all users who were voted by more than 70% of trees as a fake) were calculated with a step of 1% according to the result of the classifier. As the network was being constructed, the fakes were identified, removed and the network's metrics were being measured at every step (Table 1).

As a result of the tests, it was found that as the highly probable fake accounts were being removed, the less integrated participants lost links with the most part of networks that reflected increased component number. Network size also decreased significantly. Cohesion of the most part of the network, expressed by modularity index didn't change as the fake accounts are excluded, but the number of clusters within the largest connected component decreased. This is explained by the disconnection of small clusters from the connected component. Therefore fake accounts don't influence the cohesion/disconnection in the network.

The impact of fakes on the integration of poorly involved users into the network is lower than impact of a randomly taken account. This conclusion resulted from the comparison the network obtained after removing accounts with a 70% threshold value of the model, and 30 networks constructed by random removal of nodes quantitatively equal to excluded artificial accounts. Minimal number of components in the networks of randomly removed nodes was 7336, that is 2.5 times higher than the number of components after fakes were removed.

The level of assortativity and transitivity in the network increases with removal of fake accounts. Thus fakes are strong link concentrators distributed throughout the network, therefore observable levels of assortativity and transitivity are overestimated. This conclusion is also supported by comparison with the networks of randomly deleted members, where network parameters are less different from the entire graph.

Local transitivity value for certain users (Spearman's correlation between metrics of the exhaustive network and corrected according to specific nodes dropped to 0.98) and eigenvector centrality (up to 0.97) vary as fake accounts are removed. Average number friendship links and the ninth decile of distribution reduced, and nonparametric measures of distribution (excluding the ninth decile) increased as fake accounts were being removed. It is explained by the fact that fakes often become either hubs (but limited by the maximal number of friends equal to 10000) or, conversely, accounts poorly involved in the network. Therefore distribution of friendship link numbers of users greatly deforms as fake accounts are included in the analysis.

Table 1. Network metrics were calculated as accounts (recognized by the classifier as a fake class) were being removed

Threshold % of fakes, as higher values an account are excluded	Number of online accounts	Number of links in the network	Number of connected components	Modularity of the largest connected component	Number of clusters of the largest connected component	Assortativity of the network	Transitivity of the network
100	600315	23113829	1	0.40	185	0.16	0.09
99	600150	23096184	9	0.40	201	0.16	0.09
98	599213	23004474	84	0.40	139	0.16	0.09
97	597873	22862227	167	0.40	135	0.16	0.09
96	596640	22722786	284	0.40	151	0.16	0.09
95	594897	22539385	443	0.40	120	0.16	0.09
94	591937	22334431	603	0.40	152	0.17	0.09
93	588803	22118519	818	0.40	120	0.17	0.09
92	585849	21907134	949	0.40	126	0.17	0.09
91	582260	21695578	1107	0.40	118	0.17	0.09
90	579011	21470725	1230	0.40	216	0.16	0.09
89	575550	21256290	1364	0.40	214	0.16	0.09
88	572047	21056993	1540	0.40	139	0.16	0.09
87	568851	20873389	1683	0.41	123	0.16	0.09
86	565412	20666763	1822	0.41	118	0.16	0.09
85	562185	20472632	1972	0.41	104	0.16	0.09
84	558931	20270449	2106	0.41	101	0.16	0.09
83	555702	20096617	2226	0.41	108	0.15	0.08
82	552402	19928804	2337	0.41	103	0.15	0.08
81	549299	19757009	2451	0.41	99	0.15	0.08
80	546020	19593964	2543	0.41	93	0.15	0.08
79	542792	19427574	2599	0.41	80	0.14	0.08

(continued)

Table 1. (continued)

Threshold % of fakes, as higher values an account are excluded	Number of online accounts	Number of links in the network	Number of connected components	Modularity of the largest connected component	Number of clusters of the largest connected component	Assortativity of the network	Transitivity of the network
78	539440	19259315	2788	0.40	96	0.14	0.08
77	536072	19098666	2842	0.40	89	0.14	0.08
76	532674	18934999	2896	0.41	76	0.13	0.08
75	529462	18811865	2909	0.40	78	0.13	0.07
74	526119	18676798	2933	0.40	54	0.13	0.07
73	522606	18541846	2989	0.40	60	0.13	0.07
72	519002	18421021	2963	0.41	46	0.12	0.07
71	515359	18298964	2953	0.41	51	0.12	0.07
70	511297	18195034	2893	0.41	52	0.12	0.07

4   Conclusions

The study of local and urban networks of Internet users require a researcher to take into account disadvantages of big data such as their possible incompleteness and unreliability. If the first type of disadvantages can be attributed to an accidental or intentional omission of a part of personal data by users (for instance, city of residence), the second is related, first of all, to the presence of a large number of artificial accounts in networks creating "noise" in the data. Incompleteness and unreliability of the data cause changes in the network topology and subsequently a displacement of the network characteristics. Due to this, methods of network correction are used (supplementing missing user data or, on the contrary, "cleaning" the network of fakes). One of the ways to detect fake accounts is the classifier developed in the present work on the basis of random forest algorithm.

The proposed classifier correctly recognizes 92% of users (15.2% of fakes were recognized as real users, 5.7% of real users were falsely recognized as fakes). This is based on static as well as behavioral properties to reveal profile authenticity [2]: information put into the profile fields, network and behavioral metrics (transitivity, number of friends and subscribers, group membership, location in network segment, etc.).

The present work confirms findings of previous studies of other social networks: artificial accounts are greatly integrated into the network of real users. Fakes add friends using the snowballing principle for more contacts. Moreover, they act as link concentrators in the network: as fake accounts are being removed, the less integrated members lose links with most part of the network, this is seen in the growth of the number of components, and the network itself significantly decreases in size. Fakes more likely become hubs or are poorly involved in the network accounts. Therefore distribution of the number of friendship links of users is strongly deformed as the fake accounts are including into the analysis. The presence of fake accounts also overestimates levels of assortativity (the tendency to form friendship links with those who have a similar number of friends) and transitivity (the proportion of closed triads, where all three are friends). Thus a significant number of artificial profiles unsupported by real users really influence the topology of the network and, consequently, on how information will be distributed. Therefore correct investigation of various processes, as well as network structure on social networking sites should be preceded by the identification and removal of fake accounts among them.

The topic of fake agents in a network is in itself of scientific interest and has prospects for further investigation. The increase in the number of fakes and their real impact on both structure of network and processes of distribution of information within it reflect the current trends in the development of online communities, having a direct impact on non-virtual reality. Despite the fact that in the paper fakes are considered a "noise" in data that is necessary to eliminate in order to formulate correct conclusions on the network under study, fakes can be the object of research in themselves. The great variability of behaviors demonstrated by artificial agents determines the variety of methods and approaches for their study. In particular, outside the paper there are questions of identity and situations when real people create fake accounts in order to show another side of themselves different from real life. In such situation fake is a way of playing other social roles and scenarios (including deviant ones) that are inaccessible to an individual in offline. This can act as a significant socializing factor. This approach to the problem allows applying classical sociological theories, for example, E. Goffman's dramaturgy.

Acknowledgements. This research was financially supported by the Russian Government Program of Competitive Growth of Kazan Federal University, state assignment of Ministry of Education and Science, grant agreement No. 34.5517.2017/6.7 and by RFBR, grant No. 15-29-01173.

References

1. Adewole, K.S., Anuar, N.B., Kamsin, A., Varathan, K.D., Razak, S.A.: Malicious accounts: dark of the social networks. J. Netw. Comput. Appl. **79**, 41–67 (2017). https://doi.org/10.1016/j.jnca.2016.11.030
2. Alymov, A.S., Baranyuk, V.V., Smirnova, O.S.: Detecting bot programs that mimic people's behavior in the social network "VKontakte". Int. J. Open Inf. Technol. **8**, 55–60 (2016). (in Russian)
3. Boshmaf, Y., Muslukhov, I., Beznosov, K., Ripeanu, M.: The socialbot network: when bots socialize for fame and money. In: Proceedings of the 27th Annual Computer Security Applications Conference, pp. 93–102 (2011)
4. Cao, Q., Sirivianos, M., Yang, X., Pregueiro, T.: Aiding the detection of fake accounts in large scale social online services. In: Proceedings of the 9th USENIX conference on Networked Systems Design and Implementation, pp. 1–15 (2012)
5. Chen, C.-M., Guan, D., Su, Q.-K.: Feature set identification for detecting suspicious URLs using Bayesian classification in social networks. Inf. Sci. **289**, 133–147 (2014)
6. Conover, M., Ratkiewicz, J., Francisco, M., Gonçalves, B., Menczer, F., Flammini, A.: Political polarization on twitter. In: Proceedings of the 5th International AAAI Conference on Weblogs and Social Media, pp. 89–96 (2011)
7. Conti, M., Poovendran, R., Secchiero, M.: Fakebook: detecting fake profiles in on-line social networks. In: Proceedings of the 2012 International Conference on Advances in Social Networks Analysis and Mining (ASONAM 2012), pp. 1071–1078 (2012)
8. Cresci, S., Di Pietro, R., Petrocchi, M., Spognardi, A., Tesconi, M.: Fame for sale: efficient detection of fake twitter followers. Decis. Support Syst. **80**, 56–71 (2015). https://doi.org/10.1016/j.dss.2015.09.003
9. Davydov, L.: On the use of social networks as a tool for creating political authority's image. Int. J. Environ. Sci. Educ. **11**(18), 12423–12430 (2016)
10. El Azab, A., Idrees, A.M., Mahmoud, A.M., Hefny, H.: Fake account detection in twitter based on minimum weighted feature set. Int. Sch. Sci. Res. Innov. **10**(1), 13–18 (2016)
11. Ferrara, E., Varol, O., Davis, C., Menczer, F., Flammini, A.: The rise of social bots. Commun. ACM **59**(7), 96–104 (2016). https://doi.org/10.1145/2818717
12. Fire, M., Kagan, D., Elyashar, A., Elovici, Y.: Friend or foe? Fake profile identification in online social networks. Soc. Netw. Anal. Min. **4**(1), 1–23 (2014)
13. Fire, M., Katz, G., Elovici, Y.: Strangers intrusion detection—detecting spammers and fake profiles in social networks based on topology anomalies. ASE Hum. J. **1**(1), 26–39 (2012)
14. GitHub: Access to VK (Vkontakte) API via R. https://github.com/Dementiy/vkR. Accessed 10 Jan 2018
15. Top Websites Ranking. https://www.similarweb.com/top-websites. Accessed 10 Jan 2018

16. Xiao, C., Freeman, D.M., Hwa, T.: Detecting clusters of fake accounts in online social networks. In: Proceedings of the 8th ACM Workshop on Artificial Intelligence and Security, pp. 91–101 (2015). https://doi.org/10.1145/2808769.2808779
17. Yang, Z., Wilson, C., Wang, X., Gao, T., Zhao, B. Y., Dai, Y.: Uncovering social network sybils in the wild. In: Internet Measurement Conference, pp. 259–268 (2011)
18. Zhu, Y., Wang, X., Zhong, E., Liu, N., Li, H., Yang, Q.: Discovering spammers in social networks. In: Proceedings of the Twenty-Sixth AAAI Conference on Artificial Intelligence, pp. 171–177 (2012)

The Method for Prediction the Distribution of Information in Social Networks Based on the Attributes

Ilya Viksnin$^{(\boxtimes)}$ ⓘ, Liubov Iurtaeva ⓘ, Nikita Tursukov ⓘ,
and Ruslan Gataullin ⓘ

ITMO University, Saint Petersburg, Russia
wixnin@mas-lab.ru

Abstract. Social networks are important part of society. Analysis of information flows and activity of users may provide different opportunities for scientist. However, existing methods and models for prediction of information flow couldn't provide sufficient level of accuracy. Proposed method of information flow analysis is based on machine learning algorithms. First stage of research aims to analyze the features, that could be useful for describing activity of users and information in social networks. Data was assembled from social network "VKontakte". Data includes main information about selected features for each person. On the second stage were conducted experiments, based on machine learning methods. Three main approaches were implemented in research - naive Bayes classifier, logistic regression analysis and k-means clustering. A comparison of different machine learning methods was conducted on last stage. Best results of predictions were reached by usage of naive Bayes classifier. Proposed method for prediction of information flow is usable for organizing users' protection from different type of information attacks.

Keywords: Information flow · Social networks · Machine learning

1 Introduction

Main goal of social networks is interaction people. Developer of such networks create different tools to simplify search of other people with same interests and to improve communication mechanisms within groups. Today functionality of social networks provides much more things than only pure communication. Some shops, newspapers and other organizations consider social networks as main opportunity to increase count of clients or, sometimes, as only market for their products.

This way many companies are trying to give for such groups improved mechanisms for work with public. One of the most popular tool is parser. Parser allows to gather basic information about people behavior. Gathered information may be used for designing marketing company, preparation of targeted advertising and so on. However, this is not only the one way to use such information - it seems easy to affect people due to knowledge of their interests, habits and tendency. To organize monitoring and

D. A. Alexandrov et al. (Eds.): DTGS 2018, CCIS 858, pp. 503–515, 2018.
https://doi.org/10.1007/978-3-030-02843-5_42

counteractions against such attacks it should be clarified ways of information spreading in social networks.

Main goal of current research is to improve quality of existing methods for prediction information flow between people in social networks. To reach this goal, authors defined tasks:

1. define main components of method;
2. assemble data set from social network;
3. select main features from elements of social networks;
4. conduct experiments.

In this paper under the elements of the social network refers to network users.

2 Literature Review

Paper [1] describes the dissemination of information through the social network Flickr. Photo hosting allows to post photos. Network tools allow to create connections between people (friends) and add photos to favorites. Model considered in the paper [1, 2] describes the dissemination of information based only on the availability of friendly indicators and user preferences, so such methods will not be able to work properly in larger social networks.

According to the ideas in [3] there are two seminal models, namely Independent Cascades (IC) [5–7] and Linear Threshold (LT) [8–10]. They assume the existence of a static graph structure underlying the diffusion and focus on the structure of the process. They are based on a directed graph where each node can be activated or not with a monotonicity assumption, i.e. activated nodes cannot deactivate. The IC model requires a diffusion probability to be associated to each edge whereas LT requires an influence degree to be defined on each edge and an influence threshold for each node. For both models, the diffusion process proceeds iteratively in a synchronous way along a discrete time-axis, starting from a set of initially activated nodes, commonly named early adopters.

In paper [4] authors used a successful method of evaluating the trust of users to each other. For each of the 6 million users, authors computed the value of each influence measure and compared them. Rather than comparing the values directly, authors used the relative order of users' ranks as a measure of difference. In order to do this, authors sorted users by each measure, so that the rank of 1 indicates the most influential user and increasing rank indicates a less influential user [11, 12]. Users with the same influence value receive the average of the rank amongst them. Once every user is assigned a rank for each influence measure, authors are ready to quantify how a user's rank varies across different measures and examine what kinds of users are ranked high for a given measure.

In paper [13] the developed model of distribution showed satisfactory results. Model shows the dynamics of distribution among users by analyzing their interaction, behavior and properties of information. Taking into account shortcomings listed in the second chapter of the article, a new model was developed.

According to the developed model vertex i which connected with j active neighbors at time t activates if the condition (1) execute.

$$\sum_{j=1}^{n} D_{ij} * A_i * L_t > f_i \tag{1}$$

where Dij – the influence of the neighbor j to the node i, Ai – the activity of the vertex i, Lt – the relevance of the information at time t.

The coefficient D is calculated according to the following rule (2).

$$D_{ij} = \frac{Like_{ij} + Repost_{ij} + Friends_{ij}}{Like_i + Repost_i + Friends_i} \tag{2}$$

where $Like_{ij}$—the number of "likes" on node i from node j, $Repost_{ij}$—the number of "repost" on node i from node j, $Friends_{ij}$—the number of common friends, $Like_i$—the number of all "likes" at node i, $Repost_j$—the number of all "repost" at node i, $Friends_i$—the number of all friends at node i.

The coefficient A is calculated according to the following rule (3).

$$A_i = \frac{Repost_i}{Repost} \tag{3}$$

where Repost—the number of "Repost" all adjacent to the vertex i.

The coefficient L is calculated according to the following rule (4, 5).

$$L_t = LP_{t-1} - LP_t \tag{4}$$

$$LP_t = \frac{Like_{t-1} + Repost_{t-1}}{PosLike_{t-1} + PosRepost_{t-1}} \tag{5}$$

$Like_t$—the number of "likes" for news at the time t, $Repost_t$—the number of "repost" for news at the time t, $PosLike_t$—the possible number of "likes" for news at the time t, $PosRepost_t$—the possible number of "repost" for news at the time t.

When calculating the coefficients weight of each of mark "likes" is equal to 2, the mark "repost" is equal to 4, friend is equal to 1.

The percentage of successful predictions is 13%.

In this paper, an attempt to improve the efficiency of the model developed in [13] was implemented. The greatest efficiency is achieved through the use of machine learning methods. Comparison of efficiency was carried out on the dataset collected from one group of the social network "VKontakte".

3 Data Set

Users of social networks may be classified on base of their characteristics. Characteristics of users may report about basic behavior trends of users. It seems necessary to describe main rules and characteristics of elements presented in social networks. Authors have selected social network Vkontakte to conduct experiments.

Social network Vkontakte bases on some rules:

1. each user has personal page;
2. each user can subscribe on news from other users;
3. each user can put "Like" and "Share" on information from other users;
4. users can comment each note;
5. some pages are known as groups - on such pages users may write some notes about different topics.

Information about persons used for classification may be divided in such groups:

1. information about users and their interaction:
   a. information about subscribes;
   b. information about marks "Like" (authors, date);
   c. information about marks "Share" (authors, date);
   d. information about comments.
2. information about notes:
   a. publication time;
   b. type of note.

Interaction of people may change during the time. Thus, information used for prediction should be actual. Moreover, authors restrict subject of research by only one group and all users, which have subscribed on this group. This approach decreases requirements to computing power.

Vkontakte has an API that can be used to collect information from social network. To gain all available information is important to have structure for storage big data. Each user has not only statical structure like name, birthday and so on, but also a dynamically data like "Like", "Share" and so on. One of the challenges is providing short time from creation a request till presentation of results. Time for answering on requests should be acceptable for researchers (less than 1 s for one request). Implementation via MySQL [14] couldn't provide acceptable time of work - answers were preparing in 1 to 10 s. To solve this problem, authors have selected graph database platform Neo4j [15]. Classical table implementation of database will store excess information, so it's not useful for current research.

For qualitative analysis of selected machine learning algorithm, it is necessary to select important parameters and present the data in the form of a certain structure.

The dissemination of information is realized by setting users mark "Repost", that is, in fact the model must solve one point problem, which is to predict the installation of this mark within one pair of users. In the future, the model should iteratively aggregate the obtained data into a common database for prediction.

Empirically parameters were chosen for analysis of the distribution of k-th user's post by i-th user are shown in Table 1.

Table 1. Parameters for analysis.

	User i	User k	Relation i => k	Relation k => i	Analyzed post
Number of "Like"	+	+	+	+	
Number of "Repost"	+	+	+	+	
Number of comments	+	+	+	+	
Number of posts	+	+			
Number of common friends			+	+	
Content category					+
Publication time					+

Subject matter of distributed content has a great influence on the dissemination of information. In this regard, the following categories of content were formed for greater accuracy of prediction: amusement information, political content, news and other.

Determining the type of content is a very difficult task, at the moment a lot of scientists are conducting research on this topic. In this paper, the definition of the content type is an auxiliary part, so a primitive algorithm was developed to determine the category of content. With the help of experts' evaluation for each category (category 1–3), a sample of words, most often found in the records of this category, was created. Further for each post the number of matches of words with sample from each category was counted. The post belongs to the category with the highest number of matches. If there was no match, the post fell into the "other" category.

To make a prediction about information flow between two users is necessary to have information about their previously interaction. Thus, information about characteristics of each user, their communication and mutual "Like" and "Share" is required. Database should be structured before analysis. Therefore, authors create row for each pairs of users, contained information about their interaction, after that all rows with all possible pairs will be put in one table in database.

Let's introduce the following symbols:

1. user from start of analysis is known as ring 0;
2. subscribers of user (ring 0) are known as ring 1;
3. subscribers of users from ring 1 are known as ring 2.

Algorithm of filling such table is shown of Fig. 1. First step of analysis will start from ring 0 (i = 0). Second step is to analyze last ten notes on the page (j < 10). For each note of users from ring i is providing analysis of connection between subscribers

(k) of current user. Obviously, k < n, where n - count of subscribers of current user. Each record will produced one row in table. Rings of users should be analysis from ring 0 to ring 2 and all rings should be sequentially analyzed. Data set formatting is over after users from ring 2 analysis.

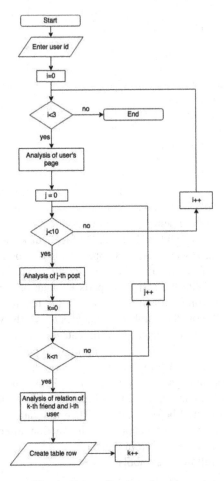

Fig. 1. Data collection algorithm.

Thus, table with whole data will be filled. JSON file contains hundreds of entries with following form:

```
{
    id_post: '{{index(600)}}',
    id_i: '{{5}}',
    id_k: '{{56}}',
    common_friends: '{{20}}',
    likes_i: '{{80}}',
    likes_k: '{{52}}',
    repost_i: '{{3}}',
    repost_k: '{{16}}',
    comments_i: '{{31}}',
    comments_k: '{{90}}',
    likes_ik: '{{24}}',
    likes_ki: '{{45}}',
    repost_ik: '{{2}}',
    repost_ki: '{{4}}',
    comments_ik: '{{1}}',
    comments_ki: '{{10}}',
    category_post: '{{2}}',
    time: '{{18}}',
    post_i: '{{10}}',
    post_k: '{{43}}',
}
```

These numbers are an example of analyzed parameters value for one pair of users and one record from the experiment.

The collected and formalized data are used for training classifiers and testing using machine learning algorithms. The training sample is 75% to build a model, the remaining 25% is a test sample designed to evaluate the performance of the classifier.

4 Experiments

The models and methods considered in the second chapter have the following disadvantages:

1. For prediction it is necessary to select coefficients for such parameters as the number of "Like" and "Repost" marks manually, based on statistical data and expert experience;
2. It is necessary to determine the threshold value for the probability of occurrence of the mark "Repost". Finding data to select is difficult. In this regard, experts are forced to select values from a random range and analyze the impact of this value on the result.

Machine learning algorithms solve these problems with greater speed and accuracy. Thus, the authors use the following classification methods to determine the best accuracy parameter:

1. logistic regression analysis;
2. k-means clustering;
3. naive Bayes classifier.

With the help of classifiers, the sample is divided into two classes: the class of observations for which the "repost" was made and the class of observations for which the "repost" was not made.

Observation Y, which characterizes the factors of the record, is as follows:

$$Y = \{X_1, X_2, \ldots, X_n, C_m\} \tag{6}$$

where X_n is the attribute variable,
n is the number of independent attributes,
C_m is the class variable,
m is the number of classes equal 2.

The conditional probability that the observation of Y belongs to the class Cm is calculated by the formula:

$$P(C_m|Y) = \frac{P(X_1|C_m) \cdot P(X_2|C_m) \cdot \ldots \cdot P(X_n|C_m) \cdot P(C_m)}{P(Y)} \tag{7}$$

The accuracy of the classification is calculated as the percentage of the correctly classified data compared to the true or absolute value and is determined by the Eq. (8):

$$Accuracy = \frac{P}{N} * 100\% \tag{8}$$

where P - the number of record-connection pairs of users for whom the classifier has made the right decision,

N - the size of training sample.

The informative value of each parameter was calculated in the analysis by linear regression method. Then was allocated 10 options with the highest information content.

By means of the R language the informative features were calculated. The informativity of the j-th feature is calculated by the to Eq. (9):

$$I(x_j) = 1 + \sum_{i=1}^{G} \left(P_i \sum_{k=1}^{K} \left(P_{i,k} * log_k P_{i,k} \right) \right), \tag{9}$$

where G is the number of feature gradations, K is the number of classes.

Informativity $I(x_j)$ is the normalized value that varies from 0 to 1.

P_i is the probability of i-th gradations of the feature by the Eq. (10):

$$P_i = \frac{\sum_{k=1}^{K} m_{i,k}}{N}, \tag{10}$$

where $m_{i,k}$ is the appearance frequency of i-th gradations in that class, N is the total number of observations.

$P_{i,k}$ is the probability of i-th gradations of the feature in k-the class by the equation:

$$P_{i,k} = \frac{m_{i,k}}{\sum_{k=1}^{K} m_{i,k}}.$$ (11)

The results are shown in Table 2.

Table 2. Informative attributes.

	User i	User k	Relation i => k	Relation k => i	Analyzed post
Number of "Like"	0,5561	0,5219	0,2338	0,6432	
Number of "Repost"	0,5357	0,5126	0,3554	0,8894	
Number of comments	0,1164	0,0998	0,2787	0,4945	
Number of posts	0,2976	0,2842			
Number of common friends			0,4123	0,4123	
Content category					0,6598
Publication time					0,0029

First of all, three classifiers were analyzed with an initial set of parameters. Than this classifier was run with a reduced number of parameters. The reduced list of parameters does not include the parameters with the least informative, such as number of all comments on both user pages and publication time. The results are shown in Tables 3 and 4.

Table 3. Classification result with initial set of parameters.

Method	Accuracy
Logistic regression	0,189
K-means clustering	0,25
Naive Bayes classifier	0,45

Table 4. Classification result with reduced list of parameters.

Method	Accuracy
Logistic regression	0,201
K-means clustering	0,31
Naive Bayes classifier	0,46

According to Table 4 naive Bayes classifier shows better accuracy. Maximum accuracy of prediction is 46%.

Accuracy values can be easily calculated using an confusion matrix (Table 5). With a small number of classes (no more than 100–150), this approach allows to visualize the performance of the classifier.

Table 5. Confusion matrix for Naive Bayes classifier method.

	TRUE "repost"	TRUE "not repost"
Prediction "repost"	0,16	0,43
Prediction "not repost"	0,09	0,32

The confusion matrix is a matrix of size N by N, where N is the number of classes. Columns of the matrix reserved for expert solutions and rows reserved for decisions of a classifier. In the process of classifying the case from the test sample, the number appears at the intersection of the string class returned by the classifier and the column class to which the case actually belongs.

According to Table 5, the classifier determines the majority of "Repost" marks correctly. The diagonal elements of the confusion matrix are explicitly expressed, which means that the selected attributes can accurately classify data.

Visualization of model's results is presented in Figs. 2 and 3. Graphical distribution of information is made by graph. Graph center is initial user of the social network, the rest of the graph nodes are connected between the user and each other.

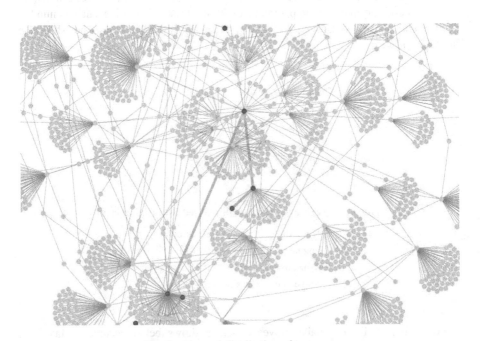

Fig. 2. The real distribution of test post.

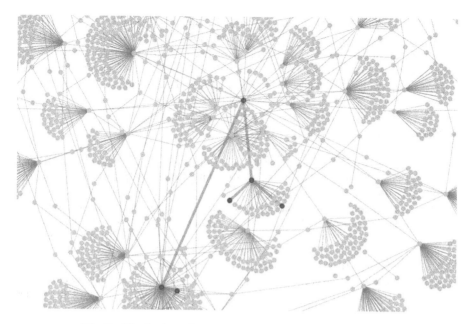

Fig. 3. Distribution of test post according to developed method.

Connection between nodes is friendly relationship between users. The model provides for researcher a visualization of the actual and calculated distribution of any post.

Final result is visualized on researcher's web-page and allow to see both the distribution of information and short information about each of the user (node of the graph). In addition to the graphical representation, information about users is presented in the form of a text table.

The visualization is implemented using the programming language JavaScript and D3.js [21], allowing to process and present data in a graphical format. The interface is the php web page. Main element constitutes a graph that displays users and their relationships, also there is input form that allows to consider a user. The form contains a field for entering a user's ID on social network and textbox for entering post or part of post on page. After confirmation of data entry, the resulting graphs showing the real information diffusion (Fig. 2) and calculated model information distribution (Fig. 3) are loaded.

5   Conclusion

In this paper, authors have improved a mathematical model of information diffusion in social networks. Introduced improvements allow to increase quality of predictions. Accuracy of predictions increased by 3 times (46%). So authors have reached main goal. Throw the research were assembled data from social network Vkontakte, selected main parameters of diffusion and conducted experiments.

Unfortunately, some information in Vkontakte and other social networks is private, thus, it's impossible to estimate full social graph. However, results of improved method are better, than of basic method. In the future authors plan to create cross-identification methods for different social networks to solve these challenges. Moreover, authors will propose methods to block negative information in social network.

References

1. Cha, M., Mislove, A., Gummadi, K.P.: A measurement-driven analysis of information propagation in the flickr social network. In: Proceedings of the 18th International Conference on World Wide Web, pp. 721–730 (2009)
2. Mislove, A., Koppula, H., Gummadi, K., Druschel, P., Bhattacharjee, B.: Growth of the flickr social network. In: ACM SIGCOMM Workshop on Online Social Networks (2008)
3. Guille, A., Hacid, H., Favre, C., Djamel, A.: Zighed: information diffusion in online social networks: a survey. ACM SIGMOD Record **42**(2), 17–28 (2013)
4. Wang, F., Wang, H., Xu, K.: Diffusive logistic model towards predicting information diffusion in online social networks. In: ICDCS 2012 Workshops, pp. 133–139 (2012)
5. Cha, M., Haddadi, H., Gummadi, K.P.: Measuring user influence in twitter: the million follower fallacy. In: Proceedings of the Fourth International AAAI Conference on Weblogs and Social Media, pp. 10–17 (2010)
6. Alvanaki, F.: See what's enblogue: real-time emergent topic identification in social media. In: EDBT, pp. 336–347 (2012)
7. Becker, H., Naaman, M., Gravano, L.: Learning similarity metrics for event identification in social media. In: WSDM, pp. 291–300 (2010)
8. Garofalakis, M.: Distributed data streams. In: Encyclopedia of Database Systems, pp. 883–890 (2009)
9. Budak, C., Agrawal, D., Abbadi, A.: Structural trend analysis for online social networks. PVLDB **4**(10), 646–656 (2011)
10. Leskovec, J., Backstrom, L., Kleinberg, J.: Meme-tracking and the dynamics of the news cycle. In: KDD, pp. 497–506 (2009)
11. Gruhl, D., Guha, R., Liben-Nowell D., Tomkins A.: Information diffusion through blogspace. In: Proceedings of of the 13rd International Conference on World Wide Web (WWW), pp. 491–501 (2004)
12. Draief, M., Massouli, L.: Epidemics and Rumours in Complex Networks. Cambridge University Press, New York (2010)
13. Viksnin, I., Iurtaeva, L., Tursukov, N., Muradov, A: The model of information diffusion in social networking service. In: Proceedings of the 20th Conference of Open Innovations Association FRUCT, pp. 731–734 (2017)
14. Greenspan J., Brad B.R: MySQL/PHP Database Applications. Wiley, New York (2001)
15. Webber, J.: A programmatic introduction to Neo4j. In: Proceedings of the 3rd Annual Conference on Systems, Programming, and Applications: Software for Humanity. ACM (2012)
16. Masse, M.: REST API design rulebook: designing consistent RESTful web service interfaces. O'Reilly Media Inc, Sebastopol, California (2011)
17. Tranmer, M., Elliot, M.: Multiple linear regression. In: CCSR Working Paper (2008)
18. Likas, A., Vlassis N., Verbeek J.: The global k-means clustering algorithm. Pattern Recogn., 451–461 (2003)

19. Rish, I.: An empirical study of the naive Bayes classifier. In: IJCAI 2001 Workshop on Empirical Methods in Artificial Intelligence, vol. 3, issue 22, pp. 41–46 (2001)
20. Rish I., Hellerstein J., Jayram T.: An analysis of data characteristics that affect naive Bayes performance. Technical Report RC21993, IBM T.J. Watson Research Center (2001)
21. Rauschmayer, A.: Speaking JavaScript: An In-Depth Guide for Programmers. O'Reilly Media Inc, Sebastopol, California (2018)

Data Mining for Prediction of Length of Stay of Cardiovascular Accident Inpatients

Cristiana Silva[1], Daniela Oliveira[2], Hugo Peixoto[2],
José Machado[2(✉)], and António Abelha[2]

[1] Department of Information, University of Minho, Braga, Portugal
a71665@alunos.uminho.pt
[2] Algoritmi Research Center, Department of Information, University of Minho,
Braga, Portugal
id7220@alunos.uminho.pt,
{hpeixoto,jmac,abelha}@di.uminho.pt

Abstract. The healthcare sector generates large amounts of data on a daily basis. This data holds valuable knowledge that, beyond supporting a wide range of medical and healthcare functions such as clinical decision support, can be used for improving profits and cutting down on wasted overhead. The evaluation and analysis of stored clinical data may lead to the discovery of trends and patterns that can significantly enhance overall understanding of disease progression and clinical management. Data mining techniques aim precisely at the extraction of useful knowledge from raw data. This work describes an implementation of a data mining project approach to predict the hospitalization period of cardiovascular accident patients. This provides an effective tool for the hospital cost containment and management efficiency. The data used for this project contains information about patients hospitalized in Cardiovascular Accident's unit in 2016 for having suffered a stroke. The Weka software was used as the machine learning toolkit.

Keywords: Data mining · Weka · Prediction · Cardiovascular accident

1 Introduction

We live in a world where vast amounts of data are collected daily. This explosively growing, widely available, and gigantic body of data makes our time no longer the "information age" but the "data age" [1]. Hospitals itself are nowadays collecting vast amounts of data related to patient records [2]. All this data holds valuable knowledge that can be used to improve hospital decision making [3, 4]. Therefore, analyzing such data in order to extract useful knowledge from it has become an important need. This is possible through powerful and adaptable data mining tools which aim precisely at the extraction of useful knowledge from raw data.

The project of this work primarily consists in the implementation of data mining techniques to predict the hospital Length Of Stay (LOS) of cardiovascular accident (CVA) patients based on indicators that are commonly available at the hospitalization

© Springer Nature Switzerland AG 2018
D. A. Alexandrov et al. (Eds.): DTGS 2018, CCIS 858, pp. 516–527, 2018.
https://doi.org/10.1007/978-3-030-02843-5_43

process (e.g., age, gender, risk factors, stroke subtypes). For this purpose, it was developed two predictive models through classification learning techniques.

LOS is used to describe the duration of a single episode of hospitalization, that is, the time between the admission and discharge dates. It is useful to predict a patient's expected LOS or to model LOS in order to determine the factors that affect it [5, 6]. This model can be an effective tool for hospitals to forecast the discharge dates of admitted patients with a high level of certainty and therefore improve the scheduling of elective admissions, leading to a reduction in the variance of hospital bed occupancy. These fluctuations prevent the hospital from having an efficient scheduling of resource allocation and management, resulting in short supply for the required resources or in the opposite scenario, that is, the supply being over the demand. The prediction of a patient's LOS can therefore enable more efficient utilization of manpower and facilities in the hospital, resulting in a higher average bed occupancy and, consequently, in cutting down on wasted overhead and improving profits [3, 7].

The clinical data used for this matter was obtained from one single hospital and contains information about patients who were hospitalized in CVA's unit in 2016 for having suffered a stroke.

For the purpose of this work, the Waikato Environment for Knowledge Analysis (Weka) was utilized as the machine learning toolkit.

2 Background

Today's data flood has outpaced human's capability to process, analyze, store and understand all the datasets. Powerful and versatile tools are increasingly needed to automatically uncover valuable information from the tremendous amounts of data generated from trillions of connected components (people and devices) and to transform such data into organized knowledge than can help improve quality of life and make the world a better place [1, 8]. Many forward-looking companies are using machine learning and data mining tools to analyze their databases for interesting and useful patterns. Products and services are recommended based on our habits [9]. Several banks, using patterns discovered in loan and credit histories, have derived better loan approval and bankruptcy prediction methods [10, 11].

The healthcare industry itself generates large amounts of data on a daily basis for various reasons, from simple record keeping to improving patient care with foreknowledge of the subject's own medical history, not to mention the information required for the organization's day-to-day management operations. Each person's data is compared and analyzed alongside thousands of others, highlighting specific threats and issues through patterns that emerge along the process. This enables sophisticated predictive modelling to take place [12–14].

2.1 Data Mining: The Heart of KDD

Knowledge Discovery in Databases (KDD) is the nontrivial extraction of implicit, previously unknown, and potentially useful information from data [10]. Its main goal is to turn a large collection of data into knowledge through the discovery of interesting patterns [15, 16]. Given a set of facts (data), a pattern is a collection or class of facts sharing something in common, describing relationships among a subset of that data with some level of certainty. A pattern that is interesting and certain enough, according to user's criteria, is recognized as knowledge [10].

This being said, KDD shares the same ultimate goal as the data mining process, since the second is an essential element of the first. The typical data mining process requires the previous transference of data originally collected in production systems into a data warehouse, data cleaning and consistency check. While KDD consists of the whole process from data preprocessing to the pattern discovery and evaluation, data mining, an essential step in the process of KDD, is the search itself for relationships and global patterns that exist in large databases but are 'hidden' among the vast amount of data, such as a relationship between patient data and its hospitalization period (see Fig. 1) [1, 16–18].

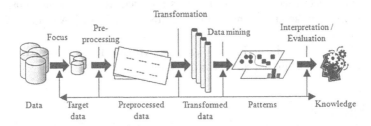

Fig. 1. Step of the KDD process. Adapted from [18]

When it comes to discovering pattern classes in the data mining process, in practice, the two primary goals consist of prediction and description. While the first consists of pattern identification and involves the usage of a certain number of variables/fields in the dataset to predict unknown or future values of other variables of interest, the second consists of class identification (clustering) and is focused on grouping individuals that share certain characteristics together, finding patterns that describe the data to be interpreted by humans [10]. These types of learning are also called supervised and un-supervised learning, respectively [19].

After a predictive model is built and validated, it is deemed able to generalize the knowledge it learned from historical data to predict the future [9]. In this way, for example, it can be used to predict the diagnosis for a certain patient based on existing clinical data from other previous patients with similar features. Models like these implement a classification function, in which the result is a class or a categorical label. Predictive models can also be used to predict numeric or continuous values by implementing a regression function [20].

2.2   Classification

Classification is probably the oldest and most widely-used of all the KDD approaches. In a classification problem, typically there are labeled examples (historical data) which consist of the predictor attributes and the target attribute (dependent variable which value is a class label). The unlabeled examples consist of the predictors attributes only.

As mentioned above, classification is learning a function that maps the unlabeled examples into one of several predefined categorical class labels [19, 21].

It is a two-step process consisting of training and testing. The training step is where the classification model is build, by analyzing training data (usually a large portion of the dataset). A classification model consists of classification rules that are created through a classification algorithm (classifier) that, in turn, entails a set of heuristics and calculations. In the testing step is where the classifier is examined for accuracy or by its ability to classify unknown individuals, by using testing data. Its accuracy depends on the degree to which classifying rules are true, being that classification rules with over 90% accuracy are regarded as solid rules [22].

3 Related Work

The matter of this work has been broadly studied since the advantages of knowing how long patients will stay in a hospital are overall recognized. Thus, there are several studies trying to address this problem by building prediction models. Even though many studies have been developed towards the predictions of LOS related other health problems (e.g., congestive heart failure [3], end stage renal disease [23], burn [24]), or not related to any specific health issue [7, 25], only a few are directly related to the prediction of LOS for stroke patients.

In [5], a group of 330 patients who suffered a first-ever ischemic stroke of this type and were consecutively admitted to a medical center in southern Taiwan were followed, prospectively. The purpose of this study was to identify the major predictors of LOS from the information available at the time of admission. Univariate and multiple regression analysis were used for this purpose. The median LOS was 7 days (mean, 11 days; range, 1–122 days). The main explanatory factors for LOS were identified as being the NIHSS score, modified Barthel Index score at admission, small-vessel occlusion stroke, gender and smoking. The main conclusion was that the severity of stroke, as rated by the total score on NIHSS, is an important factor that influences LOS after stroke hospitalization.

A similar study was presented in [26] where a group of 295 first-ever stroke patients were subjects of assessment in order to identify the factors that influence both acute and total LOS. Once again, a multiple regression analysis was performed for this purpose. The mean LOS was 12 days and the mean total was 29 days. Stroke severity measured with NIHSS was identified as being a strong predictor of both acute and total LOS. Also, while prestroke dementia and smoking revealed to have a negative impact in acute LOS, prestroke activities of daily living dependency was identified as a predictor of shorter total LOS.

4 Methods

The available clinical data for this project included 477 cardiovascular accident cases consecutively admitted at a CVA's unit in 2016. The dataset was obtained from a data warehouse in a comma separated value (csv) format and contained several attributes such as patient's gender, age, risk factors (presence or absence of history of hypertension, hypocoagulation, diabetes, atrial fibrillation, previous antiagregation, previous stroke, and smoking), provenance (whether the patient arrived to the hospital on its own, in an ambulance, through another hospital, or though Urgent Patient Orientation Centers), stroke's subtypes, clinical classification, previous and exit ranking (degree of disability), treatments, procedures, complications, and destinations. It also contained the time symptom-door, that is, the time between the moment the patient has the first symptom and the moment he enters the hospital, time door-neurology and time door-CT, that is, the time between the moment he enters the hospital and the moment he enters the neurology department and the moment that he develops a CT exam, respectively.

Since the purpose of this work was to predict LOS for a certain patient at the CVA unit's time of admission, it was only taken into consideration information available at that moment, that is, factors that can be assessed the moment the patient enters hospitalization. Even though some factors during hospitalization may have a major impact in its duration, the goal of this study is to provide a way for clinic professionals to make an estimation right away, being this information extremely useful for the hospital administration as well as the patient's relatives. In this sense, based on knowledge acquired from the previous research, the predictor variables, that is, the possible explanatory factors for LOS available at the time of admission, were prospectively selected.

4.1 Data Preprocessing

In the data cleaning process, all the missing values were removed. These unknown values were represented by either the value NULL in some classes or the value 0 in others. Since there was a vast amount of unknown values, especially for the time symptom-door and time door-neurology, numerous cases were eliminated from the dataset. This led to a final number of 211 cases used in this study. Consequently, it was necessary a relevance analysis since some of the classes contained the same value for all the cases or the majority of them. In this sense, all the valueless factors were removed from the dataset such as the different stroke subtypes and some risk factors.

The data transformation process was performed using normalization, which involved scaling all values to make them fall within a small specified range ([0–1]). This was performed at a stage where it wasn't established whether the final purpose would be a classification or regression prediction, for which normalization, is strictly necessary.

4.2 Modeling

WEKA software was used for the modeling process, has the capacity to read ".csv" files, change the classes' data type and then store these files in attribute-relation file format (arff) which is Weka's own format. However, in this project, the data was converted to arff format before it was loaded into Weka software, so the various attributes could be easily classified as being real (numeric) or nominal (categorical). Initially, the only numeric attributes were age, time symptom-door, time door-neurology, and LOS.

At the modeling stage, after a few attempts of adopting a regression approach in Weka, which was not giving satisfying results, the target attribute was converted into categorical classes in order to obtain better outcomes. Instead of predicting a numeric value (LOS in days), the goal became the prediction of a class (LOS in period of days).

Although LOS had a range of 0–116 days, it had a mean value of 13 days. This was taken into consideration for the definition of datasets with different intervals of days. Numerous possibilities were tested by comparing several learning methods such as ZeroR, IBk, and Random Forest. Since accuracy is not the ideal metric to use when working with an imbalanced dataset [27], which is the case, the evaluation was made with four performance measures based on the values of the confusion table: true positives (TP), false positives (FP), true negatives (TN), and false negatives (FN). The mentioned measures are [7, 27]: accuracy – correctly classified instances ((TP + TN)/ (TP + TN + FP + FN)); kappa statistic - accuracy normalized by the imbalance of the classes in the data to see if the result is indeed a true outcome or occurring by chance; precision - measure of a classifier exactness (TP/(TP + FP)); recall/sensitivity - measure of a classifier completeness (TP/(TP + FN)).

The error rates were not taken into consideration since these are used for numeric prediction rather than classification.

It was also necessary to check which factors had a negative influence in the final result in order to determine what would be the predictor variables for LOS. Each one of the various attributes were removed from the datasets, one at a time, and the best classifiers determined in the previous step were applied each time. If the removal of a certain attribute resulted in better metrics, it wouldn't be retrieved to the dataset.

After the final datasets and the corresponding classifiers had been selected, the sampling methods, more specifically cross-validation, percentage split, and supplied test set, were evaluated.

5 Results and Discussion

In this section, it is presented the results for the practical steps enumerated in the previous section, as well as its respective discussion.

Some of the results for the best datasets mentioned in the previous section where different category labels were applied to the target attribute, are presented in Table 1. In this table, the selected measures are displayed for each dataset and classifier.

Table 1. Results for prediction of LOS with different datasets

Datasets	Classifier	Accuracy	Kappa statistic	Precision	Sensitivity
A. 4 intervals (0–20–40–60–116 days)	ZeroR	68,72%	0	0,472	0,687
	IBk	91,00%	0,8161	0,912	0,910
	RandomForest	90,05%	0,7851	0,9	0,9
B. 2 intervals (0–7–116 days)	ZeroR	53,55%	0	0.287	0,536
	IBk	81,99%	0,6370	0,82	0,82
	RandomForest	81,52%	0,6241	0,822	0,815
C. 3 intervals (0–7–30–116 days)	ZeroR	46,45%	0	0, 216	0,464
	IBk	82,46%	0,7236	0,825	0,825
	RandomForest	80,57%	0,6911	0,807	0,806
D. 4 intervals (0–10–20–60–116 days)	ZeroR	58,29%	0	0,340	0,583
	IBk	81,99%	0,6892	0,825	0,820
	RandomForest	84,83%	0,7278	0,849	0,848
E. 3 intervals (0–20–40–60 days)	ZeroR	70,73%	0	0,5	0,707
	IBk	89,27%	0,7637	0,893	0,893
	RandomForest	89,76%	0,7548	0,899	0,898

By analyzing Table 1, it's clear that the best dataset is A since it presents the best overall values for the present measures. However, in reality, it would be more useful to be able to predict LOS for a period whose limit was shorter than 20 days. Dataset D also presents decent overall results and allows the prediction of LOS for a period limit of 10 days. This being said, datasets A and E were both selected to further assessment.

It is important that, since only a rare number of cases were within the range of 60–116 hospitalization days, the dataset E was created to evaluate whether the removal of these cases from the first dataset would improve the results. Since the opposite occurred and, in reality, it's actually useful to know if a patient is expected to stay for that long, dataset E was discarded.

In Table 2, some of the results for the selected datasets when comparing several learning methods are presented.

Table 2. Results for prediction of LOS with different learning methods

Dataset	Measure	Classifier				
		IBk	KStar	J48	LMT	Random Forest
A	Accuracy	91,00%	86,26%	81,99%	81,52%	90,05%
	Kappa statistic	0,8161	0,7137	0,6203	0,6256	0,7851
	Precision	0,912	0,862	0,815	0,823	0,900
	Sensitivity	0,910	0,863	0,820	0,815	0,900
D	Accuracy	81,99%	81,99%	66,35%	76,77%	84,83%
	Kappa statistic	0,6892	0,6827	0,3822	0,5848	0,7278
	Precision	0,825	0,822	0,661	0,765	0,849
	Sensitivity	0,825	0,820	0,664	0,768	0,848

As it can be seen in the table above, the best classifiers were IBk for dataset A with an accuracy of 91% and Random Forest for dataset D with an accuracy of 84.83%.

The accuracy results for the attributes assessment as mentioned in the previous section, are presented in Table 3. All measurements were taken into consideration.

Table 3. Results for predictions of LOS with different datasets

	Accuracy			Accuracy	
Attribute	A	D	Attribute	A	D
Gender	87,20%	83,41%	Atrial fibrilation	90,52%	84,36%
Age	88,15%	86,26%	Prev. antiagregation	88,15%	85,78%
Provenance	90,52%	87,68%	Smoking	91,47%	88,15%
Previous ranking	88,15%	85,30%	Previous stroke	91,00%	86,26%
Clinical classif.	88,62%	82,94%	Time symptom-door	90,52%	77,25%
Diabetes	85,78%	86,26%	Time door-neurology	89,43%	84,36%

The final predictor variables for LOS in each dataset were then determined as well as new values for accuracy. The determined attributes for the new dataset A2 were all the factors except for smoking, which resulted in a accuracy of 91.47%. On the other hand, the determined attributes for dataset D2 were all the factor except for age, provenance, and smoking, which resulted in a accuracy of 88.15%.

In Table 4, some of the accuracy results for different sampling methods are displayed. By its analyzation, it is visible that 10-fold cross validation was the best sampling method for both datasets, by maintaining the same accuracy results as before.

Table 4. Results for prediction of LOS with different sampling methods

Accuracy	Cross-validation			Percentage split		
Dataset	6-fold	8-fold	10-fold	66%	75%	80%
A2	86,73%	84,36%	91,47%	77,78%	83,02%	85,71%
D2	83,89%	84,36%	88,15%	76,39%	79,25%	83,33%

In order to evaluate the supplied test set sampling method and verify if there was overfitting or not, datasets A and D were distributed into two sets: training set (70% of the data) and test set (30% of the data). The best obtained accuracy results were 90.48% with KStar classifier for dataset A2 and 82.54% with Random Forest classifier for dataset E2. Even though accuracy values decreased in a visible way, it is due to the natural data variance. It wasn't a substantial decrease that could raise any concerns.

In Table 5, the accuracy values tell us that the first model correctly identifies 91.47% of the cases while the second model correctly identifies 88.16% of them. The value for both precision and sensitivity is 0.915 in dataset A2, which means that the first model is 91.5% exact and complete, presenting low false positives and negatives. The same stands for dataset E2, for which the precision and sensitivity values are 0.883 and 0.882.

Table 5. Results of the best models for datasets A2 and E2

Dataset	Accuracy	Precision	Recall
A2	91,47%	0,915	0,915
E2	88,15%	0,883	0,882

Even though these values are slightly lower, it's still a solid outcome for the model's positive predictive value and true positive rate. In this classification problem, the statistic, precision and sensitivity values were, in general, proportionally equivalent to the accuracy values, which facilitated the classifiers and sampling methods assessment and selection for each dataset.

By analyzing the confusion matrix illustrated in Table 6, it can be seen that the majority of the instances were well classified in both models since they are mostly found in the diagonal elements. There was a small number of false positives and negatives. In both datasets, the class which was the least well classified was naturally the first class since it is the most popular class. It presents 9 FP and 8 FN for dataset A2 (interval of days from 0 to 20), and 13 FP and 10 FN for dataset E2 (interval of days from 0 to 10). False positives are slightly more serious in the context of this work, since they mean that the hospital will be expecting a less hospitalization period than it actually is predominated to be, which can result in lack of resources. On the other hand, false negatives mean that the hospital will prepare itself for a longer hospitalization period that will not happen, resulting in wasted overhead.

Table 6. Confusion matrix of the best models for datasets A2 and E2

Dataset A2				Dataset E2			
137	4	4	0	**113**	1	9	0
6	**34**	0	0	4	**17**	1	0
2	0	**17**	1	8	0	**51**	1
1	0	0	**5**	1	0	0	**5**

It was not made an attempt of deleting random instances since the quantity of data was already much reduced. However, it would be a legitimate method for possibly getting better accuracy and overall measures.

From the above-mentioned results, it can be concluded that it isn't truthful to define a certain classifier as the best one for any predictive classification of data because each problem has an adequate classifier that will perform better than others, even though it might not be the case for other datasets. It was also possible to conclude that classifiers of a particular group don't necessarily give similar accuracies. Additionally, it became clear that measures and more importantly, the appropriate classifier, vary according to the dataset being used, specifically the number of attributes, number of instances, and the categorical classes defined for the target attribute. It was also possible to realize that a categorical prediction allowed the obtainment of better results than a numeric one.

Finally, the selected predictor variables didn't corroborate what was theoretically expected from the state of the art research. In [5, 26], smoking was one of the variables defined as being the explanatory factors for LOS, which was the only variable excluded from both datasets in this study. However, gender and the severity of the stroke were declared as being important factors, which happened in this case also, since previous ranking stands for the degree of disability the patient presents when he initiates hospitalization.

6 Conclusions

This project primarily consisted in the implementation of data mining techniques to predict the hospital Length Of Stay (LOS) of cardiovascular accident (CVA) patients based on indicators that are commonly available at the hospitalization process (e.g., age, gender, risk factors, CVA's type). For this purpose, it was developed two predictive models, through classification learning techniques.

The best learning models were obtained by the IBk and Random Forest methods, which presented high accuracy values for two datasets with different categorical classes (91.47% and 88.16%, respectively) and overall measures such as precision and sensitivity. The number of false positives and negatives was quite acceptable, which is essential to determine how much faith the system or user should put into this model.

Since the goal of this predictive model is not directly related to the patient health and more related to the hospital management, false positives or negatives are not so serious as they usually would be in the medical field, specially the second ones.

However, the lack of clinic available resources can represent a serious threat for patient health. In this case, either the hospital will prepare itself for a longer hospitalization period that will not happen, resulting in wasted overhead, or it will be expecting a less hospitalization period than it actually is predominated to be, which can result in lack of resources.

These models were obtained through an extensive analysis procedure that revealed the following influential input attributes: gender, previous ranking, clinical classification, diabetes, atrial fibrillation, previous antiagregation, previous stroke, time symptom-door and time door-neurology. For one of the datasets, it was also age and provenance. This showed that these predictor variables are not certain for every problem similar to this.

All the extracted knowledge confirmed that the obtained predictive model is credible and with potential value for supporting decisions of hospital managers. These models can be used by other researchers in order to improve their work, possibly in other fields of study. However, it has to be taken into consideration that each problem needs its individual assessment and intensive analysis of different methods.

Acknowledgments. This work has been supported by Compete: POCI-01-0145-FEDER-007043 and FCT within the Project Scope UID/CEC/00319/2013.

References

1. Han, J., Kamber, M., Pei, J.: Data Mining: Concepts and Techniques. Morgan Kaufman (2011). https://doi.org/10.1016/c2009-0-61819-5
2. Oliveira, D., Duarte, J., Abelha, A., Machado, J.: Improving nursing practice through interoperability and intelligence. In: Proceedings of 5th International Conference on Future Internet of Things and Cloud Workshops—FiCloudW, pp. 194–199 (2017). https://doi.org/10.1109/ficloudw.2017.92
3. Turgeman, L., May, J., Sciulli, R.: Insights from a machine learning model for predicting the hospital Length of Stay (LOS) at the time of admission. Expert Syst. Appl. **78**, 376–385 (2017). https://doi.org/10.1016/j.eswa.2017.02.023
4. Miranda, M., Abelha, A., Santos, M., Machado, J., Neves, J.: A group decision support system for staging of cancer. In: Weerasinghe, D. (ed.) eHealth 2008. LNICST, vol. 0001, pp. 114–121. Springer, Heidelberg (2009). https://doi.org/10.1007/978-3-642-00413-1_14
5. Chang, K., Tseng, M., Weng, H., Lin, Y., Liou, C., Tan, T.: Prediction of length of stay of first-ever ischemic stroke. Stroke **33**(11), 2670–2674 (2002). https://doi.org/10.1161/01. STR.0000034396.68980.39
6. Portela, F., et al.: Predict hourly patient discharge probability in intensive care units using data mining. Indian J. Sci. Technol. **8**(32) (2015). https://doi.org/10.17485/ijst/2015/v8i32/ 92043
7. Azari, A., Janeja, V., Mohseni, A.: Healthcare data mining. Int. J. Knowl. Discov. Bioinform. **3**(3), 44–66 (2012). https://doi.org/10.4018/jkdb.2012070103
8. Fan, W., Bifet, A.: Mining big data: current status, and forecast to the future. ACM SIGKDD Explor. Newsl. **14**(2) (2013). https://doi.org/10.1145/2481244.2481246
9. Guazzelli, A.: Predicting the future, part 2: predictive modeling techniques. IBM DeveloperWorks (2012). https://www.ibm.com/developerworks/library/ba-predictive-analytics2/index.html
10. Kantardzic, M.: Data Mining. Wiley, Hoboken (2011). https://doi.org/10.1002/ 9781118029145
11. Foster, D., Stone, R.: Variable selection in data mining. J. Am. Stat. Assoc. **99**(466), 303–313 (2004). https://doi.org/10.1198/016214504000000287
12. Marr, B.: How Big Data Is Changing Healthcare. Forbes (2015). https://www.forbes.com/ sites/bernardmarr/2015/04/21/how-big-data-is-changing-healthcare/#266cc7012873
13. Machado, J., Abelha, A., Neves, J., Santos, M.: Ambient intelligence in medicine. In: Proceedings of IEEE Biomedical Circuits and Systems Conference, pp. 94–97 (2006). https://doi.org/10.1109/biocas.2006.4600316
14. Duarte, J., Portela, C.F., Abelha, A., Machado, J., Santos, M.F.: Electronic health record in dermatology service. In: Cruz-Cunha, M.M., Varajão, J., Powell, P., Martinho, R. (eds.) CENTERIS 2011. CCIS, vol. 221, pp. 156–164. Springer, Heidelberg (2011). https://doi. org/10.1007/978-3-642-24352-3_17
15. Prather, J., Lobach, D., Goodwin, L., Hales, J., Hage, M., Hammond, W.: Medical data mining: knowledge discovery in a clinical data warehouse. Proc. Conf. Am. Med. Inform. Assoc. AMIA Fall Symp. **89**(10), 101–105 (1997)
16. Holsheimer, M., Siebes, A.: Data Mining—The Search for Knowledge in Databases. CWI Report (1991)
17. Neves, J., et al.: A deep-big data approach to health care in the AI age. Mob. Netw. Appl. **23**, 1–6 (2018). https://doi.org/10.1007/s11036-018-1071-6

18. Fayyad, U., Piatetsky-Shapiro, G., Smyth, P.: Knowledge discovery and data mining: towards a unifying framework. In: Proceedings of International Conference on Knowledge Discovery and Data Mining, pp. 82–88 (1996)
19. Eapen, A.: Application of Data mining in Medical Applications. UWSpace, pp. 1–117 (2004)
20. Chapple, M.: Defining the Regression Statistical Model (2016). https://www.lifewire.com/regression-1019655
21. Fonseca, F., Peixoto, H., Miranda, F., Machado, J., Abelha, A.: Step towards prediction of perineal tear. Procedia Comput. Sci. **113**, Elsevier (2017). https://doi.org/10.1016/j.procs.2017.08.284
22. Yoo, I., Alafaireet, P., Marinov, M., Pena-Hernandez, K., Gopidi, R., Chang, J., Hua, L.: Data mining in healthcare and biomedicine: a survey of the literature. J. Med. Syst. **36**(4), 2431–2448 (2012). https://doi.org/10.1007/s10916-011-9710-5
23. Yeh, J., Wu, T., Tsao, C.: Using data mining techniques to predict hospitalization of hemodialysis patients. Decis. Support Syst. **50**(2), 439–448 (2011). https://doi.org/10.1016/j.dss.2010.11.001
24. Yang, C., Wei, C., Yuan, C., Schoung, J.: Predicting the length of hospital stay of burn patients: comparisons of prediction accuracy among different clinical stages. Decis. Support Syst. **50**(1), 325–335 (2010). https://doi.org/10.1016/j.dss.2010.09.001
25. Tanuja, S., Acharya, D., Shailesh, K.: Comparison of different data mining techniques to predict hospital length of stay. J. Pharm. Biomed. Sci. **7**(7), 1–4 (2011)
26. Appelros, P.: Prediction of length of stay for stroke patients. Acta Neurol. Scand. **116**(1), 15–19 (2007). https://doi.org/10.1111/j.1600-0404.2006.00756.x
27. Brownlee, J.: 8 Tactics to combat imbalanced classes in your machine learning dataset (2015). https://machinelearningmastery.com/tactics-to-combat-imbalanced-classes-in-your-machine-learning-dataset/

Multiparameter and Index Evaluation
of Voluntary Distributed Computing Projects

Vladimir N. Yakimets[1,2] (iD) and Ilya I. Kurochkin[1(✉)] (iD)

[1] Institute for Information Transmission Problems of Russian Academy
of Sciences, Moscow, Russia
iakimets@mail.ru, kurochkin@iitp.ru
[2] The Russian Presidential Academy
of National Economy and Public Administration, Moscow, Russia

Abstract. In 2014–2015 years the very first sociological study of Russian crunchers [20] – volunteers who provide their computing resources for solving laborious tasks was conducted by authors. The study covered almost 650 people, which is a representative sample (more than 16% of total sample of about 4000 crunchers). A detailed analysis of that survey data led the authors to the idea of developing a new approach to evaluation of VDC projects. It is based on expert assessments of project quality on many criteria such as clarity of concept and vision, sound scientific platform, as well as existence of visualized results, availability of tools for encouraging crunchers, and so on. A new tool for assessing the quality of VDC projects (the YaK-index) is proposed and described in this paper. It was applied for evaluating some VDC projects to identify their strong and weak features, to make recommendations for improving their efficiency, to enhance the attractiveness for those interested in the VDC, and to create conditions for providing comparable information to the leadership of VDC projects. This paper describes the YaK-index idea and methodology, some stages of its development. Examples of visualization of comparable results of evaluating for a number of projects are given.

Keywords: Voluntary distributed computing (VDC) · The VDC project
Crunchers · Evaluation index of the VDC project
Characteristics for assessing the quality of VDC projects

1 Introduction

The use of distributed computing systems for high-performance computing is an alternative to calculations on supercomputers and other multiprocessor computer systems. Distributed computing systems or grid systems have a number of features, such as heterogeneity of computing nodes, their geographical distance, unstable network topology and high probability of disconnection of a computing node or communication channel. But even with such features, the computing potential of the grid system can be huge because of the large number (hundreds of thousands) of compute nodes. There are software platforms for organizing distributed computing, such as HTCondor [1], Legion [2], BOINC [3]. At the moment, the most common platform for organizing

© Springer Nature Switzerland AG 2018
D. A. Alexandrov et al. (Eds.): DTGS 2018, CCIS 858, pp. 528–542, 2018.
https://doi.org/10.1007/978-3-030-02843-5_44

distributed computing is BOINC (Berkeley Open Infrastructure for Network Computing) [4]. This is open non-commercial software for organizing distributed computing on personal computers.

Grid systems that consist of personal computers, laptops, smartphones and tablets are called desktop grid systems. Desktop grid systems are divided into 2 types: enterprise and public. Enterprise desktop grid systems are deployed within organizations to perform calculations in their interests [5]. Public grid systems attract the computing power of volunteers. As a rule, the organizers of public grid systems are scientific or educational organizations. A public computing grid system is called a voluntary distributed computing project. Based on the BOINC platform, several dozens of projects have been deployed in the interests of leading academic and scientific organizations [4].

The capacity of the computing grid system can be increased in two ways: increasing the efficiency of existing computing nodes and increasing the number of compute nodes. Increasing the efficiency of computing nodes is accomplished by setting up a load balancing system [6], fine-tuning the replication parameters [7], and increasing the load of computing nodes [8, 9]. The increase in the number of computing nodes for enterprise desktop grid systems is carried out with the help of administrative influence.

2 Theoretical Grounding

For public projects of voluntary distributed computing, the task is to attract new volunteers and their computing power and/or to retain the VDC project participants. To develop a set of measures for attracting and retaining volunteers in a VDC project, you need to know not only the statistical parameters, such as the number of volunteers and the computing power of their computers, but also the motivation of volunteers and their expectations. It is necessary also to interact with the community of volunteers to draw their attention to the VDC project.

The vast majority of scientific articles on the VDC projects are published in English. The English-language sites dominate, including those associated with the platform BOINC [4]. It should be noted that in English and Russian literature a majority of publications and articles on Internet resources provide a description of the individual VDC projects, their status, scientific and technical achievements [10–12]. Significantly less common are scientific papers which characterize organization of VDC activities and cruncher involvement in VDC projects [13–15]. And it is quite rare to see papers which examine various aspects of citizen participation in VDC projects [16, 17]. One of the first attempts of more or less systematic study of the conditions and characteristics of crunchers involvement in VDC projects in Russia, as well as their motivations and preferences has become a sociological study among 650 Russian crunchers [20]. Findings of that sociological survey were published in [18, 19]. Analysis of these data and a thorough discussion of the findings on a number of domestic forums and Internet resources, created the prerequisites and forced the authors to develop a methodology for an index evaluating of VDC projects on the basis of many parameters, including such as assessment of the project concept, description its goals and objectives, quality of visualizing the project findings, availability of tools for encouraging crunchers to participate, and so on. Based on a multiparameter "portrait" of the VDC project the actors involved into its activities will have a chance to see strong (with the best estimates) and weak (with low estimates) characteristics of the project and then decide what should be improved. It is clear that not all weak sides of the project can be improved at once. Some next stages of evaluation can be implemented. Therefore in addition to the above multiparameter estimates an index was proposed to give the VDC project team an opportunity to monitor changes of characteristics values and decide what next steps can be applied. For instance, if there is an increment of index due to changes introduced then decisions made on improvements were true. In case when value of the index was decreased means that wrong decisions on changes have been made.

Initially, the websites of a number of VDC projects based on BOINC platform [4] were studied. The list of the VDC projects analyzed among others includes:

- SETI@home, engaged in the processing of radio telescope signals to search for radio signals from extraterrestrial civilizations [12];
- Einstein@home, involved in testing Einstein's hypothesis about the existence of gravitational waves, as well as now this project is engaged in the search of pulsars according radio and gamma-ray telescopes [11];
- POGS@home, aimed at building a multispectral atlas (from near infrared to ultraviolet radiation), as well as at determining the rate of star formation, the stellar mass of galaxies, the distribution of dust and its mass in the galaxy and etc. [10];
- SAT@home, associated with searching for solutions to such complex problems as inversion of discrete functions, discrete optimization, bioinformatics, etc.), which can be effectively reduced to the problem of the feasibility of Boolean formulas [14];
- Some other VDC projects were studied too – Asteroids@home, LHC@home, Rosetta@home, MilkyWay@home, Folding@home, Gerasim@home [13] and etc.

A new tool (YaK-index) was developed to assess the quality of the VDC projects implementation. It was applied to a number of the above-mentioned projects in order to identify their strong and weak features, make recommendations to increase their efficiency, as well as to increase attractiveness for people interested in the VDC, and to provide comparable information for the organizers of the VDC projects.

3   Methodology for the Index Evaluation of VDC Projects

The methodology for the index evaluation of VDC projects includes the following main stages:

1. Creating an index model;
2. Collecting information to describe the most important elements of VDC projects;
3. Conducting surveys of participants of selected VDC projects to calculate the values of the YaK index;
4. Calculating YaK-index values and visualizing the results.

3.1   Model of the YaK-Index of the VDC Projects

We introduce the notation:

$i = \overline{1, n}$ - the ordinal number of the important characteristics of the VDC project (hereinafter referred to as characteristics), it is assumed that n equal to 7–9, that is, from 7 to 9 estimated characteristics of each VDC project will be taken into account;

$s = \overline{1, S}$ - the ordinal number of the VDC project, $S = 34$;

R^s - YaK-index of the VDC project s;

x_i^s - availability of characteristic i of the VDC project s (0 – if not present; 1 – if available);

α_i^s - the mean weighting factor (significance) of characteristic i from all respondents of s-th the VDC project, $0 \le \alpha_i^s < 1, \sum_{i=1}^{n} \alpha_i^s = 1$;

ρ_i^s - an mean expert assessment of the quality of i-th characteristic from all respondents of s-th VDC project.

The scale values vary from -2 to 2. A linguistic interpretation of these values is given in the questionnaire. If necessary $\rho_i^s \in \{-2, -1, 0, 1, 2\}$ can be converted into the set $\rho_i^s \in \{1, 2, 3, 4, 5\}$.

Identically for all n characteristics it is mapped one-to-one in a numerical set from the set of possible linguistic estimates. The maximum value of the numeric scale is m. In our case, it is assumed that m = 5. But it is possible to normalize the index values so that they vary from 0 to 1.

There are two possibilities for calculating the value R^s:

1. When the weights of characteristics for a VDC project are individual and independent of what such weights are for all other VDC projects.
2. When for all VDC projects the same vector of weights is defined.

In the first case, the index R^s is calculated as follows:

$$R^s = \frac{\sum_{i=1}^{n} \alpha_i^s \bullet x_i^s \bullet \rho_i^s}{n_1^s m}$$

Here n_1^s is the number of characteristics for VDC project s, $n_1^s \le n$.
In the second case

$$R^s = \frac{\sum_{i=1}^{n} \alpha_i \bullet x_i^s \bullet \rho_i^s}{n_1^s m}.$$

3.2   Collecting Information for Describing the Most Important Elements of VDC Projects

Since the index evaluation of the VDC projects is carried out for the first time, it is necessary to implement a number of preparatory activities related to the determining characteristics (parameters) that are relevant for each VDC project, identifying the significance of such characteristics, and developing a questionnaire for obtaining expert judgements on characteristics for each project.

The list of characteristics of the VDC projects, which is advisable to use in the assessment process was determined during special expert on-line sessions with the participation of the most active crunchers of the Russian VDC projects.

As a result, 9 characteristics were selected to assess the features of VDC projects:

1. The clear concept and vision of the project;
2. Scientific component of the project;
3. The quality of scientific and scientific-popular publications about project;
4. Design of the project (site, certificate, screensaver);
5. Informativity of materials on the project site;
6. Visualization of the project results (photo, video, infographic);
7. Organization of feedback (forums, chat rooms, etc.);
8. Stimulation of the cruncher participation (competitions, scoring, prizes);
9. Simplicity of joining the project.

In agreement with the crunchers participating in online sessions, it was decided to identify weights of the VDC projects characteristics simultaneously with the assessment of the values of these characteristics for the projects under evaluation. Respondents were asked to determine the weight of each characteristic using a scale from 0 to 10 points. It was assumed that the weight value "0" corresponds to the lack of characteristics for this project.

3.3   Conducting Surveys of Participants of Some VDC Projects for Calculating Its YaK-Index Values

A special questionnaire (in Russian and English) [21] was developed for interviewing participants of various VDC projects to collect information from the Russian and international community of crunchers. The questionnaire was published and links to it were allocated on the resources of the crunchers interaction. To evaluate the characteristics of the VDC project, it was suggested to use a 5-point scale (with the following linguistic interpretation): "+2" is excellent; "+1" is good; "0" is normal; "−1" - it is necessary to improve; "−2" is bad.

The status characteristics of the respondents (administration, team captain, cruncher, observer, donor) as well as the duration of their involvement in the project (up to 1 year, up to 2 years, 3–4 years, more than 5 years) were requested to point out in the questionnaire. In total, about 250 respondents responded to two versions of the questionnaire (in Russian and English). In this paper the average estimates, as well as the values of the YaK-index, were calculated only for 10 projects for which more than 10 questionnaires were filled, including Asteroids@home, Einstein@home,

Folding@home, Gerasim@home, LHC@home, MilkyWay@home, POGS@home, Rosetta@home, SAT@home and SETI@home.

3.4   Visualization of Survey Results

Questionnaires from all 250 respondents (for all projects) were used to determine the averaged weights of each characteristic. It should be mentioned that the average weight of a characteristic for all projects was not significantly different from the average value of it for an individual project.

To visualize the projects characteristics weights a radar diagram was used (Fig. 1). On Fig. 2 visualize estimates of the all characteristics are arranged in descending order to average weight.

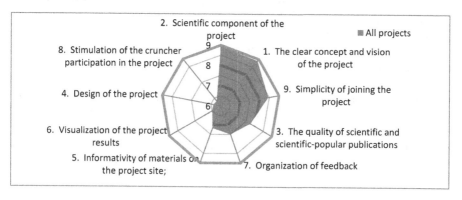

Fig. 1. Ranked weights of characteristics for all projects.

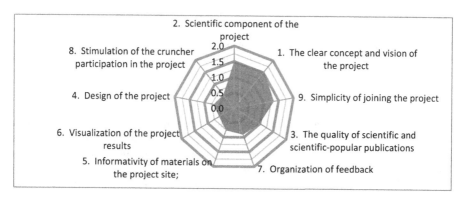

Fig. 2. Estimates of the characteristics of all projects, taking into account their ranking by weight.

First, let's present estimates of large international VDC projects:

- SETI@home (Berkeley University of California) works in the field of astrophysics. Project power – 774.47 TeraFLOPS. The number of users is 141,546 (1,659,008). The number of nodes: 162,987 (4,091,510) [12].
- Einstein@home (American Physical Society, US National Science Foundation, Max Planck Society) is also focused on astrophysics. Project power - 770.720 TeraFLOPS. The number of users is 27,860 (441,167). Number of nodes: 51,322 (1,585,760) [11].
- POGS@home (developed and coordinated by the International Research Center for Radio Astronomy Studies, Australia, Perth). It is engaged in processing data from telescopes of the world in different ranges of the electromagnetic spectrum in order to create a multifrequency (ultraviolet-optical-infrared spectra) atlas of near neighborhoods of the universe. The physical parameters (the stellar mass of galaxies, the absorption of radiation by dust, the mass of the dust component, the rate of star formation) are determined using the technique of searching for the optimum for the distribution of spectral energy. As of February 14, 2014, the project involved 7,937 users (more than 18,000 computers) from 80 countries, delivering about 43 TeraFLOPS [10].
- SAT@home (Institute of System Dynamics and Control Theory, Siberian Affiliation of RAS, Institute for Information Transmission Problems, RAS). It is engaged in searching for solutions to such complex problems as inversion of discrete functions, discrete optimization, bioinformatics, etc., which can be effectively reduced to the problem of the feasibility of Boolean formulas [14, 16].

4   Results for Selected VDC Projects

4.1   SETI@home

This is one of the longest and most popular projects of voluntary distributed computing – the project has been working for 19 years, and its audience is over one million volunteers around the world. The success of the SETI@home project and the successful concept of distributed computing enabled the creators of the Berkeley University to improve the project software to the BOINC distributed computing platform. Since 1999, the project has solved many different computing tasks. However, over time, the attention of creators and project administrators to motivating volunteers decreased. In part, this can be explained by the high scientific authority of the creators and administrators of the project, as well as the status of "project number 1" on the BOINC platform. Characteristic weights of the project SETI@home almost coincide with the weights for all projects (Fig. 3).

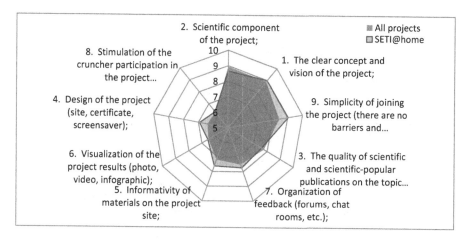

Fig. 3. Weights of characteristics for the project SETI@home.

4.2 Einstein@home

Comparing Figs. 4 and 6, we note that the weights of the characteristics of the projects SETI@home and Einstein@home are higher than the values of the averaged weights for all projects except for one – stimulation of the participation of the crunchers in the project. But the actual evaluation of the characteristics of the two projects differ significantly. The project Einstein@home has almost all its characteristics higher (Fig. 5) than the estimates for all projects. The estimates of five characteristics of the SETI@home project are below the estimates for all projects, and four others (concept, simplicity of joining, feedbacks and design) are higher.

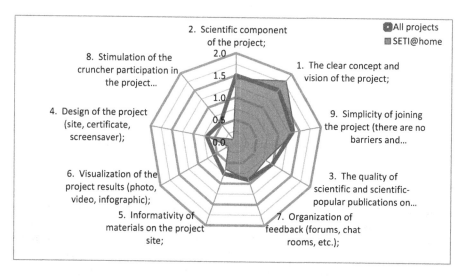

Fig. 4. Evaluation of the characteristics of the project SETI@home.

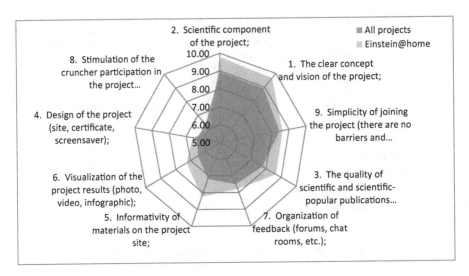

Fig. 5. Weights of characteristics for the project Einstein@home.

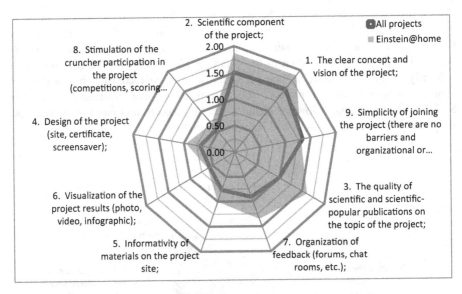

Fig. 6. Evaluation of the characteristics of the project Einstein@home.

4.3   POGS@home

TheSkyNet POGS is a relatively young international project that was created to process data from various telescopes of the world in different ranges of the electromagnetic spectrum [10]. The administration of the project takes great care to interact with the community of crunchers. The project implements the viewing and visualization of personal results, created a complex system of virtual prizes, regularly held competitions timed to commemorative dates. This project can be called one of the best in the visual component and the interaction with the crunchers (Figs. 7 and 8).

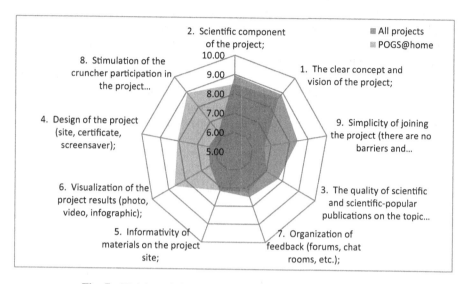

Fig. 7. Weights of characteristics for the project POGS@home.

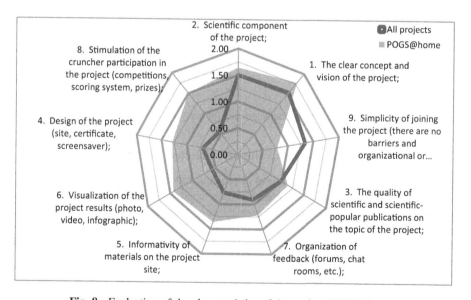

Fig. 8. Evaluation of the characteristics of the project POGS@home.

4.4   SAT@home

For the SAT@home project, we note that the weights of the characteristics are very similar to the weights for all projects (Fig. 9). A distinctive feature is that only two characteristics of SAT@home (simplicity of joining and organization of feedback) turned out to be slightly higher than estimates for all projects (Fig. 10), and in general the estimates of the characteristics of this project are inferior to similar estimates of Einstein@home (compare Figs. 10 and 6). Estimates of the characteristics of the SETI@home and SAT@home projects (Figs. 4 and 10) are similar, but it is noteworthy that the SAT@home project has significantly less appreciated the design intent, its scientific component and concept hence, we can conclude that the SAT@home project team should pay special attention to the development of these aspects.

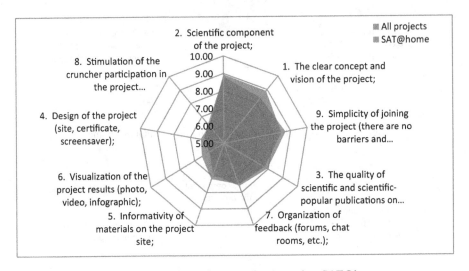

Fig. 9. Weights of characteristics for the project SAT@home.

4.5   Calculating the YaK-Index Values for Selected VDC Projects

Using the calculated average (for subset of projects under consideration) and individual values of characteristics weights for each project separately, as well as expert estimates of the characteristics, the YaK-index values were calculated (Table 1). It should be noted that for the comparative analysis of projects, a YaK-index with averaged characteristics should be used, and for the dynamics of changing the YaK-index within a single project, it is necessary to use the YaK-index weighted for a particular project.

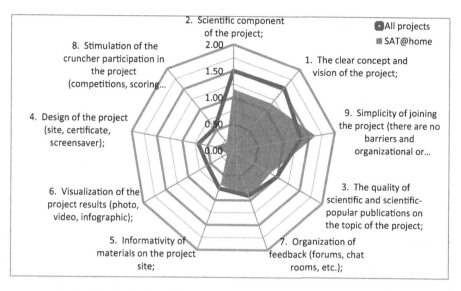

Fig. 10. Evaluation of the characteristics of the project SAT@home.

Table 1. YaK-index.

№	Project title	YaK-index (with average weights of characteristics)	YaK-index (with individual weights of characteristics)
1	SAT@home	0.58	0.57
2	SETI@home	0.60	0.61
3	Einstein@home	0.65	0.69
4	Rosetta@home	0.61	0.63
5	Gerasim@home	0.59	0.61
6	POGS@home	0.66	0.69
7	Asteroids@home	0.62	0.62
8	LHC@home	0.64	0.64
9	MilkyWay@home	0.60	0.61
10	Folding@home	0.65	0.68

Judging by the magnitude of the YaK-index values, all 10 VDC projects have a certain capabilities for development. So, in the case of using individual characteristics scales (the right column), the highest values of the index (0.69) have both the Einstein@home project and the POGS@home project. The lowest values got the SAT@home project. The teams of the best two projects, referring to the values of the characteristics weights (Figs. 5 and 7), can determine which characteristics of their projects they should pay more attention to in order to increase the values of the YaK-index. Thus, for the POGS@home project, it is necessary to carry out activities related to the simplification of joining the project as its assessment by the project participants is the lowest one (slightly more than 0.5). In addition, there are capabilities for improving two more characteristics - the quality of scientific and popular science materials on the project and the organization of feedback on the site.

For the project Einstein@home, judging by Figs. 5 and 6, an increase of the YaK-index values is possible when both a visualization of the project results and a stimulation of the participation of crunchers in the project are improved.

The lowest values of the YaK-index in both cases (the right and the second from the right columns of the table) were obtained by the SAT@home project (0.57 and 0.58). This is just a bit over half of the maximum possible values of the index. It is clear that this project is "younger" than the rest ones. Nevertheless, by comparing the radar diagrams with weights and estimates of characteristics, we can recommend to the project teams to pay attention to the scientific component and description of the project's concept, as well as to visualizing the results and design of the project site.

5 Conclusions

The contents of VDC-projects are significantly differ from each other. They have different scales of research, sometimes very different periods of implementation. They use diverse research tools. A common feature for them is the availability of crunchers, whose participation is essential in the implementation of projects. The involvement of crunchers in the activities of the project depends to a large extent on a number of parameters characterizing the project itself and how its work is organized. Using the techniques of sociology, we developed a tool to survey participants and organizers of a number of VDC projects. Using the Toolkit, we determine the list of the most important characteristics of VDC projects that are essential for crunchers involved in their activities, as well as to assess the significance of such characteristics for different projects.

A new approach to the evaluation of VDC projects was developed, consisting of 2 complementary parts:

1. Multiparameter evaluation of VDC projects by crunchers and other participants by using questionnaires. Following the processing of individual evaluations by respondents on special scales, average project performance values for each of the parameters were calculated. This made it possible to graphically create a comprehensive visualization of multidimensional "portrait" for each VDC project.
2. Calculation of the aggregated index, when the average estimates were "weighed" taking into account the coefficients of their significance.

Multiparameter assessment provided a visualization of multidimensional "portrait" of VDC-project, highlighting its strengths and weaknesses. On the basis of such data, the project team can develop proposals to constructively impact on the identified weaknesses of the project. Such proposals could contribute to the improvement of the VDC project.

An index approach was used in order to fix the consequences of the proposals application. Then multi-dimensional assessment was repeated and if the calculated index value for the individual VDC -project increased, it means that the decisions had been constructive.

When the index value decreased, it was necessary to reconsider the decisions and develop other proposals.

Both multidimensional "portrait" (9 parameters) and index evaluation of the VDC-project complement each other. Such evaluation results are an important tool for the project team, helping to improve project performance and management.

Acknowledgments. This work was funded by Russian Science Foundation (№16-11-10352).

References

1. Litzkow, M.J., Livny, M., Mutka, M.W.: Condor-a hunter of idle workstations. In: 8th International Conference on Distributed Computing Systems, 1988, pp. 104–111. IEEE. (1988)
2. Grimshaw, A.S., Wulf, W.A.: The legion vision of a worldwide virtual computer. Commun. ACM **40**(1), 39–45 (1997)
3. Anderson, D.P.: Boinc: a system for public-resource computing and storage. In: Proceedings of the Fifth IEEE/ACM International Workshop on Grid Computing 2004, pp. 4–10. IEEE. (2004)
4. The server of statistics of voluntary distributed computing projects on the BOINC platform. http://boincstats.com. Accessed 30 Jan 2018
5. Ivashko, E.E.: Enterprise desktop grids. Programmnye Sistemy: Teoriya i Prilozheniya [Program Systems: Theory and Applications] **1**, 19 (2014)
6. Kim, J.S., Keleher, P., Marsh, M., Bhattacharjee, B., Sussman, A.: Using content-addressable networks for load balancing in desktop grids. In: Proceedings of the 16th International Symposium on High Performance Distributed Computing, pp. 189–198. ACM (2007)
7. Chernov, I., Nikitina, N.: Virtual screening in a desktop grid: replication and the optimal quorum. In: Malyshkin, V. (ed.) PaCT 2015. LNCS, vol. 9251, pp. 258–267. Springer, Cham (2015). https://doi.org/10.1007/978-3-319-21909-7_25
8. Ben-Yehuda, O.A., Schuster, A., Sharov, A., Silberstein, M., Iosup, A.: Expert: pareto-efficient task replication on grids and a cloud. In: 2012 IEEE 26th International on Parallel & Distributed Processing Symposium (IPDPS), pp. 167–178. IEEE (2012)
9. Bridgewater, J., Boykin, P. O., Roychowdhury, V.: Balanced overlay networks (BON): an overlay technology for decentralized load balancing. IEEE Trans. Parallel Distrib. Syst. **18**(8) (2007)
10. Homepage of the Sky Net POGS project. http://pogs.theskynet.org/pogs/. Accessed 30 Jan 2018
11. Homepage of the Einstein@home project. https://einsteinathome.org/ru/. Accessed 30 Jan 2018
12. Homepage of the SETI@home project. http://setiathome.berkeley.edu/. Accessed 30 Jan 2018
13. Vatutin, E.I., Titov, V.S.: Voluntary distributed computing for solving discrete combinatorial optimization problems using Gerasim@home project. In: Distributed Computing and Grid-Technologies in Science and Education: Book of Abstracts of the 6th International Conference. Dubna: JINR, pp. 60–61 (2014)
14. Posypkin, M., Semenov, A., Zaikin, O.: Using BOINC desktop grid to solve large scale SAT problems. Comput. Sci. **13**(1), 25 (2012)

15. Lombraña González, D., et al.: LHC@ Home: a volunteer computing system for massive numerical simulations of beam dynamics and high energy physics events. In: Conference Proceedings, vol. 1205201, no. IPAC-2012-MOPPD061, pp. 505–507 (2012)
16. Zaikin, O.S., Posypkin, M.A., Semenov, A.A., Khrapov, N.P.: Experience in organizing volunteer computing: a case study of the OPTIMA@home and SAT@home projects. Vestnik of Lobachevsky State University of Nizhniy Novgorod, no. 5–2, pp. 340–347 (2012). (in Russian)
17. Tishchenko, V., Prochko, I., L, A.: Russian participants in BOINC-based volunteer computing projects. The activity statistics. Comput. Res. Model. 7(3), 727–734 (2015). (in Russian)
18. Clary, E.G., et al.: Understanding and assessing the motivations of volunteers: a functional approach. J. Pers. Soc. Psychol. 74(6), 1516 (1998)
19. Webpage of World Community Grid project. 2013 Member Study: Findings and Next Steps. https://www.worldcommunitygrid.org/about_us/viewNewsArticle.do?articleId=323&utm_source=email&utm_medium=email&utm_campaign=user_study_20130815. Accessed 30 Jan 2018
20. Yakimets, V.N., Kurochkin I.I.: Voluntary distributed computing in Russia: a sociological analysis. In: Proceedings of the XVIII Joint Conference Internet and Contemporary Society' IMS-2015. ITMO University, St. Petersburg, pp. 345–352, 23 June 2015. (in Russian)
21. Kurochkin I.I., Yakimets V.N.: Evaluation of the voluntary distributed computing project SAT@home. National Supercomputer Forum (NSCF-2016), Pereslavl-Zalessky, Russia, 29 November–2 December 2016. http://2016.nscf.ru/TesisAll/09_Gridi_iz_rabochix_stanciy_i_kombinirovannie_gridi/611_KyrochkinII.pdf. Accessed 30 Jan 2018. (in Russian)

Author Index